The Trials of
HARRY S. TRUMAN

The Extraordinary Presidency of an Ordinary Man, 1945–1953

Jeffrey Frank

Simon & Schuster
New York London Toronto Sydney New Delhi

Simon & Schuster
1230 Avenue of the Americas
New York, NY 10020

First Simon & Schuster hardcover edition March 2022

SIMON & SCHUSTER and colophon are registered
trademarks of Simon & Schuster, Inc.

For information about special discounts for bulk purchases,
please contact Simon & Schuster Special Sales at 1-866-506-1949
or business@simonandschuster.com.

The Simon & Schuster Speakers Bureau can bring authors
to your live event. For more information or to book an event,
contact the Simon & Schuster Speakers Bureau at 1-866-248-3049
or visit our website at www.simonspeakers.com.

Interior design by Lewelin Polanco

Manufactured in the United States of America

10 9 8 7 6 5 4 3 2 1

Library of Congress Cataloging-in-Publication Data is available.

ISBN 978-1-5011-0289-9
ISBN 978-1-5011-0291-2 (ebook)

for Thomas Adam Frank, and his mother, Diana

Contents

Prologue The Missourian   ix

1. President Truman   1
2. Terminal   15
3. An Unsteady Alliance   30
4. "The Basic Power of the Universe"   44
5. Truman's "Conniver"   58
6. Churchill Makes Mischief   71
7. The Quick and the Dead   82
8. A Season of Disharmony   96
9. The Doctrine's Dilemma   106
10. Wealth of a Nation   122
11. Strange Interludes   133
12. A Cemetery for Dead Cats   141
13. Minority Reports   150
14. The Frontiers of Hazard   165
15. The Scrapper   175
16. Office Politics   188
17. "First Lightning"   204
18. "A New Fanatic Faith"   216
19. A "Border Incident"   229
20. "The Second Hand of Destiny"   246
21. A Meeting on a Small Island   263

22. *Mense Horribilis* 278

23. "Voice of God" 299

24. "The Mess in Washington" 313

25. Dubious Battles 327

26. Bad Chemistry 340

27. The Bitter End 351

Epilogue Citizen Truman 363

Acknowledgments 381
Notes 385
Sources 471
Illustration Credits 499
Index 501

The Missourian

The first time you are in Washington I wish you would come in and see me. There are several things I want to talk to you about.

—Harry Truman to Harry L. Hopkins, August 18, 1945

1. When Harry S. Truman became President of the United States, after the death of Franklin D. Roosevelt, he was sixty years old and, outwardly, the portrait of a Midwestern striver: a bit too well dressed, in natty suits, fedoras or Stetsons, and two-tone shoes. His thick glasses, at certain angles, could give his eyes a sudden, unsettling enlargement. His face—the face of a sympathetic small-town banker—appeared gray in newsreels, but was actually a weather-beaten red, the complexion of a retired farmer. That was not surprising, because he was someone who, for a decade, had plowed the fields and raised livestock on his family's farm. Roy Roberts, the *Kansas City Star*'s managing editor and not a Truman admirer, was struck by the idea that someone who not so long before "was still looking at the rear end of a horse" should find himself leading the world's most powerful nation. "What a story in democracy," he wrote, and added, "What a test of democracy, if it works." What a test indeed.

Truman's nearly eight years as president—a time of exalted national goals, virulent anti-Communism, and accelerated social change—would encompass a lot: the end of wars in Europe and the Pacific; the emergence of the United States, ready or not, as the world's preeminent military and economic power; the first use of an atomic bomb, and the development of far more destructive weapons; the beginning of a long "cold war" with the Soviet Union, and an unwinnable "hot war" in the Far East. He was prepared for none of this—although, having been a United States senator for ten years and a vice president for about three months, he had some idea how an operation like the Executive Branch functioned. But this was a bigger job than any he'd ever held—immeasurably so—and he wondered if he was up to it.

Having suddenly been handed the role of world leader, he knew that he had to take his rightful place, as Roosevelt's successor, alongside the British prime minister Winston Churchill and the Soviet chairman Joseph Stalin. That was daunting. Churchill and Stalin had led their nations during a monstrous war while Truman was representing a semi-rural American state with a population under four million. Nor would it be easy to lead a nation of a hundred and forty million diverse people. Truman pretty much supported the New Deal, though not with the zeal of Roosevelt's East Coast men—who knew that he wasn't one of them. He believed that leaders needed to be resolute, and considered indecisiveness something of a character flaw, but this made him inclined to decide questions quickly, intuitively—making what he called "jump decisions," with all the risks of undue haste.

Every administration has personnel problems, but Truman seemed to have more of them than usual. His first two secretaries of defense showed signs of mental instability. His first appointment as secretary of state, the cunning, and nervously high-strung James Francis Byrnes—Jimmy Byrnes—thought he should have been president; his eccentric secretary of commerce, Henry Agard Wallace, thought the same thing about himself. Truman's fallings-out within his own administration were often followed by rancorous recriminations, and he fired so many top officials that, as he neared the end of his second term, the *Washington Post* counted the number and labeled him the "champion axman among Presidents." That statistic bespoke Truman's insecurities as well as his imperfect knowledge of the people who surrounded him, many of whom he'd first met when, without warning, he found himself holding the nation's highest office.

He was deferential, too much so, toward the generals and admirals of World War II, particularly the three five-stars: George Catlett Marshall, who would hold two major cabinet posts; Dwight D. Eisenhower, whom Truman turned to until they turned on each other; and, until things went very wrong, the vainglorious and charismatic Douglas MacArthur, the Pacific commander. He relied inordinately on the honorable and steadfast Dean Gooderham Acheson, his fourth, and final, secretary of state, whose certainties about the postwar world would lead Truman into some dangerous policy cul-de-sacs. To better understand Truman, it helps to see how he was affected, and guided, by these men (there were no women) and quite a few others: antagonistic members of Congress, some principled and others consumed by partisanship; atomic scientists and engineers; a generation of unusually powerful newspaper columnists who disdained Truman, the parvenu, and didn't hide it; and a coterie of Missourians—friends, cronies, and assorted hangers-on who sullied his reputation by casting doubt on his probity. One also needs to know the leaders of the Grand Alliance, not only Churchill and Stalin, but Roosevelt, whose absence was sharply felt during some of the most critical moments of Truman's White House years.

Truman liked to be known for directness and honesty—it became a trademark of sorts—but he could fudge, and even lie, when he felt cornered or embarrassed. He was not a hater, but he had a sharp temper and could be a topnotch grudge-holder, especially if someone offended his wife, Bess, or his daughter, Margaret—Mary Margaret, whom her father called "Marg" or "Margie," with a hard g. He saw himself as a defender of the Bill of Rights and talked, privately, about the danger of the FBI becoming a domestic "Gestapo." Yet, by executive order, he established a "loyalty" program that affected more than two million federal workers, and didn't entertain many second thoughts about its malign collateral damage.

Truman was the only president never to attend college, and certain gaps in his education were evident in what could be unusual readings of history. But he was highly intelligent, shrewd, and able to give close attention to the unending influx of papers that piled up on his desk. He was also a diligent student of the presidency, and his respect for it was such that he sometimes referred to "the President's

xii   THE TRIALS OF HARRY S. TRUMAN

office," as if it were a place apart. "He wouldn't be asking what I ought to do, but what should the *President* do," an aide said. He was rarely introspective, or reflective, and could be jingoistic and reactive, but then he'd come out with a burst of insightfulness or good humor. He could laugh with others, and at himself: "I have appointed a Secretary for Columnists," he wrote in his diary. "His duties are to listen to all radio commentators, read all columnists in the newspapers from ivory tower to lowest gossip, coordinate them and give me the results so I can run the United States and the World as it should be." He was the most approachable of postwar presidents, and the least self-important: "There were several thousand people at the airport in Paducah, all of whom wanted to see Jumbo, the Cardiff giant, the President of the United States," he wrote, after a visit to Kentucky. "It is a most amazing spectacle, this worship of high office." He never shed the romantic idea that America was a land of community, democratic values, opportunity, and don't-fence-me-in freedom. Yet he once said that it might someday be necessary for the government to seize control of the press, much as he would one day seize the nation's steel mills.

Since Truman's death, in late 1972, a consensus has built among historians that he was a "near great" president, with full-fledged greatness usually reserved for the likes of George Washington or Abraham Lincoln, and perhaps Franklin Roosevelt, although those rankings, always in flux, can be a little silly. Truman's standing reflects the applauded events of his time in office, including the postwar rebuilding of Europe through the Marshall Plan; the founding of the United Nations; establishing a stable North Atlantic military alliance; recognition of Israel. As a domestic leader, he wanted programs to expand the social and economic benefits of the New Deal—an impulse that led to several attempts to create a national health insurance program—and he was committed to equality for African Americans. He believed that he understood the "common, everyday citizen" as well as anyone in public life, and on that score may very well have been right.

But when Truman left office, his approval rating, after many climbs and dips, stood at a record low of 31 percent, and at one point fell to sixteen percent. There were good reasons for that, just as there are good reasons why his ranking has climbed sharply. Reassessments never end, and those numbers are bound to see further permutations as the past is approached from different vantage points. As the historian Amos Elon wrote, "Hindsight is not necessarily the best guide to understanding what really happened." That shifting picture of the past is what draws us to what seems, at first, the familiar story of the Truman presidency, and to watch it unfold—and surprise—as its protagonists face the astounding problems of their time.

2. The journalist John Gunther, in his 1947 time capsule, *Inside U.S.A.*, recalled the pre-presidential Truman as a "trim, small, graying man with shiny spectacles and an alert inquisitiveness." Gunther described him standing by a wall map in his Senate office and, "as affectionately as a father poring over the photograph of a beloved child, pointed out various lights and shadows, bumps and hollows, in the Missouri landscape political and otherwise." Missouri has 114 counties, but Truman was most familiar with the landscape of Jackson County, in the western part of the state. He knew the territory the way William Faulkner knew his imagined Yoknapatawpha County. The roots of Truman's life, his outlook, and his family, can be found there, particularly within a thirty-five-mile radius that encompasses the city of Independence and parts of Kansas City.

It's most useful to know just a few things about Truman's childhood and young manhood. One is that his father, John Anderson Truman, born in 1851, had a quick, fighting temper, and that his life turned into a series of disappointments and unrealized ambitions. He was a farmer, a livestock trader, a speculator in grain futures, a local road overseer, and a dabbler in Democratic Party politics. In late December 1881, he married Martha Ellen Young, a red-headed farmer's daughter who'd reached the spinsterish age of twenty-nine. In their wedding photograph, one sees two determined people: John is seated and Martha, who at five-foot-six was two inches taller than her husband, is standing to his right. She's the one likely to hold your attention. What can't be seen beyond the portrait of a strong nineteenth-century farmwoman is how unusual she was for her place and time. For one thing, she'd been to college—Central Female College, a Baptist institution in Lexington, Missouri—where she studied music, art, and literature. Books and music were embedded in her. She was particularly attentive to her first child, Harry S. (the stand-alone initial honors the names of two grandparents), born on May 8, 1884, in Lamar, Missouri. Two more children followed: John Vivian (known as Vivian), born in 1886, and Mary Jane, in 1889.

John and Martha had grown up during a time of warfare along the Kansas-Missouri border, serial conflicts that were among the most vicious ever fought on American ground. In the 1850s, guerrilla bands—Kansas "jayhawkers," who supported the antislavery Free-Stater cause, and the pro-slavery Missouri "bushwhackers"—engaged in robbery, murder, and a variety of atrocities, none of which surpassed a massacre in Lawrence, Kansas, where, on August 21, 1854, a psychopathic former schoolteacher, William Clarke Quantrill, who was to become a Confederate guerrilla leader, told his men to "Kill every male and burn every house." Before Quantrill and his raiders escaped across the Missouri border, they had murdered nearly 200 men and boys and burned 185 buildings. The fighting and lawlessness only brushed the six-hundred-acre Young family farm, in Grandview, though it was situated just forty miles from Lawrence. The Trumans and Youngs were farmers, after all, not soldiers, but also Missourians with Confederate sympathies, which were passed down to their children, and baked into them.

Harry loved to read, though it's hard to believe his claim that, when he was thirteen, he'd been through "all the books in his home town library including the International and Britanica [sic] Encyclopedia." His mother gave him a set of illustrated books called *Great Men and Famous Women*, which influenced him well past boyhood. He admired Hannibal, Cyrus the Great, George Washington, Robert E. Lee—an eclectic grouping—and had a special affinity for Gustavus Adolphus, the King of Sweden during the Thirty Years' War. "They may look like an ill-considered group," he once said, "but if you notice, they have two things in common: each of them is the best in his line, and they all have that mysterious power that makes men ready to follow them into hell, if necessary." As a reader, he was handicapped by a mysterious condition which an ophthalmologist called "flat eyeball," an acute sort of myopia that Truman called a "deformity." His doctor prescribed thick lenses, and told Truman to avoid rough sports so as not to risk breaking his glasses.

Harry went to school twenty miles from the Grandview farm, in Independence, where, as a *Kansas City Star* story put it, "his closest friends were a studious group. . . . During the Passover they would go to Abie Viner's house and eat unleavened bread." He gave serious attention to the piano and studied the music of Mozart, Chopin, Beethoven, and Liszt. Charles Ross, another friend and classmate, who later became Truman's press secretary, remembered the sports-avoiding pianist walking to his teacher's house, carrying a music roll: "Mothers held him up as a model, so he took a lot of kidding. It required a lot of courage for a kid to take music lessons in a town like Independence." After high school, he worked in various low-paying jobs: as a timekeeper for a construction company, in the mailroom of the *Kansas City Star*, and as a clerk in the Union National Bank. His father, who had some local political connections, helped him get a page's job at the Democratic National Convention, which convened in Kansas City in 1900, when William Jennings Bryan was nominated for the second time. "He had the most remarkable voice," Truman recalled. "He could get up and tear the hide off the Republicans better than any man ever I heard." Soon after his twenty-first birthday, Harry and some of his friends joined Battery B, a new Missouri National Guard unit, in Kansas City, which might have been a lark, but turned out otherwise.

Out of financial necessity, the Truman family in 1906 moved back to the Grandview farm. Harry, who gave up city life, and a hundred-dollar-a-month job at the Union National Bank, wrote that, during the next ten years, "I had the best time I ever had in my life," and perhaps he did. But the farmhouse was small and dark; there was no electricity, and the only source of heat was a living-room stove. You either froze on below-zero winter mornings or baked in the heat of a Missouri summer. "Just think of me arising at 5:00 a.m. and making three fires on these chilly mornings," he wrote to Bess

Wallace, his future wife, in the winter of 1913. "I sleep with the windows up and shake for thirty minutes every morning when there's a fire already going." A visitor, poking around, and climbing a narrow, back staircase, will see that Harry and his brother, Vivian, must have shared a small second-floor bedroom, as well as a chamber pot that probably was stored under their bed. Harry's parents slept in the front of the house, which had a separate entrance, and his sister had a room of her own.

The farm did well—agriculture was enormously profitable in that time and place—though it probably never earned fifteen thousand dollars in one year, as Truman claimed. But it made enough so that Truman could afford a 1911 Stafford automobile. The car was a great help in Harry's nine-year, and apparently chaste, courtship of the former Elizabeth ("Bess") Virginia Wallace, whom he'd first noticed in Sunday school, in Independence, when he was six or seven. "I saw there the prettiest sweetest little girl I'd ever seen," he wrote in his diary. "I was too backward to even look at her very much and I didn't speak to her for five years. . . . If I succeeded in carrying her books to school or back home for her I had a big day." With jumbled tenses, and Victorian delicacy, he added "I'd never had another and never have."

America entered the war in Europe in April 1917, and Harry, the National Guard member, enlisted that August. The following March, he was shipped overseas, to France, where, despite poor eyesight, he was chosen to lead Battery D of the 129th Field Artillery. With the rank of captain, Truman, a Baptist and Mason, realized that he had a talent to command, in this case men he called "the wild Irish and German Catholics from . . . Kansas City." Bess by then had agreed to marry him, but they decided to wait until the war was over. "I didn't think it was right to get married and maybe come home a cripple and have the most beautiful and sweetest girl in the world tied down," Harry wrote in his diary. He promised that he "wouldn't look at the French mademoiselles," and would return "reasonably pure."

Truman's devotion to Bess was matched, perhaps overmatched, by the powerful, almost obsessive attentiveness of her mother, Margaret (Madge) Gates Wallace, who reacted to the prospect of Bess's marriage with passive-aggressive opposition. Margaret Truman thought that it came from seeing her father as "the farmer who was threatening to take her daughter away from her." Madge Wallace is sometimes portrayed as a model of nightmare mother-in-lawness, but whether or not she liked Harry (opinions differ because no one knows), she was a wounded, angry, difficult woman. She'd never gotten over the suicide, in June 1903, of David W. Wallace, her forty-three-year-old husband. The news was recounted in several regional newspapers, including the *Jackson Examiner*, which reported, with grotesque granularity, that he'd "stood in the center of the bathroom floor, placed the muzzle of the revolver back of the left ear and fired. The bullet came out over the right eye and fell into the bath tub."

That family history shamed Madge, who became something of a recluse, and may explain why she clung to her only daughter, born in 1885. After Bess and Harry were married, in 1919, at Trinity Episcopal Church in Independence, they moved to 219 North Delaware Street, a fourteen-room, two-story house built by Bess's grandparents. When the newlyweds settled in, on the second floor, Bess's grandmother and one of three younger brothers were already in residence. So was Madge.

Having been to war, and having led men with different backgrounds, gave Truman the self-confidence to see him through a number of business ventures, none of which did well. One was a partnership with a friend, Edward (Eddie) Jacobson, with whom he'd run a profitable Army base canteen—"a fine Jewish boy in my battery who had been in merchantile [sic] business in Kansas City." The friendship would endure, but the Truman & Jacobson Haberdashery, which they opened in downtown Kansas City in 1919, went bust within two years. Like John Truman, his son kept looking for ways to become successful in a relative hurry.

3. Truman may never have had a political epiphany, but he was attracted to the sociability of politics and acquired a patron: T. J. (Thomas Joseph) Pendergast, a former saloonkeeper who controlled the Democratic political machine in Kansas City. "I'm the boss," T.J. once said. "I know all the angles of organizing and every man I meet becomes my friend." Tom Pendergast became a "friend" to Truman, who'd had a wartime friendship with a Pendergast nephew, but Truman had other plusses: He was a farmer, a veteran, had local roots (the Trumans and Wallaces had relatives all over Jackson County), and was considered basically honest, though increasingly indebted to a corrupt political machine. He was also a joiner. Over the years, along with becoming a Mason (reaching the level of 33rd degree), he'd become, among other affiliations, an Elk, a Lion, and an American Legionnaire. He paid ten dollars to join the Ku Klux Klan, although when a Klansman informed Truman that the Klan was less interested in patronage than in keeping Roman Catholics from advancing in Jackson County, he changed his mind. As Richard Lawrence Miller noted, in his thorough book on Truman's early political life, he never officially became a member.

Boss Pendergast offered Truman his political start in 1922, when the party needed a candidate for eastern judge in Jackson County's three-man court. The post didn't require judicial qualifications, of which Truman had none, but it did require administrative talent, which he possessed in large measure, as well as a capacity to focus on such fine points as the best mixture of concrete and gravel required to build superior, hard-surfaced roads. Although he lost his next election, in 1924, he stayed in public life, as the president of the National Old Trails Road Association, and talked about the importance of good roads. He won the higher post of presiding judge in 1926, and again in 1930, with the *Kansas City Star* writing that he'd given the county "an able, honest and efficient administration."

But that had a two-term limit, and as 1934 approached, when Truman would turn fifty, he saw himself at a turning point. After a talk with Pendergast, he considered a new direction: to run for a safe seat in Congress (Pendergast had helped to gerrymander the district) or become a tax collector. "Congressman pays $7,500 and has to live in Washington six months a year," he told Bess. "Collector will pay $10,000 and stay at home; a political sky high career ends with eight years Collector. I have an opportunity to be a power in the nation as Congressman, I don't have to make a decision until next year. Think about it." Though he'd asked Bess for her opinion, he seems never to have seriously considered anything but Congress. Pendergast, though, reneged, and offered the congressional seat to someone else.

Then another opportunity came along: a chance, though not a very good chance, to win a United States Senate seat, when the machine's first two choices backed out. Truman's eventual, narrow win became possible when a third candidate entered the Democratic primary, but success came with a cost to his reputation. After he arrived in Washington, he was called a "Pendergast office boy," or "bellhop," or someone who'd get "calluses on his ears listening on the long distance telephone to his boss," labels that were shed slowly. He didn't try to hide his connection. Almost as soon as Truman was sworn in, a large, framed photograph of T.J. was hung in the senator's private office.

Truman very much liked being a United States senator. He thrived in an informal club that welcomed a certain breed of political man, mostly Democrats, most from small towns, who rotated in and out with each election cycle. They found in one another's company a nurturing refuge, sometimes at "Board of Education" meetings in the hideaway office of Congressman Sam Rayburn, of Bonham, Texas, who would become House speaker in 1940. Its members, some leading a virtual bachelor's life, included Vice President John Nance ("Cactus Jack") Garner, of Uvalde, Texas, who'd been a senator when Roosevelt chose him as a running mate in 1932; Senator Alben Barkley, of Paducah, Kentucky, the majority leader; and Leslie L. Biffle, of Pigott, Arkansas, the fifty-year-old secretary of the Senate, who had no official power but whose presence could be felt in the currents, and undercurrents, of the Capitol building, someone who'd mastered an ability to whisper without moving his lips. "One had to be an adopted member of the group for quite a while to realize that anything was going on under the easy gossip and badinage," Dean Acheson observed. "Then one discovered that almost everything was going on." They enjoyed poker, bourbon, with its mystical additive, "branch water" (which might come from the tap in John Nance Garner's washroom). They liked gossip, and politics, but their interests did not extend much beyond Capitol Hill and their constituents. They were content with the pleasure of their own company, and with the respect that came with the offices they held. In a letter to Bess, Truman described lonely stretches of time, broken up by visits to Griffith Stadium, the home of the Senators, the city's baseball club, or a stop at the Metropolitan Theater, at 9th and F Streets, which, before the war, offered live stage shows along with movies:

> *You were anxious about my evenings. I haven't had any this last week as we've worked every night. . . . [Senator Sherman] Minton and I went to a picture show. . . . We went to the ball game yesterday on a couple of free tickets he had, and Washington won five to two. They've been constant losers. I went up to the Metropolitan by myself and saw* Man about Town. *(Its cast included Jack Benny, Dorothy Lamour, and Eddie "Rochester" Anderson.) It is a very funny show. The nigger steals the screen.*

As that last sentence suggests, Truman was a man with casual prejudices, some that he tried to rid himself of and some that he simply couldn't.

By 1940, near the end of Truman's first term, Boss Pendergast was no longer a factor. He'd been in and out of the penitentiary, for income tax evasion, and Truman faced another three-way primary, this time against two of the men who'd helped send his patron to prison: Governor Lloyd Stark, and the prosecutor, Maurice Milligan, whose brother, Jacob, had run against Truman in 1934. To add to Truman's long odds, Roosevelt favored Stark. The Pendergast aroma could hurt Roosevelt's chance of carrying Missouri, and he let Truman know that if he'd be good enough to drop out, and avoid a nasty primary fight, he could be appointed to the Interstate Commerce Commission. "I sent word that I would run if I only got one vote—mine," Truman told Jonathan Daniels, a onetime aide and early biographer, though it's difficult to believe that he'd been so defiant of the President. Truman got career-saving help from an energetic Irishman, Robert E. Hannegan, of St. Louis, chairman of the Democratic City Committee, from which came the city's real power.

His victory was suspiciously narrow, dependent on thousands of tainted votes from St. Louis. But a win by any margin left Truman gushing with relief that he could return to the companionable Senate: "I'll never forget Tuesday night if I live to be a thousand—which I won't," he told Bess. "My sweet daughter and my sweetheart were in such misery it was torture to me. I wished then I'd never have made the fight. But it was a good fight." It was also a good fight for Hannegan, who, helped by Senator Truman, was soon rewarded with the post of collector of internal revenue for St. Louis, a seven-thousand-a-year federal job, with benefits, an appointment that the *St. Louis Post-Dispatch* called "preposterous."

After that, Truman was less a provincial back-bencher and more a legislator determined to accomplish something meaningful. With support from colleagues, he chaired a new committee—the Senate Special Committee to Investigate the National Defense Program—to examine defense budgets, cost overruns, and potential cheating by contractors, and brought to the task the focus that he'd demonstrated when he oversaw road construction in Jackson County. The Truman Committee, as it came to be known, began its work ten months before Japan attacked Pearl Harbor; before wrapping up, it had saved the nation many millions of dollars. *Time* magazine, in a 1943 cover story titled "Billion-Dollar Watchdog," described Truman as "the committee's energetic generalissimo," and his committee as giving "red faces to Cabinet members, war agency heads, generals, admirals, big businessmen, little businessmen, labor leaders."

In mid-1943, the committee's tenacious investigators stumbled upon the secret atom bomb project after noticing some unusually high expenditures in Pasco, Washington, for something called the "Manhattan Engineer District"—the Manhattan Project. That led Senator Truman to telephone Henry L. Stimson, the secretary of war, to ask what was going on. Stimson, then seventy-six, a Republican with a pedigree of public service and a reputation for rectitude, attempted to deflect Truman, telling him that he "was one of the very few men who knew what that was about and what it was intended for, and I simply couldn't tell." In their conversation, which Stimson recorded, Truman said, "You assure that this is for a specific purpose

THE TRIALS OF HARRY S. TRUMAN

and you think it's all right; that's all I need to know," and Stimson replied, "Not only for a specific purpose, but a unique purpose." Truman said "he trusted me implicitly," Stimson wrote in his diary.

But Truman could get peevish when he didn't get his way, and he wanted to know more. After all, he was a United States senator! In March 1944, he told Stimson that his committee had information that the work at Pasco "is being carried out in a wasteful manner," and that, unless it got a proper briefing, it might have to be investigated. Stimson, in his diary, took note of Truman's "ugly letter" and called him "a nuisance and a pretty untrustworthy man. He talks smoothly but he acts meanly." After Stimson informed Truman that, in refusing to share his secrets, he was "merely carrying out the express directions of the President," Truman dropped the subject.

4. Washington is a city of secrecy and untruths, all the more so during wartime. "The amount of bare-faced lying that was done in Washington in those days is beyond estimate," the educator-scientist James B. Conant recalled. "One just didn't ask an old friend whom one met at the Cosmos Club what he was doing." Certainly, the topmost secret was the development of an atomic bomb, but something else, something much harder to hide, concerned Roosevelt's health. One had only to see him at close range to suspect that he wasn't well; friends who hadn't been near him for a while were, as one put it, "shocked and horrified" by his appearance. "His shirt collar hung so loose on his neck that you could have put your hand inside it," a visitor recalled. There had been occasional newspaper stories that he was under the weather, but his White House doctor, Rear Admiral Ross T. McIntire, either lied or revealed diagnostic ineptitude when he said in early 1944 that his patient had "one of the best years since he entered the White House," and moreover that his "stamina is far above the average." These fictions were rarely questioned; no one wanted America's enemies to know that the President was enfeebled. McIntire, though, knew that Roosevelt was suffering from advanced cardiovascular disease; his assistant, Dr. Howard G. Bruenn, knew that the prognosis was exceedingly grim.

In April,1944, Roosevelt spent a month at Hobcaw Barony, a twenty-three-thousand-acre coastal plantation in Georgetown, South Carolina, owned by the seventy-three-year-old financier Bernard M. Baruch, the son of a Confederate surgeon, who enjoyed acting the role of a Southern plantation owner and loved being in the center of things (and letting everyone know it). When Roosevelt reappeared in Washington, on May 8, rumors pursued him, among them that he'd had a secret operation, or had met Churchill in London, on the eve of an anticipated Allied invasion of Europe. By June 6, the actual date for Operation Overlord, Roosevelt was back at work and pretending to mull whether to run for a fourth term.

He waited until July 11—just eight days before the Democratic Convention opened in Chicago—to reveal his unsurprising intentions to reporters who'd gathered around his office desk. He was a heavy smoker, mostly of Camels, and after he'd fitted his latest cigarette in a favorite ivory holder and had it lighted by Stephen T. Early, his press secretary, he read aloud from a letter he'd purportedly written to Robert Hannegan, who'd recently become the national Democratic Party chairman: "If the people command me to continue in this office and in this war," Roosevelt read, he was willing. He uttered these words with a straight face before he concluded, saying, "And now, if you will go out quietly—" The reporters laughed, but had one more question: "Have you found a candidate for Vice President yet?" To which Roosevelt replied, "Well, that sounds like an unfriendly question. I won't answer it."

It *was* a mildly unfriendly question. By then, Roosevelt, through indecision or the pleasures of secrecy, was tormenting the two leading candidates for the job: Henry Wallace, the incumbent, who'd replaced John Nance Garner in 1940, and the former South Carolina senator James F. Byrnes, whom Roosevelt had asked to head the Office of Economic Stabilization, and then, in May 1943, to reorganize management of the home front by establishing the Office of War Mobilization. That gave Byrnes control of rents, rationing, and the distribution of supplies, an assignment so big that journalists began referring to him as the "assistant president." Interest in the vice presidency was considerable because of the pronounced awareness that the job came with the Damoclesian possibility of succession.

Roosevelt's most awkward task was getting rid of Wallace, then fifty-five and looking slightly in need of a haircut. Before the vice presidency, Wallace had served seven years as secretary of agriculture, and before that had built the Hi-Bred Corn Company, of Des Moines, Iowa, which made him wealthy. He had been a cause for worry ever since Roosevelt, in 1940, had overruled party leaders to put him on the ticket. There was something about him, a penumbra of dreaminess, that made the very thought of a *President* Wallace alarming. The social critic Dwight Macdonald was struck by how Wallace's Presbyterian upbringing incorporated elements of Buddhism, Judaism, Zoroastrianism, Islam, and Christian Science, as well as spiritualism, numerology, and astrology. It was also hard to miss Wallace's pronounced sympathy for the Soviet Union. You did not have to be a Cold-Warrior-in-waiting to find such views troublesome, and more so because of the dreadful worry that Roosevelt would not complete his term.

Byrnes believed that, despite Wallace's incumbency, Roosevelt had promised *him* the vice presidency. But there was considerable resistance to Byrnes. Leaders of organized labor mistrusted his commitment to the rights of workers, and Roosevelt worried that "the colored question would come up and then we'd have a lot of trouble." The "colored question" was a euphemism for Byrnes's unyielding segregationist views, which troubled a lot of people, even in an era when segregation was unexceptional. Walter White, who'd led the NAACP for two decades, regarded Byrnes as a hated enemy because of what White called his "unrelenting, skilled, and uniformly successful opposition to every measure sought by Negroes," from a federal anti-lynching bill to gaining access to public accommodations and transportation. There was, in addition, an actuarial objection: Roosevelt wanted someone younger than himself, and Byrnes, at sixty-five, was three years his senior.

Byrnes's career would be unimaginable in the résumé-driven world of modern Washington, but he'd demonstrated that, in pre–World War II America, one could go far with a generous helping of intelligence and aspiration. He looked like someone's idea of a jaunty Irishman: A 1940 *Saturday Evening Post* profile described him as a short, slight man with an "odd, sharply angular face from which his sharp eyes peer out with an expression of quizzical geniality." He'd been reared in Charleston, where his mother took in sewing to support the household. His formal education ended when he left school at the age of fourteen, but his mother taught him shorthand, which he mastered well enough to become a court reporter—a job that led him to study for the bar exam. The *New York Times* editor Turner Catledge, who was born and reared in Mississippi and felt a kinship with Byrnes, called him the "smartest politician I knew." He liked to drop by for a drink at Byrnes's office, or his apartment in the Shoreham Hotel, for what they called "bullbat time"—named for a Southern bird that comes out around twilight. Sometimes the two Southerners would sing hymns and old ballads. Catledge recalled that Byrnes took shorthand notes of every conversation, and "then he'd review them at night." Byrnes's biographer David Robertson called the shorthand a "defensive" tactic, "more a private language to himself than a record to be shared with others."

Byrnes had served seven terms in the House, beginning in 1910, and was elected to the Senate in 1930. Roosevelt had considered him for the vice presidency once before, in 1940. But Byrnes's chances were damaged by his having left the Catholic Church and becoming an Episcopalian, which risked alienating both Catholic and non-Catholic voters. In 1941, Roosevelt appointed him to the Supreme Court—a great leap for someone who'd never finished secondary school or sat on the bench. Byrnes, though, was bored by the judiciary, and sixteen months later, having left no discernible mark on the court and with the nation at war, he was brought into the administration by Roosevelt. Byrnes's impressive record seemed to qualify him for the vice presidency, apart from all that made him an unacceptable pick.

The Bronx political boss Ed Flynn, who'd been New York's secretary of state when FDR was governor, was among the first to urge Roosevelt to jettison Wallace, and to see that Senator Truman offered many advantages. His labor record was better than Byrnes's,

his border state background much safer, and everyone had heard of
the Truman Committee. Above all, he was unlikely to do much damage to the ticket. Roosevelt had also been thinking along those lines,
and the newspapers had begun to pick up the speculation. Truman,
aware of this talk, proclaimed his disinterest, which may have been
the most effective way to campaign for the job.

Roosevelt sometimes dodged arguments by smiling and nodding
and saying things like "Thanks for taking the trouble to come in and
give me your slant on this," but he'd gotten into a difficult spot by
making promises that he needed to break. He asked Samuel Rosenman, a senior adviser, to tell Wallace he was out—that "I'd like to
have him as my running mate, but I simply cannot risk creating a
permanent split in the party." He asked Postmaster General Frank
Walker, a longtime confidant, to tell Byrnes the same thing—that
"I'm sorry it has to be that way." Before the end of what turned into
a long dinner discussion on a hot July night, during which many
names were proposed, Roosevelt, as if the thought had just occurred
to him, said, "Boys, I guess it's Truman."

When the Democratic National Convention opened in Chicago,
on Monday, July 17, the twenty-year-old Margaret Truman wrote
in her diary, "We are on our way to Chicago. Hope it will be fun,
but probably not very exciting." Roosevelt, meanwhile, had set off
on a journey west in his private railroad car, the *Ferdinand Magellan*, a specially constructed Pullman that was outfitted with armored
plating, three-inch bulletproof glass, a bath, and an elevator that
enabled him to board in his wheelchair. By then, he'd let the convention's chairman know, in his circuitous way, that he wouldn't be
supporting Wallace: "If I were a delegate," he wrote, he, personally,
would vote for Wallace's renomination, but, stepping back from any
responsibility, he added, "Obviously the convention must do the deciding," and he hoped that it would give "great consideration to the
pros and cons of its choice." On that same Monday, with Truman
still insisting that he had no designs on the vice presidency, Byrnes
told Truman that *he* was Roosevelt's choice, and asked Truman to
nominate him. By the next day, though, Truman no longer sounded
uninterested in the job for himself. After the Missouri caucus voted,

unanimously, to draft him, Margaret in her diary wrote, "Ye Gods!" But while Byrnes apparently believed that he remained Roosevelt's first choice, there was at least one big problem—"one thing we forgot," Hannegan told him. "The President said, 'Clear it with Sidney'"—Sidney Hillman, who ran the influential political action committee for the Congress of Industrial Organizations (CIO). Hannegan later denied that the words "clear it with Sidney," or any variation, were ever uttered by Roosevelt, but uttered or not, labor leaders, had made clear that they couldn't support Byrnes, after which, as his friend Turner Catledge wrote in the *Times*, "his stock appeared to slip markedly."

Truman later told Jonathan Daniels that, when Hannegan informed him that Roosevelt wanted him on the ticket, he'd replied, "Tell him to go to hell. I'm for Jimmy Byrnes." That was Truman at his most inflated. The likely version is that Roosevelt, speaking by telephone in a voice loud enough to be heard by everyone in a hotel room, said he wanted Truman on the ticket to avoid a party split. Truman's initial response, which can be read in many ways, was something like "Oh, shit," but he certainly offered no objection. In his diary he wrote that he was "forced into it by Pres. Roosevelt himself," and that became the version he decided to stick with.

On Wednesday, July 19, Byrnes formally, and sulkily, withdrew his name "in deference to the wishes of the President," and Roosevelt the next day was renominated, for a fourth term. Truman watched the balloting from a box, alongside Bess and Margaret, though he took a break to get a hot dog. Alistair Cooke, the American correspondent of the *Manchester Guardian*, was at a lunch counter when the nomination was settled, and recalled, "Next to me was a lobster in steel-rimmed glasses—a solid, square little man in a sky-blue double-breasted suit and polka-dot tie. In one hand he had a Coke bottle and in the other a hotdog dripping mustard like butterscotch sauce." When a voice in the hall kept asking "the next Vice President" to come to the rostrum and the organist started to play the "Missouri Waltz," the man in the blue jacket "jammed the bottle on the counter, took a final lick at the mustard, dumped the hotdog in a trash basket and said, 'By golly, that's me!'" Hold that picture—that snapshot of a sixty-year-old legislator from Jackson County who'd just been nominated for the nation's second-highest office—and then try to forget it.

5. Before the 1944 convention, Roosevelt and Truman had barely been acquainted. Years before, when the Roosevelts invited Senator and Mrs. Truman to one of their nonstop White House dinners, Bess stayed home. She didn't say so publicly, but Washington's fast lane made her uncomfortable. Her absence surely went unnoticed in a crowd that included members of Congress, many with their wives, as well as cabinet officers, and Richard E. Byrd, the polar explorer—a "very spiffy affair," Truman thought. Insofar as socializing with Roosevelt went, that was about it. In fact, after the convention, by my count, Truman and Roosevelt saw each other eight times, but—with just one exception—only in the company of many others.

"I don't think I saw Roosevelt but twice as Vice-President except at Cabinet meetings," Truman told Jonathan Daniels, adding that "Cabinet members, if they had anything to discuss, tried to see him privately after the meetings." He complained to Henry Wallace that Roosevelt never took him into his confidence—"They didn't tell me anything about what was going on." According to James Roosevelt, the President's oldest son, "Father felt Harry had done some good work in the Senate, but he still regarded him as a . . . small-town Midwesterner who in no way was big enough to become president. I don't think Father thought about him that much." Truman could not have forgotten that Roosevelt had nearly ordered him to withdraw from his 1940 Senate race, which helps to explain why, even after 1945, he'd refer to Roosevelt as a "fakir" (a favorite, albeit misused, Truman word) or a self-promoter or an "egotist." Truman kept these views fairly private; like other politicians, he could bubble with admiration when it suited him. For all that, he was susceptible to Roosevelt's charm.

They had their first, and only, face-to-face meal well before the election, on a hot, humid August 18: "The Pres. took his coat off and I had to," Truman wrote to Margaret. "Told him if I'd known that was what he intended to do I'd have put on a clean shirt and he said he had that very morning." They sat on the South Lawn, under a magnolia tree that was supposedly uprooted from Tennessee, where it had been planted by Andrew Jackson to honor his late wife. An AP photograph shows FDR, in a white shirt and polka-dot bowtie, looking pretty much like his best old self. They discussed the post-war jobs outlook, some pending bills, and the upcoming campaign. Lunch lasted seventy minutes.

Truman recounted more of this for Bess and Margaret: how he'd arrived five minutes early, how Roosevelt was so nice that "You'd have thought I was the long lost brother or the returned Prodigal." Truman told Roosevelt how much he appreciated him for "putting the finger on me for V.P." Then "the movie men and then the flash-light boys" worked until the President "got tired or hungry and said 'now boys one more, that's enough.'" The President's daughter, Anna Roosevelt Boettiger, who took on the role of hostess when her mother was away, had expected Bess to be there. When Tru-man explained that she was in Missouri, Roosevelt, who guessed the truth, told him that Eleanor had once been very timid and that, when he first ran for governor of New York, she wouldn't go to political meetings or make speeches. "Now," he said, "she talks all the time." FDR also gave him "a lot of hooey" about what Truman could do in the fall presidential campaign.

"He's still the leader he's always been, and don't let anybody kid you about it," Truman told reporters after the meal. "He's keen as a briar." He was more honest with his friend Harry Hawkins Vaughan, with whom he'd served during the war, and who, on the path to becoming Truman's perpetual buddy, was working in Truman's Sen-ate office. "His hands are shaking and he talks with considerable difficulty," he told Vaughan. "It doesn't seem to be any mental lapse of any kind, but physically he's just going to pieces." Roosevelt, he thought, "talked like a phonograph record played at the wrong speed." He didn't say anything about this to Bess, who would only have worried about the implications for her husband. The subject of Roosevelt's health was always raised gingerly by reporters, but inti-mations of mortality were in the air. On October 8, Wendell Willkie, the 1940 Republican presidential nominee, died, of a heart ailment. He was fifty-two, ten years younger than Roosevelt.

Truman wasn't much of a campaigner, though perhaps not as shaky as William Shannon and Robert Allen made him out to be when they wrote that he "read his ghostwritten speeches slowly and mechanically, as if he were translating them from Hindustani as he went along." He was better without a script, though he could be loose with facts. One October day, in El Paso, Texas, he seemed to blame World War I on Warren G. Harding, who'd succeeded Woodrow Wilson, in 1921—two years after the Armistice. "You can't afford to take a chance on another Harding," Truman said. He could sometimes seem recessive in the company of more colorful politicians. An aide to the New York mayor Fiorello La Guardia recalled Truman visiting City Hall, in the fall of 1944, after delivering a campaign speech. La Guardia sometimes liked to keep visitors waiting, and the aide remembered being "surprised to find Truman standing shyly alone, his hands thrust into his pockets, staring out of the window toward the cross section of Broadway and Chambers Street."

On November 8, 1944, the Roosevelt-Truman ticket defeated the Republicans—New York governor Thomas E. Dewey and Ohio governor John W. Bricker—by an electoral landslide and a margin of three million votes. In Kansas City, radio listeners who tuned in to hear from Roosevelt's running mate, instead heard Mozart's Ninth Sonata. Then the announcer introduced the piano player: Truman. "Here was a man waiting to be Vice President," a newspaperman recalled, "and he was playing Mozart instead of biting his nails. He played it very nicely."

The inaugural ceremony, on the South Portico of the White House, was a minimalist affair, unfollowed by parades. It was a cold day; in 1937, the inaugural date had been switched from March to January. Some eight thousand guests, some in galoshes, stood on the snow-covered South Lawn, and thousands more watched from outside the distant gates. Truman was sworn in by Henry Wallace, who'd agreed to join the cabinet, as secretary of commerce. Roosevelt, bareheaded, was given the oath by Chief Justice Harlan F. Stone. He never smiled, and seemed, to Truman, to be in pain. The

New York Times reporter Cabell Phillips recalled Roosevelt "standing gaunt, gray, and hollow-eyed . . . supported by his son James," a sight that made onlookers uneasy. He spoke for six minutes, one of the shortest inaugural addresses ever. The ceremony was followed by a buffet lunch for favored invitees, among them Bernard Baruch, Edith (Mrs. Woodrow) Wilson, thirteen Roosevelt grandchildren, and Helen Keller, who, although she could neither see nor hear, admired a blue plume on a hat worn by Grace Tully, Roosevelt's personal secretary. The President stayed for about twenty minutes, leaving hand-shaking duties to Eleanor and the Trumans.

Two days later, Roosevelt set off by rail, sea, and air, to Yalta, in the Crimea, for a meeting with Churchill and Stalin, travel plans that were kept secret. His entourage included his daughter, Anna; Jimmy Byrnes, whose invitation may have been a form of apology; and the Bronx boss Ed Flynn, whose presence was altogether baffling. Truman on January 22 received a "highly confidential" memorandum from Roosevelt, telling him "If you have any urgent messages which you wish to get to me, I suggest you send them through the White House Map Room. However, only *absolutely urgent* messages should be sent." He furthermore told Truman to keep his radio messages "as brief as possible"; long messages might have to be sent by pouch. In other words, please don't bother me.

Years later, Truman recalled a fantasy version of Roosevelt, someone who'd confided in him, and with whom he'd chatted about books and historical arcana. "We discussed such episodes in history as the turning back of the Turks at Vienna, and how Genghis Khan was stopped before he could reach Austria," Truman wrote. "These were the things we talked about when we were through with our business. Roosevelt was just as interested as I was in history, and knew more about certain phases of it than I did." It's fair to assume that Truman yearned for such a connection, because he made it up with such conviction.

───❧───

Truman discovered that a vice president's life was sweet, and even Bess began to be drawn to the pleasures of flattering attention. By tradition, a president didn't accept invitations to private functions, which made the Trumans the ranking "diners out," a role they didn't shy from. "Not since the days of Charlie Curtis"—Herbert Hoover's vice president—"have we had a 'social' V.P.—and the town's hostesses are licking their chops," the *Washington Post* reported, explaining how things had changed for the worse, in 1933, when the John Nance Garners settled in. "Everyone knew they never stepped out of the Washington Hotel after 9 o'clock," and after that came the war and Vice President Wallace. Then along came "the likeable Mr. Truman (whose natty scrubbed looks are quite a contrast to that of his two predecessors)."

The Trumans may have reached a social apogee on February 17, 1945, when Evalyn Walsh McLean invited a hundred and fifty people to meet them. Mrs. McLean, the fifty-eight-year-old widow of Edward McLean, a former owner of the *Washington Post* and the *Cincinnati Enquirer*, could lure just about anyone to Friendship House, at 3308 R Street. (The original Friendship House, an estate on upper Wisconsin Avenue, was demolished during the war and became the apartment complex called McLean Gardens.) Evalyn McLean owned the Hope Diamond, a deep blue gem with a convoluted international provenance, a stone that later went on view at the Smithsonian Institution.

This was not Truman's bourbon-and-branch-water crowd, although a number of his Senate colleagues made it onto Mrs. McLean's guest list. So did Supreme Court justices, military officers, and ambassadors, as well as Lauritz Melchior of the Metropolitan Opera and J. Edgar Hoover, the director of the FBI. The *Kansas City Star* announced the McLean party on its front page, where, under the headline "Social Spotlight Falls on the Missouri Plowboy," it also hinted at the possible abuse of ration tickets at "one of the most sumptuous feasts since the war." Mrs. George Mesta—Perle Mesta, an Oklahoma oilman's daughter who became known as the "hostess with the mostest"—showed her competitive social muscle by giving a dinner for the Trumans at the Sulgrave Club, with an orchestra, a ventriloquist, and the operatic soprano Rosa Ponselle, who persuaded the vice president to become her accompanist after she climbed onto a piano and attempted to sing like the torch singer Helen Morgan. In March, a correspondent for the *Chicago Tribune* wrote that Truman had "shed the customary cocoon of Vice Presidential anonymity and emerged as the capital's No. 1 social butterfly," and that, since the inauguration, his name had appeared more often on the society pages than that of any other Washingtonian. That statistic would have been hard to verify in the pre-Google age, but Truman was increasingly found in company in which he'd never before been found.

His role as the city's number one diner-out included a benefit for the National Press Club Servicemen's Canteen, where the movie star Lauren Bacall "perched" on a piano while the vice president played a serenade and a Marine allegedly "sighed" to a sailor, "Wow, she's really a sizzler!" A photograph of Bacall, her legs well displayed, smiling down at the piano player, did not please Bess. Truman was also getting friendly attention from, among others, the *Christian Science Monitor* columnist Roscoe Drummond, who wrote, "While he does not count himself a heavy thinker, Mr. Truman knows what is going on in Washington, has a genuine grasp of national affairs and is an informed interpreter of Administration policy." Drummond could be an observant reporter, but, like so many of his colleagues, he could also be solicitous of people in power.

From February 4 to 11, while the Trumans were immersed in social Washington, Roosevelt was in Yalta, in the Crimea, a locale chosen because Stalin had refused to travel far from home. It had been an arduous journey. "If we had spent ten years on research we could not have found a worse place in the world than Yalta," Churchill said. Dr. Howard Bruenn was to write that conditions at the Livadia Palace, the site for talks, were "wholly unsanitary, as the Germans had left the building infested with vermin."

The three had met once before, in Tehran, in November 1943, when the liberation of Europe was still a year off. Now they knew that the war with Germany was nearly won and that victory over Japan was inevitable, although at an uncertain cost. What remained was the aftermath, including questions of reparations, a new "world security" organization—the United Nations—and the possible dismemberment of Germany. In Tehran, Roosevelt had said, "You either have to castrate the German people or you have got to treat them in such a manner so that they just can't go on reproducing people who want to continue the way they have in the past." The future of Poland, its boundaries and governance, was an issue contentious enough to come up for discussion at seven of the eight plenary sessions. The agenda of a London-based Polish government-in-exile, formed during the war, was very different from that of the pro-Soviet "Lublin" government. Although it was finally agreed that the "London Poles" should have a role in the government, it was an agreement that Stalin would never honor. Roosevelt understood, and Truman was to learn, that Stalin regarded Poland's geography as inseparable from Russia's security.

Roosevelt's voyage home included more meetings: with King Farouk, of Egypt; Haile Selassie, of Ethiopia; and, in the Suez Canal, with the first Saudi king, Abdul Aziz ibn Saud. It also included a death at sea: Roosevelt's devoted, and protective, appointments secretary, General Edwin "Pa" Watson. The ship docked in Newport News, Virginia, on February 27, and, at six the next morning, Roosevelt arrived, by train, at the Bureau of Printing and Engraving "station," near the White House—an arrival preceded by rumors that it was the President who'd died at sea.

At noon the next day—March 1—Roosevelt went to the Capitol, to report to Congress. He delivered an odd, almost conversational speech, which he began by referring to the polio he'd contracted in 1921 and his decision not to stand while he spoke. "I know that you will realize it makes it a lot easier for me in not having to carry about ten pounds of steel on the bottom of my legs," he said. A couple of times, he appeared to lose his place and wandered away from the text. The cadences were Roosevelt's, but the words were not delivered by the vigorous man who'd led the nation since 1933. Mrs. Roosevelt saw the decision to sit in the well of the House as significant: It meant that her husband "had accepted a certain degree of invalidism." A decade later, Truman said it was *his* suggestion that Roosevelt stay seated. Such a conversation, though not disprovable, is inconceivable. It was a way for Truman, with the same imagination that recalled him bullshitting with Roosevelt about history, to burnish the past.

At the March 21 White House Correspondents' dinner, the *New York Times* correspondent Allen Drury thought Truman "looked spick and span in a dark suit with a handkerchief, carefully folded so that exactly four corners showed, stuck in his breast pocket, beginning to seem, already, like a man who is getting a great deal of experience in the social life"; and that Roosevelt, who seemed to enjoy the entertainment by Danny Kaye, Jimmy Durante, and Fanny Brice, looked "old and thin and scrawny-necked." The President the next day left for Warm Springs, Georgia, where for twenty years he'd been treated for the effects of infantile paralysis. His only contact with the vice president came after Truman, on April 5, asked for a bit of friendly patronage: "Hope you are having a good rest. Hate to bother you," Truman wrote. He thought that his friend Bob Hannegan was "entitled to recognition" for his good campaign work, that Roosevelt should appoint him postmaster general, and that Frank Walker, who held the post, should become federal loan administrator. Roosevelt, at his noncommittal best, replied two days later: "I think your idea has a lot of merit in it and as soon as I get back I will talk with Frank."

6. On April 11, 1945, Truman wrote home to say how busy he was, having to answer letters and greet people—"just as fast as they can go through the office without seeming to hurry them." As for his sole constitutional duty, to preside over the Senate, "it's my job to get 'em prayed for . . . and then get the business to going by staying in the chair for an hour." As vice president, he was entitled to an office, on the Senate side of the Capitol, but he still liked to end his afternoons by making his way to the House and to Speaker Rayburn's "Board of Education" hideaway. There, somebody would pour bourbon and branch water, and life was good.

The next day, April 12, a Thursday, Truman started another letter home, urging his mother and sister to "Turn on your radio tomorrow night . . . at 9:30 your time and you'll hear Harry make a Jefferson Day address to the nation." His more limited task was to introduce Roosevelt, who was to deliver the radio speech. Truman had otherwise been looking forward to a poker game that evening at the Statler Hotel, a prospect to make him smile. But there was a last-minute change in the schedule. Edward McKim, another Truman war buddy, who was to join the game, heard from Harry Vaughan, who informed him that the vice president had gotten a call from the White House. "He'll have to answer that," Vaughan said, "but we'll be a little bit late."

The call was from Steve Early, Roosevelt's press secretary, who wanted Truman to telephone the White House "right away." Early asked him to come to 1600 Pennsylvania Avenue "as quickly and as *quietly*" as possible, after which a member of Truman's staff watched his smile vanish: "He just jammed his hat on his head and rushed out. He just said, 'I'm going to the White House' and he was through the door like a flash." By then, Early had telephoned the three major wire services with a "Flash," the designation for news of utmost urgency. First reports were that, at about 1 p.m., on this mild spring day, while sitting for a portrait inside the Little White House, his retreat at Warm Springs, Roosevelt had said, "I have a terrific headache"—probably his last words. Two hours later, at the age of sixty-three, Roosevelt was dead of what was described as a massive cerebral hemorrhage.

It was nearly dark when Truman was driven to the White House grounds, followed, as Jonathan Daniels later wrote, "by the personages who constituted the government of the United States," who raced past the guarded gate. Truman was taken to Mrs. Roosevelt's second-floor sitting room, where, when Truman asked what he could do, Mrs. Roosevelt replied, "Tell us what *we* can do." That Truman-Roosevelt exchange, which appears in most accounts of those moments, was followed by practical matters, among them that Truman had to be sworn in as soon as possible. He telephoned Bess, who was at their second-story apartment, at 4701 Connecticut Avenue. He told her the President was dead and that he was sending a car. Bess and Margaret were quickly en route, but the six-mile drive from upper Connecticut Avenue to the White House added more delay—"quite a long wait," Secretary of War Stimson thought.

Truman, neatly dressed as always, wore a light gray business suit and a blue bow tie, with a blue-and-white handkerchief showing from a pocket. Close by were members of the Roosevelt cabinet—most of whom would soon be gone—and such familiar faces as Les Biffle, the secretary of the Senate. Truman looked nervous and pale and held on to a small Bible that had come from Roosevelt's office. Standing across from Chief Justice Stone, who wore a black suit, he raised his right hand, then lowered it to grip the Bible. At first, he seemed unable to repeat the oath. Then he reached into a pocket for a slip of paper, a cheat sheet with the words he needed to recite. He stood stiffly, the Bible in his left hand, and when he'd finished, with the words "So help me God!" he shook Stone's hand. Stone said simply, "Mr. President." Bess Truman was weeping, and it doesn't take a mind reader to know that the tears were not entirely for the dead president and his family.

He became "President Truman" at 7:09 p.m., and after that met with the cabinet officers. At first no one said anything, but Henry Morgenthau Jr., the treasury secretary for most of Roosevelt's three terms, aimed a nod of his head at Secretary of State Edward R. Stettinius, the ranking cabinet officer—a nudge that he ought to say something. Stettinius, who'd been appointed by Roosevelt just three months before, said they all supported Truman. Secretary of Labor Frances Perkins, who was close to the Roosevelt family, was "quietly praying," and sobbed throughout the meeting. Before Stimson left, he spoke briefly to Truman. Considering their terse communications over the past eighteen months, it was not a complete surprise when the secretary of war said that they needed to talk "about an immense project that was under way." But there was no time then to get into that. The Trumans soon led a procession, which raced out to their Connecticut Avenue apartment, where the President ate a roast beef sandwich in a neighbor's apartment.

On Friday morning, Jonathan Daniels came to the Oval Office with papers that, on an ordinary day, he would have given to Roosevelt, who would have been at the two-pillared "Resolute" desk where Truman was sitting. "The desk had been swept clean of the toys and bric-a-brac which Roosevelt had left when he went off to Warm Springs," Daniels recalled. "It seemed still Roosevelt's desk and Roosevelt's room. It seemed to me, indeed, almost Roosevelt's sun which came in the wide south windows and touched Truman's thick glasses. I remember that his eyes were magnified by them. Also, I remember that he swung around in the President's chair as if he were testing it."

In the afternoon, Truman went to the Capitol, for a lunch that he'd asked Les Biffle to arrange. The Vermont senator George Aiken, a Republican, recalled that Truman "hung on to me and the tears ran right down his cheek. He kept saying, 'I am not big enough for this job, I'm not big enough for this job.'" To reporters who'd trailed him to the Capitol, Truman asked, "Have you ever had a bull or a load of hay fall on you? Well, I felt as though the moon and the stars and all the planets fell on me last night when I got the news." He added, "I don't know if you newspaper men ever pray. But if you do, please pray for me." That appeal, much quoted and repeated, was Truman at his most modest, stunned, and frightened. It reflected the mood of the city. "It was almost . . . a physical shock to the entire community, that permeated the atmosphere in a way that I've never known before or since," a Pentagon official recalled. "Even the declaration of war didn't compare, the shock waves, that seemed to be going around us everywhere with our war leader suddenly dead." Federal workers, finding it hard to concentrate, began taking annual leave. Distracted elevator operators in government buildings were letting people off at the wrong floor.

When Truman returned to the White House, another visitor was waiting for him: Jimmy Byrnes who, just before Roosevelt died, had resigned his post at the Office of War Mobilization and returned to his home, in Spartanburg, South Carolina. "I greeted him as an old friend," Truman recalled, and during the half hour they spent together, he asked Byrnes about the Yalta conference. Despite the invitation to Yalta, Byrnes remained bitter about the way he'd been treated by Roosevelt. "He has not hesitated to gut every friend he had," Byrnes told a friend. After Byrnes heard the news, he'd hurried back to Washington. "It is a world tragedy," he said to reporters. "At the moment my personal regret is such that I would not trust myself to make a statement. I am so distressed." One can read that as an expression of grief, but Byrnes's distress certainly encompassed the ache that one feels at an important missed chance: his absence from the line of succession. He said he was ready to give the new president any assistance he might want. "I'm just private citizen James F. Byrnes," he told reporters, trying to sound like an ingenuous volunteer.

That pose wasn't likely to last. Newspaper stories were already suggesting that Byrnes would become a high-level adviser, as Harry Hopkins had been to Roosevelt, or that he'd replace Secretary of State Stettinius, who was widely regarded as an affable amateur, though one who, with his strong features and white hair, had been favored since birth with the countenance of a serious man. Byrnes, in Yalta, had been little more than spectator, kibitzer, and, with his shorthand skills, a note-taker. But simply having been there, with Roosevelt, gave him a cloak of gravitas. He quickly prepared for Truman a morocco-bound volume of his shorthand summaries, entitled *The Crimean Conference*, which he labeled "Top Secret." It included a memorandum that described Roosevelt's willingness to admit two Soviet republics—Ukraine and White Russia—to the future United Nations, thus giving the Soviets three Communist-bloc votes in the General Assembly. Byrnes's excited advice was that this information "should be kept under lock and key" lest it fall into the hands of "the columnists," and "start a war on several fronts."

Roscoe Drummond, with a well-aimed dart of flattery, wrote that bringing Byrnes into the administration's "inner counsels" suggested "both wisdom and bigness" on Truman's part. Byrnes and Truman had never been intimate friends, and uneasy feelings between them had lingered since the convention. But from the time that Truman had arrived in Washington as a freshman senator, in 1935, Byrnes had seemed to him an impressive figure, a self-confident leader. Truman once called him "the best all-round official" he'd ever met. No one doubted the hold that Byrnes seemed to have on people for whom he worked, and the insinuating charm he possessed.

∽∞∽

The train from Warm Springs, bearing Roosevelt's coffin, arrived at Union Station on an unseasonably warm and humid Saturday morning, and was carried to the White House on a horse-drawn caisson. A late-afternoon service in the East Room was attended by two hundred people, who sat in gold-backed chairs. Robert Sherwood, the playwright and Roosevelt speechwriter, noticed that when Truman entered the room, no one stood—not out of disrespect, Sherwood believed, but because those present "could not yet associate him with his high office; all they could think of was that the President was dead." Everyone stood for Eleanor Roosevelt, dressed in black, who was with Anna and Elliott Roosevelt, the only one of the four Roosevelt sons to make it home from overseas duty. An empty wheelchair was off to the side.

The three Trumans—Harry, Bess, and Margaret—were joined by Truman's friend Harry Vaughan. After the Inaugural, Vaughan was transferred from Truman's Senate office to become the first-ever vice-presidential military aide, with the rank of colonel. On this occasion, Colonel Vaughan wore heavy gold *fourragère*, a noisy sartorial display. Harry Hopkins, who'd been Roosevelt's closest aide and was being treated at the Mayo Clinic for stomach cancer, appeared, Sherwood recalled, "like death . . . a dreadful cold white," and looked as if he was about to faint. The service, which included two hymns, was over in twenty-three minutes. As the Truman family walked to a waiting car that would take them to their apartment, the new president realized that he'd forgotten his hat. That's what aides were for: Harry Vaughan soon came running, hat in hand.

At a little past 10 p.m., along with the official party, the Trumans boarded an overnight train to Hyde Park, where Roosevelt was to be buried on Sunday morning. Harry Hopkins was too exhausted to make the trip, but there were no other obvious absences. As the train headed north, Byrnes was busy, giving Truman his impressions of Yalta, but also staking a claim on a return to power. Gertrude Lash, whose husband was close to Mrs. Roosevelt, noticed that Byrnes "never left Truman's side." Francis Biddle, the attorney general, recalled approaching Truman in the train and seeing that Byrnes, along with Hannegan, "clung to him as if they were afraid that he might be captured by someone else." In Truman's eyes, Byrnes was a man who'd not only been the "assistant president" but, perhaps as well as anyone, understood Washington, and the nature of its intrigues, through which Byrnes had suffered and advanced. Unlike Truman,

Byrnes already knew about the atomic bomb, which he'd regarded with a crafty politician's worry that, if it didn't work, his Office of War Mobilization might be blamed for a two-billion-dollar failure. "I know little of the project," he'd written to Roosevelt, in March, as if to make sure his ass was covered, "except that it is supported by eminent scientists," and that "even eminent scientists may continue a project rather than concede its failure."

The next day—Monday, April 16—the neophyte president addressed a joint session of Congress. He spoke slowly, and with firm intent. With his unmistakable border-state twang, soft and slightly high-pitched, it was far from the resonant voice to which the nation had grown accustomed. He called Roosevelt "a great man who loved, and was beloved by, all humanity," and said that "no man could possibly fill the tremendous void left by the passing of that noble soul." The applause was loudest when he said that the war would continue "until no vestige of resistance remains." Afterward, in a letter home, he told his mother and sister that he was frightened—"almost as scared" as he'd been when he was told that Roosevelt was dead—but "it seemed to go over all right," and "maybe it will come out all right."

7. How it came out is the subject of this book, and at the heart of the narrative is Harry S. Truman, a complicated man concealed behind a mask of down-home forthrightness and folksy language, who'd say something was "right good" rather than just "good." There was a peppiness to him—the newsreels caught that. He walked with a rapid, soldierly gait, eyes straight ahead, often smiling, managing to exude confidence despite what a top aide called a "wholesome sense of inadequacy" and a belief that "nobody is really big enough to be President." He started off like someone who'd made a wrong turn into the wrong place—an alien among the Ivy Leaguers of New Deal Washington, or a scrappy artillery captain among the illustrious generals of World War II. He understood that he could never emulate Roosevelt, and privately said that most of the people around FDR were "crackpots and the lunatic fringe"—certainly people who made him feel uncomfortable. "I want to keep my feet on the ground," he told an aide, and didn't "feel comfortable unless I know where I am going."

He was, inescapably, someone who'd stepped out of the nation's rural past and found himself in a dizzying mid-twentieth-century world, like a character from a Mark Twain fable: *A Missouri Farmer in FDR's Court*. That's the Truman celebrated in national memory, an ordinary man who rose greatly to an occasion: solid, plainspoken, unbendable, proof that individuals, even if they lacked the captivating personalities found in *Great Men and Famous Women*, could alter their times. It's true that, out of the disorder that followed victories in Europe and the Pacific, Truman and his circle *did* alter their times, even if not always for the best.

They did so even though Truman himself bore little resemblance to the commanding figures he admired, or aspired to follow. He could connect to crowds from the back of a train, but seemed to shrink, almost nervously, when he spoke to the nation on radio or television. Perhaps that didn't matter, or not all the time. His presence wasn't always required for great things to be accomplished. For instance, the Marshall Plan, a great success of the Truman era, had many fathers—advocates, visionaries, idealists, and planners—while Truman's role was decidedly passive. The order to drop an atomic bomb—widely regarded as the most momentous of Truman's decisions—transformed the concept of warfare, and much more. But loosing that first atom bomb, on Hiroshima, was also an inescapable choice, an unremarkable decision for a wartime leader. That is, one may debate the necessity, and morality, of simply *using* atomic weapons, but after years of planning and expense, not to mention the political realities that Jimmy Byrnes recognized, it's implausible that any president—particularly a novice like Truman—could have halted its deployment against a hated enemy, moreover an enemy that could still inflict many more casualties on American soldiers. "I couldn't worry about what history would say about my personal morality," Truman later wrote. "I did what I thought was right." His remarks on that subject, over the years, would reveal troubled, even ambivalent feelings, but never any serious doubt.

The greatest test of Truman's leadership would come when he committed the nation to a new kind of war, on the Korean peninsula. The deepening involvement and changing objectives in what became an inconclusive, and ruinous, three-year conflict were entirely escapable. It became the tragic misjudgment of the Truman presidency, a failure of vision and direction, although it did show off Truman's ability to make major decisions, sometimes in a hurry. There were certainly good reasons to challenge Communist North Korea after it attacked the South, in June 1950, among them a belief that Stalin was behind it, aiming to expand Soviet control, and that something should be done to thwart that ambition. It was also seen as a first test of the United Nations' ability to repel unprovoked aggression.

But what Truman was eager to characterize as a UN "police action" became, almost overnight, an American war. The conflict, which exploded with uncontrollable force, would result in more than thirty-seven thousand American deaths, a far greater loss of Korean life, and the obliteration from the air of much of Korea, then an unadvanced nation, with a population of about thirty million, scattered among towns and villages. The goal of pushing the northern invaders back across the Thirty-Eighth Parallel—the de facto border between North and South—was soon revised. In a breathtaking escalation of purpose, Truman soon described America's first "limited" Asian ground war in existential terms: "We know," he said, "that what is at stake here is nothing less than our own national security and the peace of the world."

To go to war seven thousand miles away, in a country that posed only an abstract threat, required of Truman not only a suspension of disbelief but credulous faith in his advisers. Their outlook, a dread that any hint of weakness might be interpreted as appeasement, had been shaped by the events leading up to World War II. No one felt that more acutely than Secretary of State Acheson, who surrounded himself with like-minded men, which didn't leave much room for vigorous debate, or for consideration of what might go wrong, not only then but in the future. Acheson's perspective, along with an absence of steadying presidential leadership, was most keenly felt in the late fall of 1950, when the war took an ominous turn and

Truman seemed overwhelmed, even unnerved. That's about when General Eisenhower, in a diary entry, wrote "Goddamit—is there no desire to *know* where we are going?" Not without sympathy, he added "And poor H.S.T., a fine man who, in the middle of a stormy lake, knows nothing of swimming. Yet a lot of drowning people are forced to look to him as a lifeguard. If his wisdom could only equal his good intent!!"

After a successful, creative beginning—a time of the Marshall Plan, and a military alliance among North Atlantic nations—that stormy lake would engulf the last years of Truman's presidency. Yet even as he was worn down, he remained the man whom Winston Churchill met for the first time in July 1945, on the outskirts of Berlin: not a simple person, though someone who sometimes saw things in simple terms, as if the world could be understood as a place like Jackson County, only bigger, and with more dialects. Charles McMoran Wilson, the prime minister's doctor, had asked Churchill if he thought Truman had any "real ability." Lord Moran's recollection was vivid: "The P.M. stood over me. The white of his eyes showed above his pupils, his lips pouted. Looking down at me as if he were saying something he did not want to be repeated: 'I should think he has,' he said. 'At any rate, he is a man of immense determination. He takes no notice of delicate ground, he just plants his foot down firmly on it.' And to illustrate this the P.M. jumped a little off the wooden floor and brought his bare feet down with a smack."

That's not a bad way to start thinking about Harry Truman, from the time when he'd just taken on his enormous new task: as a determined man, a man of limited imagination and experience, who happened to be a good man, and who managed to hold tight for nearly eight years as he was hurled through the mid-twentieth century, and wouldn't, or couldn't, let go.

ONE

President Truman

> Just two months ago today, I was a reasonably happy and con-
> tented Vice President. But things have changed so much it
> hardly seems real. I sit here in this old house and work on for-
> eign affairs, read reports, and work on speeches—all the while
> listening to the ghosts walk up and down the hallway.
>
> —Harry Truman, June 1945

> Don't shoot the piano player—he's doing the best he can.
>
> —Harry Truman, October 1945 (overheard)

1. A few days after Truman's swearing-in, Eben Ayers, a former newspaperman who'd come to work in the White House press office just before Roosevelt's death, told his diary, "Confusion and uncertainty prevail." He worried that the late, notorious T. J. Pendergast, to whom Truman once owed so much, might still cast a shadow of disrepute over the White House. He was also reacting to this new crowd, people unknown to him, such as Harry Vaughan, Truman's military aide and faithful friend, "a man of bouncing en-thusiasms and earthy comedy." It was not quite twenty-five years since the short, scandal-burdened presidency of Warren G. Harding, and Ayers feared a return to low standards. "I have no desire to remain here," he wrote, "if we are to have a Democratic Harding Administration." Ayers was letting his Northeastern prejudices show, but he wasn't alone in harboring suspicions about this new, seem-ingly rough-hewn bunch, so unlike the Roosevelt crowd, and what it might say about the new president—a stranger to the executive branch. "It was a dreadful time," one correspondent recalled. "Here was a man who came into the White House almost as though he had been picked at random from off the street, with *absolutely* no useable background and no useable information."

Sympathy for Truman would have been a more appropriate reaction. The job was, without a pause, crushing, inescapable. Decisions needed to be made rather than debated on the floor of the Senate. Truman worried about his family—especially about Margaret, and how the change in their lives would affect her—but even about the Connecticut Avenue apartment they'd just vacated. "I've paid the rent for this month and will pay for another month if they don't get the old White House redecorated by that time," he wrote to his mother and sister four days after being sworn in. The rent! For their five-room corner apartment, it was $120 a month. The Trumans hadn't entirely moved out, and, in the meantime, were living in Blair House, across Lafayette Square from the White House, where Mrs. Roosevelt would stay for a few more days, while she packed.

He thought about his general unreadiness—and who to blame for it. He told John McCloy, the assistant secretary of war, that Roosevelt had said, "Harry, I want you to follow these things more closely because I feel that I may not last through." McCloy recorded this in his diary, although with skepticism, noting that others close to Roosevelt said "this was the first time they had even heard anyone say that the President had intimated any such thing." It was alarmingly obvious that Truman didn't know a lot that he ought to have known, and that there was no crash course for presidents. The situation left Truman especially vulnerable to missteps in foreign policy. While Roosevelt had been surrounded with advisers whom he trusted, and with whom he was comfortable, Truman hadn't given the subject a lot of thought and had no foreign policy team that he could call his own. Nor did he have much of an idea what Roosevelt had been up to. "I was handicapped by lack of knowledge of both foreign and domestic affairs—due principally to Mr. Roosevelt's inability to pass on responsibility," Truman wrote in his diary, on May 6. "He was always careful to see that no credit went to anyone else for accomplishment."

One of Truman's first tutors was W. Averell Harriman, an intense, and nervous, chain-smoker, the son of the railroad oligarch Edward Henry Harriman. He had striking good looks, was a first-rate polo player, and, with a fortune estimated at about forty million dollars, could have led the life of the idle rich. But he'd known the Roosevelts, Eleanor and Franklin, since his student days at Groton, and was drawn to politics and public life. Since 1940, when he was recruited by Roosevelt to help oversee the Lend-Lease program, he'd held a number of high-level jobs. In 1943, he became ambassador to the Soviet Union, a job, as the *New Yorker*'s E. J. Kahn Jr. wrote, for which he was "abnormally equipped with energy, curiosity, ambition, and money." Harriman had been an effective, self-confident minister, one who tended to rely on personal diplomacy—"A country's policies can only work out successfully if you get to the right people," he said. He claimed that no other foreigner had spent as much time with Stalin as he had.

The news from Warm Springs had reached Moscow at about 2 a.m. on April 13, and Harriman, knowing that Stalin kept late hours, had set out immediately for the Kremlin, and Stalin's suite of offices, which seemed to a visitor like an ornate maze, a succession of reception rooms. Stalin seemed to him genuinely distraught. "He greeted me in silence and stood holding my hand for about thirty seconds before asking me to sit down," Harriman recalled. Harriman tried to assure him that Truman would continue Roosevelt's foreign policy and that he was "a man of action and not of words"—someone he would like.

But in the two months after Yalta, Harriman had become increasingly mistrustful of Russia, so much so that, a few days before Roosevelt's death, he'd begun a cable to Secretary of State Stettinius, setting down his concerns. It continued for eight typed pages, and grew increasingly harsh: The Russians were consumed by "suspicion and resentment," and "hadn't carried out all the military agreements made at Yalta", since then, "the Soviet government has retaliated in the most definite way against one or all of the positions we have taken in both large and small matters." He suggested that he, personally, inform Stalin, with whom he'd had some "very rough talks," to change course. If not, "the friendly hand that we have offered them"—namely Lend-Lease—"will be withdrawn." Harriman must have had second thoughts, because he didn't send the cable; after Roosevelt's death, he decided to take his views directly to Truman.

By the time Harriman got to Washington, the handholding in Moscow had been forgotten. He talked to Truman as if the President were a schoolboy just learning the fundamentals. He told Truman that he'd hurried back out of a "fear that you did not understand, as I had seen Roosevelt understand, that Stalin is breaking his agreements." He worried that Truman couldn't have had time "to catch up with all the recent cables." Truman told Harriman that he'd done his homework—read, and absorbed, the correspondence between Stalin and Roosevelt, as well as the Yalta agreements—an improbable accomplishment, even for a speed-reader with perfect eyesight. Harriman said he was "greatly relieved to discover that you have read them all and that we see eye to eye on the situation," but he was not entirely relieved: During their first conversation, and subsequent ones, Harriman feared that Truman "was being overhumble," and worried "that he would not grasp control of the presidency, that he might be indecisive." He "kept saying—too often, I thought—that he was not equipped for the job, that he lacked experience and did not fully understand the issues." But Harriman soon became persuaded that the President "showed the right kind of humility," and "the capacity to make decisions."

Truman's reaction was gratitude. "I am glad," he told Harriman, "that you are going to be available to our delegation in San Francisco. And keep on sending me long messages." He assured Harriman that he wasn't all that worried about the Russians—"Anyway, [they] need us more than we need them," he said.

Truman's antipathetic view of Russia, though not entirely consistent, seemed to be entrenched, its origins obscure. He'd told Stettinius that "we must stand up to the Russians at this point . . . we must not be easy with them," and had remarked to Henry Wallace that they were "like people from across the tracks whose manners were very bad," a view that certainly appalled Wallace. Those opinions were reinforced by Harriman, who saw the Russians as "these barbarians," and help to explain Truman's diplomatic debut: a testy, off-key meeting with Vyacheslav Molotov, the Russian foreign minister, who'd stopped in Washington before flying on to San Francisco, for the first United Nations conference. That in itself reflected a Soviet change of heart. Stalin had originally refused to send Molotov as a delegate, but Harriman apparently had persuaded him to change his mind. That was interpreted as a friendly gesture, though it was also a way for Stalin to get a reliable secondhand impression of Truman.

Molotov was no ordinary foreign minister. As Milovan Djilas, a Yugoslav revolutionary-turned-dissident, pointed out, he was the only Politburo member who addressed Stalin with the familiar pronoun *ty*. He was short on charm—he seemed unsure of himself and stuttered—but he was born with a talent for infinite patience, which gave an impression of impenetrability; he was, Djilas wrote, "deliberate, composed and tenacious." Molotov arrived in Washington on April 22, in the late afternoon, after an unusually long flight: Due to wartime restrictions inside the Soviet Union—no beacons or landing lights—he was limited to daytime flying, which lengthened the journey by four days. When he saw Truman the next day, the President had already absorbed advice from Harriman, Stettinius, and army chief of staff George Marshall, among others, which reinforced his sentiments. Charles (Chip) Bohlen, a Russian expert and Roosevelt's interpreter at Yalta, watched with evident pleasure as the conversation with Molotov turned sour.

At one point, the well-coached Truman told Molotov that keeping commitments was not a problem for the United States but that the Soviet Union was taking too long to honor *its* agreements, particularly a promise, made in Yalta, to bring the "London" Poles into the Polish government. When Molotov said that the Poles had not been cooperating with the Red Army, Bohlen recalled, Truman "firmly and briskly" said he wasn't interested in propaganda—that he merely wanted Molotov "to inform Stalin of his concerns." When Molotov tried to change the subject, Truman interrupted him, and finally cut short their conversation, saying, "That will be all, Mr. Molotov. I would appreciate it if you would transmit my views to Marshal Stalin." In his memoirs, Truman made this back-and-forth sound even harsher, with Molotov saying, "I have never been talked to like that in my life," and Truman replying, "Carry out your agreements and you won't get talked to like that."

Hearing this from someone who'd been president for less than two weeks, Molotov may have been more mystified than insulted—and surprised that Truman was trying to sound as if he'd mastered the tortuous history affecting Poland and Russia. "At our first meeting," Molotov recalled, "he began talking to me in such an imperious tone!" Rather stupid, he thought—"he wanted to show who was boss." Bohlen remembered Molotov leaving in a hurry, but Molotov later claimed to remember something else: a change in Truman's tone as he "talked modestly about himself" and said, "There are millions like me in America, but I am the President."

When Molotov reported to Moscow, he must have emphasized the stridency, because Truman the next day received a mild scolding from Stalin, who suggested, in pure Stalinese, that the President needed to remember that Poland and the Soviet Union had a common border, and that, as he'd pointed out to Roosevelt, in Yalta, security was his primary focus—that Poland had twice been used as a corridor to invade Russia. "You evidently do not agree that the Soviet Union is entitled to seek in Poland a Government that would be friendly to it," Stalin's cable said. "This is rendered imperative . . . by the Soviet people's blood freely shed on the fields of Poland for the liberation of that country." Stalin's claim on Poland was strengthened by the irresistible fact that Poland was already an occupied country.

Whatever was actually uttered, Truman had the all-too-human penchant for inflating himself after the fact. In this case, he sketched a self-portrait of a tough, no-nonsense executive. "I gave it to him straight," he told Joseph E. Davies, a former ambassador to Russia. It was a "one-two to the jaw." He informed Davies that what "the Soviets best understood was 'the tough method,'" and that "Molotov was shaken and went pale." One-two to the jaw or not, an aide later wrote, Truman's memory of conversations with those with whom he disagreed "frequently did not square with the recollections of others who were present." Robert L. Dennison, who later became a naval aide to Truman, was one of those who recognized the habit: "I have been with the President on occasions when he had what appeared to me to be a perfectly normal and amiable conversation with a caller. After the caller left, he would say to me, in effect, 'I certainly set him straight,' or, 'I let him have it.'" Dennison supposed that he "may have been commenting on what he wished he had said, or perhaps his words were too subtle for me to understand."

⌬

On April 24, right after Molotov left for San Francisco, Truman received a note from Secretary of War Stimson, saying "I think it is very important that I should have a talk with you as soon as possible on a highly secret matter." That "matter" was the atom bomb, and Stimson had prepared a memo that, in dramatic language, recounted its history and declared that "within four months we shall in all probability have completed the most terrible weapon ever known in human history, one bomb of which could destroy a whole city."

The next day, Stimson and General Leslie R. Groves, who had directed the Manhattan Project, made their way to the White House. They spent about forty-five minutes with Truman, trying to explain the power of this new device, which had never been tested, had cost a fortune, and had taken years to build, with operations in Oak Ridge, Tennessee, Pasco, Washington, and an archipelago of university laboratories that included Columbia, the University of Chicago, and Berkeley. Its most celebrated lab, attached to the University of California, was in the New Mexico mountain town of Los Alamos, near Santa Fe. The first detonation, code-named "Trinity," was to take place sometime in the next few months, in the New Mexico desert.

The project—Stimson referred to it as "S.1," with the "S" standing for "Special"—had its doubters. Admiral William Leahy, whose formal title, under Roosevelt, was "chief of staff to the commander in chief," called it "the biggest fool thing we have ever done. The bomb will never go off, and I speak as an expert in explosives." On the other hand, it was possible to imagine that it might be *at least* as powerful as Stimson believed. Jimmy Byrnes, putting aside his own doubts, at one point told Truman that "we were perfecting an explosive great enough to destroy the whole world." Truman remembered how, when he'd chaired the Truman Committee, Stimson had rebuffed him. Stimson remembered too: "[Truman] said that he understood now perfectly why it was inadvisable for me to have taken any other course than I had taken," Stimson wrote in his diary. His first impression of Truman, as president, was positive. He liked the "promptness and snappiness with which he took up each matter and decided it." Stimson missed Roosevelt's leadership qualities, but not his "long drawn out 'soliloquies.'"

2. On May 8, 1945, which happened to be Truman's sixty-first birthday, Generaloberst Alfred Jodl, the chief of staff of the German High Command, signed Germany's unconditional surrender, in a red school building in Reims, France. General Dwight D. Eisenhower, the supreme commander of the Allied forces, had by then visited the Buchenwald concentration camp and seen, as he put it, "indescribable horror," and that "evidence of bestiality and cruelty is so overpowering as to leave no doubt . . . about the normal practices of the Germans in these camps." Jodl was the Nazi soldier closest to Hitler, and Eisenhower's revulsion was such that he avoided meeting him, and thus any chance of having to shake his hand.

News of the surrender brought out cheering crowds in Europe's capitals. In New York, the celebrations lasted until Mayor Fiorello La Guardia urged people to go home, or return to work. In Washington, the mood was more subdued, if only because any attempt at joyful spontaneity would have seemed a little forced—"an overanticipated thrill" in the words of Isaiah Berlin, the British philosopher and historian, whose job at the British Embassy was to report on the American political scene. Stimson said that Japan's "fading power for evil must and shall be utterly destroyed," and he warned that the Germans "must be watched lest they again poison civilization."

Truman knew that the occasion required a speech—yet another address to the nation, and, ready or not, he did his best. Looking a little uncertain, and in a voice that sounded nervously mechanical, his short talk began, "This is a solemn but a glorious hour. I only wish that Franklin D. Roosevelt had lived to witness this day." He continued, "If I could give you a single watchword for the coming months, that word is—work, work, and more work. . . . Our victory is but half-won. The West is free, but the East is still in bondage to the treacherous tyranny of the Japanese." The coming Sunday was Mother's Day, which Truman proclaimed as a time to "acknowledge anew our gratitude, love, and devotion to the mothers of America," as well as a day for prayer and thanksgiving.

The Mother's Day designation had a special meaning because, three days later, Martha Ellen Young Truman, the President's ninety-two-year-old mother, would visit Washington, accompanied by the President's fifty-six-year-old sister, Mary Jane. It would be Martha Truman's first flight—on the same four-engine plane that Roosevelt used. It was her first time in Washington, as well as the first time that she'd seen her firstborn son since he'd become president. When Truman met the plane, he went aboard for a private welcome, and, perhaps, to warn his mother that a swarm of photographers was outside, waiting for them. "Oh fiddlesticks!" Martha Truman reportedly—and may actually—have said. "If I'd known that I wouldn't have come."

The visit was a brief respite. It had been just a month since Roosevelt's death, and change was about to come, speedily. Although Truman was Roosevelt's constitutional heir, no one thought that things would continue as they had. The quick appointment of Robert Hannegan as postmaster general, replacing Frank Walker, made that clear. For the holdovers, getting used to the Truman presidency took some effort. Truman had supported the New Deal, but he was never a full-throated New Dealer. "I don't want any experiments; the American people have been through a lot of experiments and they want a rest from experiments," he told an aide. He disliked words like "progressive" and "liberal," and thought a phrase like "forward-looking" expressed it better.

Those who'd been closest to Roosevelt found the transition especially hard, even wrenching. They had only to read the newspapers to know what lay ahead—that, and hear about Truman's indiscretions, which had a way of leaking out. He'd carelessly told Henry

Wallace that he had "no confidence in the State Department what-soever" and was "going to get new leadership as soon as possible." He also let slip that he wasn't eager to keep Francis Biddle, at Justice, or Frances Perkins at the Labor Department, and their fates too quickly became the subject of Washington gossip. Secretary of State Stettinius couldn't avoid newspaper stories saying that Jimmy Byrnes would soon replace him, and while he was not the brightest man in Washington, he knew that he was being undermined. The undermining was being carried out by such people as the very powerful political commentator Walter Lippmann, who was certain that the inexperienced secretary of state would soon resign and be "given another post of distinction and usefulness." Byrnes, who could read the same stories and felt entitled to any chance to better himself, could not always bring himself to call Truman "Mr. President," or even some workaround. In their correspondence, he sometimes used the salutation "Dear Harry," less a sign of disrespect than of bewilderment at their new circumstances.

On May 23, Truman began his press conference by saying, "Well, I have some Cabinet changes I wanted to tell you about. Mr. Biddle's resignation has been accepted, and Tom Clark of Texas will be appointed in his place as Attorney General." Frances Perkins had also resigned, he said, along with the secretary of agriculture. There'd been rumors that Truman would replace Treasury Secretary Henry Morgenthau, but when Truman was asked whether Morgenthau had offered his resignation, he said, "No, he did not, and if he had, I wouldn't accept it." Did he contemplate any change in the State Department? "I do not," Truman said. Were any of the resignations offered at his request? "They were not," Truman said.

Almost nothing that Truman said that day was true. Francis Biddle knew—and knew that Truman knew—that his fate was tied to Missouri loyalties, and was proof of the saying that all politics is local: Then-Senator Truman had once tried to block the reappointment of Maurice Milligan, the Kansas City U.S. attorney who'd led the prosecution of T. J. Pendergast, and Biddle, the attorney general, had refused to go along. Truman not only fired Biddle, but the dismissal had come in a phone call from Steve Early, the former

Roosevelt press secretary. Biddle was appalled—not at being fired, but that "the manner of my dismissal was abrupt and undignified." He'd asked for an appointment with Truman who, to his credit, agreed to see him.

Nor had Biddle wanted Tom Clark, then the head of the Criminal Division, to succeed him; in fact, he'd been so displeased by Clark's performance that he'd wanted to fire him. Truman later remembered it differently—claiming that Biddle had recommended Clark's appointment. What's probably the truth is that, six days after Roosevelt's death, Sam Rayburn, the House speaker, sent a note to his friend Harry Truman that invoked the persuasive elements of friendship, patronage, and local politics. The speaker told the President that "in case an Attorney General was to be named there is one man who has my complete confidence and endorsement"—Tom Clark, who "knows how to work on the team." Rayburn didn't need to spell out the meaning of "team"; Truman surely knew that Clark had been a protégé of Truman's Missouri ally Bob Hannegan.

Morgenthau should have known that he'd be leaving. His relationship with Roosevelt had been an easy one. They'd been neighbors in Hyde Park, FDR called him "Henny Penny," and his wife, Ellie, was a friend of Eleanor Roosevelt's. Morgenthau could see that Truman "has a lot of nervous energy and seems to be inclined to make very quick decisions," but he was burdened by a shield of obtuseness, which led to colossal misreadings of Truman's moods, even as those moods were recorded in Morgenthau's diaristic accounts. Following one conversation, right after Germany's surrender, Morgenthau left "with the distinct feeling that the man likes me and has confidence in me, and I must say that my confidence in him continues to grow. He gives me the impression of being completely frank"—which was certainly the impression that Truman cultivated. He had no idea that Truman would refer to him as a "block head, nut—I wonder why F.D.R. kept him around." Truman certainly didn't believe Morgenthau was a blockhead, and everyone knew that he was friendly with the Roosevelts, but that was the sort of language that Truman used about people he didn't much care for.

Morgenthau, like Stettinius, soon became aware of maneuverings that affected him, and he tried to pry information out of Truman by volunteering to exchange private intelligence. In a visit to the Oval Office, he said, "The talk around town is that you are going to put Stettinius out. Now, I am not asking you whether you are or not, but if you have it in mind, I would like to talk to you about his successor." When Truman told him to go ahead, Morgenthau put his foot in it: "I don't know whether you are thinking about putting Byrnes in or not," he said, "but I want to say in the first place, so that you completely understand me, I can't get along with him." He continued, "If the other people around you were honest, they would tell you the same thing."

Truman, who was an enthusiastic poker player, kept his Byrnes card facedown.

"Oh, I know Mr. Byrnes. He is a conniver," Truman said.

"That's just what he is. I just don't think he would work on anybody's team. Just because he has gone on a trip to Russia doesn't make him an expert on foreign affairs."

"You don't know how difficult the thing has been for me," Truman said, shaking his head.

Truman can't be blamed for avoiding straight answers. Replacing any senior cabinet officer would be seen as a major shakeup, and it was not Truman's style to hurt people. But these Roosevelt appointments were not his people, and the White House was not yet his territory as the Senate had been.

Secretary of State Stettinius was in San Francisco, for the first United Nations conference, when he got the anticipated news from the occasional Truman errand boy and lobbyist George E. Allen—"the laughing lobbyist," in columnist Doris Fleeson's words—a chubby, ingratiating Mississippian described as a "court jester, adviser, and wire-puller." Allen knew how to pour it on, and told Stettinius that he'd "done a magnificent job here and the only thing that can happen to you is to be something bigger than Secretary of State"—even President. When Stettinius asked what he was talking about, Allen said he meant Stettinius would become the first United States delegate to the United Nations.

These personnel shifts would reveal a definite westward shift, away from Roosevelt's Hudson River and toward the Mississippi. Six of FDR's ten cabinet members were from New York, with none from the South or the West Coast. Roosevelt's circle had included several women, while Truman's confidants were uniformly men—many of them Missourians, some dating back to his time in the National Guard, most of whom were regarded by people like the Eastern columnists Joseph and Stewart Alsop with unconcealed snobbery, as "the sort to be conspicuous good fellows at a State convention of the Legion." Isaiah Berlin, whose circle included the Alsops and Chip Bohlen, reported home that "the men whom the new President has chosen for his personal staff are of blameless enough reputation but dim and provincial to a degree. . . . a collection, at best, of worthy and honourable mediocrities." Frances Perkins, the only woman in the cabinet, was born with the handicap of being female. It's not that Truman didn't *like* women, but that, as one adviser put it, he was "rarely relaxed and comfortable in their presence." Perkins had wanted to resign for some time, but Roosevelt had said, "Oh, you can't leave me, you've got to stay here, Frances," after which she could only obey.

The new press secretary was another Missourian, in this case a boyhood friend, Charles Ross, a reporter and editorial writer at the *St. Louis Post-Dispatch*, a Pulitzer Prize winner—and by no means a mediocrity. Ross, who suffered from arthritis and heart ailments, often had a cigarette dangling from his lips; he favored a lugubrious expression and was, in one description, a "stooped, lean, tired figure, with sad spaniel eyes and enormous pouches under them." He was trusted by reporters and knew Truman well enough to address him with uncommon directness.

Ross was also perfect choice for a press corps that was getting used to Truman. The President for his part mostly enjoyed reporters, although he could rage at some of the columnists, and assumed, often with good reason, that newspaper owners—Hearst and Scripps Howard and, above all, Robert "Colonel" McCormick's *Chicago Tribune*—were against him. But he was relaxed with beat reporters, many of whom came from backgrounds very much like his; on some level, these were his people. He liked joking with them, and liked the laughter. Before the formal questioning began, he might say, "I just want to get the ordeal over with," or "Let the vultures in." Because he sometimes spoke rapidly, and journalists, not yet using tape recorders, were forced to take notes, he was sometimes asked, "Are you going to go slow today?" To that, he once replied, "I haven't very much to give you today, but I'll be very slow. I understand the longer I string it out, the fewer questions I'll have to answer, and you'll all say 'Thank you' sooner."

In early June, less than two months into his presidency, Truman wrote to Bess to say, "Well I'm getting better organized now. My office force soon will be shaken down and so will my Cabinet when I've gotten State straightened out"—replacing Stettinius with Byrnes. He hadn't given much thought to replacing Secretary of War Stimson or navy secretary James Forrestal, but he wanted Bess to know that he was on top of things, adding, "I shall let [them] alone until the Japanese are out of the picture." He ended on a note of good-humored hope, or perhaps self-mockery, when he went on to say, "It won't be long until I can sit back and study the whole picture and tell 'em what is to be done in each department. When things come to that stage there'll be no more to this job than there was to running Jackson County and not any more worry."

TWO

Terminal

I am getting ready to go see Stalin & Churchill, and it is a chore. I have to take my tuxedo, tails, negro preacher coat, high hat, low hat and hard hat as well as sundry other things. I have a brief case all filled up with information on past conferences and suggestions on what I'm to do and say. Wish I didn't have to go, but I do and it can't be stopped now.

—**Harry Truman, in a letter home, July 3, 1945**

1. On May 13, 1945, a warm and damp Washington day, Joseph E. Davies, the former ambassador to the Soviet Union, telephoned the White House to say it was urgent that he see the President. He was "gravely concerned and alarmed over the Russian situation," he said, but it's fair to say that Davies never stopped being gravely concerned and alarmed about Soviet-American relations, so much so that, after he'd heard Truman's account of his encounter with Molotov, he'd written a note to the foreign minister—"My dear friend"—that amounted to an apology: "I feel sure that as you and Marshal [Stalin] come to know our President Truman better . . . a concert of action and purpose will be assured." He told Molotov that he had faced a "difficult situation . . . with ability and dignity."

Truman welcomed the sixty-eight-year-old Davies, who'd been the first chairman of the Federal Trade Commission. He'd become a very rich Washington lawyer in 1935, when he married Marjorie Merriweather Post, the breakfast-cereal heiress, whose homes included Washington's Hillwood mansion and the Mar-a-Lago estate in Palm Beach, Florida. Davies's ambassadorial duties began in 1937, and he'd used his experience, which lasted two years, to produce *Mission to Moscow*, published in 1942. The book became a best seller, and the basis of a Warner Bros. film, in which Walter Huston played Davies and Davies, appearing as himself, introduced the movie.

The film undoubtedly strengthened American support for the Soviet Union, then an essential ally in the fight against Nazi Germany. It was said, though never confirmed, that President Roosevelt himself had asked Jack Warner to make it. The book, though, did not do much to enhance Davies's reputation, and is best remembered for his impression of Stalin, as someone with "a strong mind which is composed and wise," and whose "brown eye is exceedingly kindly and gentle. A child would like to sit in his lap and a dog would sidle up to him." George Kennan, who was on the embassy staff when Davies began his stint, saw him as "a shallow and politically ambitious man, who knows nothing about Russia," but in the spring of 1945, Davies was still someone to be reckoned with.

When Davies arrived in the President's private office, on the second floor, Truman, in shirtsleeves, said that he too was disturbed by the Russian situation, such as renewed tension over the future of Poland. He complained that the newspapers—"these damn sheets"—made everything more difficult. Davies told Truman that "he and he alone could really save the situation," and urged him to meet with Stalin. He suggested Alaska or Siberia, or "on a warship somewhere in that neighborhood," and offered to cable Molotov to help arrange it. Their conversation continued until seven-thirty, at which point Truman asked Davies to stay for dinner. They had "a jolly time," Davies recalled, at a table that included Bess and Margaret, as well as Truman's mother and sister, who'd been in town since Mother's Day, and Madge Gates Wallace, who would spend many of her remaining years with her daughter and son-in-law.

Davies was about to learn that plans for another meeting of the Grand Alliance were already in the works, and a week later, Truman asked him to take on some advance work—as an emissary to Churchill. That was a curious choice, not least because Davies's empathetic view of Russia was so at variance with that of the British prime minister, who had already begun using the phrase "Iron Curtain."

Truman was in a talkative mood, and told his visitor about the still-top-secret atomic bomb. "I was startled, shocked, and amazed," Davies wrote in his diary.

Truman had also decided to send Harry Hopkins as his envoy to Stalin, although Hopkins, on most days, felt too poorly even to get out of bed. When Churchill's doctor saw Hopkins in Yalta, in February, he'd thought that "physically he is only half in this world." But Stalin was known to trust Hopkins, whom he'd met in 1941. Chip Bohlen recalled him saying that Hopkins was the first American to whom he'd spoken "*po dushe*"—"from the soul." Truman told Stettinius that "he had great confidence that Harry would be able to straighten things out with Stalin."

Part of Hopkins's errand was no doubt to make diplomatic repairs, but there were substantive matters to pursue, such as the ever-elusive Polish compromise, which had stalled the talks in San Francisco, and getting agreement on a site for another Big Three conference—preferably Berlin. The arduous journeys to Tehran and Yalta had drained Roosevelt and Churchill. "Twice running we have come to meet [Stalin]," Churchill had written to Truman in early May, and suggested that they meet at "some unshattered town in Germany, if such can be found." He gave this future meeting the appropriate, and somewhat ominous, name "Terminal," which may have reflected his gloomy suspicions about Russia's military and political ambitions in Europe.

Truman, in his diary, sounded oddly unrealistic about Hopkins's assignment, writing that he wanted him to "make it clear to Uncle Joe Stalin that I knew what I wanted—and that I intended to get it—peace for the world for at least 90 years. That Poland, Rumania, Bulgaria, Czvekosvakia [sic], Austria, Yugo-Slavia [sic], Latvia, Lithuania, Estonia et al made no difference to U.S. interests only so far as World Peace is concerned." He added that "Uncle Joe should make some sort of gesture—whether he means it or not to keep it before our public that he intends to keep his word." As it happened, Stalin complained about American "misdeeds," and seemed almost baffled by the concept of a "free Poland," but Hopkins, joined by Harriman and Bohlen, soldiered on. At one point, Stalin informed his visitors that Hitler was alive—that he hadn't shot himself inside the Reich Chancellery, on April 30—and, furthermore, that Joseph Goebbels, the Reich's propaganda minister, and others, might also be alive and "in hiding." Upon hearing that, Hopkins said he hoped that Hitler could be tracked down "wherever he might be." Stalin said that submarines might be transporting gold to Japan, "with the connivance of Switzerland," and that Hitler could have fled to Japan. Harriman reported to Truman that the talks had gone about as well as could be expected, although Stalin "never will fully understand our interest in a free Poland as a matter of principle."

Joseph Davies had been instructed to inform Churchill that Truman wanted a pre-conference tête-à-tête with Stalin because Churchill already had "the benefit of frequent contacts and friendly association" with Soviet leaders. Churchill at first expressed no objection to Truman meeting first with Stalin. Then he began having second, and third, thoughts—becoming "quite emotional," Davies thought. He had to face a parliamentary election in July, with voting to begin on July 5, and worried that this perceived change in his status might hurt him. The PM had already sensed a gravitational shift in the alignment of power, away from him. To an observer in Tehran and Yalta, it looked as if Roosevelt and Stalin enjoyed "ribbing" Churchill, sometimes to the point of angering him. Churchill was especially concerned about the "grave dangers which would arise with the withdrawal of American troops from Europe," a view that Davies had conveyed to Truman, along with his opinion that Churchill's anti-Soviet outlook "placed not only the future, but possibly the immediate Peace in real danger."

2. The White House, in mid-June, announced that the next Big Three meeting would run sometime between July 5 and July 26. The site was to be Potsdam, situated twelve miles southwest of Berlin, in the Russian occupation sector, a city once known for its parks and grand houses. The city's name became history's shorthand for the longest, and strangest, of the three Grand Alliance conferences.

Truman knew that the title "President" could not close the gap in stature and authority that came from having led a nation through the deadliest war in history, as Churchill and Stalin had done. Churchill was said to view Stalin as "one of the great figures of history," much the way that Churchill saw himself. In an upended time, in which Truman had become the leader of the world's most powerful nation, he could only try to demonstrate confidence and sureness, as he had when he flew to San Francisco, on June 26, for the formal signing of the UN charter. As an unseen band played "Hail to the Chief," Truman walked to the stage and told delegates from some fifty nations, "You have created a great instrument for peace and security and human progress in the world. The world must now use it!" There, for one happy, spontaneous, presidential moment, he departed from his script to say, "Oh, what a great day in history this can be!"

While Truman was there, Edward Stettinius, the wounded secretary of state, finally got his chance for a face-to-face talk about what lay ahead for him, and to tell the President that he worried whether Jimmy Byrnes, his unannounced successor, could work with others.

"Jimmy Byrnes will work with you harmoniously and satisfactorily," Truman said. "I shall insist upon it. That will be part of the understanding."

"Are you going to make it clear I have succeeded as Secretary of State?" Stettinius asked.

"Yes," Truman replied, "you have done a magnificent job and I shall say so." The next day, Truman traveled to Independence, and kept his word: He said that the forty-four-year-old Stettinius had carried out his work "with distinction," and that he intended to nominate him to be the chief representative to the United Nations.

On June 30, Truman formally nominated Byrnes as secretary of state, an appointment the Senate approved, in a unanimous vote, without a committee hearing. With that, Byrnes moved to the head of the line of presidential succession—where Truman had stood the year before, and which, it was pointed out, "alters completely the necessary qualifications of the Secretary of State." It took the Presidential Succession Act of 1947 to bring the House speaker and the president pro tempore of the Senate to the front of the queue.

In the next day's *New York Times*, the Washington correspondent Cabell Phillips wrote that Truman "continues to grow to those exacting proportions demanded by the high office he inherited." When Phillips wrote about "mounting confidence" that Truman's tenure would be marked by "soundness of judgment and clear-headed progressiveness," it sounded as if he was trying to persuade himself that Roosevelt's unexpected successor could do the job.

Truman was undoubtedly cheered by such favorable report cards. His buoyant spirits were evident at his next press conference, on July 5, two days before he was to leave for Europe, when he showed up wearing a white-and-black seersucker suit with a green necktie. "Take the bars down," he said, as the press corps filed in. As he sipped a glass of water, he said, "Just taking a little something for my nerves!" Reporters laughed. The President then removed from a drawer what appeared to be a sword—an ivory baton, encrusted with gold and diamonds. "That's the Reichsmarschall's baton," Charlie Ross informed reporters—war booty presented to Truman by the general who'd captured Hermann Göring, the Luftwaffe commander. Truman said that Göring had wept when the baton was taken from him, and that it would go to the war museum at West Point, to be put on display alongside such treasures as the golden 7.65mm Walther PP given to Hitler by Carl Walther on the occasion of Hitler's fiftieth birthday.

The President also announced that Treasury Secretary Henry Morgenthau was resigning. "I have a successor in mind, but he will not be announced until I get back from Europe," he said. The unsurprising choice was Fred Vinson, the son of the Louisa, Kentucky, town jailer, who'd served several terms in Congress, before resigning, in 1943, to run the Office of Economic Stabilization. He was described as a "tax expert," but was, above all, Truman's genial good friend and a favorite poker companion. That left Truman with just four of the ten cabinet members he'd inherited from Roosevelt: Secretary of War Stimson, Commerce Secretary Henry Wallace, Navy Secretary James Forrestal, and Interior Secretary Harold Ickes.

On July 7, 1945, a Saturday morning, Truman sailed from Norfolk on the navy heavy cruiser USS *Augusta*. When he considered what lay ahead, his mood was no longer cheerful. "Talked to Bess last night and the night before," he wrote in his journal. "She wasn't happy about my going to see Mr. Russia and Mr. Great Britain—neither am I." He went on to write, "How I hate this trip! But I have to make it—win lose or draw—and we must win." What he meant by "win" was not spelled out. It was the sort of sea journey that Roosevelt would have loved. "We have just enough work to keep us busy and not too much to prevent a rest," H. Freeman (Doc) Matthews, who ran the State Department's Office of European Affairs, wrote to his wife, naming some of his shipmates: Byrnes; Benjamin Cohen, an aide to the new secretary of state; Chip Bohlen; and Admiral William Leahy, who'd been Roosevelt's chief of staff and had been asked to stay on as Truman's. "[We] usually meet for an hour in the morning and another in the afternoon preparing for meeting and between times Chip, Ben & I work up some papers. Before dinner the President comes to the mess for a highball with us and after dinner (at 6 p.m. incidentally) we have movies in his cabin which is large and roomy. I'm seeing all the good pictures we missed." Truman had time to enjoy target practice with five-inch, eight-inch, and forty-millimeter guns. "Right interesting to an artillery man," he wrote home.

Truman had asked the State Department and the Pentagon to summarize what they thought he needed to know, and used his shipboard time like a diligent student. "He squeezed facts and opinions out of us all day long," Admiral Leahy later remarked, exaggerating the duration of Truman's concentration, though not his determination. Truman felt the strain of having to catch up: "Have been going through some very hectic days," he'd told his diary, on June 1. "Eyes troubling somewhat. Too much reading 'fine print.' Nearly every memorandum has a catch in it and it has been necessary to read at least a thousand of 'em and as many reports. Most of it at night."

At one point during the eight-day crossing, Truman led correspondents from the three major wire services ("the three ghouls," Leahy called them) up and down ladders, from the boiler room to the control towers, to the sick bay to the kitchen, taking time for meals with officers and seamen. He conferred every day with Byrnes and Leahy, to discuss not only the somewhat spare agenda in Potsdam, but the terms of Japan's anticipated surrender. Cordell Hull, Stettinius's predecessor as secretary of state, had urged Byrnes to insist on unconditional surrender, meaning that the emperor, and Japan's ruling class, "must be stripped of all extraordinary privileges and placed on a level before the law with everyone else." The poet Archibald MacLeish, who was working for the State Department as a public information officer, also favored that condition. "What has made Japan dangerous in the past and will make her dangerous in the future if we permit it, is, in large part, the Japanese cult of Emperor worship," he argued in a memo. Byrnes wanted Truman to insist that the emperor's abdication was non-negotiable, to see that any concession would smack of "appeasement," although "appeasement" was not a useful term when referring to an enemy that was, by almost any measure, already beaten. But with no one aboard to argue, as Kai Bird observed, in his biography of Stimson's deputy, John McCloy, Truman left unaltered the draft of the surrender proclamation, which, in its final form, became the "Potsdam Declaration."

The *Augusta* docked on July 15, in Antwerp, Belgium, where Truman was greeted first by General Eisenhower, who'd become military governor of the American occupation sector in Germany. The President was driven to Brussels, and flown to Berlin-Gatow Airport, in a Douglas C-54 Skymaster. Berliners that day saw the power of the occupiers, not only the twelve P-47 Thunderbolts that accompanied Truman's plane, but the fourteen giant transports that circled the city. Truman's C-54 took a roundabout path so that he could view the battlefields in northern France, Belgium, and Germany. Stimson went from side to side, peering from the plane's windows, while Byrnes and army chief of staff George Marshall seemed uninterested in aerial sightseeing. From the air, the cities of Kassel and Magdeburg looked obliterated—not a house standing—while the countryside, according to the logbook, "seemed to be under cultivation and, with its numerous black-green wooded hills . . . presented a beautiful appearance." The devastation of Europe wasn't always visible; cities that had escaped heavy bombing still had to cope with illness and food shortages. At a Washington dinner party, someone asked the columnist Marquis Childs, who'd recently been in Eastern Europe, "What is Belgrade like?" and he replied "Like North Dakota bombed."

3. Potsdam offered another, frustrating opportunity to solve several disputes that were bound to keep lingering, such as the once and future boundaries of Germany and Poland. At times the conference came to resemble an appalling dinner party, giving the victorious hosts a chance to dress up and strut.

Two of the victorious hosts were no longer in peak form. Churchill, at seventy, was weary, not only from the years of war but from bouts of pneumonia, and efforts to keep his parliamentary majority. Voting had already begun, with the results due on July 25, and the PM was right to be worried: On July 4, at a rally in Walthamstow, in northern London, he'd heard the most enthusiastic booing of the campaign. Facing the possibility of defeat, Churchill asked Clement Attlee, the leader of the opposition Labour Party, to attend the conference as a "friend and counselor" of the British government. Stalin had no immediate political worries—after all, he'd maintained control of the Soviet Union, since 1929, with a network of secret police, domestic terror, and, in the late 1930s, the purge trials that got rid, permanently, of many political opponents. But he too was exhausted by a war in which the number of Soviet dead had exceeded twenty million, and, at sixty-six, he was far from robust.

Potsdam was moderately shattered (a castle built by Frederick the Great had recently been demolished by a British air raid), but among its intact buildings were six royal and imperial palaces, some of them failed emulations of Versailles. One of these, Schloss Cecilienhof, an attempt to evoke an English country house, with Tudor trimmings, was selected as the meeting place. The three leaders were to stay in Potsdam's once-prosperous Babelsberg neighborhood, on Lake Griebnitz, situated about a mile and a half from the Schloss. Babelsberg had remained fairly intact and, at first glance, looked much like the unshattered place where, in another time, the once-renowned

UFA film studios had produced Fritz Lang's *Metropolis* and Josef von Sternberg's *The Blue Angel*, and, in the mid-1930s, with the rise of Nazism, Leni Riefenstahl's *Triumph of the Will*. One could easily imagine a good life among the well-to-do, many of them high-ranking Nazis, and the filmmakers who worked for them. Each large villa came with a Steinway or Bechstein grand piano. Joan Bright Astley, who worked for Churchill's war cabinet, saw the enclave as "an oasis of material comfort in a desert of devastation."

Some thirty-eight houses were assigned to the Americans, and maintained by household staffs, who watched over amenities that included barber service, laundry facilities, and toothbrushes wrapped in cellophane. Truman's "Little White House," painted yellow and overgrown with vines, was a twenty-three-room, three-story stucco villa, at 2 Kaiserstrasse, and like the other houses was set close to the road, with rear gardens that stretched to the lake. Doc Matthews, who roomed there with Chip Bohlen, wrote home to say that the house "used to belong to a big Nazi movie producer who has long since disappeared"—probably to a "labor battalion," in Siberia. "His wife works in the neighborhood as a charwoman now and is glad to do so for she gets more rations that way." Stimson thought that "except for the heat and mosquitoes"—Berlin and environs were going through an intense hot spell—his quarters were "fairly comfortable." The Russians had installed two new bathrooms. They'd also very likely bugged the house, as they'd done during the conferences in Tehran and Yalta. The interior, the Baltimore *Sun*'s Price Day wrote, showed off "overdone lampshades, sentimental lithographs, statues of women and children, too many stuffed birds and a bewilderment of ornate clocks."

Churchill arrived two hours after Truman, and settled in two blocks away, at 23 Ringstrasse—"a beautiful house . . . surrounded on every side by forests," he told his wife, Clementine, though he too complained about the heat. Stalin had been delayed by a heart ailment of uncertain severity. His arrival, a day later, solved the matter that had vexed Churchill during his conversations with Davies: There would be no Stalin-Truman meeting before Churchill got his à deux chance. That was to come the next day, July 16, at 11 a.m., an early hour for a late-riser like Churchill.

"Well, I gave him as cordial a reception as I could—being naturally (I hope) a polite and agreeable person," Truman wrote home. He was determined not to be impressed by Churchill's celebrity, or smothered by his charm: "I am sure we can get along if he doesn't try to give me too much soft soap." Afterward, he judged the prime minister to be "a most charming and a very clever person—meaning clever in the English not the Kentucky sense. He gave me a lot of hooey about how great my country is and how he loved Roosevelt and how he intended to love me etc etc."

Churchill's impression of Truman was less guarded: "Winston has fallen for the President" was how Charles McMoran Wilson—Lord Moran, the Prime Minister's doctor—saw it. The prime minister seemed to think that Truman had fallen for him too, but those early conversations were uncomfortable, especially when Churchill began referring to "the melancholy financial position of Great Britain," an admission that his country was broke. "We should require time to get on our feet again," he told Truman, sounding less like the leader who'd given courage and hope to a beleaguered nation, and more like an American senator seeking disaster relief after a tornado had ripped through his state.

Soon after Churchill left, Truman ventured out to see Berlin—"to do a little sightseeing," as Byrnes put it—to inspect the wreckage of Germany's defeat. He was accompanied by Byrnes and Leahy, and their excursion quickly grew to ten cars, motoring past what remained: the Victory Column, erected after the Franco-Prussian War, in 1870; most of the Brandenburg Gate; then, along Unter den Linden, to the kaiser's palace. German civilians, who watched with passive curiosity, noticed a tall, uniformed man in the lead car—Major General Floyd L. Parks, commander of the city's American Sector. No one seemed interested in Truman, the man in the blue suit and tan Stetson, who rode in the second car, an open convertible. Churchill, who'd decided to tour Berlin in another caravan, did not go unrecognized: Some onlookers turned away, some smiled, and one older man shook his fist and said, "There he is, the old one." The two motorcades met briefly when they crossed the Unter den Linden.

It was not hard to feel some sympathy for the battered Germans.

Admiral Leahy's antipathy toward Russia was such that he wanted to blame most of the destruction on Russian artillery, explaining that "it was not hard to distinguish between the effects of artillery and of aerial bombing," as if flattening the city by air had been a gentler path to ruin. Leahy regarded the Germans, unlike the Russians, as "a highly cultured and proud people who are racial kinsmen of the English and the Americans" and just happened to have "followed false leaders to their destruction."

The drive had a dreamlike quality. Churchill's chief military adviser, Lord Alanbrooke—General Alan Brooke—"found it hard to believe that after all these years' struggles, I was driving through Berlin!" Lord Ismay—General Hastings Lionel "Pug" Ismay, Churchill's chief of staff—noted that the "only Germans to be seen were a few old men and women pushing wheelbarrows, perambulators and hand-carts piled up with their pathetic possessions. . . . There was a smell of death and decay, and one wondered how many corpses still lay in the ruins."

Both motorcades stopped on Wilhelmstrasse, where the passengers observed the smoked walls of the Reich Chancellery and what was left of the balcony—the "Hitler balcony." The Chancellery appeared at first to be a pile of rubble (the balcony had collapsed over an entrance), but John McCloy thought it was still "an impressive affair even in its present state of serious destruction." Truman wanted to go in—it was, after all, where the Reich, and its fuehrer, had met their end—but, at Byrnes's urging, he stayed in the car. Truman's reflections, in all their banality, have been quoted in many histories: "It is a demonstration of what can happen when a man overreaches himself. I never saw such destruction. I don't know whether they learned anything from it or not."

As for the wasteland that had once been the lively city of Berlin, Truman showed little curiosity; the depressing picture that stayed with him was "the long, never-ending procession of old men, women, and children wandering aimlessly . . . carrying, pushing, or pulling what was left of their belongings. In that two-hour drive I saw evidence of a great world tragedy." Churchill, who'd seen firsthand the bombing of British cities, couldn't resist a closer inspection of the bunker, and followed a Russian soldier down a flight of stairs. He turned back when told that there were two more flights, dissuaded by the impending upstairs climb but also by the smell—of corpses, and garbage—the stink becoming more intense in temperatures that exceeded ninety degrees Fahrenheit. Outside, perspiring and wiping his forehead, Churchill sat in an adjoining courtyard, which was covered with shell splinters. "Hitler must have come out here to get some air, and heard the guns getting nearer and nearer," Churchill said, as if to himself, adding that "it was from here that Hitler planned to govern the world." These thoughts made him smile. "That is why England is where she is," he added, contentedly. "I'll tell Stalin about this."

A White House aide, George McKee Elsey, a twenty-seven-year-old former duty officer, made the full descent to Hitler's study, where a large marble-topped table had been shattered. He couldn't resist picking up some of Hitler's stationery, as well as a "pocketful of Nazi medals." John McCloy took possession of a chair from Eva Braun's bedroom, a "gift" presented by General Parks. McCloy realized that he didn't know how to get it home, "and I feel as if I were very much of a 'looter,'" but Parks and his MPs "took two others so I felt less guilty." Joseph Davies, whom Truman had invited to attend the conference, took a stack of dinner invites that had belonged to Hermann Göring's family. He filled in the date, and sent invitations from Hermann and Emmy Göring to various members of the American delegation, a macabre, and slightly unsettling, prank.

This contagious search for keepsakes went well beyond Berlin. By the time of the Potsdam conference, the ruins of Hitler's mountain retreat in Berchtesgaden had been visited by GIs and nurses, as well as generals and congressmen, many writing their names on the walls. A corporal named Edward Kilitsky, a Third Army soldier, picked up a set of dishes from the SS barracks and sent them to relatives, in Philadelphia, who posed for a newspaper photographer with their Nazi dinnerware.

4. On the day that the war's victors went sightseeing in Berlin, the world's first atomic bomb was exploded in the American Southwest. The brief, blazing light from the Trinity test, in New

Mexico, could be seen as far away as Albuquerque and El Paso. A story, on page thirty-four, of the *El Paso Herald-Post*, said it was caused by an army ammunition explosion and that many "saw a flash light up the sky, like daylight, and felt earth tremors." A newspaper reported that "a blind woman . . . saw the light." Stimson, in Potsdam, got the report at about 7:30 p.m., in a cable from his assistant, George L. Harrison, a former New York Life Insurance executive. Stimson took the cable immediately to Truman's villa, at 2 Kaiserstrasse, where he showed it to the President and Byrnes, "who of course were greatly interested, although the information was still in very general terms." The cable said:

> *Operated on this morning. Diagnosis not yet complete but results seem satisfactory and already exceed expectations. Local press release necessary as interest extends great distance. . . . I will keep you posted.*

McCloy thought "the whole thing seems ominous," and Truman's reliance on Byrnes and Leahy worried him. "It is not a particularly intellectually-minded group the President has about him," he thought, "though Byrnes is astute and experienced. There will be some Missouri and old Leahy in our policies from now on—I do not know how enlightened it will be." Then: "It amazes me how the power to dispose the world reposes in these three men gathered here—God give them light!" A more detailed account, carried to Potsdam five days later by an army courier, included an arresting description of the explosion written by a brigadier general, Thomas F. Farrell:

> *The whole country was lighted by a searing light with the intensity many times that of the midday sun. It was golden, purple, violet, gray, and blue. It lighted every peak, crevasse and ridge of the nearby mountain range with a clarity and beauty that cannot be described but must be seen to be imagined.*

Stimson took this more detailed description to Truman's Babelsberg villa, and afterward observed that "the President was tremendously pepped up by it and spoke to me of it again and again when I saw him. He said it gave him an entirely new feeling of confidence." It seemed to give Truman a feeling of superstitious awe, which he waited several days to record, in his diary: "We have discovered the most terrible bomb in the history of the world. It may be the fire destruction prophesied in the Euphrates Valley era, after Noah and his fabulous ark." When Churchill read General Farrell's description, his excitement seemed insuppressible. He waved a cigar and said to the American secretary of war, "Stimson, what was gunpowder? Trivial. What was electricity? Meaningless. This atomic bomb is the second coming in wrath." The world seemed to have been rearranged: "We now had something in our hands which would redress the balance with the Russians!" To Lord Alanbrooke, Churchill sounded transported, and even a little bloodthirsty: "Now we could say if you insist on doing this or that, 'Well we can just blot out Moscow, then Stalingrad, then Kiev, then Kuibyshev, Karkhov, Stalingrad [sic], Sebastopol etc etc. And now where are the Russians!!!"

When McCloy later observed Truman and Churchill, he thought that the news had even affected their body language, and that they had begun to act like "little boys with a big red apple secreted on their person." In motion-picture images from that time, one can see Truman, with a confident expression, wearing a Stetson, advancing with a sure-footed stride.

THREE

An Unsteady Alliance

Let us define the western borders of Poland, and we shall then be clearer on the question of Germany. I find it very hard to say what Germany is just now.

—Joseph Stalin, July 18, 1945

1. The White House aide George Elsey remembered how, in the late morning of July 17, as Stalin stepped out of his armored limousine at Truman's yellow stucco villa, Truman's friend and aide (General) Harry Vaughan came out the front door, bounded down the half-dozen steps, and headed straight for the generalissimo—the title that Marshal Stalin had recently awarded himself—his right arm extended as if "to shake the hand of a fellow Rotarian." Stalin was "startled [and] froze in his tracks. His escorts bristled," but he nonetheless shook Vaughan's hand, and was led inside to Truman, who was at his desk. Truman recalled looking up, and "there stood Stalin in the doorway," as if he'd just materialized. Then, "after the usual polite remarks, we got down to business," although the "business" seemed to be Truman's eagerness to demonstrate his readiness. "I told Stalin that I am no diplomat but usually said yes or no to questions after hearing all the argument. It pleased him. I asked him if he had the agenda for the meeting. He said he had and that he had some more questions to present. I told him to fire away. He did and it is dynamite—but I have some dynamite too which I'm not exploding now"—a not-so-sly private reference to the Trinity test. "I can deal with Stalin," he continued. "He is honest—but smart as hell."

Over the years, that appraisal of Stalin's intelligence wouldn't change, but Truman's view of him would veer from ingenuous (the benign, ironic "Uncle Joe" appellation, dating from Roosevelt's time) to mistrustful, hostile, and grudgingly impressed. He somehow managed to separate his suspicion of "the Russians," and the presumed malignance of the Politburo, from the Stalin he'd met in Germany. Henry Wallace remembered Truman saying to him that "the 'old man' had a good heart." Truman never seemed particularly curious about Stalin's homicidal past, such as his role in the state-enforced starvation of millions of Ukrainians—the *Holodomor*—in the early 1930s, or the murderous purges of party unfaithful. Nor, for all the writerly flair that Truman could occasionally muster, were there many personal impressions, though he "most especially noticed" Stalin's "eyes, his face and his expression," and he was surprised at how short Stalin was, shortness being a subject that he touched on often enough to suggest that Truman was sensitive about his own height. He'd once said that "the whole Roosevelt family is very short," although Franklin Roosevelt was six-foot-two. He thought that the five-foot-ten Theodore Roosevelt, whom he once saw in the flesh, "was a very small man, he was only about 5 foot six inches tall, and he had a cushion in the bottom of the car so he could stand up and look taller than he really was." A few days before the end of the Potsdam conference, he made the curious remark that "It is always easy to understand and to get along with big men. It is only the 'little fellow' who are hard to deal with. That is because of their egotism and desire to show off their knowledge and 'strut their stuff.' " Years later, when Truman referred to Stalin as "that little son-of-a-bitch," he was still engaged in competitive measurements, insisting that he "was a good six inches shorter than I am and even Churchill was only three inches taller than Joe! Yet I was the little man in stature and intellect! So the press said." Truman was five-foot-nine; Stalin was probably five-foot-six, and Churchill's height was about the same as Stalin's.

The onetime ambassador Andrei Gromyko was struck that Stalin "was always unhurried," and recalled that "I never saw him increase his pace, and it seemed to me that time itself slowed down when he was at work." Others noticed that, close up, one could see that Stalin's face was pockmarked and his teeth discolored, or that "the impressive part of him was a very large head." Such particulars came from people like Milovan Djilas, who noticed that Stalin would toy with his pipe—an English Dunhill, which he'd sometimes fill with tobacco from the Herzegovina Flor cigarettes he smoked. After Stalin's death, Djilas felt free to write that "his hair was sparse, though his scalp was not completely bald. . . . His teeth were black and irregular, turned inward. Not even his mustache was thick or firm." Unlike Joseph Davies, who was struck by Stalin's "exceedingly kindly and gentle" brown eyes, Djilas was drawn to "those yellow eyes and a mixture of sternness and roguishness." Yet Churchill's daughter, Mary, remembered Stalin as "small, dapper and rather twinkly." Truman was determined to shrink Churchill and Stalin to ordinary dimensions, and wrote home that "old fat Winston" was "as windy as old [William] Langer"—a Republican senator from North Dakota. He saw Stalin as a type, akin to a political boss from Jackson County, later remarking to Jonathan Daniels, "He was as near like Tom Pendergast as any man I know."

Stalin apologized for his late arrival (that vague heart ailment), and Truman, with Midwestern hospitality, asked him to stay for lunch. When Stalin replied that it wasn't possible, Truman had the obvious rejoinder: "You could if you wanted to." Stalin stayed, and lunchtime conversation, as Jimmy Byrnes recalled, was "general in nature and cordial in spirit." The question of Hitler's death came up, as it had when Stalin met with Harry Hopkins, and Stalin still said he believed Hitler was alive, and possibly in Spain or Argentina. Truman, who found Stalin to be "in a good humor" and "extremely polite," knew that he ought to inform his guest about the Trinity test, but he'd told Churchill "I think I had best just tell him after one of our meetings that we have an entirely novel form of bomb."

2. Schloss Cecilienhof, built for Crown Prince William in 1917, had nearly two hundred rooms in four wings. The Russians had refurbished three dozen of them, along with planting a Soviet Red Star, made of geraniums, in the central courtyard, a floral arrangement that endures to this day. The palace was surrounded by a park that contained the rough graves of soldiers who'd been shot in nearby skirmishes. In one section, headstones commemorated the departed dogs and cats of the crown prince's household.

A contemporary visitor is likely to be surprised by the intimacy of the oak-paneled conference hall, and the tight seating around the circular table: fifteen men (the three leaders, their foreign secretaries, interpreters, and ambassadors) used straight-backed chairs; Truman, Stalin, and Churchill had the luxury of armrests. Military and civilian advisers sat behind the leaders, and lower-level staff sat behind *them*, taking notes. The plenary sessions, usually held in the late afternoon, could be brief, sometimes less than two hours. When discussions were tedious, delays for translation made them more so. They could stall over minor points, such as the distinction between "reparations" and "booty" when it came to the disposition of the German fleet. A number of topics from the Yalta conference were revisited: national boundaries (Poland's in particular), German war reparations, and Nazi war crimes. There was quick agreement to establish a Council of Foreign Ministers, a subject that had been discussed in Yalta. The ministers could meet periodically and, because they served at the pleasure of their governments, might not bind any nation to much of anything.

There was considerable secrecy, and a need-to-know atmosphere. Even Secretary of War Stimson felt excluded—"crippled by not knowing what happens in the meetings in the late afternoon and evening." He resented the influence of Byrnes, who "gave me the impression that he was hugging matters . . . pretty close to his bosom." When Stimson asked Byrnes if there were minutes "which I could have the privilege of looking over," Byrnes replied that they wouldn't be transcribed until the conference was over. In fact, there were no designated stenographers, and, as a result, there are no wholly reliable records of what was said, though the rough Soviet transcripts and the Potsdam volumes, contained in *Foreign Relations of the United States*, track pretty closely.

Truman was asked to preside over the plenary sessions, as Roosevelt had in Tehran and Yalta. It was not an unfamiliar task for a veteran legislator, but Washington hadn't prepared him for anything like Potsdam: "It makes presiding over the Senate seem tame," he told Bess. "I was so scared I didn't know whether things were going according to Hoyle or not." Nor was Potsdam prepared for Truman's occasional rawness, his out-of-placeness. Yet if he lacked the easy assurance of Roosevelt, his stubbornness and outward steadiness had another kind of value. "So I preside," he told his mother. "Churchill talks all the time and Stalin just grunts but you know what he means."

He didn't confess how homesick he was, but he couldn't hide how he hated it when the day's mail came without news from home. "I've only had one letter from you since I left," he wrote to Bess, on July 18, a day when the temperature fell by fifteen degrees, and gray skies moved in. "I look carefully through every pouch that comes— but so far not much luck." At midnight on July 18 (late afternoon in Missouri), as he was intensely missing the voices of home, he spoke to Bess by radio-telephone.

Truman thought his international debut had been a success. "They all say I took 'em for a ride when I got down to presiding," he told his mother and sister. "It was a nerve wracking experience but it had to be done." He told Bess that "Admiral Leahy said he'd never seen an abler job and Byrnes and my fellows seemed to be walking on air." Byrnes, though, thought it had not gone all that well, and that Truman had "got very snappy with Stalin." The columnist Drew Pearson was informed, undoubtedly by Byrnes, that Truman spoke "as if he were lecturing a schoolroom," while making clear that "I don't expect to stay here all summer." That account is supported by a July 20 letter to Bess, in which Truman portrayed himself in a favorite, pugilistic pose: "We had a tough meeting yesterday. I reared up on my hind legs and told 'em where to get off and they got off. I have to make it perfectly plain to them at least once a day that so far as this President is concerned Santa Claus is dead and that my first interest is U.S.A., then I want the Jap War won and I want 'em both in it. Then I want peace—world peace and will do what can be done by us to get it. But certainly am not going to . . . pay reparations, feed the world, and get nothing for it but a nose thumbing." He concluded, "They are beginning to awake to the fact that I mean business."

Truman had somehow got the idea that Stalin "seems to like it when I hit him with a hammer." That sounded tough, but there is little in the limited transcripts of that day's meeting to suggest that sort of hectoring by Truman, although at one point he insisted that he expected the Yalta agreements to be carried out "to the letter." Yet whatever Truman actually said, and in what tone, there must have been *something* to trouble Joseph Davies, who, the State Department's Doc Matthews recalled, passed a note to the President saying, "I think Stalin's feelings are hurt. Do be kind to him."

Churchill's interpreter A. H. Birse thought that Truman's manner "was that of a polite but determined chairman of a Board Meeting." Alexander Cadogan, the British permanent under secretary of state, appreciated Truman's directness—"most quick and businesslike," he thought—in contrast to Churchill, who seemed unusually distracted, very likely because of the upcoming parliamentary vote. He'd been that way since leaving London, Cadogan thought—"has refused to do any work or read anything," and worse, refused to stay quiet when he doesn't understand what's being discussed. "Instead of that, he butts in on every occasion and talks the most irrelevant rubbish, and risks giving away our case at every point." He thought Truman looked "noticeably restless" during some of Churchill's "more repetitious speeches." It seemed to Archibald Clark-Kerr, the British ambassador to Russia, that Churchill was sometimes reduced to pure emotion, someone who could "transform his face from the rosiest, happiest, the most laughing, dimpled and mischievous baby's bottom into the face of an angry, and outraged bullfrog!"

Stalin was the most disciplined of the three, a State Department official thought, demonstrating a "well-ordered mind—things stored there in proper sequence and order"; Doc Matthews, who'd met Stalin in Yalta, got an impression of "great power and ruthlessness." He might listen passively until something interested him, at which point "he would hold forth, sometimes sharply, sometimes pleadingly or cynically, sometimes with flashing anger." Stalin's doggedness could at times be matched by Truman's, as when the three principals began a baffling dialogue on what Churchill called "the meaning of 'Germany'"—whether it should be thought of "in the same sense as before the war."

Truman: How is this question understood by the Soviet delegation?

Stalin: Germany is what she has become after the war. There is
no other Germany. That is how I understand the question.

Truman: Is it possible to speak of Germany as she had been before the war, in 1937?

Stalin: As she is in 1945.

Truman: She lost everything in 1945; actually, Germany no longer exists.

Stalin: Germany is, as we say, a geographical concept. Let's take
it this way for the time being. We cannot abstract ourselves
from the results of the war.

Truman: Yes, but there must be some definition of the concept of
"Germany." I believe the Germany of 1886 or of 1937 is not
the same thing as Germany today, in 1945.

3. Churchill, who'd once been a journalist, had urged
Truman and Stalin to ban the press. He characterized the hundred
or so reporters in Berlin as a "prowling army . . . carrying 'very dangerous weapons,' attacking our fortress," and volunteered to talk
to them, "to stroke down their plumage." To Clementine he wrote,
"We are besieged in our impenetrable compound by a host of reporters who are furious at not being able to overrun us. It is impossible
to conduct grave affairs except in silence and secrecy." Charlie Ross,
the President's press secretary and another former newspaperman,
was no help to reporters, who might have done more to defog the
proceedings. Even for the participants there was no real freedom of
movement outside the meeting rooms. "One has to walk rather like
a tiger, round and round one's cage," Alexander Cadogan thought.
"If one goes outside the British Sector, one is challenged at every
yard by Russian sentries with tommy-guns." The barrier to press
coverage, a *New York Times* account noted, threatened "to have the
unfortunate result of creating the impression that [the leaders] have
gathered for a round of social activity to celebrate victory rather
than to plan the peace."

That impression was aided by the three principals, who dressed for state dinners as if the conference were a costume ball. Churchill would wear an admiral's uniform, complete with a ribbon of decorations, an outfit to which the First Lord of the Admiralty was entitled. Stalin liked to put on a white military coat with star-studded epaulets, and gold stripes running up his dark trousers. Truman, in the spirit of Americans abroad since the day of John Adams, wore dark suits, though he also made use of his tan Stetson if the occasion allowed.

Each leader took a turn at hosting a dinner. Truman went first, on July 19, at the Little White House, on 2 Kaiserstrasse, serving a meal that reflected the abundance of postwar America, with a menu that included *pâté de foie gras*, caviar, *perch sauté meunière*, filet mignon, ice cream and chocolate sauce, along with vodka, several wines, and liquors, and fresh vegetables flown in from the *Augusta*, still docked in Antwerp. Toasts were raised for the King of England, the three leaders, even the foreign ministers. "Stalin," Truman wrote home, "felt so friendly that he toasted the pianist when he played a Tskowsky (you spell it) piece especially for him. The old man loves music. He told me he'd import the greatest Russian pianist for me tomorrow. Our boy was good. His name is List and he played Chopin, Von Weber, Schubert, and all of them."

"Our boy" was Army Staff Sergeant Eugene List, a twenty-seven-year-old concert pianist, who'd been drafted as a rifleman. "The whole thing had an air of unreality about it," List wrote, in an unpublished memoir. "I remember concentrating with all my might on the eighty-eight keys of the piano, which represented something familiar and real that I could hold on to. But now and then, as I played, I would glance up and there would be Churchill or I would glance up and there would be Stalin. It was like a wild dream." List, and nineteen-year-old Private First Class Stuart Canin, a violinist, played during dinner, and after the meal, on a veranda overlooking Lake Griebnitz. "It was then," List wrote, that "Stuart and I found ourselves all too soon running out of music we could play together"— which left it up to List, as a soloist. "At what I thought was the end of that already incredible evening," he continued, "Stalin sprang up

and said, 'I want to propose a toast to the pianist!' I had been performing professionally since I was ten, but now I was petrified. President Truman motioned me forward, and someone placed a glass of
vodka in my hand. There I was, face to face with Stalin, what does
one say?"

List told Stalin that, when he was sixteen, he'd played the Shosta-
kovich Concerto, with Leopold Stokowski, and the Philadelphia Orchestra, "and Stalin seemed pleased!" Churchill asked List to play
the "Missouri Waltz" (not a Truman favorite), which List was able
to improvise—"with Stalin leaning on the piano and puffing on his
pipe." After that, someone asked Truman to play, and, List wrote, he
"gave a very good account of himself in the Paderewski Minuet"—
the Minuet in G. Before the Potsdam conference was over, List had
played five times for the presidential party, on the back porch of the
Little White House, which faced Lake Griebnitz. Truman, at least
once, helped out as a page-turner. "Imagine having the President of
the United States turn pages for you!" List wrote to his wife. "Isn't
that really something?" He was impressed by Truman's musicality:
"He loves music and what's more he understands it."

When someone asked Truman where the next conference would
be held, Truman replied "Washington," and Churchill said London,
while Stalin said, "Well, you know there are also palaces in Japan."
Truman still just wanted it to be over. "Well I'm hoping to get done
in a week," he told Bess, with unfounded optimism. "I'm sick of
the whole business—but we'll bring home the bacon." At the third,
and final, dinner, hosted by Churchill, Truman responded to com-
pliments from the prime minister, who said that everyone had been
struck by his "sincerity, frankness and powers of decision," and Stalin, who said that "honesty adorns the man." Truman said "what a
great pleasure and privilege it was for . . . a country boy from Missouri, to be associated with two such great figures as the Prime Minister and Marshal Stalin." Playing the part of a modest newcomer
was a way for Truman to edge toward equality.

Truman waited until the eighth plenary session adjourned, on
July 24, to tell Stalin about the Trinity test. He'd wanted to do it
"nonchalantly," and had told Chip Bohlen that he'd rely solely on

the Russian translator so as not to signal that anything special was being said. Nonchalant or not, many in the conference room were discreetly staring. Anthony Eden, the British foreign minister, recalled that he and Churchill were "covertly watching," and "had some doubts whether Stalin had taken it in." Truman thought that the generalissimo "showed no unusual interest. All he said was that he was glad to hear it and hoped we would make 'good use of it against the Japanese.'"

The Russians weren't fooled. "We got the point at once," Molotov was to write. In the privacy of his villa, Stalin said that he'd spoken to Igor Kurchatov, the Soviet nuclear physicist, and "We will no doubt have our own bomb before long."

"And the Americans have been doing all this work on the atom bomb without telling us," Molotov pointed out.

"Roosevelt clearly felt no need to put us in the picture," Stalin said. "He could simply have told me the atom bomb was going through its experimental stages. We were supposed to be allies." He intended to tell Kurchatov to "speed things up."

4. When Truman had arrived in Berlin, he'd told General Eisenhower that one objective was to enlist Russia in the war against Japan; Stalin had already agreed to that, in Yalta. Eisenhower, though, urged him, as navy secretary James Forrestal noted, "not to assume that he had to give anything away to do this, that the Russians were desperately anxious to get into the Eastern war and that . . . there was no question but that Japan was already thoroughly beaten." Truman in any case had second thoughts about a Russian role as soon as he'd gotten reports of the Trinity test, which offered the promise that the war in the Pacific could be quickly won without outside help.

Truman had also brought to Berlin a proposal of his own: to put the world's inland waterways—canals and rivers—under international control, so that, as he saw it, there could be free passage to all the seas of the world. His reading of history, he explained, had convinced him that the major wars of the previous two centuries had originated between the eastern frontier of France and the western frontier of Russia. He then distributed a two-paragraph memorandum on the subject, which included setting up "interim navigation agencies for the Danube and the Rhine."

Truman's reading of history tended to be highly personal, and in this case, very much focused on the American experience—even the Missouri experience—which he saw as a model for the world. He pointed out that rivers and canals had opened up the continental United States, and said, "I do not want to fight another war in twenty years because of a quarrel on the Danube." When Truman asked for a response to his memorandum, Stalin replied that it dealt only with the Danube and the Rhine and that he was more concerned with access to the Black Sea Straits, which, under the 1936 Montreux Convention, was controlled by Turkey. When Truman said he hoped these matters could be considered together, Stalin couldn't suppress his impatience: He wanted to end the discussion. "Our ideas differ widely," he said. "Perhaps we can pass over this point now."

Truman, though, was not about to let it go; he was no longer the junior senator from Missouri, whose persistence could be ignored. Truman had an idée fixe—that national boundaries should give way to such well-traveled waterways as the Panama and Suez Canals. If the goal was not achievable, if the idea seemed pointless, Potsdam was nonetheless an ideal forum in which to present it—and a way for Truman to put his imprint on these historic moments. Because mockery was out of the question, the proposal was handed off, in all seriousness, to the Foreign Ministers Council.

Churchill meanwhile had the British election on his mind. The July 25 session adjourned at noon because the prime minister and Eden needed to return to London, to await the results. "We shall be back the day after tomorrow—or at least some of us will," Churchill said—with a chuckle, or so Doc Matthews recalled. "We have been going at it hammer and tongs in the last few days and it looks as if we may finish up Sunday," Truman wrote, longingly, to Bess, on the day of Churchill's departure. But Churchill, whose Tory government suffered a substantial defeat, never returned to Berlin. The results were soon clear, and at 7:30 p.m., on July 26, the king invited Clement

Attlee for form a new government. The new PM chose Ernest Bevin, a former dockworker and labor organizer, to replace Eden as foreign minister. "It's too bad about Churchill," Truman wrote home, "but it may turn out to be all right for the world."

Truman, though, discovered that he missed Churchill. "He knew his English language," he told Margaret, "and after he'd talked half an hour, there'd be at least one gem of a sentence and two thoughts maybe, which could have been expressed in four minutes." He continued, "Anyway, he is a likable person, and these two"—Attlee and Bevin, who made their first joint appearance on July 28—"are sourpusses." Attlee, he continued, "is an Oxford graduate and talks with that deep-throated swallowing enunciation, same as Eden does. But I understand him reasonably well. Bevin is a tough guy. He doesn't know, of course, that your dad has been dealing with that sort all his life, from building trades to coal miners." The conference was winding down. After a short July 28 session, which adjourned at midnight, Stalin became "indisposed," and two more days passed without a plenary session. Truman found time to write to Churchill, telling him it was a "shock" to learn the result of the English election, and that "We miss you very much here . . . but we wish you the happiest possible existence from now to the last call." He added the somewhat self-celebratory thought that "we shall always remember that you held the barbarians until we could prepare."

The conferees became a little punchy during a discussion of German war crimes, when Attlee objected to Molotov's suggestion that the phrase "such as Goering, etc." should be added after the word "criminals." It was difficult, Attlee argued, to pre-select the defendants—they might want to add more names. Stalin, reasonably enough, said that the phrase "such as" left the list open-ended. "Every country has its favorite Nazi war criminal," he said. Byrnes, in apparent agreement with Attlee, said that "if the Conference failed to include these favorites, it would be difficult to explain why they were not on the list." When Attlee observed that there was some doubt as to whether Hitler was alive, "and he was not on the list," Stalin replied that "Hitler was not at our disposal," but he was willing to make that concession: Hitler should be added to the list, Stalin said, at which point laughter broke out. A Russian interpreter observed that "Stalin gave Hitler a gift of many years of semi-mythical life after death."

None of this diminished Truman's interest in bringing open access to inland waterways, which he again insisted "had been a hot bed for breeding wars during European history," and that it was a matter of "vital importance." On August 1, the final day of the conference, Truman still couldn't let it go: All he wanted in the final communiqué was "a factual statement" that the waterways proposal had been referred to the foreign ministers. "There was already enough in the protocol"—the first draft—Stalin said. That's when Truman lost patience: "I have accepted a number of compromises during this conference to conform with your views," he told Stalin, "and I make a personal request now that you yield on this point."

Stalin seemed to understand most of what Truman was saying, and even before his translator was done, he interrupted to say, "*Nyet*!" Then he added, in English, "No. I say 'no!'" A diplomat who had been sitting behind Truman and Byrnes, recalled that "Truman could not mistake the rebuff. His face flushed, and he turned to the American delegation and said, loud enough to be overheard, 'I cannot understand that man!'" He was also overheard saying, "Jimmy, do you realize that we have been here seventeen whole days? Why, in seventeen days you can decide anything!"

It was past midnight when the conference ended, which might explain the sour notes and short tempers. The lack of any meaningful accomplishment didn't help matters. After more than two weeks, and so many hours of laborious discussion, the future of Poland remained pretty much up to the Soviet Union, just as it had after the Yalta meeting; the question of war reparations, if any, remained unsettled; the status of Berlin was unclear, and the whereabouts of the post-suicidal Adolf Hitler remained a subject for fantasists. One could already see fissures in the alliance with Soviet Russia. Years later, Chip Bohlen talked with Charles Mee, the author of a fine book on Potsdam, about Truman's waterways obsession—a subject, Mee wrote, that "was still faintly embarrassing." With a shrug, Bohlen said, "Well, that was the President's own idea. . . . Everyone has these little flights of fancy; sometimes they simply go so far beyond the realm of the possible that it is best just to let them pass."

∞

If Truman was a familiar sort to the Americans, to the Old World he sometimes seemed a semi-exotic creature, whose unembarrassed declarations and cheerful resilience concealed his difficulty in sensing the motives, and agendas, of others. Truman was used to speaking not only American English, but a language shorn of diplomatic nuance and evasion, and it gave him good reason to hate being stuck in the tiring, argumentative, unresolved Potsdam discussions. Archibald Clark-Kerr, the British ambassador to Moscow, was struck by the stylistic shift from Roosevelt. "The prestige, the cocksureness," he thought, had been replaced by "drabness, bewilderment and an acute sense of inferiority, which were painful to watch." For all that, Clark-Kerr, with patronizing smugness, found Truman to be "endearing and disarming in his utter simplicity and modesty." Such attempts to assess Truman missed a lot—that he was both simpler and more complicated than he appeared to people like the blinkered Clark-Kerr. The essential Truman, rarely visible inside Schloss Cecilienhof, was on view during a break in the conference, on a ninety-seven-degree day in the Rhine Valley, when he visited American troops. He shook hands with GIs, played the piano—in "a jazzy style"—and ate fried chicken and ice cream. He wanted the soldiers to know that he was one of them. "My one regret in the later unpleasantness is that I was not allowed to wear a uniform," he said, sounding as if he meant it, and which, at that moment, he may have. That too was Truman, unguarded, far from home, embracing sentiments that the Old World might observe, but could not understand.

FOUR

"The Basic Power of the Universe"

In this last great action of the Second World War we were given final proof that war is death.

—Henry L. Stimson

1. There was never a doubt that what Secretary of War Stimson liked to call "S-1" and the British referred to as "Tube Alloys" (or, when it was still possible to joke, "Myrna Alloys"), would be used against Japan, and on July 25, while Truman was still in Potsdam, he gave the order forever associated with his presidency: to drop the "first special bomb" on a Japanese target, sometime after August 3, with visual targeting. "The target will be a purely military one and we will issue a warning statement asking the Japs to surrender and save lives," Truman wrote in his diary. "I'm sure they will not do that, but we will have given them the chance."

Japan got the warning—the "Potsdam Declaration"—a day after the order went to Carl A. Spaatz, the commanding general in the Pacific. Unless Japan met the demand for unconditional surrender, it said, the Allies would launch the "inevitable and complete destruction of the Japanese armed forces" and "the utter devastation of the Japanese homeland." The ultimatum's provisions included an occupation, "stern justice" for war criminals, establishment of democratic values, and a promise that sounded almost conciliatory: "We do not intend that the Japanese shall be enslaved as a race or destroyed as a nation." It didn't mention the future of the emperor. As expected, the terms of the Potsdam Declaration were quickly rejected.

"The final decision of where and when to use the atomic bomb was up to me," Truman wrote in his memoirs, which he meant to be his last word on the decision. He repeated himself a page later: "I had made the decision." In theory, Truman could have decided *not* to use the bomb, but that would have meant reversing a decision that, as a practical matter, had been made for him. In any case, dropping the first atomic weapon was what Truman and his advisers had anticipated and wanted. The "Interim Committee," the innocuous name for a group whose temporary duties were to consider the bomb's implications and purpose, completed its work on June 1, 1945, and recommended using it "as soon as possible," against a military target, with no warning about its power. "So far as I can remember, the question as to whether the atomic bomb should be dropped . . . was never voted on or seriously discussed in any meeting . . . that I attended," Assistant Secretary of State William Clayton, a member of the Interim Committee, recalled. "I think it was just accepted as settled policy." The physicist Arthur Holly Compton thought "it seemed to be a foregone conclusion that the bomb would be used."

As to *where* it should be dropped, the "Target Committee," when it met on May 10 and 11, put Kyoto, once Japan's capital and the emperor's residence for a thousand years, in the number one spot. "From the psychological point of view," the committee concluded, "there is the advantage that Kyoto is an intellectual center . . . and the people there are more apt to appreciate the significance of such a weapon." Striking Kyoto from the list became a personal mission for Secretary of War Stimson, who argued, with some passion, that the city was not a military target but "exclusively a place of homes and art and shrines." Stimson made the case to Truman that, if Kyoto was destroyed, "the bitterness which would be caused by such a wanton act might make it impossible during the long post-war period to reconcile the Japanese to us in that area rather than to the Russians." That apparently persuaded Truman, whose July 25 diary entry said, "Even if the Japs are savages, ruthless, merciless and fanatic, we as the leader of the world for the common welfare cannot drop this terrible bomb on the old capital . . . "—Kyoto—"or the new"—Tokyo. "He & I are in accord." Four cities remained on the target list: Hiroshima, Kokura, Niigata, and Nagasaki.

Despite suggestions that the weapon should be demonstrated in an isolated spot (Stimson, on July 2, had asked Truman if it was worth trying to "warn Japan into surrender"), the President was persuaded by General Marshall, Byrnes, and others, that dropping the bomb on a city would end the fighting sooner, and that, by avoiding a land invasion, it would spare a half-million American lives. That number, which Truman would cite for years, was something of a fiction. Estimates of potential battle casualties have fluctuated, but Barton J. Bernstein has argued, persuasively, that the more realistic cost of an invasion of mainland Japan, lasting four months, was a quarter-million casualties, with a death toll much lower than that. But no matter the number, Truman understood that it was a president's duty to protect American soldiers; momentum overcame doubt and hesitation. Not least of the reasons to go forward was a natural, if chilly, curiosity to see if, and how, the "gadget" (the bomb's laboratory nickname) worked in an actual war. There was also an awareness that simply possessing such an instrument of war would be useful in future dealings with Russia. Byrnes seemed to refer to that when he remarked to Joseph Davies that "'the New Mexico situation' had given us great power, and that in the last analysis, it would control." But it takes several leaps back in history to be persuaded that, at that time and place—and after Russia had agreed to join the war against Japan—intimidation of the Soviet Union was an urgent question.

By any rational measure, Japan had already been defeated. In March 1945, in the deadliest aerial bombardment in history, some three hundred B-29s, under the direction of the air force general Curtis LeMay, dropped nearly two thousand tons of incendiary bombs on Tokyo, killing close to a hundred thousand people and leaving at least a million homeless. In early July, navy secretary James Forrestal learned from "highly reliable" Japanese sources that the Japanese realized that they'd lost "and are only seeking a face-saving way out." The bombing raids, Forrestal continued, "have knocked out a large portion of their ability to make war and . . . the people of many cities have become homeless mobs." It is sometimes pointed out that the United States Strategic Bombing Survey, a year later, concluded that Japan would have given up by the end of 1945, and perhaps sooner, "even if the atomic bombs had not been dropped, even if Russia had not entered the war, and even if no invasion had been planned or contemplated." But Truman and his generals didn't possess that useful future intelligence in the summer of 1945.

2. Truman wanted to be far from Germany when news of the bomb broke, knowing it could come as early as August 3. "I don't want to have to answer any questions from Stalin," he told his aide George Elsey, and he made his escape from Berlin on August 2, at eight in the morning. "I am very sure no one wants to go back to that awful city," he wrote in his diary. He was in a hurry to get home—so eager to return that he turned down invitations to visit Denmark, France, and Norway. But he had one more stop, three hours later: His plane landed close to Mill Dock, Plymouth, where the *Augusta* was now anchored. Nearby was the HMS *Renown*, a British battle cruiser, whose passengers included George VI, who'd traveled by train from London to welcome the President. The king, wearing his navy uniform, personally greeted Truman when he was piped aboard, accompanied by Byrnes and Admiral Leahy.

King George knew all about the Tube Alloys—"our new terrific explosion," Truman called it—and, when he asked Leahy for his opinion, Leahy replied, as he had before, "I do not think it will be as effective as is expected. It sounds like a professor's dream to me!" The king disagreed, Leahy recalled: "Jestingly he said to me, 'Admiral, would you like to lay a little bet on that?'" Truman's spare account of meeting George VI includes the anodyne assessment that "I found him to be well-informed on all that was taking place, and he gave me the impression of a man with great common sense." Truman enjoyed lunch enough to remember the menu—"a nice and appetizing lunch—soup, fish, lamb chops, peas, potatoes and ice cream with chocolate sauce." During the meal, they "talked of most everything, and nothing much." The king's private secretary, Sir Alan Lascelles, later chatted with the diplomat and diarist Harold Nicolson. "He tells me that . . . all went very well indeed," Nicolson wrote. "Truman is short, square, simple and looks one straight in the face." By contrast, "the Secretary of State is a chatterbox. At luncheon . . . Byrnes began discussing in front of the waiters the impending release of the atomic bomb. As this was top-secret, the King was appalled. 'I think, Mr. Byrnes', he said, 'that we should discuss this interesting subject over our coffee.'"

Just after 3 p.m., the king paid a reciprocal call on the *Augusta*. He spent half an hour in the President's quarters, during which, in Truman's words, they "put on the formalities." The king signed the ship's guest book, collected autographs for his daughters, Elizabeth and Margaret, "took a snort of Haig & Haig," and signed a card for Truman's daughter before returning to the *Renown*. Truman and his companions saw the king off at 3:34 p.m., and fifteen minutes later, the *Augusta* set sail for Newport News, at maximum speed. All in all, Truman spent about five hours in the United Kingdom.

⸺⸺⸺⸺⸺

Four days later, aboard the *Augusta,* Truman was eating lunch with the crew, in the enlisted men's mess, when the ship's captain, Frank E. Graham, brought him a message from Stimson, confirming that "Little Boy," a ninety-seven-hundred-pound fission bomb, had been dropped on its target:

> HIROSHIMA WAS BOMBED VISUALLY WITH ONLY ONE TENTH COVER AT SEVEN FIFTEEN P M WASHINGTON TIME AUGUST FIVE. . . . RESULTS CLEAR CUT SUCCESSFUL IN ALL RESPECTS. VISIBLE EFFECTS GREATER THAN IN ANY TEST.

Truman turned to shake Graham's hand. "This is the greatest thing in history," he said. Ten minutes later, another report came from Stimson:

COMPLETE SUCCESS, EVEN MORE CONSPICUOUS THAN
IN EARLIER TEST, IS INDICATED BY FIRST REPORTS.

After reading this second message, Truman, jubilant, almost giddy, spoke to the nearby sailors and said "It's time for us to get on home!" The United Press's Merriman Smith, recalling that moment, wrote that "as the noise in the mess hall died down and the sailors listened expectantly," Truman announced "our first assault on Japan with a terrifically powerful new weapon, which used an explosive twenty thousand times as powerful as a ton of TNT." After Truman left the mess hall, where "the crew cheered and clapped," he went to the wardroom, where he gave the news to the ship's officers: "Keep your seats, gentlemen. I have an announcement to make to you," he said, sounding both tense and excited. "Mr. Truman almost ran as he walked about the ship spreading the news," Smith recalled. "He was not actually laughing, but there was a broad, proud smile on his face. . . . When the President . . . shouted his good tidings, an awful load lifted from our backs."

In a presidential statement, prepared in advance and released in Washington, Truman declared that this new bomb "is a harnessing of the basic power of the universe," and that "we have spent two billion dollars on the greatest scientific gamble in history—and won." It included another demand for immediate surrender: "We are now prepared to obliterate more rapidly and completely every productive enterprise the Japanese have above ground in any city," it said. "If they do not now accept our terms they may expect a rain of ruin from the air, the like of which has never been seen on this earth." Truman couldn't speak to the nation from the *Augusta*, but a record of sorts was made: He was filmed aboard the ship, reading part of the statement, in a slow, and almost machine-like voice, his index finger guiding him through the text.

The statement was written by a public-relations man named Arthur W. Page, a Bell System employee, who was a friend and Long Island neighbor of Stimson's. Page had met twice with the Interim Committee, but even with this peripheral role, he'd felt the stress of having to keep their big secret. His military aide, Page recalled, "couldn't tell his wife what he did. I think she thought he was going crazy." Because press secretary Charlie Ross was traveling with Truman, Eben Ayers, his deputy, made the announcement in Washington, and became a little puffed up by his role. "This was a historic day, perhaps one of the most historic and significant in modern times," Ayers wrote in his diary. "It was made historic by an announcement, which I had the distinction of making."

3. The *Augusta* docked in Newport News in the late afternoon of August 7, at which point Truman traveled by car to Washington, arriving at the White House a little before eleven. Despite the late hour, quite a few members of his staff were there to greet him. Ayers thought his boss looked "fit and somewhat tanned" from the voyage, and "seemed delighted to be back and glad to see us." Surrounded by people he trusted, who, in every sense, spoke his language, Truman could once again be at ease, and less careful with every utterance. He could also return to being an early riser after a month spent with late-risers Churchill and Stalin.

A troupe of aides followed Truman upstairs to his study, on the residence floor, where he stopped to play a few bars on his piano and telephone Bess. She was in Missouri, but planned to return to Washington the next day. After drinks were ordered, Truman talked about Potsdam, and the interesting people he'd met—Stalin, Churchill, and Attlee, but especially Stalin. "The President seemed to have been favorably impressed with him and to like him," Ayers thought. "Stalin was one, he said, who if he said something one time would say the same thing the next time; in other words he could be depended upon." He'd become no fonder of Molotov—a "regular Slav," he told Henry Wallace, "obstinate and bull-headed."

Not much was yet known about what had just happened to Hiroshima. The War Department "as yet was unable to make an accurate report" because of an "impenetrable cloud of dust and smoke," leaving to the imagination how the blast, beyond that opaque veil, had affected those on the ground. This not-knowing led Tokyo Radio to report that "practically all living things, human and animal, were literally seared to death." But enough was known to realize that something had altered the direction of human history. A *Herald Tribune* editorialist wrote that an American air crew had "produced what must without doubt be the greatest simultaneous slaughter in the whole history of mankind," and asked, "Will the obliteration of one city suffice? Or will we have to repeat the horror?" Edward R. Murrow, on his CBS Radio broadcast, quoted the chemist George Kistiakowsky, who, after witnessing the July 16 Trinity test, had said, "I am sure that at the end of the world—in the last millisecond of the earth's existence—the last man will see what we saw." Beyond such apocalyptic musings, victory over Japan was certain. But there was not yet an offer to surrender.

On August 9, the egg-shaped "Fat Man," a plutonium device weighing nearly eleven thousand pounds, was dropped on Nagasaki. Although Fat Man was slightly more powerful than Little Boy, fewer people died in Nagasaki—perhaps half as many as the estimated seventy thousand killed in the initial blast in Hiroshima. Most of the damage came in a residential neighborhood, although, once again, for several hours, it was impossible to see much; a cloud of smoke, twenty thousand feet high, hid the city from aerial view. "We gave the Japanese three days in which to make up their minds to surrender, and the bombing would have been held off another two days had weather permitted," Truman wrote in his memoirs. "During those three days, we indicated that we meant business." During those days, the Twentieth Air Force sent out hundreds of B-29 bombers, for conventional bombardment.

The Nagasaki mission seems to have gone forward without a direct presidential order. After the first atomic bombing of Japan was set in motion with the July 25 directive to General Spaatz, no one was prepared to halt or delay the second one. As far as General Groves was concerned, Truman's approach, after Hiroshima, "was one of noninterference—basically a decision not to upset the existing plans." The Princeton historian Michael D. Gordin points out that, although Truman was the last link in the chain of command, Groves had "stacked the deck so that everyone involved . . . had a vested interest in seeing those bombs used as quickly and as often as necessary (or possible)."

Truman addressed the nation on that August 9 to report on the Potsdam conference, the war's progress, and, because he was unable to let go of the subject, his dream of access to inland waterways, with "free and unrestricted navigation." He once more said that Japan's only option was surrender. Otherwise, although he realized "the tragic significance of the atomic bomb. . . . We shall continue to use it until we completely destroy Japan's power to make war." At one point, Truman's language had an uncharacteristic coarseness: "The Japs will soon learn some more of the other military secrets agreed upon at Berlin," he said. "They will learn them firsthand—and they will not like them."

One of Truman's listeners, in Paris, was the American hostess Susan Mary Jay (later Susan Mary Alsop), who wrote to her friend Marietta Tree, in Washington, to say, "Every time I look at a picture of President Truman, I think what an honest, decent face he has but how incongruous it was to hear from that flat, unimpressive voice those bloodcurdling words about the power of the atomic bomb. One felt that such news should come with a clash of cymbals and the vocabulary of the three witches from *Macbeth*. Truman looks like my dentist in Washington, and the tone was the same as Dr. Osborne's 'Open just a little wider, please.'"

After Nagasaki, and Russia's declaration of war against Japan, it was hard to avoid a feeling that Japan was like a half-conscious boxer, bleeding on the ropes, and that the pounding ought to be stopped. Bishop G. Bromley Oxnam, president of the Federal Council of Churches of Christ in America, and John Foster Dulles, chairman of the Council's Commission on a Just and Durable Peace, urged a suspension of the aerial attack. Speaking from the pulpit of Trinity Church, in lower Manhattan, a minister said that victory gained by the atom bomb would come "at the price of world-wide moral revulsion against us."

On August 10, through its government radio, Japan made clear that it was ready to surrender if Emperor Hirohito could remain on the throne. "Some of those around the President wanted to demand his execution," Admiral Leahy recalled. "If they had prevailed, we might still be at war with Japan." The wait for the inevitable moment of surrender took more than eighty hours, the terms evolving in painful slow motion, in communications transmitted through neutral Switzerland. Then, on the morning of August 14, Charlie Ross told reporters that "it looked as if at last we are nearing the end of our long vigil"; the first official word of surrender reached Secretary of State Byrnes at about 3 p.m.

A formal announcement was set for seven o'clock, but before that Truman had several visitors, including, at midday, a strange entr'acte: a limousine from the British Embassy brought the Duke of Windsor, the instantly recognizable older brother of George VI, who, after abdicating the throne, at the end of 1936, had lived a life of inconsequence and whose loyalty to the Allied cause was, at the very least, suspect. He stayed with the President for about half an hour. At 6:57 p.m., reporters crowded into Truman's office, where the President, standing at his desk, and smiling broadly, said, "Ladies and gentlemen, this is a great day, a day we have been waiting for since December 7, 1941." He said that the Japanese had accepted the terms of surrender, with "no qualification," and that General Douglas MacArthur, the supreme Allied commander in the Pacific, who was already designated to oversee the occupation of Japan, would receive the surrender. The emperor would live on.

Truman said that "V-J Day" celebrations would have to wait until the formal surrender was signed by the Japanese—that would be September 2. But it was impossible to suppress the celebratory urges of large crowds in big cities. The *Herald Tribune* reported that Times Square, "the mecca of extroverts," was ready, with a crowd of a half million "who boiled over with a frenetic madness the moment the announcement came." In less than an hour, this "roaring, writhing, spectacle of elation" had doubled in size, and soon it doubled again. "Pedestrians went crazy and leaped onto the running boards of cars . . . while they shrieked at the top of their lungs." The celebration far outdid V-E Day.

When Truman made his short announcement, it was 6 p.m. in Grandview, Missouri, where an enterprising journalist had staked out Martha Ellen Young Truman's house. When her telephone rang, the President's ninety-two-year-old mother answered with a hesitant "hello" and then, "Yes, I'm all right." Only one side of the conversation was overheard: "Yes, I've been listening to the radio. No, I'm all alone. Mary's gone to the city. No, she'll be all right. I told her to call the Secret Service man if there was any crowd. . . . I heard the Englishman"—Clement Attlee—"speak. I'm glad they accepted the surrender terms. . . . Yes, I'm all right. . . . Now, you come and see me if you can." Then she turned and went into the living room. "That was Harry," she explained. "I knew he'd call. He always calls after something that happens is over. He said the announcement he made was all that was necessary. The Englishman talked and told the whole story. There wasn't any need of Harry going on the air. He's not one to want all the glory." She later said, "I'm glad Harry decided to end the war. He's no slow person. He gets where he's going in short order." The "Englishman" had said, "The last of our enemies is laid low."

4.   A word like "conscience" was rarely used in connection with an all-out war against a hated enemy, but the atomic bombings of two Japanese cities nagged at Truman, as it had at Stimson—which is not to say that Truman ever confessed any doubts. Rather, he was determined to let history understand his reasoning—that he wanted "to shorten the agony of war, in order to save the lives of thousands and thousands of young Americans." He'd also say that he was determined to spare civilians, a subject he addressed in the July 25 diary entry that recorded his order to drop the Hiroshima bomb: "I have told the Sec. of War, Mr. Stimson, to use it so that military objectives and soldiers and sailors are the target and not women and children." Truman may have fudged the date of that note, but not by much. In his memoirs, he wrote, "I had told Stimson that the bomb should be dropped as nearly as possible upon a war production center of prime military importance," and went on to describe Hiroshima as "a military base," chosen to avoid civilian casualties "insofar as possible."

Truman certainly *wanted* to believe that, but Hiroshima was not a significant military target, although an army headquarters was situated there. Most of those killed in Hiroshima and Nagasaki were noncombatants; out of some seventy thousand who perished in Hiroshima, probably no more than seven thousand were military personnel. Truman later attempted to persuade himself, or history, that he'd tried to avoid using the bomb at all. "I pleaded with the Japanese in my speech announcing Germany's surrender, begging them to surrender too," he later wrote, although there had been little pleading in his reference to "the treacherous tyranny of the Japanese." He made the dubious claim that, as late as June 18, 1945, the decision to deploy was not yet final.

Truman returned to the subject at the Gridiron Club in mid-December 1945, an annual evening at which guests, mostly politicians and journalists, are forced to endure skits and songs that aim to be biting and clever. The Gridiron dinner had just been revived, after going dark for four and a half wartime years, and when Truman had finished joking about his treatment by the press ("Walter Lippmann had said I'm great—and a damn fool"), he became serious: "You know the most terrible decision a man ever had to make was made by me at Potsdam," he said. "It was a decision to loose the most terrible of all destructive forces for the wholesale slaughter of human beings. The Secretary of War, Mr. Stimson, and I weighed that decision most prayerfully. But the President had to decide. It occurred to me that a quarter of a million of the flower of our young manhood was worth a couple of Japanese cities and I still think they were and are." He continued, "But I couldn't help but think of the necessity of blotting out women and children and non-combatants. We gave them fair warning and asked them to quit. We picked a couple of cities where war work was the principle industry, and dropped bombs."

Truman was never less than prickly on this subject, as he was after a conversation with J. Robert Oppenheimer, the physicist who'd had much to do with the bomb's development. "He came to my office," Truman wrote, a year later, to Dean Acheson, the former assistant secretary of state whom Byrnes had asked to serve as under secretary, "and spent most of his time ringing [sic] his hands and telling me they had blood on them because of the discovery of atomic energy." Truman said he had no sympathy, and called Oppenheimer a

" 'cry baby' scientist." Yet in a conversation with the historian Arthur Schlesinger Jr. and the theologian Reinhold Niebuhr, in 1951, he said, "The worst thing I ever did was to give the order which killed all those people over there. It was terrible; but I had no alternative; and I would give such an order again if it ever became necessary." That was not exactly regret, but it does suggest that living with that decision was not so easy to shrug off.

Truman told Henry Wallace that, after Nagasaki, he'd given orders to stop the atomic bombing. "He said the thought of wiping out another 100,000 people was too horrible," a Wallace diary entry said. "He didn't like the idea of killing, as he said, 'all those kids.' " But even though Japan's surrender was imminent, and even though General Marshall had ordered General Groves to hold off on using another atom bomb "without express authority from the President," it might not have ended then. If Japan's capitulation hadn't come quickly, a third bomb very likely would have been loaded onto one of the B-29 Superfortresses based on Tinian Island, been ready on or about August 18, and dropped on Tokyo.

5. Soon after V-J Day, a Hollywood studio began to make a film about the bomb's development. Its impetus came from the actress Donna Reed, whose high school chemistry teacher had worked on the Manhattan Project, in Oak Ridge, Tennessee, and whose husband, an agent, contacted Louis B. Mayer, the head of Metro-Goldwyn-Mayer. In order to win government approval, a movie-industry delegation met with President Truman, who unintentionally gave the film a title when he told them, "Make a good picture. One that will tell the people that the decision is theirs to make. . . . this is the beginning or the end!"

The Beginning or the End was released in early 1947, and was a box-office, and artistic, failure. Bosley Crowther, the *New York Times* movie critic, said it was "so laced with sentiment of the silliest and most theatrical nature that much of its impressiveness is marred." Crowther may been struck by such devices as an imaginary conversation between Truman and Charlie Ross:

The President: Sit down Charlie. The time has come for you . . . to know our nation's top secret. It must remain just that— top secret.

Ross: Of course!

The President: We have just developed the most fearful weapon ever forged by man—an atomic bomb.

Ross: Even the word is frightening.

Neither Hollywood nor the movie audience seemed ready to consider that, whether or not the bomb's use was justified, something fundamental had changed, that there was no going back, and that, as David Lilienthal, who later became the first chairman of the Atomic Energy Commission, wondered, "Isn't the real danger to civilization to be found in the recognition that warfare is no longer conflict within limits imposed by morality, but without limit, without moral containment?"

FIVE

Truman's "Conniver"

"Don't ever let anybody talk to you about foreign affairs."
—President Truman, in a letter to his mother
and sister, September 1945

1. Unlike Roosevelt, who took charge of his own foreign policy, Truman came to rely, almost entirely, on the counsel of others—people who'd been around, who knew more about the world than he did, the "striped-pants boys" at the State Department, a Truman phrase that bespoke a sourly dismissive, class-conscious animosity toward his own foreign service. He listened to military men, such as General Marshall, and Admiral Leahy, the seventy-year-old chief of staff he'd inherited from FDR. He respected Secretary of War Stimson, who'd soon be leaving the cabinet, and who had urged Truman to show mercy to vanquished Japan, saying, "When you punish your dog you don't keep souring on him all day after the punishment is over; if you want to keep his affection, punishment takes care of itself." There was also a steady, and not always helpful, parade through Truman's office, from old friends in Congress to cronies, such as the omnipresent General Harry Vaughan.

In the first months of Truman's presidency, no one was as influential as James Francis Byrnes, the secretary of state, though there were reasons to wonder how long that could last. Among students of Washington intrigue, there was a belief that Byrnes had never recovered from being passed over for the vice presidency, and that, when Roosevelt died, as Joe Alsop later wrote, he was like "the head boy in a school who found himself, by a bizarre chapter of accidents, under the leadership of the man who had been the smallest and least-regarded boy in his class." Byrnes had never considered Truman a rival, and yet, by stealth or circumstance—and the manipulations of Roosevelt—Truman had bested the man he referred to, only partly in jest, as "my able and conniving Secretary of State."

Byrnes's failings, like Truman's, included inexperience and relative ignorance of the world, but Byrnes nonetheless managed to give the impression that he grasped the subtleties of history and foreign policy. Simply having once been at Roosevelt's side gave him a certain authority. As Britain's the *Spectator* put it in early July, Truman "must be given a little time . . . to play himself in," adding that "it is fortunate that the second-highest level continuity is provided in the person of Mr. J.F. Byrnes, who was present with President Roosevelt at Yalta as unofficial adviser." During his three weeks in Potsdam, Byrnes enjoyed his proximity to world leaders; it was almost a badge of honor that Stalin called him "the most honest horse thief he had ever met." Byrnes's appointments, which included Dean Acheson, as under-secretary, did promise continuity, but Byrnes himself bore little resemblance to the diplomats and analysts who'd made their careers in the Foreign Service.

Inside the State Department, the ornate, granite French Second Empire building across from the White House (it's now the Eisenhower Executive Office Building), Byrnes tended to keep to himself. Acheson, his deputy, recalled that he operated "entirely personally with a very small number of people." He usually took lunch at his desk and made long working days even longer by calling meetings that might go on until 7 or 8 p.m. George Curry, who later helped Byrnes with his autobiography, recalled that those late sessions, which often turned into debates, would find Byrnes "rocking in his chair, his coat open and his hands frequently pulling at his belt," a characteristic gesture. He seemed to listen, and yet, as someone who knew him said, "you never knew you had made an impression until you saw it in the cables." Soon after Byrnes was sworn in, Truman thought, "My but he has a keen mind! And he is an honest man. But," he added, "all country politicians are alike. They are sure all other politicians are circuitous in their dealings. When they are told the straight truth, unvarnished it is never believed—an asset sometimes." That curiously skeptical, and insightful, assessment of the "country politician" at State was bound to change, though not for the better, not least because Byrnes could act as if he carried Truman's foreign policy in a side pocket. Truman was very much aware of this, and it irked him. "More and more during the fall of 1945," he recalled, "I came to feel that. . . . Byrnes was beginning to think of himself as an Assistant President in full charge of foreign policy."

Byrnes's chance to continue some of what had begun in Potsdam came with the initial get-together of the Foreign Ministers Council. This "Little Three"—Byrnes, Molotov, and Ernest Bevin, along with representatives from France and the Chiang Kai-shek government in China—met in October 1945, in London, a conference that was judged, at best, to be a waste of time.

Other difficulties accompanied this line of work: In late November 1945, Byrnes and Truman were flummoxed when Major General Patrick J. Hurley, the American ambassador to China, suddenly, and loudly, resigned. He quit his post while accusing State Department diplomats of pro-Communist sympathies, seeking the ruination of Chiang Kai-shek, and warning that American policies in Asia were leading to a third world war. This ultimately incoherent tantrum set off a political eruption, which Truman hoped to stamp out by asking George Marshall, who had just retired as army chief of staff, to step in as a special envoy to China. "No man probably had more fully deserved an honorable and restful retirement than Marshall," Truman would write, and yet he unhesitatingly called him at his home in Leesburg, Virginia, and made his request, without preliminaries— and to the dismay of Mrs. Marshall.

Byrnes was quick to defend his State Department, and interest in Hurley began to fade. Byrnes's special difficulties with Truman began when the ministers met again, in Moscow, in December. Byrnes had pushed for this second round, even though it overlapped with the Christmas holidays, and this time he wanted it to include only himself, Molotov, and Bevin, who, according to Averell Harriman, thought it was too rushed and "hated the idea."

The Moscow meetings addressed some questions that would never find practical answers, among them how to control the peaceful uses of atomic energy. The existence of an American atom bomb gnawed at Stalin, who told Igor Kurchatov, the Soviet nuclear scientist, that "Hiroshima has shaken the whole world. The balance has been destroyed." In a rare interview, with the *Sunday Times* of London, Stalin tried to shrug off the idea that this imbalance worried him. "Atomic bombs are intended for intimidating the weak-nerved," he told the newspaper's Alexander Werth, "but they cannot decide the outcome of war, since atom bombs are by no means sufficient for this purpose." Nor had Russia and the United States gotten any closer to finding common ground on Poland's future, or even on what seemed to be peripheral issues, such as the future of the divided Korean peninsula, and while Byrnes was able to reach minor treaty agreements, particularly with Romania and Bulgaria, nothing was bound to loosen the Soviet hold in Eastern Europe.

Byrnes's performance in Moscow was described, in contemptuous detail, by George Kennan, the forty-year-old deputy head of mission. With a kind of schadenfreude, Kennan watched Byrnes being outmatched by Molotov, whose eyes were "flashing with satisfaction and confidence . . . clearly enjoying every minute of the proceedings." He was merciless in his dissection of Byrnes, whom he saw as someone whose main purpose was to reach some sort of agreement—"he doesn't much care what . . . for its political effect at home. The Russians know this." Kennan was also embarrassed by Byrnes's social gaffes, details of which he saved for his memoirs. The visiting ministers had been invited to a special performance at the Bolshoi Ballet, for Prokofiev's *Cinderella*, which recently had its premiere. Every seat was filled, except those being held for the American secretary of state and his party. After fifteen minutes, Kennan worried that Byrnes might have forgotten about the ballet. He asked an aide to find out what was causing the delay, and was told, "They are only sitting up in his room at the embassy telling stories and having drinks and no one dares go in and interrupt them." Kennan hurried to a telephone, and was told, by an amused Russian, "They have just left." Byrnes arrived five minutes later, having kept several thousand people waiting for half an hour.

Kennan was an unusual sort of public man, an "alienated loner," in the superb portrait of the era's "wise men" by Walter Isaacson and Evan Thomas: bald and slight, very bright, sharply aware of social embarrassment. One acquaintance was struck by his eyes, "which are most unusual: large, intense, wide-set." A newspaperman saw him as "slender and good-looking in a refined and sensitive way. His eyes are blue, his chin well-formed, his mouth highly expressive, chilling or charming as its owner decrees." In Moscow and, later, at the State Department, he could be a difficult man, untroubled by asking touchy questions, but he also showed himself to be enormously perceptive and spookily prescient, qualities that eluded Byrnes, whose missteps in Russia were nothing compared to his missteps with Truman.

2. After declaring that the meetings with Bevin and Molotov had been "very constructive" and had succeeded in creating a "friendly spirit" for addressing the world's problems—an exaggeration on both counts—Byrnes left Moscow on December 27. At sixty-three, he gave an impression of vigor and liveliness, and after a long plane trip he was usually less fatigued than many younger men. But Moscow had been grueling. "The working hours of the Soviets were hard on me," Byrnes wrote, in a memorandum to himself. "I like to work in the morning and sleep at night. The Soviets like to sleep in the morning and work at night. . . . Frequently I found myself humming 'Nobody Knows the Trouble I See.'"

As Byrnes began the long journey home, he found it hard to sleep on the plane. He kept reliving the days in Moscow, and the "enormous nervous strain" of negotiating with the Russians. He had other things on his mind too, including a radio address that he planned to deliver on December 30, the day after his return. But he hadn't cleared the speech with Truman, and seemed to believe that he needn't make a great effort to keep the President informed. Harriman, who'd sat in on the Moscow meetings, wondered about that. After the first negotiating session, he'd asked Byrnes if he should draft a report for Truman, or if Byrnes preferred to do it himself. "He said that he was not going to send any telegrams," Harriman recalled. "I argued that this was customary, but he remained adamant. 'The President has given me complete authority.'" Byrnes also surprised Harriman with his suspiciousness: "I can't trust the White House to prevent leaks," he'd said. Harriman's diagnosis—not his alone—was that Byrnes "was always jealous of Truman." The President's special assistant John Steelman was sure of it: "I used to sit in the cabinet and watch Mr. Byrnes and Mr. [Henry] Wallace both look at the President, and I always felt that I could tell what they were both thinking—each one thinking, 'I ought to be sitting there, in that chair.'"

Byrnes hadn't entirely brushed aside his responsibility to serve the President. He *had* tried to cable a communiqué to Washington, a seventeen-page report, sent on December 27 by the Army Signal Corps. But because it was the holiday season, and offices were empty, it took longer than usual to get a document encrypted. Byrnes was told that Acheson had made special arrangements to transmit the communiqué to Truman, but Truman didn't receive it right away. He'd already left Washington for Independence—a journey undertaken in winter weather so foul that commercial flights had been canceled.

Truman's Missouri holiday turned out to be unusually rotten. He was so determined to get home for Christmas that only a refusal to fly by the Army Transport Command would have kept him away. After a four-hour delay, and a takeoff through slush and a sleet storm, with de-icing equipment throwing chunks of ice back from the propellers, his plane, the *Sacred Cow*, made it to Kansas City in six hours. When he reached Independence, and the big house on North Delaware Street, exhausted, Bess said, "So you've finally arrived. I guess you couldn't think of any more reasons to stay away. As far as I'm concerned, you might as well have stayed in Washington." By the time Truman was on his way back East, a day later, he felt so miserable that, when he got to his desk in the White House, he didn't try to disguise his mood. He wrote what must have been an unusually bitter letter to Bess—so much so that he telephoned Margaret and asked her to retrieve it from the post office, and burn it. "I did as I was told," she later wrote. "I took it home and burned it in the backyard incinerator."

History mourns the loss of that letter, but a more measured one that Truman wrote in its place still revealed a rare record of marital squabbling, and anguish. "When you told me I might as well have stayed in Washington so far as you were concerned I gave up, cussed [Senator Arthur] Vandenberg, told the Secretary of Agriculture to give all the damned cotton away for all I cared," he wrote. "You can never appreciate what it means to come home as I did the other evening after doing at least 100 things I didn't want to do and have the only person in the world whose approval and good opinion I value, look at me like I'm something the cat dragged in and tell me I've come in at last because I couldn't find any reason to stay away. I wonder why we are made so that what we really think and feel we cover up?" Almost abjectly he added, "No one ever needed help and assistance as I do now. If I can get the use of the best brains in the country and a little bit of help from those I have on a pedestal at home, the job will be done."

After that, Truman didn't want to spend time alone at the White House. He went from there to the Washington Navy Yard, to board what Henry Wallace called "the fanciest presidential yacht which has ever been in use"—the 243-foot *Williamsburg*, built by the Bath Iron Works in 1933. There, in the late afternoon of December 28, the dispirited Truman joined some of his favorite shipmates—among them Charlie Ross, Harry Vaughan, Admiral Leahy, and a recent addition, another Missourian, Clark Clifford, who'd become his assistant naval aide, though he wouldn't remain in that job for long. Truman planned to use some of the time aboard to work on his January State of the Union speech, but throwing himself into work didn't do much to improve his mood.

3. Byrnes's plane landed at Washington's National Airport on December 29, after a flight that took about sixty hours. Among those waiting for him were his wife, the former Maude Busch, whom he'd married in 1906; the British ambassador—the Earl of Halifax—and Acheson, who knew that Truman would regard Byrnes's itinerary as a violation of "proper procedure," which was to report first to the President and wait for his approval before delivering a radio talk. "He was tired," Acheson recalled. "His radio speech required further work." He informed Byrnes "as well as I could" about "some of the matters on which the President would want enlightenment."

Byrnes now faced the prospect of having to leave at once for Quantico, Virginia, where the *Williamsburg* was moored. His first response was "Goddammit to hell, I can't do that. I've got to work on this speech." But he knew better than to refuse a president, even Harry Truman, and after stopping at the Shoreham Hotel for a quick meal, a bath, and a change of clothes, he was on his way again. That was a wise decision: Truman by then was inclined to think that he should order Byrnes to cancel his radio speech.

Although Byrnes's Moscow communiqué had finally reached the President, there was no mistaking Truman's annoyance at what appeared to be his secretary of state's casual attitude. Nor was he impressed by Byrnes's report, which informed him that, after talking with Stalin, "I now hope that we can make forward steps toward settling the Rumanian-Bulgarian problems," that they had "discussed the Chinese situation, Iran and atomic energy," and that "as a result of our conversation, I hope that we will . . . be able to reach some agreement on these issues." That was followed by more fuzziness and vague optimism: "We are in general accord as to Far Eastern issues. The situation is encouraging and I hope that today we can reach final agreement on the questions outstanding and wind up our work tomorrow." In his memoirs, Truman wrote that Byrnes's report contained "very little that the newspaper correspondents had not already reported from Moscow," and, above all, "this was not what I considered a proper account by a Cabinet member to the President. It was more like one partner in a business telling the other that his business trip was progressing well and not to worry."

Truman's aide John Steelman recalled Truman telling Charlie Ross, "Get ahold of Byrnes and tell him to come on this boat . . . if he has to swim. Tell him I said to be here, and I don't mean maybe." His impatience hinted at more trouble to come. Other hints could be found in Admiral Leahy's diary, in which, on December 26, referring to the Moscow meetings, he'd written, "From information available to me I am of the opinion that Mr. Byrnes has made conces-sions to expediency that are destructive of the President's announced intentions." While Byrnes was still en route from Moscow, Leahy characterized the foreign ministers' statement on agreements with Romania and Bulgaria, which demanded no more than inclusion of two opposition leaders in a new government, as "an appeasement document which gives the Soviet everything they want and preserves to America nothing." Moreover, the President "informs me that he was not consulted by Secretary Byrnes in the agreements made at the Moscow conference."

Leahy's diplomatic experience was mostly limited to the time he'd spent, from 1940 to 1942, as ambassador to Vichy France, an as-signment that included Roosevelt's instructions to cultivate Marshal Philippe Pétain, the World War I hero who became a Nazi collabo-rator. Roosevelt had been fond of Leahy—their friendship extended back to World War I—and rescued his career by making him his chief of staff. The columnist Marquis Childs believed that, after Roo-sevelt's death, Leahy never felt entirely at home in the White House, but Truman valued his dour affect and private counsel, which, to the annoyance of some of Truman's senior staff, occasionally drifted into domestic matters. Leahy would continue to refer to Byrnes's "ap-peasement attitude" and a "policy of appeasement." Those views, and Leahy's intense anti-Soviet feelings, certainly left their mark. Years later, when Truman was interviewed by Jonathan Daniels, he used almost identical language, saying "I told [Byrnes] . . . that his appeasement policy was not mine. I was not going to have a policy announced and then be told about it." That was not a conversation that Byrnes recalled, and it very likely never happened.

When Byrnes, on that December 29, 1945, was taken by sea-plane to the *Williamsburg*, he found himself in the company of some of the men around Truman, few of whom he knew. He did know Leahy—they'd both served under Roosevelt, and hadn't much liked each other—but not these Missourians, people like Vaughan and Ross and Clifford. Even if Byrnes could satisfy Truman on any single point, Leahy was not about to be satisfied: "I repeatedly asked Mr. Byrnes for information as to what benefits accrue to the United States," he noted in his diary, and "was unable to get a satisfactory reply." Steelman remembered that Leahy had been "unmerciful"; he would ask about the Moscow meeting, and when Byrnes replied, "the admiral would probably tell him, 'No, that isn't the way it happened, I happen to have the reports here, and furthermore you did so-and-so, and so-and-so.' . . . Oh, he just tore into him." (The "reports," if that account is accurate, would have come from Harriman or Kennan, or both.) Truman spent more than an hour with Byrnes, in private, Steelman recalled, "and he got the trimming of his life," not only from the President but from others on board. But perhaps Truman's trimming was mild. Memory may be flexible. After their shipboard conversation, Truman told Charlie Ross that he'd approved Byrnes's radio speech.

Truman also invited Byrnes to join the evening poker game, though he must have known, after years of acquaintanceship, that Byrnes was not a poker player. Byrnes said that he needed to work on his radio talk, and would have to leave the ship in the morning. When Truman asked him to return after delivering the speech, Byrnes was again left with no choice. To follow Byrnes's schedule over these few days—from Moscow to Washington to Quantico to Washington and back again—is to feel sympathy for a tired employee and a boss who, by design or obliviousness, was subjecting him to a mild form of torture. On the day that Byrnes left the *Williamsburg*, Leahy recorded that the Quantico region was experiencing "cold, bleak winter weather with some fog."

4. Consciously or not—Palmetto accent or not—Byrnes sometimes managed an approximate imitation of Roosevelt when he spoke, sonorously, in a formal setting, although his intonation sometimes wavered strangely, making him sound like someone who had just mastered English pronunciation. In his speech, broadcast by NBC, he declared that the United States had not shared atomic secrets, would never do so without proper safeguards, and said that General MacArthur's role as the supreme commander of conquered Japan was unaffected. As for treaty agreements with Romania and Bulgaria, he pointed out that both nations shared a common border

with the Soviet Union, and had been allied with the Axis powers. "It must be recognized that the Soviet government has a very real interest in the character of the government of these states," he said, which was Stalin's view, but had also been Roosevelt's view.

Byrnes returned to the *Williamsburg* on New Year's Eve, where the holiday was about to be celebrated, with inescapable cheer. A White House announcement said that when 1946 arrived, Truman's party and the ship's officers were singing "Auld Lang Syne," accompanied by an improvised three-piece band made up of enlisted men who, among other unavoidable tunes, played "Deep in the Heart of Texas," "There's a Long, Long Trail," and "As the Caissons Go Rolling Along." It was still cold—"icy winds swept down the Potomac River," the *Herald Tribune* reported. All attempts at cheeriness may not have reached Truman, who spent much of New Year's Day in the stateroom, working on his State of the Union speech. The ship's phones weren't hooked up, and the day before, Truman had had to ask a White House operator to read a wholly impersonal message to Bess that said, "Things are on the mend outside the country and we hope to improve them at home." Byrnes was still out of sorts, wishing he were home, in South Carolina. What made it worse, although he did not know it, he was on his way to alienating Truman for good. Truman later told Jonathan Daniels that "Byrnes lost his nerve in Moscow."

Byrnes's memory of those three days in late December bore little resemblance to what Truman remembered, or what Admiral Leahy witnessed. In Byrnes's recollection, Truman had said "he understood and expressed pleasure at the progress we had made" in Moscow, and "urged me to make the radio report, and insisted that I stay for dinner." He would have preferred to rest, "but because of [Truman's] cordiality I accepted the invitation to join him in ushering out the old year." As Robert Messer points out, in his informative study of Truman, Byrnes, and the early Cold War, critics of Byrnes's conduct in Moscow overlook that Truman "only afterward complained that Byrnes had not kept him informed, [and] at no time evidenced the least interest in what was happening there." The piling on of Byrnes, then and in retrospect, was somewhat unfair. It was, after all, no fault of Byrnes's that his cable took so long to reach the

President. Although treaties affecting Bulgaria and Rumania didn't offer the prospect of any real change, Soviet influence in the region was already entrenched and unlikely to become less so. As for the future of atomic energy, who could object to the unremarkable idea, proposed by the American delegation, to establish a UN commission to deal with the question, and of "extending between all nations the exchange of basic scientific information for peaceful ends"? Rather, what's most obvious in Byrnes's lengthy cable is its emptiness, its blindness to the preliminaries of the coming Cold War.

In a city whose inhabitants feasted on rumors, Byrnes's future was a favorite topic in the first months of the new year. Drew Pearson, on January 8, reported that "fast-moving, hard-working" Byrnes didn't always remember that Truman was someone "who likes to know, sometimes in detail, what's going on." Other reporters had caught on that something wasn't quite right, and at a press conference in mid-March, Truman started off by saying, "I want to make it strong and emphatic, as there still seem to be rumors about that there has been a rift between the Secretary of State and myself, that there is no such rift, never has been one, and never will be, I hope." When a reporter said "these rumors about Secretary Byrnes apparently don't just come from spontaneous combustion," Truman replied, "Yes they do—yes they do. . . . They have no foundation in fact whatever, and never have had; and I don't know what else they could come from except spontaneous combustion, and somebody just wants to tell a big lie."

But Truman wasn't being honest, and his increasing estrangement from his secretary of state came out in an unsent letter that he wrote on January 5. Starting with the salutation "My dear Jim," it went at once to the heart of the matter:

> *I have been considering some of our difficulties. As you know I would like to pursue a policy of delegating authority to the members of the Cabinet. . . . But in doing that and in carrying out that policy I do not intend to turn over the complete authority of the President nor to forgo the President's prerogative to make the final decision.*

Therefore it is absolutely necessary that the President should be kept fully informed on what is taking place. This is vitally necessary when negotiations are taking place in a foreign capital.

Truman went on to say that he'd been kept "completely in the dark on the whole conference until I requested you to come to the *Williamsburg* and inform me." His tone then took a sudden, ominous turn, possibly reflecting the influence of Admiral Leahy:

There isn't a doubt in my mind that Russia intends an invasion of Turkey and the seizure of the Black Sea Straits to the Mediterranean. Unless Russia is faced with an iron fist and strong language another war is in the making.

That led Truman back to the subject of inland waterways—"we should continue to insist on the internationalization of the Kiel Canal, the Rhine-Danube waterway and the Black Sea Straits"—and then, as if America's power was infinite and irresistible, he added that "we should rehabilitate China and create a strong central government there. We should do the same for Korea. Then we should insist on the return of our ships from Russia and force a settlement of the Lend-Lease Debt of Russia." He concluded by saying, "I'm tired of babying the Soviets."

Truman was wise enough to keep the letter to himself, although he made it public a few years later. At the end of 1945, which the radio commentator Elmer Davis called "probably the most decisive year in American history—perhaps the most decisive year in all human history"—its querulousness, the inflammatory suspicion that Russia was about to seize the Black Sea Straits and invade Turkey, would only have led more people to question Truman's ability to navigate the future with the confidence and cunning of a Roosevelt. His petulant tone, revealing a clear understanding of his unsatisfactory relationship with his senior cabinet officer, was a reminder that Truman was in great need of a more capable guide, and partner, than James Francis Byrnes.

SIX

Churchill
Makes Mischief

> *Q:* Mr. President, do you support the State Department's pol-
> icy that the United States should—
> *The President.* The State Department doesn't have a policy un-
> less I support it. [Laughter] Finish your question—I'm sorry.
>
> **—Presidential News Conference, January 31, 1946**

1. In Washington, that cruel city where flatterers, journalists, and hangers-on may accrue unusual power, it did not take
long for second thoughts to set in. The very idea of Harry Truman as
the nation's leader was so off-putting to many of the city's insiders
that even his wardrobe became a target. Truman, it was said, dressed
"like he had just come off of Main Street in Independence . . . everything was a little too precise." Some of his shoes had mesh in them!
The *Harper's* magazine editor John Fischer, in early 1946, wrote,
"There is hardly a man in Congress who doesn't believe in his heart
that he would make a better chief executive than Good Old Harry,"
and Isaiah Berlin told a friend that the "boiling indignation" that
Roosevelt once aroused had been replaced by a "cynical disillusioned
acceptance of machine politics and the poor perplexed little man of
the White House." Truman, he thought, seems "a pathetic figure,"
a view that may have been influenced by Berlin's own postwar melancholy.

A more sympathetic view of Truman was held by Dean Acheson,
Byrnes's deputy since August 1945, whose future with Truman would

turn out to be very bright. The fifty-two-year-old Acheson, a Washington lawyer who'd served in the State Department since 1941, had happened to talk to Vice President Truman just before Roosevelt died. A couple of weeks later, in a letter to his son, David, he said that Truman had impressed him. While he acknowledged "the limitations upon his judgment and wisdom that the limitations of his experience produce," he believed that "he will learn fast and will inspire confidence." Above all, he judged Truman to be "straight-forward, decisive, simple, entirely honest." Acheson recalled these impressions, with retrospective satisfaction, in his autobiography, published nearly a quarter century later.

Truman didn't miss much when it came to his reputation, and to suggestions that he wasn't up to the job; in a letter to Bess, he referred to "conspirators in the 'Palace Guard.'" He was sensitive to any intimation that he wasn't wholly in charge. But there was no escaping that his policies, or those coming from the State Department, were still unformed—particularly those affecting relations with the Soviet Union, as both countries pulled back from their wartime alliance. Truman and Stalin never came close to understanding each other, although Truman once observed, astutely, that "a dictatorship is the hardest thing in God's world to hold together because it is made up entirely of conspiracies from the inside." Stalin seemed to regard Truman as a little man with a big bomb, a Roosevelt manqué, a provincial obsessed with international waterways. Stalin may have reminded Truman of Boss Pendergast, but Pendergast was no Stalin and Stalin was nothing like any Missouri political boss. Nor, considering Stalin's record of pitilessness, was he any sort of "Uncle Joe," but rather someone who, as Churchill thought, left "the impression of a cold and deep wisdom and a complete absence of illusion of any sort."

Truman could nonetheless entertain the illusion that Stalin was "a prisoner of the Politburo," the man described by Harry Hopkins as "a forthright, rough, tough Russian," who always put Russia first, but "can be talked to frankly." This was also the Stalin who adhered to an ideology deadened by suffocating language, an outlook broadcast over Moscow Radio, on February 9, 1946, when the overarching theme was a determination to catch up with, and surpass, the West—to "leap into an advanced country from an agriculture country." If one interpreted Stalin's hour-long speech that way, and many did, it became a clear warning of Soviet ambitions. It prompted the State Department to ask George Kennan, who'd become deputy chief of mission in Moscow, for his analysis of Soviet aims, a task that Kennan turned into a major homework assignment: an eight-thousand-word cable, the so-called "Long Telegram," which argued that the Soviet Union needed to be reined in, prevented from extending its power beyond its borders—"contained." It was a view that would metamorphose into the Truman era's foreign policy

Russia's expansive goals were a topic at Georgetown dinner parties. Guests at Joe Alsop's house one January night, in 1946, included Chip Bohlen, who was now running the Russia desk at State; Supreme Court justice Hugo Black; Henry Wallace; Grace Tully, who'd been Roosevelt's private secretary; and the Gauds, a couple originally from South Carolina. William Gaud, who worked with navy secretary Forrestal, thought the United States ought to "kick the Russians in the balls," and should be checked at every opportunity. Alsop agreed with that, while Wallace argued that some accommodation was needed, that the Russians should have access through the Dardanelles Strait, in northwestern Turkey—that they'd been promised that after World War I. Justice Black agreed with Wallace, but Gaud called it "crap." When Wallace offered the rejoinder that Gaud's opinion was crap, Gaud said, "Well, then, we are even"—none of this close to the sparkling dialogue of Georgetown legend. Alsop that night insisted that Russia was expanding much as Nazi Germany had. A war with Russia, he added, was inevitable, and the quicker it came the better.

In that atmosphere, even the President might spout off, alarmingly. During a White House staff meeting in February, Truman pulled some telegrams and cables from a folder on his desk and remarked, as Eben Ayers noted in his diary, "that we were going to war with Russia or words to that effect." Those thoughts— that war with Russia was unavoidable—were shared by Winston Churchill, six months out of office. Depending upon his mood, Churchill sometimes talked about England starting that war, as if to get it over with—knowing that it would have required the unprovoked United States to join in. That scenario assumed a quick victory, an assumption that depended on America's sole ownership of the atomic bomb. In the early post-war years, that nuclear monopoly affected international relations in much the way that a large star would alter the orbits of the planets.

2. Truman was always ready to listen to Churchill, though he was not much concerned by some of Churchill's concerns, such as the rapid pace of American demobilization. Rather, he'd been feeling pressure to bring America's soldiers home—some of the pressure coming from the soldiers themselves. The broadcaster Elmer Davis, in early January 1946, told his listeners how five thousand protesting soldiers, in Frankfurt, had to be stopped by paratroopers, who'd pointed rifles at the protesters, and that in Yokohama, Japan, soldiers chanted "we want to go home" to the visiting secretary of war, Robert P. Patterson, Henry Stimson's successor. Davis reported this along with the observation that without an army "as big as may be needed," the administration could not be expected to pursue the "vigorous foreign policy . . . that we need, in these times."

Churchill was now the leader of the British opposition, but his new status left him out of sorts—still so stunned by the July 25 election that, as the Earl of Halifax had been told, "He could only think and talk about where he could get a house or find a car!" He was, though, about to cash in, having signed contracts, including one with *Life* magazine, to write about the war. David Reynolds, in his engaging account of Churchill's writing life, has pointed out that if Churchill had not been turned out of office, he might never have produced his wordy but indispensable six-volume history.

With the luxury of free time, and fighting off the depression that plagued him, Churchill, accompanied by Clementine, came to the United States in early January 1946, intending to stay for about nine weeks. This presented a minor diplomatic dilemma—namely, what was to be done with him? He was a distinguished visitor, but there was no compelling reason for his visit. One commitment to speak had come at Truman's urging: the former PM had agreed to give a talk, on March 5, in Fulton, Missouri, at Westminster College, Harry Vaughan's alma mater. Nothing was said about his proposed subject, but it was not hard to guess at the themes, and because Truman had told Churchill, "I would be most pleased to introduce you," the un-delivered speech kept growing in importance.

The Churchills were to spend most of their stateside time with a Canadian acquaintance, in Miami, where the former PM painted, went to an occasional cocktail party, flashed the V-sign to random crowds, and swam. Winston and Clementine welcomed visitors—among them Byrnes and Bernard Baruch—and managed a short jaunt to Havana, on February 7, where they dined at the United States Embassy. Afterward, Ambassador Raymond Henry Norweb informed Truman that Churchill had spoken "rather intimately of some major issues preoccupying his mind," and that his "greatest fear . . . is that Russia will not only master the secret of atomic war-fare but will not hesitate to employ it for her own ends." Churchill also told Norweb that "it would appear to be his lifetime fate to issue 'clarion calls' regarding the dangers he foresees."

Although Churchill was now a former world leader without a leading role, his heroic persona was intact when he flew to Washing-ton, on February 10, for dinner with Truman. When his borrowed B-17 Flying Fortress landed at National Airport, in wintry sleet, five hundred people were waiting, hoping for a glimpse of this already historic figure. Churchill did not disappoint; he was in full costume, carrying a lit cigar and wearing a black homburg. There was no sign that he'd just been through a bumpy, five-hour flight, during which the pilot hit an air pocket that threw passengers out of their seats and broke tumblers, while crockery flew about the cabin.

Charlie Ross told reporters the next day that the main dinner topic had been the upcoming trip to Missouri. The original plan had been for Truman and Churchill to fly out, but Churchill sug-gested that they travel by train. "Will you please wire me whether this change commends itself to you," he asked. It suited Truman, and so, on March 4, the two of them, and their accompanying staffs, along with about sixty journalists, departed from Union Station. The *Ferdinand Magellan* was back in service. The elevator that Roosevelt used to board his special Pullman car had been removed, but the *Magellan* was otherwise much as it had been since its inaugural run, in 1943, in all its cramped, slightly claustrophobic luxury.

Churchill knew that his upcoming address—he'd given it a Churchillian title, "The Sinews of Peace"—was likely to stir things up. He had tried to keep his government informed, though he'd not given Prime Minister Attlee or Foreign Secretary Bevin a preview. Truman denied knowing in advance what Churchill planned to say, but that was probably an untruth. Churchill informed Attlee, in a telegram, that he'd shown Truman a mimeographed copy of the final draft, and that Truman "told me that he thought it was admirable and would do nothing but good though it would make a stir." Byrnes, who'd also seen it, suggested no alterations, and Admiral Leahy was "enthusiastic." More than enthusiastic: Leahy knew that the subject would be "the necessity for full military collaboration between Great Britain and the U.S." until the United Nations grew stronger. He foresaw "forceful objections by the Soviet to our having such a bilateral military association," but, after reading the speech, "I could find no fault."

Going over the speech would have been one of the few serious intervals during a trip in which Truman, at one point, accepted an invitation to pilot the diesel locomotive. Churchill showed off his knowledge of Americana, taking note of Civil War battle sites as they rode through Maryland and West Virginia. At Harpers Ferry, where the Confederate general "Stonewall" Jackson had seized the Union general George McClellan's supplies, he recalled a visit to Shangri-La, Roosevelt's cabin in Catoctin Mountain Park (now Camp David), and how, passing through Frederick, Maryland, he'd wanted to see the house that belonged to Barbara Fritchie, the celebrated Unionist. Churchill could recite John Greenleaf Whittier's poem about Fritchie ("shoot if you must this old gray head, but spare your country's flag"), and, it was reported, did so, flawlessly, as they rode west.

In the combined conference and dining room of the *Ferdinand Magellan*, as Truman and Churchill became more relaxed, the guests—among them Harry Vaughan, Charlie Ross, and Clark Clifford—lounged on sofas and in easy chairs, watching the late-winter landscape, while Churchill told stories, some sounding more than a little stale, as when, holding a whiskey and soda, he said, "You know, when I was a young subaltern in the South African War, the water was not fit to drink. To make it palatable, we had to put a bit of whiskey in it."

By the second evening, Truman and Churchill were on a Harry-and-Winston basis. "Don't think I ever had a more pleasant holiday," Truman reflected, in his diary. "We organized a low limit poker game and the wise cracks would make Bob Hope laugh. My sides are sore." It was Churchill who'd suggested switching from gin rummy to poker, knowing that Truman liked to play for relaxation, fellowship, and amusement. Truman's games observed certain customs, among them a hundred-dollar limit on what a member of the White House staff could lose. (Outsiders, such as journalists, were bound by different rules.) Anyone losing that hundred would go on "poverty" status—which allowed an impoverished player to take seed money from the pot, if the pot could support it. But although Truman was "a good and even possibly a very good" player, one participant recalled, he was liable to give his emotions too large a role. He favored anarchic variations, the sort that drove purists mad, such as "seven card, low hole card wild, high low," with all its wild-card possibilities, a system that, in Ross's view, Churchill "couldn't seem to get the hang of." These games sometimes had a three-raise limit, but for outsiders, not bound by "poverty poker" rules, losses could mount up. The second night's game lasted until about 1:30 a.m., and Churchill, who, Ross thought, "took a boy's delight in the game," called a straight a "sequence" and a jack a "knave," came out a little behind.

The rail trip ended in Jefferson City, Missouri; from there the travelers went by car to Fulton. If Churchill was nervous, Truman had reason to be nervous too. Clement Attlee thought it was of "vital importance" for the United States to avoid being "maneuvered into a position where they were lined up in a bloc against Russia to implement Britain's European policy." But that's what Churchill wanted, and what, only partially disguised within a fusillade of Churchillian prose, he said in Fulton, before an audience of nearly three thousand, seated in the campus gymnasium. The speech contained passages that glowed purple, as when he said,

The awful ruin of Europe, with all its vanished glories, and of large parts of Asia glares us in the eyes. When the designs of wicked men or the aggressive urge of mighty States dissolve over large areas the frame of civilized society, humble folk are confronted with difficulties with which they cannot cope. For them is all distorted, all is broken, even ground to pulp.

Truman's presence, Churchill said, would "dignify and magnify" his remarks; it certainly magnified their significance. The President occasionally applauded the speaker's observations, and, because he was seated just to the former PM's right, everyone could see him clapping. Truman didn't neglect Stalin: "I became very fond of both of them," he said, when he introduced Churchill. "They are men and they are leaders in this world today, when we need leadership." Churchill managed only to say, "I have a strong admiration and regard for the valiant Russian people and for my wartime colleague, Marshal Stalin." But that was about the only good word he had for Stalin as he continued, speaking with reverberating cadences and tricolon constructions. He called for "a special relationship" with the United States, meaning not only a "growing friendship and mutual understanding between our two vast but kindred systems of society," but military cooperation. Getting a little carried away by the concept of this binational friendship, he foresaw "the principle of common citizenship," although he was prepared to leave that "to destiny, whose outstretched arm many of us can already clearly see."

Most famously, and quotably, Churchill spoke about Europe's postwar future, saying that "an iron curtain has descended across the Continent"—not the first time he'd used that phrase, but the most attention-getting—and (his arm rising and falling) declared that "behind that line lie all the capitals of the ancient states of Central and Eastern Europe. . . . and all are subject . . . to a very high and, in some cases, increasing measure of control from Moscow." He was sure that "there is nothing" the Russians "admire so much as strength," and in that spirit said it would be "criminal madness" to give the "secret knowledge or experience of the atomic bomb" to the embryonic United Nations. Lest one forget his prewar foresight, he said, "Last time I saw it all coming and I cried aloud to my own fellow-countrymen and to the world . . . but no one would listen and one by one we were all sucked into the awful whirlpool."

That night, in Washington, the Achesons gave a dinner party, where conversation naturally turned to the Fulton speech. When Alice Acheson said that Churchill wanted a military alliance with the United States, against Russia, Richard Casey, the Australian ambassador, and his wife, Ethel, became enthusiastic. Henry Wallace, also at the table, was not at all enthusiastic; it was not, he said, a primary objective of the United States to save the British Empire. At that, as Wallace recalled, "Mrs. Casey placed her hands on her hips and went almost into a frenzy. She proclaimed that the purpose was to save the world—not the British Empire." The ambassador, who'd been a member of Churchill's War Cabinet, said the Russians were beasts. When Wallace brought up the idea of disarmament, Casey said, "You might as well talk about a trip to the moon."

4. The Fulton speech, as expected, did stir things up. Three senators issued a joint statement of protest; the *Herald Tribune* declared that Churchill had "flung a block-buster into the disordered and tottering streets of man"; James Roosevelt, the eldest of the late President's four sons, said, "It is up to us and to every peace-loving man and woman in the entire world to stand up now and repudiate the words, the schemes and the political allies of the Hon. Winston Churchill." It was not surprising, then, that Truman would be tempted to dissemble. At a March 8 press conference, he said, "I didn't know what would be in Mr. Churchill's speech. This is a country of free speech. Mr. Churchill had a perfect right to say what he pleased. . . . I had told him if he would come over here and give the lecture at that little college, that I would be glad to introduce him." When Truman was asked for his opinion of the speech, he replied, "I have no comment."

But as criticism intensified, Truman told Acheson to avoid a New York reception for Churchill. It was as if he finally realized that what a foreign leader had said at "that little college," as the President sat nearby, could reverberate in unexpected ways—that his command of the nation's foreign policy could slip away in a way that a more experienced leader would not have allowed.

If Truman hadn't known what was coming, what did that say about his grasp of the job? If he *did* know, had he endorsed Churchill's outlook? Stalin seemed to think so. On March 13, in an interview with *Pravda*, he called Churchill's speech "a dangerous act," and, moreover, said that "Churchill and his friends remind one of Hitler and his friends." The Fulton speech, he said, was "a call to war with the Soviet Union."

Those were very harsh words, and Truman, realizing this, wrote to Stalin to say that he hoped for a better relationship between their countries. He invited Stalin to visit Missouri and make a speech of his own, with "exactly the same kind of reception." Furthermore, he would personally introduce him just as he'd introduced Churchill. The letter was carried to Moscow, in April, by a new American ambassador, Lieutenant General Walter Bedell ("Beetle") Smith, General Eisenhower's former chief of staff, who had just replaced a worn-out Averell Harriman.

When General Smith saw Stalin on April 5 (it turned out to be his only formal meeting with the generalissimo during the three years he'd spend in Moscow), he recalled that "Stalin listened impassively, and nodded," finally saying, "I would like very much to visit the United States, but age has taken its toll. My doctors tell me that I must not travel long distances and I am kept on a strict diet. . . . A man must conserve his strength. President Roosevelt . . . did not save his strength. If he had, he would probably be alive today." Stalin said that a speech like Churchill's, if directed against the United States, would never have been permitted in Russia.

⁂

On a Friday night in late March, about two weeks after the Fulton speech, Charlie Ross was still at work inside the White House, where, at about 9 p.m., he saw Truman. They were separated by rank—President and press secretary—but they'd known each other since high school, so it was not strange for the distance between them sometimes to melt away. Bess was in Independence, and Truman was working on a Jackson Day speech, while waiting for his twenty-two-year-old daughter to return from a night out. Margaret for years had been studying music, hoping for a professional career as a singer. Truman wasn't enthusiastic. "If she wants to be a warbler," he told his mother and sister, "and has the talent and will to do the hard work necessary to accomplish her purpose, I don't suppose I should kick." Nor did he like the idea of Margaret moving to New York to study music, "but I don't want her to be a Washington socialite and she doesn't want to be." He promised his support if she finished college, but had also remarked, "I'd rather have grandchildren in the family than a prima donna." She'd soon graduate from the George Washington University, majoring in history and international relations, and, as her father knew, would also soon be on her own.

"We had a drink together," Ross wrote in his diary. "He seemed lonesome." Ross too was a little glum: here he was, working hard, stuck indoors during that sweet time of the year, when the cherry blossoms were out around the Tidal Basin. Two days later, Truman dined with some of his staff, and held forth on some of his favorite subjects: Mark Twain, Independence, the Mormon Church (Joseph Smith had once said that the Second Coming of Christ would occur in Jackson County), and his own reading, which, he said, included the Book of Mormon, the Koran, *The Decline and Fall of the Roman Empire*, and "all the books in the Independence library." Of the Soviet Union, he said, with some certainty, "Russia couldn't turn a wheel in the next ten years without our aid."

SEVEN

The Quick and the Dead

Many years ago, a very wise man named Bernard Baruch took me aside and put his arm around my shoulder. "Harpo, my boy," he said, "I'm going to give you three pieces of advice, three things you should always remember."

My heart jumped and I glowed with expectation. I was going to hear the magic password to a rich full life from the master himself. "Yes, sir?" I said. And he told me the three things.

I regret that I've forgotten what they were.

—Harpo Marx

1. President Truman might appear relaxed when he sipped a late-night bourbon, or played poker with his aides, but now and then, in the privacy of his diary, he'd just let loose, as he did, probably in the early fall of 1945, when labor unions were threatening disruptive strikes, the Grand Alliance was crumbling, and the mere existence of nuclear weapons was an inescapable worry. Of the strikers, he wrote, "Declare an emergency—call out the troops. . . . If any leader interferes court martial him. [Illegible] ought to have been shot in 1942, but Franklin didn't have the guts to do it." As for that other matter: "Get plenty of Atomic Bombs on hand—drop one on Stalin, put the United Nations to work and eventually set up a free world." It wasn't the only time Truman would record such flare-ups.

It was a way to take his political id off the leash of responsibility, and to punish imagined and real malefactors. But such dark moods were brief, and rarely supplanted his innate good nature.

Truman was never able to ignore the disquieting presence of atomic arms. A month after Hiroshima, he promised to make a recommendation to Congress on the future of nuclear energy, and later that September, he met with members of his cabinet to get their thoughts on whether to share scientific information with the Russians. That he would solicit so many views, vapid and thoughtful, suggests how perplexed he was by the responsibility for this thing, this mortal threat that posed so many novel questions. The occasionally tormented Henry Stimson, the outgoing secretary of war, said that "world peace rests on whether or not we and the Russians can find a working pattern of understanding"; and Vannevar Bush, who'd headed the National Defense Research Council, said the Russians would probably catch up within five years, which was not a prediction that Truman welcomed. Under Secretary of State Dean Acheson argued, in a memorandum, that the theoretical knowledge was widely known, and because engineering a bomb was only a matter of time, "a policy of secrecy is both futile and dangerous."

On October 2, Truman sent his promised Special Message to Congress, asking for legislation to control the domestic development and use of nuclear energy. Its fifteen hundred words included the rosy thought that "the hope of civilization lies in international arrangements looking, if possible, to the renunciation of the use of the bomb," and to a guarantee that it would not be used as "an instrument of destruction." Yet, after six months as president, Truman was still unguarded enough to suddenly, unpredictably, say something silly, something he couldn't possibly mean, as he did just five days later, at a fishing camp called Reelfoot Lake, near Tiptonville, Tennessee. He was there for a brief rest, on his way to dedicate a nearby dam, and Charlie Ross had invited the traveling press to stop by to sip some twenty-year-old Jack Daniel's. The socializing turned into an impromptu news conference, during which Truman acknowledged that the "scientific knowledge that resulted in the atomic bomb" was no secret, but "the know-how of putting that knowledge practically to work that is our secret; just the same as know-how in the construction of the B-29." A few questions followed:

Q: You mean, then, that we will not share that knowledge with our allies?

The President: Just the same as we haven't shared our engineering knowledge, or any of our engineering secrets. But so far as the scientific knowledge is concerned, they all know that, anyway.

Q: But so far as the bomb secret is concerned, we will not share that?

The President: Not the know-how of putting it together, let's put it that way.

When Charlie Ross said, "This isn't a press conference, it's off-the-record," Truman corrected him: "Well, Charlie, it's all right, let them use it."

Reporters did use it, and on the printed page it sounded as if Truman hadn't realized that Great Britain and Canada had been partners in the Manhattan Project. Although he certainly knew better, his remarks, in context or out, reflected his real inclination: to hold on to this slippery, unkeepable secret as long as America had sole possession of the bomb, and the technology to make more of them. But what he'd said impelled Prime Minister Clement Attlee to travel to Washington, where he was joined by the Canadian PM, Mackenzie King. During meetings over several days in November, the three allies came to the unsurprising conclusion that "faced with the terrible realities of the application of science to destruction," there was an "overwhelming need to maintain the rule of law among nations"—which meant giving full support to the United Nations. There was no mention of a top-secret 1943 meeting between Roosevelt and Churchill, who'd agreed that the still-untested bomb would be used only with mutual consent, an agreement to which Truman did not feel bound.

In the six years that Attlee served as prime minister, he would make just one more trip to Washington—five years later, and once again driven by unspoken nervousness about Truman's approach to the atomic bomb.

2. A first-term Connecticut senator, Brien McMahon, was among the first elected officials to see that the bomb couldn't be treated as if it was simply the biggest-ever explosive, another weapon in the arsenal of the military establishment. On the day that Fat Man was dropped on Nagasaki, McMahon sent a telegram to Truman, saying that the bomb "points up with horrible emphasis the necessity for using our skill and money to help instead of ruining mankind." It is no understatement to say that McMahon was obsessed by the subject, and was determined to master it, to "learn all that I could about the development of nuclear physics." By early September 1945, he was at work on legislation that emphasized civilian authority over the use and development of atomic energy. A competing bill, which favored control by the military establishment, was sponsored by Congressman Andrew Jackson May, of Kentucky, and Senator Edwin C. Johnson from Colorado, who was better known for condemning the actress Ingrid Bergman's affair with the director Roberto Rossellini. The May-Johnson bill was widely opposed by, among others, the scientific community.

Truman favored McMahon's approach, and the senator began to see the President with some frequency, which not many freshman legislators could have managed. The new president and the freshman senator got along well, and Washington then was small enough, and relaxed enough, for Truman to drop by the McMahon home, on Woodland Drive, in the city's Kalorama neighborhood. McMahon wasn't daunted by what lay ahead. Ten years earlier, at age thirty-two—when he was the youngest person ever put in charge of the Justice Department's Criminal Division—he'd been intimidated and shot at when he led the government's attempt to enforce the Wagner National Labor Relations Act in the coal country of "Bloody" Harlan County, Kentucky. It seemed to mark him. A decade later, after he was elected to the Senate, a newspaper story described him as "a short well-groomed gentleman who really looks important." He was a serious, ambitious, and sometimes pompous young man. "Even though he was so young," an aide recalled, "he always tried to make himself older."

With Truman's encouragement, McMahon spent months on a bill—the Atomic Energy Act of 1946—that transferred the responsibilities of the Manhattan Project, overseen by General Leslie Groves, to an all-civilian Atomic Energy Commission, to be appointed by the President. General Groves and the Pentagon opposed that change. Admiral Leahy correctly sensed an implicit distrust of the armed services—remarking, within earshot of navy secretary James Forrestal, that the act would be mean turning over "one of the most effective weapons of war to a civil commission which would dole out its product, if it decided to make any, as it saw fit." The atomic scientists who'd designed and built the bomb were eager to ensure precisely that result. McMahon's daughter, Patricia, remembered active lobbying at their home, on Woodland Drive—"guys coming to the house young, science-type guys, frayed collars," who didn't want the military in control. "They knew it was not a good match."

Truman was basically satisfied by the bill that emerged in early 1946, and heaped praise on McMahon, for whom "there beckons a place of honor in history." On June 1, after six months of testimony and debate, the Senate voted, unanimously, to pass what was sometimes called the "McMahon Act," and sent it to the House, where it passed two months later. The act also established congressional oversight, with an eighteen-member Joint Committee on Atomic Energy. It was unusual to give the chairmanship of such an important committee to a freshman senator, and General Groves, for one, took special, skeptical note of that. "I have never been able to learn," he later wrote, "who it was on the White House staff that put the idea across that the chairman in this instance should be Senator McMahon, despite his lack of seniority. I have always doubted whether President Truman was particularly interested in which course was taken."

There seems to be no written record, but it undoubtedly was Truman himself who "put the idea across," having found a determined and reliable ally in McMahon. He did so despite a number of other domestic distractions that spring: the Churchill visit, in early March, and, in late April, the death of Chief Justice Harlan Stone, of a cerebral hemorrhage. Truman filled the post of chief justice by doing what he often did: naming a friend, in this case Fred Vinson, a poker companion, and, recently, his treasury secretary. The vacated Treasury post went to another old friend, John W. Snyder, a former St. Louis banker.

3. Simply being the bomb's custodian—faced with the "terrible position we are all in because of this discovery," as Under Secretary of State Dean Acheson put it—heightened a wish for international control. President Truman had endorsed that notion after his meetings with Prime Ministers Attlee and King. At a Navy Day celebration, in early January 1946, he said, "The highest hope of the American people is that world cooperation for peace will soon reach such a state of perfection that atomic methods of destruction can be definitely and effectively outlawed forever," though his sincerity was undercut by the such phrases as "highest hope" and "state of perfection."

Secretary of State Byrnes, who'd discussed atomic energy controls at the foreign ministers' conference in Moscow, took the initiative by asking Acheson to chair a committee to study the international question. That assignment led Acheson to talk to his friend David Lilienthal, the chairman of the Tennessee Valley Authority, a thoughtful, sometimes combative Midwesterner, the child of Jewish immigrants, who'd graduated from DePauw University, in Indiana, with a Phi Beta Kappa key and a reputation as a pretty good light-heavyweight boxer. During a forty-five-minute conversation, Acheson was disarmingly indiscreet: Neither Truman nor Byrnes, he told Lilienthal, seemed to grasp what was involved in "the most serious cloud hanging over the world." Furthermore, "commitments, on paper and in communiques, have been made and are being made . . . without a knowledge of what the hell it is all about—literally!" In any case, he said, the status quo was unacceptable. Acheson had more on his mind: Four days later, he asked Lilienthal to become the "directing head" of an advisory group, which would include Harvard's president, James B. Conant, General Groves, and Acheson, as well as business executives and scientists, among them the physicist J. Robert Oppenheimer. Lilienthal agreed—hesitatingly.

The Acheson-Lilienthal Committee, as it came to be known, worked quickly and, in less than two months, came up with the outline of an expansive, even radical, proposal, mostly written by Oppenheimer, to establish worldwide control of atomic materiel, energy, and weapons, and to set up an international Atomic Development Authority. What was needed, Oppenheimer later wrote, was "a quite new approach to international problems," a realization that "the security of all peoples would be jeopardized by a failure to establish new systems of openness and cooperation between the nations." Then, in mid-March 1946, their work-in-progress was interrupted by what Lilienthal saw as "a crazy kind of finale—or is it the curtain-raiser?" That was a recommendation, by Byrnes, that Truman appoint the financier Bernard Baruch to the new United Nations Atomic Energy Commission, which would make Baruch the public face of the Acheson-Lilienthal report, someone who could bring to the task what a generous writer called a "booming, resonant, expressive voice, loaded with maleness and information." In a way this was no surprise. Baruch and Byrnes, both South Carolinians, had known each other for a long time. Baruch had been a donor to Byrnes's senatorial campaigns, and when Byrnes lost out on the vice presidency, in 1944, Baruch had attempted to console him, not entirely successfully, writing that "I am well aware of the hurts and rebuffs you have experienced, undeserved as I know them to be." Baruch, someone who thought a great deal about himself, added, "In times like these, however, none of us can think of himself." But it was, if measured by Baruch's qualifications, nonetheless a curious appointment.

Acheson thought Baruch's reputation was "entirely self-propagated." Lilienthal, who intuited that Baruch was unlikely to be an enthusiastic ally of their work, was horrified. "When I read this news," he wrote in his diary, "I was quite sick." At seventy-five, almost deaf in one ear, Baruch seemed older than his chronological age. Although he would live nearly twenty more years, he required a full-time nurse-housekeeper-companion. His stamina was limited: "I can only work between the hours of ten and twelve in the morning and from 2:30 to 4:30 in the afternoon," he informed Byrnes. Night sessions were out of the question. "He is really quite an old man," Lilienthal, who was forty-seven, thought. During meetings, he found it painful to watch Baruch fidget with his hearing aid and sag as the afternoon proceeded." Lilienthal was further discouraged when he learned that Baruch wanted to bring in some Wall Street friends as "alternates and co-workers," among them Herbert Bayard Swope, a Baruch assistant during World War I, when Baruch served on the War Industries Board. Swope was also the uncredited author of Baruch's most quotable phrases. He was well equipped for the task, having been editor of the *New York World*, a remarkable newspaper that, before it expired, in 1931, was home to, among others, the critic Alexander Woollcott, the novelist James M. Cain, and the opinion writer Walter Lippmann.

With his new title, Baruch couldn't hide his pleasure, or his bubbling vanity. "It is a mystery to me why they took me out of the domestic and international fields of economics, where I had such vast experience, and put me in another field where I know nothing," he said. Yet, as his biographer Jordan A. Schwartz observed, it wasn't all that mysterious. Truman may have seen Baruch as a "stuffed shirt" and an "old goat" and thought "there never was a greater egotist," but he saw his value. He wanted the American representative to the UN to be someone people would recognize and, out of habit, admire. Baruch, anyone could see, was well cast in the role of a wise elder. The journalist Helen Lawrenson, a former romantic interest, whose *Esquire* magazine debut, "Latins Are Lousy Lovers," made her famous, described him as a man with "proud bearing, thick white hair, a strong, aquiline nose, crafty blue eyes... always the most distinguished-looking man in any group." She also saw Baruch as an "obsessive conniver and manipulator who liked to be described as a mysterious Richelieu-like figure behind the scenes, a secret string-puller, and a major self-promoter." The columnist Marquis Childs saw Baruch more clearly, as someone with a deep attraction to power: "Only the snapping turtle mouth now and then gave it away."

Baruch enjoyed the attention, a higher grade than he'd gotten two years earlier, when he'd provided room and board for President Roosevelt, at his Hobcaw Barony estate. On the afternoon of March 26, 1946, savoring his role, he met with Truman for nearly an hour. As he left the White House, the waiting pack of reporters asked if he'd read the draft of the still-secret Acheson-Lilienthal report. "Frankly, I did," Baruch replied. What were his thoughts? At that, he laughed and said, "I can't hear you," which may have been true, although there was no way to know if the nearly deaf Baruch had read, or absorbed, anything in the eighty-page policy report. Baruch "wasn't much on technical scientific stuff," Schwartz wrote, "but he could smell his way through it."

Baruch's big moment, one of the biggest of his life, came on June 14, 1946, in a speech at the UN's temporary home, a gussied-up gymnasium on the Bronx campus of Hunter College. Days before, Lilienthal and Acheson had gone over the text, and found it "rather confused and badly organized." Byrnes had then admitted, to Acheson, that bringing in Baruch was "the worst mistake I have ever made." But to Lilienthal's relief, the speech that Baruch delivered, the work of the talented Swope, was much better than the version he'd read, and Baruch did a first-rate job of impersonating a senior statesman. Seated, and reading from his text, as he spoke to "my fellow citizens of the world," he used language that sometimes rose to the occasion. That was especially true of the beginning: "We are here to make a choice between the quick and the dead," he said—using "quick" in its Biblical sense, meaning "alive," and quoting either the New Testament or, perhaps, *Hamlet*, where Laertes says, "Now pile your dust upon the quick and the dead." The speech sometimes strained at the rhetorical leash, as when he said, "Behind the black portent of the new atomic age lies a hope which, seized upon with faith, can work our salvation." But the plan it seemed to sketch out was immediately praised as imaginative and bold.

The "plan," though, was not actually a plan. It included demands that would never be met, such as the unilateral destruction of America's atomic weapons and inspections by the Atomic Development Authority. Another doomed proviso said that no nation could veto any attempt to enforce the agreement. There was no mistaking that the veto issue was aimed at the Soviet Union, and that, as the Soviet delegate, Andrei Gromyko, made clear, the Russians would never agree to it. Despite these diplomatic cul-de-sacs, Baruch managed to hit it off with Gromyko, and invited him, along with a number of others, including Trygve Lie, the UN secretary-general, to the Joe Louis–Billy Conn heavyweight rematch, at Yankee Stadium. There, by one account, "they all appeared to have a rollicking good time." Admiral Leahy watched the fight on an eighteen-square-inch television, at Washington's Statler Hotel, and noted in his diary that "the negro won by a knock-out in the eighth round."

———— ✕✕✕ ————

On the day of Baruch's speech, Truman did not seem conversant with this still-unfamiliar subject:

> *Q:* Mr. President, do you have any comment on the statement which Mr. Baruch is making today on the atomic energy control—
>
> *The President:* Mr. Baruch has been informed of the policy of the President with regard to atomic energy, and I haven't seen his statement, but I imagine he is following the policy as it was outlined to him by myself and the Secretary of State.
>
> *Q:* Mr. President, is that policy outlined in the so-called Acheson-Lilienthal report?
>
> *The President:* No. It's the policy outlined in the directive which I sent to Mr. Baruch.

But after a year in office Truman was mastering the art of ducking uncomfortable questions, deploying "no comment" as if he'd just discovered the phrase. After a conference, during which he'd replied five times with a "no comment," Charlie Ross noted, with the satisfaction of a trainer, that "this is a technique that some of us have been urging upon him for a good while. He has been too free in answering badgering questions. Even some of the newspapermen have been wanting him to be a little more reticent in his own interest."

4.   With exquisitely awkward timing, the United States, on July 1, 1946, began a series of nuclear tests near Bikini Atoll, in the South Pacific. This followed the "quick and dead" speech by two weeks, and came a month before Truman signed the Atomic Energy Act of 1946, which was passed by Congress on August 1.

"Operation Crossroads," which had been in the works for months, and postponed at least once, was intended to observe what would happen when bombs were dropped on warships or exploded under water. The operation, overseen by a Joint Army/Navy task force and involving some forty thousand people, did not make much military, diplomatic, or economic sense, although there was no denying the power of curiosity—to learn what these explosives could do to inanimate objects and small animals. Its pointlessness was understood by Lippmann, who noted that it involved areas in which the United States had undoubted superiority: sea power and atomic bombs. Pitting these against each other, he wrote, "is somewhat as if Joe Louis were trying to find out whether he can break his own right arm with his own left hand." Robert Oppenheimer tried to persuade Truman to call off, or postpone, Operation Crossroads, pointing out that "attempts to simulate combat conditions in a single test must necessarily be crude," and that "more useful information could be obtained by model tests and by calculations." Jimmy Byrnes, at a cabinet meeting on March 22, also urged Truman to cancel the exercise, calling it "extremely unwise"—more so because he'd soon be attending a multi-nation peace conference in Paris. He worried that the tests would be seen as just a "big show on the strength of the atomic dictator."

Truman refused to consider canceling. "This test will cost a hundred million dollars, and if the tests are cancelled this amount of money will be wasted," he'd said. He did say that, after the first of the three planned detonations, he'd decide about the next two, but by mid-April, he was in "complete agreement" with the military's view that the tests "are of vital importance in obtaining information for the national defense," and that Operation Crossroads should be seen as "in the nature of a laboratory experiment."

Before the Bikini tests could begin, though, there was a hitch: The 165 men, women, and children who lived on Bikini Island ("dusky Micronesians" in contemporary accounts) and their leader, King Juda, had to be moved 130 miles southeast, to Rongerik Atoll, where the navy had built a new village. The populace was reported to have accepted these changed circumstances with humility. King Juda in any case was quoted saying (the translation from Marshalese was described as "approximate") that "if it is for the good of mankind that this thing be done, then we will be glad to help. We will put our trust in God." It is not difficult to read between those docile lines, whether or not they, or anything close to them, were actually spoken.

"Abel" became the world's fourth atomic bomb blast—after Trinity, Hiroshima, and Nagasaki. When it went off, on July 1, it impressed the *New York Times*' William L. Laurence, who called it an "awesome, spine-chilling spectacle, boiling, angry super volcano." Senator Leverett Saltonstall, a Massachusetts Republican, part of a small delegation of officials and scientists chosen by Truman as witnesses, felt a small tremor before seeing "a white cloud with a beautiful silver white mushroom top." Navy Secretary Forrestal felt the blast from a distance of eleven miles, and watched a "vast cone of smoke . . . suffused with streaks of rose-purple light." It was not as destructive as many had hoped. Out of some ninety ships in the Bikini Lagoon (submarines, battleships, cruisers, destroyers, landing craft, some of Japanese and German origin), most remained upright; five were sunk, six were wrecked, and about half were damaged, some negligibly. Three thousand goats, sheep, pigs, and mice imported to the South Pacific did not fare so well. Many fell ill, and died slowly, of radioactive poisoning, while others perished instantly.

A few days before "Baker," the second test, on July 25, Admiral W. H. ("Spike") Blandy, who commanded the Joint Task Force, went to see King Juda on Rongerik Atoll, where an interpreter explained that the admiral was another kind of king, someone who "commands thousands of men and hundreds of ships." Blandy said it was a great honor to visit King Juda and his people, and he thanked them for their "kindness and cooperation." King Juda was introduced to Senator Carl Hatch, a New Mexico Democrat, who headed the congressional delegation and was identified as a "direct representative of the President." Hatch told the King, "You have made a true contribution to the progress of mankind all over the world and the President of the United States extends to you, King Juda, his thanks for all you have done." The king may not have understood what Hatch was saying, or have had any idea what this "President" was, or cared, but the Americans started piling on gifts: tobacco, a pipe, a cigarette holder and cigarettes for the king; chocolate, soft drinks, and salted nuts for the villagers; and a globe of the Earth for the village schoolteacher, along with an attempt to explain what it was. Senator Hatch thought the king would be pleased with some military gold braid.

The king was invited to watch Baker, which was to be set off under water. The AP reporter Don Whitehead was aboard a B-29 when the world's fifth atomic bomb produced "a gigantic dome-shaped mushroom of smoke, vapor, and water." A young navy doctor, David Bradley, was simply depressed at what he'd witnessed: "The whole business must seem like a very bad dream to the regular Navy men: decks you can't stay on for more than a few minutes but which seem like other decks; air you can't breathe without gas masks but which smells like all other air; water you can't swim in, and good tuna and jacks you can't eat. It's a fouled-up world." King Juda watched from the upper deck of the flagship *Mount McKinley*, and was heard muttering the words "big boom."

The Bikini tests (a third one, "Charlie," was canceled) came while arguments on controlling the atom continued at the United Nations, inside Manhattan's Henry Hudson Hotel. Andrei Gromyko, as expected, rejected the American plan—particularly the limitation of veto powers. *Pravda* said the testing "did not bring about the end of the world, but it blew up something more essential than a pair of old ships" —that it undermined confidence in the seriousness of the American proposals. *Pravda* was not a source to be trusted, and its motives were suspect, but it was hard to dispute this particular assertion. When Truman's cabinet met, at the end of July, the spare minutes noted that Forrestal "provided a colorful description of the bomb explosion." Truman that day seemed more interested in various legislative matters, especially a question concerning mineral rights held by the government.

Truman was certainly sincere, even farsighted, in his support of the "McMahon Act"—particularly in his commitment to civilian custody of the domestic atomic stockpile. But while he endorsed the concept of international control and cooperation, he never had much faith in the idea of sharing nuclear technology—of giving away the "know-how," even if overseen by some UN body. Perhaps it is unfair to say that Truman wanted some sort of charade at the United Nations, but that was what he got from the doddering Baruch, despite a memorable performance in June. Everyone seemed aware of the danger that would someday accompany an international arms competition, but preferred that to putting national autonomy at risk.

One night in late July, Lilienthal met Oppenheimer at Washington's National Airport, where Oppenheimer had arrived on a late flight from New York. They talked well past one in the morning. Lilienthal, who was already being mentioned as the first chairman of the Atomic Energy Commission, sounded discouraged, though not yet ready to give up on the idea of international nuclear control. But he found Oppenheimer "in deep despair." In his diary, he wrote, "When I said that there are some situations in which one cannot acknowledge despair, he took me to task for this, in a gentle but firm way, saying that it was this sense of a 'reservoir of hope' that was quite wrong, for it does not exist."

EIGHT

A Season of Disharmony

The situation where Byrnes is away from Washington all the time, being his own negotiator, is very bad indeed. With Truman what he is, there is simply no one to take a general view of our interests and our policy. That's why the policies we have are made in bits and pieces—now in one department, now in another; now in one bureau, now in another.

—Walter Lippmann, in a letter to John J. McCloy

1. The murder, by the Third Reich, of six million men, women, and children, most of them Jews, was chillingly recalled in early September 1946, as the trial of twenty-four top Nazis concluded, in Nuremberg. Some of the accused, knowing their probable fates, were angry; others, such as Walther Funk, the former Reichsbank chief, wept, insisting that they'd known nothing. Hans Frank, aka the "Butcher of Warsaw," blamed Hitler, and called him a coward for having committed suicide. A month later, the defendants were sentenced—twelve by hanging—and as they stood and listened to their fates, in translation, some flung away their headsets, although Hans Frank, who'd slashed his wrists in a suicide attempt, found it hard to use his left hand. Hitler's deputy, Martin Bormann, was tried in absentia; Hermann Göring managed to commit suicide, with a cyanide capsule. An imaginary Hitler lived on, not only in the mischievous suggestions by Stalin, but in published accounts that the fuehrer and Eva Braun had in fact escaped to Argentina, transported by submarine, and had set up house on a German-owned estate in Patagonia. Officers in the former German Navy dismissed these stories, and rumors, but they persisted. In early September, security officers from the four occupying powers began what was termed a "manhunt"—from Berlin to Tokyo to Buenos Aires—on the chance that Hitler had not died in his bunker.

The executions, on October 16, two weeks after the sentencing, were carried out behind prison walls. Those who waited outside could hear shouts and, by one account, "a thudding like the springing of a heavy trap door," as the men were led to the gallows, one by one, between 1 a.m. and 2:45 a.m. The trial and executions troubled Ohio's Senator Robert Taft, who, speaking at Kenyon College, said they violated "that fundamental principle of American law that a man cannot be tried under an ex post facto statute." He added that "vengeance is seldom justice," but the distinction was a little too fine for that time. President Truman, a few days later, said that other ex-Nazis, including industrialists, politicians, and police officials—"these remaining malefactors [who] played their miserable roles at lower levels"—would face their fate.

In America, the summer of 1946 had marked the first full year of peace since 1940. People took to the Labor Day weekend as if to reclaim lost time. Park officials in Chicago predicted that a million and a half people would be out and about; thousands more crowded bus and railroad stations, while those fortunate enough to own a car (private auto production, prohibited during the war, had started up again in 1945) took to the road. Weather on the East Coast was fair and comfortable, and Atlantic City expected a record four hundred thousand visitors. New Yorkers discovered that there was space to be had on ships bound for Bermuda or Puerto Rico, but the Pennsylvania Railroad needed to add forty-seven extra sections; bus and rail passengers traveling to and from Washington and New York got used to standing room. Pan American World Airways reported that bookings to London—a flight that, with refueling stops, took more than seventeen hours—were sold out, and the company announced plans to fly an eighty-passenger version of the B-29 Superfortress, offering coast-to-coast service in six hours. It was as if the nation were engulfed in the rare serenity that comes when every threat seems manageable.

Harry Truman, in mid-August, began a stag vacation, an eighteen-day cruise aboard the *Williamsburg*, covering two thousand miles, its route taking him from the Potomac River to Quonset Point, Rhode Island, to Bermuda and back to American soil on September 1. Along the way, various advisers boarded and disembarked, but the full-time voyagers, apart from the Secret Service, included a few regulars: Charlie Ross, Harry Vaughan, John Snyder, and Clark Clifford, who'd gone from assistant naval aide to naval aide, although he'd never been to sea. In late June, Clifford got a big promotion, to White House special counsel, the job once held by Samuel Rosenman. The title was misleading; there were no legal chores (those were handled by the Justice Department), but Rosenman, who'd quit the New York Supreme Court to work as a speechwriter for Roosevelt, had wanted to be called something more prestigious than "assistant." For Clifford, who would also write speeches, it was a leap in a career that had quickly taken him from practicing law in St. Louis to the White House. "His manner is one of bland and affable confidence—when he talks, he clasps his hands together, in a faintly sacerdotal gesture," Stewart Alsop wrote, admiringly, but not everyone was won over. "His face is too handsome, his blond hair too evenly waved, his smile too dazzling, his voice too resonant, his manner too patently sincere, his family background, childhood, college record, romantic courtship, and legal career are all too storybookish to be real," Robert S. Allen and William V. Shannon wrote in their gossipy book about the early Truman years.

The *Williamsburg* was escorted by the USS *Weiss*, which carried journalists, who lived in cramped corners while Truman and his privileged companions swam, fished, and watched movies—among them Bob Hope's *Monsieur Beaucaire* and Orson Welles's domestic-Nazi melodrama *The Stranger*. Truman's daily walks took him around the deck, sometimes accompanied by the genial Harry Vaughan. Toward the end of the journey, when the *Williamsburg* anchored at Hampton Roads, Virginia, reporters on the *Weiss* could see men on the sundeck playing a volleyball variant, employing a medicine ball, and watched with amusement when the heavy ball landed in the water.

The *Chicago Tribune*'s Walter Trohan, observing Truman and his friend John Snyder, recalled, "It was a very curious thing, the two of them . . . would sit there with their arms around each other like a couple of boys on the levee of the Mississippi watching it go by. Just a manner of deep personal friendship, not even talking. They just liked each other's company, as young lads do."

It wasn't all sunshine and sea breezes, though; there was no escape from domestic politics. At one point, advisers briefed Truman about the upcoming midterm elections, which many predicted would go badly for the Democrats. Truman also used some of his shipboard time to mull his five appointments to the new Atomic Energy Commission. David Lilienthal was to be its first chairman. By the time of Lilienthal's confirmation hearings, in the fall of 1946, one witness called the AEC "possibly the most important federal bureau in the history of the republic."

2. As the summer of 1946 was ending, Secretary of State Byrnes was still at the Paris peace conference—it was to last until October—where he signed treaties affecting monetary and territorial issues with Italy, Finland, Romania, Hungary, and Bulgaria. Meanwhile, in Washington, Commerce Secretary Henry Wallace had urged Truman to make more of an effort to reach a peaceful accommodation with Stalin. When other nations eventually get their own atomic bombs, Wallace wrote to the President, the result will be a "neurotic, fear-ridden, itching-trigger psychology in all the peoples of the world."

But a private letter to Truman was one thing; expressing these thoughts in public was almost guaranteed to cause difficulties, and Wallace did just that, on September 12, at a political rally, in Madison Square Garden. He said, "We should recognize that we have no more business in the political affairs of Eastern Europe than Russia has in the political affairs of Latin America, Western Europe, and the United States," and warned that "the tougher we get, the tougher the Russians will get." As for the unsettled nuclear arms question, "not only should individual nations be prohibited from manufacturing atomic bombs, guided missiles, and military aircraft for bombing purposes, but no nation should be allowed to spend on its military establishment more than perhaps fifteen per cent of its budget."

Spectators at the Garden were raucous, and left-wing—"a Stalinoid audience," the critic-essayist Dwight Macdonald wrote. They liked what Wallace had to say, and booed any mention of Truman's name. Wallace had made some elisions in his prepared text, and among the sentences dropped were those critical of Russia. No longer would he say that the Russians "should stop conniving against us in certain areas of the world," and that they "should stop teaching that their form of Communism must, by force, if necessary, ultimately triumph over democratic capitalism." When Wallace was later asked why he'd made those cuts, he said, forthrightly, "Because I felt I had been booed enough." All this might have been ignored were it not that Wallace informed the crowd that Truman had read his speech beforehand and had told him it "represented the policy of his administration." At the word "Truman," the crowd hissed again.

The transcript of Wallace's remarks had been available hours before the Garden rally, in time for Truman to be asked about them at an afternoon news conference:

> *Q:* In the middle of the [Wallace] speech are these words, "When President Truman read these words, he said that they represented the policy of this administration."
> *The President:* That is correct.
> *Q:* My question is, does that apply just to that paragraph, or to the whole speech?
> *The President:* I approved the whole speech.

Truman had wanted to deny it. Before he met with reporters, he'd told Eben Ayers, the deputy press secretary, that he'd never given his approval. But Charlie Ross, who knew better, urged Truman to tell the "whole truth"; and Truman agreed. It didn't take long for Wallace's speech to become an enormous embarrassment for the President who, in Walter Lippmann's deadly phrase, had shown himself to be "a bit slow to catch on."

Because Byrnes was in Europe, and his deputy, Dean Acheson, was also away, William Clayton, the Under Secretary of State for Economic Affairs, had been left in charge. Clayton regarded the Wallace speech as an emergency—all the more so because he'd read it just an hour before it was to be delivered. Because no one at State seemed aware that Truman, at his press conference, had already acknowledged seeing the speech, what followed was an episode of interoffice hysteria, and pleas for someone to make Wallace cut the line about getting Truman's approval. Byrnes would feel "the ground had been cut out from under him," Clayton believed, and he called Charlie Ross to say that a deletion was "imperative." But it was too late to fix what had been broken. In the White House, there was a feeling that Truman had been "trapped" by reporters' questions, but trapped or not, Admiral Leahy told Truman that Wallace, whom Leahy regarded as "pink" and an "honest 'fellow traveler,'" couldn't stay in the cabinet unless the nation's foreign policy was to be "radically changed."

Much of this behind-the-scenes intrigue made its way to James Reston, whose front-page *New York Times* story appeared on Saturday morning, two days after Wallace spoke. That afternoon, Truman called reporters to his office and read a word-parsing statement—namely that there'd been "a natural misunderstanding," that he had answered "extemporaneously," and that his answer "did not convey the thought that I intended it to convey. . . . I did not intend to indicate that I approved the speech as constituting a statement of the foreign policy of this country." Coming from a man "in a less exalted position," Dwight Macdonald wrote, that statement "would be called a lie."

Truman's muddled explanations didn't solve his personnel problem. He hoped Byrnes would be able to restrain himself, he told Will Clayton, but Byrnes was too coldly furious to stay calm. In a cable to Clayton, he wrote, "At this time I have not determined whether I will communicate with the President on the subject." Justice Robert Jackson, who'd been on temporary leave to become the lead prosecutor in Nuremberg, had just seen Byrnes, in Paris, and got the impression that Byrnes's words were now "at a discount and the stupid handling of the situation by the White House had created an impossible situation for him." Wallace waited two days—until Monday—to issue *his* statement, and then made matters worse: He not only stood by what he'd said at the Garden, but added that "I intend to continue my efforts for a just and lasting peace and I shall within the near future speak on this subject again." He'd tried to assure Truman that he hadn't intended to damage Byrnes, but he'd already said too much: as Admiral Leahy knew, a cabinet divided against itself could not function. Truman also talked to Byrnes, in Paris, and tried to explain what had happened—that he'd been "pressed for time," and that he'd had "other most important people" coming by to see him. "I wish my Cabinet members would stay in their own fields and attend to their own business," Truman said. "Wallace has a habit of attending to every member's business but his own."

Wallace returned to the White House on Wednesday, September 18, with photographers snapping every step. By then, Byrnes had sent his angriest cable yet, telling Truman, "You and I spent fifteen months building a bipartisan policy. We did a fine job convincing the world that it was a permanent policy upon which the world could rely. Wallace destroyed it in a day." Byrnes's cross mood led to a threat to resign if Truman couldn't make Wallace shut up about foreign policy "while he is a member of your Cabinet."

Wallace spent two and a half hours with the President, and when he left, reporters were still there. "Did the President tell you you had to be quiet or resign?" he was asked. "No." Was he told to stop making foreign-policy speeches? Wallace said, "I found the President is confident that we can keep peace with Russia." In his diary, though, Wallace wrote that Truman told him that Byrnes "had been giving him hell" and "threatened to leave Paris at once and come home" unless he silenced himself. "Never was there such a mess and it is partly of my making," Truman told his mother and sister. "But when I make a mistake it is a good one." He'd come to believe that Wallace was not as "fundamentally sound intellectually" as he'd once thought.

Byrnes's loyal assistant, Walter Brown, thought Byrnes's threat to resign was unwise; he'd urged him to let the matter play out—sure that, sooner or later, Truman would ask Wallace to leave. Brown was right. Having to choose between two cabinet officers, neither one very loyal, both of whom had coveted the vice presidency, Truman fired Wallace, during a short telephone call, on September 20, a Friday. "Of course I hated to do it," he wrote home, adding that when he'd told Wallace, "he was so nice about it I almost backed out!" Reporters were told that Truman had made the decision "independently," overnight, and that the conversation with Wallace had been brief, and harmonious, which wasn't true. Wallace's formal note to the President began with the disrespectful salutation "Dear Harry," followed by "As you requested, here is my resignation," and continued, "I shall continue to fight for peace." That turned out to be the least of it.

Truman needed to escape, and at about noon, the next day, he went to the Navy Yard, where the *Williamsburg* was docked, and where he planned to spend that night and part of Sunday. He cheerfully informed his shipmates that he'd asked Averell Harriman to replace Wallace as commerce secretary, and that Harriman's reply had been "Hell, yes." But it was obvious that Truman was in a blue mood. After all, he knew that he hadn't read a speech that he should have read, and had tried to duck the consequences—and because of that, Wallace's public career seemed to be over. Dean Acheson thought Truman's mistake was to see the differences between Byrnes and Wallace as "a personal quarrel that could be patched up," and that he'd become ensnared because sometimes he hurried to answer a question before hearing it—that "President Truman's mind is not so quick as his tongue."

By Monday, though, Truman's mood began to improve; "It was clear," Charlie Ross observed, "that he felt a great sense of relief." As he conferred with Ross and others, Ross pointed out that the break with Wallace had been "bound to come sooner or later," and that it was "impossible to keep on driving two horses going in opposite directions." Truman agreed that the atmosphere had been cleared, and that a "good deal of the tension that had been present in Cabinet meetings would now be ended." Now, he said, with a burst of optimism, he could count on teamwork as they pursued "peace in the world and full production at home." It was the sort of occasion that prompted the increasingly weary Ross to jot, in a journal, "What a strange job is that of the press secretary. There is no other in the world, I am sure."

3. Democrats had controlled Congress since 1933, when Roosevelt started his first term. Republicans were expected to gain seats in the 1946 midterms, but Truman seemed confident that the Democrats would keep their congressional majorities. At least that was the impression Admiral Leahy got during an "aperient and interesting gossipy talk" with Truman, Majority Leader Alben Barkley, Harry Vaughan, and Chief Justice Fred Vinson. Republicans, though—with the campaign slogan "Had Enough?"—were more attuned to the public's mood. The party took back thirteen Senate seats and fifty-five House seats—enough to give them majorities in both houses of Congress for the first time since 1928. At the annual Gridiron Club dinner, the club's president, Raymond P. Brandt, of the *St. Louis Post-Dispatch*, delivered the traditional "Speech in the Dark," and recalled that Truman had once called 1946 a year of decision. "Well," Brandt said, "the voters decided."

The unambiguous results left the unelected president looking so weak that some wondered if he could continue to govern. The freshman senator J. William Fulbright, an Arkansas Democrat, suggested that Truman appoint a Republican as secretary of state and then resign—letting the designated appointee succeed him. The *Chicago Sun-Times*, a Democratic newspaper, liked that suggestion; so did the *Atlanta Constitution*, in a page-one editorial, which pointed out that the Fulbright proposal offered a chance to avoid the inaction of a hopelessly divided government. The popular choice for secretary of state was the Michigan Republican Senator Arthur Vandenberg, now the chairman of the Foreign Relations Committee, who, since the end of the war, had shown a capacity for creative bipartisanship. Those in favor of a Vandenberg succession were willing to overlook that this next president would take office without the bother of primaries, conventions, or an actual election.

More Truman disparagement came from President Roosevelt's son Elliott, who, with his third wife (of five), the actress and television personality Faye Emerson, had just returned from Russia and Po-land. They'd seen Stalin, in the Kremlin, on his sixty-eighth birth-day, and interviewed him for *Look* magazine, a conversation during which, Elliott wrote, the generalissimo appeared thinner than when he'd last seen him, at the Tehran conference, but "the eyes were the same. . . . They have the same snap and sparkle of tolerant good humor." Elliott asked Stalin whether he viewed the American mid-term results as "a swing away . . . from belief in the policies of Roo-sevelt," and Stalin replied, carefully, that the election suggested the Truman government was "wasting the moral and political capital created by the late President." Truman was disturbed enough by this criticism to call President Roosevelt's onetime confidant Frank Walker, to ask if Elliott's comments reflected his mother's views. "Would you mind having a talk with her?" he asked. Walker did so, but didn't tell Truman everything that Eleanor Roosevelt had told him: "In general I think President Truman is doing . . . as well as could be expected," she'd said. "Of course, I don't know whether he was well enough equipped to take over a job like this, but if Franklin had to handle the present situation I'm not sure he could do so." She also told Walker, "I don't think he can be elected in 1948."

Truman was in Independence when the midterm results came in, and, accompanied by Bess and Margaret, returned by rail to Wash-ington. On his arrival at Union Station, only one high-ranking offi-cial was there to welcome him: Acheson, the under secretary of state. "It had for years been a Cabinet custom," Acheson later wrote, "to meet President Roosevelt's private car on his return from happier elections and escort him to the White House." He'd never imagined that "the President would be left to creep unnoticed back to the capi-tal. So I met his train." He recalled that "to my great surprise, I found that I was the sole person on the platform. Not even a reporter was there. . . . I was the reception committee." Whatever Acheson had expected, he was undoubtedly aware that even a weakened president is still the most important person in town, and was wise enough to know that the future lasts a long time, and that Truman would re-member who stood by him when it mattered most.

NINE

The Doctrine's Dilemma

"You ask me whether there is any 'precedent' for the action we are taking. . . . I am afraid we cannot rely upon 'precedents' in facing the utterly unprecedented condition in the world today."

—Senator Arthur Vandenberg, to a constituent, on May 12, 1947

1. Well before 6 a.m. on January 6, 1947, Truman was up and about, as was his habit, and in a cheerful mood because, after breakfast and the newspapers, he'd be meeting Bess and Margaret at Union Station—two miles away, or thirty-five minutes on foot. "It was a good walk," he told his diary. "Sure is fine to have them back." They'd been together for Christmas, in Independence, but only briefly—as briefly as the year before, though this time without the discord. He'd flown out on Christmas Day, and returned to Washington, alone, on December 26, having to face the new year with a Republican Congress. That was not a happy prospect. When he chatted with aides, he could sound discouraged enough to say that he just wanted to get the country "on an even keel," after which "anybody could run the show."

He didn't mean it, but there was lot he would have liked to hand over to someone else. "This great white jail is a hell of a place in which to be alone," he told his diary. "While I work from early morning until late at night, it is a ghostly place. The floors pop and crack all night long." Yet he could appreciate his rare vantage point—his participation in the continuum of history. He was prone to read the American past in his own way, and with abundant sympathy for his predecessors, even those with sinking reputations: "Anyone with imagination can see old Jim Buchanan walking up and down worrying about conditions not of his making. Then there's Van Buren who inherited a terrible mess from his predecessor as did poor old James Madison. Of course Andrew Johnson was the worst mistreated of any of them." He added that "the tortured souls who were and are misrepresented in history are the ones who come back."

If those tortured souls were imaginary, the "cracks and pops" were not. After a recent state dinner, with entertainment provided by Eugene List, the pianist who'd played in Potsdam ("He played the great A-flat waltz, Opus 42," Truman wrote home), building engineers told Truman that a chain holding the center chandelier was stretching, a hint of other, more serious structural problems.

At least his intermittently uncomfortable relationship with Jimmy Byrnes was coming to an end. In the spring of 1946, Byrnes had written Truman to say that he hoped to leave—that he was worn out and that, since becoming secretary of state, he'd "found it necessary to work long hours, six and at times seven days a week" and, moreover, that his doctor had "advised that I must 'slow down.'" In that letter, dated April 16, he'd said that he wanted to be out by July 1. But Byrnes changed his mind. He wanted to deal with various questions at the next foreign ministers conference, in Paris, and then he stayed on through the summer and in the weeks after Henry Wallace was fired. He waited until the end of the year to write another resignation letter, and Truman this time promptly accepted.

Few were going to miss him, particularly as an administrator. To Dean Acheson, who'd been under secretary for nearly eighteen months, it was as if Byrnes's State Department "consisted of about six people and he would work with them all the time, and what the rest of the Department did was no concern of his and he did not want to be bothered about it." Acheson later said, "He had a great tendency to read a telegram and very often he would pick up his pencil and start drafting the answer, and you would say, 'There are fifty people who ought to work on this before it comes to you. Now, don't do that.' But he would say, 'I'm doing it in shorthand and it does not take much time.' He would get absorbed by the conference of foreign ministers or the treaties with satellites or whatever it would be—everything else would go."

The timing of Byrnes's departure was hastened by a newspaper story; James Reston had learned about the first letter and was writing about the second one. Knowing that, Byrnes hurried to the White House—"all out of breath," Truman noted, and angry too—"morally certain that the information had leaked at the White House." That, Truman wrote in his diary, wasn't so. The news of Byrnes's resignation—the *New York Times* story was published on January 8, 1947—came just as *Time* magazine, with exceptionally bad timing, chose Byrnes as its Man of the Year, in a cover story that credited "this small-town lawyer and congressional cloakroom compromiser" for having made clear "that the U.S. had planted the weight of its power in the path of the Russian advance." It also portrayed Byrnes as a man who "lacks the born statesman's personal dignity."

Although he was supposedly quitting "on the advice of his physicians," those who knew Byrnes knew that he was a still-robust sixty-four. Proof of that would come a few years later, with yet another political career—as governor of South Carolina—and a public life that would extend almost to his ninetieth birthday. If Truman, in his diary, sounded sorry, it was a perfunctory sorrow: "I am very sorry Mr. Byrnes decided to quit. I'm sure he'll regret it—and I know I do. He is a good negotiator—a very good one," he wrote, adding, "But of course I don't want to be the cause of his death and his Dr. told him in March 1946 that he must slow down. So much for that." To Byrnes, Truman wrote, with not a syllable of sincerity, that he'd accepted his resignation "with great reluctance and heartfelt regret."

The truth was that Truman was not only glad to replace Byrnes, but had long since—longer than Byrnes knew—recruited his successor, whose appointment was announced along with Byrnes's departure. Eight months earlier, in May 1946, Truman had offered the post to General George C. Marshall, who, he told his diary, was "the ablest man in the whole gallery." Truman's admiration for the army chief of staff seemed to have no bounds. "The more I see and talk to him the more certain I am he's the great one of the age," he added a few months later. In his memoirs, he described Marshall as "one of the most astute and profound men I have ever known," and added "He talked very little but listened carefully to everything that was said. Sometimes he would sit for an hour with little or no expression on his face"—others detected a "one-sided half-smile"—"but when he had heard enough, he would come up with a statement of his own that invariably cut to the very bone of the matter under discussion."

Acheson too seemed to regard Marshall with something like awe: "The moment General Marshall entered a room, everyone in it felt his presence," he later wrote. "It was a striking and communicated force." An even giddier impression was made on Susan Mary Alsop, who'd met Marshall in Paris, at a dinner, and wrote to a friend, "He is most un-disappointing. Cool, shrewd, appraising eyes, speaking little, his tremendous impressiveness makes everyone else seem small around him."

Truman's inexhaustible reservoir of faith in Marshall was what had led him, in November 1945, to ask him to step in after Ambassador Patrick Hurley suddenly resigned. Marshall would go on to spend thirteen months in China, pursuing an arduous, and ambitious, mission for which he was not prepared and was, almost certainly, destined to fail: to persuade Chiang and the Communist leader Mao Zedong, whose forces had been at war for more than two decades, to form a coalition government. It didn't seem an impossible task; Chiang and Mao were in agreement on the importance of modernizing China, and had been allies in the war against Japan. Marshall, who'd served a tour of duty there in 1927, seemed to come tantalizingly close, getting both sides to agree, in principle, to a cease-fire. An impressed American correspondent wrote that Marshall "revealed such a lively, pellucid memory" that, even though he said nothing on the record, "I would still be hopeful about the results of his mission here." But little inside China was the way it appeared to Western eyes, and given the distrust, and deep political differences, between the two factions, Marshall's goal was unreachable. Of his efforts, James Reston wrote, gently, "It cannot be said that his mission to China was a spectacular success."

To tender this fresh job offer to Marshall, Truman employed a singular emissary: General Eisenhower, whom he'd informed, as Eisenhower, knowingly, recalled, that Byrnes "was going to be quite ill, or something like that." When Eisenhower saw Marshall and asked if he'd take the job at State, Marshall replied, "Great goodness Eisenhower, I'd take any job in the world just to get out of this one!" That makes for an amusing story, but it was probably no less true for that. After six years as army chief of staff, and more than a year pursuing an increasingly futile goal in China, he was more than ready to come home.

Marshall's jolly willingness to serve was another reason for Truman's better mood on January 6, 1947, when he met Bess and Margaret at Union Station. "This gives me a wonderful ace in the hole because I have been terribly worried," he'd told Eisenhower when the general reported back. To his mother and sister, he wrote, "I am hoping that Gen. Marshall will take the striped pants boys for a ride. There are more tea hounds and S.O.B.s in that place than in all the rest put together with the possible exception of the place Henry Wallace filled up with them." Averell Harriman, he added, "is straightening that one out." After nearly two years as President, the mindset of Jackson County still affected Truman's outlook and fed his suppressed suspicions. He still seemed unable to shake the idea of a State Department populated by "striped-pants boys" and "tea hounds" and run-of-the-mill sons of bitches. Byrnes felt some of that too; as he left the department, he remarked, "Any man who would want to be Secretary of State would go to hell for pleasure."

2. During Dean Acheson's year and a half as under secretary, his job had become much larger than his title. Scotty Reston, for whom Acheson was a valuable source (the two were regular lunch companions), portrayed him in a magazine story as the "No. 1 No. 2 Man in Washington." During the 562 days that Byrnes served in the cabinet, he was away for 350, enough for someone to quip that

"Washington fiddles while Byrnes roams." When Byrnes was out of town, Acheson, as acting secretary, spent a lot of time with Truman, with whom he slowly, and surely, established himself as someone deeply informed and unflaggingly steadfast.

David Lilienthal, who sometimes saw Dean and Alice Acheson socially, was struck by the under secretary's improved mood after Byrnes quit. "Dean spent a good deal of the time bubbling over with his enthusiasm, rapture almost, about General Marshall," he noted, after a dinner party at the Achesons'. "He has admired him for a long time. But to work with him is such a joy that he can hardly talk about anything else." Byrnes's management style, he added, "had about driven Dean crazy." Acheson had been particularly frustrated by, as he put it, having "no real place in the line of authority." With General Marshall in charge, all that changed. "When he spoke to me, he told me that he expected me to run the Department of State, that was *my* responsibility," Acheson recalled. "He was quite clear that he did not want to be engaged in what he called interminable discussion about things."

There were, naturally, questions as to whether Marshall was suited for a diplomatic job, along with a worry that giving him the post might alter the idea that the military was "the servant and not the master of our foreign policy." That didn't turn out to be much of a worry, although Marshall brought to the State Department the sort of organization that he'd employed when he was army chief of staff. He saw the post of under secretary as equivalent to a deputy chief of staff. "Avoid trivia," Marshall said during an early staff meeting. One of his first decisions was to ask George Kennan, who'd recently been called back from Moscow, to set up and run the new Policy Planning Staff, a small group to review and set longer-range strategy—as Acheson put it "to look ahead, not into the distant future, but beyond the vision of the operating officers caught in the smoke and crises of current battle." Kennan enthusiasts by then included navy secretary Forrestal, who'd circulated the so-called "Long Telegram," and Walter Bedell Smith, who'd been an aide to Marshall during the war and told his former boss that Kennan "knows more about the Soviet Union, I believe, than any other American." The Policy Planning Staff's mission would be defined as it evolved. As the historian

John Lewis Gaddis pointed out, in his authoritative book on Kennan, "There was no competition: grand strategy was a new concept in Washington." Kennan got an office next to Marshall's, a guarantee of unhampered access.

There was, though, competition of a sort—across the street, from the White House, where a freshly baked study of Soviet aims had been prepared at Truman's request. Truman hadn't been wholly satisfied by Kennan's "long telegram" and, according to his daughter, wanted "even more comprehensive reports, written from the White House point of view." To get this something more, he'd asked Clark Clifford, the new special counsel, to prepare a fresh look at the Soviet threat.

Such an assignment would have been a daunting task for any serious student of Soviet Russia. It was a curious assignment for a personable Missouri lawyer who knew very little about the subject, but had won Truman's favor and wanted to keep it. Clifford might have tried to carry out this assignment by himself were it not for the propinquity of the bright, willing aide George M. Elsey, another former naval officer who, at twenty-eight, had gone from the Map Room to become Clifford's assistant—and, unlike Clifford, could include attendance at the Potsdam conference on his résumé. Together, in the summer of 1946, Clifford and Elsey worked on giving Truman what he'd asked for, whatever that might be.

Elsey approached this commission with enthusiasm and persistence, starting with form letters, signed by Clifford, which he'd sent to a number of administration officials. By July 1946, Elsey had begun to synthesize the replies—a mix of fact and opinion regarding Soviet Russia, compiled from sources in the State Department, the Pentagon, the intelligence community, even the White House. Neither Elsey nor Clifford seemed troubled by the risk of circularity—seeking official views from officials to augment other official views. By the late summer of 1946, Elsey had completed his work. At about 5 p.m. on September 24, under Clifford's signature, their report, a hundred pages long and titled "American Relations with the Soviet Union," went to the President's desk.

The tone of the Clifford-Elsey analysis was stern, and dark—far surpassing Kennan in its darkness. After calling relations with the Soviet Union the "gravest problem facing the United States today," it went on to say that "the solution of that problem may determine whether or not there will be a third World War" and that the Soviets were "on a course of aggrandizement designed to lead to eventual world domination by the U.S.S.R." It set down a list of broken agreements and hostile ambitions, along with the assertion that "the language of military power is the only language the disciples of power politics understand," and, furthermore, that, for the Russians, "compromises and concessions are considered . . to be evidences of weakness." Yet it left room for a hope that Soviet leaders—even though they "profess to believe that the conflict between capitalism and communism is irreconcilable"—also realize that "we are too strong to be beaten and too determined to be frightened." Truman read it that night, and according to Margaret Truman and Clark Clifford, regarded it with mild horror—as if those pages, if exposed to sunlight, could explode. Early the next morning, he called Clifford at home and asked, "How many copies of this report do you have?"

"Ten," Clifford replied. (Clifford, in *his* memoir, said that he had twenty copies.)

"I want the other nine," Truman demanded. "Get them right in here."

Clifford and his cargo reached the President's desk in less than an hour, at which point Truman told him, "This has got to be put under lock and key," and that, if the report leaked, "it would blow the roof off the White House, it would blow the roof off the Kremlin. We'd have the most serious situation on our hands that has yet occurred in my Administration." That's when "the President took the reports from me," Clifford recalled, "and neither I nor Elsey nor anyone else, ever saw them again." The next morning, Clifford called Elsey to say, "The Boss doesn't want it known that there is such a report. . . . Absolute secrecy is necessary." Elsey, though, had already given a copy to Admiral Leahy, whose first response was that "it ought to come right out and say the Russians are sons of bitches!"

With the distance of years, the report, which lacked the sophistication, and depth, of Kennan's analysis, reads like many slapdash, alarmist newspaper columns of the time. As if to demonstrate toughness, its author ("Clifford," but actually Elsey) sounded at times ready for war, even nuclear war, and discussed that prospect with bland assurance: "Whether it would actually be in this country's interest to employ atomic and biological weapons against the Soviet Union in the event of hostilities is a question that would require careful consideration in the light of the circumstances prevailing at the time," it said. That such boilerplate could have been written by a trusted adviser, and that the President could have taken it seriously enough to squirrel it away, was a reminder that the Truman administration, or at least the President and the men in his circle, were still a wobbly group, finding their way, determined to make sense of a world that few seemed to know very well.

3. Although "domino theory" would wait until the Eisenhower era to make its way into the political phrasebook, it was already commonplace to view the nations of the postwar world as potential chess pieces, or dominos. That outlook was encouraged by people like Walter Lippmann, who warned that Russia wanted to "take the Balkans, Turkey, Iran, Iraq—the whole region—out of the British sphere of influence and to absorb it into the Soviet sphere." By the beginning of 1947, Britain's "sphere of influence" was near the vanishing point. In February, Lord Halifax, the British ambassador, informed Secretary of State Marshall that his country intended to end its military support for Greece and Turkey, a decision that Marshall saw as "tantamount to British abdication from the Middle East." With no other country able to act as an economic guarantor, a consensus quickly built that Britain, as the State Department speechwriter Joseph M. Jones was to write, had "handed the job of world leadership, with all its burdens and all its glory, to the United States." Truman had only to look at the floor-mounted globe in his office—General Eisenhower, who'd used it during the war, had given it to him, in Frankfurt—to see where Russia might push fresh territorial claims.

Truman thought he understood the temptation of the Turkish Straits, which linked Asia to Europe. The subject, after all, had been discussed, at length and not always amicably, in Potsdam. A few months earlier, the Soviet Union had asked for new terms—increased control of the Straits—at the expense of Turkey. Truman and his counselors believed that would further weaken Greece, already enfeebled by a civil war between government forces and Communist rebels. Joseph Jones recalled a meeting at which Truman pulled out a map and said it was time to take a firm position—"that we might as well find out now as in five or ten years whether the Russians were bent on world conquest." No one was rude enough to point out that, when something happens on a map, anything is possible.

On February 27, 1947, six days after Marshall was informed that Greece and Turkey could no longer count on England's financial support, Marshall and Acheson walked across 17th Street to the White House, to meet with Truman and congressional leaders, and to make a case for sending American aid—as much as four hundred million dollars. When Truman, in Acheson's recollection, "flubbed his opening statement," the under secretary asked to jump in, after which he poured it on: Soviet pressure, Acheson said, was being felt in the Urals, Iran, and northern Greece, which could mean opening "three continents to Soviet penetration." He compared these potential targets to "apples in a barrel infected by one rotten one," and said that "the corruption of Greece would infect Iran, would also carry infection to Africa through Asia Minor and Egypt, and to Europe through Italy and France, already threatened by the strongest domestic Communist parties in Western Europe." Running short on disease metaphors, Acheson said they faced "a situation which has not been paralleled since ancient history. . . . Not since Athens and Sparta, not since Rome and Carthage have we had such a polarization of power."

In Acheson's recollection, a long silence followed this extravagant historical parallel. Then Senator Vandenberg, the chairman of the Foreign Relations Committee, turned to Truman and said, "Mr. President, if you will say that to the Congress and the country, I will support you and I believe that most of its members will do the same." There was a story, often repeated, that, as he was leaving, Vandenberg added, "Mr. President, the only way you are ever going to get this is to make a speech and scare hell out of the country." Admiral Leahy was not enthusiastic. He not only anticipated a "violent reaction . . . against entangling political involvement in Europe in violation of a traditional American policy," but had a very different idea of what was of most importance to the United States: he wanted Marshall to pay more attention to China, where Leahy had spent time as a young man and where the fighting between the forces of Chiang and Mao was to continue for another two years. He felt strongly—and, as it turned out, correctly—that "a stable, non-Soviet government" in China was of far more value. When Truman found time to write home, he said that "foreign affairs are in the usual turmoil," and that he was "spending every day with Marshall . . . and hoping we can get a lasting peace." He added, "It looks not so good though right now."

Truman almost never seemed to doubt, or question, what was being urged by Acheson and Marshall. Theirs was an outlook that suited him, and encouraged what was becoming his idealized view of America's role in a changed world. His memoirs contain a number of passages in which he recalled acting with resolve, prepared to show the willingness of a muscular nation to defend a weak one. All this was prelude to what became known as the Truman Doctrine, a template for action—the idea, as Truman soon put it, that "wherever aggression direct or indirect, threatened the peace, the security of the United States was involved." Acheson (quoting Joseph Jones) later wrote that everyone in Truman's circle was "aware that a major turning point in American history was taking place. The convergence of massive historical trends upon that moment was so real as to be almost tangible." The burdens of world leadership came with that convergence, but Truman and his advisers had the luxury of inflating the Soviet menace while projecting unflinching firmness. The United States, after all, was still the only nation to possess an unmatchable weapon.

Truman believed that he needed to appeal, in person, to Congress. Elsey worried that it wasn't the right time to give an "all out" speech—that the public wasn't prepared for such a change in policy, that it was being done too hastily, and that the Russians hadn't provided an "adequate pretext." A better subject, Elsey thought, might be what he called "U.S. Responsibility for European Reconstruction." Clifford, who'd been asked to pitch in on a speech that would be written by Jones, disagreed. Elsey's "methodical mind," he thought, made him too cautious, and he decided to do what he could to make the speech as "strong as possible, both in style and content."

George Kennan, who'd taken up his duties with the Policy Planning Staff just a few weeks earlier, was worried by what he saw unfolding. He'd read an early draft of Truman's speech and, Jones recalled, "to say that he found objections to it is to put it mildly." Kennan thought this new path was being proclaimed "in terms more grandiose and more sweeping" than anything he'd envisaged. He didn't think that the Russians, even if their goal *was* world conquest, were up to the task—that economic difficulties and other problems would inevitably defeat such ambition. Nor was Kennan aware of serious Communist penetration in Turkey—"no comparable guerrilla movement"—though he agreed that aid to Greece would support stability there, and he said as much to Acheson. Clifford wanted to toughen the speech, which Acheson was not inclined to do, but even without that, the policy was set.

Like many bad writers, Clifford was impressed by his way with words. The senior aide John Steelman, who was unimpressed, said, "He was not as competent as he was able to get the press to say." Clifford, though, was particularly proud of his attempted contributions, and of language more Cliffordian than Churchillian, such as "The seeds of totalitarian regimes are nurtured by misery and want. They spread and grow in the evil soil of poverty and strife." But that's how speeches get written, and Truman's went through many drafts, with many suggestions from several consultants. As for delivering a speech, a Senate colleague once teased Truman about his lack of talent: "I need not tell you," he said, as he introduced him, "that Harry Truman is not an orator. He can demonstrate that for himself." Truman, though, had improved his radio personality with help from a coach, the Cox radio executive Leonard Reinsch, who got him to slow down, to work on dramatic pauses, and to raise his voice level. "Boy, does he work at it!" Reinsch said. Acheson knew that Truman had "difficulty in reading aloud long words, long sentences, and long paragraphs," and George Elsey asked the Signal Corps to prepare large cue cards so that Truman could look up from his script.

In its final form, the speech that Truman delivered, on March 12, to a joint session of Congress and a radio audience, was mostly shorn of Cliffordisms. It had been almost two years since Roosevelt's death, but Americans were still unaccustomed to a voice variously described as "flat," or "Midwestern," or "nasal," or "clipped." Vocal training helped with the delivery, which took nineteen minutes, but not the speech itself. At the start, it sounded almost like a plea to help the Grecian needy—simply because they were needy: "Lack of sufficient natural resources has always forced the Greek people to work hard to make both ends meet," Truman said. It became tied up in qualifiers—a "would" here, an "if" there, and a "might well" when needed: "If Greece should fall under the control of an armed minority, the effect upon its neighbor, Turkey, would be immediate and serious. Confusion and disorder might well spread throughout the entire Middle East." With the plea that Greece needed the infusion of a benefactor's money, Truman said, in what became the most quoted passage, "it must be the policy of the United States to support free peoples who are resisting attempted subjugation by armed minorities or outside pressures. I believe that we must assist free peoples to work out their own destinies in their own way." That got a standing ovation. Truman later recalled making last-minute changes, replacing the word "should" with "must" in those two sentences, because "I wanted no hedging in this speech. . . . It had to be clear and free of hesitation or double talk." He was describing the actions of the resolute leader that he wanted to be.

There was not yet talk about a "Cold War," an expression first used by Bernard Baruch, soon after Truman's speech—a linguistic gift from Herbert Bayard Swope. Baruch was willing to give Swope public credit for that one, but was less willing to cede ownership to another cherished phrase—"Every man has a right to his own opinion, but no man has a right to be wrong in his facts"—a variation of which has been attributed to Daniel Patrick Moynihan.

4. When congressional hearings began, a week later, Acheson told the House Foreign Affairs Committee that Greece was near collapse and needed American assistance to prevent a "chain

reaction" of totalitarianism from sweeping through the region. The aid program, he said, would help avert a future war. When Acheson said that the United States did not intend to send troops, and that there was no intention to assist just *any* nation that asked for help, the Ohio senator Robert Taft wasn't persuaded. He called Truman's speech "a complete departure from previous American policy," and saw the loans to Greece and Turkey as signaling acceptance of the principle "of dividing the world into zones of political influence, Communist and non-Communist." This was a Taft theme; he'd been widely ignored, months before, when he warned that the United States had "accepted the philosophy of force as the controlling factor in international relations."

This new direction also troubled those who wondered why the United States should pick up after the British. World leadership had a nice ring, but apart from the glory of it all, there were practical drawbacks. It would have sounded heartless to say such a thing, but shoring up a fragile nation could be much like adopting a family that no one truly cared about. Joseph Jones described Truman as someone who "recognized that a full turn in history was necessary and called the turn." It was certainly a turn in Truman's reputation. The idea that "he's not big enough for the job" was being supplanted by a view that he seemed "destined to have a very definite niche in history," as the *Washington Post*'s Edward Folliard wrote, adding that "in generations to come, American schoolchildren will be required to bone up on the Truman Doctrine, the epochal policy he laid before Congress." Epochal or not, the *Wall Street Journal*'s Vermont Royster, in a column published the next day, wrote that the President had "asked the United States to embark on a long road from which there is no turning," and that he had taken the words of the Monroe Doctrine, from 1823, and "applied them to the world"—a policy bound to have consequences that Royster did not need to spell out.

That's what worried George Kennan: that the American aid plan had been "put in the framework of a universal policy rather than in that of a specific decision addressed to a specific set of circumstances." It implied that what had been decided for Greece was something that the United States would be prepared to do for any other country, provided only that this other country faced the threat of, in the words of Truman's speech, "subjugation by armed minorities or by outside pressures." But, Kennan continued, "it seemed to me highly uncertain that we would invariably find it in our interests or within our means to extend assistance to countries that found themselves in this extremity." Years later, in the early stages of the Vietnam War, Kennan returned to this subject, writing that he'd always been struck by what he called the "persistent urge to seek universal formulae or doctrines in which to clothe and justify particular actions."

As soon as he finished his speech, the President, along with Leahy, Clifford, Vaughan, Ross, and Steelman, hurried to National Airport, for a flight to Key West, the westernmost of the populated islands in the Florida Keys. It was Truman's second time there; his first, on the recommendation of his doctor, followed the distressing 1946 midterms. From then on, Key West became Truman's place to rest and escape, in the company of the men who often surrounded him. Truman stayed in the recently vacated quarters of the commandant of the Naval Operating Base, a rambling, ten-room structure, near the water, that became known as the Little White House. From a sunny deck chair, he'd sometimes hold forth, as one staff member put it, on "sea shell collections, stories of Missouri, or stagecoach days, almost anything and everything." He'd go for short swims, lasting about ten minutes, "swimming neither far nor fast, but pleasant splashing." He'd be encircled by three or four Secret Service agents who would watch for sharks or barracuda, although they usually don't enter shallow water. On March 13, right after settling in, he wrote to his daughter, now twenty-three, telling her how tired he'd been— "worn to a frazzle"—and that the "terrible decision I had to make had been over my head for about six weeks." He went on to write "there is no difference in totalitarian or police states, call them what you will, Nazi, Fascist, Communist or Argentine Republics," and didn't hide his heightened scorn for left-leaning advisers he'd once listened to—"The American Crackpots' Association, represented by

Joe Davies, Henry Wallace, Claude Pepper and the actors and artists in immoral Greenwich Village." Having got that off his chest, he finished up saying, "Your Pop had to tell the world just that in polite language."

Truman was still in Key West on March 16, when his daughter made her radio debut, with the Detroit Symphony. After college, Margaret's focus had been on serious voice training; most recently, she'd been studying with a Mrs. Thomas J. Strickler, the wife of one of her father's World War I friends. The Detroit concert was sung before an audience made up mostly of reporters and a few critics, as well as Mrs. Strickler. Getting through it might have been as difficult for the President as it was for his daughter. Margaret, who was getting over a bout of laryngitis, recalled being "numb with nervousness and a huge dose of penicillin." The *New York World-Telegram*'s Harriet Van Horne had observed her beforehand, as she sat alone, on the stage of the Music Hall, "a tense figure huddled in a gray squirrel coat, with her blue chiffon skirts gathered about her." She thought that the President's daughter seemed nervous as she sponged her palms, smoothed her skirts, and, at one point, "looked at the ceiling in a prayerful attitude."

The program was aired by the American Broadcasting Company, and reached an estimated fifteen million people, among them Truman, who was in the living room of the Key West house when he heard his daughter sing "The Last Rose of Summer," a Mexican folk song, and Félicien David's "*Charmant Oiseau.*" Afterward, he telephoned Margaret, in Detroit, and then his mother, in Grandview, who was bedridden with a fractured hip; then he talked to Bess, who was at the White House, with *her* mother, Madge Gates Wallace. "It was a great relief to have it over," Truman said, in a letter home. Between his daughter's trial and his recent address to the nation, he'd been very much on edge. Someone in the living room of the Little White House started talking just before the broadcast from Detroit began and, Truman, with furious impatience, thought, "I wanted to shoot him."

TEN

Wealth of a Nation

> *The President:* I have no objection to any method that will
> save the grain to get to these hungry people. I am trying to
> keep people from starving to death this winter, that's all.
>
> *Q:* Mr. President, if you ate more poultry, wouldn't you have
> fewer chickens to eat the grain?
>
> *The President:* Now that's like which came first, the chicken
> or the egg. Can't answer a question like that. Can't answer
> that question.
>
> **—President Truman, on a program to help needy nations**

1. In the middle of May 1947, the President, "with great regret," accepted Dean Acheson's resignation. It wasn't a fraught resignation, as Jimmy Byrnes's had been the year before. Rather, as Truman and Secretary of State Marshall knew, it had been planned since February. Acheson had never been happier, but he'd decided to return to his old law firm, Covington & Burling, because he needed to earn more money: During six years in the State Department, as assistant secretary and under secretary, his annual salary had never risen above twelve thousand dollars. He'd be leaving the department, James Reston wrote, while his authority and prestige were high, and his stature on Capitol Hill had "grown immeasurably." With those kind words, there were more kind words left over for General Marshall, Byrnes's successor, who'd "shown a remarkable grasp of complex issues," a phrase redolent with the expectation that Reston would continue to cultivate his best sources as he became, in *Newsweek*'s phrase, "the perfect information broker for the Cold War."

Acheson would stay until June 30, and, because the Republicans were favored to win the White House in 1948, it seemed to him unlikely that he'd return to government service anytime soon. Marshall, by early February, had already recruited Acheson's replacement: fifty-one-year-old Robert Abercrombie Lovett, a partner at Brown Brothers-Harriman and a former assistant secretary of war for air. Lovett had been eating breakfast at home, in Locust Valley, on the North Shore of Long Island, when Truman telephoned and told him that Marshall had accepted the job "on the condition . . . that you'd come down and be his Under-Secretary." Marshall had admired Lovett's strengthening of the army air forces during the war. Of Marshall, Lovett later said "I was absolutely devoted to him."

Lovett, slim and bald, described as having "a brooding priest-like face" that was "faintly hollowed by nervous energy," also possessed a sense of humor, or an appreciation of irony, and had the endearing habit of asking his secretary to ration his cigarettes—one every two hours—the better to rein in his heavy smoking. He arrived during an enormous change of emphasis in America's foreign policy. This shift had been announced, like a smoke signal in newsprint, by Walter Lippmann, in an April 1947 column that bore the title "Cassandra Speaking." Cassandra was, of course, Lippmann, in his best "the-crisis-is-developing" voice; he was, he wrote, "saying only what informed and responsible men say when they do not have to keep up appearances in public": that "none of the leading nations of Europe . . . has any reasonable prospect of recovery with the means at its disposal" and that a "European economic collapse is the threat that hangs over us and all the world." What was needed, then, was something much bigger than anything that had gone before. Senator Alben Barkley, of Kentucky, the minority leader, picked up the theme in a speech to the Society for the Advancement of Management, where he said that the United States might need to provide "millions, even billions" to rebuild Europe. That was provocative enough for Senator Vandenberg to telephone Acheson and Marshall, neither of whom wanted to injure their useful alliance with the chairman of the Foreign Relations Committee. Acheson, it was said, was "very much aware of the fact that Congress was not in the mood to support another dose of what . . . the economizers in Congress would call 'Operation Rathole.'"

Acheson expanded on this theme in May, when he spoke to the Delta Council, an economic development group, in Cleveland, Mississippi. The speech, most of it written by Joseph Jones, referred, in nonspecific terms, to an aid program more ambitious than the one for Greece and Turkey. He said that "the devastation of war has brought us back to elementals"—the need for food and fuel—and that when people and nations "exist in narrow economic margins," a principal American aim was to "widen these margins." Jones had sent a draft to Lippmann, an acknowledgment of the columnist's sovereign power over public opinion, and asked him to please note that there'd already been too much emphasis on the military aspects of the Truman Doctrine. "Mr. Acheson hopes to bring discussion back on a level where it belongs," Jones suggested, while adding that the Delta Council speech "outlines a positive economic program." Scotty Reston got the message right away, and told his readers that the words of the Truman Doctrine had been "set to a new tune." His analysis ran as a news story on an inside page and addressed the idea that the United States might even help rebuild the defeated Axis powers.

Europe's future was the topic during an Acheson lunch with three British journalists in early June. Soon after they'd left his office, the press officer at the British Embassy asked one of them, the BBC's Leonard Miall, if he'd seen a copy of a commencement speech that Acheson's boss, General Marshall, was about to deliver at Harvard. When Miall replied that he wasn't aware of it—it hadn't come up during lunch—the press officer said, "Well, if I were you, I would have a look at it. It is very interesting stuff." Miall hurried to get the advance text and recalled that "there were none of the trappings of it being an important speech. There were none of the double-spacing and things by which you recognize that this was a very important démarche." Miall by coincidence belonged to a car pool that included Charles P. Kindleberger, an MIT economist who'd been involved with Marshall's upcoming speech—and never mentioned it during their trans-Potomac commutes. Even in peacetime, Washington remained a city of meaningful gossip and calculated silence. Miall, however, soon knew enough to tell his BBC listeners about an initiative that he saw as representing uncommon generosity and farsightedness, although he overlooked its potential to sharpen differences between Russia and the West.

Marshall, at Harvard, was to receive an honorary degree along with a group that included T. S. Eliot, class of '10; J. Robert Oppenheimer, class of '26; and General of the Army Omar N. Bradley. The ceremonies were held on a breezy, sunny June 5, before an audience of about seven thousand, who applauded as the university's president, James B. Conant, led the honorees through the Yard, and nearby streets, to Memorial Hall. What struck those present was the low-keyness of Marshall's speech, how it almost got lost among the rituals and witty remarks. After some fumbled business with his reading glasses, Marshall, who wore a gray suit, said that he was "touched by the great distinction and honor" and then, glasses in place, went on to read his talk, in a hard-to-hear monotone. "I need not tell you that the world situation is very serious," he began, and went on to say, among other things, that "our policy is directed not against any country or doctrine but against hunger, poverty, desperation and chaos," and that its purpose ought to be the "emergence of political and social conditions in which free institutions can exist." Yet it was easy to miss the point. Congress had recently approved a $350 million contribution to war-damaged countries, and the United States would undoubtedly do more, but few realized, on that June 5, that what Marshall called "our policy" was something much bigger and bolder than anything that had gone before.

Some early newspaper accounts had difficulty deciding what Marshall was talking about, though the *Boston Globe*'s story said the speech "may be the touchstone of new State Department policy." The *Herald Tribune* saw it as a call for "augmented American aid to Europe" as well as a program "formulated and agreed upon by the European countries," and the *New York Times* gave considerably more attention to a Soviet-backed coup in Hungary. Marshall's speech was addressed under a small headline: "As 'Cure' For Ills/ Only Then Can Our/Aid Be Integrated,/Says The Secretary." The usually well-informed Reston seemed more interested in the "crisis" facing the future of bipartisan foreign policy. It took a little longer for the Alsop brothers to inform their audience that Marshall had introduced the "general shape of a great program," and for Lippmann, with ominous impatience, to write that, although time was running short, Americans could still be persuaded to make financial sacrifices "in their own interest and in that of civilization in general."

Someone following this closely might have noticed that the day after Marshall spoke, General Eisenhower, now the army chief of staff, gave a speech that sounded remarkably like Marshall's—almost a Midwestern echo. Eisenhower had accompanied Truman to Missouri for a reunion of the Middle West 35th Division, which had served in both world wars, and to mark the third anniversary of the Normandy landing. Truman was seated in a box toward the rear of the Municipal Auditorium (Admiral Leahy was at his side) when Eisenhower declared that "Human misery, begotten of hunger and want, multiplied by hopelessness, sharpened by fomenters of unrest, cannot long continue on so vast a scale without collapse of the civilized structure in civilized areas." He also said that "without the United States, civilization, as we know it, will perish." There's no record of Marshall and Eisenhower having worked out this sequence of speeches, but it's hard to believe that there was no coordination with the State Department. Little attention, in any case, was paid.

When Truman spoke the next day, he said the nation's task was to help "less fortunate peoples who are earnestly striving to improve or reconstruct the institutions of free and independent nations"—a reaffirmation of the Truman Doctrine. His emphasis, though, was on post–New Deal domestic goals: a national health program, an increase in the minimum wage and Social Security benefits, conserving "our precious resources," and providing low-cost energy. He also marched alongside comrades from Battery D of the 129th Field Artillery, and, at the corner of Twentieth Street and Grand Avenue, left his car to lead the marchers on a steep climb to the two-hundred-foot-tall Liberty Memorial, which honors the dead of World War I. It was a very warm day—"so hot that all my clothing was wet at the end of the review," Admiral Leahy recalled. Truman was smiling, looking exceedingly happy, and it's not taking historical liberties to suggest that he might have remembered his younger self, returning, uninjured, a quarter century before, renewing his pursuit of Bess Wallace, and starting another life, away from the Grandview farm.

2. Although the European recovery proposal became known as the "Marshall Plan," no single person deserves credit, and, in any case, as Marshall acknowledged, "the idea wasn't so much." The State Department's William Clayton, who'd headed the American delegation on the Committee for Economic Cooperation for Europe, thought it was like "one of those inventions that several people come up with at the same time," while noting that he'd been in a position "that would naturally make me the person to start the Marshall Plan." In May 1947, Clayton wrote a memorandum arguing that "without further prompt and substantial aid from the United States, economic, social and political disintegration will overwhelm Europe." George Kennan, running State's Policy Planning Staff, claimed to be "intimately connected" with the idea of massive aid to Europe, and gave some credit to Lippmann for "many of the thoughts which were later embodied" in Marshall's speech—ideas that Kennan and the columnist had discussed over lunch and that Lippmann ("Cassandra") had written about.

When Charles Bohlen accompanied Marshall to Moscow, for a foreign ministers' conference in the spring of 1947, Marshall had talked to him about "finding some initiative to prevent the complete breakdown of Western Europe," and soon afterward, Marshall concluded a radio speech by saying that the recovery of Europe had been slower than expected: "The patient is sinking while the doctors deliberate." He later described the Harvard speech, for which Bohlen wrote the chief draft, as a three-way collaboration—between Bohlen, Kennan, and himself: "I cut out part of Kennan's speech and part of Bohlen's speech and part of my speech and put the three together, and that was the beginning of the talk." Truman was to write that Acheson's speech to the Delta Council "might be called the prologue to the Marshall Plan," but, if that's so, should credit go to Marshall, who announced the policy, or to Acheson, who delivered that speech, or to Joseph Jones, who wrote and promoted it? Marshall for that matter didn't think Acheson, who was leaving the State Department on July 1, had all that much to do with it.

President Truman apparently hadn't read Marshall's entire speech, and reporters didn't ask about it for at least two weeks after it was delivered. Nor did the President show much early enthusiasm for the idea. That may have been premeditated reticence, along with Truman's excellent political antenna—his awareness, after the 1946 midterms, of how difficult it would be to ask a Republican Congress for an enormous aid program so soon after urging help for Greece and Turkey. Truman also understood how helpful it would be to have the plan introduced by Marshall. "If we try to make this a Truman accomplishment, it will sink," he told Clark Clifford. Something called the "Marshall Plan" would do "a whole hell of a lot better in Congress." Clifford recalled that Truman, referring to the Republican majority, told him, "Anything going up there bearing my name will quiver a couple of times, turn belly up, and die."

Acheson found it hard to believe that Truman and Marshall hadn't discussed the Harvard talk beforehand—that the Secretary of State "went off to deliver so momentous a speech with an incomplete text and never informed the Department of its final form." Yet that appears to be just what Marshall did. It wasn't until June 16, eleven days *after* the speech, that he brought up the subject with Truman, a conversation he recounted in a memorandum that he sent to Acheson and Lovett—his outgoing and incoming deputies. Truman, he told them, had "congratulated me on my Harvard speech and said he thought I had said just the right thing." He said that he, in turn, had "apologized for not consulting . . . [Truman] . . . and explained that I had not finished the draft until I went to the plane," to which Truman said "not to concern myself about that. I assured him it would not happen again." Truman asked Marshall about getting together, on the *Williamsburg*, with Treasury Secretary Snyder, Senator Vandenberg, and, possibly, Senator Tom Connally, the ranking member of the Foreign Relations Committee, to "spend an evening talking things over"—just the sort of thing, with its potential for dithering, that Marshall dreaded.

The former chairman of the Truman Committee worried about the cost—enough so that, on June 22, he appointed three separate committees—the most influential being the Committee on Foreign Aid, chaired by Averell Harriman—to study what the nation could afford. He acknowledged that the impact of foreign aid on the domestic economy was of "grave concern to every American," but insisted that recovery abroad was essential to "a peace founded on democracy and freedom." There were obvious advantages to opening markets in a region that, for all practical purposes, had disappeared after 1939.

The plan's political success was helped by Russia's predictable opposition, which grew steadily; and then, furiously. Although Marshall, at Harvard, had talked about Europe and "free institutions," he hadn't foreclosed the possibility that the Soviet Union and its East European satellites could receive American aid. But as Kennan and others foresaw, Russian leaders were bound to be suspicious: American dollars could affect not only the economies, but the governance, of Czechoslovakia, Bulgaria, Yugoslavia, and other vulnerable nations. Furthermore, the proposal was likely to revive Germany, an unappealing prospect for a nation that, during the war, had suffered the losses that Russia had. William L. Shirer, who had witnessed, and chronicled, the rise of Nazi Germany, was skeptical of the idea that "if we only make Germany productive and prosperous, she will automatically become democratic and peaceful." It was unjust, he wrote, to put Germany's industrial revival "ahead of reconstruction of Germany's victims."

Andrei Y. Vishinsky, the Russian deputy foreign minister—the most visible prosecutor during the Soviet purge trials—attacked "the so-called Truman Doctrine and Marshall Plan." During a September speech at the United Nations that lasted more than ninety theatrical minutes, Vishinsky blamed the United States for fomenting another world conflict—pitting the "war-mongering propagandists" against the "peace-loving nations." His clanking language reflected a world dividing into two camps. So did an essay titled "The Sources of Soviet Conduct," published in the July 1947 issue of the quarterly *Foreign Affairs*. The author was identified only as "X," but those in the know recognized the substance of George Kennan's 1946 "long telegram," which had argued for "containing" the Soviet Union. All these words, spoken and written, were like an overture to the arrival of the Cold War, the Herbert Bayard Swope (or George Orwell) coinage, which, after it was appropriated by Lippmann, in columns and a book, quickly made its way into postwar language.

By the time President Truman, five days before Christmas 1947, formally asked Congress to approve the European Recovery Act—the Marshall Plan—he was embracing it with affection and unswerving commitment and privately referred to it as "a historical State Document." Based on the recommendations of Harriman's committee, the Act called for a seventeen-billion-dollar recovery program, extending over four years, intended to restore the economies of sixteen countries and, at the same time, help protect them from the advance of Communism. To win passage, it needed the support of Senator Vandenberg, who spent many nights at Blair House, working side by side with Marshall. Marshall himself later said "I worked on that as hard as though I was running for the Senate or the presidency." Members of the House Select Committee on Foreign Aid toured Europe from August to October 1947, and the misery they encountered left its mark. The first-term California congressman Richard Nixon recorded his impressions in a diary: "Hamburg, Berlin and the other German cities looked up at us just like great gaunt skeletons," a typical entry said. "We could not understand how it was possible that three million people could be living . . . there like a bunch of starved rats in the ruins."

Truman inflated his role in the history of the Marshall Plan—writing, for instance, that he and Marshall had been of one mind since the morning of April 26, 1947, when Marshall, after fifty-three days of negotiations in Moscow, returned to Washington and "confirmed my conviction that there was no time to lose in finding a method for the revival of Europe." In fact, on that April 26, Truman had interrupted a Potomac cruise to greet the secretary of state's plane at National Airport; fifteen minutes later, he was on his way back to the *Williamsburg*. Though they saw each other during the next few days, Marshall was more focused on his Moscow talks, and even managed a trip to Pinehurst, North Carolina, to spend a night with his wife. During an evening session with Truman and several top legislators, and a cabinet lunch, on April 28, Marshall reported that the Moscow negotiations had been very difficult: Stalin had complained about a loan request being ignored, and Marshall had reproached the generalissimo for an "attitude of contemptuousness" toward a number of American proposals. To reporters, in an off-the-record session, he'd said that Stalin had "looked pretty bad, as if he had somehow shrunk into his clothes."

Truman, though, deserves to be celebrated for the plan, which, above all, was a reflection of his irresistible belief that American good-heartedness was a renewable resource. "Never before in history," he would write, "has one nation faced so vast an undertaking as that confronting the United States of repairing and salvaging the victors as well as the vanquished." And he added, because it was his story too, "Marshall and I were in perfect agreement."

4. The idea that "history was moving with 20th Century acceleration" was part of a *Time* magazine cover story on Arnold Toynbee, then a relatively unknown British historian. His ambitious *A Study of History*, published in six successive volumes, since 1934, had set out to analyze the rise and fall of twenty-six civilizations, most of which had gone extinct, or dormant. The magazine's cover showed a pensive Toynbee against a background of steep cliffs, with figures, who represented various doomed societies, tumbling down, presumably into oblivion. The article was written by Whittaker Chambers, a *Time* senior editor and repentant ex-Communist (he would soon become famous for other reasons), who called Toynbee's project "the most provocative work of historical theory written in England since Karl Marx's 'Capital.'" The story appeared in March 1947, soon after England decided to cut off aid to Greece and Turkey, and before the Truman Doctrine speech to Congress. Anyone familiar with Chambers will recognize his passionate, anti-Red voice in the declaration that Americans had "grasped the fact that this was no merely political or military crisis; it was a crisis in Western civilization itself."

The magazine received fourteen thousand requests for reprints, and an abridgement of the first six volumes of *A Study of History* sold more than a hundred thousand copies in one year. This overnight popularization did not encompass the newly famous Toynbee's dark side, which he was about to reveal in a short, disturbing book called *Civilization on Trial*: He would call the Truman Doctrine a "turning point" that might be seen as an "impulsion away from" attempts to achieve "political world unity." Toynbee went on to imagine that what came next could lead mankind to a "knock-out blow," by which he meant "one more world war, fought with atomic and other, perhaps not less deadly, new weapons." How mad! How gloomy and alarming!

Nothing could have been further from a foreign policy that was still driven by Woodrow Wilson's democratic idealism—a stubborn determination to remake the Old World, with a democratic design. Out of that impulse—generous, self-interested, and indifferent to the alarms it might set off beyond America's orbit—came the European Recovery Act, the most significant, and lasting, achievement of the Truman administration. It was a fascinating experiment, conducted in a postwar laboratory: For a brief time, until the threat it posed to Communism's fanciful ideas became real, the Marshall Plan offered an appealing answer to a novel historical question: How would a nation that possessed unlimited wealth and military strength choose to use that remarkable, and extraordinary, power?

ELEVEN

Strange Interludes

The night, though already arrived, was but beginning. The prowler and the gangs, the murderers and the thieves, who would soon emerge into the open, were still waiting for the deeper darkness. [He] came to a sign that flashed on and off, repeating tantalizingly:

ROOMS FOR THE UNPROTECTED

$20 A NIGHT

—A. E. van Vogt, *The World of Null-A* (1948)

"I'm just the girl who takes the nine o'clock conference, and I need my job, and if I do too much thinking and talking I'll lose it."

"What're you afraid of—thought control police?"

"Sure. We all are."

—Pat Frank, *An Affair of State* (1948)

1. In 1917, the year that thirty-three-year-old Harry Truman enlisted in the army, the twenty-two-year-old John Edgar Hoover changed jobs—transferring from the Library of Congress, where he'd worked with its card-indexing system, to the Justice Department, where he applied the methodology that he'd learned at the library. Hoover, who was bright and put in long hours, stood out among his coworkers. In 1924, he was asked to run the Bureau of Investigation, an agency empowered by the Commerce Clause of the Constitution to cross state lines, in pursuit of spies and "white slavers." When Truman began his first Senate term, in 1935, the BOI was renamed the Federal Bureau of Investigation, by which time Hoover and his "G-men," who combated anarchists, gangsters, Nazis, and Communists, were famous. The Bureau's promoters included several radio programs (*Gangbusters*, the best known, went on the air in 1936) and, most effectively, J. Edgar Hoover himself— dark-eyed, squat (five-foot-seven), unsmiling, yet strangely photogenic.

Truman and Hoover were wary of each other; one could sense the bad chemistry almost by looking at them. In 1942, they'd had a little run-in, a controversy furthered by the treacherous New York gossip columnist Walter Winchell, who'd written that restraints on the FBI had prevented the Bureau from uncovering Japan's plans to attack Pearl Harbor. Truman then chaired an interstate commerce subcommittee on wiretapping legislation, and thought that notion was silly. "On the contrary," Truman said, on the Senate floor, "a study of the record will show that wiretapping and interception of messages were fully practiced" before Pearl Harbor, " . . . as if there had been a law saying 'Go out and wiretap as much as you can.'" Alben Barkley, of Kentucky, then the Senate majority leader, and a Truman friend, said that he'd never heard "of anybody stupid enough to think that the debacle at Pearl Harbor was caused by the failure of Congress to pass wiretapping legislation." Barkley urged his colleagues to ignore "the little pin pricks" of "irresponsible" columnists, such as Winchell, whom the *Chicago Tribune* referred to as Hoover's "Stork Club playmate." The FBI director, who took notice if someone used the word "stupid" in connection with the Bureau, said that the FBI didn't have jurisdiction over the territory of Hawaii. But he was wrong, and soon admitted it.

After the war, Hoover turned his attention to domestic subversion, and whenever he spoke, he could be counted on to say something bleak, but newsworthy. He did so in late March 1947, in a rare public appearance, on Capitol Hill, telling the House Committee on Un-American Activities that the Communist Party was "better organized than were the Nazis in occupied countries," and that the Party's "most effective foes can be the real liberals and progressives who understand their devious machinations." He praised the House committee for revealing "the diabolic machinations of sinister figures engaged in un-American activities." Speaking later to the newsreel cameras, and sounding not unlike Dean Acheson vis-à-vis a Red infection of Greece and Turkey, Hoover said that Communist ideology is "akin to disease that spreads like an epidemic and like an epidemic a quarantine is necessary to keep it from infecting the nation." The idea of Reds lurking among us inspired reveries of carnage for Mickey Spillane, a former fighter pilot who'd been writing comic books for a living until he invented a private eye named Mike Hammer. "I pumped slugs in the nastiest bunch of bastards you ever saw and here I am calmer than I've ever been and happy too," Hammer says in *One Lonely Night*. "They were Commies."

There was an element of exaggeration in such reactions. The Party's political power was minuscule; its largest popular vote— 102,991—came at the height of the national economic panic, in 1932. But Hoover's remarks came just a week after the "Truman Doctrine" speech, and days after the President, on March 22, issued Executive Order 9835, which established the Federal Employee Loyalty Program. The program's goal was to screen current and prospective government workers because, Truman said, "the presence of disloyal men and women constitutes a threat to our democratic processes." A number of newspaper stories used the word "purge" to describe what many suspected was sure to come next.

The loyalty program, which adopted the recommendations of the five-month-old President's Temporary Commission on Employee Loyalty, was a strange interlude in postwar America, and an odious time in the Truman presidency. The federal workforce employed more than two million men and women, with a half-million more hired each year. Truman planned to ask Congress for twenty-five million dollars to cover the program's cost, saying that the nation needed "maximum protection . . . against the infiltration of disloyal persons into the ranks of its employees." But having committed the administration, Truman's private beliefs remain something of a mystery, though it's not difficult to understand why he issued Executive Order 9835. As one Loyalty Board veteran observed, it was "a reply to critics in and out of Congress who charged that he was 'soft' on Communists, that government service was honeycombed with subversives." Such beliefs had an odd staying power. General Patrick Hurley had made the accusation when he resigned as ambassador to China, in late 1945, and one didn't need a lot of evidence after February 1946, when more than twenty men suspected of spying for Russia were rounded up in Ottawa by Canadian Mounted Police.

Truman sometimes seemed uncomfortable with what he'd set in motion. Clark Clifford recalled that, soon after issuing the loyalty order, Truman came to his office—an unusual occurrence—and said, "Let's be sure that we hold the F.B.I. down. If we leave them to their own devices and give them what they want, they will become an American Gestapo." He complained to Bess that "Edgar Hoover would give his right eye to take over [the Secret Service] and all Congressmen and Senators are afraid of him. I'm not and he knows it. If I can prevent it there'll be no NKVD or Gestapo in this country. Edgar Hoover's organization would make a good start toward a citizen spy system. Not for me." Truman no doubt believed in those democratic virtues, but he tended to say that sort of thing only to those whom he wholly trusted.

Over the years, Truman said so little about the loyalty program that one might suspect he was ashamed of it. In his memoirs, he never quite said what he thought, or simply declared that Communism was a nasty business, which had introduced the world "to the outrage of brain-washing." He also wrote "it is essential for the investigative authorities to have sources of information which they cannot reveal," adding the disclaimer that "when it comes to an individual being charged with a crime, under our procedure he has a right to be confronted with his accusers."

Executive Order 9835 did not actually guarantee that right. Rather, the program metamorphosed into something that was intrusive, oppressive, and semipermanent, starting with new strata of federal bureaucracy: more than six thousand FBI agents, civil service investigators, their clerks, and support staff. By mid-August 1947, acting on instructions from the Civil Service Commission, all two million federal employees began to be fingerprinted, and were filling out forms that asked, among other things, for their connections to any organization. This material went to the FBI to be checked against Bureau files. The Supreme Court Justice Robert Jackson, who'd been Roosevelt's attorney general before his appointment to the court, was among those who didn't much like what was going on—and said so. "We must all agree," he said, "that FBI reports are not evidence but information"—much of it unverifiable. The FBI, and its director, had come to possess a considerable amount of unverifiable information, and, as Justice Jackson understood, information was power.

After the issuance of Executive Order 9835, many civil servants, not surprisingly, began their workdays with a feeling of uneasiness. The program, vague in places, left government workers vulnerable to seemingly irregular associations, unconventional friends, or the mischief of a vengeful colleague. Everyone seemed to know someone who was frightened, who worried that *something* from the past might come out. If "derogatory information" turned up, one could face the scrutiny of a "full field investigation," involving the Civil Service Commission, the FBI, the military, and any "appropriate government investigative or intelligence agency." Investigators were urged to focus on various categories of activities, beyond such obvious ones as sabotage and espionage. Some categories were described in language that hinted at a "disloyal state of mind," which altered substantially traditional concepts not only of free speech but of free thought. Alan Barth, for thirty years a *Washington Post* editorialist, wrote that it was "no overstatement to say that the loyalty program fundamentally alters the traditional American relationship of the individual to the State—a relationship that is the key characteristic of a free society. . . . The inevitable effect is a corruption of the traditional American right of privacy and the development of a dangerous police power." Barth was never an FBI target (he wrote respectfully of Hoover), but his daughter, Flora Barth Wolf, remembers the mood in the house whenever her mother talked to *her* mother: "She believed that the F.B.I. was listening on the phone. She indulged my grandmother and talked about what my brother and I had for breakfast. And she'd say goodbye to her and goodbye to 'you too' who was on the line."

The large net cast by the order included membership, or "sympathetic association," with any group designated as subversive by the Attorney General's List of Subversive Organizations, a creation of Tom Clark's Justice Department. The List grew to some three hundred, and included the American Civil Liberties Union along with such diverse, and curious, entries as the League of Women Shoppers. The FBI had the extra task of coming up with its own Security Index—people to be tracked down in case of a national emergency. The result was not quite panic, but rather a glum uncertainty that helped establish the conditions for panic and dislocation. Soon after Truman issued the order, the *Washington Post*'s Jerry Kluttz, who wrote the paper's "Federal Diary" column, visited the Munitions Building, the workplace for six thousand Veterans Administration personnel, and spent part of a morning in the cafeteria, where he sensed a mood of nervous apprehension. "Any employee who happened by and stopped for a moment to buy an apple or chocolate bar," he wrote, "was collared by a strong-arm investigator."

Most federal employees, if they became targets, could appeal an adverse finding to a Loyalty Review Board, another new entity. But the process, no matter how discreetly handled, could be humiliating; and because "disloyalty" was such a fluid term, an inquiry could go beyond expected boundaries. Eleanor Bontecue was a lawyer in the Justice Department and War Department in the mid- to late-1940s. Her indispensable 1953 book on the program pointed out that some loyalty board members were deeply suspicious of whites who associated with African Americans; they might inquire as to how a person felt about "mixing white and Negro blood in the Red Cross blood bank." Other questions could be creepily personal, for instance whether a couple's "marriage relation" began before the wedding. Loyalty boards were interested in reading habits (the novelists Howard Fast and Upton Sinclair were worrisome); possession of recordings by the prodigiously gifted Paul Robeson, an admirer of Soviet Russia, was an alarm bell.

Eleanor Roosevelt gave Truman her sharp opinion after ten State Department employees were fired, in October 1947, for having "indirect association with representatives of foreign governments." The department had recently warned employees that, in cases of reasonable doubt, "the department will be given the benefit of the doubt, and the person will be deemed a security risk." Seven of the fired employees weren't told what they'd been charged with, and weren't allowed simply to resign, which left a permanent blot on their records. Mrs. Roosevelt told Truman that those dismissals had compelled her to write: "I have been getting from all of my friends, Republicans and Democrats alike, such violent reactions to the Loyalty Tests." Truman, the next day, in a thousand-word public statement, tried to assure government employees that they needn't fear "witch hunts" or "kangaroo courts," and that "rumor, gossip, or suspicion will not be sufficient to lead to the dismissal of an employee for disloyalty." Apparently referring to the State Department firings, he said that he'd ordered government agencies to grant hearings to fired workers— though not, in fact, every agency and not in cases where it might be "necessary to exercise extraordinary powers" granted by Congress."

In about two weeks, Truman replied directly to Mrs. Roosevelt, in a tone of distant formality. He'd read her letter with "sympathetic reactions to the ideas you express," and knew that "the overwhelming number of civil servants in the United States are not only faithful and loyal, but devoted patriots." He acknowledged that it was "contrary to American tradition to inquire into the political or philosophical views of anyone," and that "all of us feel . . . a certain repugnance to this program." Yet he insisted that "there were certain indications of a small infiltration of seriously disloyal people into certain sensitive parts of the government," and that "we all must remind ourselves that no one has a constitutional right to work for the government." The right to a government job, as Truman certainly knew, wasn't an issue. He also knew that the publicity surrounding this case wasn't good for the administration. The State Department eventually permitted the seven fired employees to resign, without prejudice.

In the summer of Executive Order 9835, Truman felt more alone than ever. He still awoke early, often before dawn, and still went on walks at 120 paces a minute. In the summer, as with all summers,

Bess preferred living in her mother's house, on North Delaware Street. Margaret, at twenty-three, had moved to New York, in pursuit of a professional career as a singer. She briefly considered using "Margaret Wallace" as a stage name, the better to disassociate herself from the White House and establish her own identity.

One early morning, Truman found himself thinking about the absent Bess. He recalled musical shows that they'd seen together, and suddenly felt shaken by sentimental recollection: "'The Girl from Utah' left the greatest impression on me because of the song 'They'll Never Believe Me,'" he wrote to Bess. "You'd just said you'd take a chance on me. Wasn't it a terrible chance? Never did I think I'd get you into all the trouble you're in now. Well you didn't have to take the chance did you?"

TWELVE

A Cemetery
for Dead Cats

> When Secretary Forrestal is really interested in a cause, he
> doesn't sleep, and doesn't let others sleep.
>
> —James F. Byrnes

1. Soon after Senator Truman became President Roosevelt's running mate, he published an article in *Collier's* entitled "Our Armed Forces MUST Be Unified," which recommended consolidating the army and navy to "put our defensive and offensive strength under one tent." As the former chairman of the Truman Committee, he thought he understood military waste and overlap, and could say, with some authority, that "our scrambled professional military setup has been an open invitation to catastrophe."

As President, he continued to push for it, although it was a sensitive topic, especially for the navy, whose leaders worried that the army, with a force twice as large, would dominate the military establishment. It was not a matter to stir the public's imagination, but was a propellent for something much larger: a rethinking and reshuffling of the nation's military and foreign-policy establishment. In its final form, a civilian secretary of defense would replace the navy secretary and the secretary of war; a National Security Council would coordinate foreign and military policy for the executive branch; and the Office of Strategic Services would be replaced by an intelligence service modeled after the British version, or at least the British version before it began to leak state secrets. A lot of this had been outlined in a report by Ferdinand Eberstadt, a New York lawyer and investment banker, but the prime mover was James Forrestal, who was Eberstadt's good friend and onetime Wall Street colleague.

The Truman aide George Elsey believed that, without Forrestal's "adamantine insistence," there would not have been a National Security Council, or a secretary of defense. That's an exaggeration. From the time of Truman's 1945 message to Congress, which said, "When we were attacked four years ago . . . we certainly paid a high price for not having" a unified military," to the Eberstadt Report, and numerous congressional hearings, most of this restructuring had been inevitable. But, as Elsey said, "What Forrestal kept pressing for . . . was the absolute necessity of some kind of governmental machinery which would attempt to bridge the gap between military and foreign policy." As Forrestal was to put it, "The military functions and the civilian decisions march together." Bridging that gap would not be easy going; every department had a stake. Secretary of State Marshall, at a cabinet meeting, said the language being proposed gave him the impression that a National Security Council "would be determining the entire foreign policy of the United States," and while Forrestal tried to reassure him, there were grounds for worry.

What became the National Security Act of 1947 was much more than a reorganization of the Executive Branch. It was also a prelude to rethinking the nation's active, perhaps unwelcome, role in the affairs of other nations. Secretary of War Robert Patterson said as much when he testified about the proposed legislation, in the spring of 1947, and declared that "the maintenance of the future peace of the world will depend on the attitude and polices of the United States." Clare Hoffman, a Michigan Republican, who chaired the House Committee on Expenditures in the Executive Branch, had then asked, "What you mean is if we become powerful enough, we are acting as master policeman and no one else will dare start a war?"

Patterson replied, "I think that if we have adequate military strength, no nation will dare attack us or will commence a major war anywhere. I believe that."

"That is to say, we become boss policeman."

Patterson wouldn't have put it that way: "I think the whole world knows that the intentions of the United States are peaceful and not aggressive," a view, or belief, with which Truman wholly agreed.

2. James Vincent Forrestal, who was destined to become one of Truman's unhappiest appointments, had worked in Washington since 1940, recruited during Roosevelt's prewar mobilization effort, and befriended by Harry Hopkins. He became under secretary of the navy, and then navy secretary, in 1944, when his predecessor, Frank Knox, died suddenly. By 1947, he was the only remaining member of the Roosevelt cabinet, which, as Morgenthau, Perkins, Biddle, Ickes, Wallace, and others had learned, was not a distinction to be sought. When Truman talked to him about becoming the nation's first secretary of defense, Forrestal wrote to Robert Sherwood, the playwright and Roosevelt speechwriter, that "this office will probably be the greatest cemetery for dead cats in history," a puzzling but vivid image.

Born in 1892 and reared in the Hudson River town of Beacon, Forrestal was the son of first- and second-generation Irish immigrants. He attended Princeton, but left the college a year before graduation; during Word War I, he was a navy aviator, though not a pilot. After a brief career in journalism, he found his vocation on Wall Street, beginning as a bond salesman for the investment bank William A. Read & Co., where he moved rapidly upward to become president of the firm, now called Dillon, Read & Co. In 1926, he married Josephine Ogden, a twenty-six-year-old West Virginian, who'd been a chorus girl in the Ziegfeld Follies and an editor at *Vogue*. In an early portrait by Cecil Beaton, one can see slender, dark-haired Josephine in all her flapper beauty.

While Harry Truman, in the 1920s, was pursuing political office in Jackson County, the Forrestals were being seen in all the best places in Manhattan and Long Island. As Townsend Hoopes and Douglas Brinkley write, in their excellent biography, Jim and "Jo," as she was known to her friends, moved in circles that included George Gershwin, Robert Benchley, John O'Hara, and John Dos Passos. He is thought to have been a model for Roger Thurloe, the protagonist in one of Dos Passos's late, lesser novels, *The Great Days*, described as "a small man [with] a remarkably fast bouncy stride," and a habit of compulsively scratching the back of his head.

Something about Forrestal stayed with people. He "exerted an almost magnetic attraction" on most men and women, an early biographer wrote. "The way he carried himself, together with the broken nose"—Forrestal had been an amateur boxer—"tight mouth, and piercing eyes" produced a lasting impression. Arthur Krock, the *New York Times* Washington bureau chief, who'd known Forrestal since the 1930s, saw him as someone who could "invest any social gathering with a rare degree of wit and gaiety." Like a journalistic godfather, Krock sometimes used his column to boost him, even for the presidency. Social Washington was fascinated, sometimes gushingly so, by the Forrestals, who'd bought one of Georgetown's grand residences, Prospect House, built in 1788 by a Revolutionary War general. The society columnist Mary Van Rensselaer Thayer wrote that Jo Forrestal called her husband "Forrestal" and "unlike most wives is continually amazed by his kaleidoscopic activities." Robert Lovett, the under secretary of state and a Wall Street friend, believed that what Forrestal really wanted was a life of "prosperous obscurity."

What was left out, in an age when journalists still practiced discretion, was that Jim and Jo's personal life was a nightmare. They were "a lively, kinetic couple" in public, a friend recalled, but it was a malignant liveliness. The Lovetts were sure that Jo had suffered some sort of breakdown after the move to Washington. She drank too much, and her behavior was a constant source of mortification, such as her late appearance at a dinner the Forrestals gave for Churchill's son, Randolph, when, looking at the guests from the top of a staircase, she said, very loudly, "Good Lord, what in the world do all you people have to say to each other?" It was only when things had gone very wrong that Arthur Krock revealed that his wife (though not, apparently, Krock himself) "had begun to detect inner disturbances in Forrestal."

Between Truman and Forrestal was a perpetual risk of miscommunication. That could lead to a baffling conversation like the one that occurred at the end of a cabinet meeting, in the early summer of 1947, when Forrestal asked Truman the sort of hypothetical question that he sometimes liked to pose: "What does this country do, politically or militarily, if it is confronted during this summer with a Russian *démarche* accompanied by simultaneous coups in France and Italy?" Truman replied that "we would have to face that situation when it arose," and that "the answer would have to be found in history—of the struggle between the Romans and Carthage, between Athens and Sparta, between Alexander the Great and the Persians, between France and England, between England and Germany." Forrestal could not summon up that sort of Trumanesque history, and didn't seem to know what to make of it.

What made it harder for Truman was Forrestal's intensity—a nervous personality that combined rigidity with indecisiveness. In photographs, Forrestal is rarely smiling, and gives the impression of a man unable to bend. At the Pentagon, as navy secretary, he'd been known as a difficult, exhausting boss, described, in a *Time* cover story, as "articulate, blunt Jim Forrestal . . . a quietly cynical man," who could be seen "gazing skeptically over the top of his pipe and only occasionally flaring into tightlipped, concise profanity." Robert L. Dennison, the assistant chief of naval operations, recalled that "he'd go out late in the afternoon and play golf, expect the men to stay there, and then he'd come back and work until all hours of the night without any regard for these people."

Truman's first choice as secretary of defense had been Robert Patterson, the secretary of war, the office overseeing the army and the air force. But Patterson was determined to leave Washington; his wife had been urging him to return to law, and a possible judgeship. "I couldn't bring myself to force him to stay," Truman thought, which left the navy secretary, in effect, as first runner-up.

The Truman cabinet, even without Forrestal, was not a congenial, cohesive group. The concerns of a General Marshall were far from those of Truman's friends and loyalists, such as the Missourian John Snyder at Treasury or Tom Clark at Justice. So it was a comfort for the President to find a place for someone as agreeable as Rear Admiral Sidney W. Souers, another Missourian, whom Truman appointed as the first director of the Central Intelligence Group—the CIG—the precursor to the Central Intelligence Agency. Described as "a pleasant, very shrewd man with an anonymous sort of face and a wispy mustache," Souers had been recruited by Clark Clifford, who later wrote that "I turned first to the man I knew best in the intelligence community, my friend from St. Louis," although Souers did not belong to an "intelligence community," and Clifford was not conversant with that "community." Souers had been a reservist during the war, and his background was in real estate, insurance, and running a self-service grocery chain called Piggly Wiggly. But personal chemistry is a mysterious thing, and in a short time, Truman fell for Souers, with an affection that was instantaneous, genuine, and deep. Stuart Symington, another Missourian, who became the first air force secretary, recalled that Truman "became devoted to Souers, without reservation, Sid saw him day after day, about every day, you know. . . . He loved the President, and respected the President. It was mutual." Those were not feelings that Truman had, or could have had, for Jim Forrestal, whose chilly, sardonic affect could be off-putting and whose loyalty to the President was occasionally in question.

Truman's view of defense policy was much the same as Forrestal's. A visitor to Forrestal's Pentagon office could see a framed printed card that said, "We will never have universal peace until the strongest army and the strongest navy are in the hands of the most powerful nation." He had been an early champion of George Kennan's ideas on Soviet "containment." But it should also have been obvious that Forrestal's ambivalence when it came to unifying the armed services might cause difficulties; his former assistant, John T. Connor, knew that he was intent on preserving the "integrity and spirit of the Navy." Forrestal had raised the question with Truman in the summer of 1945, but came away believing that the President sounded less interested in efficiency, and more in "the destruction of 'political cliques that run the Army and Navy.'" Most of Truman's thinking, Forrestal believed, had come from his experience in the Missouri National Guard. Yet he found things to admire in Truman. When former Secretary of State Byrnes informed him that "Stalin did not like Truman and had told him so," Forrestal replied that Truman was "the first one who had ever said 'no' to anything Stalin asked."

Dead cats aside, Forrestal did not even seem sold on the expanded Pentagon job. When he'd testified before the Senate Military Affairs Committee, in 1945, he'd warned about creating a "position that concentrates power beyond the capacity of any one man to use that power and certainly beyond the capacity to obtain and digest the knowledge upon which its use could be based." Stuart Symington said that Forrestal wanted to limit the defense secretary's authority, but realized that one needed more power to do the job properly—a fatal contradiction of goals.

3. Truman formally nominated Forrestal as the nation's first secretary of defense on July 26, 1947—the day that he signed the National Security Act. It was not a propitious time. Mary Jane Truman had called her brother at nine that morning and told him "mamma is sinking swiftly." Truman had gotten similar calls before, and his mother had rallied before, but this time the news sounded especially dire. He ordered a plane, with a scheduled takeoff at 12:30.

Forrestal was with Truman, at the White House, as they waited for delivery of the bill, which had just been passed by Congress and was slowed by problems at the printing office. As the physical copy of the bill made its way, by car, from the Capitol, their conversation was strained. Forrestal must have sensed the rawness of Truman's worry as, for forty-five minutes, they tried to fill the silences. At one point, Forrestal suddenly asked Truman how he accounted for Hitler's decision to go to war in 1939, when "he actually had in his hands all the cards necessary to dominate Europe." Truman replied that Hitler had "simply become drunk with power," and had made two big mistakes: attacking Poland, and not invading England after the fall of France. Forrestal thought that Truman's analysis was faulty, that it "illustrated the work that we had to do to impress on him the fact that the crossing of a body of water"—the English Channel—"is not a casual business." But Forrestal was wise enough to keep his opinion to himself, and at that moment, as they conversed, almost disjointedly, the President and his incoming secretary of defense could not have been more removed from each other, either in mood or sympathetic understanding.

When the bill still hadn't arrived, Truman finally asked that it be delivered to him at the airport. He would sign it there, before his plane took off for Missouri. In his diary, he recalled something of that late morning: "Finally recieved [sic] bill at airport. Signed it and appointed Forestal [sic]. All favor him. Took off at 12:30. . . . At 1:30 Washington time recieved [sic] message my mother has passed on. Terrible shock. No one knew it." Truman believes that he may have known about the news from Missouri just before the message arrived: "I'd been dozing and dreamed she'd said 'Goodbye, Harry. Be a good boy,'" was how he remembered it. "When Dr. Graham came in to my room on the Sacred Cow I knew what he would say," Truman told his daughter. "I knew she was gone when I saw her in that dream. She was saying goodbye to me."

Four hours later, the President arrived in Grandview, the hamlet where he'd been reared and where, for ten years, he'd plowed the fields and shared a small upstairs room with his brother, Vivian. He met Mary Jane and Vivian, and the three siblings drove five miles to the village of Belton, to choose a casket. "Spent Sunday morning and afternoon at Grandview," Truman wrote in his diary. "Mamma had been placed in casket we had decided upon and returned to her cottage. I couldn't look at her dead. I wanted to remember [her] alive when she was at her best. This was a terrible day. Arose at 6:15[,] had breakfast, fixed up by Bess at seven. Didn't sleep much Saturday night or Sunday night. So took a nap after breakfast. Had a time doing it."

There were still official duties; Charlie Ross called to say that the Mexican ambassador wanted to fly out to pay his respects. "I took a short nap, had lunch at 12:00 and went to Grandview, arriving at 1:00," the diary continued. "All the cousins on both sides came. About fifty of them. The Baptist preacher Wellborn Bowman conducted the service. It was as mamma wanted it. We went to Forest Hill and the preacher did it excellently at the grave. Along the road all cars, trucks and pedestrians stood with hats off. It made me want to weep—but I couldn't in public. I've read thousands of messages from all over the world in the White House study and I can shed tears as I please—no one's looking."

Three days later, Truman called in reporters. "I wanted to say to you personally a thing or two that I couldn't very well say any other way," he said. "I wanted to express to you all, and to your editors and your publishers, appreciation for the kindness to me during the last week. I was particularly anxious to tell the photographers how nice they were to me, and to the family, and I didn't know any other way to do it but just call you in and tell you. I had no news to give you, or anything else to say to you, except just that, and I felt like I owed it to you. You have been exceedingly nice to me all during the whole business, and I hope you will believe it when I say to you that it is from the heart when I tell you that."

The death of Martha Ellen Young Truman was no sudden shock. She'd been confined to bed since fracturing a hip several months before; her vitality was ebbing. But despite earlier alarms that the end was near, the President was shaken. His devotion to his mother was intense, so much so that he might write home several times a week; it was why he telephoned home when Japan surrendered. The loss came at a time in his presidency when the absence of such a personage, one whose belief in him had been total and loving, was disorienting. The creation of a new, and complex, national security apparatus, demonstrated Truman's ability to make clear, unambiguous decisions, but not the talent to get across to the country a clear sense of his goals. It's unlikely, though, that anyone then could have anticipated the assault of changing circumstance.

THIRTEEN

Minority Reports

As usual it has been a trying week. What with Palestine and the Jews and Negroes and the South.

—Harry Truman, in a letter to Mary Jane Truman,
March 26, 1948

1. Clark Clifford, who made a habit of taking credit for the work of others, liked to see himself as a political strategist in much the way that he saw himself a geopolitical thinker, and he usually managed to carry it off. "His is the kind of intelligence that produces perfectly parsed sentences and balanced paragraphs even in social conversation," Stewart Alsop wrote. "In the mind's ear one can hear even the semicolons and parentheses click into place." In the fall of 1947, Clifford wrote or, more precisely, claimed authorship of a thirty-two-page memorandum, which, he admitted, was "based solely on an appraisal of the politically advantageous course to follow." For instance, to the Republicans' charge that the administration was indifferent to the threat of native-born Communism, the President "adroitly stole their thunder by initiating his own Government employee loyalty investigation procedure." It dissected the country into interest groups—among them "The Farmer," "The Negro," "The Jew," and even "The Alien Group," which favored expanded immigration quotas. Most of this disarmingly cynical document was actually written by James H. Rowe, an assistant in the budget office, who took a fairly modest view of his handiwork: "There is nothing new; it is old-hat. I think it is objective," he wrote, in a cover note, before the manuscript was seized by Clifford.

When it came to "The Negro," Rowe-Clifford believed that Truman could win the votes of Northern blacks without much risk of losing the white South, which had voted Democratic since the Civil War. But that was a bad bet. White Southerners wanted to believe that a man from rural Missouri, whose ancestors had supported the Confederacy, was one of them. But Truman was not one of them. He was, rather, someone torn, trying to work out where he stood as he dealt with his background and upbringing—his inescapable assumptions about race, which included white superiority—and his attachment to what he saw as the promise of American equality. Mary Jane Truman told a white reporter, "Harry is no more for nigger equality than any of us," but she wasn't being fair to her brother, who separated social equality, which seemed to him undesirable, from economic opportunity, which he thought necessary. At the same time, he seemed uninterested in how social and economic equality might be connected. In a speech Truman delivered in Sedalia, Missouri, in 1940—described as a "tribute to the Negro"—he said, "Their social life, will, naturally, remain their own," but "in all matters of progress and welfare, of economic opportunity and equal rights before law, Negroes deserve every aid and protection." A month later, speaking to the National Colored Democratic Association, in Chicago, he said, "I am not appealing for social equality of the Negro. The Negro himself knows better than that, and the highest type of Negro leaders say quite frankly they prefer the society of their own people. Negroes want justice, not social relations."

That outlook, which, to modern ears, sounds unblinkingly racist, and yet was meant to win black votes in Jackson County, was pretty much what Truman always believed. But, as President, he pretty much stopped saying it, and began to sound more like someone determined to speak for history. He did this—an evolutionary leap—when he spoke to the NAACP, on June 29, 1947, at the Lincoln Memorial, standing alongside such antagonists of the Old South as Eleanor Roosevelt, Supreme Court Justice Hugo Black, and Walter White, the president of the NAACP.

This question had already given President Truman some vexed moments. In October 1945, six months after Roosevelt's death,

Bess Truman had agreed to be the guest of honor at a Daughters of the American Revolution tea, despite a decision by the DAR to ban the pianist Hazel Scott, an African American, from performing at DAR Constitution Hall. The DAR had been through this before, in 1939, when it banned an African American opera star, the contralto Marian Anderson: Eleanor Roosevelt then resigned from the DAR, and Anderson went on to give a celebrated concert, before seventy-five thousand people, at the Lincoln Memorial, a performance that began with the words "My Country, 'tis of Thee." Hazel Scott, at twenty-five, was known for performing swing versions of the classics, but to get a sense of her unusual, even astonishing, talent, one ought to watch one of her many film clips.

Scott had recently married the New York congressman Adam Clayton Powell Jr. (one of two African Americans in Congress), and Powell quickly got involved in his wife's behalf: He wired Mrs. Truman, with copies to the President and the New York congressional delegation, asking her "to have the American decency" not to attend the DAR tea. Truman's office replied to Powell, saying, "Artistic talent is not the exclusive property of any one race or group," and acknowledging that the war in Europe had been fought against countries "which made racial discrimination their state policy." Having said that, though, the White House was unwilling to interfere in the management of "a private enterprise." When Truman recounted this for his mother and sister, he sounded not at all sympathetic, telling them that "a highbrow preacher from N.Y. has been annoying us. He's a congressman, a smart aleck and a rabble rouser. He got nowhere."

After Powell referred to Bess as the "last lady," which guaranteed that he would never be welcome in the White House, Truman was said to have joked that he wanted the jovial Mississippian George Allen, still in Truman's clubby inner circle, to look up that "damn nigger preacher" who'd said things about "the Madam" and kick him around. Margaret Truman was to write that her father knew he'd made a mistake—"He was far more inclined to condemn the D.A.R.," she insisted. She also recognized that the episode had damaged her mother: "There could not have been a worse beginning to her first ladyship. . . . She had been maneuvered into a comparison with Eleanor Roosevelt and had come out a dismal second on the public opinion charts."

By the time Truman spoke at the Lincoln Memorial, his emotional connection to this cause was real enough. He'd been disturbed by reports of violence against blacks, mostly in the South—lynchings and fatal beatings that went unpunished—and by one sickening incident in particular: the intentional blinding of Sergeant Isaac Woodard Jr., on February 12, 1946. Woodard, a decorated soldier, had served in the Philippines, a member of a segregated support unit during New Guinea maritime landing operations. After three years, he was on his way home, by Greyhound, from Augusta, Georgia, to Winnsboro, South Carolina. According to Sergeant Woodard's affidavit, he'd asked the bus driver to wait while he used a rest-stop bathroom. "Go ahead and get off and hurry back," the driver said, but only after first saying no, cursing Woodard, and being cursed back. An hour later, the driver stopped again and went to fetch the police. During a skirmish outside the bus, a local policeman "began punching me in my eyes with the end of his billy," and, in Woodard's words, drove a baton "into my eyeballs."

Truman learned about the mutilation of Sergeant Woodard months later, from the NAACP's Walter White. But the story was becoming a widely publicized horror, thanks in large part to Orson Welles, who then was broadcasting regular fifteen-minute commentaries on ABC radio. He began his July 16, 1946, broadcast by reading every word of Woodard's affidavit. Truman wrote to Tom Clark, the attorney general, that he was "very much alarmed at the increased racial feeling all over the country." He realized that the Justice Department was looking into lynchings, in Tennessee and Georgia, but he thought that wasn't going to be enough—that "this is going to require the inauguration of some sort of policy." To David K. Niles, an administrative assistant overseeing civil rights, he sent a note saying, "I am very much in earnest on this thing and I'd like very much to have you push it with everything you have."

A year later, on the mid-summer day that Truman spoke in front of Lincoln's giant statue, he sounded like a different man, though when he gave his sister a preview of what was ahead, he was almost apologetic: "I've got to make a speech to the Society [*sic*] for the Advancement of Colored People tomorrow and I wish I didn't have to make it," he wrote to Mary Jane. "Mrs. R[Roosevelt], Walter White, Wayne Morse, senator from Oregon, + your brother are the speakers. Walter White is white in color, has gray hair and blue eyes, but he is a Negro. Mrs. Roosevelt has spent her public life stirring up trouble between whites and blacks—and I'm in the middle. Mama won't like what I say because I wind up quoting old Abe. But I believe what I say and I'm hopeful we may implement it."

Truman's "old Abe" quotation was unlikely offend anyone; few could object to the hope that "if it shall please the Divine Being who determines the destinies of nations, we shall remain a united people." Loud applause came when Truman spelled it out, saying, "The only limit to an American's achievement should be his ability, his industry, and his character," and "our immediate task is to remove the last remnants of the barriers which stand between millions of our citizens and their birthright. There is no justifiable reason for discrimination because of ancestry, or religion, or race, or color." When he'd finished, he turned to Walter White and said, "I said what I did because I mean every word of it—and I am going to prove that I do mean it." If he actually *had* meant every word, that would have been an extraordinary transformation, but he was nonetheless determined to earn the goodwill he felt that day.

He soon turned to Charles Edward Wilson, a New Yorker whose biography was at least as remarkable as Truman's: He'd left school (PS 32) when he was twelve, to work as an office boy for Sprague Electrical Works, and eventually became president of General Electric. Truman asked Wilson to chair a committee to consider the challenge of inequality. In a relatively short time—by October 1947—Wilson's group was able to produce a 178-page report titled "To Secure These Rights," a document that overcame its committee origins to offer a generous, thoughtful, and detailed examination of race in America—from disparities in employment and education to the prevalence of police brutality. At one point, it addressed the peculiar fact that, for black Americans, "Washington is not just the nation's capital. It is the point at which all public transportation into the South becomes 'Jim Crow.' " Walter White called the report "the most courageous and specific document of its kind in American history."

On February 2, 1948, Truman sent Congress a civil rights message, along with a program that included a Federal Fair Employment Practices Act, an anti-lynching law, an anti–poll tax bill, and an end to segregated interstate travel. It did not go over well in the South. Cecil Wyche, a South Carolina judge, who was deer-hunting in the low country of the state, remarked to his companions, "Well, boys, they've fired on Fort Sumter again." A Mississippi congressman, Thomas G. Abernethy, called it a declaration of war on Southern traditions: "They have put the odorous issue squarely under the nose of every Southern leader of the Democratic Party. We either live with the stench or we don't." In that spirit, the editors of the *Jackson Daily News*, wrote "Here's telling President Truman that the Democratic Party in Mississippi is through with him, now, hereafter and forever," and said the state would send a delegation to the Democratic National Convention, in July, to oppose Truman's nomination. There was immediate talk of Southern Democrats supporting their own presidential candidate and withholding electoral votes from Truman—enough to send the next presidential election into the House of Representatives.

South Carolina's governor, Strom Thurmond, said that a Fair Employment Practices Commission resembled something "patterned after a Russian law written by Joseph Stalin about 1920," and he swiftly became the leader of the Southern resistance. "I am through with him," Thurmond said of Truman, and on March 17, 1948, he spoke to a party rally, in Columbia, in defense of "our way of life since Reconstruction." He explained that "the laws dealing with the separation of the race are necessary to maintain public peace and order . . . essential to the protection of the racial integrity and purity of the white and Negro races alike." He'd never dreamed that a Democratic President would "stab us in the back."

Two days later, at Washington's Mayflower Hotel, Truman spoke at the Jefferson-Jackson Day Dinner, the informal start of the 1948 presidential campaign. The hundred-dollar-a-plate meal was boycotted by a group of Southerners because "of the presence of Negroes"—about a dozen. In its description of the event, the *New Republic* magazine, where Henry Wallace had just become editor, described a discouraging scene: "The President's uninspired words and his even more than usually monotonous tone produced only a few outbursts of mild applause." The writer of the unsigned comment added that "if Harry Truman didn't know how much his stock was slipping, he was the only top Democrat . . . who was still in the dark," and concluded, "The condemned man ate a hearty dinner."

Willingly or not, Truman had found himself assuming an unfamiliar role: as a champion of African Americans. While he could not put aside his ancestral biases, he knew that he could never ally himself with the Confederate wing of his party—people like Governor Thurmond, who was bad enough, and Theodore G. Bilbo, the unfettered racist governor of Mississippi. Truman was never in a hurry when it came to the changes that real racial equality would bring, but injustice, and unfairness, grated on him, the cruelties inflicted on blacks angered him, and he wanted no part of any of that.

2. Henry Wallace had been an angry man since Truman fired him, in the late summer of 1946. His humiliating fall—from Roosevelt's vice president, to Truman's commerce secretary, to dismissal from the cabinet, to nominal magazine editor—took just eighteen months. It came as no surprise when, at the end of 1947, he announced that he intended to run for president as an independent, and would take on the "bipartisan reactionary war policy" of the major political parties. He'd been making speeches and holding rallies for some time, although Wallace himself was the lesser attraction. Rather, a Wallace rally was a chance to watch the comic actor Zero Mostel, who, dressed as Sherlock Holmes, might mock the House Committee by performing, "Who's gonna investigate the man who investigates the man who investigates me?" Or to hear "The House I Live In" sung by Paul Robeson—"This giant of a man," one awed spectator wrote, "you could see his big, poetic eyes and his barrel chest." If it was hard to take Wallace seriously, it was harder to ignore a special congressional election in the Bronx, in February 1948, where a candidate supported by Wallace and the Communist-backed American Labor Party managed a victory that the *Herald Tribune* called an "earthquake." It wasn't that exactly, but rather an anomalous contest, in a heavily Jewish district, where the contentious question of establishing a new Jewish state, situated in Palestine, had played a role. It didn't take a Clifford memorandum to understand that "The Jew" was key to carrying New York State, and that elections in that era were rarely won without New York's electoral votes.

Truman's connection to American Jews was, in its way, as complicated as his relationship with African Americans. It was an ideal subject for Drew Pearson, whose widely syndicated "Washington Merry-Go-Round" was fed by a large network of sources, not all of them trustworthy—someone who single-handedly represented what Truman, in choleric moments, called the "sabotage press." On March 11, 1948, a Pearson column said that Truman had discussed Palestine with a "New York publisher" and editor (neither identified), and then, "pounding his desk, he made remarks about 'the—New York Jews.' . . . 'They're disloyal to their country. Disloyal!' he cried."

The next day, Truman began a press conference by reacting to the latest Pearson: "I had thought I wouldn't have to add another liar's star to that fellow's crown, but I will have to do it. That is just a lie out of the whole cloth. That is as emphatic as I can put it."

"May we quote you on that, sir?" he was asked.

"Verbatim, if you like," Truman replied.

"All Jews? The Jews?"

"Jews," Truman repeated. "Jews in New York are disloyal, which is a lie out of the whole cloth. It makes good reading in a political year."

The truth, though, was that Truman *had* met with a New York publisher, the *New York Times'* Arthur H. Sulzberger, and that, in Sulzberger's words, the President was "bitter" about the British, who had governed Palestine under a League of Nations mandate since 1922. He was also bitter about the political activism of New York Jews. When Sulzberger had interrupted to say, "Wouldn't you make that New York Zionists, Mr. President, because I am bitter about them too?" Truman replied, "Of course, that is what I mean." Sulzberger sent a private memorandum about this conversation to Charles Merz, the newspaper's editorial page editor, and added, "It seems that some of his best friends are Jews!" The real subject, in any case, was not disloyalty as it's commonly understood, but the intense interest of American Jews in Palestine.

The British mandate was set to expire in May 1948. After that, most of Truman's advisers favored some sort of UN trusteeship for Palestine, even though the UN was ill-equipped for such a task. A trusteeship, though, would be a lot less troublesome than carving out a new nation. A new nation would require the messiness of a partition between Muslims and the Jewish settlers who kept arriving, in boatloads. Loy A. Henderson, the director of near Eastern and African affairs at the State Department, was very much against partition. The defense secretary, James Forrestal, agreed with Henderson, and told a House Armed Services subcommittee in January that oil was "the life blood of a war machine," that domestic oil reserves were being depleted four times as quickly as they were being replenished, and that the Arab response to partition would make the pipelines to the Persian Gulf less secure.

While the concerns of the foreign-policy establishment were based on that sort of worry, they were not entirely separate from free-floating anti-Zionist sentiments that bubbled up in the State Department and other agencies. Forrestal had telephoned his old friend Bob Lovett, the under secretary of state, to inform him that he'd asked Truman "not to see any more of these Jews; also, we should do nothing which would prejudice the other countries." Lovett took note of this call in his daybook, but did not record his reaction.

Truman himself, as Sulzberger had suggested, could sound casually anti-Semitic, as when he supposedly remarked to Henry Wallace that "Jesus Christ couldn't please them when he was here on earth, so how could anyone expect that I would have any luck?" Truman was not an anti-Semite, but Zionists annoyed him, and Jewish Americans in general were getting on his nerves. But the counterforce of events moved him to take a position on Israel that was opposed by people whose advice he usually followed, such as Admiral Leahy, who saw a partition of Palestine leading to a "world wide war between Moslems and Christians," and especially Secretary of State Marshall, whose influence with Truman was almost always decisive. But one should never underestimate the power of Truman's emotions. He had neither Roosevelt's charm nor his cold-bloodedness, and it was hard to turn away from the war's visible aftermath: Jewish refugees who'd been liberated from the death camps in Poland and were drawn to the powerful idea of settling in Palestine, the site of ancient Israel. How could a prosperous, democratic nation turn away from that?

On July 11, 1947, a Chesapeake Bay steamer, the former SS *President Warfield*, left France and set a course for Palestine, carrying forty-five hundred unwelcome immigrants, among them Holocaust survivors and orphans who, as the *Herald Tribune* put it, "have passports to nowhere." The ship, renamed *Exodus 1947*, was intercepted a week later by three British warships, acting for the Mandate government of Palestine, with the intent of transporting its human cargo back to France. A twenty-four-year-old American seaman was clubbed to death by British troops as they tried to board the ship, a death that led to a mass funeral in Haifa, and got the close attention of Under Secretary Lovett's office, which prepared a press release, just in case it was needed.

On July 21, Truman noted in his diary that Henry Morgenthau, the former treasury secretary, wanted to talk "about Jewish ship in Palistine [sic]. Told him I would talk to Gen[eral] Marshall about it." The visit annoyed Truman: "He'd no business, whatever to call me. The Jews have no sense of proportion nor do they have any judgement on world affairs." With rising indignation—working himself up to a fleeting state of outrage was a Truman trait—he added, "The Jews, I find are very, very selfish. They care not how many Estonians, Latvians, Finns, Poles, Yugoslavs or Greeks get murdered or mistreated as D[isplaced] P[ersons] as long as the Jews get special treatment. Yet when they have power, physical, financial or political neither Hitler nor Stalin has anything on them for cruelty or mistreatment to the underdog." He continued, in a more ecumenical tone: "Put an underdog on top and it makes no difference whether his name is Russian, Jewish, Negro, Management, Labor, Mormon, Baptist he goes haywire." When Truman got in these moods, it was easy to believe that Drew Pearson had accurately reported his burst of temper, while not quite understanding his state of mind. With over a hundred thousand persons, mostly Jewish, in American refugee camps after the war, Acheson later said, "It was our responsibility."

The journey of *Exodus 1947* continued: In September, it sailed to Hamburg, Germany, where the passengers were interned and where, impelled by enraged memory, a swastika was painted on the Union Jack. The British Foreign Office asserted that Secretary of State Marshall's office had no opinion on the matter, but that wasn't true; the British had been urged by Marshall to reconsider. Over the next few months, the passengers of *Exodus 1947* made their way to Palestine, through secret ports, and on small fishing boats. Leon Uris's 1958 best-selling novel, *Exodus*, and a 1960 film, starring Paul Newman, which gave highly romanticized versions of what happened, left out the sequel: an unresolved future, with no obvious compromise in sight.

Loy Henderson, who became something of a villain to those who favored a Jewish state, recalled being summoned to the White House on the day, in late 1947, that a special UN Committee on Palestine came out in favor of a partitioned state. Henderson faced several aides, particularly Clifford, whose questioning was sharp enough to make him feel like a hostile witness. Clifford could, and did, exaggerate his own status, but the relative informality of the Truman White House allowed someone like the White House counsel to attend meetings at which he had no obvious role. Henderson recalled being asked about "the sources" of his views: "Were they merely my opinions which might be based on prejudice or bias?" Finally, "it seemed to me that the group was trying to humiliate and break me down in the presence of the President. . . . The cross-questioning became more and more rough and finally the President stood up. 'Oh, hell,' he muttered, 'I'm leaving.'" Henderson, at that point, was unable to decipher Truman's true feelings.

Truman's appointments secretary, Matthew Connelly, thought

that the President had acted out of humanitarian impulses, yet was not innocent of politics. "I raised the question with Mr. Truman, 'How many Arab votes are there in the United States?'" Truman's outlook was certainly influenced by his friend Eddie Jacobson, with whom he'd served in the National Guard and become a business partner when they opened a retail store—Truman & Jacobson Haberdashery—in downtown Kansas City. Margaret Truman thought that Jacobson's influence has been much exaggerated. "The whole thing is absurd," she declared, with unmistakable annoyance, and finality, in the biography she wrote of her father. "Eddie Jacobson was one of the hundreds of army friends my father made during World War I." After the store went bankrupt, in 1919, she wrote, "Dad saw comparatively little of him. I don't believe they ever discussed politics, except in the most offhand fashion."

But Margaret, or her ghostwriter, Thomas Fleming, too glibly tried to diminish the Truman-Jacobson friendship, much as she'd exaggerated the number of her father's army friends. "I was always glad to see him," Truman later wrote of Jacobson. "Not only had we shared so much of the past, but I have always had the warmest feelings toward him. It would be hard to find a truer friend." Jacobson even visited Truman in Key West, an invitation that was rarely extended to outsiders, and in a series of filmed interviews that Truman gave in 1963 and 1964, he called Jacobson "one of the finest people I've ever had anything to do with," and said that, as business associates, "he and I completely understood each other and we offset each other."

Jacobson visited the White House a number of times, and while Truman was usually happy to see him, he was not happy when Jacobson showed up, uninvited, on March 13, 1948. Truman knew that Jacobson was there to talk about Palestine; he intended to tell him "I wanted to let the matter run its course in the United Nations." The visit lasted about forty-five minutes, and as Truman recalled (a story repeated in most Truman biographies, complete with its unlikely dialogue), Jacobson pointed to a sculpture of Andrew Jackson and said, "I have never met the man who has been my hero all my life. But I have studied his past as you have studied Jackson's." His hero, he said, was Chaim Weizmann, the seventy-three-year-old future president of Israel—"perhaps the greatest Jew who ever lived," Jacobson said. "He is an old man and a very sick man. He has traveled thousands of miles to see you, and now you are putting off seeing him. That isn't like you."

It's a lovely story, but, according to Abraham Granoff, a Kansas City lawyer who'd once accompanied Jacobson to the White House, "it's more or less fiction"—including Jacobson's purported affection for Weizmann: "I don't think Weizmann's name ever passed our lips before this incident came up," he recalled. But the President agreed to see Weizmann, and told Jacobson (in several accounts) something like "All right you baldheaded son-of-a-bitch, let him come." Five days later, on March 18, Weizmann visited the White House, arriving through the east entrance, unobserved by reporters, and spoke to Truman for about fifteen minutes. No official record of their conversation exists.

Truman later recalled that he hadn't learned how to pronounce Chaim—*high-yem*—and called him "Cham" instead. "He was a wonderful man, one of the wisest men I've ever met," he said, and remembered that "we had a long, long conversation." Truman could be a charming storyteller, and in his sentimental version of what happened, he called in Jacobson after Weizmann had left, and said, "You two Jews have put it over on me, and I'm glad you have because I like you both."

3. The new Jewish state—Israel—was proclaimed, in Palestine, on May 14, 1948, after which the United States announced that it would grant de facto recognition. That came as a surprise to delegates at the UN, who were meeting at Flushing Meadows Park, in Queens. It also followed, by two days, another unpleasant meeting in Truman's office, in which Clifford once more assumed the role of advocate—acting, he recalled, at Truman's request.

Marshall wasn't pleased to see Clifford—perfectly groomed, dressed as if for a court appearance. When Clifford urged "prompt recognition" of Israel, Marshall's face reddened. "I don't even know why Clifford is here," the secretary of state said. "He is a domestic adviser, and this is a foreign policy matter." As Clifford recalled it, Truman then said, "Well, General, he's here because I asked him to be here." Marshall later wrote a memorandum in which he said that if Truman went ahead with his Israel plans, "the great dignity of the office of the President would be seriously diminished," and that "the counsel offered by Mr. Clifford was based on domestic political considerations." He repeated something that he'd also said aloud: "that if the President were to follow Mr. Clifford's advice and if in the elections I were to vote, I would vote against the President." George Elsey's notes say "CMC [Clifford] was enraged—& Marshall glared at CMC." Clifford later wrote that Marshall never spoke to him again.

Robert Lovett, who was there and also believed that the administration's policy was being guided by domestic politics, did not glare at Clifford. Lovett was known for his tact as well as a deft use of humor, and glaring wasn't his style. After the meeting broke up, he telephoned Clifford, and suggested that they find a way to cool things down. Five days later, Lovett set down his own misgivings in a memorandum: "Clifford told me that the President was under unbearable pressure to recognize the Jewish state promptly," he wrote. "My protests against the precipitate action and warnings as to consequences with the Arab world appear to have been outweighed by considerations unknown to me, but I can only conclude that the President's political advisers, having failed . . . to make the President a father of the new state, have determined at least to make him the midwife." Whatever Clifford's deep beliefs, loyalty to the President wasn't among them. He confided to George Elsey that he didn't know "whether Truman could even be nominated, let alone elected," and "very privately, *very* privately, he wondered whether Truman was 'deserving of four years more.'"

With no turning back, the administration hastened to invite Weizmann, now the de facto head of state, to visit Washington. Journalists, with an unslaked appetite for White House intrigue, saw that Marshall had lost this argument, and perhaps more: They could write that the secretary of state no longer had his hands firmly on the wheel of foreign policy and, if that was so, who exactly was in charge?

How Truman made his decisions—what advice he got, and from whom—could be hard to track, no doubt because it was hard to find a consistent pattern. For all his admiration of General Marshall, he remained curiously suspicious of his own State Department. "I had thought when General Marshall went over there he'd set them right," he'd written to his sister, in late March 1947, but "the 3rd & 4th levels over there are still the same striped pants conspirators." Along with his discomfort with the professional diplomatic world, where his unanchored opining was a poor fit, was a seeming over-reliance on advisers with military résumés—among them Marshall, Admiral Leahy, and General Walter Bedell Smith, the ambassador to Russia. That didn't escape the attention of a group of clergy, educators, and scientists, including Albert Einstein, who, in early 1948, warned that they exerted a "dangerous influence" over foreign policy. When a *Washington Post* editorial suggested it was time to "liquidate" Leahy's job, the admiral took affronted note in his diary, writing, with just a whiff of anti-Semitism, that "Mr. Meyer"—Eugene Meyer, the publisher of the *Post*—"and Mr. Einstein who have a common racial origin seem to be in agreement in this matter." Truman, in any case, valued Leahy, and was not about to listen to the carping of professional opinion-writers.

During an off-the-record conversation with the *New York Times'* Arthur Krock, Truman confessed to a growing sense of being walled in—and feeling, more than ever, that he needed to remember that "two persons are sitting at this desk. One is Harry Truman, and other is the President of the United States, and I have to be sure that Harry Truman remembers on all occasions that the President is there too."

The birth of the Israeli state, in the years right after the war, had very little to do with State Department protocols or the cool arithmetic of Middle Eastern oil, but rather with an inner tug-of-war between the President's private feelings and the assertive counsel of his close advisers. It had touched something raw inside Harry Truman, the other person always sitting at that desk.

FOURTEEN

The Frontiers of Hazard

Our Russian "friends" seem most ungrateful for the contribution which your great country and mine made to save them. I sometimes think we made a mistake—and then I remember Hitler. He had no heart at all. I believe that Joe Stalin has one but the Polit bureau [sic] won't let him use it.

—President Truman to Winston Churchill,
October 14, 1947

1. In late February 1948, Truman was back in Key West, where, as the White House travel log phrased it, he spent time "sunning, swimming and exercising" with his companions. A more candid entry could have added that he was escaping from the discontents of Southern Democrats, partition in Palestine, and reports that the "action committee" of Czechoslovakia's Communist premier had effectively dismembered what had been a fragile ruling coalition and seized control of the government. A visitor to Prague, a few months earlier, would have found a city that appeared prosperous, so unlike the rest of Europe, yet whose people recognized the threatening presence of Soviet agents. Jan Masaryk, the son of Tomas Masaryk, the country's founder and first elected president, had been expected to follow his father's path. The putsch, in the nascent stage of the Cold War, put an end to the innocent hope that Czechoslovakia, having experienced more than its share of betrayals, might find its way to some sort of middle ground between Soviet Communism and

Western democracy. Some remembered that Jan Masaryk had received the longest, and loudest, applause at the first UN conference, in San Francisco, when he'd said, "Let us please stop talking about the next world war."

The news from Czechoslovakia so disturbed Senator Vandenberg, the chairman of the Foreign Relations Committee, that he pushed for accelerated passage of the European Recovery Act—the Marshall Plan—which had been the subject of repetitive hearings since late December. "There is only one voice left in the world . . . to hearten the determination of other nations and other peoples in Western Europe to survive in their own choice of their own way of life," he said, from the floor of the Senate. "Whatever our answer is to be, let it be made as swiftly as prudence will permit. The exposed frontiers of hazard move almost hourly to the west." Vandenberg had asked not to be interrupted while he spoke, and when he was done, senators of both parties rose and applauded. Secretary of State Marshall told Truman, in a memorandum, that the Communists "have succeeded, by terror and the threat of force, in establishing a Communist dictatorship," and that quick passage of the act, without "crippling amendments," was essential.

All this was on Truman's mind when, on March 5, a few hours before he returned to Washington, he wrote a woeful letter to his daughter. It was time, he told her, to have "a record for yourself regarding these times," even if it might seem "a terrible bore," though he surely believed it would not be a bore. His tone was both angry and nervous, as suited someone who'd been thrown thoroughly off balance and wasn't sure what response, if any, to make. "We made agreements on China, Korea and other places none of which has Russia kept," he told the twenty-four-year-old Margaret. "So that now we are faced with exactly the same situation with which Britain + France were faced in 1938/39 with Hitler. A totalitarian state is no different whether you call it Nazi, Fascist, Communist or Franco's Spain." From there, he turned to his personal reading of European history, which sometimes could be difficult to follow: "The oligarchy in Russia is no different from the Czars, Louis XIV, Napoleon,

Charles I and Cromwell," he wrote. "It is a Frankenstein dictatorship worse than any of the others. Hitler included." He continued:
"A decision will have to be made. I am going to make it." The nature
of that decision wasn't spelled out, but it sounded portentous, and
he made it sound more so by adding "Things look black."

On the day of that March 5 letter, General Lucius Dubignon
Clay, the military governor of Occupied Germany, sent a curiously
worded "EYES ONLY" cable to the director of the Pentagon's intelligence division—a message bound to alarm anyone who saw it.
Under Secretary of State Lovett got the impression that Clay was
"drawn as tight as a steel spring," and his cable made the rounds in in
Washington; Secretary of Defense Forrestal, who was often on edge
in any case, copied the text into his diary, under the heading "War—
Likelihood in near Future—Message from Clay." Clay's cable said
that, until recently, he'd thought that war was unlikely for at least a
decade, but now felt "a subtle change in Soviet attitude which I cannot define but which now gives me a feeling that it may come with
dramatic suddenness." This was pure instinct, he admitted, "a feeling of a new tenseness in every Soviet individual with whom we have
official relations," but even in the absence of supporting data, "my
feeling is real." The uneasiness was contagious. According to Gallup,
Americans, by a large majority, believed that the Soviet Union was
determined to rule the world and would, if it could, destroy Chris-
tianity.

On March 10, five days after Clay's cable, Jan Masaryk, the nation's future leader, jumped, or was pushed, from a third-floor window of his apartment, in the Czech Foreign Ministry. Whether it was
suicide or murder, as many suspected, has never been definitively
settled, although the evidence points strongly toward murder. The
next day, in the auditorium of the State Department, Secretary Marshall, who'd developed a tic that tugged at a corner of his mouth,
sat on the edge of a table and talked to several dozen reporters.
He had nothing cheerful to say. He'd told the House Foreign Affairs Committee in January that Russia threatened the stability of
the world, and that there were "barefaced efforts to overthrow the

governments of France and Italy." He called the world situation "very, very serious," said that Czechoslovakia, two weeks after the Communist takeover, was under a "reign of terror," and that the death of Masaryk "indicates very plainly what is going on." Protocol let Marshall decide what could be quoted, so his words were no slip, and meant more because they were spoken by someone widely viewed as a calming influence on an excitable president. Marshall's language was so arresting that he got a gentle scolding from the *New York Times'* James Reston, who agreed that the turmoil in Czechoslovakia was deplorable, but not in the same league as Robespierre's original Reign of Terror. He quoted one "observer" who compared Marshall to a man who stands up in a theater and announces, "I advise everybody here to be very calm because the whole block around this theater is on fire."

That afternoon, during a Truman news conference, a questioner asked about the death of Masaryk. "Of course, I was well acquainted with Mr. Masaryk," Truman said, although they could only have met once, at the first UN conference, "and feel very badly, and am very sorry that he is dead, and shall express my sympathy to his family." He said that he didn't want to make "any official statement on his death or its cause," and that "we should be careful, as General Marshall said, not to let any passions get the better of us until we know the facts." One could be sure, though, that he wanted to say more, and four days later, Charlie Ross told reporters that Truman intended to address a joint session of Congress on March 17. It was clear that the President had come to some sort of decision, or realization, in a hurry.

2. The coup in Czechoslovakia, and the death of Masaryk, were but the latest installments in a slow-motion crisis that had intensified after the Truman Doctrine speech in March 1947, and the introduction, three months later, of the Marshall Plan. It was noteworthy that Truman's upcoming speech was being rushed, and that it would be broadcast nationwide. Truman also planned to speak afterward, in New York, at the Friendly Sons of St. Patrick's

Day dinner, where he could count on a rousing reception. Truman told his staff that the country would be "sunk" if Congress didn't act on what he intended to propose, including reinstatement of the military draft and an endorsement of a mutual defense agreement that was recently signed, in Brussels, by five European nations. Truman didn't elaborate, but Secretary Marshall and others knew that the Brussels Pact was bound to affect the foreign and defense policies of the United States.

The speech that Truman delivered on March 17, 1948, came on one of those Washington days that begin with a sense of impending crisis, with an almost obligatory front-page *New York Times* headline: "Tense Capital Awaits Truman Speech . . . on State of World." James Forrestal found the morning papers "full of rumors and portents of war," and thought that "if all Europe lies flat while the Russian mob tramps over it, we will then be faced with a war under difficult circumstances, and with a very good chance of losing it." Eben Ayers, the deputy press secretary, heard a trace of grandiosity when Truman informed his staff that he was about to make a big decision "on matters of principle, that he did not care what happened to him," as if the big decision might affect only his reputation. Truman acknowledged that General Marshall had worried that he might "pull the trigger"—start a war—but said "it was better to do that than to be caught, as we were in the last war, without having warned the Congress and the people."

When Truman, a year earlier, in the same setting, announced his intention to aid Greece and Turkey, he'd sounded determined, and committed to putting up economic barriers to encroaching Communism. This time, he seemed ready to do battle with this hostile world—perhaps a little too ready. One may read his speech as a public version of the letter he'd written to his daughter—alarmist, almost fearful, despite the unmatched power of the United States military. It was also an echo of what former secretary of war Robert Patterson had said, in the spring of 1947, when, testifying about the National Security Act, he'd declared that "the maintenance of the future peace of the world will depend on the attitude and polices of the United States."

The President hurried through his speech, which he began by saying, "There is an increasing threat to nations which are striving to maintain a form of government which grants freedom to its citizens," and that "it is of vital importance that we act now, in order to preserve the conditions under which we can achieve lasting peace based on freedom and justice." He went on to say that the "Soviet Union and its agents have destroyed the independence and democratic character of a whole series of nations in Eastern and Central Europe," and that the "tragic death of the Republic of Czechoslovakia has sent a shock throughout the civilized world." For emphasis, he added that the Russians were seeking "Communist control and police-state" rule in Europe, and that "this ruthless course of action" had created a "critical situation in Europe today." He did not use a phrase like "reign of terror," as Marshall had, but in asking Congress to reinstate the military draft, he said, "We must be prepared to pay the price for peace, or assuredly we shall pay the price of war." He had planned to call for quick passage of the European Recovery Act, but before he spoke, the Senate, with a push from Vandenberg, had already voted its approval, 69 to 17. The House would soon do the same, in a voice vote.

Truman finished in about eighteen minutes. He never looked up. His audience, which interrupted with applause only three times, reacted with silence when he veered close to issuing a battle cry, saying, "There are times in world history when it is far wiser to act than to hesitate," and "there is some risk involved in action—there always is. But there is far more risk in failure to act." On a scale of bellicosity, though, Truman's speech was a relatively subdued preamble to what was said that night, at the Friendly Sons of St. Patrick's Day dinner. There, in the ballroom of the Hotel Astor, Truman sat next to the archbishop of New York, Francis Spellman, whom the pope, in 1946, had elevated to the College of Cardinals. It was as if, after dark, the spirit of the day had been transported, from the Fifth Avenue parade, the saloons, and inebriated crowds, dressed in green, to the nearly three thousand people in this large room, the tables decorated with flags and green leaves, each place setting accompanied by a green hat and green carnation. The President's flag, the flag of Eire, and the papal flag hung above the dais, where Truman returned to some of the themes he'd addressed earlier that day: The United States had taken on the role of "the principal protector of the free word" and the "faith and strength of the United States are mighty forces for the prevention of war and the establishment of peace." He wanted to sound forceful, and couldn't resist tossing in something about Henry Wallace, now a presidential candidate, who'd accused Truman of "laying the foundation" for war with Russia. Wallace's name hadn't appeared in the advance text, but reporters had been alerted, by Truman himself, that the interpolation was coming: "I do not want and I will not accept the political support of Henry Wallace and his Communists," Truman said, the "his" an outright slur. "These are days of high prices for everything," he added, "but any price for Wallace and his Communists is too much for me to pay. I'll not buy it."

Cardinal Spellman, in his choice of words and phrases, outdid Truman, saying that, in Europe, "we witnessed the killing and enslavement of whole peoples by Communists, who, with the shedding of blood, became as if drunken with it." Spellman's imagery then became gaudy: The world "hangs crucified on its cross of sin— crucified by nails of greed, anarchy, cruelty, and atheism," and "in this hour of dreadful desperate need we are permitting Soviet Russia to continue her policy of persecution and slaughter and dooming our neighbor-nations and ourselves to reap a rotted harvest of appeasement." At the end of the evening the presidential party took the train to Washington.

The next morning, at a White House staff meeting, Truman was in high spirits. He joked about tipping off reporters that a Wallace remark was coming; Charlie Ross, he said, "has found the leak in the White House." As for the politics of his St. Patrick's Day speeches, Clark Clifford (or James Rowe) had already noted, in their lengthy political memo, that "there is considerable political advantage to the Administration in its battle with the Kremlin. . . . The nation is already united behind the President on this issue. The worse matters get . . . the more is there a sense of crisis. In time of crisis the American citizen tends to back up his President."

3. Berlin, in the spring of 1948, was no longer a site of postwar harmony among the victors, if it ever had been, but rather an unwelcome Western island situated inside the Russian zone of Occupied Germany. Since the end of the war, there'd been hassles at border crossings and outbreaks of violence that the Russians were unable, or unwilling, to control. Admiral Leahy was receiving reports—unconfirmed, but taken seriously—that Russia was preparing for military moves in Western Europe. The Western powers, meanwhile, planned to combine the three Western zones, and establish the deutschmark as a stable currency. That wasn't a military threat, but a promise of something more worrisome: a prosperous West Germany, the reverse image of the Communist East.

On March 31, 1948, the Soviet Command announced that American military trains passing through the Soviet zone were required to submit to inspection, and began to stop passenger trains leaving Belin. On June 20, the Russians made a more aggressive move: to further isolate Berlin by blockading roads, rails, and waterways, leaving only three air corridors unimpeded. The Soviet blockade created a crisis that could have escalated into a shooting war that no one wanted, fought over a city that was considered indefensible. Admiral Leahy judged the American military situation in Berlin to be "hopeless because sufficient force is not available anywhere for us and we have no information to indicate that the U.S.S.R. is suffering from internal weakness." Although Truman told Senator Connally, the ranking member of the Foreign Relations Committee, "We aren't going to stand for it," the American response was calm. Six days after the blockade began, Secretary Marshall, who'd been admitted to Walter Reed Army Medical Center for a checkup, asserted a principle without making a threat: "We are in Berlin as a result of agreements . . . on the areas of occupation . . . and we intend to stay."

The United States managed to stay, and avoid war, with the help of an airborne operation, approved by Truman, the first of its kind,

which was able to bring food and fuel to the more than two million Berliners. Flying from Frankfurt to Berlin's Tempelhof Airport,
planes often landed just minutes apart, a logistical feat that came
with the perpetual risk that things could go wrong. Sometimes they
did go wrong. Less than two weeks after the airlift began, three men
died in a fatal crash; during fifteen months of what the Germans
called *die Luftbrücke*—"the air bridge"—about a hundred more,
mostly Britons and Americans, were killed in accidents. General
Clay was sure that the airlift could continue "indefinitely"—unless,
that is, the Russians tried to stop it in ways that went beyond occasional outbreaks of aerial gamesmanship. In late July, the West began
a counter-blockade, which blocked traffic to and from the Soviet
zone.

On days of high tension, it was possible to imagine another war.
Given Russia's proximity, and superiority in manpower, it was difficult to imagine such a conflict being fought without nuclear weapons.
The Joint Chiefs had updated the strategy for nuclear conflict with
Russia, arriving at a war plan called TROJAN which included a target list of seventy cities, twenty of them considered first-priority and
which, the Chiefs estimated, would require 133 atomic weapons.

The most recent demonstration of the American nuclear monopoly had come in May 1948, with a new round of tests on Eniwetok
Atoll—the first since 1946's Operation Crossroads. Three "improved" weapons were detonated and were witnessed by military
personnel and scientists, among them the Atomic Energy Commission's Robert Fox Bacher, a Cornell physics professor and Los Alamos veteran. When the five members of the commission reported
back to Truman, Bacher began to say what an extraordinary sight
it had been, going on until Truman interrupted him. "I wanted to
go out and see that," he said. As Bacher continued, Truman rubbed
the back of his neck and said, "Why, that's enough to wipe out a
good part of the world. If we could just have Stalin and his boys
see one of these things, there wouldn't be any question about another war." He continued, "Of course, I don't like the idea of such
things at all. I gave the order for the others and I don't want to have
to do that again, ever. What I hope you will work hard at is the

peaceful things about it, not the destructive. But until we are sure about peace, there's nothing else to do." As Truman spoke, David Lilienthal, the commission's chairman, found it painful to look at his face, "so marked" by weariness.

When Truman said, "I gave the order for the others," it was a way of saying that he didn't intend to alter custody arrangements for atomic weapons—that he wouldn't transfer responsibility from the civilian Atomic Energy Commission back to the military, which Forrestal and others had been urging. He didn't want "to have some dashing lieutenant colonel decide when would be the proper time to drop one."

Lilienthal wanted to reassure Truman that the peaceful uses of nuclear energy were on the minds of the commissioners. "Mr. President," he said, "you couldn't have picked a less bloodthirsty six men if you had tried for a long time."

"That's why I believe in a civilian Commission," Truman replied. "I feel just like you about it. But we have this to do, and you have made fine progress."

Before the commissioners made their exit, Lilienthal remarked on how well the five had managed to work together, to which Truman responded with an appealing, generous homily: "I told you that poor men couldn't make a good law succeed, and that good men could make even a poor law succeed," he said. "I appointed good men."

FIFTEEN

The Scrapper

I'm a homegrown American farm product. . . . And I'm proud
of the breed I represent—the completely unterrified form of
American democracy.

—Harry Truman, at the State Fairgrounds in Raleigh,
North Carolina, on October 19, 1948

1. The 1948 presidential race is remembered for the
zest with which Harry Truman pursued his first, and last, run for
the presidency, and for its surprise ending, which Truman always
said was no surprise to him. He seemed remarkably able to shrug
off the possibility that he might not even be nominated (a fanciful
substitute was General Eisenhower), and to appear unrattled by the
stress and the unwelcome surprises that come with the job. Doctors
at Walter Reed had discovered a worrisome swelling in Secretary
of State Marshall's right kidney, a potential medical emergency that
could not be ignored. Defense Secretary Forrestal was showing signs
of unsteadiness, and was rumored to have placed a discreet bet on
Truman's probable opponent, Governor Thomas E. Dewey. That
rumor was probably spread by Harry Vaughan, who was said to have
it in for Forrestal. Even the White House, with creaking floors and
falling plaster, was a worry: "Now my bath room is about to fall
into the Red Parlor," Truman wrote to Mary Jane, with only slight
exaggeration.

In early June 1948, Truman escaped from Washington with a two-
week pre-campaign trip aboard the *Ferdinand Magellan*, to "find out
what people are thinking about," and to be cheered by the applause

of strangers. "If I felt any better I couldn't stand it," he said before the train pulled out of Union Station, where Marshall and Forrestal were among those who'd come to see him off. The traveling entourage included Charlie Ross, Harry Vaughan, and Clark Clifford, with Bess and Margaret planning to board the train in Omaha. The *Washington Post*'s Edward Folliard, who was fond of Truman, observed "an entirely different man from the one his countrymen have come to know from the radio networks and the newsreels," someone who'd become a better politician: "There is a melody in his voice, a pace and a sincerity that are utterly lacking when he has a manuscript before him." The excursion gave Truman a chance to greet local office-holders, tell stories about his Missouri boyhood, and celebrate the Democrats as the party of the farmer, the workingman, and whoever qualified as an "ordinary American." This relaxed, even improvisational approach brought with it imprudent moments, as when, in Eugene, Oregon, referring to the Potsdam conference, he said, "I went there with the kindliest feelings in the world toward Russia. I got very well acquainted with Joe Stalin, and I like old Joe—he is a decent fellow. But Joe is a prisoner of the politburo. He can't do what he wants to." That phrase—"I like old Joe"—was unlikely to be forgotten, and was the sort of remark that inspired cracks like "To err is Truman."

He attacked the Republican Congress, a reliable target, and said it will "go down in history as the special-privilege Congress." That was enough for Senator Vandenberg to reply that Truman, unlike Congress, was taking a "self-serving political vacation," and to point out that, thanks to congressional Republicans, Truman had gotten his way on the big things: aid to Greece and Turkey and passage of the Marshall Plan. When Senator Taft accused "our gallivanting president" of "blackguarding Congress at every whistle stop in the West"—a reference to the small towns that trains raced through, often with no more than a warning whistle—Truman seized on that phrase, and said, "Before this campaign is over, I expect to visit every whistle stop in the United States." But then Truman wasn't aiming for an elevated dialogue. He'd admitted as much to General Marshall when he'd told him not to pay attention to anything he said during a campaign: "It's going to be a rough fight with no holds barred, but this is home politics and need not concern you."

2. Republicans met during the last week of June, in Philadelphia. After three ballots, they chose Governor Dewey over Senator Taft, his chief competitor, and Dewey chose Earl Warren, the California governor, to complete the ticket. The tone of the first presidential campaign since the war did not suggest that much had changed in the level of discourse. Clare Boothe Luce, the former two-term congresswoman, playwright, and wife of the *Time* magazine founder Henry Luce, showed off her writerly talent, and rhetorical wickedness, when she described a tripartite Democratic Party made up of the "lynch-loving, white-shirted race-supremacists of the Bilbo ilk"; the "Moscow wing," which was "masterminded by Stalin's Mortimer Snerd, Henry Wallace"; and the "Pendergast wing," run by the "wampum and boodle boys." She reminded delegates what "the little New Dealer" had said about Stalin: "Good old Joe!"

It was being said that the President was a little man unable to handle his big job; Walter Lippmann said that his whistle-stop tour was proof to the country "how small a part Mr. Truman plays in the great office which he holds." Truman's overall approval was down to 36 percent, and his party was being pulled apart, losing both Henry Wallace voters and Southern Democrats. Many appeared ready to abandon him; he was being faulted for inept leadership, "narrow intelligence," and the influence of the "Missouri Gang." Truman seemed very much alone, cheering himself on in a hopeless cause—an election very few thought he had a chance of winning. For other Democratic office-holders, the 1946 Republican sweep seemed predictive of more trouble. In this climate, there were still pleas for someone—*anyone*— to replace Truman before the Democrats convened in mid-July.

Eisenhower's stubborn enthusiasts hadn't given up, although the general, who'd never declared a party affiliation, had other plans. He was about to retire as army chief of staff and become president of Columbia University. His fans included at least two of President

Roosevelt's four sons, the liberal Americans for Democratic Action, and the right-leaning *Manchester Union Leader* in New Hampshire, whose publisher, Leonard Finder, had written an "open letter" to Eisenhower in which he said it was the general's duty to run. Eisenhower replied that, while he respected the political profession (though, in truth, he didn't), "my decision to remove myself completely from the political scene is definite and positive." Eisenhower meant it, and told James Forrestal, a friend, that he'd worked hard on his letter. Yet he was vain enough to worry that some might interpret it as a "refusal to respond to duty, around which," he told Forrestal, his entire life had been built. Forrestal, for his part, was said to have replied, "Ike, with that puss you can't miss being President."

Truman kept his unhappiest thoughts mostly to himself. One mid-June day, sitting on the South Porch of the White House, he reflected on the clamor of politics: "A mocking bird imitates robins, jays, red birds, crows, hawks—but has no individual note of his own. A lot of people like that." In a letter to Mary Jane, he referred to people "whose definition of loyalty is loyalty to themselves. . . . Take the Roosevelt clan as an example." The matriarch of the Roosevelt clan was embarrassed by her anti-Truman children and, in her newspaper column, wrote that her sons "are grown men and I decided long ago that once children were grown they must be allowed to lead their own lives." The Roosevelt name still had worldwide cachet, so much so that, when Secretary of State Marshall, on March 26, learned that Franklin Jr. was about to urge an Eisenhower draft, he worried about its impact on foreign policy. Through Marshall's hurried intercession, Eisenhower was persuaded to telephone Roosevelt's namesake, to warn him that "any action of this kind now, in the middle of very delicate situations in various parts of the world, could have the most dangerous consequences." Franklin Jr. nonetheless endorsed Eisenhower later that day.

Pondering what appeared to him to be a broken party, Walter Lippmann concluded that the only hope for a Democratic victory lay with the reluctant Eisenhower. Otherwise, Democrats would need a plausible alternative to Truman—a caretaker who, after Truman's certain defeat in November, could watch over the party's recovery.

Lippmann's choice for the role of party concierge was Alben Barkley, the seventy-year-old minority leader, who wanted the presidential nomination for himself. That suggestion struck A. J. Liebling as "what must surely be the first printed appeal to a major party to throw an election." In a letter to Churchill, Truman, feeling battered from several sides, made a rare admission: "I am going through a terrible political 'trial by fire,' " he said. "Too bad it must happen at this time." By that he meant the situation in Berlin: " 'Communism'—so called, is our next great problem. I hope we can solve it without the 'blood and tears' the other two cost." The Berlin airlift was still going well, although, just days before the Democratic Convention, a C-47 food plane struck a low mountain peak near Frankfurt, killing two air force officers and a civilian passenger.

Barkley, recalling the mood in Philadelphia, said "You could cut the gloom with a corn knife." It struck the *Washington Post*'s Folliard as feeling "creepy" and "funereal," and it was otherwise noticed that a number of well-known Democrats, among them Mrs. Roosevelt, had gone missing. Truman was finding it difficult to recruit a running mate. He asked Justice William Douglas and told him he "owes it to the country to accept." When Douglas turned him down—he didn't intend to quit the court to take a flier on something with such a chancy future—Truman relegated him to the category of "crackpots whose word is worth less than Jimmy Roosevelt's," and added the thought that "no professional liberal is intellectually honest." Truman found himself more or less forced to run with his old friend Barkley, who imagined he might get the nomination for himself and had agreed to give the keynote address. Among Barkley's promoters was Leslie Biffle, the secretary of the Senate, whom Truman suspected of double-dealing. "My 'good' friend, Leslie Biffle, spends all his time as sergeant-at-arms at the Convention running Barkley for President," a diary entry read. Barkley, whose self-importance sometimes competed with his good-natured pomposity, later quoted himself telling supporters, "If anybody puts my name in nomination, I will arise and renounce it," but no one did nominate him, so only Barkley knew if he meant it. He did show off his septuagenarian fitness when a hotel elevator broke down and he walked up eight flights to his room.

Truman reminded himself to "call old man Barkley and smooth his feathers so he'll go ahead and make the keynote speech," and the keynote, delivered on July 12, the convention's first night, was a great success. In an era without much air-conditioning, the hall was hellishly hot, though not so hot as to calm the enthusiasm for Barkley, visible from the floor as a florid man in a white suit. Delegates shouted "Pour it on, Barkley! Pour it on!" and Barkley loved it. When he was done, after speaking for more than an hour, he sulked; he didn't like being portrayed as too eager, or too old, and it was reported that he might regard an offer to join the ticket as coming too late. "I don't want any warmed-over biscuits after they have been passed around to everybody else," he said. But few doubted that Barkley would seize the biscuit were it offered, which it was—and then, unhesitatingly, he did.

Both nominating conventions were televised, and the four networks—NBC, CBS, ABC, and DuMont—reached an audience of about ten million, all in the East. Five o'clock shadows were noticeable; some of the men resisted using lipstick. But for the first time, people at home, including the President, could experience the boredom, perspiration, and tantrums of a political convention. "I watch the demonstration on television," Truman wrote in his diary, on July 13, the day before he was to be nominated. "Having been in on numerous demonstrations, I'm not fooled. I can see everything taking place on the platform. The 'actors' forget that." Then, in a spurt of displeasure, he added, "Barkley in his good speech mentions me only casually by name."

It was raining in Philadelphia when Truman's train arrived, on July 14, late in the afternoon. As the evening wore on, he stayed out of sight, on a freight-loading platform at the rear of the convention hall, where he could watch passing trains and listen to speeches. The convention came to angry life when delegates considered a civil rights plank. Despite what Truman had said to the NAACP at the Lincoln Memorial a year earlier, he wanted the convention to consider an innocuous affirmation, not a troublesome plank that called for "the right of full and equal political participation" and "the right of equal opportunity of employment," words that were bound to end any pretense of political harmony. Its author was the thirty-seven-year-old mayor of Minneapolis, Hubert Horatio Humphrey, a Senate candidate, and a pharmacist by training. His declaration that "the time has arrived for the Democratic party to get out of the shadow of states' rights and walk forthrightly into the bright sunshine of human rights" was enough to nudge the Mississippi delegation and half the Alabama delegation to walk out. Senator Lister Hill, of Alabama, remained inside the hall, where he shouted, "You shall not crucify the South on this cross of civil rights." Truman had to wait nearly four hours for the delegates to nominate him.

Joe Alsop recalled the 1948 convention as "one of the outwardly saddest and generally most dank political gatherings I have watched," although with vivid moments. "The most somber of all of these" came toward the end of the session, with the President still outside the hall, "wearing a pressed white linen suit and waiting, completely alone." Alsop continued: "Truman appeared to be as jaunty as ever, but at long intervals he took a pull on a half bottle of liquid that was in his pocket. The president, I learned later, had a stomach ailment that night, and, in all likelihood, this was some form of medicine." Joe and his brother Stewart decided not to report "seeing the president of the United States reduced to such a lonely plight." Also left unsaid was the possibility that Truman was having a nip of spirits, though, given Truman's limited, but regular, intake of bourbon, it was not unlikely. The bottle might also have contained what Truman called "snake oil," a home remedy prescribed by the White House doctor, Wallace Graham, who'd once told his patient that when he was "under a lot of stress," his lungs produced "a little more fluid than usual."

It was nearly 2 a.m. on Wednesday (or Thursday, July 15) when Truman, having won the nomination, reached the microphones. With much of the nation asleep, and speaking from notes, he said, "Senator Barkley and I will win this election and make these Republicans like it—don't you forget that! We will do that because they are wrong and we are right." He promised to call Congress back to Washington on July 26—"Turnip Day" in Missouri—to deal with civil rights, aid to education, and more. (The reference was to a Missouri saying: "On the twenty-sixth of July, sow your turnips, wet or dry.") If his words were angry, they were probably directed as much toward those Democrats who'd wanted to replace him with someone like Eisenhower, and toward the Southerners who'd walked out, as toward the Republicans who intended to defeat him. Truman that night was declaring his independence, taking the stage in his most genuine role, as a scrappy champion of the American underdog, an identity that no Republican could possibly assume.

With elegant timing, when Turnip Day arrived, Truman signed Executive Orders 9980 and 9981, which ordered the desegregation of the federal workforce and committed the federal government to integrating the military services. These changes wouldn't be felt overnight; desegregation of the military would wait until the Eisenhower administration. But the signings did announce that the old order was on its way out, and it was Truman who'd made the announcement.

3. Two days later, six thousand Southern Democrats, from thirteen states, convened in Birmingham, Alabama, and nominated Governor Thurmond as the "states-rights" Presidential candidate. Henry Wallace's minuscule Progressive Party met in late July, in Philadelphia. Wallace's would-be vice president was Senator Glen Taylor, of Idaho, whose career had reached its pinnacle the previous November, when, wearing a white sombrero, he rode up the steps of the Capitol, on a sorrel horse named Nugget. Truman told his staff, "We are going to be on the road most of the time from Labor Day to the end of the campaign. . . . I know I can take it. I'm only afraid that it'll kill some of my staff—and I like you all very much and I don't want to do that."

By mid-September, aboard the *Ferdinand Magellan*, Truman was averaging about one speech per waking hour, and creating a portrait of himself that would outlast the campaign. "I'm going to fight hard," he said, "and I'm going to give 'em hell." If the traveling press corps saw a man isolated in a custom-built car, Truman could only see enthusiastic crowds. On occasion, he might say (as rendered by the *New Yorker*'s Richard Rovere), "And now, howja like to meet ma family?" Then he'd invite Bess to the rear platform, saying, "This is the Boss," followed by Margaret, saying, "This is the boss' boss." (In some regions it would be "And now I'd like *for* you to meet Miss Margaret.") Sometimes he'd invite people to come aboard, a practice that the Secret Service hated. In nostalgic memory, especially in a time when candidates hurry from venue to venue by jet plane, a campaign by rail is something to be savored, although not by those who were along for the ride. "The only thing is you can't take a bath," the *Christian Science Monitor*'s Richard Strout recalled when he talked about life aboard a campaign train. "You get kind of high after the third week, you know, but it was a traveling circus."

After Labor Day, the poll-taker Elmo Roper reported that Dewey "is almost as good as elected to the Presidency." Therefore, he wrote, "I can think of nothing duller or more intellectually barren" than to treat the remaining eight weeks of the campaign as some sort of horse race. Roper sounded ready to change professions, writing that "I do not wholly approve of Presidential predicting under any circumstances. It has become a stunt." It was "virtually certain," the *New York Times* reported, that the states' rights Democrats, supporting Governor Thurmond, would win at least forty-five electoral votes from eleven states. (It turned out to be four states, and thirty-nine electoral votes.)

Truman's frenetic campaigning became a way to relax, to close off the world, though he never lost sight of what was happening beyond the windows of the *Ferdinand Magellan*. In early September, when the situation in Berlin deteriorated—riots and the kidnappings of Westerners, instigated by the Communists—he returned to Washington to meet with Marshall, Forrestal, and the National Security Council. Marshall often looked fatigued, his face flushed. He'd been making regular trips from his home, in Leesburg, Virginia, to Walter Reed, where his swollen kidney had been monitored since June; by September, it was twice its normal size, and doctors told him it had to be removed—an operation that Marshall decided to delay so that he could attend United Nations General Assembly meetings in Paris, which were supposed to continue past October.

Truman met with reporters on September 9, and more or less ducked questions on the clashes in Berlin, much as Marshall had

done the day before. "We have been trying to negotiate all our difficulties," the President said. "We have been negotiating ever since the
war ended, and we are going to continue negotiating, hoping to get a
settlement. You can't settle it in any other way." In his diary, two days
later, he wrote, "Spend a most pleasant day talking of world affairs,
western trip, speeches, prima donnas in government, etc." It did not
take long for his mood to change: "Have a terrific day," he wrote in
his diary, though he didn't mean that in a good way: "Forestal [*sic*],
Bradley . . . Symington brief me on bases, bombs, Moscow, Lenin-
grad, etc." Then, once again, he considered the worst: "I have a
terrible feeling afterward that we are very close to war. I hope not."
Lunch with Secretary Marshall was slightly reassuring: "feel better
although Berlin is a mess. My staff is a turmoil." Marshall was sure
that the "present tension in Berlin" and "Russian desperation" had
been set off by the reception, in Europe, of the European Recovery
Act. Before he left for Paris, according to his biographer Ed Cray, he
"apparently" told Truman, during an unannounced meeting, that he
needed an operation and planned to retire in January. There was no
public announcement, though; the reelection campaign was already
shaky enough.

In light of discouraging polls and rumors of war, two of Truman's speechwriters, David Noyes and Albert Z. Carr, thought that
something dramatic was needed to give the campaign a boost. Carr
was sure that "the theme of peace, which had been systematically
woven into [Truman's] speeches, was invariably popular," and the
two of them came up with a scheme that involved sending Fred Vinson, the chief justice, to confer with Stalin, the chief Communist.
Vinson was reluctant, but Truman liked the idea, and preparations
went ahead swiftly. Broadcast time for a "non-political" presidential
speech, for what could have been an electrifying radio event, was
quickly cleared on CBS.

It made a kind of sense. Truman and Vinson, both from rural
districts in border states, had been friends and poker-playing companions since the mid-1930s. Stalin, it was thought, might welcome
this show of peaceful intent. But the idea of sending someone so
unready as Vinson on a diplomatic mission, in a time of international

friction, had not been fully thought through. Furthermore, Truman had not only bypassed the United Nations, but Britain and France, who shared responsibility for Occupied Berlin. Worse than that, he hadn't informed his secretary of state, who was back in Paris, attending the UN meetings.

The Vinson-to-Moscow idea led to a bureaucratic panic greater than the panic, two years earlier, when Truman endorsed—and then didn't endorse—Henry Wallace's speech at Madison Square Garden. This time, when Under Secretary of State Lovett learned about the Vinson plan, he called the White House and, as he jotted in his logbook, said, "Mr. President, I've got to see you right away, urgent." Lovett, worried that the story might leak, told his driver to go as fast as he could: "Wham, he throws on this red light and the siren and away we go"—the first time he'd used the red flasher in an official car. When he saw Truman, on October 5, a Tuesday morning, he said, "This is utterly impossible. You are not only going to lose the Secretary of State but are going to lose the whole mission." Truman, with typical patience, replied, "Well you tell me about it." Truman soon canceled the Vinson plan, and hurried to mend matters with Marshall, in a teletype conversation.

Marshall flew back to Washington, where he told reporters that he'd been called home by the President and that there was "no foundation" to reports of any split. As for the Vinson plan, which by then had got out, Marshall said, with laconic avoidance, that he and the President had discussed it, by teletype, and that was when Truman "decided it would not be advisable to take this action. The matter was then dropped."

Truman, who'd been off campaigning in Buffalo, got back to Washington barely in time to meet Marshall, whose plane had circled National Airport until the President arrived. "I am grateful to you," Marshall said when they greeted each other, perhaps as much in appreciation of Truman's personal welcome as of his quick abandonment of Vinson's voyage. The only hint of Marshall's annoyance came when reporters asked him if he'd be returning the next day to the White House, and Marshall, making it clear that he was speaking off the record, said, "I hope not."

Truman tried to portray what had happened as merely an earnest search for peace in a troubled world, but Lovett had his suspicions. He thought that Clark Clifford might have been an instigator, acting on a belief that Truman was, at bottom, a naïf: "That's the first and only time that I know of where a fast one was tried and the President just didn't understand it." Lovett still worried that Truman might say something silly, and asked John Snyder, the treasury secretary and a close Truman friend, "how the President could be protected from that sort of thing." Could Snyder accompany Truman, "to avoid a recurrence"? Snyder, though, said he was too busy to get involved.

It didn't quite end there. Lovett soon heard that Truman was "going to try something else, along the lines of the Vinson affair, something like a bilingual conversation between him and the gentleman (Stalin)." That information must have come from Senators Vandenberg or Connally. They'd recently seen Truman, and he'd asked what they thought about him making a "person-to-person phone call to Stalin"—realizing, perhaps, that a station-to-station call to the Kremlin might not get through. The senators discouraged him. "You don't know any Russian and he doesn't know any English," Connally said. "Besides there's the question of authenticity. After you finish talking, what will you have?" Connally thought that Truman looked disappointed, and recalled that, as they left, Vandenberg said, "He must be feeling desperate about the campaign." Although Truman certainly hadn't thought it through, he no doubt hoped that *something* good might come of it, not least, as Vandenberg observed, a helpful bump in his poll numbers.

On September 28, in Dexter, Iowa, before a farm audience estimated at between sixty and eighty thousand, Truman called his opponents "gluttons of privilege" who have "stuck a pitchfork in the farmer's back," and said that Republicans were beholden to Wall Street masters who were "cold and cunning men." That was a not-bad rejoinder to Senator Taft, who had said that Truman wanted Congress to pass a "police state program."

Three days before the vote, Truman campaigned in Queens, and said, "You can throw the Gallup Poll right into the ashcan." By then, he seemed almost to have lost sight of the idea that he was competing for the presidency—to have decided simply to enjoy the contest as a contest, as if he were once more running for a Jackson County judgeship, a liberation of the spirit. On Election Day, he went to the Elm Hotel in Excelsior Springs, thirty-two miles from Independence. By then, all he wanted was a hot mineral-water bath and a chance to be alone. He ate a ham-and-cheese sandwich, drank buttermilk, and by 7 p.m. was in bed, and asleep, though it could not have been a very sound sleep, no matter what he later claimed. He woke up at midnight, to listen to a radio broadcast, and slept, until four-thirty, after which he got up, shaved, and dressed. At 5 a.m., he listened to the news again. "The news was good," he told Charlie Ross, "and so I decided to come in to town."

Office Politics

The difficulty has been the removal of those human frictions
that are inevitable in government, or, for that matter, in the
military world, that are not removable either by law or directive (in both cases the solutions are apt to come unstuck by
Thursday).

—James Forrestal, in a letter to Roscoe Drummond,
on December 23, 1948

1. Four days after the election, when the city could ex-
hale, more than two hundred showed up for a formal dance at the
Sulgrave Club, a Beaux Arts–style mansion near Dupont Circle.
There, mixing on the dance floor, in motion with cabinet officers,
the military, and diplomats, one could spot Clark and Marnie Clifford, the very image of glamor and success, Washington-style, as well
as Jim and Jo Forrestal, showing no sign of the ruinous strains on
their marriage. Changes were coming, as they did after every election, though not right away. Truman knew that Secretary of State
Marshall was planning to step down. Everyone knew that Forrestal's
future was shaky; he'd never belonged to the small group that Truman most relied on. He was often the subject of barely coded news
stories, filled with anonymous darts, suggesting, as one put it, that he
was "expected to take the 'graceful way out' by resigning," and that
the White House "already was looking for a successor."

The President was not among the dancers at the Sulgrave. Rather,
he'd left right away for Key West, his fifth visit, after a welcome in
Union Station that he judged to be "the greatest in the history of

this old capital." Before leaving, Truman held a short cabinet meeting, and asked for suggestions to include in his State of the Union
speech. It was to be his longest stay yet in the Keys, about two weeks,
and he began it by growing a sort-of beard—chin whiskers, with a
mustache on the way. When a reporter asked about his visible gray
stubble—"What is that, a Van Dyke?"—Truman replied, "No, it's
not a Van Dyke, it's a Jeff Davis." He asked "Where are your cameras?" knowing that a "lid" was on, meaning there would be no
photographic record of his unshavenness. Even Clark Clifford, usually dressed with lawyerly correctness, was going barefoot, in worn
slacks, looking so unkempt that Truman started calling him "Jeeter,"
after a character in Erskine Caldwell's *Tobacco Road*. Many of his
usual companions were already on hand, and were soon joined
by two more from the bourbon-and-branch-water crowd—Vice
President-elect Barkley, who nearly ran over a cat, and Leslie Biffle.

Truman was a man at rest, one day wearing seersucker slacks and a
white linen sports shirt that pulled up when he raised his arms—"it fits
me quick," he said—and sometimes the garish Hawaiian shirts which
were almost an act of defiance. His morning walks usually took him
off the naval compound and into town, from the Green Street gate to
Simonton, then to Southard, and back to the base. He liked to go near
the water, and could stray over to touristy Duval Street. The weather
was in the low eighties, and, as if to mark this hiatus as a special occasion, Truman for the first time invited the traveling press to join him
on what was being called "Truman Beach," a rocky stretch that had
once been accessible from the Little White House. "He had on his
swim trunks for his daily sun bath and swim," the wire-service reporter
Robert G. Nixon recalled. "He was pretty full of himself, naturally."

Naturally.

Truman didn't gloat, at least not in the spirit of, say, Kipling's
Stalky; there was no *"Ti-ra-ra-la-i-tu! I gloat! Hear me!"* He did,
though, take pleasure in recalling the words of those who'd got it
wrong, and he savored the "Dewey Defeats Truman" headline that
ran in early editions of the *Chicago Tribune*, which beame a treasure
for collectors of political ephemera. In their *Herald Tribune* column
published the morning after the vote, but overtaken by inconvenient

deadlines, the Alsop brothers had written that "events will not wait patiently" until Dewey was sworn in, and they warned about the hazards of "flying dual-control." And Truman did draft a note to the pollster Elmo Roper, to inform him that "candidates make election contests, not pole [*sic*] takers or press comments by paid column writers." He had every right to wallow in victory: He'd not only won the presidency, by sizable electoral- and popular-vote margins—without help from the Solid South or New York—but Democrats once again held majorities in both houses of Congress. "You've got to give the little man credit," Senator Vandenberg told his staff on the morning after. "Everyone had counted him out but he came up fighting and won the battle. He did it all by himself. That's the kind of courage the American people admire." Truman couldn't forget what the smart columnists had written about the smallness of his presidency, and the impossible odds against its success; he'd refer to the Alsop brothers as the "sop sisters," and remarked that Walter Lippmann "should be working from a latrine" rather than an ivory tower. He didn't keep a list of enemies, but he knew who his allies were, he knew who held him in contempt; and he didn't forget. And he knew, as Vandenberg and others had recognized, that he'd done it pretty much alone, without much help from what his deputy press secretary, Eben Ayers, referred to as "Wednesday morning Democrats."

That meant a lot: He was no longer a president-by-happenstance— owing everything to the mortality of Roosevelt—but because millions of Americans had voted for him, and, in doing so, had given him more authority, and confidence, a new, if still unacknowledged, sensation. There was no way to foresee that the election marked a dividing line in the Truman presidency: that after nearly four years, when so much had gone so well, the supply of good fortune, for the President and the country, might be running low.

⸎

The Key West interlude ended on November 21, when the Trumans returned to Washington, although not to the White House, which, on November 7, had been closed for repairs and was off-limits to tourists and social occasions. A ceiling in the East Room was now supported by scaffolding, and the marble grand staircase used for receptions was at risk of crumbling. Congress needed to appropriate money for renovations, and there were suggestions that the hundred-and-fifty-year-old mansion might become a museum—that something more modern could take its place. The Trumans in any case would take up residence across Lafayette Square, in Blair House, with access to the adjacent Lee House. While repairs went on, the Oval Office would remain a working office. Truman could walk to work, though the walks were halted by the Secret Service when a sightseeing business started selling president-watching tickets. Truman missed having that bit of exercise.

In his State of the Union message, delivered in early January 1949, Truman announced a "Fair Deal," in which he urged more economic equality, including the idea that "our economic system should rest on a democratic foundation and that wealth should be created for the benefit of all." He asked for a national health insurance program: "We need—and we must have without further delay—a system of prepaid medical insurance which will enable every American to afford good medical care," he said, adding, "In a nation as rich as ours, it is a shocking fact that tens of millions lack adequate medical care."

That was not a surprising, or new, policy. In November 1945—just seven months after being sworn in—Truman had asked Congress for a compulsory medical insurance plan. When that enlisted little support, he tried again in the spring of 1947, in a message to Congress, looking for a program "to make available enough medical services to go around, and to see that everybody has a chance to obtain those services." What might have been called "Trumancare" would have cost six to seven billion dollars, paid for by a 3 percent payroll tax. Like its 1945 ancestor, it was dead from the moment of its arrival at the Senate's Labor and Public Welfare Subcommittee. At the start of his full term, though, Truman was not about to give up on that elusive goal.

White House renovations ruled out its being used for a reception after the inauguration, on January 20, the first peacetime swearing-in ceremony in eight years. That day bore little resemblance to the somber, even gloomy ceremony four years earlier, on the South Portico of the White House, when the exhausted Franklin Roosevelt had seemed barely present. The mood, in the Washington of early 1949, was one of gaiety and celebration. There were enough private parties to entertain an estimated million out-of-town visitors, and a pre-inaugural gala included a cast of movie and radio celebrities— among them Abbott and Costello, Lena Horne, Alice Faye, who sang "I'm Just Wild About Harry," and the comedienne Joan Davis, who joked that she'd sat next to a senator "who from force of habit refused to pass anything." Truman got his public gloat, at an electoral college dinner, where he mimicked the NBC radio commentator H. V. Kaltenborn's on-air predictions of defeat, saying, in Kaltenborn's recognizably clipped voice, "Mr. Truman is a million votes ahead in the popular vote, but when the complete returns are in he will be defeated by an overwhelming majority." The crowd loved it, Truman loved doing it, and no one seemed to have any memory of the Truman who'd been headed for the forgotten pages of history.

Before the swearing-in, Truman attended a fifteen-minute prayer service at St. John's Episcopal Church, situated across Lafayette Square from the White House, taking his seat in Pew 63, the spot reserved for presidents since the time of James Madison. Along with the Truman family, and a few regular parishioners, the pews were filled by Truman people, among them Barkley, Chief Justice Vinson, Attorney General Tom Clark, and Forrestal, increasingly disconnected, although two weeks earlier, the President and Bess had come to dinner at Prospect House, an occasion that included Vinson and General Eisenhower.

Since Secretary of State Marshall returned from Paris, in late November, he'd spent much time at Walter Reed, where a non-cancerous kidney had been removed on December 3. For much of December, the newspapers had been filled with speculation about a successor. That had never been a question for Truman, nor, as it turned out, for Dean Acheson, who'd spent the last sixteen months at his law firm, Covington & Burling. Days before Marshall's operation, Acheson had gone to see Truman on at least three occasions, during which Truman had asked him to become the next secretary of state. "You had better be sitting down when you hear what I have to say," Truman had said, with a big smile, when he offered Acheson the job. Acheson was joyful at the prospect of returning to the State Department. "It has taken years and years, but now I am on my own," he told a friend. Truman announced the appointment on January 7, when Marshall and his deputy, Bob Lovett, formally resigned. On January 20, Acheson was also in a pew at St. John's as churchgoers sang "O God, Our Help in Ages Past," and read, responsively, the 122nd Psalm: "Peace be within thy walls/and prosperity within thy palaces."

At half-past twelve, on a platform on the east side of the Capitol, Truman was sworn in by Vinson, after which he kissed the Bible. Truman and Barkley wore tall silk hats; the Supreme Court justices wore skullcaps. The sun was bright, but a chilly wind swept through. Podium-watchers saw Vinson clapping his hands in time to "Hail to the Chief," and Harry Vaughan popping peanuts into his mouth.

Truman's speech was emphatically pedestrian, a missed opportunity for a president who'd been given a chance to start over, to say something memorable, to expand on some of his Fair Deal ambitions, and chose instead a piling on of woolly platitude. ("Communism is based on the belief that man is so weak and inadequate that he . . . requires the rule of strong masters," while "Democracy is based on the conviction that man has the moral and intellectual capacity, as well as the inalienable right, to govern himself.") The speech is remembered, if that is the word, for the fourth point of what Truman called "four major courses of action," which was a promise to make the "benefits of our scientific advances and industrial progress available for the improvement and growth of underdeveloped areas." He concluded with the thought that "each period of our national history has had its special challenges. Those that confront us now are as momentous as any in the past," and "I say to all men, what we have achieved in liberty, we will surpass in greater liberty." When he was finished, and began shaking hands all around, it looked to some as if Forrestal was being blocked by Treasury Secretary Snyder and Archbishop Patrick O'Boyle, who had stepped forward to deliver the benediction.

The ceremony was followed by the biggest-ever inaugural parade. As if to make up for the austerity of 1944, it lasted for three hours,

showing off floats that included a model of the Empire State Building, a miniature Mardi Gras, Missouri mules, cowboys, Clydesdale
horses, women in skimpy clothes and goose bumps, the marching
bands of the four armed services, and hundreds of aircraft, including
the gargantuan, six-engine B-36 bomber, swooping past. In homage
to Captain Truman, the boys of Battery D paraded, some of whom,
three decades after the Great War, relied on walking canes. General
Eisenhower, who was now installed as the president of Columbia
University, had started the afternoon as a passenger in army secretary
Kenneth Royall's car, but got out to march past the reviewing stand.
When Truman spotted him (in full uniform, his five stars brightly
visible), the President lifted his tall silk hat and waved to the general.
When Strom Thurmond's car drove by, and the former Dixiecrat
doffed his cap, Truman seemed to be looking elsewhere.

3. Truman's regard for Marshall had been such that Marshall told his biographer, Forrest Pogue, "I could get him to approve
anything, but I knew enough to know I didn't have the whole field."
That was overstating it—Marshall didn't get his way on Palestine—
but there was enough truth in it for Kenneth Royall to say that if
Marshall "even intimated any course, that was likely to be the law
of the land."

It was different with Acheson; Truman was never in his thrall,
though he never doubted that Acheson fit the part. An anonymous
Republican congressman once remarked, not entirely in jest, that if
Truman had been ordered to paint a foreign minister, he would have
produced a portrait of Dean Gooderham Acheson, who, in the words
of his son, David, was "a tall, handsome man, 6-feet-1 in height,"
looking more English than American. But more than that, Truman
respected Acheson, trusted him, and had come to rely on him during
Jimmy Byrnes's frequent absences, when Acheson was acting secretary. "The President was almost always inclined to deciding in favor
of the view which I presented, not because I presented it but because
the other view was so silly," Acheson later said. When it came to
foreign policy, Truman was uncomfortable with sustained analysis,

and appreciated Acheson's seeming grasp of the modern world, his stern anti-Communism, and his talent for assessing problems and proposing solutions. In that way, they understood, and benefited, from each other. At fifty-five, Acheson was nine years younger than Truman. He'd gone to Groton, then Yale (class of '15), where his crew coach was Averell Harriman. He received a law degree from Harvard, where one of his professors, the future Supreme Court justice Felix Frankfurter, recommended him as a clerk to Justice Louis D. Brandeis. But Acheson and Truman overcame the crevasse between the Ivy League and Jackson County, and their relationship, which would come close to friendship, was to last beyond the Truman presidency.

The *New Yorker*'s Philip Hamburger was struck by Acheson's "forbidding" features—"his penetrating, almost popping eyes." David Acheson thought his father's mustache "was perhaps his chief vanity," so much so that he attended to it with great care: "To give his mustache the necessary insouciance, he turned the ends up a bit, not in vertical pikes, like Kaiser Wilhelm II, but in a modified guardsman style. . . . To proof the mustache ends against gravity, Dad applied a little bit of Pinaud's mustache wax a couple of times a week." Hamburger went so far as to write that "in the morning light, his big reddish-gray mustache . . . has a personality of its own."

Acheson came by his Englishness through his father, Edward Campion Acheson, who was born in Woolwich, England, and became an Episcopal bishop in Connecticut. His mother, Eleanor Gertrude Gooderham, was Canadian. His slightly foreign affect could be off-putting. "I look at that fellow," the Nebraska senator Hugh Butler said, "I watch his smart-aleck manner and his British clothes and that New Dealism, everlasting New Dealism in everything he says and does, and I want to shout, 'Get out, Get out. You stand for everything that has been wrong with the United States.'" But Acheson had important allies in Congress, and in the press—the *New York Times'* James Reston, in particular, although Reston once told his publisher that Acheson "can be as mean as a polecat one day and generous and philosophic the next." The British journalist and broadcaster Malcolm Muggeridge began his flatteries near the day of Acheson's appointment, when he wrote, in the London *Telegraph*, that he "is too intelligent to be at all a fanatic and too personally disinterested to be an opportunist," and described him as a "brilliant raconteur, whose wit is quick and rapier-like and never deserts him." Acheson, susceptible to such blandishment, wrote Muggeridge to say that "I suppose I cannot say that so kind and flattering analysis seemed to me good but I *can* say that I got very great pleasure and lift of spirits from it."

Acheson sometimes regarded Truman as a beginner, and there were times when he wished, as others did, that he would learn the delicate art of careful parsing and precise avoidance. Among friends, he'd refer to Truman's tendency to sometimes say too much. When someone, at a dinner party, remarked that he liked Truman's spontaneity, Acheson motioned toward his gray hair and said: "That's Truman's spontaneity for me." But he never patronized Truman, nor suggested that anyone but Truman was in charge of the nation's foreign policy, which is not the same as saying that Truman actually *framed* policy. It is hard to separate Acheson's influence from what became the Truman Doctrine, in March 1947, or the outlook that would lead to America's involvement in a war on the Korean peninsula, in 1950. George Kennan was to say that Truman "had, in effect, only one foreign policy advisor, namely Mr. Acheson, and was entirely dependent on what advice the latter gave."

If Truman could have redone his first year as president, Acheson, or someone very much like him, would have been at his side, in Potsdam, or when he accompanied Churchill to Fulton, Missouri—in other words, someone other than James F. Byrnes, who, he would later say, was "conniving to run the Presidency over my head." Acheson's views were not always sound—far from it—but his steady role as a foreign policy guide would have lasting importance, and it is impossible to imagine Truman's presidency, and America's postwar history, without him.

4. While Acheson drew closer to Truman, the awkward, often unspoken, tension between Truman and Forrestal had not diminished. Truman once asked Captain Robert Dennison, who'd succeeded Clifford as his naval aide, "Do you know who the Secretary of Defense is?"

"Yes, sir," Dennison replied, sensing that the question wasn't as simple as it sounded. "It's James Forrestal."

"You're wrong," Truman said. "I'm the Secretary of Defense. Jim calls me ten times a day to ask me to make decisions that are completely within his competence, and it's getting more burdensome all the time."

The standoff in Berlin hadn't improved Forrestal's standing. In mid-July, after a meeting with Marshall and Forrestal, Truman wrote in his diary that "Jim wants to hedge—he always does. He's constantly sending me alibi memos which I return with directions and the facts. We'll stay in Berlin—come what may. . . . I have to listen to a rehash of what I know already and reiterate my 'stay in Berlin' decision." In a spurt of irritation, laced with self-approval, he added, "I don't pass the buck, nor do I alibi out of any decision I make." Forrestal's colleagues and friends could see the strain, and worry, on his face. It was hard not to notice how, during meals, he'd repeatedly dip his fingers into a finger bowl and lick his lips.

A few days after the election, Forrestal took a hurried trip to Western Europe, traveling from Paris to London to Frankfurt to Berlin, where he discussed defense ties with the five Brussels Pact nations. The security of the North Atlantic had been addressed five months earlier when the Senate, by a 64–4 margin, passed the "Vandenberg Resolution," a nonbinding affirmation of the principle of "associating" American military power with friendly alliances—a program parallel to the Marshall Plan. Forrestal, in Berlin, had his own survival on his mind. He told reporters that his future was up to Truman, but "I have informed him that I will be unable to remain throughout his entire administration." When Truman, in Key West, was asked about Forrestal's curious remark, he said "I have no comment."

Forrestal was back in Washington on the night of November 16, and would have seen Truman's chilly "no comment" in that morning's paper. Right away, he telephoned the President and asked to see him. "Why don't you come down for lunch?" Truman suggested. Forrestal left for Florida early the next day, and when reporters asked again about his plans, he sounded like someone who wanted to stay in the Pentagon. "I am at the service of the President," he said. "The Cabinet is singularly and peculiarly his business."

Exhausted from his hurried round-trip, Forrestal had hoped for a serious talk about his future. What he found, when he arrived in Key West a little past noon, was a president who was becoming more thoroughly tanned, surrounded by his men, some sunbathing in lounge chairs, all of whom hurried to get their work done in the morning so that afternoons would be free for volleyball and evenings free for poker. Truman's whiskery stubble had lasted until the morning of November 12, when Bess and Margaret arrived; then, the subtropical mood began to recede.

Forrestal had brought along three aides, but they weren't seated with him at the small table in the garden of the Little White House. The lunch with Truman, which did include two Florida politicians—Governor-elect Fuller Warren and Senator Claude Pepper—lasted about forty-five minutes, after which, Charlie Ross told reporters, "Secretary Forrestal gave President Truman a memorandum on what he had seen abroad, and an oral report. I am told that was the only topic of their conversation." What about the situation regarding Forrestal's future? "There is no situation," Ross replied. "I am told that the tenure of Mr. Forrestal in the Cabinet did not come up." Truman later told some of his aides that Forrestal had seemed "perfectly satisfied and happy" and had never uttered a word about resigning.

If Truman really meant that, he'd been astonishingly unobservant. Despite Forrestal's disclaimers, he'd given many signals that he wanted to settle the question of his future; he'd been around long enough—from Wall Street to Roosevelt's Washington—to be sensitive to every perceived slight and hint of disapproval. When he returned to Washington, a little after nine that night, he felt even more adrift within the Truman orbit.

Forrestal sometimes tried to escape the pressure of his job, and his uncertain status, by playing a round of golf at the Chevy Chase Club. But that was not an occasion for a relaxed foursome, but rather something to be pursued with speed, and in silence. He favored a twosome, and was said to hold a speed record for getting through eighteen holes. "Jim was all drive; there was no surcease in him," the historian Arthur Schlesinger Jr., who'd struck up a late acquaintanceship with Forrestal, thought. Eisenhower saw Forrestal as someone not only worn by the burden of work, and interservice rivalries, but untrusting of his Pentagon colleagues—undone by "his terrific, almost tragic disappointment in the failures of professional men to 'get together.'" Eisenhower drafted a "personal and secret" memorandum for Forrestal, whom he regarded as a friend. He called it a "sketchy outline" of a program to fix what he saw as a stalemate in the nation's security establishment—one that would require a "certain amount of Presidential intervention." Its chief purpose was to relieve the pressure on Forrestal by giving him a deputy and a White House liaison. But while Truman agreed to appoint an under secretary, the service heads were still in charge of their domains. In case of a dispute, Forrestal's role was still little more than that of an umpire, although an umpire who lacked the power to enforce his rulings.

But Forrestal's problems, and disappointments, went beyond a difficult job and a difficult marriage. Since his appointment as defense secretary, in the summer of 1947, he'd been attacked by Walter Winchell and, above all, by Drew Pearson, who saw him, in the words of a Pearson associate, as "the arch representative of Wall Street imperialism and of a world view that war with the Soviet Union was inevitable." These attacks rose to the level of vendetta, such as the suggestion, promoted by Pearson, that Forrestal had shown cowardice when his wife was the target of a Manhattan street robbery in 1937. The holdup had been tabloid-worthy because some fifty thousand dollars in jewelry was taken, and because Jo had returned home at about 2:30 a.m., after a night in the Persian Room at the Plaza (a "swank nightspot"), escorted by the ex-husband of the heiress Dorothy Schiff. According to Pearson, Jim watched from an upstairs window and, rather than trying to help his wife, "slipped out the back entrance, vaulted the rear fence, ran down an alley, and caught a taxi to his club where he spent the remainder of the night." Attorney General Tom Clark, a supposed friend, informed Pearson that Forrestal had asked his advice on whether to sue Pearson and had been "as nervous as a whore in church."

Ferdinand Eberstadt realized that his old friend was close to a breakdown. On a winter day when he couldn't reach Forrestal at the Pentagon, he went to 3508 Prospect Street. The house was dark, with all the blinds drawn. When Forrestal came to the door, he told Eberstadt to keep quiet because "they are watching this house and they have wired it."

Even before Eisenhower's intercession, Truman knew that the job had become too much for Forrestal. Washington, then as now, is an incubator of rumors and damaging gossip, and one did not have to rely on Drew Pearson to believe that Forrestal was a deeply troubled man. He'd begun to telephone the President several times a day, repeating himself; he told Truman's friend John Snyder, the treasury secretary, that his telephone was being tapped, and that he was being followed by Zionist and Communist agents. Snyder felt obligated to report this to the President, who later wrote, without embellishment, "When I saw Jim Forrestal was cracking up under the pressures of the reorganization of the Defense Department, I looked around for a successor"—someone who "could relieve Forrestal and do the unification job that needed to be done."

A last round of Forrestal-is-out stories appeared in late winter. Anonymous sources—identified as "persons high in the President's councils," among them, undoubtedly, Harry Vaughan—made it known that, as one story put it, they were "anxious to get rid of the Defense Secretary and put in his place a more active member of the Democratic Party." Truman had not looked very hard for a successor. His choice, announced on the day of Forrestal's resignation, was Louis Johnson, a founder of Steptoe & Johnson, one of Washington's weighty law firms, who'd long coveted the job. He'd felt let down, even angry, when President Roosevelt, in 1940, gave the War Department post to Henry Stimson. Johnson had been an assistant secretary of war before Pearl Harbor and a national commander of the American Legion, but his most important qualification was having chaired the Democratic National Finance Committee, which raised a million and a half dollars for the Truman-Barkley campaign. "Big, beefy" Johnson was fifty-eight, a bald, jowly man weighing two hundred pounds—strong enough, it was said, to lift the rear end of a

Model T. Ford—described in an otherwise friendly magazine profile as a "highly ambitious political stalwart and feudist." Johnson had also been one of Pearson's informants.

On Tuesday, March 1, Forrestal was told to come to the White House. He spent nearly two hours with Truman, during which he was asked to submit a letter of resignation, a chore that Forrestal was unable to complete without summoning outside help. Two days later, his forced resignation was announced, accompanied by a generous "Dear Jim" letter from Truman that tried to make it sound as if the decision had been Forrestal's alone. Truman later said that Forrestal "wanted to resign long before he did, and I kept him from it," which is doubtful, and that "he, himself, recommended Louis Johnson as his successor," which is difficult to believe. Johnson, years later, made the same dubious claim.

The changeover was to take effect before the end of the month, and the ceremonies of leave-taking began in earnest on March 23, when Forrestal was given a dinner in his honor in the Sapphire Room of the Mayflower Hotel. Truman arrived late—at about half-past nine—and began by talking about himself: "I am sincerely sorry that I couldn't be here for the whole evening, but I couldn't make it. I have, as you know, too much to do for one man, and in addition to that my daughter came home for the weekend today, and I stayed at home and had dinner with her." As for the guest of honor, he said, a little mysteriously, "Eventually I had to accept his resignation for his own welfare, because he was making a tremendous sacrifice by staying on the job," and concluded by saying, "Jim, I want to congratulate you on a great public career. I hope I am as well thought of, when I go out of office, as you are."

Truman got a call from Forrestal on the morning of March 28, the day that Johnson was to move into the Pentagon, where he'd commandeered the largest office—Room 3E880 on the outer ring on the Potomac River side—as well as the nine-by-five-foot walnut desk that had belonged to General John Pershing and a table that had been General George B. McClellan's desk during the Civil War. "I could only hear one end of the conversation," Robert Dennison, the naval aide, recalled, "and the President said, 'Yes, Jim, and that's the way I want it,' and so on. Then when he hung up, he said, 'That was Forrestal wanting to know whether I *really* wanted him to be relieved by Louis Johnson this noon'"—almost as if he were seeking a stay of execution.

Johnson was sworn in by Chief Justice Vinson, a Pentagon ceremony watched by a crowd that included most of the military high command. Absent was Jo Forrestal, who'd been living in Paris. Forrestal, standing behind Vinson, appeared weary, but was afterward taken to the White House, for a surprise: Truman awarded him the Distinguished Service Medal, the nation's highest civilian honor. After reading a citation, Truman pinned the medal to his chest. Forrestal started to say something, but murmured only "It's beyond my . . ." and couldn't finish. "You deserve it, Jim," Truman said. Forrestal might have been less moved had he known that, three days earlier, Truman had given Admiral Leahy, who was also present, his *third* Distinguished Service Medal.

He returned to the Mayflower for another testimonial dinner, this one honoring Louis Johnson. When the correspondent Robert Nixon caught up with Forrestal, "I asked him what were his plans and so forth. You could not believe the expression on his face at this gathering . . . It was ghastly, he looked like a man who just could not believe it." The next morning, the House Armed Services Committee met to salute Forrestal, to tell him that their regard was "indelibly inscribed in our hearts." Forrestal said he was "too much overcome." His next destination was Hobe Sound, Florida, where Robert Lovett had a house, and where Forrestal's friends wanted him to rest and play golf.

Forrestal didn't stay long. On April 5, he returned to Washington, and checked into the Naval Medical Center in Bethesda, for what was described as a "routine medical checkup and physical examination." A day later, a "high-ranking" Pentagon source said Forrestal was suffering a nervous breakdown, although "nervous exhaustion" was the preferred term. Doctors said they were "very much encouraged" by his response to treatment, although he'd lost twenty-five pounds and had "marked low blood pressure, a secondary anemia, and a neuromuscular weakness" associated with exhaustion. Drew Pearson began his April 10 radio broadcast saying, "I regret to report that James Forrestal . . . is out of his mind and apparently has been partly so for some weeks."

Forrestal spent six weeks on the sixteenth floor of the hospital, an isolated, frightened man. He believed that he was being watched by NKVD-trained secret police, or by Zionist agents plotting to kill him. Truman came to the hospital on April 23 and managed to stop at several sickbeds, among them one for Les Biffle, who was suffering from pneumonia; Admiral Leahy, now officially retired and recovering from a prostate operation; and Forrestal. According to a White House announcement, Truman found that these "very important patients" were "coming along fine." On May 22, 1949, Forrestal was in room 1618, apparently reading Sophocles's *Ajax*. From there, wearing a dressing gown, he made his way to a nearby pantry, where he was able to pry open a screen held in place by thumb latches and, from this sixteenth-floor window, jump.

Forrestal's suicide was the first by an American official of such high rank. It came on the night of the Gridiron Club dinner, at the Statler Hotel, where much of official Washington, including Truman and Barkley, were dressed in white tie and watched satirical skits, including one in black dialect performed by imitators of the popular *Amos 'n' Andy* radio program. Charlie Ross, who'd been among the guests, was told about Forrestal's death in a telephone call that came between 2 and 3 a.m. By the time Ross got to the White House, a presidential proclamation had already been prepared. Truman had planned to attend another Gridiron event—a Sunday afternoon reception, which included an encore of the Saturday skits—but, on Ross's recommendation, decided to skip it.

David Lawrence, in the next day's *Evening Star*, wrote that "the vicious rules of politics in America killed a great public servant"—a column that dwelled on Forrestal's visit to Key West the previous November, when there'd been no chance to speak privately with Truman. The column upset Truman. He remarked to aides that Lawrence was "trying to make out that he had killed Forrestal." It was a miserable coda to the life of a man who, like the protagonist in Dos Passos's *The Great Days*, had said "I expect to remain a victim of the Washington scene."

"First Lightning"

We are like the man who lives in a tar-paper shack and develops a flame-thrower to protect himself.

—Ralph Lapp, in June 1950

1. President Truman once boasted that the United States "could lick Russia," and found it hard to let go of a belief that the Russians would never catch up with Western technology. "You can understand the Russian situation if you understand Jackson County," he told his early biographer Jonathan Daniels. "You only have to recognize that the people of Jackson County came out of the dark ages in 900 A.D. while Moscow came out of the dark ages only in 1917."

Truman had other reasons to feel confident about being able to "lick Russia." The Berlin blockade had come to an end in early May, after eleven months, and with no benefit to Russia. The West's counter-blockade had further strained the economies of Eastern Europe, and to that was added the imminent birth of a new, partitioned half nation: the Federal Republic of Germany, administered by the United States, Great Britain, and France. On the other side of this divide lay a German-speaking extension of the Communist bloc, a depressing laboratory of Red misrule.

The blockade ended a month after the signing of the North Atlantic treaty, which realized the ambitions of the Vandenberg Resolution, and committed the United States, Canada, and ten Western European nations to the "collective defense and the preservation of peace, security and freedom in the North Atlantic Community." Joining such a military alliance, in peacetime, was something new for

Americans. At a signing ceremony, in Washington, Truman said, "We hope to create a shield against aggression and the fear of aggression," but he also tried to make it sound ordinary, even a little homey: "We are like a group of householders, living in the same locality, who decide to express their community of interests by entering into a formal association for their mutual self-protection." But the North Atlantic Treaty Organization (NATO) was a neighborhood-watch group in which each "household" was bound to come to the defense of any house under attack. It succeeded, for decades, in maintaining tense stability in Western Europe—an enduring achievement of Truman's time in office.

Truman could almost always project calm and good humor, even when he was frightened by what he faced, day by day—as when when he wrote his "things-look-black" letter to Margaret, after Jan Masaryk's death. In late August 1949, he unnerved White House staffers by remarking, almost casually, and not for the first time, that "we are now nearer to war than we have been at any time." Although Josip Broz Tito, the president of Yugoslavia, had broken with Stalin eighteen months earlier—the first Soviet bloc leader to do so—pressure from Russia hadn't abated, and Truman, with his geographical passion, sometimes regarding the globe in his office, liked to point out that recent wars, except for the last one, had started in that vicinity. Something else, though, had put Truman on edge that August, something that shook his faith in Soviet technological ineptitude and his certainty that Russia would "never" be able to build a nuclear bomb. By then, Truman knew that Russia had detonated a small atomic device, at a Kazakhstan test site called Semipalatinsk-21, though the White House waited nearly a month to issue a statement. "We have evidence," it said, on September 23, "that within recent weeks an atomic explosion occurred in the U.S.S.R."

The passive phrasing suggested a reluctance to admit that the Soviets had developed an atomic *weapon* rather than a mere explosive. Defense Secretary Johnson, as he hurried away from quote hungry reporters, advised them, "Don't overplay it." Dean Acheson broke through that semantic barrier, saying that he assumed the Russians had made a "weapon" and had exploded it. There was no reason to think that everything would change, he added, just because Russia had found the key to releasing atomic energy. But a lot *had* changed. Vannevar Bush, in 1945, believed it would take Russia five to ten years to make an A-bomb, General Leslie Groves thought it would take twenty, and now that they'd tried one out, no one seemed to know if it was their only bomb or if more were squirreled away. An unnamed official said the test had been discovered only through a "miracle of intelligence," but it was less a miracle than the success of a long-range detection system that had been proposed by Lewis L. Strauss, a member of the Atomic Energy Commission.

Soviet scientists called their bomb "First Lightning," and the news was agitating. Film records of the aftermath in Hiroshima and Nagasaki were still censored, but one didn't need photographs to learn about the effects of a weapon powerful enough to level much of a city in an instant, and its radioactive aftermath. In John Hersey's portrait of Hiroshima's survivors, which appeared in the August 31, 1946, issue of the *New Yorker* and became a best-selling book, one could linger over grisly details, such as how "the fluid from their melted eyes had run down their cheeks." In 1947, the *Bulletin of the Atomic Scientists*, founded two years earlier, published its first "Doomsday Clock"—a conceit predicting the imminence of an atomic war—and set it at seven minutes to midnight. A popular NBC radio drama, *Dimension X*, began a 1950 episode with the voice of a narrator saying, "It was in the year 1991 that man disappeared from the face of the earth. The third atomic war had ended at last, leaving the land a mass of red radioactive dust, filling the air with gamma rays so deadly that life on the surface was no longer possible."

The possibility of atomic warfare had become much more real. One heard this unease from the North Carolina–born preacher Billy Graham, as he began the two-month "Christ for Greater Los Angeles" campaign that, with an assist from the Hearst newspaper chain, would make him famous. Graham, then thirty years old, advertised himself as "America's Sensational Young Evangelist" in "The Largest Tent in the World . . . a Canvas Cathedral with the Steeple of Light"—a Hollywood searchlight. Audiences for these tent revivals were drawn in by Graham's oratorical talent, but also by his magnetic appeal—looking, as his biographer Marshall Frady put it, like some "blond, gallant, crystal-eyed prince out of a Nordic fairy tale." When the Los Angeles crusade debuted on September 25, two days after the White House announced the Russian test, Graham dwelled on the subject, with considerable embellishment: "Mr. Truman said . . . that we must be prepared for *any* eventuality at *any* hour," he said, excitedly. "Today Moscow announced that Russia has been piling up bombs for over two years, and gigantic plants have been turning out atomic bombs! Radio warnings have been issued from behind the Iron Curtain, and our own president declares, 'We must be prepared!'" Graham then uttered what became a signature line: "I am persuaded that time is desperately short!"—along with a more specific warning: "God is giving us a desperate choice, a choice of either revival or judgment. There is no alternative! If Sodom and Gomorrah could not get away with sin, if Pompeii and Rome could not escape, neither can Los Angeles!"

On New Year's Day, 1950, three months after the Los Angeles crusade, Graham sent a telegram to Truman, asking him to call for a "Day of Prayer." The telegram was not acknowledged by the White House (Truman seemed to have no idea who Graham was), but the young evangelist appeared to believe that a meeting with the President was bound to occur, and he wasn't wrong.

2. Truman waited until October 6 to hold his next news conference, during which he sounded eager to change the subject:

> *Q:* Mr. President, you referred in the statement . . . to evidence of an atomic explosion in Russia. Have you, since that time, received any further evidence or details of that explosion?
> *The President:* I made all the statement that I intend to make, on the subject, in that statement that was made on the 23d of September.

Truman then referred to Bernard Baruch's 1946 speech to the United Nations, which he called "the most important proposition in the history of the world with regard to that atomic situation," adding that "the Russians didn't see fit to accept our proposition." Then he said, inaccurately, that the United States had been willing "to turn over to the United Nations the atomic control of the world. No other nation in the history of the world, with the most terrible weapon in its possession, has ever been known to do anything of that sort."

Reporters persisted:

Q: Mr. President, there is a report that Russia is about to come up with some new proposal for disarmament. Would you look forward to hearing what that is?

The President: Not necessarily.

Q: It will make no change?

The President: Any number of proposals that couldn't be accepted, and this will probably be in the same class. . . .

Q: If we don't get an agreement with Russia, is it possible for an arms race in this thing?

The President: I hope there won't have to be an arms race.

There was already, though, an undeniable arms competition, and an uneasy inevitability about its future: the development of more powerful bombs, particularly a thermonuclear device that would use deuterium, an isotope of hydrogen, as an explosive. This so-called "Super" wasn't a new concept; during the war, several atomic scientists, among them Enrico Fermi and J. Robert Oppenheimer, thought it should be pursued in peacetime. Its most probable design, by 1949, was based on the calculations of Edward Teller, a Hungarian-born physicist whose name would become widely known, and Stanislaw Ulam, a Polish-born mathematician who deserved equal billing but rarely got it. This theoretical bomb was a secret until November 1949, when Senator Edwin C. Johnson, a Colorado Democrat and a member of the Joint Congressional Atomic Energy Committee, appeared on the DuMont television network and, to Truman's great displeasure, revealed that American scientists had *already* designed a bomb six times as powerful as the plutonium device dropped on

Nagasaki, and were still far from satisfied. "They want one that has a thousand times the effect of that terrible bomb," Senator Johnson said. After that, Truman summoned Brien McMahon, chairman of the Joint Committee, and the attorney general, J. Howard McGrath, and told them to, please, do what they could to stop the "loose talk."

That thousand-fold claim, although hard to absorb, was no exaggeration; the bomb's power, in theory, was open-ended. "The fact that no limits exist to the destructiveness of this weapon makes its very existence and the knowledge of its construction a danger to humanity as a whole," the nuclear physicists Enrico Fermi and Isidor Rabi said. "It is necessarily an evil thing considered in any light." Albert Einstein believed that a Super was a catastrophe-in-waiting. He told Eleanor Roosevelt, who'd gotten her own television program, on NBC, that a hydrogen bomb might be able to irradiate the entire atmosphere and thus cause the "annihilation of any life on earth." It sounded, the Alsop brothers wrote, "like a Walpurgis night dream of total destruction." In early January 1950, the influential brothers published the first of several scary columns on the subject, one of which said, "The ability to build such a bomb is, in theory, the ability to blow up the earth." Those columns infuriated Truman. "I don't know where the 'Sop Sisters' got their information," he told Senator McMahon, "but evidently somebody thinks it is proper to talk to lying scoundrels."

A decision on whether or not to build and test a Super was up to the President, and Truman was feeling immense pressure, from several sources: the Defense Department wanted to go ahead, but the Atomic Energy Commission opposed it, by a three-to-two margin, with David Lilienthal and Lewis Strauss on opposite sides. The AEC's General Advisory Committee, which gave technical advice, was likewise opposed to a weapon whose only purpose, they believed, was to destroy large cities and "slaughter a vast number of civilians." The push to go forward came from, among others, Harold C. Urey, who'd worked on the Manhattan Project and won a Nobel Prize in the chemistry of heavy hydrogen. At a Roosevelt Day dinner, in New York, in January 1950, he said, "I do not think we should intentionally lose the armaments race," adding, with a better-dead-than-Red flourish, that "to do this will be to lose our liberties, and with Patrick Henry, I value my liberties more than my life." As if to add to the alarm he was fomenting, he added that "we may already have lost the armaments race." Urey's remarks got more attention when he testified before the Senate Foreign Relations Committee and posited the idea that the Soviets might use tramp steamers to carry atomic bombs to ports all over Europe.

Ernest O. Lawrence and Luis Alvarez, at the AEC Radiation Laboratory of the University of California at Berkeley, met with Brien McMahon, who, after the Russian test, had become a strong advocate of the Super. Between September 1949 and June 1950, McMahon saw Truman at least eight times, including a dinner in McMahon's honor, at the 1925 F Street Club. In late November 1949, McMahon wrote a long memorandum to Truman, which sounded both reasonable and, unavoidably, in a Strangelovian sense, insane: "There is no moral dividing line that I can see between a big explosion which causes heavy damage and many smaller explosions causing equal or still greater damage. . . . What, then, is the distinction between the 1,000 square miles which one super might scorch and the 1,000 square miles which 143 fission bombs might destroy?" He added that "an attacker who dropped a half-dozen supers on an enemy's largest industrial areas would free up the hundreds of fission bombs otherwise needed." McMahon was also able to see the strangeness of viewing fission bombs, of the sort dropped on Japan, as relatively puny.

Truman took his time. Lilienthal had resigned from the AEC, but was staying on until the hydrogen-bomb question was settled. He was encouraged after a conversation with Truman in November, during which he told the President that McMahon and his committee would "try to put on a blitz to get a quick decision," and Truman had replied, smiling, "I don't blitz easily." But that was Truman— often eager to assert what he saw as his stout independence. In fact, although Truman said nothing publicly while the question was discussed, and re-discussed, within the administration, he'd privately made his decision. "I am sure his mind was made up at the very beginning, but nevertheless he had those processes carried out in an orderly way," said Admiral Sidney Souers, who'd left the Central Intelligence Group to become the executive secretary to the National Security Council. As for Souers's continuing relationship with Truman, he said, "Admiral Leahy and I were his chief constables." Even so, facing so much paperwork and disagreement, Truman took one more judicious step: On November 19, he informed Admiral Souers that he'd designated Lilienthal, Acheson, and Louis Johnson to serve as a "special committee" of the NSC, and to make a final recommendation on the Super.

This little committee had neither collegiality nor focus. Johnson, who had always favored building the bomb, and Lilienthal, who did not, would never agree. Acheson and Johnson had developed a passionate mutual dislike, which Acheson blamed on what he called the "acerbity of Louis Johnson's nature," but the differences between them were also affected by a competition for influence with the President, which Acheson, who was cleverer than Johnson, and whose pull with Truman was unmatched by anyone else, was destined to win. The Special Committee met just twice; their first meeting, three days before Christmas, turned into an argument between Lilienthal and Johnson while Acheson and Lilienthal talked about re-exploring the fading chance of international cooperation.

Acheson, in recognition of Truman's determination to preserve American military superiority, always knew what Truman would decide—it didn't need to be said. Louis Johnson knew it too, but wanted to make sure: without informing Acheson or Lilienthal, he'd forwarded to Truman a memorandum from General Omar Bradley, the first chairman of the Joint Chiefs of Staff, who'd made a simple and, for Truman, persuasive, argument for a hydrogen bomb: Beyond the "imperative necessity of determining the feasibility of a thermonuclear explosion," Bradley wrote, "possession of a thermonuclear weapon by the USSR without such possession by the United States would be intolerable."

The showdown, which wasn't much of a showdown, came when the Special Committee held its second, and final, meeting on a Monday morning, January 31, 1950, in Acheson's former office in the old State Department building. Acheson spoke of "stubborn facts," among them that delaying American research would do nothing to delay Soviet research. To Acheson's mild surprise, Lilienthal was no longer objecting, at least not formally, although there was something he wanted to say, directly, to Truman. Why not see him now? Johnson suggested, with sudden agreeableness. He'd already booked an appointment, for himself, at 12:30, and was willing to share his time. Every hour of delay, Johnson said, increased the pressure on Truman. "We must protect the President," he said. As for any disagreements among them, Johnson said, "the thing to do was to play it down, make it just one of those things." With that, the briefly amicable Special Committee, accompanied by Souers, walked across the street to the White House.

The group stayed in Truman's office for about seven minutes. In that time, Acheson informed the President that they'd reached agreement, and handed him a sheet of paper, which outlined their rationale, along with a statement for the press. When Acheson said that Lilienthal had something he wanted to say, Truman said *he* had something to say too, and went first: He'd always believed such weapons should never be used, and didn't believe that the United States would ever use them, but, because of Russia's behavior, he saw no alternative to building them. Then Lilienthal, the lame-duck commissioner, got his chance. He had "grave reservations" about the Super, he said, and was concerned that Truman's decision, no matter how carefully worded, would be seen as confirming the status quo—that it would magnify "some of the weaknesses that were growing greater every month, namely our chief reliance upon atomic weapons in the defense of this country and Europe."

Truman cut him off—he had more to add. All this could have been discussed quietly, he said, if Senator Johnson hadn't gone on television, in November, and blabbed. Since then, there had been "so much talk in the Congress and everywhere and people are so excited" that there was no alternative to making an H-bomb—and that was what he was going to say. Truman recalled White House meetings when the subject had been whether to send aid to Greece and Turkey. Back then, in 1947, "everybody predicted the end of the world if we went ahead, but we did go ahead and the world didn't come to an end." Although the two cases could not have been less alike, and Truman had reshaped this recent history to suit him, the comparison gave him confidence that, once again, he'd made the correct decision. Admiral Souers later recalled a more from-the-gut moment: when the Commission first told Truman about the H-bomb, he'd said, "What the hell are we waiting for? Let's get on with it."

In a short written statement—118 words—Truman said it was his responsibility, as commander in chief, "to see to it that our country is able to defend itself against any possible aggressor," and he was therefore directing the Atomic Energy Commission to continue its work on the research and development of atomic weapons, "including the so-called hydrogen or super-bomb." This, he added, would go forward "until a satisfactory plan for international control of atomic energy is achieved."

J. Robert Oppenheimer too always knew how this would be decided. As a scientist, he recognized an irresistible momentum: "When you see something that is technically sweet, you go ahead and do it and you argue about what to do about it only after you have had your technical success. That is the way it was with the atomic bomb." Truman's own, unwavering leaning toward American strength was augmented by people like Lewis Strauss, who'd made the attractive argument, sounding much like General Bradley, that it would be "unwise to renounce unilaterally any weapon which an enemy can reasonably be expected to possess."

Two days after Truman endorsed the Super, Lilienthal got enough of a shock to write in his diary that "the roof fell in today, you might say." The reference was to a British scientist named Klaus Fuchs, who'd worked at Los Alamos during the war, and was about to be arraigned, in London, for passing atomic secrets, including secrets of the H-bomb, to the Russians. Lilienthal saw this as "a world catastrophe, and a sad day for the human race." He'd heard that when Truman got this news, he told Admiral Souers to "tie on your hat."

3. Any hope of shielding the American public from the implications of the superbomb had long since vanished. There had been Senator Johnson's words, plus a stream of leaks, which many suspected came from inside the Joint Committee, along with those columns by the energetic Alsop brothers. The morning after the announcement, Truman met in his office with reporters, who wanted to know more about the "decision to produce the superbomb." But he wasn't budging, and wasn't good-humored about it.

> Q: Mr. President, Senator McMahon has indicated that he is about to make a speech asking for a nationwide public discussion of the issues raised by the superbomb. To do that, facts about it are necessary. Can we look forward to having some disclosures further than that—
>
> The President: No, you cannot look forward to anything except what was stated.

When McMahon, later that day, spoke on the floor of the Senate, he sounded like a man pulled in at least two directions. He remained loyal to the President, saying that, in the "world which we inhabit today," Truman had no choice but to approve a bomb that could deliver "chunks of the sun." But in his speech, which was not at all routine, and on which he'd worked for some time, he asked for "a moral crusade for peace," and the revival of the Acheson-Lilienthal proposal for international control of atomic energy. Before he was done, he'd twice quoted Bernard Baruch's "quick and the dead" UN speech, which he called "one of the greatest addresses known to English language," and made the daring suggestion that the United States commit fifty billion dollars, over five years, toward a "global Marshall Plan" to assure effective arms control. It would, he argued, cost no more than two-thirds of the annual arms budget, and if it succeeded, would be an incredible bargain. When he was finished, many of his fellow senators stood in admiration. Herbert H. Lehman, of New York, called it "a great speech; a great public document," and Paul Douglas, of Illinois, called it "extraordinarily brilliant, moving, of the highest statesmanship in Christian ethics." Then Douglas went to McMahon's side and clasped his hand.

Truman was unmoved by McMahon's big ideas. "The Baruch

position is just the same now as it was the day it was made," he said, a week later. "No reason to reconsider it. It is just as good today as it ever was." He also said, "We are attempting to get international control of atomic energy and trying our best to get a peace in the world that will be good for everybody. That's all we are after. That's all we have ever wanted. That is the fundamental basis of our foreign policy."

This was certainly an opportune time to try to head off a thermonuclear arms race, although it cannot be said that the postwar history of arms control would have taken a different course if Truman had done what some in Washington were urging: attempt a new sort of bargain with the Russians—to call off development of the H-bomb in return for a commitment to enforceable international controls. One of these was Senator Vandenberg, who, the day after Truman announced the intention to go ahead, suggested going to the UN and making just that offer. It was "not precisely a revolutionary or dangerous proposal" was how James Reston, the voice of establishment Washington, put it. But even if Stalin had agreed—a doubtful proposition—and even if a reliable, and trustworthy, method for international safeguards could have been developed, Truman was still not ready to step away from a familiar path: to live with the risk of a permanent and dangerous balance of power. Furthermore, he'd persuaded himself that "everything pertaining to the hydrogen bomb was at this time still in the realm of the uncertain. It was all theory and assumption." That wasn't true, but believing that made it easier for Truman to decide.

EIGHTEEN

"A New Fanatic Faith"

A country which in 1900 had no thought that its prosperity and way of life could be in any way threatened by the outside world had arrived by 1950 at a point where it seemed to be able to think of little else but this danger.

—George Kennan

1. President Truman appeared to be in fine spirits in the late winter of 1950, when he gave a one-on-one interview to Arthur Krock, the *New York Times'* Washington Bureau chief, who rewarded him with a deferential front-page story. "In the age of atomic energy," it began, "and in the shadow of a hydrogen detonant . . . a serene President . . . sits in the White House with undiminished confidence in the triumphs of humanity's better nature." And more: "He sits in the center of a troubled and frightened world," striving to steer the right course in the current "penumbra of doubt and fear." Truman, Krock informed his readers, was "the kind of American who must be observed at first-hand," just as he, Krock, was doing, "free to speak with the candor and natural piety of his make-up, to be wholly understood." Through all that Krockian prose, which obeyed the convention of "indirect discourse"—no verbatim quotes could be used without permission—the authentic Truman nonetheless came through. He recalled his first days as president—"without a single member of the Cabinet who was devoted to him personally"—and revived the notion of dispatching Chief Justice Vinson to "straighten out Stalin," in Krock's paraphrase. Truman also talked about "Congressional spy hunts," and Washington's atmosphere of "hysteria," which put him in mind of the Alien and Sedition Acts and the "Know-Nothing" movement of the 1850s. There was no mention of Senator Joseph McCarthy, of Wisconsin, who'd just delivered a speech in Wheeling, West Virginia, that, without evidence, warned of Communist infestation in the State Department, and claimed the senator had a list of names. But Truman's allusion to McCarthy, as well as the House Committee on Un-American Activities, was unmistakable.

The forty-year-old McCarthy—a "heavy-shouldered, black-browed man," in William S. White's pithy description—had been elected to the Senate in the 1946 midterms, the year that John F. Kennedy, of Massachusetts, and Richard M. Nixon, of California, won House seats. But until his Wheeling speech, he'd shown little overt interest in Communism, or the purported misdeeds of the State Department; nor had he revealed his aptitude for reckless, casual cruelty. After Wheeling, when the *Milwaukee Journal* editor Paul Ringler said to him, "Joe, I don't believe you've got a goddamn thing to prove the things you've been saying," Ringler recalled McCarthy replying, "I just want you to know I've got a pailful of shit and I'm going to use it where it does me the most good." McCarthy repeatedly dipped into his pail of shit. Ten days after the Wheeling speech, he took to the Senate floor, for six hours, to dilate on the claim that the State Department was home to an espionage ring. He was just getting started. As Richard Rovere put it, "He was a political speculator, a prospector who drilled Communism and saw it come up a gusher."

McCarthy had a lot of fresh material to work with. Four months earlier, after decades of fighting, the Communist leader Mao Zedong announced the birth of the People's Republic of China. McCarthy, and his allies on the right, recalled, with suspicion, General Marshall's failed mission to negotiate an end to China's civil war and denounced what they saw as a betrayal of America's wartime ally, Chiang Kai-shek, who had decamped to the offshore island of Formosa (Taiwan). That violent, complicated history was sometimes summed up with a question—"Who lost China?"—although China had been "lost" without much help from outsiders. While China suffered through a Great Terror that, by the end of 1951, led to the murder of nearly two million people, the West could only watch, and argue about what might have been done to help Chiang, and whether to recognize the new government as legitimate.

McCarthy had other, more potent domestic issues: Russia's nuclear bomb, the exposure of the atom spy Klaus Fuchs, and the evergreen case of Alger Hiss, a former State Department employee, whose name, since the summer of 1948, had been synonymous with suspicions about spies and fifth-columnists. A month before McCarthy's Wheeling speech, Hiss had been sentenced to prison on two perjury counts: lying about passing classified documents to the Russians and denying that he'd known his accuser, the *Time* magazine editor Whittaker Chambers.

Although the Hiss case lacked the high stakes of atomic secrets (the documents were not particularly sensitive) or the half-billion Chinese who'd fallen under Communist rule, it provided compelling drama, including the mystery of a central character who wasn't what he'd appeared to be and who, Zelig-like, had been an aide to Secretary of State Stettinius, in Yalta, and then secretary general of the first United Nations conference, in San Francisco. The Hiss case also ensnared Dean Acheson, who'd been friendly with Hiss, whose brother worked in Acheson's law firm. When Acheson was asked about Hiss, he'd replied, as the son of an Episcopal bishop, by urging his questioners to consult the Gospel according to Saint Matthew. "I do not," he said, "intend to turn my back on Alger Hiss." McCarthy then called Acheson a man who'd "proclaimed his loyalty to a man guilty of what has always been considered as the most abominable of all crimes."

Truman's reaction to the attack on his secretary of state was to be forthright and loyal—among his most appealing qualities. In Key West, in late March 1950, after a picnic lunch with the White House press corps, he praised Acheson and said, "McCarthy's antics are the best asset that the Kremlin can have." After reporters pleaded for permission to quote him directly ("Brother, will that hit page one tomorrow!" one said), Truman offered a milder version, omitting McCarthy's name: "The greatest asset that the Kremlin has is the partisan attempt in the Senate to sabotage the bipartisan foreign policy of the United States." He did, however, single out the Senate minority leader, Kenneth Wherry, of Nebraska, saying, "To try to sabotage the foreign policy of the United States is just as bad in this cold war as it would be to shoot our soldiers in the back in a hot war. I am fed up with what is going on, and I am giving you the facts as I see them." McCarthy didn't care. "It couldn't be any worse. . . . I wish someone had sabotaged it sooner."

Truman had been pleased enough with that day's performance to send the transcript to Acheson, with a hopeful note: "I think we have these 'animals' on the run. Privately, I refer to McCarthy as a pathological liar and Wherry as the blockheaded undertaker from Nebraska. Of course we can't do that publicly, but there's no doubt that's exactly what they are." A couple of weeks later, Truman instructed an aide to talk to the House Majority Leader John W. McCormack, and to employ anti-McCarthy language when he did so: "Roman Holiday in the House. Hoax," Truman's scribbled note said. "Fraud + Deceit. Use it often." McCarthy, though, had a lot more in his pail.

2. The administration's commitment to more powerful nuclear weapons had come with an apparent benefit: by avoiding major increases in manpower and equipment, the defense budget could reflect Truman's frugal instincts, a carryover from his Senate days. At the end of the war, the size of the military, including support staff, stood at about twelve million men and women. By the summer of 1947, those numbers had shrunk, to some 1.5 million. Military spending, at its wartime peak, had been eighty-two billion dollars. It fell to thirteen billion, a drop that led General Marshall to complain, privately, to the columnist Marquis Childs that billions of dollars' worth of supplies were being buried, or dumped in the ocean. "What am I to do?" he'd said. "This is an advertisement to the world that we are giving up our positions of strength everywhere."

These economies had the enthusiastic support of Louis Johnson, who liked that nuclear weapons were cheaper than large armies and battleships. Less than a month after being sworn in as defense secretary, in the spring of 1949, he canceled a super-carrier, the USS *United States*, a decision which led, quickly, to the resignation of the navy secretary, John L. Sullivan, who, in an acrimonious farewell, said that Johnson had acted "drastically and arbitrarily," and had not even found time to listen to his opinion. The ship's cancellation was interpreted as another commitment to the idea that wars of the future would be very different from what had gone before—that there would be less reliance on conventional arms and armies. Atomic bombs could be delivered by a new fleet of Convair B-36s, the largest propeller-driven planes ever built, with a range of ten thousand miles—a feat that no super-carrier could hope to match. It was said that, in the future, a surprise strategic attack, with hydrogen bombs, could be carried out by pilot-less aircraft or submarine-launched guided missiles.

Johnson had promised Truman to hold defense spending to thirteen billion dollars, and Truman and Johnson were inclined to shrug off warnings that, in a time of relative peace, and given America's nuclear superiority, a diminishment of manpower would put the nation's security at risk. The most vehement opposition to the defense cuts came, not surprisingly, from the Alsop brothers, who went on the attack, in a sequence of columns that were repetitive, brooding, and, when it came to Louis Johnson, vituperative. James Forrestal had been a personal friend, and the brothers saw him as a "a tragic hero of the post-war years," a man "whipped onwards by the fierce whip of an intense patriotism," someone who'd borne the burden of foresight. Their loathing of Johnson became increasingly personal. They wrote about his "smarmy assurances," his "concealed disarmament program," and said that behind his defense economies "lurks . . the specter of our eventual defeat in the world struggle with the Soviet Union."

Stewart Alsop took special note of the antagonism between Johnson and Acheson, which he called a "great subterranean struggle." Their very different personalities—supercilious Acheson, bombastic Johnson—caused problems enough, but there was furthermore something erratic about Johnson's behavior. What most aggravated him was a suspicion that Acheson was out to sabotage his defense budget. Johnson went so far as to order restrictions on contacts between State and Defense employees, and to insist that General James H. Burns, his liaison to State, talk only to H. Freeman (Doc) Matthews, the deputy under secretary. Acheson later recalled that "any other discussions over the telephone, in person, or in any other way that he found out about, was verboten, and he raised hell."

Johnson's no-talking policy was unsustainable. It fell apart, abruptly, during a March, 1950 State-Defense meeting attended by Acheson, Johnson, and a number of senior advisers, including Paul Nitze, who'd come to Washington from Wall Street a decade earlier and, in early 1950, replaced George Kennan as head of the Policy Planning Staff. Nitze recalled Johnson showing up in "a towering rage" and complaining about "a conspiracy to subvert his attempts to hold the Defense budget down to twelve and a half billion dollars." Acheson remembered Johnson "leaning back with the front legs of his chair off the ground" and coming down "with a crash," after which he "whacked the table and just blew up in the most violent way." After Johnson said, "I won't have anything to do with this conspiracy," he ordered his entourage, which included General Omar Bradley, the Joint Chiefs chairman, to follow him out the door. Most did leave, Acheson remembered, although they left behind General Burns who "put his head in his hands and wept in shame." Johnson left no written recollection of that meeting. Doc Matthews thought that he "must have been off his rocker at that time."

Johnson was not off his rocker, though he was unwell: He was suffering from blood clots on the brain, for which he was later treated at the Mayo Clinic; and he'd always been combative, suspicious, and quick to lose his hot temper. Dean Acheson, in his memoirs, promoted the "off-his-rocker" theory, writing that "evidence accumulated to convince me that Louis Johnson was mentally ill. His conduct became too outrageous to be explained by mere cussedness."

Johnson certainly knew what was going on. What he termed a "conspiracy" began with a Truman directive, on January 31—the day Truman announced that America should go forward with the research and development of a thermonuclear bomb. Truman had ordered a State-Defense Review Group to reexamine "our objectives in peace and war" in light of Russia's "probable" nuclear capability and "possible" ability to build a thermonuclear bomb. That directive would lead to what became known as National Security Council Paper (NSC) 68, a twenty-three-thousand-word policy guidepost that described, in vivid language, a hazardous postwar world and proposed large increases in military spending. Its recommendations were secret, but not for long. "It can be confidently reported," Stewart Alsop wrote, in March, that a "root-and-branch review policy," initiated by Dean Acheson, was under way and that Truman would have to choose between that and Johnson's "phony reassurances."

When Johnson blew up, a summary of the State-Defense review had been on Truman's desk for more than a week, and was tangible proof that Johnson's suspicions of Acheson were justified. Had Johnson stayed in the room, he'd have heard more about the latest draft of the National Security Council's tour d'horizon, with its focus on the Soviet Union. "Unlike previous aspirants to hegemony," it said, the Soviet Union "is animated by a new fanatic faith, antithetical to our own, and seeks to impose its absolute authority over the rest of the world." The Soviet empire, it continued, was increasing military spending "to support its design for world domination," and the United States needed "a rapid and sustained build-up of the political, economic, and military strength of the free world"—in other words, a defense budget that bore no resemblance to the present one. NSC-68 could be read as a lesson in how American foreign policy was being formed—shaped by the expanding influence of the nation's defense and intelligence agencies.

Authorial credit for this desk-bound muscularity belonged to Nitze, but it reflected Acheson's belief that "the cold war is in fact a real war in which the survival of the free world is at stake." It was a reminder that, with George Marshall gone, someone like George Kennan no longer fit in. Kennan had worried about the nation "drifting toward a morbid preoccupation with the fact that the Russians conceivably could drop atomic bombs on this country, regardless of . . . whether it would be profitable or otherwise for them to do so." Real security, he believed, "must rest on the *intentions*, rather than the capabilities of other nations." That kind of thinking is why Kennan, at the end of 1949, began a leave that took him, and these unwelcome opinions, to the Institute for Advanced Study at Princeton, and why Acheson wanted to replace him with someone like Nitze, who saw things his way. Personnel shifts like that meant that within the Acheson State Department—and therefore within the Truman administration—fresh discussion about the direction of American policy was a rarity.

NSC-68 (its formal title was "United States Objectives and Programs for National Security"), reached Truman's desk on April 7, 1950, and remained classified until 1975. Modern readers may find it difficult to appreciate its "secret" classification. Those able to make their way through its sixty-six pages will be struck more by its repetitiveness than by any encounter with rigid analysis. Dean Acheson, always jealous of his reputation, was aware of its flaws. One can imagine him smiling when, writing his memoirs, he quoted the remark of an unnamed policy veteran that "when he first read NSC-68 he thought that it was 'the most ponderous expression of elementary ideas' he had ever come across," adding something from Oliver Wendell Holmes Jr.—that there are times when "we need education in the obvious more than investigation of the obscure." Nor did Acheson have a problem admitting that the purpose of NSC-68 was to "bludgeon the mass mind of 'top government.'"

Truman may never have read all of NSC-68, though he was certainly aware of its gist; he referred it to the National Security Council, with a request for more information on "the implications of the conclusions." He wanted the report, which was infused with the same gloomy spirit as the 1946 Clifford-Elsey report, to get "no publicity," though its essence had already leaked out. NSC-68 undeniably provided a rationale for the administration's direction and decisions, but not a universal rationale. How, for instance, to react to Communist aggression in a small Asian country, in circumstances that posed no obvious threat to the United States? Was that part of a design for world domination?

3. When Truman talked to Arthur Krock in February 1950, he said—not for the first or last time—that the only agreement

Russia kept after Yalta was to join the war against Japan. He never stopped seeing Russia as a country inhabited by semi-primitives, incapable of advanced thought, a people that somehow had managed to explode a nuclear *something*. At the same time, he was unembarrassed at regarding Stalin as "Uncle Joe," kin to the roguish politicians he'd known in Jackson County, and held on to the dubious idea that the Politburo, not Stalin, made the big decisions and was to blame for Soviet duplicity. Acheson was inclined to view the Soviet Union as more powerful, and aggressive, than it actually was, and his suspicions about Soviet intentions bolstered Truman's.

With so much worldwide potential for trouble—in Europe, Iran, the new Red China, and the Middle East—Acheson did not expect the next batch to come from Korea, a nation about the size of Utah, with a history that dated back centuries, to the age of the Three Kingdoms. "Never has fate been secreted in so unlikely a receptacle," Acheson was to think, as he became familiar with the country's past, or at least its most recent hundred years or so.

In the nineteenth century, Korea had been bedeviled by Japanese incursions, and, early in the twentieth century, the "Japan-Korea Protocol" diluted the Korean government's authority. Any hope for independence ended in 1910, when Japan simply annexed Korea, beginning an occupation that was to last until the end of the Pacific war. Korea's right to independence had been affirmed in late 1943, when Roosevelt, Churchill, and Chiang Kai-shek met in Cairo; the promise was repeated, in 1945, in the Potsdam Declaration. After the war, the Allies came up with a plan for a four-power Korean "trusteeship," an idea roundly hated by Koreans, for it seemed to once more rule out a unified, independent government. The reality of two Koreas took shape as the Russian and American military settled in, on the both sides of the thirty-eighth North Latitude—the 38th Parallel—an arbitrary dividing line that a Department of Defense paper aptly described as "a geographical artificiality violating the natural integrity of a singularly homogeneous nation."

The United States' role in turning this arbitrary line into something more permanent was the handiwork of two army colonels, Charles H. "Tick" Bonesteel, a West Point man, and David Dean

Rusk, a former professor of government, who worked with the Operations Division of the War Department. These two officers, working late, had been studying a *National Geographic* map, looking for an identifiable natural boundary that could include Seoul, the Korean capital. As Thomas J. Schoenbaum wrote, in his thorough study of Rusk's public career, "This latitudinal line . . . arbitrarily selected by tired men in the middle of the night would become the boundary between North and South Korea." To the surprise of the Americans, the Russians accepted the line, but, as Schoenbaum suggested, they should have known that the 38th Parallel had once been an "administrative line for Japan—the boundary between two zones of occupation during World War II." Unwittingly, then, Rusk and Bonesteel had selected a border that the Russians would seize upon as "a division of Korea into two geographic spheres of influence."

The Russians, north of the Parallel, supported a repressive Communist regime, led by Kim Il-Sung, who'd led a unit of the wartime Soviet army. The United States, in the south, backed a somewhat less repressive, non-Communist regime, led by Syngman Rhee, an American-educated (Princeton, Harvard) Christian, who'd lived for forty-odd years in the United States. Korea was not a country to which Americans had ever paid much attention, despite occasional oubreaks of fighting along the border. Few could have found Korea on a map.

A prescient CIA report warned, in 1947, that, since V-J Day, "Soviet tactics have clearly demonstrated that the USSR is intent of securing all of Korea as a satellite." It pointed out that the Russians didn't need to occupy the North in order to control it—that "the machine they have built in the north to carry out their policies" was enough. That was certainly the case in 1948, when Truman said the United States should aim for a settlement "which would enable the U.S. to withdraw from Korea as soon as possible with a minimum of bad effects." By end of the year, Soviet troops had pulled out of the peninsula; the Americans, apart from a small number of advisers, were gone by the early summer of 1949. But after those withdrawals, the Russian "machine" vis-à-vis the South, was in a stronger position than before. Truman that summer asked Congress to appropriate a hundred and fifty million dollars for Korea's economic recovery, saying that the country "has become a testing ground [for the] practical value of the ideals and principles of democracy," in contrast to "the practices of communism which have been imposed upon the people of north Korea." That was a typical expression of American goals in a region little understood, and where ideas about democratic ideals didn't mean very much.

Korea was not foremost in Acheson's mind when he gave a speech at the National Press Club on January 12, 1950, when the United States was content to let Syngman Rhee carry on the fight to hold the non-Communist South. Acheson's focus, as it had been all along, was on the Soviet role in the spread of Communism, which he viewed as a long struggle that, absent the approach recommended in NSC-68, might have a catastrophic dénouement. "Communism," he said at the Press Club, "is the most subtle instrument of Soviet foreign policy that has ever been devised . . . the spearhead of Russian imperialism."

Acheson was particularly concerned with what he called the "dismemberment" of China, and believed that Russia coveted contiguous Manchuria and Mongolia, with the aim of "attaching them to the Soviet Union." Almost as an aside, he discussed what he called the "defensive perimeter," and suggested that the United States was unable, or unwilling, to defend certain areas of the Pacific, including Korea. While saying it would be "utter defeatism and madness" simply to pull out of Korea, he emphasized the folly of military involvement: "It must be clear that no person can guarantee these areas against military attack," he said. "But it must also be clear that such a guarantee is hardly sensible or necessary within the realm of practical relationship."

That was not a remarkable assertion. When the Pentagon, in early 1949, asked General Douglas MacArthur for his opinion, the Pacific supreme commander who had settled, contentedly, into the role of Liberator of Japan, favored the early withdrawal of American troops. Much like Acheson, he said it was "not within the capabilities of the United States to establish Korean security forces capable of meeting successfully a full-scale invasion from North Korea supported by Communist-inspired internal disorder."

Acheson later tried to rearrange the words of his Press Club speech, but was not persuasive when he tried to take them back. Years later, when he was asked if he'd consulted beforehand with the Defense Department, he conceded that he hadn't, and that he probably should have checked with the Pentagon: "It was my decision, and I did it perhaps without adequate thought." Like Formosa, Korea's "importance was of a negative sort," Acheson said. "It was not important to us to have its use. It was important to us that it not be used by a hostile power."

If Acheson had had an intimation that war would soon come to Korea, he would not have said what he did. American intelligence, though, was unaware that, in March 1949, Kim Il-Sung had visited Moscow, and spent seventy-five minutes with Stalin, looking for Soviet support in a future invasion; Kim had "brought with him concrete plans for an attack," Nikita Khrushchev, a witness to the 1949 conversation with Stalin, recalled. Kim had never abandoned his goal of unifying Korea, and leading one nation of his design.

Acheson, though, was far more concerned about the future of France's colonial territory, the Associated States of Indochina—the kingdoms of Cambodia, Laos, and Vietnam, which were about to be recognized by the United States and England. France for years had been at war with the anti-colonial Viet Minh, led by Ho Chi Minh, a Communist and nationalist, an American ally in the war against Japan. In the opinion of the State Department, what was needed in Vietnam was a *non-Communist*, nationalist leader. Yet in a report to the National Security Council, the department saw no promising path to this ideal future, apart from suggesting that State and Defense should give priority to "all practicable measures" to prevent Communist expansion in Southeast Asia. In May 1950, Acheson met with the French foreign minister, Robert Schuman, and afterward announced that the United States would send seventy-five million dollars to French Indochina, to combat the threat of "Soviet imperialism."

The *New York Times'* roving correspondent C. L. Sulzberger was among those who realized that something of great importance was happening. "In an undeliberate, haphazard way," he wrote, in May

1950, the United States was "in the process of elaborating what is the equivalent of a 'Truman Doctrine' for Southeast Asia"—believing that, without such a commitment, "the Communist tide will spread contagiously." Sulzberger didn't mention Korea, and didn't need to repeat the core principle of the Doctrine, as stated by Truman in his 1947 speech to Congress: that "wherever aggression direct or indirect, threatened the peace, the security of the United States was involved." It was enough to suggest that Constable America was still walking the beat, and that those rounds were about to encompass a much larger, and distant, part of a dangerous neighborhood.

NINETEEN

A "Border Incident"

The war came early one morning in June of 1950, and by the time the North Koreans occupied our capital city, Seoul, we had already left our university.

—Richard E. Kim, *The Martyred*

1. On June 24, 1950, a Saturday, Joe Alsop gave a dinner party at the yellow cinder-block-and-brick house that he'd designed at 2720 Dumbarton Street, and although Washington was no place to be on the last weekend in June (on this particular day, the temperature had reached ninety-six degrees), an Alsop dinner, with its promise of spirited talk and gossip, was hard to resist. The Supreme Court justice Felix Frankfurter, a Georgetown neighbor, was there. So was Dean Rusk, now an up-and-coming State Department officer, and Frank Pace Jr., a thirty-seven-year-old former Budget Office director who'd recently been appointed as army secretary. Alsop recalled that "we had finished a very jolly dinner and were engaged in lively discussion when my Filipino butler Jose announced a telephone call for 'Mr. Rush'"—a mispronounced "Rusk."

Alsop watched Rusk's face "turn the color of an old-fashioned white bed sheet," and remembered him informing the dinner guests that North Korean troops had crossed into the South—a "rather serious border incident," as he put it. Pace and others "promptly turned ashen-faced" and left. The remaining guests settled down to argue whether, as Alsop wrote, "this was it," with "it" being the imagined spark that would set off an international explosion. The news had just come to the State Department in a radio message from John Muccio, the American ambassador to Korea.

President Truman was in Missouri. After a stop at the new Friendship Airport, near Baltimore, which he dedicated "to the cause of peace in the world," he'd gone on to Independence, to be with summer-in-Washington-averse Bess. Louis Johnson, the defense secretary, and General Omar Bradley, the Joint Chiefs chairman, had just returned from Japan, where they'd seen General MacArthur, the SCAP—the supreme commander for the Allied Powers and Japan's de facto viceroy. It was not a social visit. MacArthur never went out at night—to conserve every molecule of his mental and physical energy—and had declined a dinner invitation from Johnson that came almost as an order. General Lawton Collins, the army chief of staff, was at his beach cottage on the Chesapeake Bay, and Dean Acheson was at Harewood, his farm in Sandy Springs, Maryland, a once-pastoral area that has long since become part of the extended Washington suburbs. His weekend had been spent with carpentry—"turning a table leg on a lathe or running a corner board through a joiner," activities that relaxed him; after dinner, he'd "turned in to read myself to sleep." That came to a halt when he got a telephone call from Muccio, in Seoul, where it was Sunday afternoon. (Korea was thirteen hours ahead of Washington, on Daylight Savings Time.) Muccio informed Acheson that the "border incident," which had begun at dawn that morning, was actually a heavy attack, unlike patrol forays of the past.

Acheson telephoned Truman at about 11 p.m. (10 p.m. in Missouri), and got the President's approval to present a resolution on Korea to the United Nations, an organization that Acheson, privately, regarded with disdain. Truman thought he ought to return to Washington right away, but Acheson talked him out of it, saying, "There's not a thing to do, you stay there until at least tomorrow, and we'll be in touch, but you can't do a thing tonight." There was, though, one thing that Truman *could* do, Acheson said: let Frank Pace know that he wanted "the fullest cooperation between the departments." That should not have been necessary, but Louis Johnson's simmering hostility toward Acheson, and his "no-talking" edict, were still a problem. Johnson and Acheson had barely spoken in months, and Truman had been overheard saying, "If this keeps up we're going to have a new Secretary of Defense."

It wasn't another Pearl Harbor. It didn't touch American soil and had no chance of doing so. Nor did it fall within the "defensive perimeter" that Acheson had described six months earlier. It was certainly an act of war, carried out by a Russian client state, although, as the historian Bruce Cumings has argued, "it was immediately clear that this war was a matter of 'Koreans invading Korea'; it was not aggression across generally accepted international lines." In fact, there's still much unknown about what led to the attack. The enormous amount of written material on this period suggests that Stalin had wanted to avoid war with the West, but was willing to gamble that the United States would not want to face the logistical and political difficulties of war in a place that American leaders seemed to consider beyond the "defensive perimeter." It is also likely that Stalin's approval of Kim's military operation, which came in early 1950, was influenced by Acheson's January 12 Press Club speech. The timing certainly suggests that, without that unintentional encouragement, Stalin would not have supported the attack. But the invasion probably wouldn't have happened if the Guomindang, Chiang Kai-shek's Nationalist Party, had been victorious in China's civil war. As Chen Jian, a scholar of modern Chinese history, has pointed out, establishment of the People's Republic helped persuade Communists and Communist sympathizers "throughout the world, especially in East Asia, that history indeed was on their side."

It *was* a night recalled with great clarity. John D. Hickerson, an assistant secretary of state, had been at home, in the Cleveland Park neighborhood of Northwest Washington. He was used to getting calls at night and on weekends, and if the phone rang after 9 p.m., his habit was to grab his car keys, in case he needed to make the short drive down Rock Creek Parkway to the State Department. That night, Hickerson heard from the watch officer, who said, "There's a development and I think that you would want to come in right away."

There wasn't much that Hickerson could do on that Saturday night, but the same was true for a striver like Rusk, who'd come straight to the office from the Alsop dinner. In April, Rusk had asked for what seemed like a demotion: to leave his post as "deputy under secretary for substantive matters" (Acheson's phrase) to become assistant secretary for Far Eastern affairs. This title better suited the former Colonel Rusk, who'd long had an interest in the region. Acheson had regarded Rusk's request as a favor, a way to replace one of those assistant secretaries being blamed for the "loss" of China.

2. In Tokyo, General MacArthur, as the proconsul of Japan, lived inside the American Embassy. He was an intimidating figure, even from a distance of seven thousand miles, and much more so at close range. When Truman adviser Albert Z. Carr visited Tokyo, one officer told him, "He is greater than Napoleon. He combines the qualities of ten men. He is a great soldier, a great statesman, a great political philosopher, a great economist, a great student of literature, and a great historian." His loyal adjutants have tried to portray him as a man with a lightning-quick understanding of events. Major General Courtney Whitney, whose loyalty bordered on reverence, recalled phoning early on Sunday morning, seeing MacArthur in his gray, West Point bathrobe, and that "it took only a moment for the import of the news to sink in." In MacArthur's recollection, written years later, the news came by telephone, which "rang with the note of urgency that can sound only in the hush of a darkened room." He was told that thousands of "Red Korean troops . . . were moving southward with a speed and power that was sweeping aside all opposition," and it *did* recall Pearl Harbor: "It was the same fell note of the war cry that was again ringing in my ears. It couldn't be, I told myself. Not again!"

But MacArthur was flummoxed by this sudden development. His wartime reflexes were gone. His biographer William Manchester has suggested that "he appeared to be trying to convince himself that there would be no need for action." John Foster Dulles, who was sometimes recruited for diplomatic assignments (he'd worked on the United Nations charter, had been Thomas Dewey's foreign policy adviser, and would become secretary of state under President Eisenhower), was in Tokyo to negotiate a benign peace treaty with Japan. When Dulles got word of the attack, from a State Department officer, he couldn't persuade anyone on MacArthur's staff to telephone the general; everyone, he later said, was afraid to disturb him on a Sunday—family time when he liked to watch the films of West Point football games that were flown out to him. Army Lieutenant Alexander Haig, the duty officer for Major General Edward Almond, MacArthur's chief of staff, was probably the first military officer in Tokyo to learn, from Muccio, that a war had begun, but Haig was nervous about calling the "volcanic" Almond. He did, though, make the call and tell Almond that Muccio regarded the invasion as genuine.

Dulles finally made the MacArthur call himself. Later that day, he went to see the general, in his office on the sixth floor of the Dai-ichi Mutual Life Insurance Building. Dulles was accompanied by John W. Allison, the director of the State Department's Office of Northeast Asian Affairs, who remembered that MacArthur "was magnificent as he strode up and down his huge office, his khaki shirt open at the neck, and his famous corncob pipe gripped between his teeth." But the general called the reports from Korea "fragmentary and inconclusive," and said, "This is probably only a reconnaissance in force. If Washington only will not hobble me, I can handle it with one arm tied behind my back."

The next day, Dulles had dinner with MacArthur and his wife, Jean. There was no mention of Korea, and after the meal, the guests, including several enlisted men, retired to the ballroom, for a movie—a western, which MacArthur watched from a rocking chair. When MacArthur saw Dulles off, the general said, "Anyone who wants to commit U.S. troops to fight in Korea should have his head examined."

Although there was artillery fire on the outskirts of Seoul, and reports that the city was being evacuated, it wasn't until Tuesday, June 27, that MacArthur's headquarters viewed the Sunday attack as far more serious than just another incident along the 38th Parallel. Seoul fell the next day; its defenders on the south side of the Han

River watched, helpless, when the main crossing—the Han River Bridge—was dynamited, with no warning, by the retreating army, leaving hundreds of military personnel and civilians stranded on the collapsing bridge. As many as eight hundred were killed by the explosion, or drowned, a devastating event in the history of the war. While it halted the north's advance, a blitzkrieg with Russian-built T-34 tanks, it left tens of thousands at the mercy of an army about to inflict enormous suffering. By the end of June, the military historian Roy Appleman wrote, everything north of the Han was lost.

"It is strange to recall," the State Department's Doc Matthews was to write, "how difficult it was in the first two or three days to get General MacArthur, sitting in 'splendid isolation' in Tokyo, to take Korea seriously." General Eisenhower, in a note to his friend General Alfred Gruenther, referred to MacArthur, and not admiringly: "Has it occurred to you that the G-2 [military intelligence] Division in Japan is headed by the same man who headed the G-2 Division in the Philippines in 1941?"—when the islands fell to Japan. "Is it possible that he is not very alert? This is something that might cause you and your associates a little head scratching."

3. Truman, on Sunday, had gone ahead with plans to visit his brother, Vivian, on the Grandview farm, and to see his sister, Mary Jane. But he didn't stay for Sunday dinner. The Korean situation kept nagging at him—"thought Acheson might call, which he did," he noted in his diary. The UN Security Council, having been called into emergency session at Lake Success, New York, voted 9–0 to approve a resolution, presented by the United States, that called the attack "a breach of the peace." It asked for an immediate cease-fire and withdrawal of North Korea's forces back to the 38th Parallel, and urged members to "furnish such assistance to the Republic of Korea as may be necessary to repel the armed attack." That rare show of unanimity was only possible because the Soviet representative had been boycotting the UN, to protest the seating of Nationalist China on the Security Council. Reporters, in Independence, knowing that something important was happening, were outside the

Truman house, which was encircled by an iron fence to protect the shrubbery. When Acheson telephoned again, Truman decided to return at once to Washington. "Don't make it alarmist," Truman told the waiting reporters. "It could be a dangerous situation, but I hope it isn't."

Truman's plane landed late that Sunday afternoon. During the flight, he mulled recent history—or, as he recalled it five years later, what he saw as the appetite of totalitarian powers for Western democracies. "I felt certain that if South Korea was allowed to fall, Communist leaders would be emboldened to override nations closer to our own shores," he wrote. More than that, "If this was allowed to go unchallenged it would mean a third world war, just as similar incidents had brought on the second world war." In connecting the Korean attack to the risk of another world war (a linkage that newspaper stories did not shy from), Truman managed to work himself up to the point of seeing the invasion not only as a test of national will, but of personal backbone. He was met at the airport by Acheson, Johnson, and James E. Webb, the under secretary of state, who remembered that Acheson climbed into the backseat with Truman, while he and Johnson took the jump seats. Webb recalled that Truman's first words were "By God, I don't believe they can support this military action across the trans-Siberian Railroad and I'm gonna let them have it." At that, "Louie stuck out his hand to shake hands—'yessir, we'll let 'em have it.'"

Acheson had prepared for the meeting at Blair House by giving himself time to "ruminate," to let "various possibilities, like glass fragments in a kaleidoscope, form a series of patterns of action and then draw conclusions from them." He recalled thinking that "if Korean force proved unequal to the job, as seemed probable, only American military intervention could do it," and that, right away, he'd viewed the attack as "an open, undisguised challenge to our internationally accepted position as the protector of South Korea, an area of great importance to the security of American-occupied Japan." That retrospective outlook simultaneously reshaped his own publicly stated views on the "defensive perimeter" and pretty much came out of nowhere. In this reshaping, he wrote of "the shadow cast by power"—an elegant phrase to describe what he saw as America's postwar burden.

During the Sunday war council, which continued until 11 p.m., Acheson gave Truman what he characterized as "a darkening report of great confusion," and among his recommendations, short of war, was that General MacArthur should be ordered to supply Korea with more arms and equipment; that the air force should protect Gimpo, the Seoul airport, during an evacuation of American civilians; and that the Seventh Fleet should be moved to prevent China from attacking Formosa, while also blocking Formosa from attacking the mainland—the kind of trouble no one sought. While Acheson was at it, he wanted more financial aid for Bao Dai, the faltering last emperor of Vietnam, along with a military mission to the region. Louis Johnson, suspending his feud with the secretary of state, said that he liked what Acheson had just said.

General Collins, the army chief of staff, said that the military situation in Korea was "bad," and that South Korea's chief of staff "has no fight left in him." If the United States intended to commit ground troops, he said, "we must mobilize." Everyone around the table knew that the depleted state of the armed forces posed a serious problem. Truman, though, seemed unable to acknowledge the predicament when, with no one objecting, he said that he'd "done everything he could for five years to prevent this kind of situation." He wondered about mobilizing the National Guard and asked General Bradley if he thought that was necessary; if so, it meant asking Congress for funds. Bradley replied that if ground forces were sent to Korea, without general mobilization, other commitments would suffer. Acheson then suggested that mobilization plans be held "in reserve."

Truman wanted the Joint Chiefs to think about mobilization. "We must do everything we can for the Korean situation," he said, adding that the viability of the United Nations was at stake. "I don't want to go to war," he said. Truman knew that the quandary he suddenly faced was, at least partly, of his own making. To do nothing about such a brazen Communist military adventure meant ignoring the administration's policy blueprint, set forth in NSC-68—and that meant risking American prestige, and possibly surrendering not only

Korea but Formosa. If he chose military engagement, with available manpower, there was no way to predict, or control, what might come next. Acheson said it was "important for us to do something even if the effort were not successful." That was a curious argument, but Defense Secretary Johnson agreed, saying that "even if we lose Korea this action would save the situation."

In less than forty-eight hours, a small, divided Far East nation had come to assume enormous significance. Foster Dulles added his view in a worrying wire to Acheson: "To sit idly by while Korea is overrun by unprovoked armed attack would start a disastrous chain of events leading most probably to world war." An intelligence report prepared for the State Department asserted that "the North Korean Government is completely under Kremlin control and there is no possibility that the North Koreans acted without prior instruction from Moscow." Acheson didn't doubt these assessments, although they were not wholly accurate. "It seemed close to certain," he recalled, "that the attack had been mounted, supplied, and instigated by the Soviet Union and that it would not be stopped by anything short of force." That was a view that Truman and Acheson continued to hold, but in fact, while the Russians had helped supply the North with tanks and other weaponry, and had a malevolent rooting interest in the outcome, Stalin's actual role was relatively modest. He'd supported Kim's plan to attack and hoped that, if carried out with overwhelming force, it might settle things quickly; and he was clever enough to see how an Asian war might ensnare the United States. But Russian soldiers were not on the ground, fighting American soldiers, which had been Stalin's chief worry when he acquiesced to Kim's war plans. Soviet aerial involvement would come later.

Truman, on Monday, June 26, met with representatives of the South Korean Mission, and told them, possibly to their mystification, that Americans admired the Korean people "and their struggle in adversity." He said "I tell you two things"—that, in 1777, when things looked bad at Valley Forge, "some friends came and helped," and that, in 1917, when Europeans were in despair, "some friends went over and helped them." On Tuesday, in the late morning, Truman saw a group of senators and congressmen who'd been invited to a "very important meeting on Korea." After Acheson summarized what was happening, Senator Tom Connally, of Texas, the chairman of the Foreign Relations Committee, said this would be the "clearest test case the United Nation has ever faced." Truman by then had further clarified his own thinking. "If we let Korea down, the Soviets will keep right on going and swallow up one piece of Asia after another," he said. "If we were to let Asia go, the Near East would collapse and no telling what would happen in Europe." That sort of formulation reflected Acheson's viewpoint, and Acheson, in his statements, reinforced Truman's leanings. Truman gave his guests a preview of a much-worked-on public statement, which he read aloud. It said that he'd "ordered United States air and sea forces to give the Korean Government troops cover and support," and that "the attack upon Korea makes it plain beyond all doubt that communism has passed beyond the use of subversion to conquer independent nations and will now use armed invasion and war." A few moments of silence followed, after which Acheson pointed out that the President's public announcement did not mention the Soviet Union—only "communism"—so that Russia could still back down "without losing too much face."

That announcement, along with news that MacArthur had taken command of the Seventh Fleet, was widely applauded. Clark Clifford, who'd left the White House in late 1949 to start a career as a high-priced Washington lawyer, sounded excited by the prospect of a little war in which he had no part. "The old fire horse got a whiff of smoke," he said, in a note to Truman that called his decision "magnificent." He suggested that Truman ask the UN "to issue an order giving the North Korean forces forty-eight hours to withdraw"; if they refused, "military forces of member nations . . . will bomb military objectives." There were, though, dissents. The *Chicago Tribune*, consistent with its anti-interventionist tradition, called Truman's statement "an illegal declaration of war," and argued that "the essence of the Truman policy is to give Russia a free hand in choosing when war will come and where." Senator Taft, after saying that he had no choice but to back the President, had second thoughts: There was "no legal authority" for Truman's action, he said, and if Congress let it go unchallenged, "we will have finally terminated for all time the right of Congress to declare war as provided by the Constitution." He also saw the Korea crisis as a result of a "bungling and inconsistent foreign policy"—especially what the Republican right saw as a passive China policy that they blamed for Mao Zedong's Communist victory and the routing of Chiang Kai-shek. Taft said—and would say again—that Acheson should resign.

There was nothing inconsistent about Acheson's role as a prime mover of administration foreign policy. As James Reston saw it, from the moment that North Korea crossed the 38th Parallel, Acheson argued that "the whole moral basis of American foreign policy, and the confidence of the world in the United States, in the United Nations, and in the whole collective security system was at stake." With self-assurance and calm encouragement, he tried to guide Truman's decision-making in a war that, at its outset, had great popular support. A Gallup survey found that eight of ten voters agreed with Truman that the American response would further "the cause of peace for the world."

4. On June 29, two days after announcing a commitment to provide "cover and support," Truman held a press conference, during which he said several things that he might not have said had he been more careful, or would have said only if he'd been less liberal about granting permission to quote him freely. It began with an apparently simple question:

> Q: Mr. President, everybody is asking in this country, are we or are we not at war?
> The President: We are not at war.
> Q: Mr. President, another question that is being asked is, are we going to use ground troops in Korea?
> The President: No comment on that.
> Q: Mr. President, in that connection it has been asked whether there might be any possibility of having to use the atomic bomb?
> The President: No comment.

Q: Could you elaborate sir, a little more on the reason for this move, and the peace angle on it?

The President: The Republic of Korea was set up with the United Nations help. It is a recognized government by the members of the United Nations. It was unlawfully attacked by a bunch of bandits which are neighbors of North Korea. The United Nations Security Council held a meeting and passed on the situation and asked the members to go to the relief of the Korean Republic. And the members of the United Nations are going to the relief of the Korean Republic to suppress a bandit raid on the Republic of Korea.

Q: Mr. President, would it be correct, against your explanation, to call this a police action under the United Nations?

The President: Yes. That is exactly what it amounts to.

Having introduced the term "police action"—even though it was a reporter, not Truman, who did the introducing—and suggesting that neighboring "bandits" were to blame, and offering "no comment" on the prospect of using a nuclear bomb, there were, unsurprisingly, more questions:

Q: When you refer to police action on behalf of Korea, you mean United Nations?

The President: That is correct. That is correct.

Q: Mr. President, your "no comment" on the atomic bomb might be subject to misinterpretation. Has there been any change—

The President: No comment will be made on any matter of strategy. I don't expect to comment on any matter of strategy.

That press conference came at about the time that MacArthur made his first post-attack trip to Korea. Along for the 120-mile flight were five members of his staff and four Tokyo-based correspondents, who filed reports that could only bolster a MacArthur mystique that included such physical objects as "his famed Bataan" (a Lockheed C-121A Constellation), his corncob pipe (one of his corncobs is encased inside the War Memorial in Seoul), and his "scrambled eggs" cap (the military nickname for golden oak-leaf trimming on the visors of dress hats).

When they were on the ground, a mile from Seoul, General Whitney recalled that "MacArthur took his pipe from his mouth and jabbed its stem toward a hill a little way ahead," suggesting that they move closer. In the distance, they could see Seoul burning. On the return to Tokyo, MacArthur scribbled out a distressing message for his superiors in Washington. The note arrived at 1:31 a.m., and, among other things, said that "the Korean Army and coastal forces are in confusion, have not seriously fought and lack leadership through their own means," and that their army "is entirely incapable of counteraction and there is grave danger of a further breakthrough. If the enemy advance continues much further, it will seriously threaten the fall of the Republic." It continued: "The only assurance for the holding of the present line, and the ability to regain later the lost ground is through the introduction of U.S. ground combat forces into the Korean battle area." Acheson got a similarly urgent report from William Sebald, the State Department's highest-ranking person in Tokyo, after Ambassador Muccio had said the situation was "desperate and rapidly deteriorating" and "strongly urged all out effort before situation out of hand." That was no exaggeration. Of ninety-eight thousand men in the Republic of Korea Army on June 25, at the end of the month, U.S. Army headquarters could account for only twenty-two thousand south of the Han.

To MacArthur's annoyance, General Collins responded to his demand for ground combat forces in a teleconference—a cumbersome two-way teletype—and informed him that this required Truman's approval. "Time is of the essence," MacArthur replied, "and a clear-cut decision without delay is imperative." Rusk too was eager for the Americans to step in with force. The doubters included Louis Johnson, Army Secretary Pace, and Admiral Forrest Sherman, the chief of naval operations, who worried about "the hazards involved in fighting Asiatics on the Asiatic mainland." Acheson, though, was not discouraged. Nor was Truman, who had more faith in the United Nations than Acheson, and explained his thinking to his aide George Elsey: "Okay, now we started the United Nations. It was our idea, and in this first big test we just couldn't let them down. If a collective system under the U.N. can work, it must be made to work, and *now* is the time to call their bluff."

Early in the morning of June 30, Truman asked Pace and Johnson to look at MacArthur's request, and to consider an offer from Chiang Kai-shek to send an additional thirty-three thousand soldiers from Formosa, if the United States would arrange for their transport. "What that will do to Mao Tse-tung we do not know," the President said. "We must be careful not to cause a general Asiatic war." Without explaining his reasoning, he added, "Russia is figuring on an attack in the Black Sea and toward the Persian Gulf. Both are prizes Russia has wanted since Ivan the Terrible, who is now their hero along with Lenin and Stalin." The decision to send the thirty thousand United States troops to Korea was made later that day, during a meeting that lasted about half an hour. Acheson, wisely, put a stop to Chiang's offer, pointing out that using Nationalist troops might very well persuade Communist China to reply in kind.

Truman said that he would give General MacArthur "full authority to use the ground forces under his command, with no limit on the number of divisions to be sent to Korea." He also agreed to a naval blockade of North Korea. The White House statement was a masterly example of the use of language to disguise the scope of a military commitment: "In keeping with the United Nations Security Council's request for support . . . in repelling the North Korean invaders and restoring peace in Korea," it said, "the President announced that he had authorized the United States Air Force to conduct missions on specific military targets in northern Korea wherever militarily necessary, and had ordered a naval blockade of the entire Korean coast. General MacArthur has been authorized to use certain supporting ground units."

Later that June 30, Truman saw Foster Dulles, who'd just returned from Tokyo. Dulles described MacArthur's disengagement when word had come of the North Korean incursion, and said he'd "like to have MacArthur hauled back to the United States." Truman replied that he couldn't recall him "without causing a tremendous reaction in this country where he has been built up to heroic stature."

That may have understated MacArthur's stature. "It was not easy to draft a cable to General MacArthur," Robert Cutler, who had served in the War Department's Legislative and Liaison Division, said. "He was regarded in the Pentagon and elsewhere, not as a Person but as a Personage." As Matthew Ridgway, the deputy army chief of staff, put it, there was "an almost superstitious awe of this larger-than-life military figure who had so often been right when everyone else had been wrong."

Yet General Eisenhower, who'd been MacArthur's chief of staff in the Philippines in the 1930s, doubted not only his perspicacity but his ability as a commander. He thought MacArthur, at seventy, was too old, and described him to General Ridgway "as 'an untouchable' whose actions you cannot predict, and who will himself decide what information he wants Washington to have and what he will withhold." Less gently, he'd once remarked, "I just can't understand how such a damn fool could have gotten to be a general." A lot about MacArthur irked Truman, although he confined those opinions to his diary, where he regarded him as "a play actor and a bunco man," and didn't "see how a country can produce such men as Robert E. Lee, John J. Pershing, Eisenhower, & Bradley and at the same time produce Custers, Pattons, and MacArthurs." Truman's early animus was not unprompted. He disapproved of MacArthur's political ambitions—that, in 1944, he'd lent his name to a dubious presidential candidacy, and did so again, in 1948, from Japan, ending that effort only after losing the Wisconsin primary. To Truman, there was something unbecoming about a man in uniform pursuing the presidency, an ambition that MacArthur had not yet abandoned. Yet for all that, Truman also deferred to the Personage who'd been first in his class at West Point, a military aide to Theodore Roosevelt, and chief of staff of the celebrated "Rainbow Division" in 1917, when Harry Truman was a mere field artillery captain.

On that same post-invasion June 30, Truman agreed to adopt the open-ended conclusions of NSC-68—its ultimate cost to be determined—"as a statement of policy to be followed over the next four or five years." It was a lot to deal with. Eben Ayers, the deputy press secretary, saw that Truman was already in need of a respite.

He'd found the time to play poker before lunch, with Ayers acting as banker and bookkeeper, and to play again in the late afternoon, after which the President slept until nearly dinnertime. Then, Ayers noted in his diary, "we played cards until after 1:00 a.m."

5. Truman was proud of being able to make decisions quickly—"jump decisions," he called them—based on the recommendations of advisers he most trusted, as well as "his own deep hunches," as the *New York Times'* Anthony Leviero explained it. "You've got to make it now," Truman believed, "and then if it's wrong, maybe tomorrow you can make a better one." He said, "If your heart's right and you know the history and the background of these things, it'll be right. You'll find nine times in ten the decision off the cuff, in the long run, is the correct one."

Jump decisions, though, had drawbacks. They could mean, as the magazine journalist Robert Bendiner wrote, that Truman would give someone like Acheson "an automatic go-ahead without trying to weigh for himself the problems involved." They could mean a failure to think through the possible consequences of a quick yes or no, which was not a problem for those who bore no direct responsibility—consultant outsiders like Foster Dulles, or members of Congress, or newspaper columnists, who could change their minds, and change them again, without penalties. The *Wall Street Journal*'s Vermont Royster, who'd questioned the wisdom of the Truman Doctrine three years earlier, pointed out that "actual thinking about" the Korea decision, its costs and risks, "was in a time span of less than 24 hours"—so hurried that Truman's advisers "are only just now beginning to calculate all the risks." That sort of haste bothered the President's critics who, Bendiner wrote, believed that Truman had "almost no capacity for abstract thought, that where judgments from the White House are in fact his own, they are almost always personal or political in the narrowest sense of the word."

As Truman took rapid steps toward war, he did so without convening the cabinet or the National Security Council; nor, although he consulted a number of high-ranking military men, had he involved the Joint Chiefs. On July 3, when he met, at Blair House, with members of Congress and senior advisers, it was generally agreed that he shouldn't ask for a resolution of congressional support: That "would be practically asking for a declaration of war," the Senate majority leader, Scott W. Lucas, of Illinois, said. Acheson thought any initiative should come from Congress, such as a resolution in which Congress would "commend the action by the United States rather than action by the President."

George Elsey recalled the President bending over the globe in his office and once more articulating his worldview: "Korea is the Greece of the Far East. If we are tough enough now, if we stand up to [the Communists] like we did in Greece three years ago, they won't take any next steps. But if we just stand by, they'll move into Iran and they'll take over the whole Middle East. There is no telling what they'll do if we don't put up a fight now." This sharp divide between yes and no, or black and white, could give some decisions a sharper focus, but could also narrow Truman's view of the world, even to the point of blurring the identity, and motives, of "they" and "them." Truman liked the term "bandits," which evoked a picture of lawless guerrillas; Acheson too was quick to agree with a reporter's characterization of the North Korean government as a "gang of armed marauders which have possession of a certain amount of territory." It was a strange unwillingness to acknowledge that they were actually facing the well-equipped army of a hostile power. Soon after the deployment of American ground troops, there were signs that the United States, the supremely powerful victor of World War II, might not be able to win quickly, and decisively, when it came to fighting a small, poor nation, though one with the advantages of patience, discipline, and, as everyone knew, a powerful ally, just across the Yalu River.

TWENTY

"The Second Hand of Destiny"

Every war is ironic because every war is worse than expected. Every war constitutes an irony of situation because its means are so melodramatically disproportionate to its presumed ends.

—Paul Fussell, *The Great War and Modern Memory*

1. Official Washington was excited. "These are the rush-rush early days of the last war here," a newspaper story began. "The Potomac fever registers as soon as you pick up a telephone." The Alsop brothers, writing about "our momentous Korean decision," quoted an unnamed official who saw the attack on South Korea as "an event like Hitler's re-occupation of the Rhineland." James Reston discovered "a transformation in the spirit" of the government, and quoted some anonymous soul saying that Truman's decision "has untied a thousand knots." On July 7, 1950, by a 7–0 vote, with three abstentions and the continued boycott by the Soviet Union, the UN Security Council authorized the United States to set up a unified command in Korea. Truman then gave General MacArthur an augmented title: commander in chief of the United Nations Command, or the hard-to-digest acronym CINCUNC. Twenty-one countries agreed to send personnel to Korea, but it was difficult to mask this as anything but an American war. Fifty percent of the troops were Americans, with 40 percent from the Republic of Korea. Some countries sent none. The French representative said the "bitter struggle" in Indochina was enough to contend with.

In early July, President Truman invited Admiral Leahy, his former chief of staff, to a Cabinet meeting. Leahy was slightly baffled by Truman's objectives in Korea: "He seemed to wish to talk to somebody in whom he had confidence," he thought. Leahy, furthermore, was apprehensive. He worried that the Defense Department might take command of the war, bypassing the President, and couldn't understand Truman's optimism. While Joint Chiefs chairman Omar Bradley thought that they would keep "holding on," Leahy foresaw "another 'Dunkirk' before adequate American reinforcements can arrive."

The first American battle of the war was fought on July 5, by a task force that traveled from Japan to Pusan, on Korea's south coast. Their hazy orders were to stall a much larger North Korean force: "When you get to Pusan, head for Taejon"—a city south of Seoul. "Block the main road as far north as possible." Then, contact a general, and "if you can't locate him, go to Taejon and beyond if you can. Sorry I can't give you more information. . . . Good luck to you, and God bless you and your men." Task Force Smith (named for its leader, Lieutenant Colonel Charles B. Smith) was unarmored, and outnumbered by more than ten to one. Facing Soviet-built T-34 tanks, it didn't stand a chance. Out of 440 soldiers, assisted by the 52nd Field Artillery Battalion, 181 were killed, wounded, or missing; the rest retreated. The first GI to die, cut down by machine-gun fire, was Private Kenneth Shadrick, a nineteen-year-old coal miner's son, from a West Virginia mountain hollow called Skin Fork. T. R. Fehrenbach, who served in Korea, in the 2nd Infantry Division, and wrote the riveting memoir *This Kind of War*, recalled that, in those first days, casualties among high-ranking officers were in greater proportion than in any fighting since the Civil War. American soldiers were unprepared for their sudden assignment. As Dean Rusk later said, "We sent some poor devils who had been on garrison duty in Japan without hard field training and that sort of thing—just simply quickly flew them over and put them onto the battlefield."

In what the military historian David Rees called "the frantic race in space and time between the North Korean advance and the United Nations build-up for the prize of Pusan," in the far south, Communist forces soon took control of about 95 percent of the Korean peninsula—everything outside the "Pusan Perimeter." MacArthur kept asking for more troops, more materiel, and more logistical support. His pleas, accompanied by intimations of imminent disaster, were something of an art form. In a telegram, sent on July 9, he wrote that "the situation . . . is critical. . . . We are endeavoring by all means now avail[able] here to build up the force nec[essary]to hold the enemy but to date our efforts against his armor and mechanized forces have been ineffective." He warned of an unseen force that "assumes the aspect of a combination of Soviet leadership and technical guidance with Chinese Communist ground elements."

Truman sent Army chief of staff Lawton Collins and air force chief of staff Hoyt Vandenberg to Tokyo to get a firsthand report from MacArthur. The CINCUNC was ready. He informed his visitors that he regarded Korea as a cul-de-sac—all routes into the country depended on tunnels and bridges. "He saw a unique opportunity for the use of the atomic bomb to deal a crippling blow to these supply routes," Collins recalled. MacArthur told them, "We win here or lose everywhere; if we win here, we improve the chances of winning everywhere." Then, adding broader goals to the original mission, he said, "I intend to destroy and not to drive back the North Korean forces. I may need to occupy all of North Korea. In the aftermath of operations, the problem is to compose and unite Korea." Recalling this conversation, Collins wrote, MacArthur "always gave me the impression of addressing not just his immediate listeners but a larger audience unseen."

Soldiers on both sides of the Parallel were soon engaged in an engulfing war as battles were fought in places whose names—Taejon, Pyongtaek, the Geum River, Youngdeok, Hapcheon—were becoming familiar in the West. The United States quickly demonstrated superior airpower, with B-29 Superfortresses and a seemingly endless supply of bombs. But the war was still being fought on the ground, with all the elements of stalemate as each side advanced, and then retreated. An American general observed that the war was becoming "a sort of creeping emergency."

A visitor encounters some of this at the War Memorial, a dark giant of a building, on the site of the former Korean Army headquarters, in the Itaewon neighborhood of Seoul. Admission is free, but the War Memorial is not exactly overrun with tourists. Its overarching theme is death, and the cost of a war that, after three years, settled nothing. A visitor to its long, dim corridors, oversized rooms, and kinetic exhibits is reminded that, from first to last, Koreans saw it as a *Korean* war: Koreans fighting Koreans. In "The Reunion of the Fallen Brothers after 60 Years," a glassed-in display lets one view the disinterred remains of two Korean soldiers, identified by DNA. Military heroes are celebrated, but the videotaped testimony of veterans is anything but heroic. One, recalling a battle that left many comrades dead, says, "I was paralyzed by fear of death which could have hit me anytime just as it had hit them." Another remembers that "I got extremely terrified when I realized that I could kill people just by pulling the trigger, but pulled myself together by telling myself that I had to kill in order to live." Another room attempts to recreate the confusing sights and explosive noises of a nighttime battleground. None of the exhibits, though, attempts to depict the obliteration of Korea's towns and villages.

On the home front, J. Edgar Hoover, on July 7, informed Sidney Souers of a plan to suspend habeas corpus and detain as many as twelve thousand men and women, most of them American citizens, who could be "found to be potentially dangerous to the internal security through investigation." Souers was no longer with the NSC, but had become a "special consultant" to Truman on national security issues—an imprecise title that kept him close to his friend the President. Congressman Lloyd Bentsen, of Texas (he would become the Democratic Party's vice-presidential nominee in 1988), proposed that Truman give North Korea a week to withdraw from the South; if they refused, General MacArthur should be given a "list of principal North Korean cities which would be subjected to atomic attack by our Air Force." Another impatient Texas Democrat, the freshman Senator Lyndon B. Johnson, said that Truman should call up eight hundred thousand National Guardsmen and reservists: "We are going to be forced to do this anyway in time and the sooner the better." This oral aggression included the suggestion, from Senator Owen Brewster, a Maine Republican, to put MacArthur in charge of the atomic bomb. "The Communists should understand that we are not spending billions for bombs out of scientific curiosity," Brewster said. "Presumably they are designed to save the lives of American boys."

CBS Radio's *World News Round-Up* reported, on July 13, that Syngman Rhee, the seventy-five-year-old who'd been South Korea's unelected president since July 1948, said peace was impossible while Korea was divided by the 38th Parallel. The CBS report quoted an army spokesman who reminded listeners that the aim of the UN mission had been to push North Korean forces back across the Parallel. This so appalled the State Department's John Allison that, in a memo to Dean Rusk, he called Rhee's statement "understandable," if premature, but said the army spokesman's words were "folly," and were Allison a South Korean, he "would be strongly tempted to lay down my arms and go back to farm." American objectives seemed to be in flux. Truman, on the afternoon of July 13, was asked if he still wanted to call the conflict a "police action":

> *The President:* Yes, it is still a police action.
> *Q:* Mr. President, are we prepared to resist aggression everywhere in the world, as in Korea?
> *The President:* We will have to meet the situations as they develop. I can't answer that question.

Something essential, though, was missing: As George Kennan told Acheson, in an unasked-for letter: "We have not achieved a clear and realistic and generally accepted view of our objectives in Korea." He added that the war could "easily carry us toward real conflict with the Russians." As for Indochina, Kennan warned that "we are getting ourselves into the position of guaranteeing the French in an undertaking which neither they nor we, nor both of us together, can win."

Truman seemed, as if for the first time, to realize that victory in Korea was not going to be easy, or quick. "It looks bad in the Far

East," he wrote to Bess, on July 12. "We can't get there in force for 3 weeks and by then it may be too late. Or there'll be an explosion someplace else. Hope we can contain it and not have to order our terrible weapon turned loose." He was furthermore being subjected to dental torture—an hour each afternoon while a new dentist was "remaking my lastest [sic] upper bridge," which had just been installed "and which came out twice of its own accord."

It was time—well past time—for Truman to say something, to speak directly to his countrymen, and he finally did so on the night of July 19. In his speech, carried on radio and television, he described the fighting in Korea as a battle for the values of Western civilization: "An act of aggression such as this creates a very real danger to the security of all free nations," he said, and "this is a direct challenge to the efforts of the free nations to build the kind of world in which men can live in freedom and peace." Then he further raised the stakes, saying that the United States had committed its armed forces "because we know that what is at stake here is nothing less than our own national security and the peace of the world." He asked Congress to pass a rearmament and mobilization program, at a cost of ten billion dollars—almost double the current defense budget. "There are now statutory limits on the sizes of the armed forces," his message to Congress said, "and since we may need to exceed these limits, I recommend that they be removed." Above all, although he didn't say it, he wanted Americans to get used to the idea that what had begun as a little war with limited objectives had, in less than three weeks, drifted into a rudderless, potentially limitless conflict.

Away from the microphones, Truman might try to escape. He could even become the Truman of his youth, an autodidact who found time to conduct a mystifying dialogue on ancient history with a Missouri reporter. On the day that he called the Korean conflict a fight for Western civilization, he found time to write to the *St. Louis Post-Dispatch*'s Edward A. Harris, whom he'd known since he was a senator, to instruct him that "the wars between the Hittites and the Egyptians and between Assyria and the Hittites, between Egypt and Babylon are in the same pattern as today. . . . You don't even have to go that far to learn that real history consists of the life and actions of great men who occupied the stage at the time."

Attached to this somewhat baffling note to Harris was another, from a bemused Charlie Ross, saying, "My God, when is all this going to end?"

2. In the spring of 1948, less than two years after replacing Henry Wallace as commerce secretary, Averell Harriman moved to Paris, to administer the Marshall Plan. He returned to Washington in June, 1950, to become Truman's special assistant on foreign affairs. Walter Lippmann thought that was a grand idea; he saw Harriman in the role played by Colonel House during Woodrow Wilson's presidency, or by Harry Hopkins under Roosevelt, able to bring to the administration something missing: "direct and intimate understanding of foreign countries." In that spirit, Truman, on August 3, sent Harriman to Tokyo, for a "political brief" with MacArthur, whom Harriman had known, on a first-name basis, since 1920, when MacArthur was superintendent at West Point.

The most pressing reason for Harriman's assignment was to rein in the general, who'd recently made an unannounced trip to Formosa. MacArthur had explained that he wanted "to make a brief reconnaissance of the situation there," and dismissed the idea that the visit had any political significance or represented a conflict with his superiors in Washington. But MacArthur was a great admirer of Chiang Kai-shek, and the visit took on significance after the generalissimo issued a celebratory communiqué, saying that he and MacArthur had reached important agreements on "Sino-America military cooperation." Truman wanted Harriman to emphasize to MacArthur that Chiang couldn't be allowed to "be the cause of starting a war with the Chinese communists on the mainland." The status of Formosa was delicate enough; after all, the inclusion of Nationalist China on the UN Security Council had led to Russia's walkout.

Harriman and MacArthur spent a good deal of time together: eight and a half hours of talks, between August 6 and August 8, a dinner that included Jean MacArthur, and a day trip to Korea, where Harriman visited a command post. "Nobody shot at me," he remarked afterward. When Harriman asked if MacArthur had any doubts about the wisdom of the intervention, he replied, in Harriman's paraphrase, that it was "an historic decision which would save the world from Communist domination, and would be so recorded in history."

Harriman's report to Truman took note of MacArthur's occasional bursts of flattery, shrillness, drama, and ethnic assumptions, such as his view of how "Westerners and Orientals" look at death: "We hate to die; only face danger out of a sense of duty and through moral issues; whereas with Orientals, life begins with death," MacArthur had explained to Harriman. "They die quietly, 'folding their arms as a dove folding his wings, relaxing, and dying.'" The supreme commander, Harriman continued, then "folded his arms and sighed." He said he wanted fresh recruits, as well as "fast ships and airplanes to transport the needed troops rapidly." The idea of failure, he said, "makes me feel sick in my stomach." General Matthew Ridgway, who'd attended some of the conversations with Harriman, and who recognized MacArthur's hold on him, afterward wrote a memorandum saying "In a brilliant 2½ hour presentation . . . supported by every logical military argument of his rich experience, and delivered with all of his dramatic eloquence, General MacArthur stated his compelling need for additional combat ground forces."

Yet after they were done, something nagged at Harriman, a blurry, bad feeling: "For reasons which are rather difficult to explain," he wrote to Truman, "I did not feel that we came to a full agreement on the way we believed things should be handled on Formosa and with the Generalissimo. [MacArthur] accepted the President's position and will act accordingly, but without full conviction." Harriman pointed out the basic conflict: that Chiang wanted to use Formosa "as a stepping-stone for his re-entry to the mainland," while the United States was worried about Formosa's "falling into hostile hands," and about China entering the war.

The Formosa excursion had raised other embarrassing questions. Had MacArthur informed the State Department? Apparently not. American allies, who didn't want to be tied to the fortunes of Chiang

Kai-shek, were troubled. Acheson, uncharacteristically, was so disconcerted that he dodged reporters' questions. MacArthur, always keenly interested in his press notices, said that his Formosa visit was being "maliciously misrepresented . . . by those who invariably in the past have propagandized a policy of defeatism and appeasement in the Pacific." Certain aspects of the Formosa trip had, fortunately, gone unreported, such as how, deplaning from the *Bataan*, MacArthur had grasped the hand of Premier Chen Chang with the words "My dear Generalissimo" before figuring out which Chinese leader was which. Hearst's Bob Considine was close enough to overhear MacArthur's appreciation of the generalissimo's wife. "Look at the leg on Madame Chiang," he'd whispered to his pilot, while a band played and wind rustled Madame Chiang's split gown. "The leg of a girl of twenty."

On the day that MacArthur's latest complaint was published, Truman met with reporters:

Q: General MacArthur says there are defeatists and appeasers who are working against him. Is anybody trying to set you against General MacArthur? . . .

The President: I haven't met anybody of that sort yet. General MacArthur and I are in perfect agreement, and have been ever since he has been in the job he is now. I put him there, and I also appointed him Commander in Chief of American and Allied Forces, at the suggestion of the United Nations. I am satisfied with what he is doing.

3. The American ambassador to the UN, Warren Austin, a former Republican senator from Vermont, announced on August 17 that the United States was committed to establishing a democratic government for the entire peninsula. "The determination of the United Nations to insure that Korea shall be free, unified and independent . . . has never wavered," he told the Security Council, adding that Korea's prospects would be dark indeed if the UN supported a nation "half slave and half free." Austin's declaration, which had recast America's intentions with a Lincolnesque accent mark, was quickly toned down: Unnamed "sources" in the American delegation insisted that Truman hadn't changed the original instructions to MacArthur—to repel North Korea—and that Korea's hoped-for unification could be achieved "by negotiation." Despite that disclaimer, the service chiefs interpreted Austin's statement as a commitment to "the expulsion from Korea of the Communists as an organized political and military force." Yet, absent "official directives from higher authority," the chiefs felt stuck. A legal basis—or, more accurately, a justification for military operations north of the 38th Parallel—soon appeared, in the form of a National Security Council report (NSC- 81), which endorsed military action with a "strictly limited purpose." The authors of NSC-81 were willing to accept the risk of general war, acknowledging the unlikelihood "that the Soviet Union will passively accept" a situation in which all or most of Korea was wrested from its control. They were, however, reluctant to predict what might come next.

Then it was MacArthur's turn to make another kind of trouble. In late August, he sent a message to the Veterans of Foreign Wars, which was meant to be read at their annual encampment, in Chicago: After victory over Japan, it said, "our strategic frontier then shifted to embrace the entire Pacific Ocean, which has become a vast moat to protect us as long as we hold it." Therefore, Formosa, in the hands of an unfriendly power, would become an "enemy salient," and "could be compared to an unsinkable aircraft carrier . . . ideally located to accomplish defensive strategy." He dismissed the "threadbare argument by those who advocate appeasement and defeatism in the Pacific"—that phrase again—"that if we defend Formosa we alienate continental Asia." He warned that vacillation in the defense of the island would "shift any future battle area 5,000 miles eastward to the coasts of the American continents and our own home coast." He sent a copy to David Lawrence, telling the friendly editor of *U.S. News & World Report* that his views might help "clarify any fogginess in current American thinking."

Truman saw MacArthur's VFW letter as pure insubordination and, in a White House meeting, told Louis Johnson, "I want this letter withdrawn, and I want you to send an order to MacArthur to withdraw the letter, and that is an order from me." The defense secretary, though, resisted; MacArthur intimidated him too. Acheson, with unconcealed pleasure, later recalled that thirty minutes after the meeting broke up, Johnson was again willing to speak to him: He called to say that no one at the Pentagon could see that Truman's order made any sense—you couldn't withdraw a letter that was already public. Acheson said, "Louis, don't argue with me as to whether the President's order makes any sense or not. I heard him give it, and you accepted it; and whether it can be done or not, you'd better do it. He wants that order sent to MacArthur." Johnson thought it would be enough for MacArthur merely to say that he was speaking as "one individual only"—not for the government. But after a series of telephone calls—to Acheson again, and then to Harriman—and after meetings in several offices, Truman dictated a telegram and ordered Johnson to send it: "The President of the United States directs that you withdraw your message . . . because various features with respect to Formosa are in conflict with the Policy of the U.S. and its position in the UN." MacArthur cabled the VFW, while managing to signal that the reversal hadn't been his choice: "I regret to inform you that I have been directed to withdraw my message." By then, four hundred thousand copies of the September 1 issue of *U.S. News* had been printed and mailed.

The last thing Truman needed was a public spat with his field commander, and he tried to end it quickly. "The President regards the incident as closed," a weary Charlie Ross told reporters, on August 28, when he was asked if MacArthur would be relieved of his command. But the MacArthur incident wasn't closed, even though Truman, at his next press conference, called it a "closed incident," and tried to be generous, informing the general that General Collins and Admiral Sherman had just returned from Korea, and "their reports were satisfactory and highly gratifying to me." The VFW controversy almost drowned out the words of *another* runaway official: Francis P. Matthews, the latest secretary of the navy, who'd spoken at the Boston Naval Shipyard and said that the United States should be prepared to pay the "price of instituting war to compel cooperation for peace," an absurdist declaration that was disowned and denounced as soon as it was uttered.

As Truman faced skeptical questioning, and responsibility for a war that kept growing, he found comfort in a prayer, one that he'd recite "over and over" from his days as a "window washer, bottle duster, floor scrubber" until the present. In a remarkable look at his private beliefs, he wrote it down, perhaps never imagining that it would find its way into a book like this:

> *Help me to be, to think, to act what is right, because it is right; make me truthful, honest and honorable in all things; make me intellectually honest for the sake of right and honor and without thought of reward to me. Give me the ability to be charitable, forgiving and patient with my fellowmen—help me to understand their motives and their shortcomings—even as Thou understandest mine! Amen, Amen, Amen.*

4. Louis Johnson should have known that he was in trouble with Truman even before his appalling timidity vis-à-vis MacArthur, though he couldn't know how serious the trouble was. He didn't know that Truman, in June, accompanied by Margaret, had made a day trip to Leesburg, Virginia, to see General Marshall, and that they'd discussed China, MacArthur, Chiang Kai-shek, and the Defense Department—"a most interesting morning," Truman noted in his diary. The battering by the Alsop brothers had damaged Johnson's reputation, although the spending cuts he'd advocated had reflected Truman's wishes, and he'd also managed to alienate most of the cabinet. "Louis began to show an inordinate egotistical desire to run the whole government," Truman thought, and his territorial feud with Acheson had put him further on Truman's wrong side. That dispute entered an acute phase after Harriman overheard Johnson congratulating Senator Taft for his speech that called for Acheson's resignation and criticized Truman for not consulting Congress on Korea. After Johnson finished his telephone call, he turned to Harriman, who'd been close by, in plain sight, and said if they could just get rid of Acheson, he—Johnson—would see to it that Harriman became secretary of state. Soon after that, a presidential aide recalled, a "white-faced and upset" Harriman told Truman what he'd just witnessed.

Because Johnson had been an important Democratic fundraiser in 1948, firing him was bound to be harder than the dismissals of other senior officials. But Truman, having strongly reaffirmed his support for Johnson in early August, and, halfheartedly, later that month, had made up his mind by September. There was a pattern to these ousters: an excruciating tête-à-tête, usually after a period of public speculation—in this case a story leaked to the *Washington Post* that Johnson "is on his way out"—with each sacking showing Truman as a man in charge. Something about Truman's outward geniality made it tempting for underlings to not quite believe the ax was coming, and to push back. "Lou came in full of pep and energy," Truman told his daughter. "He didn't know anything was wrong. I told him to sit down and I said, 'Lou, I've got to ask you to quit.' He just folded up and wilted. He leaned over in his chair and I thought he was going to faint. He said, 'Mr. President, I can't talk.'" To Charlie Ross, Truman said, "I handed him a pen and told him to sign it. He broke down and cried. I waited and said, 'Lou, you've got to sign.'" He also told Ross, "This is the toughest job I have ever had to do. I feel as if I had just whipped my daughter."

It was both time-wasting and annoying to deal with such personnel problems, and Truman sometimes seemed to take a kind of malicious pleasure in this exercise of dominance. In a note to himself, he listed some of Johnson's offenses, though not the phone call overheard by Harriman: "He talked out of turn to the press, the Senate and the House—and kept it up. He talked to the lying, crazy columnists—Pearson, the Sop sisters (Alsops), Doris Fleeson, and others. He succeeded in making himself an issue both publicly and in Congress. . . . When I told him that for the good of the country he'd have to quit, he said 'You are ruining me.' That answers the question of what comes first—my sentimental attachment to Johnson or the country." He did not acknowledge that Johnson's appointment had been a mistake, motivated by politics—a debt owed to a party fundraiser. In his resignation letter, Johnson said that he'd always expected that "I would make more enemies than friends. Somewhat ruefully, I now admit I was right."

Truman wanted Johnson's replacement to be someone in whom he had absolute trust, and, unsurprisingly, he turned once more to George Marshall, even though "I felt as if I was letting him down, because I'd promised him a happy retirement"—the same thought he'd had, in late 1945, when he asked Marshall to become a special envoy in China. Marshall was vacationing in Michigan when Truman tracked him down and asked him to stop by his office. "I told him I had to get rid of Johnson," Truman recalled. He knew that Marshall was reluctant—that when he'd left the State Department, eighteen months earlier, he'd already been through major surgery. Furthermore, the 1947 National Security Act required a secretary of defense to be a civilian, with at least a ten-year break from active service (later reduced to seven years), but Truman was sure that the law could be suspended. Marshall said, "You know, Mr. President, I'll do whatever you think is necessary."

Marshall's prestige was such that, on the way to a rapid confirmation, the only hint of trouble came from Senator William Ezra Jenner, an Indiana Republican and a McCarthy ally, who asked, "Will you assure the American people unequivocally that . . . you will not be dominated by or carry out the policies of Secretary of State Acheson who will not turn his back on Alger Hiss?" Though Marshall had no idea that he would become a choice target for Jenner and McCarthy, he refused to answer.

⸺ ∽∾∽ ⸺

In late August, the New Yorker's Richard Rovere wrote, "For two or three weeks now, the fear that has haunted Washington has been the fear not of defeat in Korea or even an early war with Russia but of an unimaginably long, profitless, and perhaps inconclusive war with Communist China." The Christian Science Monitor's correspondent in Tokyo was aware of "ominous rumblings" of Chinese intervention, and the fear persisted after Acheson told reporters that China had no reason to side with North Korea—that the Chinese mainland

wasn't being threatened—although China had many reasons, ideo-
logical and geographical, to side with Kim Il-Sung. Acheson may
have believed that, but he surely knew that every sortie, by ground
or air, north of the 38th Parallel, would be regarded by China as a
provocation. When Truman, on August 31, was asked "How great
do you regard the danger of Red China becoming involved in the action in Korea?" he gave a non-answer: "I hope that there is no great
danger that Red China will become involved in this United Nations
approach to establishing peace in Korea."

Truman had much more to say on the first day of September—
his second such radio address in six weeks. This time he elevated
the Korean conflict to its highest level yet: "It is your liberty and
mine which is involved," he said. "What is at stake is the free way
of life—the right to worship as we please, the right to express our
opinions, the right to raise our children in our own way, the right
to choose our jobs, the fight to plan our future and to live without
fear. . . . Right now, the battle in Korea is the frontline in the struggle
between freedom and tyranny." He said that one and a half million
men and women were on active duty, and that "present plans" called
for doubling that number. He added that "in order to . . . meet the
danger that we face, we shall have to make many changes in our way
of living and working here at home. We shall have to give up many
things we enjoy." That turned out to be untrue; material depriva-
tions were few. He also hoped that "the people of China will not be
misled or forced into fighting against the United Nations and against
the American people," and that China, and other nations, would
resist the pull to "follow the Communist dictatorship down its dark
and bloody path."

With this pronouncement, and with the war not going well, the
stage was set for MacArthur to give his greatest late-career military
performance: an amphibious attack against the port city of Inchon,
situated twenty miles from Seoul—a sudden strike, two hundred
miles behind enemy lines. The Joint Chiefs were opposed; they
thought its risks outweighed any chance of success. MacArthur,
though, had an almost numinous belief in his instincts, and in the
value of tactical surprise. It was, furthermore, a plan that allowed

him to relive a famous World War II victory—another surprise, amphibious landing, on the Admiralty Islands, in late February 1944, when American forces encircled and isolated the Japanese Army. He knew that deference to the field commander was, as Eisenhower once put it, the "American doctrine."

The plan was presented, in the late afternoon of August 23, in MacArthur's office in the Dai-ichi Building, and while no one recorded exactly what he said, there are enough similarities in several accounts to get a good idea, down to such details as the cigarette smoke drifting across battle maps on the walls, or the timbre of the general's voice—"low and dramatically resonant," or "falling away to a whisper." He warned that "make the wrong decision here—the fatal decision of inertia—and we will be done. I can almost hear the ticking of the second hand of destiny." As Max Hastings wrote, "Against all the reasoned arguments of admirals and generals and staff officers, he deployed only the rocklike, mystic certainty of his own instinct." The Chiefs finally radioed their approval on September 8, which happened to be the same day that Dean Rusk asked the Korean ambassador, John M. Chang, if he thought the Chinese would intervene. The ambassador assured Rusk that the Chinese would not want "to make open war against the United States."

The September 15 landing was carried out by the recently activated X Corps, an amalgam of the 1st Marine Division and two army divisions, supported by air and naval personnel. It was, as David Rees wrote, "an astonishing achievement not of military logic and science, but of imagination and intuition. It was justified on no other grounds, but the most overwhelming, most simple; it succeeded and remains a Twentieth Century Cannae ever to be studied." Logic and science were essential, though; the landing required a close knowledge of the shifting tides at Inchon, and much credit for that belongs to Oliver P. Smith, the commander of the 1st Marine Division, a cautious fifty-seven-year-old Texan known as "the professor." Between September 16 and 19, UN forces then moved north, toward Pyongyang, some 120 miles from Seoul. There was little resistance; it was as if the northern fighters had melted away. All at once, the war seemed about to be over. The popular radio commentator Elmer

Davis, with his reassuring Midwest voice, said that "the war in Korea was decided by an end run—the landing at Inchon."

Two weeks later, MacArthur landed at Seoul's Gimpo Airfield, and was taken by motorcade into the city, past miles of rubble along Mapo Boulevard. Syngman Rhee had flown in from Pusan, and the two met at the Capitol—a former Japanese General Government building, a "fire-blackened, bullet-pocked shell of masonry," smelling of corpses, where, the correspondent Hugh Baillie recalled, glass shards were "tinkling down from the wrecked dome of the building." Rhee, who was more than a half foot shorter than MacArthur's six feet, looked almost frail. Both appeared deeply affected. The enemy, only ten miles away, had counterattacked that morning, but MacArthur said, "By the grace of merciful Providence, our forces fighting under the standard of that greatest hope and inspiration of mankind, have liberated this ancient capital city of Korea." He asked everyone to join him in reciting the Lord's Prayer. Rhee then took the general's hand and said, "We admire you. We love you as the savior of our race."

TWENTY-ONE

A Meeting on a Small Island

> *Mr. Rusk:* . . . there has been an effective propaganda campaign against the Rhee Government which has infected some of the U.N. delegations.
>
> *The President:* We must make it plain that we are supporting the Rhee Government and propaganda can "go to hell."
>
> —From the Wake Island conference

1. President Truman undoubtedly believed, as he later wrote, that General MacArthur "ought to know his Commander in Chief and that I ought to know the senior field commander in the Far East," which would make a face-to-face meeting worthwhile. When the notion was first discussed, aboard the *Williamsburg*, in early October 1950, the President and his companions were also aware that the midterm elections were just a month off, and that being seen with the victor of Inchon wouldn't be a bad thing. Charles S. Murphy, a North Carolinian and longtime adviser who'd replaced Clark Clifford as White House counsel, although not at the poker table, acknowledged "the feeling that this would be good public relations."

Everyone knew that, since the end of World War II, MacArthur had turned down invitations to Washington, and hadn't been back to the United States since 1936, not even for his presidential adventures in 1944 and 1948. Considering the precarious situation in Korea, there was reluctance to order him home, but George Elsey reminded Truman that, in the late summer of 1944, after the Democratic

Convention, President Roosevelt had gone to Hawaii to see Mac-Arthur and Admiral Chester W. Nimitz, the two senior Pacific commanders. Whether or not Elsey was the decisive push, that's when Truman made up his mind. "I'll go!" he said.

Truman's eagerness to meet with MacArthur could also be understood as a desire to get closer to what was often called "the situation in Korea." The war had become increasingly untethered from Washington; orders to MacArthur from the Pentagon could be ambivalent. "Your military objective is the destruction of the North Korean Armed Forces," he was told, by the Joint Chiefs, on September 27, two weeks after Inchon. In the spirit of NSC-81, MacArthur then was authorized to proceed north of the 38th Parallel, although only on the condition that "there had been no entry into North Korea by major Soviet or Chinese Communist Forces . . . nor a threat to counter our operations militarily in North Korea." Two days later, General Marshall, the new secretary of defense, sent MacArthur a top-secret, "eyes only" wire that appeared to revoke even those conditions: "We want you to feel unhampered tactically and strategically to proceed north of the 38th Parallel."

MacArthur, in his reply, seemed to believe that Marshall had given him carte blanche: "Unless and until the enemy capitulates," he wrote, "I regard all Korea as open for our military operations." When Dean Acheson later reflected on this back-and-forth, he thought it "inconceivable that General Marshall should have arrogated to himself authority to give General MacArthur dispensation to violate instructions from the Joint Chiefs of Staff." But the correspondence between MacArthur and Marshall makes it entirely conceivable that Marshall *had* given that dispensation, and that MacArthur had every reason to believe it was now his war to fight, in his own way.

The United States and China had, meanwhile, been in indirect communication, through the office of K. M. Panikkar, India's ambassador to China, who'd been passing on some ominous warnings. On September 25, Zhou Enlai, China's premier and foreign minister, told Panikkar that China would not "sit back with folded hands and let the Americans"—or any non-Koreans—"come up to their border." A week later, Zhou told Panikkar that if UN troops crossed the 38th Parallel, "we will intervene." State Department officials got a similar message, from the chargé at the American Embassy in London, but shrugged it off. Paul Nitze, the head the Policy Planning Staff, later wrote that because Panikkar had a reputation of being pro-Chinese and pro-Communist, he didn't take these warnings "at face value," though he didn't rule out that there might be something to them.

It was as if the State Department didn't want to listen. Loy Henderson, the American ambassador to India, sent a telegram to Acheson on September 27, to say that a high official in the Indian government had let him know there was "reason to believe there was real danger Peking might intervene if UN Forces cross the Parallel and that world war might result." Truman, in his memoirs, acknowledged that the State Department had "received a number of messages," but not that they were brought to his personal attention. Zhou's threat, he wrote, "was at once transmitted to General MacArthur." He did not ask why these messages, at least in summary, hadn't reached his desk.

Yet the war just then seemed to be going splendidly. On October 1, in language worked out with the State Department, MacArthur ordered North Korea's armies to surrender "forthwith," and, in language reminiscent of the demand for Japan's surrender, said that "early and total defeat and complete destruction of your armed forces" was otherwise "inevitable." MacArthur was so sure of his superior position that he didn't bother to offer terms, but rather told the Communist Army to lay down its arms and accept "such military supervision as I may direct." The quick, and predictable, reply to this ultimatum was "never," and the next day, under orders of the Eighth Army, South Korean troops moved north, crossing the 38th Parallel. Zhou Enlai then issued a new warning: The Chinese people "will not tolerate seeing their neighbors savagely invaded by imperialists," he said, and furthermore declared that the United States government was "China's most dangerous enemy." President Truman, on the day of MacArthur's broadcast, treated himself to a cruise down the Potomac. He spent hours reading newspapers and otherwise relaxing. Reporters, armed with a spyglass, could write that "Mr. Truman bared his chest to a hazy sun."

The risk of a wider war hadn't discouraged the UN General Assembly, from voting, on October 7, to support the goal of unifying Korea. The vote, opposed by the Soviet bloc, was like a roar of confidence that the war had been won—that "V-K Day," a phrase that soon appeared in headlines, was nigh. Soldiers with the 1st Cavalry Division, who'd been waiting, restlessly, in a cold rain, cheered the command to advance north. "We want to get going and get the war over," one hopeful commander said after MacArthur gave the order. At the same time, the Joint Chiefs gave MacArthur even more leeway: He was warned not to engage directly with any Chinese units—unless, that is, there was a "reasonable chance of success"—although he was told to get Pentagon approval before taking any action in Chinese territory.

On October 8, like a commander in chief rather than a field commander, MacArthur issued another ultimatum—this time to the North Korean government: surrender the "forces under your command," or else "I shall at once proceed to take such military action as may be necessary." North Korea, in reply, called for its "People's Army" to keep fighting. China's Foreign Ministry called the "American war of invasion" a "serious menace," and warned that "America and its accomplice countries . . . must be answerable for all consequences" stemming from the war. Even as Zhou's ministry issued that warning, Chinese troops were making their way, under cover, into North Korea. That was not a well-kept secret. Even the New York gossip columnist Walter Winchell, though he often made things up, wrote, on October 10, that "every Intelligence Service knows that two full Red Chinese divisions were in action against our forces," while adding the untruth that they "got such a mauling—they mutinied."

None of this discouraged Truman from asking Secretary Marshall to arrange a time and place for a Pacific meeting with General MacArthur, apparently not realizing that even Marshall found MacArthur to be a prickly case. Marshall dutifully informed MacArthur that Truman wanted to see him on October 15, in Oahu, although, depending on the situation in Korea, he was willing to shift the venue to Wake Island. MacArthur replied right away that he'd prefer Wake Island, a three-square-mile atoll occupied by the Japanese during the war and now administered by the Civil Aeronautics Administration. The White House the next day made it official: "General MacArthur and I are making a quick trip over the coming weekend to meet in the Pacific," Truman's statement said, adding that he intended to "discuss the final phase of the United Nations action in Korea."

2. Of course, MacArthur preferred Wake Island! What's puzzling is that neither Marshall, nor Acheson's State Department, nor the White House staff spoke up on behalf of the President. In the fall of 1950, when passenger jets were a decade away, Truman had agreed to a journey far more arduous than what he'd asked of his general—or what he'd ever undertaken himself: three days of travel, including more than twenty-four hours airborne, albeit in the *Independence*, a state-of-the-art four-engine Douglas DC-6. The distance from Washington to Wake Island (6,700 miles) is more than three times the island's distance from Tokyo. But Truman's eagerness to meet this illustrious soldier was a wish that could not be denied.

Truman's entourage included Omar Bradley, the Joint Chiefs chairman; Admiral Arthur W. Radford, commander of the Pacific Fleet; army secretary Frank Pace Jr.; and a number of civilians, including Averell Harriman and Dean Rusk. Among the cabinet officers who stayed behind were, most notably, Marshall, who, along with his aversion to MacArthur, said that with Generals Collins, Bradley, and MacArthur going to Wake Island, someone of authority should remain in the Pentagon; and Secretary of State Acheson, who later wrote, with undisguised revulsion, that "when the President told me of his intended pilgrimage and invited me to join him, I begged to be excused. . . . I had not been consulted in arriving at the decision to hold the meeting and offered no suggestions after it had been made. . . . I wanted no part in it, and saw no good coming from it."

Truman made a stopover in Hawaii, which included a visit to a military hospital. He must have been tired, for he tried joking with a Marine who'd lost an eye, advising him to get a job in a bank and use his glass eye to show sympathy to loan-seekers. Admiral Radford recalled that the young man, his good eye "riveted on the President," said, "Mr. President, you called this a 'police action'—it's a big war!'" Radford thought Truman "seemed really taken aback." The journey's next leg, a late flight from Hickam Field to Wake Island, took eight hours, and in the early light (it was now October 15), passengers could see abandoned Japanese tanks on the beaches and in the water, looking not unlike a grotesque species of tortoise. The *Independence* put down at the Civil Aeronautics Administration terminal at exactly 6:30 a.m. MacArthur, who didn't like to fly at night, had arrived at 6 p.m. the day before. A Pan Am Stratocruiser carrying the press and an Air Force C-121 bringing some of Truman's staff had already landed, and these arrivals were able to watch Truman's first encounter with MacArthur.

"I'm glad you are here. I have been a long time in meeting you. General," Truman said, as he stepped onto the tarmac, and into the hot humidity, typical of October weather on the island. "I hope it won't be so long next time, Mr. President," MacArthur replied. The general did not salute the President. "He shook hands, as an equal," the military historian Max Hastings wrote.

Despite the smiles and handshakes, though, MacArthur was not in a sociable mood. From the time of the summons from Washington, he'd viewed this get-together with apprehension and annoyance. "What is this meeting about?" he'd asked Harriman, while they waited for Truman's plane to arrive. When Harriman said that Truman wanted to discuss how to achieve a political victory in Korea, he thought MacArthur looked relieved. "Good," the general said. "The President wants my views." The MacArthur aide Courtney Whitney wrote that "the prospect of traveling two thousand miles from Korea for a conference that could be held by telecom or even telephone, was most distasteful to him," and his distaste grew when he learned that Truman would be accompanied by a substantial press contingent— thirty-five newspaper, radio, and television people. MacArthur acknowledged that Truman was taking time away from his own duties—and traveling a much greater distance—but that only made him think that something "really momentous was to be discussed."

John Muccio, the American ambassador in Seoul, sat next to MacArthur on the flight from Tokyo, and thought the general made clear "his disgust at 'being summoned for political reasons' when active military operations had so many calls on his time." Whitney recalled MacArthur pacing up and down the aisle, and muttering such things as "not aware that I am still fighting a war." Muccio and MacArthur were billeted in the Quonset hut where the CAA maintenance manager lived. These arrangements offended Whitney who, Muccio recalled, "was outraged. . . . that I was put in the same bungalow with MacArthur and there were two bedrooms in this with only one shower between." Like others, Muccio was struck by the general's showmanship: "I don't think MacArthur even blinked his eyes without considering whether it was to his advantage to have his eye blink or not. Everything was thought through, but it became so much a part of his nature, and his personality, that it seemed to be automatic."

The *Herald Tribune*'s Robert J. Donovan was struck by the contrast between the protagonists. "MacArthur is brilliant, theatrical, stern, eloquent, usually unapproachable," he wrote. "The President is plodding, stubborn, undramatic, shrewd and earthy." He thought that they "seemed to hit it off handsomely," a judgment reinforced by photographs that showed them "standing arm-in-arm or hand-on-shoulder laughing and chatting." Yet Donovan, who could only watch from a distance, couldn't know that certain things rankled Truman, such as MacArthur's appearance, "with his shirt unbuttoned, wearing a greasy ham and eggs cap"—he meant "scrambled eggs" cap—"that evidently had been in use for twenty years." The VFW incident, which six weeks earlier had incensed Truman, was surely not forgotten.

After introductions between Truman's staff and MacArthur's, the President and the general clambered into the backseat of the island's only passenger car, a black 1947 Chevrolet two-door sedan owned by the CAA, and headed off to a Quonset, where, as Truman remembered, they talked privately for more than an hour. Or, as MacArthur later said, they talked for about three-quarters of an hour. Or perhaps, as Courtney Whitney was to write in *his* MacArthur memoir, it was only half an hour. As for what they discussed, there were no witnesses—not even a Secret Service escort—although the driver of the Chevy overheard Truman asking about the odds of Chinese intervention. MacArthur wasn't worried; he'd assured the Joint Chiefs that there were no indications of plans to intervene. He would have more to say about that later in the morning.

MacArthur never wrote about this conversation, and much of their abbreviated talk was apparently devoted to MacArthur's thoughts about fiscal problems in the Philippines, not a subject foremost on Truman's mind. But versions of what was said leaked out. MacArthur may have expressed regret over the embarrassment caused by the VFW letter. "Oh! Think nothing more about that," Truman said, according to Whitney. During a conversation with Rusk and Harriman, MacArthur attempted to expunge the incident. When they asked if the subject of Formosa had come up with Truman, MacArthur said, "Yes. I told the President that I had supposed that my letter [to the VFW] had been right down the line of the President's policy. Had I not thought so, I would not have sent it."

Another version of their conversation was summarized in a decrypted message, dated October 21, 1950, from the Brazilian ambassador in Tokyo, Gastão do Rio Branco, to his home office. According to Rio Branco's informant, MacArthur told Truman that, if Formosa falls, "there will be nothing left for the United States to do but abandon Asia." He believed that certain leaders in Russia and China "will not have the courage to declare war," but said "it would be better to face a war now than two or three years hence," and that "there was not the least possibility of an understanding with the men in the Kremlin, as the experience of the last five years has proved." The unnamed source for Rio Branco's message—thought to be someone in the United States Secret Service, in Tokyo—also reported a "noticeable atmosphere of uncertainty and anxiety, as though some tremendous event were impending."

When army chief of staff Lawton Collins saw Rio Branco's intercepted message, he warned MacArthur that senior members of his staff with access to "the most secret information of both military and political nature are betraying their trust," and that these messages were probably being read by several foreign nations, including Russia, "thus doing irreparable harm to the security and prestige of the United States." MacArthur's response was to call Gastão do Rio Branco a "gossipy type of intriguer," and to say he'd "never known greater security safeguards to exist in any other headquarters with which I have been connected."

3. A congenial "all-hands" meeting began at 7:45 a.m. that morning, in the island's aviation shack. Truman removed his coat—a concession to the tropical weather—and MacArthur puffed on his corncob pipe. When MacArthur asked if Truman minded the pipe, he responded, "No. I suppose I've had more smoke blown in my face than any other man alive," a remark quoted in many accounts.

MacArthur dominated—simply by being MacArthur, by holding forth with the casual self-assurance of the man responsible for the triumphant Inchon landing and its aftermath. As his biographer D. Clayton James noted, he spoke more than all the other participants combined—and without resorting to the sort of monologue for which he was known. Based on a stenographic record of 485 transcript lines spoken by nine people, MacArthur's share was 243, Truman's a mere 54, with the rest trailing far behind, although Dean Rusk stood out by asking many questions. The outward amity at the table reflected an unwillingness to say anything that might challenge anyone, or go deeply into any issue; rather, as James noted, "they skipped hastily and often disconnectedly from one topic to another."

Truman asked MacArthur to assess the Korean "rehabilitation situation," a subject addressed by the UN in its vote to support the invasion across the 38th Parallel. Any postwar rebuilding needed to wait, MacArthur said, "until the military operations have ended," which he supposed would be accomplished by Thanksgiving. As for North Korea's soldiers, "they are poorly trained, led, and equipped. They are only fighting to save face." He sounded almost regretful when he said, "It just goes against my grain to destroy them, but they are obstinate." He hoped to take Pyongyang soon, and added,

"Nothing is gained by military occupation. All occupations are fail-ures." Truman nodded in agreement. "Always," he said.

After Admiral Radford said Indochina was "the most puzzling of all as to what we can do or what we should do to help the French," MacArthur said the French had been there for a "long, long time and not an ounce of aggressiveness," and "if the French won't fight, we are up against it, because the defense of Europe hinges on them." Truman reverted to the pugilistic Truman-ese he sometimes favored: "We have worked on the French tooth and nail," he said, "but the French have not been willing to listen. If the French Prime Minister comes to see me, he is going to hear some very plain talk. I am going to talk cold turkey to him. If you don't want him to hear that kind of talk, you had better keep him away from me." After Admiral Rad-ford said, "We need a little behind-the-scene stiffening of the French backbone," Truman said, "You can't do anything with the damned French."

When Truman finally asked, "What are the chances for Chinese or Soviet interference?" MacArthur replied, as he had, privately, "Had either one intervened in the first months of the war, their intervention would have been decisive and we would have had a difficult problem on our hands. But not at this time." About three hundred thousand Chinese troops were in Manchuria, he said, with about a third of them deployed along the Yalu River. "The Chinese Commies have no air umbrella," he continued. "There would be the greatest slaughter if China tried to put ground troops across. They would be destroyed. If they got fifty per cent to Pyongyang they would be doing well."

Truman appeared to accept that assessment. There is no record of the warnings from Zhou Enlai being mentioned that morning, al-though Rusk, in a brief, private conversation with MacArthur, asked about the Chinese threats. MacArthur said he couldn't understand why China had "gone out on such a limb" and must have been em-barrassed at their predicament. That Acheson, or Rusk, or some-one, hadn't urged Truman to take note of these cautions and take them seriously, is baffling. Acheson later wrote that "Chou's words were a warning not to be disregarded, but, on the other hand, not an authoritative statement of policy." In light of what came later, Acheson's absence on Wake Island could be seen as a rare dereliction of duty.

At about 9:10 a.m., after some ninety minutes of disjointed conversation, Truman, with perplexing optimism, said, "No one who was not here would believe we have covered so much ground as we have been actually able to cover." He suggested that they take a break and reconvene for a noon lunch. "In the meantime a communiqué could be prepared and talks among the members of the staff can be carried on. Then I want to award a couple of medals to a couple of people and we can all leave after luncheon." Rusk and army secretary Pace were concerned about the meeting's abrupt ending, and worried that it might encourage speculation that the whole venture was a stunt. They passed a note to Truman, suggesting that they take a little more time, but Truman's response—Rusk couldn't remember whether it was whispered or jotted down—was in effect "I want to get out of there before we get in trouble." MacArthur, in any case, didn't intend even to stick around and shoot the breeze over lunch. "If it's all right," he said, "I am anxious to get back as soon as possible and would like to leave before luncheon if that is convenient." Whatever Truman might have thought of MacArthur's rude impatience, he didn't object and ended the meeting by remarking, "This has been a most satisfactory conference."

Five minutes later, Truman and MacArthur motored to the Quonset quarters of E. E. Swafford, the Pan American World Airways manager (Pan Am had established service to the island in 1946), where Truman intended to rest briefly. Between this and MacArthur's departure, and in their few minutes alone, their conversation drifted toward American politics. In most circumstances, that would have been an odd digression, but not with these two: a soldier who wanted to be President and a politician who was naturally curious about his general's intentions. MacArthur started it: "Rather impertinently," as MacArthur put it, he asked Truman whether he intended to run for reelection in 1952, adding, as if to explain his impertinence, "The Emperor had asked me about this." Truman responded by asking

MacArthur if he saw a political future for himself. "None whatso-ever," MacArthur replied. "If you have any general running against you, his name will be Eisenhower, not MacArthur." That made Tru-man laugh. He told MacArthur that he liked Ike well enough, "But he doesn't know the first thing about politics." He added, or so MacAr-thur recalled, "Why, if Eisenhower should become President, his ad-ministration would make Grant's look like a model of perfection."

While Truman rested, MacArthur stayed inside the administra-tion building, "toying restlessly with his watch," as if he couldn't wait to be gone. Although he now seemed in a good mood, he was not forthcoming with reporters. Would he comment on the con-ference? "All the comments will have to come from the President's publicity man," he replied, an unpleasant term for Charlie Ross. At the airstrip, Truman awarded MacArthur the Distinguished Service Medal—"the fifth time I had received this decoration," he later wrote, dismissively. But he didn't object to the microphones "set up by the newsreel photographers," and, in a memoir, quoted the cita-tion, which mentioned "his judgment, his indomitable will and his unshakeable faith . . . a shining example of gallantry and tenacity."

Truman also presented MacArthur with a five-pound box of Blum's candy, handmade in San Francisco, which Charles Murphy had learned was prized by Jean MacArthur. Murphy had dispatched someone to buy the candy in Washington, but his emissary could only locate one-pound boxes. "Before I got to Hawaii, I was tell-ing this to Averell Harriman," Murphy recalled, and Harriman had said, "This is a good idea but we really ought to have a five-pound box"—which they managed to locate in Honolulu. "So, before we departed," Murphy recalled, "I went and got this five-pound box of candy and stuck it in the President's hand and he gave it to Gen-eral MacArthur." In their parting statements, Truman characterized the general as "one of America's greatest soldier-statesmen," and MacArthur said, "No field commander in the history of warfare has had more complete and admirable support than I have during the Korean operation." The *New York Times* correspondent Anthony Leviero thought that Truman had left feeling "highly pleased, like an insurance salesman who has at last signed up an important prospect while the latter appeared dubious over the extent of coverage."

As Truman boarded the *Independence*, MacArthur's final words were "Goodbye, sir, and happy landings. It's been a real honor to talk to you." Those were his final words in another sense: the two never saw or spoke to each other again. At 11:35 a.m.—it had been just five hours since their arrival—Truman and his advisers left for Hawaii, and the general's plane was off to Japan. Truman, before leaving, had been asked how it had gone, and he replied, "Perfectly. I've never had a more satisfactory conference since I've been president." Muccio thought the general, on the way back to Tokyo, was his "sparkling best, and for MacArthur, effervescent," although Rusk had irritated him. "Who was that young whippersnapper who was asking questions?" he asked. Later, though, MacArthur would write that the Wake Island conference "made me realize that a curious, and sinister, change was taking place in Washington . . . a tendency toward temporizing rather than fighting it through." He cast himself, not for the first time, as a heroic fighter in a sea of political cowardice.

A *Time* correspondent described the meeting as a "political grandstand play," but it was more than that, if not a lot more. Because no official record was kept, history has relied on several recollections, and above all on the notes taken by Vernice Anderson, the twenty-nine-year-old personal assistant to Ambassador at Large Philip C. Jessup. Anderson had been asked to come along for secretarial duties. Yet even her role was accompanied by acrimony and controversy. "She kept out of sight for the whole time as far as I can remember," Admiral Radford recalled, although it was hard to miss this young "government girl," the granddaughter of Midwestern pioneers, with dark hair and strong features—the only woman in Truman's retinue. General Whitney suggested that something sneaky was afoot: "Without our knowledge," he recalled, "this stenographer, lurking behind the door, could record only what she could hear through the small opening and what she could see by peeping through the keyhole."

Ambassador Muccio thought it had been straightforward. "There was very, very little mystery about her presence because the door was wide open and all—at least all on one side of the conference table could see her at all times," he said. Anderson remembered sitting "in an entrance area . . . with a swinging slatted door," and "since no one instructed me where to sit, I simply receded into the background into the small rear anteroom where the refreshments were." There, with the typewriter on which a communiqué was to be typed, she recalled, "I thought *everyone* knew I was there." She was proud of her work, "and since I was there with pad, pencil, and typewriter ready to assist with the communiqué, the natural thing for me to do was to write down what I heard."

Nor was Anderson the only note-taker. Colonel Laurence E. Bunker, a MacArthur aide since 1946, also took valuable, detailed notes, which correspond with Anderson's impressions and quotes. Others recalling the morning's discussion included Muccio, Bradley, Harriman, Rusk, Pace, and Colonel A. L. Hamblen, Bradley's executive officer. On the flight from Wake to Oahu, Bradley proposed that everyone work on their notes, which he'd compile as "a composite record of this event for the official record," because it had been "an extremely important and historic meeting." The final transcript (Colonel Bunker's notes were not included) came to more than five thousand words, and its portrayal of the principals should be read as the best record of what went on, as well as a chronicle of extraordinary disrespect by a general toward his commander in chief. Out of pride, or a willing suspension of disbelief, Truman seemed unable to recognize the impertinence before his eyes.

<hr />

On his way back, Truman worked on a speech—billed as a foreign policy address—that he planned to deliver from the stage of the War Memorial Opera House in San Francisco. A performance of *The Barber of Seville* had been canceled to make room for him. "I understand that there has been speculation about why I made this trip," he would say. "There is really no mystery about it. I went because I wanted to see and talk to General MacArthur." Truman would add that it was "fortunate for the world" that MacArthur, "a very great

Martha Ellen Young and John Anderson
Truman, on their wedding day, December 28,
1881, in Grandview, Missouri.

Robert Hannegan, as the chairman of the powerful St. Louis Democratic City Committee, had an essential role in Truman's early career.

Truman, in 1940, barely won his race for a second Senate term. Bess and Margaret Truman, he wrote, "were in such misery it was torture to me."

Bess and Margaret attended the 1944 Democratic National Convention, which, with President Roosevelt's connivance, nominated Truman for the vice presidency.

Truman had a rare one-on-one meeting with Roosevelt on a hot, late August day on the White House grounds.

Truman was sworn in as president at 7:09 p.m. on April 12, 1945, with his wife and daughter at his side.

Secretary of War Henry L. Stimson was eager to tell Truman about the top-secret atomic bomb.

Soon after V-E Day, Martha Truman, at ninety-three, took her first airplane journey, to Washington, to see her son.

Truman, with his close friend Brigadier General Harry Hawkins Vaughan, as they arrived at Gatow Airport, Berlin, in July 1945.

Truman (*in the Stetson*), Secretary of State James F. Byrnes, and Chief of Staff Admiral William Leahy, drive past Hitler's chancellery, as they tour the wreckage of Berlin, on July 16, 1945. Later that day, word came from New Mexico that "Trinity," the first test of an atomic weapon, had been a success.

Winston Churchill, Truman, and Joseph Stalin, after dinner on July 23, at the Churchill villa in Babelsberg.

George Catlett Marshall served as army chief of staff, then secretary of state and secretary of defense. Truman's admiration for Marshall was unbounded.

14

In March 1946, Truman and former prime minister Winston Churchill traveled to Fulton, Missouri, where Churchill delivered his "Iron Curtain" speech.

15

16

In the summer of 1946, the adviser Clark Clifford (*left*) and his assistant, George Elsey, were asked to prepare an analysis of the Soviet threat. Both enjoyed the informality of Key West.

17

James Vincent Forrestal, the nation's first secretary of defense, had a troubled tenure and a deeply troubled life.

18

No one had greater sway over Truman than Dean Acheson, who became secretary of state in 1949.

19

Truman's army buddy and former business partner Edward (Eddie) Jacobson opened his own Kansas City haberdashery. He would later influence Truman's approach to Israel.

20

Truman, on June 27, 1950, with Attorney General J. Howard McGrath (*left*) and Secretary of Defense Louis Johnson—the day he promised "cover and support" for South Korean troops.

21

Truman and Far East commander Douglas MacArthur met for the first time on Wake Island on the morning of October 15, 1950.

22

Press secretary Charlie Ross was highly regarded by White House reporters and, despite his fragile health, rarely took a day off.

23

Truman's close friendship with Chief Justice Fred Vinson was on display during Vinson's visit to Key West in 1950.

24

On November 18, 1952, an AP photographer got President-elect Eisenhower and Truman to shake hands and smile.

soldier," was leading the United Nations Command, and that he intended to ask Congress for an appropriation to pay for the reconstruction of Korea. "We must be better armed and equipped," he said, "if we are to be protected from the dangers which still face us."

Back in Washington, reality began to catch up with the time shift: it had, after all, been a fourteen-thousand-mile round-trip to conduct a rambling meeting lasting less than two hours, along with a few minutes of private talk. When White House reporters, on October 19, asked Truman if he and MacArthur were now in agreement on Formosa, he seemed agitated—maybe more than agitated, insisting that the Formosa question had been settled before they'd landed on Wake Island: "Let me tell you something that will be good for your soul," he said. "It's a pity that you columnists and reporters that represent a certain press service can't understand the ideas of two intellectually honest men when they meet." Then he said, "There is no disagreement between General MacArthur and myself."

TWENTY-TWO

Mense Horribilis

I was fearful as we climbed in the cold air, the planes bobbing slightly. Perhaps it was the day I saw my first MiG, silver, passing above us, complete in every detail, silent as a shark.

—James Salter, "Gods of Tin"

1. On the first of November, an unseasonably warm day, Truman was awakened from an afternoon nap by the sound of gunfire. Two nattily dressed Puerto Rican nationalists, acting out of murky motives, had come down from New York determined to kill him. One attacker was shot dead, just outside Blair House, in a gun battle that left a policeman dead and three others wounded: two policemen and the second assailant, who was writhing in pain. When Truman peered out an upstairs window, like a perfect target, a policeman yelled, "Get back! Get back!" Truman wasn't injured, but the assassination attempt changed the rhythms of his life; to his cousin Ethel Noland, he wrote, "I'm really a prisoner now." It bequeathed to Bess, already a worrier, a heightened nervousness that lasted for the remainder of her husband's presidency. "The S.S. say that there are more crackpots around and the 'Boss' and Margie are worried about me," Truman jotted in his diary, "so I won't take my usual walk. It's hell to be President of the Greatest Most Powerful Nation on Earth."

The fighting in Korea was entering its fifth month, and Truman could already see, as Eisenhower once remarked, that "every war is going to astonish you in the way it occurred and in the way it is carried out." He thought about going "to pay our troops there a brief

visit," or so he wrote in his memoirs, but he never pursued that notion. While such a visit might not have affected his outlook, it might
have made that pitiless conflict seem a bit less remote. From twenty
thousand feet, he would have seen that Korea was a terrible place to
fight a modern war: The six-hundred-mile peninsula is unrelentingly,
and spikily, mountainous. The winds from Siberia make the northern
winters especially bitter. Looking toward the horizon, rather than at
a wall in the Map Room, Truman might have been struck more force-
fully by the realization that the United States was many thousands of
miles distant, while North Korea had powerful allies just across the
nearly nine-hundred-mile border that it shared with China and its
twelve-mile border with the Soviet Union.

It cannot be known if the fighting could have been ended after
Inchon—whether the UN Command, in its strongest position of the
war, could have seized the chance to reach a lasting truce with the
Communists, with a return to the *status quo ante bellum*. But that
would have required UN troops to stay south of the 38th Parallel,
and General MacArthur wasn't about to halt his advance, despite
repeated warnings that China was taking this very seriously. As General Matthew Ridgway would write, MacArthur "had neither eyes
nor ears for information that might deter him from the swift at-
tainment of his objective—the destruction of the last remnants of
the North Korean People's Army and the pacification of the entire
peninsula." Against the advice of the Joint Chiefs, and as the weather
turned intensely cold, MacArthur ordered the Eighth Army and the
X Corps, the victors at Inchon, to proceed north, with the idea that
these forces could achieve a pincer operation against the enemy. Although these advancing armies were many miles apart, in unwel-
coming terrain—North Korea was at its widest just south of the
Yalu—MacArthur anticipated the war's endgame. T. R. Fehrenbach
was to write that the men marching north "had no more idea of what
awaited them than had Lieutenant Colonel Custer riding toward the
Valley of the Greasy Grass."

On the day that shots were fired outside Blair House, American
forces were within twenty-five miles of the Manchurian border, and
the order of the day was "full speed to the Yalu River." That risked

bringing Russia into the war, although Russia had already made an un-acknowledged appearance: Some of the Mikoyan-Gurevich MiG-15 jets that, for a time, outmatched anything in the Korean air, were being flown by anonymous Soviet pilots, a highly sensitive fact that was kept secret for decades. On November 8, as UN soldiers neared the border, the world's first jet-to-jet dogfight broke out during an attack on the Sinuiju bridges near the mouth of the Yalu. Chinese People's Volunteer Army (CPVA) troops were there too, fighting the UN forces. That was not much of a secret, although the number of Chinese soldiers was unknown. That led the *Wall Street Journal*'s John Chamberlain to retell the story of Cadmus, the founder of Thebes, who planted dragon's teeth that sprouted into an army.

The entrance of Chinese troops into the war was an alarming development: It was the first time, the military historian Roy Appleman noted, that the United States "found itself in military conflict with a Communist force." In retrospect, as soon as UN troops crossed the 38th Parallel, it was inevitable. With Stalin's approval, and an invitation from Kim Il-Sung to enter the conflict, China was bound to intervene.

MacArthur didn't use the word "China" when he issued a statement about facing "a new and fresh army," backed by "alien Communist forces" that lay "beyond the limits of our present sphere of military action." While neither the Eighth Army nor the X Corps knew what they were facing, MacArthur's response, from Tokyo, was to order General Edward Stratemeyer, the Far East Air Forces commander, to bomb bridges across the Yalu, on the Korean side, and to destroy factories and communications sites. Before this directive could be carried out, though, it was passed along a chain of command that eventually reached Truman: Stratemeyer notified General Hoyt Vandenberg, the air force chief of staff (a nephew of Senator Vandenberg), who informed Thomas K. Finletter, the air force secretary, who told Robert Lovett, who'd recently returned from Wall Street to become George Marshall's deputy in the Defense Department. Lovett then hurriedly informed Acheson, Marshall, and Rusk. With about three hours to go before the FEAF bombers took off—and, after a quick conference call—the operation was halted, pending consultation with the commander in chief.

Truman was in Missouri, to vote in the November 7 midterms, which would not go well for him, though not as badly as they had in 1946. When Acheson got through explaining the situation, Truman agreed to a temporary halt. When the Joint Chiefs told MacArthur to postpone the bombing mission, and insisted on knowing why he was so eager to strike those bridges, MacArthur's reply was pure MacArthur: putting a supposed life-or-death choice squarely in front of someone else—in this case Truman and the Chiefs. "Men and material in large force are pouring across all bridges over the Yalu from Manchuria," MacArthur replied. "This movement not only jeopardizes but threatens the ultimate destruction of the forces under my command. . . . I trust that the matter be immediately brought to the attention of the President as I believe your instructions may well result in a calamity of major proportion for which I cannot accept the responsibility without his personal and direct understanding of the situation." That was enough for Omar Bradley, the Joint Chiefs chairman, to telephone Truman and read to him MacArthur's calamity-of-major-proportion message. "There were grave dangers involved in a mass bombing attack on a target so close to Manchuria and to Soviet soil," Truman would recall. "But since General MacArthur was on the scene and felt so strongly that this was of unusual urgency, I told Bradley to give him the 'go-ahead.'" Acheson informed Warren Austin, the UN ambassador, that Manchuria was now considered a "privileged sanctuary" for enemy forces, and that the "hot pursuit doctrine" and "elementary principles of self-defense" would justify letting UN aircraft travel for "two or three minutes flying time" into China. The response from America's allies—Canada, the Netherlands, England, France, and Australia—was to regard this development with "greatest concern," and a fear that "great danger" might result.

North Korea was already under an intense aerial bombing attack, one that included an extensive use of napalm, a gasoline gel, developed in the 1940s by a Harvard chemistry professor, which had the advantage of sticking to its targets as they slowly burned to death. There was an element of vengeance here. General Stratemeyer noted that, following MacArthur's instructions, "every installation, facility, and village in North Korea," with the exception of two big hydroelectric power plants, had become "a military and tactical target." Seventy B-20s dropped five hundred and fifty tons of incendiary bombs on Sinuiju, a city of about a hundred thousand, which, in mid-November, was almost surgically obliterated in less than an hour. Twelve-thousand-pound bombs got their first use in Kanggye, a regional capital, close to the Chinese border, that Stratemeyer considered an important transportation and communications center. When Stratemeyer suggested to MacArthur that the Far East Air Forces could burn some other North Korean towns, MacArthur said, "Burn it if you so desire. Not only that, Strat, but burn and destroy as a lesson any other of those towns that you consider of military value to the enemy." Air Force General Curtis LeMay recalled, "We eventually burned down every town in North Korea anyway, some way or another, and some in South Korea, too. . . . Over a period of three years or so, we killed off—what—twenty per cent of the population of Korea as direct casualties of war, or from starvation and exposure?" The historian Bruce Cumings, who has never concealed his sympathy for the suffering of all Koreans, has written that MacArthur had essentially ordered the creation of "a wasteland" between the front and the Chinese border, and that the destruction of dams, and the flooding of the valleys, "accounted for the remarkable civilian death toll of more than two million."

The President had no idea what was about to happen. On November 22, the day before Thanksgiving, Harry and Bess Truman gave a pre-holiday luncheon at Blair House for Crown Prince Olav and Crown Princess Martha of Norway, along with a number of invited guests, among them the Dean Achesons and the Harry Vaughans. Three days later, on the night of November 25, what was to be a final push of UN forces toward the Yalu came to a halt, when as many as three hundred thousand CPVA soldiers came out of their hiding places, in ravines and forests, as if a "phantom force," in Ray Appleman's phrase, and attacked the divided UN forces. The assault was accompanied by the sound of what's been described as "weird bugle calls and whistles," or flutes; or bagpipes, although there were no bagpipes. It was, David Halberstam wrote, "an eerie, very foreign sound," a piercing noise that held a special, unforgettable terror for the men under fire in freezing darkness, in unfamiliar terrain. The South Korean divisions scattered. The Eighth Army, in the west, and the X Corps, in the east, separated by ravines and mountain ranges and faced with possible annihilation from an overwhelming force, looked for ways to escape, while getting deluded orders from Edward M. Almond, the X Corps commanding general. "We're still attacking and we're going all the way to the Yalu," Almond, a MacArthur acolyte, told a small combat team, before it was destroyed. "Don't let a bunch of Chinese laundrymen stop you." It was close to the Dunkirk that Admiral Leahy had once feared, intertwined with episodes of heroism and courage. Major General Oliver P. Smith, who'd commanded the Marines at Inchon, was to lead the retreat of the frostbitten 1st Marine Division, traveling single-column along a narrow, slippery, mountain road. As Max Hastings wrote in his excellent history of the war, the "two formations endured entirely separate nightmares. . . . All that they possessed in common were the horrors of weather, isolation, Chinese attack—and the threat of absolute disaster overtaking American arms."

MacArthur reported on the collapse of the UN drive, in a wire to the Pentagon, on November 28: "All hope of localization of the Korean conflict to enemy forces composed of North Korean troops with alien token elements can now be completely abandoned," he wrote. "The Chinese military forces are committed in North Korea in great and ever-increasing strength. . . . We face an entirely new war."

2. Truman absorbed the news that morning at a staff meeting, while the *New Yorker*'s John Hersey, who was in Washington to write a profile of the President, was closely observing his subject: "He had suddenly drooped a little," Hersey wrote. "It appeared that something he would have liked to forget was back in his mind, close behind his hugely magnified eyes." Hersey's account continued:

"'We have a terrific situation on our hands,' Truman said in a very quiet solemn voice. 'General Bradley called me at six-fifteen this morning. He told me that a terrible message had come from General MacArthur. MacArthur . . . says he's stymied. He says he has to go over to the defensive. It's no longer a question of a few so-called volunteers. The Chinese have come in with both feet.' . . .

"The President paused. The shock of this news made everyone sit stiff and still. Suddenly all his driven-down emotions seemed to pour into his face. His mouth drew tight, his cheeks flushed. For a moment, it almost seemed as if he would sob. Then, in a voice that was incredibly calm and quiet, considering what could be read on his face—a voice of absolute personal courage—he said, 'This is the worst situation we have had yet. We'll just have to meet it as we've met all the rest. I've talked already this morning with Bradley, Marshall, Acheson, Harriman, and Snyder, and they all agree with me that we're capable of meeting this thing. I know you fellows will work with us on it, and that we'll meet it just like we've met everything else.'" Over the next few minutes, Truman's mood shifted abruptly. At one point, he referred to Senator McCarthy's persistent besmirching of Dean Acheson, over the State Department's China policy: "Well, the liars have accomplished their purpose," he said. "I'm talking about the crowd of vilifiers who have been trying to tear us apart in this country." Then, just as quickly, his tone changed, as he said, again, "We have got to meet this thing just as we've met everything else. And we will. We will!" Truman was rattled enough to consider declaring a "complete emergency," followed by a speech to a joint session of Congress, but he was dissuaded by his advisers, who thought it could sound panicked to rush into it.

We face an entirely new war. In the afternoon of that November 28, Truman convened the National Security Council. One always imagines that these meetings advance policy, or clarify events, but it is often the case that nothing of the sort happens. So it was this time, as military and civilian officials faced one another at a table in the Cabinet Room, or stared at a map of Korea. General Bradley said the Chiefs wanted more troops from other countries—"provided they really could fight." Doubts about MacArthur were coming into the open, though expressed with delicacy. Secretary Marshall said, with considerable understatement, "There is a big gap in our lines"—between the Eighth Army and the X Corps—"and I don't know what MacArthur intends to do about that," adding, "It is his problem." Then Marshall pulled back, saying, "We have no business, here in Washington . . . asking the local commander what his tactical plans are." Vice President Barkley asked why MacArthur, just a week earlier, had said the "boys in Korea would be home by Christmas," and went on to wonder, "Did he know what was going on? If he did know, why did he say it? How in the world could a man in his position be guilty of such an indiscretion?" Truman didn't try to defend MacArthur, but said, "He made the statement; you will have to draw your own conclusion as to why he did it." He added that they had to be careful "not to pull the rug out from under him"—that "we could not cause the Commanding General in the field to lose face before the enemy." Truman, though, felt deceived. In his diary, he recalled, resentfully, that MacArthur, on Wake Island, had assured him "we had won the war and that we could send a Division"—ten to fifteen thousand men—"to Europe from Korea in January 1951."

When it was Acheson's turn, he spoke in a voice of foreboding: "We are very much closer to the danger of general war," he said. He asked everyone to remember that the Soviet Union "had always been behind every move," and that "we must all think about what happens in Korea as a world matter." He then began a curious circular rumination on what the United States wanted in Korea. "We want to terminate it," he said. "We don't want to beat China in Korea—we can't. We don't want to beat China any place—we can't." But after considering a future in which the war would turn into a "bottomless pit," he continued, "I don't know how to terminate it. . . . Our great objective must be to hold an area, to eliminate the fighting, to turn over some area to the Republic of Korea, and to *get out* so that we can get ahead with building up our own strength." So it had come to that: The United States was fighting in Korea with the goal of getting out of Korea.

On November 30, Truman held a news conference in the ornate Indian Treaty Room, at Old State, with more than two hundred reporters attending. He wore a tie that showed Paul Bunyan with a tree over his shoulder, a curiously whimsical note, and read a statement saying that the Chinese offensive "threatens not only the whole fabric of the United Nations, but all human hopes of peace and justice" and that "if the United Nations yields to the forces of aggression, no nation will be safe or secure." After that, when he probably should have thanked the reporters and left the room, he said, "All right. Ask any questions now." Those questions quickly led him to revisit treacherous territory—in particular whether, or when, the United States might use an atomic bomb. Many of his answers were untruthful, in whole or in part, as when he was asked "in what detail" he'd been informed about MacArthur's drive toward the Yalu. "Every detail," Truman replied.

Q: Did you or the State Department raise the question of whether this offensive would affect the chances of a negotiated settlement with the Peiping government?

The President: The whole matter was clearly discussed with General MacArthur every day.

Q: Mr. President, there has been some criticism of General MacArthur in the European press. . . . The particular criticism is that he exceeded his authority and went beyond the point he was supposed to go?

The President: He did nothing of the kind.

. . .

Q: Mr. President, will attacks in Manchuria depend on action in the United Nations?

The President: Yes, entirely.

Q: In other words, if the United Nations resolution should authorize General MacArthur to go further than he has, he will—

The President: We will take whatever steps are necessary to meet the military situation, just as we always have.

Q: Will that include the atomic bomb?

The President: That includes every weapon that we have.

Q: Mr. President, you said "every weapon that we have." Does that mean that there is active consideration of the use of the atomic bomb?

The President: There has always been active consideration of its use. I don't want to see it used. It is a terrible weapon, and it should not be used on innocent men, women, and children who have nothing whatever to do with this military aggression. That happens when it is used.

That sounded like a sensational development. "A whisper ran along the benches," A. J. Liebling wrote, "that Truman had said MacArthur could use the atomic bomb any time he wanted." Truman hadn't actually said that, but neither had he offered much clarity when he was asked to "retrace that reference to the atom bomb" and whether he meant it when he said "that the use of the atomic bomb is under active consideration." To that, he replied, "always has been. It is one of our weapons."

A rushed White House statement tried to say that nothing had changed: "Naturally, there has been consideration of this subject since the outbreak of the hostilities in Korea, just as there is consideration of the use of all military weapons whenever our forces are in combat." But despite the attempt to say that nuclear policy hadn't changed, it was too late to unsay what had just been said. Truman's remarks had, not surprisingly, created a disturbance at the United Nations, which Acheson said was in a "virtual state of panic," particularly among the Asian states, where there was an embedded fear, as the Saudi ambassador told Eleanor Roosevelt, that an A-bomb might once more be used "against a colored people."

The military heard a different sort of message. General Stratemeyer, for one, had taken note of Truman's declaration that "we are fighting for our own [national security and] survival," and concluded that if the President "authorizes use of the atomic weapon, MacArthur will decide where and when it will be employed." MacArthur was more than ready. From his Tokyo office, he listed for Stratemeyer his chosen targets, in order of priority: "ANTUNG, MUKDEN, PEIPING, TIENTSIN, SHANGHAI and NANKING." (Stratemeyer copied the capitalization.) MacArthur also had a short list of favored Russian targets—that is "if we get in the big one."

On the night of Truman's press conference, Acheson gave a speech, broadcast nationwide, in which he said China's "brazen act . . . even more immoral than the first" had created "a situation of unparalleled danger." He also made the oddly phrased observation that "no one can guarantee that war will not come." Truman the next day asked Congress to appropriate seventeen billion dollars for guns, tanks, and additional weaponry, plus a billion more to increase the nation's stock of atomic bombs. He felt bound to say that it "is not a war budget," which would "obviously require far more money," although, with a projected defense force of nearly three million men, it looked a lot like a budget for a nation preparing for a bigger war.

Truman was perplexed by the choices—none of them good—that he was being forced to make. The origins of this bafflement may be seen in a series of early December meetings, engulfed in pessimism. Unless the shattered X Corps could regroup, General Bradley said at the Pentagon, on December 1, "we may not have enough troops to hold a line," while Army Chief of Staff Collins thought Korea "was not worth a nickel while the Russians hold Vladivostok." Deputy Defense Secretary Lovett gingerly approached the question of withdrawal when he spoke of a "consensus" that Korea "is not a decisive area for us." Lovett could see that the loss of Korea might jeopardize Japan's future, but Western Europe was "our prime concern." The discussion, inevitably, turned to the possibility of general war—how striking China could bring in Soviet air and submarines. "The only chance then left to save us," Collins said, "is the use or threat of use of the A-bomb"—which he wanted to avoid, even if it means "that our ground forces must take some punishment from the air." It was about then that Walter Bedell Smith, who'd become the CIA director in August, mentioned a forthcoming agency analysis saying that the Russians believed "we don't intend to get into war," but were willing risk it "if they can bog us down in Asia."

At the White House, on the evening of December 2, General Marshall sounded unusually pessimistic: Within the next seventy-two hours, he said, the military situation would reach a "crash state," and that they faced the "great dilemma of determining how we could save our troops and protect our national honor at the same time." Before the meeting adjourned, Acheson suggested that now was the time to declare a national emergency. He urged Truman to freeze prices and wages, and establish "far-reaching productions controls." The President agreed with his secretary of state, as he almost always did, which set in motion preparations for a speech that he would deliver in about two weeks.

Meanwhile, the talkative MacArthur, who didn't visit Korea until December 11—more than two weeks after China's surprise offensive—and who had never spent a night in the field, continued to issue orders from Tokyo. Far from the Korean front, in the Dai-ichi cocoon, he managed to sound as if nothing was his fault, the colossal military misjudgment to divide his forces had simply happened—blame lay with circumstances he couldn't have foreseen. As he explained to the receptive editors at *U.S. News and World Report*, "When the line of battle moved northward, the area of possible detections and interdiction of enemy movements contracted." He complained that prohibiting hot pursuit by UN troops into China was "an enormous handicap, without precedent in military history." He never lost the focus on his heroic self, as when he told the wire service correspondent Hugh Baillie, "Never before has the patience of man been more sorely tried nor high standards of human behavior been more patiently and firmly upheld than during the course of the Korean campaigns." After all that, he issued a special statement that "a state of undeclared war between the Chinese Communists and the United Nations forces now exists." MacArthur's sovereign-like declaration of war preceded a wire to the Joint Chiefs in which he wrote, "This small command is facing the entire Chinese nation in an undeclared war . . . and steady attrition leading to final destruction can reasonably be expected." He asked for "ground reinforcements of the greatest magnitude."

During a morning briefing at the Pentagon on December 3, discussion turned to ways to liquidate the miserable conflict in Korea. If the Chinese refused a cease-fire offer, General Bradley asked, should they be informed that "we consider we are at war"? In that case, he said, they could bomb China, blockade the coast, and a "good many other things to bother them," though "we would probably not use the A-Bomb." Then he asked, "If we get out of Korea, are we to give up the whole of Asia?" Acheson acknowledged that, in order to win a cease-fire, the Chinese might demand a high price—they "might say we must leave Korea. They might further ask that we withdraw the Seventh Fleet from Formosa and seat them in the U.N." He recognized that "there is a danger of our becoming the greatest appeasers of all time if we abandon the Koreans and they are slaughtered," while adding that "if there is a Dunkirk and we are forced out, it is a disaster but not a disgraceful one." China was still not Acheson's primary worry: "The great trouble is that we are fighting the wrong nation. We are fighting the second team, whereas the real enemy is the Soviet Union." The sense of the meeting was summed up when General Bradley read a draft of a new order to MacArthur that "we consider the preservation of your forces is now the primary consideration."

After Acheson and Marshall left the room, some of the military men stayed to chat. General Ridgway, the deputy army chief of staff, spoke with Air Force Chief of Staff Vandenberg, whom he'd known since Vandenberg was a cadet at West Point.

"Why don't the Joint Chiefs send orders to MacArthur and *tell* him what to do?" Ridgway asked.

"What good would that do?" Vandenberg replied, shaking his head. "He wouldn't obey the orders. What *can* we do?"

"You can relieve any commander who won't obey orders, can't you?" Ridgway said, almost shouting. At that, Vandenberg walked off without saying a word.

3. What Truman had said about nuclear weapons at his November 30 press conference so stirred things up that British Prime Minister Clement Attlee hurried across the Atlantic, arriving in Washington on December 4, a day when a front-page story by James Reston, speaking for the "well-informed," announced that "every official movement in the capital today, every official report from Tokyo, and every private estimate of the situation by well-informed men reflected a sense of emergency and even of alarm. . . . Not even on the fateful night . . . when the Korean war started was the atmosphere more grim." Attlee hadn't made this journey since November 1945, when Truman appeared to have said that the nuclear "secret" belonged solely to the United States. This time, Attlee had a broader agenda: a worry that the resources being poured into Korea were coming at the expense of a rebuilt Europe.

Acheson listened, with alarm, as Attlee smoothly presented a case for rapid disentanglement from Korea, and "soon led the President well onto the flypaper." At one point, Acheson recalled, he'd "stepped on the President's foot," a nudge to suggest that the conversation slow down, which brought Acheson an annoyed glance from Attlee. But Truman didn't need Acheson's shoe to set him straight. "The British still seem to think that all should be given up in the Far East to save Europe," he wrote in his diary, the day after Attlee's arrival. "I said No!"

Discussion of the nuclear issue took only a short time. It "began disastrously," Attlee's cabinet secretary recalled, but the tone changed when Captain Truman and Major Attlee, both veterans, "were at the piano, drinking and singing First World War songs." For all their surface amiability, though, Truman would still insist that any decision on using nuclear weapons was his alone—that, in the words of a noncommittal joint communiqué, he expected to keep the PM informed "of developments which might bring about a change in the situation." In other words, nothing had changed since the fall of 1945.

There was almost nothing to cheer about during Attlee's stay, which began with a lunchtime Potomac cruise that included Acheson, Marshall, Bradley, and Charlie Ross, who took notes for a press briefing. For more than five years, Ross had been a constant Truman companion, from Potsdam to the 1948 campaign to Wake Island to the Blair House shooting to a recent army-navy football game in Philadelphia. He rarely managed to escape, although he had heart trouble, and had been hospitalized for a flare up of arthritis. "This job is like a prison," he wrote to a friend, while adding, "The work remains, of course, extraordinarily interesting," never more so than the present moment.

Ross rode back to the office with George Elsey, and when he'd settled at his desk, as forty-odd reporters waited to hear what had been discussed on the *Williamsburg*, he began by saying that he had nothing startling, nothing to set off what he called "the screaming, competitive, hurdle-the-wounded, and trample-the-dead attitude of the wire services, and of a lot of other daily reporters." The briefing included a refusal to comment on a report that a "Dunkirk" in Korea was under consideration. With patient good humor, Ross also answered questions on the shipboard seating arrangements and the lunch fare. When he was asked to read aloud from the menu, his reply gives a good idea of what was then required of a press secretary:

> *Mr. Ross:* Seafood cocktail, cream of tomato soup—croutons— them things that go in the soup—(*laughter*)—next line is ol- ives, celery, hearts, relishes and pickles; next line prime roast rib of beef—I will spell it—A-U-J-U-S—(*more laughter*); next line is braised celery; next line is broccoli-hollandaise sauce; next line is French-cut string beans; next line is hot rolls—assorted jellies; then comes lettuce romaine and chic- ory salad, with oil dressing; then comes cheese B L E U—and crackers. Then comes baked Alaska . . .
>
> *Q:* (*interposing*) Did they take a nap afterwards?
> *Mr. Ross:* I felt like it.

Then, in Ronald Farrar's fine account, a National Broadcasting Company correspondent asked him to repeat some of what he'd just said, although Ross's secretary, Myrtle Bergheim, didn't approve of those added chores. His first words were already on the wires when he lit one of his perpetual cigarettes and got ready to talk into NBC's microphone.

"Don't mumble," Bergheim said, with a smile.

"You know I *always* speak very distinctly," Ross replied.

That's when his deputy, Eben Ayers, went to check the clacking news wire. When he turned around, he saw that Ross's head had fallen to the back of his chair, and that he seemed to have passed out. With one hand, Bergheim reached for Ross; with the other hand, she called General Wallace Graham, the White House physician, whose office was a floor below, and who raced upstairs. He injected stimulators, and used a "Pulmotor" Resuscitator, but later said that death must have been instantaneous: "He was gone before I got there." The *Evening Star*'s Doris Fleeson wrote that "Charlie Ross died in battle too."

Truman and Ross had known each other since they'd attended Independence High School, class of '01, a forty-year friendship that had lasted through Truman's political life—from the Pendergast era to the presidency—and had survived Ross's career with the *St. Louis Post-Dispatch*, a newspaper that was rarely kind to Truman. Truman had already returned to Blair House when he was informed that Ross was dead, and he hastily wrote out a statement: "The friend of my youth, who became a tower of strength when the responsibilities of high office so unexpectedly fell to me, is gone. . . . I knew him as boy and as man. . . . It was characteristic of Charlie Ross that he was holding a press conference when the sudden summons came. We all knew that he was working far beyond his strength. But he would have it so." The reporters, who knew and liked Ross, waited while those sentences were typed on stencils and mimeographed for distribution; they were standing in a semicircle, in the White House press lounge, when Truman came in.

"I have a statement about Charlie Ross," Truman said, and then began to read it: "The friend of my youth, who became a tower of—" At which point his voice broke. Reporters looked up. "Aw, hell!" He threw his text down on a table. "I can't read this thing. You fellows know how I feel, anyway." With that, Farrar wrote, "the President of the United States turned and walked slowly out of the room, tears streaming down his face."

Five hours later, Margaret Truman, wearing a pink satin dress, stood on the stage of Washington's DAR Constitution Hall, in what ought to have been a happy hometown concert. In 1949, she'd begun to study with Helen Traubel, the Wagnerian soprano and Metropolitan Opera star, and in October of that year she had set off on another concert tour. In the fall of 1950, she made her first national television appearance, on Ed Sullivan's *Toast of the Town* program. Her latest circuit had brought her, on December 5, to Washington.

Truman had worried that the news about Ross might affect his daughter's performance and decided that she shouldn't be told beforehand. The Trumans attended the concert as if nothing was wrong, knowing that Margaret would worry if they weren't in their usual, visible seats, in Box 13—the presidential box. Truman's guests included Prime Minister Attlee, the British ambassador, and the ambassador's wife. Those who looked closely thought the President seemed downcast; Bess Truman appeared to have been crying. Some thirty-five hundred people in the hall brought Margaret back for four encores.

Among her father's aides, "I was closest to Charlie," Margaret later wrote. "I treated him like an uncle and he treated me like a fresh niece." She later learned that news of Ross's death had spread and supposed that it "may have made many people in the audience feel it was bad taste for me to be singing at all." Onstage, she'd "sensed there was something wrong with their reaction. At the time I blamed it on Korea. I was sure it had nothing to do with the music. In fact, I thought it was one of my better performances."

Paul Hume, the music critic of the *Washington Post*, was not impressed. His review, which appeared two days after Ross's death, said that "Miss Truman is . . . extremely attractive on the stage. Her program is usually light in nature. . . . Yet Miss Truman cannot sing very well. . . . She is flat a good deal of time." The thirty-four-year-old Hume sounded gratuitously, and determinedly, snotty as he wrote, "There are few moments . . . when one can relax and feel confident that she will make her goal, which is the end of the song," and, in case one missed the point, "She communicates almost nothing of the music she presents."

Hume may have felt it was his duty to say this, and to say it in that way, but nothing made Truman angrier than criticism directed at his wife or daughter; at that moment—after Ross's death, in the wake of the news from Korea—Hume was less the fearless critic and more the petty scold. It led in any case to one of Truman's most celebrated minor rages—"spasms" he called them—in a handwritten letter to Hume that began, "I've just read your lousy review of Margaret's concert. I've come to the conclusion that you are an eight ulcer man on four ulcer pay," and ended with the thought that if they ever met, "you'll need a new nose, a lot of beefsteak for black eyes, and perhaps a supporter below!"

This remarkable letter did not stay private for long. Hume showed it to a friend who'd reviewed the concert no more favorably for the *Washington Daily News*, and the *News* printed what the friend, in a pre-Xerox age, was able to memorize. From there it went to the front page of the *Herald Tribune*, along with a patronizing statement from Hume that "a man suffering the loss of a close friend and carrying the terrible burden of the present world crisis ought to be indulged in an occasional outburst of temper." When Margaret Truman was asked about it, she said that Hume was a fine critic and "has the perfect right to say whatever he thinks." The *Trib*'s story noted that she'd gotten a less negative notice in the *Evening Star*, and a favorable one in the *Washington Times-Herald*.

For the public, this was a brief interruption from news about the uncontrollable war in Asia. For Truman, it meant feeling more deeply the death of Charlie Ross, from whom he would take advice and who might have stopped him from sending such a letter. "He was so torn, he was torn up over Charlie," Cornelius Mara, an assistant military aide, recalled; the letter, he added, only got mailed because Truman didn't put it in his usual out-basket: "He knew that if anybody saw it they would stop it. He took it out and mailed it, on his walk." Those who knew Truman sometimes worried about his temper. David Lilienthal, the former Atomic Energy Commission chairman, thought that Truman had done "a terrible thing . . . sending another one of these inexcusably coarse and ill-tempered personal letters. . . . I worry that one of these days, that badly controlled temper might set off World War III."

Lilienthal's worries were silly but not uncommon. "It upset me," Truman wrote in his journal, "and I wrote him what I thought of him. I told him he is lower than [the Hearst columnist Westbrook] Pegler and that was intended to be an insult worse than a reflection on his ancestry. I would never reflect on a man's mother because

mothers are not to be attacked although mine has! Well I've had a
grand time this day. I've been accused of putting my 'baby' who is
the 'apple of my eye' in a bad position. I don't think that is so. She
doesn't either—thank the Almighty." As for "the jittery situation facing the country," he acknowledged that it had shaken him, adding,
alarmingly, "I've worked for peace for five years and six months and
it looks like World War III is here. I hope not—but we must meet
whatever comes—and we will."

What is so striking about these ruminations is what they reveal
of Truman's unrealistic view of American power. He held fast to the
confident, and ruinous, idea that, from a great distance—and with
no easily understood national interest at stake—the United States
could successfully wage a war and administer a lasting peace. At the
same time, he was a frightened man: unnerved by the violence that
had been set loose in Asia, and by the possibility something unknow-
able and terrible lay ahead—toying with the thought that "it looks
like World War III is here." Walter Lippmann didn't know about
the classified NSC-68 document that encouraged such ventures, but
he could see what he called the "inflated globalism" of the Truman
Doctrine—the "misinformation, miscalculation, and misjudgment at
the highest levels of decision and command"—and could imagine
that it would not end well.

4. By December 8, it was clear, as a Joint Chiefs history
observed, that "the hope of unifying Korea by force had been finally
laid to rest." During the following week, in the days before Truman
announced a national emergency, the men around him offered ideas
on how to phrase such a proclamation. To read their suggestions is
to get a sense of the sensibilities in Truman's orbit, to see how major
speeches were constructed in the 1950 White House, and to wonder
about the creeping verbiage of NSC-68, which had said, "The issues
that face us are momentous, involving the fulfillment or destruction
not only of this Republic but of civilization itself."

One early draft began, "I want to talk to you tonight about the
very serious problems that have been created for all of us by the

Chinese communists in Korea." Another said, "Tonight, I want to explain to you what this state of emergency means. It is important that all of us understand what we must do to protect our homes, our nation and everything we believe in." Paul Nitze proposed beginning, "I have today declared a national emergency. It is with a heavy heart that I have done this. The peace of the world and the security of this nation are in danger, and we must act rapidly to meet the threat." The most unusual contribution, in every sense, came from the journalist John Hersey, who was still reporting what became a five-part *New Yorker* profile of Truman. He sent along a pro bono suggestion that began, "Our way of life, which is the best the world has ever known, is in grave danger. This danger has been created by the rulers of the Soviet Union, who want to control the whole earth. The time has come to face the truth: the leaders of Russian communism want to control the whole earth. It is not enough to see this truth. We have to do something about it."

The tenth, and final, draft of the speech was finished on December 14, the day before Truman addressed his fellow citizens on television and radio. Looking and sounding less confident than his words, he said, "The future of civilization depends on what we do— on what we do now, and in the months ahead." He warned that "our homes, our nation, all the things we believe in, are in great danger." (With his pronounced Missouri accent, "believe" became "bleeve.") It was as if he were quoting from NSC-68. This danger, he continued, "has been created by the rulers of the Soviet Union," and Communist aggression was pushing the world "to the brink of a general war." Truman had not declared war, but wartime alarms were being set off, along with wage and price controls, voluntary and otherwise. To oversee an "arsenal for the defense of freedom," he established an Office of Defense Mobilization, a name that evoked the wartime Office of War Mobilization, run by "assistant president" Jimmy Byrnes. Put in charge of an office that the press called a "co-presidency" was General Electric's president, Charles E. Wilson, who three years earlier had overseen the administration's influential report on racial inequality. A *Wall Street Journal* analysis explained how the United States would probably win World War III, but quoted an unnamed general who said that if war "broke out tomorrow, the U.S. would be in an awful fix," and Stalin would win the first year "hands down." Admiral Leahy believed that Russian armies would soon invade Western Europe and that their numerical superiority promised "rapid success."

On a CBS program called *The Challenge of the Fifties—Years of Crisis*, broadcast on New Year's Eve, 1950, the commentator Eric Sevareid interviewed Acheson. As was sometimes the case, Sevareid was the more impressive figure. His Nordic aspect, brooding expressiveness, and voice of crackling certitude was particularly suited to solemn occasions. "Some Americans of authority are saying that this is America's darkest hour," Sevareid said. "Do you believe that?" Acheson replied that "a nation's darkest hour is when its citizens lose their will and their courage," and that the nation had come through other dark hours, such as the winter of Valley Forge and the night of Pearl Harbor. "We are on the side of freedom and on the side of the great spiritual values which have created our country," he said.

T. R. Fehrenbach tried to come to terms with his doubts. "Something new had happened," he wrote. "The United States had gone to war, not under enemy attack, nor to protect the lives or property of American citizens. . . . The American people had entered a war, not by the roaring demand of Congress. . . . or the public, but by executive action, at the urging of an American proconsul across the sea, to maintain the balance of power across the sea." In the bloodless prose of Washington punditry, Lippmann described the trap into which the Truman administration and the nation had stumbled: "The burden of proof is on anyone who argues that the only way to deal with a little war that has gone badly is to make it a much bigger war."

TWENTY-THREE

"Voice of God"

Senator Fulbright: Could you give us any thoughts about what you think are the basic causes of war?

Gen. MacArthur: Now, when you ask me to analyze the causes of war, I could go and show you hundreds of books that would discuss that from various angles. The remaining twilight years of my life wouldn't be long enough to put the full thesis out.

—Senate committee hearings on
"The Military Situation the Far East"

1. David Lilienthal stopped by to see Truman on the last day of January 1951, a day of sleet, freezing rain, and snarled traffic. Lilienthal thought he looked "thinner in the face than I remember him . . . dark under the eyes," but he'd put aside his worries about Truman's temperament. Rather, he found him once more to be "his familiar, relaxed, friendly, unassuming self." When Lilienthal remarked on the difficulties of the presidency, Truman said, "Well, I just do the best I can. No one has ever faced such terrible problems as we face today, such danger. I really don't think there ever has been a time quite like this. I spend long hours seeing fellows who don't agree, who ought to agree among themselves, and I have to get them to agree, or decide it myself. All day long it goes on." He continued, "I seem to take it fine—go like a steam engine all day and long into the night." As for Korea, "We're sitting on a keg of dynamite in Asia. I think we can hold them off until we get strong, and we're getting stronger every day."

Truman, outwardly, remained a model of sanguinity, even though the news continued to be bleak. Just before Christmas, Lieutenant General Walton H. Walker, the commander of the retreating Eighth Army, was killed in a freakish jeep accident; he'd been on his way to see his son, an army captain. Truman quickly replaced him with Matthew Bunker Ridgway, the fifty-five-year-old deputy army chief of staff, a "soldier's soldier," who'd commanded the 82nd Airborne Division during the war. Ridgway's nickname was "Old Iron Tits," because of two grenades he kept pinned to the harness in front of his chest, though one was actually a medical kit. Truman could not have made a better choice.

Ridgway was reluctant to criticize MacArthur, despite the SCAP's determinedly uninformed assurances about China's capabilities and intentions, but so were most military men as well as most politicians. One can measure MacArthur's personal authority by the amount of time it took Truman to react to his acts of insubordination and his attitude of lèse-majesté. Despite the general's disastrous war strategy, the President remained hesitant about suggesting that better plans were wanted. In mid-January 1951, about the time that Lilienthal popped in, he cabled MacArthur that "we need your judgement as to the maximum effort" which UN forces could provide, adding that "in the worst case . . . if we must withdraw from Korea, it [should] be clear to the world that that course is forced upon us by military necessity." Before that awkward injunction, the cable said that "this present telegram is not repeat not to be taken in any sense as a directive." A copy went to Acheson.

As a celebrity soldier, MacArthur had always attracted acolytes, such as the Republican House leader Joseph W. Martin Jr., of Massachusetts. On February 12, 1950, at a Lincoln Day dinner, in Brooklyn, Martin proposed a second Asian front, in which Chiang Kai-shek's Nationalist troops would fight alongside the UN forces. That idea had quickly been rejected at the start of the war, but Martin revived it, while saying it couldn't win support from the "same State Department crowd" that he, like some of his colleagues, blamed for China's turn to Communism. "If we want to develop a true global strategy that will wipe out the Communist threat of world domination, we must clean out the State Department from top to bottom, starting with Dean Acheson," Martin said. That was familiar language from the party's right wing, but Martin stepped over the rhetorical line when he went on to say, "If we are not in Korea to win, then the Truman administration should be indicted for the murder of thousands of American boys."

Martin was proud enough of his speech to send a copy to MacArthur, along with a note saying that he'd "deem it a great help if I could have your views on this point, either on a confidential basis or otherwise. Your admirers are legion, and the respect you command is enormous." The general replied, on March 20, with enthusiasm: A second front would "relieve the pressure on our forces in Korea." As if savoring every word for a posterity that he believed would embrace him, MacArthur added that "here we fight Europe's war with arms while the diplomats there still fight it with words," and concluded, "As you point out, we must win. There is no substitute for victory."

MacArthur knew, though, that a substitute for victory was already under serious consideration. Dean Rusk, in February, spelled it out in one of those policy memoranda in which several options are offered and only one—in this case a cease-fire and a return by all sides to the 38th Parallel—is the only realistic choice. In March, Marshall and Acheson, with the Joint Chiefs, drafted a presidential proposal that aimed to "conclude the fighting and ensure against its resumption" and "open the way for a broader settlement." When MacArthur, on March 20, was formally notified, and told to halt advances across the 38th Parallel while diplomacy was being pursued, his response—"Recommend that no further military restrictions be imposed"—was a declaration of disobedience. Three days later, following another draft of the offer to start peace talks, MacArthur did something inexcusable: He belittled China's "exaggerated and vaunted military power" and announced that he, MacArthur, was "ready to confer in the field with the commander-in-chief of the enemy forces," to see how the UN's "political objectives" might be accomplished "without further bloodshed." Or else, he said, the UN Command would "depart from its tolerant effort to contain the

war" and expand it so as to "doom Red China to the risk of imminent military collapse."

The tone of "this pronunciamento," a Joint Chiefs history observed, "practically guaranteed" its rejection, and helped convince
Truman, despite his longstanding reluctance to do or say anything
that might undermine his Pacific commander, that "the general had
to go." He'd been angry with MacArthur before, but this struck him
as another level of insolence: The general's "most extraordinary
statement," he later wrote, revealed MacArthur as someone "in open
defiance of my orders . . . a challenge to the authority of the President
under the Constitution." Margaret Truman got a firsthand glimpse
of her father's reaction: "He prevented a ceasefire proposition right
there, I was ready to kick him into the North China Sea," Truman
told his daughter. "It's the lousiest trick a commander-in-chief can
have done to him by an underling."

Truman may have decided earlier that the general had to go.
Joseph C. Goulden, in his valuable 1982 history of the war, thought
MacArthur's undoing could be traced to messages intercepted by the
National Security Agency, which recorded MacArthur telling Spanish
and Portuguese diplomats that "he could transform the Korean War
into a major conflict in which he could dispose of the 'Chinese Communist question' once and for all." Goulden's source was Charles
Burton Marshall, who served on the State Department's Policy Plan-
ning Staff. "We were in war at that time . . . so every government's
messages were being decoded," Marshall recalled. "MacArthur was
talking big in a Falstaffian way to the Spanish and the Portuguese
Ambassadors . . . that he was going to see to it that the U.S. got into
a general war against China." Paul Nitze, the director of the Policy
Planning Staff, also saw those intercepts and likewise concluded that
"MacArthur's real aim was to expand the war into China, overthrow
Mao Tse-tung, and restore Chiang Kai-shek to power." The author's
Freedom of Information Request to the National Security Agency,
asking to see those relatively ancient documents, was considered for
nearly two years, and then denied. An appeal was also denied.

MacArthur, in his memoirs, published posthumously in 1964,
revealed his version of a path to victory "in a maximum of ten days."

It would begin with "massive air attacks," and "sever Korea from Manchuria by laying a field of radioactive waste—the byproducts of atomic manufacture—across all the major lines of enemy supply." Then, with the help of Nationalist Chinese troops, he'd attack at the upper end of both coasts and "close a gigantic trap. The Chinese would soon starve or surrender." The idea of using radioactive waste as a weapon was later proposed by the Tennessee congressman Albert Gore Sr., the father of the future vice president, who urged Truman to "dehumanize a belt across the Korean peninsula by surface radiological contamination," and keep it in place so that ground troops entering the region would face "certain death or slow deformity." A disquieting *New York Times* headline said "Atomic Death Belt Urged for Korea."

2. In the late summer of 1950, Truman had set up a private intelligence channel for the war. To do the job he'd recruited Major General Frank E. Lowe, a sixty-five-year-old reserve officer, who'd been a Truman Committee investigator and, like Truman, an artillery captain during World War I. The President had armed Lowe with a letter that let him go wherever he pleased, and pretty much do whatever he wanted during the months that he spent in Korea and Japan. His reports—Lowe fired off more than eighty, sometimes more than one a day, many going no farther than the desk of Harry Vaughan—were often amplifications of MacArthur's outlook. Lowe remained a steadfast MacArthur admirer as late as mid-March 1951, when he informed Truman that the general might be on the verge of "pulling twin white rabbits out of a black silk hat," that he still inspired "extreme confidence," though "of course, we *could* wish that the United Nations would get off its hands and declare the Yalu River and the area beyond not sacrosanct." Because MacArthur still inspired such high regard, many believed that, no matter how far he overstepped, he'd face no more than a private rebuke. But circumstances had changed. Inchon was yesterday, the Communists had retaken Pyongyang, there were no more white rabbits, and Truman had run out of rebukes.

"The situation with regard to the Far Eastern General has become a political one," Truman wrote in his diary on April 5; his entry included an oddly personal digression, in which he sounded offended by MacArthur's marital history: "He has had two wives—one a social light [*sic*] he married at 42, the other a Tennessee girl he married in his middle fifties after No 1 had divorced him." Furthermore, he thought MacArthur owed him some loyalty: "I made him Allied Commander in Chief in Japan to sign the surrender documents."

At a news conference on that April 5, Truman was asked if MacArthur was "authorized to bomb bases in Manchuria," and replied, "That is a question that cannot be answered because it is a military strategy question, and it is not a question that I can answer."

The question was asked because the ordinarily sober House speaker, Sam Rayburn, after a White House meeting the day before, had said "we stand in the face of terrible danger and maybe the beginning of World War III." On the floor of the House, he'd warned of "the massing of troops in Korea and Manchuria, and not all of them Communist Chinese"—a way of saying that the Russians too had moved in. Asked about that, Truman said only, "I have no comment on Speaker Rayburn's statement, but the Speaker is a truthful man," adding "That situation has been a dangerous one for the last five years—last four years, I will say."

As usual, MacArthur was inclined to blame others. In the next morning's *Washington Post*, he was quoted telling a British correspondent, "For the first time in my military career I find myself involved in a war without a definite objective." On that same April 6, Joseph Martin, the minority leader, read aloud his recent correspondence with MacArthur. Truman confined his irate reaction to his diary: "MacArthur shoots another political bomb through . . . the leader of the Republican minority in the House. This looks like the last straw. Rank insubordination." The unnecessary inclusion of Martin's title suggests that this was written for the record, and possibly later than Friday, April 6. But whatever the timing, Truman's indignation was authentic. The VFW message sent to "newspapers and magazines particularly hostile to me" still gnawed, and so did the recollection of what MacArthur had told him on Wake Island:

"I'd flown 14404 [miles] to Wake Island to see him. . . . He told me the war in Korea was over that we could transfer a regular division to Germany Jan 1st. He was positive Red China would not come in. He expected to support our Far Eastern policy." Truman had had enough: "I call in Gen. Marshall, Dean Atcheson [sic] Mr. Harriman and Gen Bradley before Cabinet to discuss situation. I've come to the conclusion that our Big General in the Far East must be recalled."

This little group met that Friday and Saturday morning, April 7, when Truman wrote in his diary, "It is the unanimous opinion of all that MacArthur be relieved. All four so advise. I direct that order be issued, press statement prepared and suggest meeting Monday before the Cabinet meets." Truman also talked to three trusted friends—Chief Justice Vinson, Speaker Rayburn, and Vice President Barkley—with whom he discussed "the situation in Far East." He didn't tell them what was in the offing, but they surely would have been able to guess. By the time the Joint Chiefs met on Sunday, April 8, Washington was approaching another of its periodic states of agitation, with newspaper reports of an "imminent showdown" with MacArthur. Those reports were accurate. The Joint Chiefs agreed, unanimously, that MacArthur should be relieved, although it was painful to fire one of their own, especially someone with MacArthur's historic standing. His replacement was to be Matthew Ridgway, who was also rattled by the changeover. "In the Pentagon as well as in the field," he later wrote, MacArthur remained a man "who had never admitted a mistake in judgment, yet whose mistakes in judgment had been remarkably few." Yet Ridgway also came to see past MacArthur's semi-legendary reputation. When he was in his nineties, he told David Halberstam that some of the dispatches MacArthur had sent in the fall of 1950 "smacked of the purest fantasy," such as a claim that X Corps, "in great jeopardy on the east coast . . . [was] still on an offensive mission and had tied down six to eight Chinese divisions." When messages like that came in," Ridgway recalled, "it was as if madness were in the room."

Ridgway learned that he was about to take command of the Eighth Army before the news reached MacArthur. It came, he wrote, "as dramatic news often does, in a most undramatic way"—in this case, when a reporter offered congratulations. Frank Pace, the army secretary, who had traveled to Korea to personally inform Ridgway of the change, recalled that Ridgway's reaction was to say, "I can't believe it, Mr. Secretary," to which Pace had replied, "I can't either, so I'll repeat it." Then Pace went ahead and repeated it.

Late on April 10, a Tuesday night, Joseph R. Short, a conscientious, and occasionally testy, *Baltimore Sun* correspondent, who'd succeeded Charlie Ross as press secretary, asked the White House switchboard to inform the press corps of a briefing at the unusual hour of 1 a.m. The late hour would allow MacArthur to learn his fate (it would be 3 p.m. in Tokyo) while guaranteeing that the news would make it into most morning newspapers. In a statement handed to reporters, Truman said he was relieving MacArthur with "deep regret" because he was "unable to give his wholehearted support" to the government's policies." It added that "military commanders must be governed by the policies and directives issued to them in the manner provided by our laws and the Constitution."

Deputy press secretary Roger Tubby (he'd just come over from the State Department) remained at his post until the last reporter left, at about 3 a.m., after which he fell asleep on a couch. Three hours later, Tubby was up and about, stopping at a small exercise area in the West Wing where, as he remembered it, "I went into the gym to try to clear the cobwebs out of my brain, and as I was punching a heavy bag I heard a familiar chuckle behind me, and Mr. Truman said, 'Belt him a couple for me, Roger.'" In a diary entry dated April 10—although it must have been the 11th—Truman wrote, "Quite an explosion. Was expected but I had to act. Telegrams and letters of abuse by the dozens."

The initial reaction was indeed explosive, and at first overwhelmingly pro-MacArthur. Early polls suggested that the country was not only on MacArthur's side, but that Truman's approval rating had pretty much collapsed, at one point falling, briefly, to 16 percent. *Time* magazine called MacArthur "the personification of the big man" while Truman was "almost a professional little man," albeit a courageous little man. The magazine's cover was a painting of Truman with the words, "We do not want to widen the conflict." Senator McCarthy suggested that Truman was drunk when he fired MacArthur—that it was "a Communist victory won with the aid of bourbon and Benedictine," and that "the son of a bitch should be impeached." At a restaurant near the White House, Roger Tubby heard someone say "It's too bad those Puerto Ricans didn't get him!"

Yet Truman's defenders were also being heard, and their view, in time, would become history's view. On the day of the dismissal, NBC's Morgan Beatty, in a radio broadcast, said MacArthur was fired "for one reason only, namely, he made the mistake of opposing the nation's foreign policy publicly, persistently. That is not the function of a soldier." The *Herald Tribune*, a voice of moderate Republicanism, said that "he virtually forced his own removal," which touched on a suspicion, already widely held: that MacArthur, unable to resign his post in the middle of an unwinnable war, was eager to be relieved of duty.

Truman, in a radio speech, carefully addressed the dismissal, and the war: "I believe that we must try to limit the war to Korea," he said, "to make sure that the precious lives of our fighting men are not wasted; to see that the security of our country and the free world is not needlessly jeopardized; and to prevent a third world war. A number of events have made it evident that General MacArthur did not agree with that policy." During a staff meeting, he remarked that "MacArthur's going to be regarded as a worse double-crosser than [the Civil War general George] McClellan," but in his radio speech he called MacArthur "one of our greatest military commanders."

He had every reason to sound temperate. Although MacArthur had resisted the idea of a "limited war," his military superiors hadn't done much to give him clear, consistent directions. Nor had Truman ever been able to explain why, as he kept insisting, this limited war, no matter how real the dominoes, was a matter of supreme importance to the survival of Western civilization. MacArthur had badly misjudged China's strength, and objectives, but no one else of high rank, it seemed, had paid concerned attention to the warnings from China, which had been fairly unambiguous. Walter Lippmann, Truman's persistent tormenter, was quick to seize on this sensitive point: that Truman had relied on MacArthur's judgment "in a matter which belongs squarely within the responsibility of the Department of State." But Secretary of State Acheson had absented himself from responsibility for a war that he'd confidently advocated. Admiral Leahy, watching from the sidelines, thought, "It seems that at the present time the prospects for United Nations success in Korea are hopeless."

3. Jean MacArthur got the news from a radio report while the MacArthurs were entertaining lunch guests. MacArthur's faithful adjutant, Courtney Whitney, recalled that the general had been laughing at someone's remark when she walked into the room, stood behind him, and touched his shoulder. After she whispered to her husband, "MacArthur's face froze. Not a flicker of emotion crossed it. Then he looked up at his wife, who still stood with her hand on his shoulder. In a gentle voice, audible to all present, he said: 'Jeannie, we're going home at last.'" To reporters, Whitney said: "He never turned a hair. . . . I think this has been his finest hour." Whitney was prone to fawning, but General Ridgway, who was not, remembered that when he visited Tokyo the next day, MacArthur "was entirely himself—composed, quiet, temperate, friendly, and helpful to the man who was to succeed him. He made some allusions the fact that he had been summarily relieved, but there was no trace of bitterness or anger in his tone."

Sangfroid or not, the inner MacArthur was deeply upset, not only by being sacked but by the manner of the sacking. In *Reminiscences*, written years later, he complained that "no office boy, no charwoman, no servant of any sort would have been dismissed with such callous disregard for the ordinary decencies." He wanted to burnish his good name and, perhaps, avenge himself on Truman, and the Pentagon, a wish that was granted when congressional Republicans invited him to Washington, to give his side of this unfinished story, in a most public forum. Four days later, MacArthur, his wife, and Arthur MacArthur IV, his thirteen-year-old son, were aboard the *Bataan*, for the general's first visit to the United States in fourteen years.

When they landed at Washington's National Airport, a little after midnight, on April 19, several thousand people were waiting. One of the first to greet MacArthur was Defense Secretary Marshall, to whom MacArthur said, "Hello, George. How are you?" Other ranking military men were on hand—among them the Joint Chiefs. To Truman's friend, General Harry Vaughan, MacArthur said, "Glad to see you, Harry," and Vaughan replied, "Glad to see you, sir." As Vaughan made his way through the crowd, he was heard saying, "Well, that was simple." Neither Truman nor MacArthur said anything about getting together, although that would have given them a chance to discuss the ten-month-old war in which they, and the nation, were so deeply invested. Joseph Short told reporters that Truman would see the general if MacArthur asked for an appointment, and Truman acknowledged that Short wouldn't have said that without "the permission of the President." Truman and MacArthur, though, never came close to arranging even a brief consultation. The MacArthur aide, Colonel Laurence Bunker, later said that, during Truman's post-presidency, there was some discussion of a rapprochement, but Bunker seems to have relied on hearsay and the gossip of veterans. It was not something Truman sought.

It rained the next morning, but the showers were gone by noon, and it turned into a warm April day. A little past noon, twelve hours after he'd touched down, MacArthur spoke to a joint session of Congress, delivering a speech with the skill of a practiced performer. His voice at times seemed to break with emotion as he insisted, falsely, that the Chiefs had agreed with his war strategy, and as he mourned what he described as a betrayal of Korea: "The magnificence of the courage and fortitude of the Korean people defies description," he said. "Their last words to me were: 'Don't scuttle the Pacific!'" His son sat in front of the rostrum, his hands folded in his lap, occasionally twisting a finger, applauding gently when the legislators clapped and cheered. The *Herald Tribune* reported that "people were weeping openly," and that, when MacArthur was done, "a hurricane of emotion swept the chamber." The hurricane arrived with the oratorical finale, when MacArthur said, "And like the old soldier of that ballad, I now close my military career and just fade away, an old soldier who tried to do his duty as God gave him the light to see that duty. Good bye." David Lilienthal, watching on television, thought "the last ten minutes . . . was one of the two or three greatest pieces of forensics I have ever heard and seen." Admiral Leahy, who was at his son's house in Chevy Chase, judged the speech to be of "such a superlative quality of excellence" that it rivaled Churchill. Dewey Short, a right-leaning Republican congressman from Missouri, was so caught up that he said, "We saw a great hunk of God in the flesh, and we heard the voice of God." MacArthur afterward was driven through the city, where more than a half million spectators treated the day like a holiday—the "greatest crowd in Washington's history," the *Washington Post* reported.

Decades later, someone watching MacArthur before Congress, on a digital site, is likely to see something else: a seventy-one-year-old man with an undisguised comb-over, declaiming with studied theatricality. Truman may already have sensed that future; thanks to television, the daily news cycle was speeding up. Three hours after the speech, Admiral Leahy paid a call at the White House and found his former boss untroubled by the enthusiasm for MacArthur. By early May, Truman was acting as if the MacArthur episode was over. In a press conference, one could hear a return to his cheery self, the attitude of "Well, boys, what do you want now?"

> *Q:* Mr. President, General MacArthur has expressed an opinion on the question of whether or not Russia might intervene?
> *The President:* He is entitled to that opinion—he is entitled to any opinion he chooses.
> . . .
> *Q:* —were you surprised, from your knowledge of CIA and the other reports that came to you, when the Chinese Communists did come in, sir?
> *The President:* I think everybody was not exactly surprised; they were sorry to see it happen.

Q: Well, General MacArthur seems to have been surprised.
The President: He was very much surprised. [*laughter*]

〜

After two months of Senate hearings, conducted by two committees—Armed Services and Foreign Relations—the MacArthur controversy faded away. A procession of witnesses, from early May to late June, included MacArthur (who led off); the Joint Chiefs; Acheson, Marshall, and Marshall's predecessor, Louis Johnson, who used the occasion to note, not unfairly, that Acheson, at the June 1950 Blair House meeting, had made the motion to intervene in Korea, and that MacArthur had not been consulted. General Bradley, the Joint Chiefs chairman, used his testimony to warn against taking the war into China. "Red China is not the powerful nation seeking to dominate the world," he said. "Frankly, in the opinion of the Joint Chiefs of Staff, this strategy would involve us in the wrong war, at the wrong place, at the wrong time, and with the wrong enemy"—a most quotable assertion that's sometimes mistakenly applied to the war in Korea. Most Americans had stopped paying attention by the time the Armed Services Committee, on June 18, voted to wrap it up, without a formal report. Explaining that omission after so much time, and so many words (more than two million), Richard Russell, the chairman, said, "I think that the people have about made their own report in this case, and any effort on our part now to issue a report would be an anticlimax to the hearings."

The MacArthur story—what Truman might call a Washington "hullabaloo"—was not entirely over. On June 14, the reliably reckless Senator McCarthy had held forth on the Senate floor, where, for about two and a half hours, he showed off a conspiratorial imagination that was rarely captured in news accounts. He saw the dismissal of MacArthur "in the dead, vast, and middle of the night" as an alarming symptom of national decline. The United States, he said, had fallen from a "position as the most powerful Nation on earth" to one of "declared weakness by our leadership," a "planned, steady retreat from victory"—one that could only be explained by uncovering "a conspiracy so immense and an infamy so black as to dwarf any such venture in the history of man." His ripe, implausible target—the man to whom all paths of postwar betrayal led—was the "enigmatic, powerful" George Catlett Marshall.

Truman replied to this vilification in a speech delivered two weeks later, on the anniversary of the invasion of South Korea. Without uttering the name "McCarthy," he took aim at persons who were out to "destroy the trust and confidence of the people in their Government . . . by spreading fear and slander and outright lies." As he'd said before, "That political smear campaign is . . . playing right into the hands of the Russians."

MacArthur, meanwhile, had gone west, on a speaking tour, accompanied by his wife and son. Crowds were small, and after his first stops, in Texas, a former Democratic congressman, Maury Maverick, sent personal dispatches for Truman to savor. In mid-June, Maverick wired that five hundred thousand spectators had been expected to line the streets in San Antonio, but there were "altogether not over eight thousand, about fifteen thousand at speech," and that "when he started talking, people rubber-necked, and started leaving." A Dallas lawyer reported similar responses in Austin and Houston. Truman, in his diary, couldn't suppress his schadenfreude: "His Texas trip was a dud."

TWENTY-FOUR

"The Mess in Washington"

Every man who comes into the presence of a President seems to think that this is the one opportunity he may have to gain some petty advantage over some rival or to advance himself a point or two.

—Archie Butt, President Theodore Roosevelt's military aide

1. In early February 1951, at a bombing and gunnery range in Nevada, a nuclear explosion shook dishes and shattered a plate-glass window fifty miles away, in Las Vegas, a neon-lit desert city of twenty-five thousand—the first test inside the United States since Trinity, in July 1945. The final blast in the series was televised by two Los Angeles stations, which set up cameras on Mount Wilson and pointed them in the direction of Las Vegas, two hundred and fifty miles away. At about five-forty-five in the morning, according to one excited, exaggerated account, "the mountains disappeared as if by magic." The explosions left traces of radioactivity in snow that fell on Chicago, Cincinnati, Western New York, and Ottawa. The bright whiteness of the shimmering Southwest desert became a perfect backdrop to the disquiet of the times—the mise-en-scène of monster noirs in which the bomb, and its imagined side-effects, were central to the plot. "You know, every time one of those things goes off, I feel we're helping to write the first chapter of a new Genesis," someone remarks in *The Beast from 20,000 Fathoms*.

President Truman's choppy, Missouri-nasal speech, stiff facial expressions, and thick glasses were not designed for reassurance. When he addressed the subject in an unscripted talk, in San Francisco, in September, he said, "It is terrible to think of what would happen if we should have another world war. No one can imagine the destruction, the loss of life." As if relishing each unnerving syllable, he continued, "It is fantastic what can happen with the use of the new weapons that are now under construction; not only the ones we all fear the most, but there are some weapons that are fantastic in their operation. I hope we never have to use them." In case anyone missed his point, he added that these new weapons "mean that an all-out war would wipe out civilization."

A month later, Gordon Dean, a friend of Senator McMahon, who had replaced David Lilienthal as the chairman of the Atomic Energy Commission, spoke at the University of Southern California, and used his platform to welcome the advent of tactical nuclear weapons, which, when they were someday perfected, could be used to end "these endless nibbling aggressions." Dean's speech was delivered at about the time that Russia tested a second atomic bomb, and, not surprisingly, was interpreted as willingness to use such weapons in Korea. In his diary, he'd written, "We cannot forever have a stalemate in Korea"; what was needed were ways of "so effectively dealing with the Chinese troops that they can be virtually destroyed . . . by an intelligently planned atomic attack." Dean liked the word "tactical"—it was, he thought, the best term yet, and definitely superior to "junior 'small bang weapons,'" or "Nevada bombs," though he also thought a better name was needed. Truman apparently thought that these weapons were ready for use on the battlefield, and Dean knew that he needed to inform the President that "atomic artillery fired projectiles" were still on the drawing board.

2. A rare, and welcome, moment of respite came on a Sunday in early July 1951, when Truman visited Harewood, the Acheson farm in nearby Maryland, a forty-five-minute drive from Blair House. Because of the war, Truman felt tied to his office, but "that place is mighty lonely on a weekend," he told Dean and Alice Acheson. "You nice people have saved my life." Others at Harewood that day were the Achesons' son, David, a lawyer, in his late twenties; his wife, Patricia; Joint Chiefs Chairman Omar Bradley and his wife, Mary. Bess Truman was listed among the guests, but David Acheson is certain she wasn't there; at that time of year, she was likely to be in Missouri. Margaret Truman recalled that "Bess spent the summer of 1951 in Independence fretting over her mother"—Madge Gates Wallace, who was eighty-nine and in delicate health.

Truman, on that July 8, wore a tropical print sport shirt and his Key West costume: sand-colored, pleated linen slacks, polished white-and-brown wingtip shoes, and a white linen golf cap. "This was all classic Gold Coast resort dress—one missed only the palm trees and Rudy Vallee in the background," David Acheson recalled. The secretary of state asked the President if he'd like to go for a swim, and when Truman said yes, other volunteers set off, across a field, to a pool at the edge of the woods. "The President's bathing suit revealed a stocky, strong figure, clearly durable and vigorous," David Acheson remembered; he "put down his towel and glasses and plunged in." But Truman was "not quite prepared for the ice water. It was really cold, like Maine. When he came out, he let out a sort of a whoop. He said 'I can think of a number of journalists I'd like to throw in.'" After a few minutes, conversation turned to the subject of wartime leadership: what Lincoln had faced, and the pressure on Generals Grant and Sherman to turn the war around before the 1864 election.

The President needed these hours of relief; ruminations on Civil War history was no escape from the bewilderment of Korea. The morale and fighting ability of the men under General Ridgway's command had improved—Ridgway promised, "We're going the other way"—but the conflict, as David Halberstam was to put it, had become "trench warfare . . . with almost all meaning subtracted from the fighting and dying." Armistice talks had begun, in Kaesong, a castle city just south of the 38th Parallel, but there was little progress—a source of great frustration to Truman, who was prepared to increase the bombing south of the Yalu in order to force a settlement. In the privacy of his diary, Truman could let loose with an occasional "spasm." One such entry demanded that Russia "stop supplying war material to the thugs who are attacking the free world," with the alternative being "all out war," which "means that Moscow, St. Petersburg . . . Peking, Shanghai . . . and every manufacturing plant in China and the Soviet Union will be eliminated. This is the final chance for the Soviet Government to decide whether it desires to survive or not." Outwardly, where it mattered, Truman was steady and unflinching; even his critics could admire this sturdy, gray, sixty-something Midwesterner, who'd carried on with firmness, even gallantry, after Roosevelt's sudden death.

But he could still seem directionless, led by events. When it came to the misbehavior, and corruptions, of friends and acquaintances, which were becoming an issue in the late stages of his presidency, he could seem indifferent, defiantly so. To modern eyes, used to complicated corruptions, alleged and otherwise, sometimes of mammoth proportions, the "Truman scandals" appear petty, and not even particularly scandalous. The stakes were relatively small, the names mostly unknown, and the motives pathetically venal. But taken together they suggested a web of petty impropriety; and because each alleged instance of wrongdoing was tied, in some way, to the President, they summoned memories of the Pendergast era in Missouri, and the Democratic machine that had given immeasurable help to Truman's early political career.

Truman would say that an attack on the men around him was a roundabout way of attacking him, which was not always the case. Friends were friends, was his view, and you stood by friends, even if you had to lower your standards. Truman's roster of friends was still led by Harry Hawkins Vaughan, whose rank was now Major General Vaughan—the jester-companion-military aide who made regular, and unwelcome, appearances in Drew Pearson's aspersive column.

Since the late 1940s, Vaughan's name had been associated with several embarrassments, such as a Senate subcommittee's investigation of "five percenters," a term that referred to a 5 percent "commission"—basically a bribe—paid to people who could influence the allocation of government contracts. Even if Vaughan himself never, technically, accepted a bribe, he knew his way around that part of Washington, and didn't object to receiving favors, such as free passage on a United Fruit Line cargo vessel, for a family vacation in Guatemala. At the very least, Vaughan suffered from obtuseness, as if unaware of what was obvious to others: that his friendship with Truman made him a prime attraction. One White House aide thought that he "welcomed everyone, like a friendly puppy," which let lobbyists and favor-seekers take advantage. But Vaughan's puppy-ness and bonhomie concealed his occasional interference in administration business, such as his undermining of Jim Forrestal while promoting Louis Johnson, and even making forays into such patronage matters as filling a judgeship in Wisconsin.

Among Vaughan's putative friends was a Chicago perfume manufacturer, who discomfited a number of people in Truman's circle by sending freezers, a luxury item after the war, to the Truman house in Independence; to the Little White House in Key West; to John W. Snyder, the treasury secretary; to Chief Justice Vinson; and to several aides. Vaughan said, untruthfully, that the freezers were "factory rejects," although it's true that they were shoddily made. Bess Truman declared that hers was "a lemon" before she had it delivered to the town dump. In the summer of 1949, Vaughan had told a Senate subcommittee that he'd never done favors in the expectation of a reward, but he never denied doing the favors. What made all this harder was that so many of these investigations were being conducted by Democrats.

One such inquiry had begun in early 1950, when the Arkansas Senator J. William Fulbright, a member of the Banking and Currency Committee, announced a "full review" of the lending practices of the Reconstruction Finance Corporation. The RFC got its start under President Herbert Hoover, in the early days of the Depression, and was supposed to lend money to revive faltering businesses. In the postwar era, though, its mission changed. One RFC loan, for forty-four million dollars, went to the Kaiser-Frazer Corporation, a car company founded in 1947 by the auto executive Joseph W. Frazer and the industrialist Henry J. Kaiser, who'd been on a long list of Roosevelt's potential 1944 running mates. The company had said it wanted to produce a low-priced car to accompany their innovative, though unsuccessful, upmarket line, the Kaiser and Frazer. Fulbright saw it as "just a loan to a big company that needs money." It was the sort of transaction that prompted the journalist Blair Bolles, in an essay for *Harper's* magazine, to argue that Washington had supplanted Wall Street as a source of capital, and that "anybody who selfishly wanted a loan that would not benefit the nation one whit could get it from the R.F.C. if he found the right lawyer or had the support of the right politicians."

In February 1951, Fulbright's subcommittee had released an interim report, titled "Favoritism and Influence," which concluded that the RFC's problem was not bad loans but an abuse of power, and blamed Truman for ignoring the issue. Particular interest was shown in the profitable rise of a former Missourian, E. Merl Young, who began his Washington career as a government messenger, earning about a thousand dollars a year. By 1948, according to the Fulbright subcommittee, he was working for the RFC and had a hard-to-explain annual income of about sixty thousand dollars. He'd also received extravagant gifts, among them a mink coat worth $9,540—paid for by a lawyer who represented the recipient of an RFC loan. The mink coat ended up with Young's wife, Lauretta, a White House stenographer. Eventually, "five percenters," "deep freezes," and "mink coats" became shorthand for alleged squalid corruption in the Truman administration.

Fulbright understood the power of those words and headlines. "What seems to be new about these scandals," he said, "is the moral blindness or callousness which allows those in responsible positions to accept the practices which the facts reveal." Truman did not take this well. He would not have forgotten Fulbright's half-baked suggestion, made just after the disastrous 1946 midterms, that Truman should do the decent thing: appoint a Republican as secretary of state (the office-holder then next in the line of presidential succession) and resign. "You know," Truman told reporters, after Fulbright's report was released, "I spent ten years in the Senate, and I wrote a lot of reports—but I am happy to say I never wrote one like . . . this asinine report."

It could be difficult to keep track of who was being accused of what. Truman remained inclined to dismiss the subject, especially if the accused was someone with whom he was friendly—someone like William M. Boyle Jr., the Democratic National Committee chairman, who reportedly got an eight-thousand-dollar fee for helping a St. Louis printing firm get a half-million-dollar RFC loan. Boyle had been in the Missouri artillery reserve when Truman, Vaughan, and John Snyder were officers. Trying to act as if he took this seriously, Truman met with Boyle to talk it over; afterward, he said that he'd personally "examined the facts" and was sure that Boyle had done nothing wrong—an unsatisfying conclusion, even for some of the President's supporters. On August 15, 1951, at the dedication of a new American Legion headquarters in Washington, Truman used the word "scandalmongers," and, without naming names, said they "are filling the air with the most irresponsible kinds of accusations . . . trying to get us to believe that our government is riddled with communism and corruption—when the fact is that we have the finest and most loyal body of civil servants in the world."

The most potent scandal, which went beyond mere bribery, involved the enrichment of tax collectors in the Bureau of Internal Revenue, the precursor to the Internal Revenue Service. Regional collectors had never been paid well, but as tax rates climbed, they had new opportunities to supplement their income in return for "adjusting" tax bills. A case could be made—and was, by a tenacious New Republic editor-reporter named Helen Fuller—that much that went wrong could be connected to Robert Hannegan, the former Democratic Party chairman and postmaster general who, in 1940, had helped rescue Truman's senatorial career. In 1943, Hannegan had been rewarded with an appointment as U.S. revenue commissioner, with the power to hand out patronage jobs; Fuller reported that the eight most problematic collectors—each accused of bribery and misconduct—had been hired while Hannegan was in charge.

In November 1951, Truman addressed the internal revenue scandal by firing the assistant attorney general in charge of the tax division: Theron Lamar Caudle, a North Carolinian with a syrupy, mumbled drawl, who bore a striking resemblance to the actor

Raymond Burr. With Caudle gone, the "obvious next step," in the words of a Republican congressman, was to get rid of J. Howard McGrath, the attorney general. But while Truman had no particular fondness for Caudle, he liked McGrath, a former Rhode Island senator. In fact, at the 1944 Chicago convention, McGrath, who was then governor of Rhode Island, had seconded Senator Truman's vice-presidential nomination. "Son, I'll never forget you," Truman had said when McGrath walked by the Missouri delegation.

Truman finally promised "drastic action," perhaps because a Gallup survey reported that, in the 1952 election year, corruption, along with Korea, would be a winning issue for Republicans, who'd begun referring to "the mess in Washington." In February 1952, Truman finally acted—by approving the appointment of a fifty-year-old New Yorker named Newbold Morris to investigate allegations of federal corruption. Morris was the son-in-law of Judge Learned Hand, a self-described "Abraham Lincoln Republican," a former president of the New York City Council, twice an unsuccessful reform candidate for mayor, and a partner in the Wall Street law firm Lovejoy, Morris, Wasson & Huppuch—in other words, a man utterly unsuited for his new role in the equally insular, but much different, world of Harry Truman's Washington. "This is my job and I'm going to put my heart and soul into it," Morris said, when he accepted the assignment, after telling McGrath, under whom he would serve with the title of Special Assistant, "I might break some crockery down here." On his last night in Manhattan, Morris and his wife attended the opera with Mrs. August Belmont, the English-born actress-philanthropist, and the founder of the Metropolitan Opera Guild. Morris remembered that night: "As the final curtain came down on *Carmen*, I felt a sudden twinge."

That premonitory twinge might have been imaginary, but it became clear soon enough that Morris would approach his assignment with a Javert-like thoroughness, and that it was bound to end, as he was to write, without irony, with "two bodies . . . left lying on the stage as in the finale of a Shakespearean drama." When he went to see Truman, during which he told the President how much he'd enjoyed meeting Margaret at a New York lunch, he asked for an executive order directing the heads of all departments, bureaus, and agencies "to comply with my requests for personnel or papers, documents and records"; and he wanted Truman to use the phrase "prompt compliance" to show that "he and I meant business." Truman agreed to that, and pretty much gave Morris whatever he asked for. It did not seem to faze Truman when Morris said, "Mr. President, it's obviously impossible for me to investigate two and a half million government employees," but "it is feasible to look into the performance of about ten thousand employees at the top."

With striking synchronism, Morris had come to town just as the evangelist Billy Graham was in the midst of a successful crusade, at the National Guard Armory, a nightly event with overflow crowds that sometimes included members of Congress. Graham was at his oratorical prime, and, on at least one evening, warned his audience that "some of the things that are going on in this city are filthy rags and a stench in the nostrils of the Lord."

There is no evidence that Morris was moved by Graham's sermons, but by mid-March, he increased the investigative pressure, announcing that he'd prepared a special financial questionnaire for upper-level federal administrative employees, a Q&A that would be "very searching." That was one way of putting it. Before they were done, Morris and his staff had "hammered out" eleven drafts of an inquisitive fifteen-page questionnaire which asked employees not only for their professional and financial history, but to list their ownership of real estate, jewelry, furs, and other valuables; bank and brokerage accounts; unpaid debts; and gambling winnings and losses. Morris subsequently announced the appointment of *another* New York lawyer to run another staff—twenty more lawyers to analyze the data in all those questionnaires. The Attorney General was not pleased. Although he'd welcomed Morris with a six-course lunch at the 1925 F Street Club and suggested that they go on a Howard-and-Newbold basis, their working relationship had not blossomed.

McGrath was out of town when Morris, "with the help of two porters," carried six hundred copies of the questionnaires into the Justice Department. After McGrath returned, he went out of his way to avoid Morris, who telephoned—repeatedly—to ask why his questionnaire hadn't been distributed to the Justice Department staff. Nor did Morris stop there: His chief counsel informed McGrath that Morris was prepared to begin "a routine examination of the Department," which meant access to correspondence, diaries, appointment books, and phone records. McGrath would not consent to any of this. Morris didn't know, though he might have guessed, that McGrath had threatened to resign if he was forced to distribute the questionnaire to colleagues, or that he'd complained directly to the President. But, as the White House counsel Charles Murphy pointed out, in a memorandum to Truman, refusing to comply was tantamount to refusing to obey a president's executive order.

On the first of April, 1952, reporters witnessed what looked like an argument between Truman and McGrath at the Military Air Transport Terminal, where they, and other cabinet officers, were waiting to greet Queen Juliana of the Netherlands and her husband, Prince Bernhard, who were arriving for a state dinner. McGrath was observed gesticulating, Truman was looking "tight-lipped," and Joe Short, the press secretary, was pounding a palm with a fist before the President stepped away. When Truman was asked about this fascinating bit of pantomime, he said, "That is a private conversation, and it will not be quoted by me."

Two days later—two months into Morris's tenure—the dispute ended abruptly: McGrath fired Morris, in a short, clean-out-your-desk-today letter. Later that day, Truman telephoned McGrath and fired *him*, on equally short notice: He informed McGrath that he intended to announce the resignation twenty minutes hence—at his 4 p.m. news conference. When Truman met with reporters and was asked about these changed circumstances, his responses were painful:

Q: Mr. President, did Mr. McGrath fire Morris with your knowledge and approval?
The President: I saw it in the paper.
Q: I take it, Mr. President, that you didn't know about it before Mr.—
The President: It was under discussion, but I wasn't consulted when it was done.

Q: Mr. President, were you consulted before it was done, sir?

The President: They talked to me about it—I was talked to about it, but I made no suggestion or—

Q: Mr. President, would you clarify for me how you heard of Mr. Morris' being discharged?

The President: Saw it in the paper.

Q: The first you had heard?

The President: Yes—on the ticker—that's where I saw it.

Q: Mr. President, had it been decided that Mr. McGrath would resign before he fired Mr. Morris?

The President: I don't want to answer that question.

Q: Were the two events connected?

The President: I don't want to answer that question.

Q: Did you make the call [to McGrath], or did he, Mr. President?

The President: I can't answer that question.

One columnist, after calling this a "fiasco," said the "real issue is not the grafters. It is that so many of them were there so long with no one in the Administration . . . even seeming to be aware of them until hostile Congressional committees . . . began to rip things open." Nor did Truman ever seem to have his heart in taking the "drastic action" he'd promised just before hiring Newbold Morris— an "impeccable celebrity" in the words of the *Herald Tribune*. Morris seemed hurt that he didn't hear from Truman after McGrath dismissed him. "I decided that if Harry Truman really wanted to get in touch with me his secretaries would have no trouble finding me." With wounded feelings, he was soon on the train to Penn Station, and out of Truman's life for good.

Two weeks after Truman fired his attorney general, he wrote to McGrath to say, almost apologetically, that the announcement of his dismissal "made my day longer instead of shorter," and that "the happenings in the Newbold Morris case were very disturbing to me. I want you to know that my fondness for you has not changed one bit. Political situations sometimes cause one much pain." Loyalty to his troops still mattered to Harry Truman, who added that, in the future, if McGrath was interested in any other job, he would "do anything I can for you. I'll go all out." He signed the note "I am most sincerely, your friend." The Missourian in the White House could never have sent such a note to Newbold Morris.

2. Truman could be forgiven for his inattention and evasions. All this had been happening, after all, in a time when he was getting ready to announce that he wasn't going to run for another term. Many had suspected this was coming; reporters couldn't let the subject alone. In January, he'd confided his intentions to the men who'd accompanied him to Key West, and although he'd asked them to keep it to themselves, his tight little group wasn't leak-proof. He may have decided well before January. In an April 16, 1950, journal entry (one, though, likely meant for posterity), he'd written, "In my opinion eight years as President is enough and sometimes too much for any man to serve in that capacity." To that he'd appended an unrealistic appraisal of his own prospects: "I know I could be elected again and continue to break the old precedent as it was broken by F.D.R. It should not be done."

He'd also sounded amused by the political emergence of General Eisenhower, who'd gone on leave from Columbia and returned to active duty in April 1951—appointed by Truman as the first NATO commander. After Eisenhower came out as a Republican in January, Truman said, "He will stay on"—in Paris—"as long as I can keep him there, because I want him to stay. I like him. And he is doing a good job." He compared Eisenhower's presidential chances to those of General Winfield Scott, who'd run in 1852 and was defeated by Franklin Pierce, a Democrat.

Truman, though, had every reason to feel confused by Eisenhower's objectives. In mid-December, he'd written a "Dear Ike" letter, saying, "I wish you would let me know what you intend to do. It will be between us and no one else. I have the utmost confidence in your judgment and your patriotism." In a reply that demonstrated the general's talent for obfuscation, Eisenhower said he was "deeply touched" by Truman's confidence, and added a striking sentence: "It breathes your anxious concern for our country's future." His wish was "to live a semi-retired life" with his family, with a little writing and "dirt farming" on the side. "Now, I do not feel that I have any duty to seek a political nomination," he continued. "Because of this belief, I shall not do so. . . . The possibility that I will ever be drawn into political activity is so remote as to be negligible." Yet there was more to say: "This policy of complete abstention will be meticulously observed by me, unless and until extraordinary circumstances would place a mandate upon me that . . . would be deemed a duty of transcendent importance." He wrote this while his supporters were rushing to get him on the ballot in time for the March 11 New Hampshire primary, the nation's first.

Then there was the rise of Estes Kefauver, a forty-eight-year-old Tennessee senator, who, on January 23, was rude enough to announce that he'd oppose the President in New Hampshire, whether or not Truman was running. Kefauver, who liked to show off his Tennessee roots by wearing a Davy Crockett–style coonskin cap, was a big name, thanks to the work of his Senate Crime Committee, a televised tutorial on how narcotics, prostitution, and gambling had turned crime into a big business. The committee's hearings, which the *New York Times* TV critic called "nothing less than a Hollywood thriller truly brought to life," were a perfect match for a medium learning how to feast on spectacle. When Kefauver said his administration would give close attention "to the battle against corruption," few could miss the point.

Truman couldn't stand Kefauver—"Senator Cow Fever," he called him—and found him harder to take after he'd gone on to win the New Hampshire primary, by more than three thousand votes out of thirty-three thousand cast. In his first post–New Hampshire meeting with reporters, in Key West, Truman was asked if he foresaw an open nominating convention in July, and replied, "If I am interested in it, it will not be an open convention." It was as if he couldn't quite acknowledge that, in the first voting of 1952, Democratic voters had rejected a sitting president, in favor of an upstart senator.

After his second-place finish in New Hampshire, Truman, as a matter of pride, undoubtedly had fleeting doubts about his decision to step down, but not enough doubt to overcome Bess's opposition:

She didn't think *she* could survive another four years, she told him, and didn't think he could either. Truman made it official, and formal, on March 29, in front of an audience of about five thousand, at a Jefferson-Jackson Dinner, in Washington's National Guard Armory. He'd left that part out of the advance text, and his speech that night was so stale that, at one point, Libby Donahue, the White House correspondent for the left-wing newspaper *PM*, turned to Arthur Schlesinger Jr., who was at her table, and whispered, "This is the most utterly meaningless speech I have ever heard." That's about when Truman said, "I have served my country long and, I think, efficiently and honestly. I shall not accept a renomination. I do not feel that it is my duty to spend another four years in the White House." He added what he might not have said before a less partisan audience: "I stand for honest government. I have worked for it. I have probably done more for it than any other President." That was not a faithful rendition of reality, but it was Truman's reality.

The only one who looked not at all surprised was Bess, who smiled brightly. There were shouts of "No, no!" around the room, but not necessarily shouts of despair. Sitting close to the head table was Adlai Ewing Stevenson II, who, in 1948, had been elected governor of Illinois, and was overheard saying, "They applauded with really macabre enthusiasm." Stevenson had been aware of Truman's intentions since January, when Truman had begun a clandestine campaign to persuade *him* to commit to a candidacy, although the Illinois governor, a strange species of politician, had never shown any particular interest in being president.

TWENTY-FIVE

Dubious Battles

Margart Truman (to her father)*:* You know a lot of people have
said to me, "Your father sure loves a fight." True or false?
Harry Truman: Well, I never promoted a fight, but I never
ran from one if it was necessary to meet things head on.

—Interviewing her parents, in 1955,
on CBS's *Person to Person*

1. Like his father, John Truman, the President was sometimes a little too eager for a fight, and when six hundred thousand
steelworkers went on strike, on April 9, 1952, he was more than
ready for another bloodless battle. The walkout, which had been
threatened since the end of 1951, added to a landscape of labor
disarray: Some thirty thousand Western Union employees had also
struck, though not for long, and telephone workers threatened to do
the same. On the eve of the steel strike, Truman spoke to the nation
and said, "Our country faces a grave danger"—that "a prolonged
shutdown would . . . throw our domestic economy into chaos" and
could affect the supply of arms for the troops in Korea. He asked
both sides to settle, "in the national interest," knowing that so far
there'd been no willingness to compromise over the basic issues of
wages and prices. He surrendered the role of honest broker when
he said the owners were "raising all this hullabaloo in an attempt to
force the government to give them a big boost in prices."

Truman didn't doubt his authority to seize an industry that he
considered vital to the nation's security. That had been his reasoning
in 1946, when he'd been about to draft striking rail workers into

the armed forces—a presumed power that, because of a last-minute settlement, went untested. This time, Truman didn't hesitate. After signing an executive order, he told Charles Sawyer, his commerce secretary, to "take possession of and operate" the facilities of eighty-six closed steel companies—"the dirtiest job he had ever given anyone," Sawyer recalled him saying.

Senator Robert Taft, who still hoped to win his party's presidential nomination, said the government's action gave the House a "valid case" to consider impeachment, and fourteen separate impeachment resolutions were introduced. Senate Republicans called the seizure "usurpation" and "socialization," and said Truman ought to have invoked the Taft-Hartley Act, which gives a president limited power to order an eighty-day halt to a strike that can affect the nation's "health or safety."

Three of the steel companies went to court to argue that only Congress could give a president the power to seize an industry and to ask for a temporary restraining order against the seizure. When a presiding judge sided with the administration—doubting a court's power to enjoin a president—the ruling prepared the way for what was destined to become a landmark Supreme Court case: *Youngstown Sheet & Tube Company v. Sawyer*. It was a legal test that Truman believed he would win, if not on the merits then by relying on the loyalty of his four Court appointments, starting with his friend Fred Vinson, the chief justice. He also counted on former Attorney General Tom Clark, who'd joined the court in August 1949, and two onetime Democratic senators with whom Truman had served, Harold Burton and Sherman Minton. Then he'd need only one of the five Roosevelt-era justices: Felix Frankfurter, Robert Jackson, Stanley Reed, and the liberals William Douglas and Hugo Black.

Truman's concept of executive authority—the "inherent powers" of his office—were unusually broad, even farfetched. On April 17, which happened to mark Truman's three-hundredth news conference—this one with the American Society of Newspaper Editors—he was asked if he thought his "inherent powers" would also allow him to seize newspapers and radio stations. "Under similar circumstances," he replied, "the President of the United States has to act for whatever is for the best of the country. That's the answer to your question." A week later, he denied that was what he'd meant: "There has been a lot of hooey about the seizure of the press and the radio," he said, and insisted that "the thought of seizing press and radio has never occurred to me." But he didn't take back his assertion that a President, if he chose, had the power to act, unilaterally, on "whatever is for the best of the country." The language he used was beginning to sound like his early alarms about the stakes in Korea, with repeated claims that he'd acted because "we were in the midst of as great an emergency as we have ever faced."

Such exaggerations were a risk, and particularly so for Truman, whose memory and command of the facts seemed to have become less reliable. On that April 24, he led reporters down a path of partially made-up Cold War history, a rambling, disconnected monologue that began with a non-sequitur and went on to blend his commandeering of the steel industry with postwar foreign policy: "I told my advisory committee the other day that the reason for the steel seizure was the fact that we are in one of the greatest emergencies the country has ever been in, that in 1945 I had to send an ultimatum to the head of the Soviet Union to get out of Persia," Truman said. "They got out, because we were in a position then to meet a situation of that kind."

Had reporters heard correctly? Had Truman, in 1945, *really* sent a secret ultimatum to Stalin, and had Stalin then quickly backed down? "A little later on," Truman continued, "the Government of Yugoslavia decided to take Trieste. I sent for General Eisenhower, and General Marshall, and the Navy, and ordered the Mediterranean Fleet into the Adriatic Sea, and told General Eisenhower to send three divisions to northern Italy. There was no march on Trieste." He went on to praise his administration's policies—from aiding Greece and Turkey to the Berlin airlift to Korea—and said, "We are trying to arm the NATO countries so they can stand up. We are trying to prevent the Korean army that we have there, along with our allies, from being shot in the back. And that," he concluded, "can only be done by an all-out steel production."

Then he took questions from the puzzled press corps:

Q: Mr. President, on this ultimatum on Iran, I am sure there is going to be confusion. Is this something that has been published before, or are you—

The President: No, it hasn't. It's in the record, though.

Q: Was it a message from you to Stalin?

The President: It was a message from me to Stalin to get out of Persia. Unless he did get out, we would put some more people in there. And he got out.

Q: Would there be a copy of that available?

The President: No sir, there would not be.

Q: You would not release the document?

The President: No, I can't release it.

Q: Mr. President, could you tell us of the terms of it?

The President: I can't tell you any more than I have told you.

. . .

Q: Mr. President, an ultimatum is a very specific, definite word in a political sense, and it usually causes a good deal of attention. In that particular action, does it mean there was a time limit on your communique?

The President: Yes, we had a certain day in which to get out.

. . .

Q: Do you recall, or could you say how many days there were?

The President: No, I can't. You will have to look up the details.

It was not pleasant to watch a president appearing so confused about something so serious. "How could such a jumble of misinformation get into the President's mind?" the columnist Roscoe Drummond wondered. Truman had always been solid, made of durable stuff, but in the last ten months of his presidency, he was becoming more of a punching bag, concussed by politics and headlines.

Later that day, a White House spokesman tried to clarify Truman's remarks, the gist of which was that no ultimatum had ever been sent to Stalin. Nor had notes of any sort been sent directly from Truman to Stalin. Rather, through diplomatic channels at the United Nations, the Russians had been reminded of a deadline that had been agreed upon under the Anglo-Soviet-Iranian treaty of January 29, 1942. Soviet troops had left Iran by May 4, 1946.

Truman began his next news conference, on May 1, by declaring, "I don't intend to answer any questions on the steel controversy, so you won't get a book full of no comments," only to be repeatedly asked about the steel seizure and repeatedly declining to answer. Truman's jumbled answers and no-comments, though, were mercifully forgotten as *Youngstown Sheet & Tube Company v. Sawyer* moved swiftly toward a resolution before the Supreme Court. With more than three dozen attorneys present, oral arguments were presented on May 12 and May 13. The only person to speak on behalf of the steel industry was John W. Davis, who'd been the Democratic Party's presidential nominee in 1924, and lost to the incumbent, Calvin Coolidge. Davis was seventy-nine, elegantly dressed, and judged by onlookers to have been smoothly effective.

When the court ruled, three weeks later, it was not the outcome for which Truman had hoped: By six-to-three, the justices called Truman's action unconstitutional. The majority opinion, written by Justice Black, held that a president lacks the "inherent power" to act as Truman had, although Congress, "beyond question," did have that authority. The most spirited concurrence came from Justice Jackson, who wrote that "the purpose of the Constitution was not only to grant power, but to keep it from getting out of hand." He compared the seizure of the steel mills to "the prerogative exercised by George III." Only two of Truman's four appointees—Vinson and Minton—dissented. Chief Justice Vinson, looking red-faced and angry, and shaking a pencil, read his dissent aloud, a recitation that took more than an hour.

The ruling, with its mildly insulting tone, reached Truman in the early afternoon of June 2, after which Commerce Secretary Sawyer was ordered to return the mills to the steel companies. Then, as if a stopped clock resumed ticking, the strike resumed. Truman did not take it well. He asked Congress for legislation to allow the government to retake the factories, while also asking all parties "to meet as many of our urgent military requirements as possible." The

Supreme Court scholar Maeva Marcus, in his valuable book on the case, noted that Truman also began to consider the seizure provisions of the Selective Service law.

But Truman didn't take that provocative step. It was as if the fight had gone out of him. "After seven and a half years of crises, Dad was close to burnout," his daughter remembered. Bess Truman thought that he'd had "the scariest bout of presidential exhaustion yet." They'd both seen him fall asleep in a chair, which was unusual for Truman, and postpone routine work "because he was too 'shaky.'"

2. Truman couldn't escape domestic politics after his withdrawal from the presidential race. The subject was constantly on his mind. If he'd possessed the power to name a successor, it would have been Fred Vinson. He'd urged the chief justice to run, but Vinson was wise enough (after a polite period of deliberation) to say that he preferred to remain on the court. Truman was not satisfied with any of the obvious alternatives. Through a highly subjective process of elimination, Adlai Stevenson had ended up as his first choice, though not with great enthusiasm; they barely knew one another. Averell Harriman, he thought, was "the ablest of them all" (Harriman thought so too), but Truman believed that being labeled a "Wall Street banker" and "railroad tycoon" would hurt him. Senator Richard Russell, of Georgia, was "poison to Northern Democrats and honest Liberals," and more so to African Americans. As for his friend Alben Barkley, the vice president, who would be seventy-five in late November, "He wants to be President more than he wants anything else in the world," Truman wrote in his diary, adding, a little cruelly, "He can't see he shows his age. I wish he could be 64 instead of 74 at this date! It takes him five minutes to sign his name. . . . My good friend Alben would be dead in three months if he should inherit my job!"

Then there was Brien McMahon, the Connecticut senator and chairman of the Joint Committee on Atomic Energy, who was attracted to the idea of national office. He'd won his second term, in 1950, with an impressive plurality; as the legislator who'd done so much to keep the development of atomic energy in civilian hands, he'd shown political promise. He decided to run only if Truman didn't, and Truman must have confided his plans in January, because McMahon then filed for the Illinois presidential preference primary—an obvious attempt to block Kefauver, which pleased Truman. Though it had been twenty-four years since New York's Governor Al Smith, a Catholic, had lost the presidency to Herbert Hoover, Truman also had his doubts. "Brien, good luck," he said, "but those Ku-Kluckers in Southern Illinois will cut you up" McMahon soon withdrew from the Illinois primary, but thought the country was ready to elect an Irish Catholic and, in April, told the Gannett News Service that he was still available for a draft—for president or vice president—knowing that it sounded presumptuous to say it, and that he didn't think "it is at all likely."

A Stevenson candidacy had been boosted inside the White House by an informal staff cabal, led by the White House counsel Charles Murphy—Truman called him "Murph." Some of Stevenson's appeal, for Truman, apart from not being Kefauver, was his lineage: His grandfather, the first Adlai Stevenson, had been Grover Cleveland's second-term vice president. As an eight-year-old schoolboy, in 1892, Truman had worn a white cap that advertised the Cleveland-Stevenson ticket above the visor. The modern Adlai Stevenson, a short, bald, slightly overweight fifty-two-year-old with a melodious voice and a talent to charm, had impressed Illinois voters with his attempts to clean up Illinois's perpetually compromised government. "One dishonest public official is one too many" was a typical Stevenson remark.

An invitation from Truman to drop by Blair House came in January, just when Stevenson was on the cover of *Time*, the subject of a friendly portrait titled "Sir Galahad & the Pols." The magazine's story, written by T. S. Matthews, who'd known Stevenson since they were Princeton undergraduates, concluded that "in a cold season for the Democrats, Adlai Stevenson is politically hot, and Harry Truman feels the need of a little warmth." Stevenson wasn't entirely thrilled by the attention that most politicians crave, but he didn't behave like most politicians; that was part of his appeal. The *St. Louis*

Post-Dispatch columnist Marquis Childs, who was well acquainted with Stevenson, remembered, "He kept saying to me 'Why should it be me? Why do I have to run? Why do they keep telling me I have to run?'" Childs saw him as a "curious man," and "always more the man who operated outside the frame of machine politics." He was, above all, an engaging, and damaged, man who tried to bring eloquence to a profession that thrives on banality.

The damage may be blamed, in part, on a mismatched marriage: In 1928, when Adlai was twenty-eight and practicing law in Chicago, he married the twenty-one-year-old Ellen Borden, a dark-haired Chicago heiress, socialite, and a cool beauty, described by a friend as "a gay person, like a butterfly coming out of a cocoon." Ellen followed Adlai to Washington, where he worked for the State Department, and to New York, where he advised the first American delegation to the UN—and began a friendship with Eleanor Roosevelt that would endure for the rest of his life. That was not a life for Ellen Borden. Soon after Adlai won his first gubernatorial race, in 1948, the Stevensons, who by then had three sons, divorced on grounds of "incompatibility," a word that, after twenty years, pretty well summed up the void between them.

Adlai had also been damaged, in a harrowing way, when he was twelve years old: At a party given by his sister, Elizabeth (Buffie), three years his senior, an older boy informed the guests that he'd been learning about firearms. When he offered to demonstrate his knowledge, Adlai obligingly went to the basement and fetched his father's .22. According to a witness, Adlai pointed the rifle at one of the invitees, a teenager named Ruth Merin, and pulled the trigger. The bullet struck the girl in the forehead, and she instantly fell to the floor, dead. The gun had certainly been presumed to be unloaded, and it's not clear what Adlai actually intended, but he was nonetheless the one who had pointed and fired the rifle, and killed a sixteen-year-old girl.

It was not something that Stevenson talked about, or something that most of his friends knew about. His biographer, John Bartlow Martin, wrote that it was never mentioned in the family, although

Buffie recalled it, briefly, in *My Brother Adlai*, a book published after Adlai's death. "It's a hard memory to look back on and one that only those who have shared such an experience can understand," she wrote. "It's impossible for me to evaluate or describe what the psychological, emotional reactions were after the period of shock." What had won over politicians, and Illinois voters, was Stevenson's beguiling charm and, perhaps, what Martin saw as an inner sorrow that somehow served as an invisible shield. Erwin Griswold, the dean of the Harvard Law School, went so far as to protect him from a prying world: Knowing that Stevenson had flunked out, he locked his records in an office cabinet. Stevenson got his law degree from Northwestern University.

Charles Murphy's counterpart in Truman's courtship was the diplomat and banker George Ball, a Stevenson friend and former law partner, who thought Stevenson's "greatest charm was his tolerant view of the world as essentially a comic theater." Ball knew that Truman and Stevenson were very different types—"brusque and decisive" Truman as opposed to Stevenson's "subtle rendition of Prince Hamlet"—and assigned himself the role of coach. But while Stevenson knew very well why Truman had invited him to Blair House, and acknowledged that he couldn't ignore "a command from Buckingham Palace," Ball found him "stonily resistant" to the thought of becoming a candidate for president. He asked Stevenson not to dismiss the idea right away, but on the January day that they made their way to Blair House, Stevenson had already begun to list his doubts: "I'll be damned if I want to be a caretaker for the party," he said, and told Ball that "if Eisenhower runs, nobody can beat him. And anyway, wouldn't Eisenhower make a pretty good President? There's a hell of a lot of truth in the need for a change." When Stevenson and Ball arrived at the police barricades set up near Lafayette Square, the Secret Service demanded the identity of, as Ball put it, "this small, dumpy man who arrived in my old Chevrolet."

As Truman recalled their conversation, which lasted little more than an hour, "I told him that I would not run for President again and that it was my opinion he was best fitted for the place." He talked to

Stevenson about the presidency—"how it has grown into the most powerful and the greatest office in the history of the world"—and told him that "if he would agree, he could be nominated." But then "he said No! He apparently was flabbergasted." Truman later informed reporters that they'd discussed mine-safety legislation, a special concern of the governor's. (Not long before, two hundred coal miners had been killed in an explosion at the Orient Coal Mine, in West Frankfort, Illinois.) When someone asked, "You didn't offer him higher office?" the President replied, "How could I?" It should have been a sign of trouble, of hopeless miscommunication, that Truman and Stevenson couldn't even agree on what they'd said to one another. As Charles Murphy remembered it, Truman thought Stevenson, when he left, was still open to the idea of running, while Stevenson had the impression that he'd been clear in his unwillingness. When he returned to Illinois and was asked if he'd accept the nomination, he replied, "That possibility is so remote that it would be presumptuous of me to comment."

Stevenson continued to vacillate, or to duck. The Democratic Party, he remarked to friends, had "run out of poor people and run into the Korean War." But he knew that he owed the President another conversation, and asked for a second appointment—a talk, on March 4—that went no better than the first one. He'd come "to tell me," Truman recalled, "that he had made a commitment to run for reelection in Illinois and that he did not think he could go back on that commitment honorably." Truman's impression was that Stevenson had been "overcome" by Truman's assurance that he could "get him nominated whether he wanted to be or not." Stevenson argued that only Truman could defeat any Republican. "What the hell am I to do?" Truman asked his diary. "I'll know when the time comes because I am sure God Almighty will guide me."

After Stevenson and Murphy met again, on March 14, Stevenson wrote down, with pained formality, why he was disinclined to run. He cited "misgivings about my strength, wisdom and humility." Moreover, "my children seem to me altogether too young and undeveloped to subject to the pitiless exposure of a national campaign, let alone the presidency." He added that he'd gotten the impression, on March 4, that Truman "was quite reconciled to run again himself," which suggests he may not have been listening very carefully. Murphy replied at once, saying that Truman "was very much impressed by what you had to say . . . in the sense that it confirmed and strengthened the high regard he already had for you."

On April 16, some two weeks after Truman's announced withdrawal, Stevenson, in a written statement, tried again to close the door. In language distinctly his—a mixture of strained modesty along with a presumption of withheld greatness—he said, "I can hope that friends with larger ambitions for me will not think ill of me. They have paid me the greatest compliment within their gift, and they have my utmost gratitude." Stevenson sent a copy to Truman, to whom he wrote, "This is the hardest thing I have ever had to do. . . . I know you will be disappointed with me," adding, unctuously, "That you are is my greatest distress—and also my greatest honor." Truman replied six days later, with coolness, saying, "I am sorry that you felt it necessary to make this statement, although you are your own best judge of what you should do."

Despite that, George Ball hadn't given up on his friend. He urged Bernard De Voto, who wrote a column for *Harper's*, to spend time with Stevenson, in Springfield, and De Voto instantly fell for the governor, writing, among other things, that "his radio voice has the magical quality of warmth, frankness, and personal intimacy that has been missing since President Roosevelt." In mid-May, Stevenson wrote to the newspaper publisher Alicia Patterson, a friend as well as a reputed lover, to say, "I'm being pounded to death by mail, wire, telephone & quick visit on the damn nomination. . . . I wonder if I have to issue a Gen. Sherman." Truman, for his part, had wearied of Stevenson's perpetual hesitations, so much so that, on July 3, the *St. Louis Post-Dispatch* was able to report, no doubt with good sourcing, that he had "quite definitely cooled off" on Stevenson, and had told friends that he "is too damn coy." The President's pursuit of the governor never really ended, but neither was it a romance of the heart that could "cool off." It was more a coolheaded stubbornness, the sort that revealed Truman's estimable side when it came to civil rights or health insurance, but could become petty and personal when it came to partisan politics.

3. As the steel strike approached its fiftieth day, in mid-July, Truman suffered what was described as a "nervous chill," and sent for Wallace Graham, the White House doctor. His temperature climbed to a worrisome 103.6, and the next day, he was taken to Walter Reed Army Medical Center with abdominal pain, a rapid pulse, and a burning sensation during urination. His condition was serious enough for Graham to record his opinion that Truman "was very acutely ill" with a fever but "wishes only to return to his desk." Much of this was kept from the press, although the concealment was nothing to rival what was hidden during the final months of Roosevelt's presidency. Press Secretary Joe Short, on July 14, said only that Truman had a "mild virus infection" and, possibly, a "mild temperature." Asked if the President had a cold, Short replied, "Don't press me." It was probably strep throat, an illness that would have been considered serious in the years before antibiotics were widely available. But it was serious enough for Truman, who'd never been hospitalized during his presidency, to remain at Walter Reed for five days.

When Truman returned to the White House, on July 19, he appeared in good spirits, though Eben Ayers noticed that "his face seemed a little drawn and his color not as bright." He began seeing visitors again on Monday, July 21, the day that the Democratic Convention was to open in Chicago. The weather had been punishing, with the thermometer reaching a moist ninety-eight degrees and edging upward. Truman watched some of the Chicago proceedings on television. Senators Russell and Kefauver were still competing for the nomination, but it seemed increasingly likely that Stevenson—"the man we cannot permit to say no," in the words of one speaker—would be chosen in a rare, and genuine, draft.

On July 22, Robert Lovett, who'd succeeded George Marshall as secretary of of defense ten months earlier, told Truman that the steel strike was "a darn sight worse than any bombing anybody ever

launched. . . . No enemy nation could have inflicted more damage."
The government, he said, might need to build, and operate, its own
mills, and stockpile its own steel. Two days later, Truman summoned
Benjamin Fairless, the president of the United States Steel Corp.,
and Philip Murray, the president of the CIO, to the White House, to
discuss a settlement. They arrived at 10 a.m., and at 4:45 p.m., with
Murray and Fairless on either side of him, Truman announced that
the affected companies, and the strikers, had reached agreement, and
that "this should lead to a speedy resumption" of production. The
settlement terms were somewhere between the industry's early offer
and an amount recommended by the Wage Stabilization Board, and
although it's easier to see such things in retrospect, it's clear that this
compromise could have been reached long before the country had
to endure the unfolding drama, and cost, of a strike, a seizure, and
a Supreme Court fight. The timing was a little suspicious too. The
strike's sudden resolution, coming just as the Democrats were about
to nominate a candidate, suggests that petulance had overwhelmed
both Truman's common sense and the national interest.

Just after Truman announced a settlement, and prepared to leave
for Chicago, Stevenson telephoned. He said he was about to be
nominated, a denouement that Kefauver denounced as a "synthetic
draft," due to the "conniving and scheming" of the governor's allies. As Truman remembered their conversation, Stevenson asked,
"Would you object if I agreed to run?" Would it embarrass him?
"Well I blew up," Truman recalled. "I talked to him in language I
think he had never heard before." Truman said, "I have been trying
since January to get you to say that. Why would it embarrass me?"

TWENTY-SIX

Bad Chemistry

In private life Mr. Daubeny almost adulated his elder rival,—
and Mr. Mildmay never omitted an opportunity of taking
Mr. Daubeny warmly by the hand. It is not so in the United
States. There the same political enmity exists, but the political
enmity produces private hatred.

—Anthony Trollope, *Phineas Finn*

1. Adlai Stevenson's long struggle with indecision ended,
although with hiccups of self-doubt, when he was nominated, on the
third ballot. It was 1:43 a.m., on the East Coast, when Truman introduced him—"You know, it's early in the morning, and it's getting
earlier"—and promised, "We will carry on the fight." In Stevenson's
acceptance speech, on that early Saturday, he sounded close to declaring that he still didn't want to be there. "I accept your nomination
and your program," he began, and then "I should have preferred to
hear those words uttered by a stronger, wiser, and better man than
myself." During sixteen mournful minutes, he quoted the Gospel of
Matthew, and seemed to say he knew just how Jesus must have felt:
"I have asked the Merciful Father—the Father of us all—to let this
cup pass from me, but from such dreaded responsibility one does not
shrink in fear, in self-interest, or in false humility. So, 'If this cup may
not pass from me, except I drink it, Thy will be done.'" The New
York *Daily News* called him "Adelaide," but his mawkish reluctance
impressed his supporters, such as Eben Ayers, the former deputy press
secretary, for whom Stevenson's speech seemed "lofty and literary."

Truman, as sometimes happened, took offense when no offense

was intended. He complained to his diary that Stevenson had "ignored the President and the Administration. I'm not a prima donna,
thank God, and I'll give my best to elect the Democratic ticket because it is best for the United States and the world." Actually, Stevenson had not ignored Truman. As he neared the end of his acceptance,
he'd said that Truman had given a "lifetime of service and bravery
that will find him an imperishable page in the history of the Republic and of the Democratic Party." On the other hand, he didn't
mention any particular accomplishment of Truman's consequential
White House years. Stevenson's disinclination to celebrate Truman
was understandable, given that the previous months had produced
so much to skip over, from the war in Korea to bewildering domestic scandals to the administration's entanglement with the long steel
strike. Truman had no illusions about the brutality of politics, but
the words of critics still hurt, and he never stopped believing that he
deserved better and that history would treat him well.

It was not a happy convention, even apart from the funereal eloquence of the nominee. Senator McMahon, who was to have spoken
in Chicago and to have led the Connecticut delegation, had recently
been hospitalized for what was first said to be spinal surgery. He was
then reported to be gravely ill, and, with shocking suddenness, died,
of an aggressive form of lung cancer, the day after Stevenson was nominated. Truman praised his work as chairman of the Joint Committee
on Atomic Energy, but also said, and meant it, "I shall miss Brien
McMahon because he was such a good friend." He was forty-eight,
and it is impossible not to wonder what might have been next for him.

Stevenson had wanted Kefauver, the delegate runner-up, to join
him on the ticket, but that's when Truman stepped in. He'd grown
no fonder of Kefauver—the "great crime investigator," he wrote in
his diary—someone with "no reputation for anything in particular
but his being unable to understand what was going on. . . . What a
President this demagogic dumb bell would make!" Truman recalled
telling Stevenson, after the convention adjourned, that "he had the
right to choose," but "I vetoed that and persuaded him that no candidate needed to be appeased by being placed on the ticket"—a satisfying moment of political revenge.

Stevenson was urged to pick Senator John J. Sparkman, of Alabama, a segregationist, though not a Dixiecrat. After an hour and a half of meandering discussion, Truman was done. "Sparkman is your best bet," he announced. "I am going to bed." By then it was well past 4 a.m. By 7:45, Truman was on his way to Midway Airport, and thirty minutes later en route to Missouri, aboard the *Independence*, now loaded with modern gadgetry. They'd "installed a T.V. set in my quarters. Mrs. T. and the gang saw me board the plane on the T.V. set and at the same time could look out the window and see me do it!" he noted in his diary. In Independence, he said the Democrats had picked "a winning ticket," and, as for Sparkman, who was nominated by acclamation, "There's not a better fellow for the job—he's a peach."

Before leaving Chicago, Truman had written an encouraging note to Stevenson, on Blackstone Hotel stationery, and had it hand-delivered. "Last night was one of the most remarkable I've spent in all my sixty eight years," it said. "You are a brave man. You are assuming the responsibility of the most important office in the history of the world. You have the ancestral, political and the educational background to do a most wonderful job. If it is worth anything to you, you have my whole hearted support and cooperation."

Stevenson didn't get around to replying until Tuesday: "I am grateful beyond expression for your charity and good will," he wrote. "I am literally staggering under the new and unfamiliar burdens I have so abruptly assumed." He had, though, already found time to write to his friend Alicia Patterson, advising her that "The line to emphasize is that I am not Truman's candidate. He asked me and I turned it down."

2. Republicans, two weeks earlier, had convened in Chicago, and nominated General Eisenhower, whose handlers had skillfully dispatched Senator Taft. As his running mate, Eisenhower chose the California senator Richard Nixon, who was hated by Democrats, mostly for his successful Red-baiting 1950 Senate campaign, when he defeated Representative Helen Gahagan Douglas, whom he described as "pink right down to her underwear." Nixon brought youth to the ticket (he was thirty-nine), a history of Red-hunting (in particular his pursuit of Alger Hiss), and a talent for lawyerly oratory, which made the Democrats hate him all the more. He returned to his 1950 form when he introduced the phrase "Dean Acheson's College of Cowardly Containment" and, late in the campaign, said that Truman, Acheson, and Stevenson, were "traitors to the high principles in which a majority of the nation's Democrats believe," a statement that Truman, believing he had been accused of treason, never forgave.

It didn't take long for Truman to get the idea that Stevenson didn't want him around, that he was seen as a figure out of time, an unsophisticated whistle-stop politician in an age bending to the needs, and reach, of television. "Stevenson's attitude toward the President he hoped to succeed was a mystery to me for some time," Truman was to write. There was lots that irked him, such as his running mate Sparkman, in a *U.S. News & World Report* interview, calling the steel seizure "badly mishandled from the very first day," and blaming "both sides"—the unions and the steel industry. Then Stevenson had moved his campaign headquarters to Springfield, Illinois, which suggested to Truman, not wrongly, that he "was seeking to disassociate himself from the administration in Washington, and perhaps from me."

This discomfiture swelled after an editor at the *Oregon Journal*, in mid-August, asked Stevenson if he could "really clean up the mess in Washington." To that, Stevenson carelessly replied by letter, writing, "As to whether I can clean up the mess in Washington," one needed to look at what he'd accomplished in Illinois. "I can only give my best, with ruthless objectivity, as I have done here, to the pain of the politicians, the gamblers, yes, and the businessmen who liked it the old way." Stevenson's willingness to accept the "mess in Washington" phraseology was a gift to Republican speechwriters, for whom the "mess" was already a staple. In a typical formulation, Eisenhower, during an early September campaign stop in Atlanta, said, "This mess is the inevitable and sure-fire result of an administration by too many men who are too small for their jobs, too big for their breeches, and too long in power."

Truman was soon asked for his thoughts on Stevenson's back-and-forth with the Oregon newspaper:

The President: I have no comment, because I know nothing about any "mess."

Q: Mr. President, I also would like to ask you—Senator John Sparkman said that the steel strike had been mishandled. I wonder if you have any reaction to that?

The President: No comment.

Q: Are you satisfied with the way that Stevenson and Sparkman have initiated their campaign?

The President: No comment.

These "no comments" were uttered without a trace of mirth—none of the friendly laughter that marked many Truman press conferences. The Democratic Party, he said, "has to run on the record of the Roosevelt-Truman administrations, and that's all it can run on." The "mess" attacks, he insisted, baffled him. "I wondered," he later wrote, if Stevenson "had been taken in by the Republican fraudulent build-up of flyspecks on our Washington windows into a big blot or 'mess.'" But it was hard to peel off the label. "Somewhere along the line," a *Washington Post* editorial said, "the Democratic campaign managers will have to ask themselves how much President Truman's support will be worth with the head of the ticket repeatedly deploring the 'mess in Washington' and with Mr. Truman responding as if he thought the candidate were talking through his hat."

Margaret Truman was to write, with both understatement and exaggeration, that "Dad never really warmed to Adlai Stevenson, although he tried very hard to like and understand him." Truman's unfiltered opinion came out in an unsent letter, written sometime in September, in which he would have scolded Stevenson, writing, "You have treated the President as a liability" and concluded that "you are embarrassed by having the President of the United States in your corner in this campaign. Therefore I shall remain silent and stay in Washington until Nov. 4."

Truman's petulant silence would not last long. Democrats real-

ized that something was missing—the campaign needed the President, someone who could say, as Truman had, at the convention,
that Republican leaders were "men of little faith and no vision—they
wouldn't be Republicans if they weren't that way." Stevenson was
adored by his "madly for Adlai" crowds, but couldn't excite them.
Where Roosevelt had been seductive, and Truman elemental, Stevenson might show off one of his treasured phrases, such as the "yeast
which causes inflation," or "We are going to survive even with sacrifice rather than perish cheap," which were not likely to kindle anyone's emotions. It was eventually decided that he would campaign in
twenty-four states—a two-week tour that would come close to the
exhausting effort of 1948. "When it seemed to me almost too late,"
Truman recalled, "Stevenson asked me to get into the campaign . . .
and I gave it all I had." The campaign's velocity affected everyone
in Truman's orbit. On September 18, press secretary Joe Short died,
of an apparent heart attack, at his home in Alexandria, Virginia. He
was forty-eight and, like Charlie Ross, his predecessor, had rarely
taken time off. His death came on the day that Jimmy Byrnes, Roosevelt's "assistant president" and Truman's former secretary of state,
announced that he intended to vote for Eisenhower, wiping out any
residue of friendship with Truman while declaring "I shall place loyalty to my country above loyalty to a political party."

3. The chilliness between Truman and Stevenson, though,
was merely a political mésalliance, more the friction between different temperaments, a relatively minor irritation compared to the icy
hostility developing between Truman and Eisenhower, which would
effectively stamp out a respectful relationship that had lasted since
the war. In 1945, Eisenhower could say, "We've got a great leader in
this country, a man from the Midwest and a man with a whale of a
lot of common sense." In his 1948 war memoir, *Crusade in Europe*,
he recalled riding in a car with Truman, in Frankfurt, just before the
Potsdam conference, when "he suddenly turned toward me and said,
'General, there is nothing that you may want that I won't try to help
you get. That definitely and specifically includes the presidency in

1948.'" Truman would deny making that offer, but Joseph Davies, the former ambassador to Russia, offers strong evidence that he had. In a letter to his wife, written from Potsdam, in July 1945, Davies quoted Truman saying "'I told "Ike" again that he could have anything within my power to give, and that I would be glad to support him for the Presidency in 1948, if he had any such desire.' I am sure the President was sincere." As recently as the summer of 1951, Truman had been asked about the Potsdam remark and didn't quite refute it, saying, "I am just as fond of General Eisenhower as I can be. I think he is one of the great men produced by World War II, and I think I have shown that, by giving him the most important job that is available for his ability"—the NATO post.

By early 1952, soon after Eisenhower was on his way to becoming a candidate, Truman was cautioning him that politics could be a rough business for newcomers. If he opposed Eisenhower running for president, it would be "because I think very highly of him, and if he wants to get out and have all the mud and rotten eggs and rotten tomatoes thrown at him, that is his business." In May, two months before Republicans nominated Eisenhower, Truman could still say, "He's as fine a man as ever walked. . . . He's just beginning to find out what happens to a candidate."

All this goodwill turned out to be highly perishable. Republicans were confident that a winning year lay ahead, and intended to focus on "Korea, Communism, and corruption—"K1C2" in Republican shorthand. By October, the last full month of the campaign, Truman was saying that "snollygosters" had taken control of Eisenhower. (That left reporters searching for definitions of snollygoster, a term for politicians who are out only for themselves.) He was dismissive of Eisenhower's political talent: "Why, this fellow don't know any more about politics than a pig knows about Sunday." That, though, was still the language of political combat, treated only half-seriously by Truman, though it upset Eisenhower, whose face would quickly turn several shades of red when something angered him.

What Truman took most seriously was Eisenhower's willingness, in early October, to appear on a platform with Senator McCarthy, in several Wisconsin stops. Eisenhower detested McCarthy, the man who, speaking from the libel-proof Senate floor in the summer of 1951, had accused George C. Marshall, the former secretary of state and defense, of Communist sympathies, of being part of a conspiracy "to dwarf any in the previous history of man." Eisenhower had intended to speak up for Marshall, who'd done so much to advance his career. In a passage written by Emmet John Hughes, a *Time* correspondent on loan to the campaign, he was to have said, "I have been privileged for thirty-five years to know General Marshall personally. I know him, as a man and as a soldier, to be dedicated with singular selflessness and the profoundest patriotism to the service of America."

That unexceptional good opinion, uttered in that time and place, would have been understood as a reprimand to McCarthy. But those lines were excised at the last minute, and everyone knew about the excision because the *New York Times* had already printed the text of the speech. Eisenhower later denied what was obviously true: that he'd "capitulated" to the McCarthyites. He had, at the very least, capitulated to political expediency—to pressure from the Wisconsin governor Walter Kohler, among others, to cut the passage while he campaigned in Wisconsin. He'd even shaken hands with McCarthy, in full view of news photographers, visible proof of his participation in a dishonorable episode.

Charles Murphy believes that Eisenhower's silence "made President Truman as mad as anything that I know of ever. And . . . the madder he got the less he thought of General Eisenhower." Truman began to sound personally offended, which he very likely was: "What do any of us say about a fellow who joins hands with those who have tried to stab an honored chief, a friend and benefactor, in the back?" he asked. He said Eisenhower had surrendered to "moral pygmies" and "moral scoundrels," and concluded, with unusual harshness, that Eisenhower was "unfit to be President."

Nor did Truman think Eisenhower should be talking about Korea. The armistice talks, after a beginning in Kaesong, had stalled, then resumed in Panmunjom, a village north of the Parallel. Fitful progress was made on such issues as a provisional cease-fire line and the repatriation of prisoners of war, but the conflict, and the bombing of the North, continued. During an October appearance in Champaign, Illinois, Eisenhower said that fighting the war was a job for South Koreans: "Let it be Asian against Asians, with our support on the side of freedom." He acknowledged the uncomfortable possibility that the war's likely outcome would be a defeat for the UN forces—or, at best, the absence of victory: "If we cannot win the war, at least let us not shed so much of our blood in the region," Eisenhower said, although he surely knew that South Koreans had a large, if not always effective, role in the fighting, and had shed a lot of their own blood.

Truman saw Eisenhower's comments as a willingness to place personal ambition above the national interest, and, speaking in San Francisco, described the general, in his most slashing language, as "a sad and pathetic spectacle," a captive politician. Eisenhower, he said, moving their former bond to the past tense, "was my friend and a man I trusted quite completely." He pointed out that, after the war, the nation's Korean policy had been formulated by many people, including Eisenhower, who, in 1949, was army chief of staff and, like Truman and others, had once favored withdrawing American forces from the peninsula—a policy that Eisenhower had begun to criticize. "Now this decision may have been right or it may have been wrong," Truman continued, but his point was that they'd both been responsible for the nation's postwar history, and it was wrong for Eisenhower to turn on it.

In mid-October, Truman said that if Eisenhower had a remedy to end the war, "it's his duty to come and tell me what it is, and save lives right now." After all, he added, he "has been my military adviser ever since I appointed him Chief of Staff." It was as if the race was now between Eisenhower and Truman, who, Eisenhower said, was firing "salvo after red-hot salvo at me," adding that he'd been shot at by actual artillery and was "far too old to be greatly disturbed by noisy, harmless blanks"—an un-soldierly thing for a five-star general to say about a former artillery man. On October 24, in a speech written by Emmet Hughes, Eisenhower called Washington a "sorry mess," and said Korea had become "the burial ground for twenty-thousand American dead"—familiar tropes, though nonetheless effective. Then he said something new:

Where will a new administration begin? It will begin with its President taking a simple, firm resolution. That resolution will be to forego the diversions of politics and to concentrate on the job of ending the Korean War until that job is honorably done.

That job requires a personal trip to Korea.

I shall make that trip. Only in that way could I learn how best to serve the American people in the cause of peace.

I shall go to Korea.

The Stevenson adviser Jacob Arvey, listening to this on the radio, turned to his wife and said, "That's the speech that will beat us." Truman knew it too, and, in his memoirs, would write, with another seething expulsion of derision, that "no man in our national life had a better reason to know or a better opportunity to find out the nature of the enemy. No man had less right to use this crisis for political purposes." Stevenson hadn't yet decided what to say about Korea, or Eisenhower's promise to go there, apart from declaring that "an unshakable determination to stand firm" was the best path to ending the conflict. Stevenson could have helped himself by saying that he welcomed Eisenhower's pledge, and suggesting that the former supreme commander of the Allied armies might be able to accomplish something useful with a visit. Instead, he tacked on a paragraph saying that "the root of the Korean problem does not lie in Korea—it lies in Moscow." That was not an unsound assessment, but, like his "determination to stand firm," his response was unusually out of sync with the moment. Few, though, doubted Stevenson's credentials as a Cold Warrior; in a speech delivered in Detroit he'd compared Communism to a deadly illness—"a disease which may have killed more people in this world in the last five years than cancer, than tuberculosis, than heart disease—more than all of these combined." In one last lick, two days before the election, Truman declassified the 1947 document signed by then Defense Secretary James Forrestal, in which the Joint Chiefs, including Eisenhower, had recommended withdrawing American occupation forces from Korea. He'd done so, he said, to defend those who'd been subject to Eisenhower's "false and malicious attacks.

On Election Day, November 4, Truman recalled, "I voted early, before breakfast . . . in the Memorial Hall at Independence, where I had been voting for more than three decades." This year, though, it was different—"one of the few times in more than thirty years [when] my name did not appear as a candidate for some office." Bess and Margaret accompanied him on his walk to the polling place. He claimed, as always, that once a campaign was over, he stopped thinking about it: "I thought we had lost the election even before I had gone to bed."

The aftermath of what became a landslide victory for Eisenhower was unusually gloomy for someone whose cheeriness usually won out. Truman felt wounded by a columnist's assertion that without his insistent presence, Stevenson would have been better able to escape the "dead weight of the immediate past." Yet Truman seemed to find a sort of solace in defeat, remarking that that it might be a good thing for Americans to experience what life had been like under the Republicans—"to learn for themselves" what President Roosevelt and he were trying to do.

<hr />

A week after the election, an arresting headline appeared on the front page of the *Los Angeles Times*: "EYEWITNESS STORY: Island Vanishes in Pacific Blast."

That was a thrilling way to announce the world's first thermonuclear test, near Eniwetok Atoll. A sailor who'd witnessed it set down what he'd seen in a letter home—a letter published by the *Lima News* in Ohio: "I could hardly believe my eyes. A flame about two miles wide was shooting five miles into the air," along with a cloud that "looked like a head of cauliflower." The island "started to burn and it turned a brilliant red. It burned for over six hours, gradually becoming smaller. . . . An island that once had palm trees and coconuts was now nothing. A mile-wide island had actually disappeared." Another sailor wrote, "You could swear that the whole world was on fire." Edward Teller knew just what those sailors had seen. He'd been at home, watching a seismograph, waiting for a telltale blip. When he saw it, he sent a telegram to some of the old gang at Los Alamos: "It's a boy," he wrote.

TWENTY-SEVEN

The Bitter End

> I can't help but dream out loud just a little here. The Tigris and
> the Euphrates Valley can be made to bloom as it did in the time
> of Babylon and Nineveh. Israel can be made a country of milk
> and honey as it was in the time of Joshua. This is our dream of
> the future, our picture of the world we hope to have when the
> Communist threat is overcome.
>
> —President Truman, Farewell Address,
> January 15, 1953

1. After the election, President-elect Eisenhower took a
two-week holiday in Georgia, at the Augusta National Golf Club,
which would become a favorite destination during his two-term presidency. Then he flew to Washington, where an estimated half-million
applauding spectators cheered the man that millions of Americans
called "Ike." His open Cadillac convertible, along with a fifteen-car
motorcade, was accompanied by marching bands and drum major-
ettes, a parade that carried him almost to the gates of the White House.

The general wore a brown business suit and brought along
two liaisons—Joseph Dodge, a Detroit banker, and Henry Cabot
Lodge Jr., of Massachusetts, an important early supporter, who'd
just lost his Senate seat to the three-term Congressman John F. Kennedy. The President and President-elect met for about seventy minutes, a session described as cold and distant—"certainly no 'love
feast,'" as Lodge recalled it. Truman remembered that when Eisenhower "came into the President's office"—not just "my office"—"he
had a chip on his shoulder," and he'd told him "all I had in mind is

an orderly turnover to him." The "chip" may be explained by the venomous language of the recent campaign as well as the implied insult in Truman's post-election congratulatory telegram, in which he'd said that the *Independence*, the Douglas DC-6 in which he'd flown to Wake Island, "will be at your disposal if you still desire to go to Korea." Truman offered to leave pictures of Miguel Hidalgo, José de San Martín, and Simón Bolívar, after which, he recalled, "I was informed, very curtly, that I'd do well to take them with me—that the governments of these countries"—Mexico, Argentina, and Venezuela—"would, no doubt, give the new President the same pictures!" When Truman bequeathed the globe that the general had given him when they met in Germany, before the Potsdam conference, "He accepted that—not very graciously."

Truman escorted Eisenhower to the Cabinet Room, where Acheson, Harriman, and other cabinet officers were waiting. Truman handed out a memorandum on budgets and taxes, prepared by the Treasury Department, and said the meeting would demonstrate a continued commitment to national unity. "Gen. Eisenhower was overwhelmed when he found what he faced," Truman thought. "I think all this went into one ear and out the other." He was in an unforgiving mood. As he saw it, despite Eisenhower's "lifelong reputation of being a sunny and amiable man . . . those of us who knew him well were all too well aware that he was essentially a surly, angry, and disagreeable man, and I don't just mean to me, either." Acheson remembered Eisenhower "sunk back in a chair facing the President across the Cabinet table," that he "chewed the earpiece of his spectacles and occasionally asked for a memorandum on a matter that caught his attention." Not that Eisenhower was inclined to be obliging. Emmet Hughes recalled how the "mere mention of Harry Truman's name brought fast flashes of antipathy"—including wondering aloud "if I can *stand* sitting next to him" in the upcoming inaugural ceremony.

The pool photographer, Harvey Georges, of the Associated Press, recalled watching them, seated four or five feet apart, both with "very grim and determined looks on their faces." Eager for a good shot, he asked for help: " 'Mr. Presidents—I put it in the plural—may

I have a handshake?' They cooperated with that, and as soon as I saw the President's teeth in my finder, I let it go."

2. Secret arrangements, meanwhile, were being made to keep Eisenhower's promise to visit Korea. The concealment included a post-Thanksgiving pantomime in New York, where visitors, including John Foster Dulles, the secretary of state-designate, would go to Eisenhower's house, in Morningside Heights, as if the President-elect were in residence. Eisenhower was actually somewhere over the Pacific, aboard a Lockheed Constellation, on his way to the Korean peninsula. He spent three days in South Korea, where he visited a field hospital, traveled close enough to the fighting to see black smoke and hear artillery fire, inspected troops, and gazed at the chilly, mountainous terrain. He wore a hooded parka, and his face appeared blue from the cold. He spent about an hour with Syngman Rhee, in Seoul; saw his son, John, a major in the Third Infantry Division; and talked to reporters, who were under a news blackout. "We have no panaceas, no tricks of settling any problems," he said, in a statement released when he was en route to Guam. He acknowledged the strategic paradox the nation faced: "How difficult it seems to be in war of this kind to work out a plan that would bring a positive and definite victory without possibly running grave risk of enlarging the war." *A war of this kind* was a phase that encapsulated the euphemism "limited war," a term detested by Admiral Radford, the Pacific Fleet commander, who pointed out that a decision to limit a war "is not, and cannot be, the decision of one side. The enemy has a great deal to say about that."

General MacArthur had not gone silent. Since returning from Japan in April 1951, he'd taken up residence at the Waldorf Towers (also the home of former President Herbert Hoover) and become chairman of the board of Remington Rand, the business machines manufacturer. He'd kept his five-star rank, and, at least technically, remained on active duty. He'd even put himself in the running for the 1952 Republican presidential nomination, briefly entertained a hope of becoming Senator Taft's running mate, and enlivened the Republican Convention with a dark keynote speech in which he aimed to pummel the Democrats, calling them despoilers of "those very concepts of humanity and government upon which rested our past spiritual and temporal strengths," and spoke of a "deep sense of fear that our leaders in their insatiate demand for ever more personal power might destroy the Republic."

In early December, in a speech to the National Association of Manufacturers, MacArthur revealed that he had "a clear and definite solution" to the Korean conflict." Despite Eisenhower's problematic history with his onetime superior, dating back to their time in the Philippines, he responded with courtesy, saying that he looked forward to the chance to "obtain the full benefit of your thinking and expertise." MacArthur's reply, which began, "For Ike," as if he couldn't bear to refer to his former underling—a mere lieutenant colonel—as the President-elect, said, "This is the first time that the slightest official interest in my counsel has been evidenced since my return." Then, in the inflated language that MacArthur and his ghostwriters favored, he added that "a failure of policy there might doom indefinitely the progress of civilization."

Truman had other worries, and sorrows. Bess's mother, Madge Gates Wallace, who'd been an invalid for some time, died on December 5, in the White House. She was ninety. Her daughter was at her bedside, along with a nurse, a maid, and Wallace Graham, the White House physician. The President, an aide said, "got there just at the end." In a diary note written the next day, Truman said little about his uneasy relationship with Mrs. Wallace, which for more than thirty years had been burdened by memories of a place where just about everyone knew all about the Trumans, the Gateses, and the Wallaces. Rather, he let loose with what for him was an unusual explosion of bitterness toward the press:

> *She was a grand lady. When I hear these mother-in-law jokes I don't laugh. They are not funny to me, because I've had a good one. . . .*

Today we go to Missouri to bury her. [Six years ago],
I was on the same errand for my mother. The sabotage
press ... made it appear that I was wasting public money
to be decent to my mother. May God forgive them, I can't
and won't.

The same lice will do the same publicity job when I take
Mrs. Wallace, Bess and Margaret home to bury the mother-
in-law.

To hell with them. When history is written they will be the
sons of bitches—not I.

Truman didn't get around to MacArthur until he returned
from Missouri. Anyone with a "reasonable plan" for ending
the war "in an honorable way, in a way that will not lead directly into a great war," ought to present that plan "at once,"
he said, in a statement. The next day, at a press conference,
he made no effort to hide his loathing:

Q: Mr. President, have you talked to General MacArthur since
    Wake Island?
The President: No.
Q: Have you seen him since then?
The President: I made a 14,400-mile trip to get a lot of misin-
    formation. He didn't even do the courtesy, which he should
    have done, of reporting to the President when he came back
    here. I have never seen him, and I don't want to see him.
Q: You mean that would be the appropriate thing, that he should
    ask to see you?
The President: He should have come to see me and reported,
    as soon as he got here. Any decent man would have done it.

Truman noted that Eisenhower's behavior vis-à-vis the President
had been proper. "The first thing General Eisenhower did when he
came back from Europe was to report to me. And that is exactly

protocol," he said. He was not, however, prepared to ignore or forgive Eisenhower's Korean excursion: "The announcement of that
trip was a piece of demagoguery, and then of course he had to take it
after he had made the statement." Truman paused, for a brief, whispered conversation with Roger Tubby, who'd succeeded Joe Short as
press secretary; then he added what Tubby, wisely, had urged him to
add: "Well, Roger suggested that maybe some good might come out
of the trip," Truman said. "If it does, I will be the happiest man in
the world. I hope some good can come out of it."

3. As Truman began the final month of his presidency,
he didn't indulge in reflection, but, like regret, reflection had never
been his métier. In interviews with several favored journalists, the
closest he came to expressing self-doubt was when he talked about
Korea—"the most terrible" decision he'd had to make, and a "much
more important decision than the one to drop the atomic bomb."
During one valediction, he acknowledged the trap he may have
helped set, and then fallen into: After saying "We have been trying to hold the present line . . . stopping the Communists without
involving us in an all-out war in the Far East," he added, "I think
Russia would like us to get involved in such a war because it would
give then a free hand in Western Europe."

Avoidance of a wider war was a recurring theme in his leave-
taking. He didn't personally deliver his final State of the Union message; rather it was read aloud by clerks in the House and Senate. Its
eleven thousand words included an aside to Stalin: "You claim belief
in Lenin's prophecy that one stage in the development of communist
society would be war between your world and ours," it said. "But
Lenin was a pre-atomic man, who viewed society and history with
pre-atomic eyes." Referring to the recent test of a thermonuclear
weapon, he warned that "the war of the future would be one in
which man could extinguish millions of lives at one blow, demolish
the great cities of the world, wipe out the cultural achievements of
the past—and destroy the very structure of a civilization that has
been slowly and painfully built up through hundreds of generations."

A week later, Truman said farewell to the nation, in a speech that sounded as if he'd written it himself, although researchers have concluded that, at the very least, it was a collaborative venture. Its personal touches would have sounded odd coming from anyone but this Midwesterner with the soft voice and a banker's face, whose compressed words and hurried pace had become so familiar. "There are simply a few things in my heart that I want to say to you," he said. He was modest—just an ordinary American: "When Franklin Roosevelt died, I felt there must be a million men better qualified than I, to take up the Presidential task." He recalled that the surrender of Nazi Germany, the Potsdam conference, and the decision that "the atomic bomb had to be used" to end the war, happened in little more than four months. He was proud of the Marshall Plan, NATO, and urging aid for Greece and Turkey: "When history says that my term of office saw the beginning of the Cold War, it will also say that in those eight years we have set the course that can win it." When he'd finished, the two people closest to him—Bess and Margaret—joined him in view of the camera.

A tender *Herald Tribune* editorial said that Truman, as he stepped down, had "the assurance of a warm place in the people's hearts," but it was Walter Lippmann, the perpetual scold, who wrote what might be regarded as a template for the first wave of Truman appreciators, a column that began, "In the manner of his going Mr. Truman has been every inch the President, conscious of his great office and worthy of it." One could become angry with Truman, he wrote, "but neither he nor his critics and opponents were able to keep on being angry. For when he lost his temper it was a good temper that he was losing."

Truman held his final news conference on the day of his farewell address. Over nearly eight years, he'd greatly expanded the frequency of these sessions, and was in a mood to celebrate an institution that had often angered him: "This kind of news conference where reporters can ask any question they can dream up—directly to the President of the United States—illustrates how strong and how vital our democracy is," he said. "There is no other country in the world where the chief of state submits to such unlimited questioning."

Future presidents, he added, might improve the system, but "I hope they will never cut the direct line of communication between themselves and the people."

It ended with the traditional "Mr. President—thank you!" But this time it was followed by affectionate applause for this child of rural Missouri—this self-educated striver, a man determined to overcome the prejudices, ethnic and religious, of that time and place—letting him know that he was, as Lippmann put it, in his sentimental moment, someone who "has the good nature of a good man." In midcentury America, it was hard to imagine a future when those qualities could be extinguished.

4. On January 20, 1953, which turned into a mild and muggy day, Truman got up, as usual, at five-thirty, and on this morning, set about saying goodbye to White House staff—to clerks, telephone operators, and "the Secret Service boys." After these goodbyes, he met with cabinet members, and their wives, in the Red Room, one of the restored mansion's most inviting reception parlors. There, he noted, pointedly, in his diary, "we have a most pleasant visit until the General and his entourage arrive." After that, it went downhill, speedily.

The Trumans had invited the Eisenhowers to join them for coffee before the noon swearing-in ceremonies, but Eisenhower's limousine, a black Lincoln, arrived at 11:30—which left them just enough time to get to the Capitol. As the columnist Doris Fleeson described the scene, there was an "awkward moment while the staff waited to see if General Eisenhower would enter the White House to greet the man who was still President, still Commander in Chief of the Armed Services, in which the new President is still a five-star General." She continued, "Mr. Eisenhower sat still. Only after Mr. and Mrs. Truman and Margaret emerged from the White House did Mr. Eisenhower get out of his car." The CBS correspondent Eric Sevareid, another witness to this odd standoff, told the Truman biographer David McCullough that "it was a shocking moment." It left Truman little choice but to join Eisenhower in the waiting Lincoln. The

White House usher J. B. West "watched the two grim-faced men step into the special, high-roofed limousine," and thought, "I was glad I wasn't in that car."

The two-mile drive proceeded in near silence, as both passengers waved to spectators lined up along the route. "I ride with Ike in car No. 1 along with [former Speaker] Joe Martin & [Senator] Styles Bridges," Truman recalled. "Bess & Margie ride with Mrs. Ike. Conversation is general—on the crowd, the pleasant day, the orderly turnover etc. Ike finally said that Kenneth Royall"—the army secretary during Truman's first term—"tried to order him home in 1948 for the inaugural ceremony but he wouldn't come because half the people cheering me at that time had told him they were for him. I said, 'Ike I didn't ask you to come—or you'd been here.'" Truman recalled that "Bridges gasped" and that Martin "changed the subject." That conversation—Bridges's gasp and all—may have happened just as Truman recalled, but if so, they'd all gotten it wrong: Eisenhower, in 1948, *had* been in Washington, *had* taken part in the inaugural parade, and had exchanged friendly salutes with his commander in chief, who was watching from a reviewing stand.

For all the rancor between them, there'd been gestures of good intent, though even some of those were disputed. Truman wanted Major John Eisenhower to return stateside, to watch his father take the oath, and Eisenhower later wrote that when he'd asked Truman who'd ordered his son back, "I thanked him sincerely for his thoughtfulness. My son had been upset when he first received the order because, not knowing the reason, he was fearful that he might lose his assignment in his combat division." But Truman's military aide, Robert Dennison, remembered that, on the way to the Capitol, Eisenhower turned to Truman and said, "I wonder what s.o.b. ordered my son back, just to *embarrass* me," and Truman replied, "I did." No one, in any case, disputes that Eisenhower offered Truman the use of the *Ferdinand Magellan*, to take him home to Missouri, and that Truman didn't hesitate to accept.

Along with the Trumans, Eisenhowers, the Richard Nixons, and the Alben Barkleys, there were many familiar faces on the platform, among them former president Herbert Hoover and General

George C. Marshall who, in one account, "smiled in paternal fashion." Eisenhower became the thirty-fourth President of the United States at 12:32 p.m., and a moment after he'd taken the oath, Truman reached out to shake his hand. President Eisenhower began his inaugural address with a prayer that he'd written: "Give us now, we pray, the power to discern clearly right from wrong, and allow all our works and actions to be governed thereby and by the laws of this land." When he'd finished, he got another handshake from Truman, and one from Barkley and Chief Justice Vinson. Bess Truman kissed Mamie Eisenhower, who had looked close to tears. One of those in the dispersing crowd was Rosemary McMahon, the widow of the late Connecticut senator. On her way home, she spotted Alben Barkley, who was walking up an incline toward his apartment, at 2101 Connecticut Avenue. She stopped to offer him a lift, which Barkley accepted.

Truman's plans for the remainder of that day included lunch with his cabinet at the Acheson house, on P Street. Some Georgetown neighbors were standing along the block, eager to get a glimpse when he arrived with Bess and Margaret. When they spotted him, Truman got what was described as a "tumultuous ovation," long and loud enough to persuade him to say that "this is the greatest demonstration that any man could have, because I'm just Mr. Truman, a citizen from Missouri, now." The lunch was off-limits to reporters, but they could hear laughter whenever the front door opened. Only the invited guests heard Truman say, "The great thing about my low approval rating is that every year it's going to be better." When the party broke up, Acheson was persuaded to step outside. "We have had a very gay time," he told the crowd. "We told stories on each other and remembered about some of the things that have happened to us. We ended as we began, with love and devotion to our chief, his wife, and their daughter, which I believe has never been equaled."

Some reporters left to file their stories, but planned to return to Union Station in the early evening, where several thousand spectators had come to wave goodbye—"An immence [sic] crowd," Truman noted. "Took four policeman & 3 secret service men to get me to the car. Never anything like it so it is said." Eben Ayers, Charlie Ross's former deputy, who'd watched the ceremonies on television, wanted to be at the train station for a last farewell. At about five-thirty, with his wife, Mary, he'd set out from their house in Northwest Washington, taking Massachusetts Avenue to avoid the remnants of an inaugural parade that had lasted more than four and a half hours. They found a parking spot at a filling station, and pushed through the crowd that was jammed on the train's platform, finally managing to approach the *Ferdinand Magellan*, the rear car of Baltimore & Ohio's National Limited. It turned out to be worth the effort. Ayers managed to shake hands with Truman, say hello to Margaret, and greet Chief Justice Vinson and former Treasury Secretary Snyder. The crowd sang "Auld Lang Syne" as the former president stood on the car's rear platform, with Bess and Margaret beside him, like a postcard from 1948. "This is the first time you've sent me home in a blaze of glory," Truman said. "In all my career, and it has been a long one, I've never had anything like this happen. I will never forget this if I live to be a hundred, and that's what I expect to do." The *Ferdinand Magellan* left the station, at 6:30—"amid cheers & tears," Truman wrote—after which the Ayerses headed home, stopping on the way for dinner at a Hot Shoppe, on the corner of 17th and H Streets, a transition as abrupt as it is for anyone who's ever served in the White House.

At seven the next morning, during a stop in Cincinnati, Truman alighted for a rapid walk, and was immediately greeted by the expectant press. Did he feel any different? He pointed to the reporters and said, "It seems just the same where we are." The following evening, the train arrived in Independence, at the Missouri Pacific Depot on South Grand Avenue, and Truman once more attracted a crowd of several thousand. Others waited in front of the Gates-Wallace house on North Delaware Street, still a neighborhood of relatives as well as friends. "Never was such a crowd or such a welcome in Independence. Mrs. T & I were overcome," Truman wrote in his diary. "It was the pay-off for thirty years of hell and hard work."

Citizen Truman

> I recall turning to John Snyder and saying, "What a great change can come to a man in a matter of moments. An hour ago, anything I might have said would likely have been flashed around the world. Now I could talk for hours on any subject and no one would pay the slightest attention."
>
> —**Harry Truman**

1. Bess and Harry Truman lived in Independence, then a city of some thirty-seven thousand—it's now three times that—for the rest of their lives. Crowds would sometimes form in front of the Delaware Street house, hoping for a sighting of an ex-president, in his native habitat. Such glimpses were uncommon; the family home was protected by a fence and a front-gate lock controlled from inside. But Truman could sometimes be spotted on a morning walk, a sentimental, circular route that took him past the places that would "bring back wonderful recollections," such as the Presbyterian Church, at Lexington and Pleasant Streets, where, as a six-year-old, he got his first glimpse of "little golden haired" Bess.

There was no rule book for former presidents, and in any case, Truman was not bound to observe the custom of ex-presidential silence—or caution. "I am not convinced Russia has the bomb," he said less than a week after leaving office. His interlocutor, a wire-service reporter, wondered about the ethics of writing a story that seemed to him so factually wrong, but went ahead because "I was quoting the President of the United States who had just left office and who had had access to all the intelligence information possessed by this government." After the story was published, the rebukes to Truman were as fierce, and fast, as if he were still in office. Bourke B. Hickenlooper, an Iowa Republican senator and the former chairman of the Joint Congressional Committee on Atomic Energy, said that if Truman's doubts were real, he'd been guilty of "reprehensible misrepresentations" when he was president. A few days later, Truman took a vow of silence. "I'm not going to comment on public affairs now or any time in the near future," he told reporters who'd tagged along for a walk. "You boys can consider this a dry news hole." It was, as everyone knew, a vow with an early expiration date.

Truman wanted any future earnings to be for legitimate work—not for something that exploited his former office. He'd turned down offers to appear on television, and even to be Margaret's piano accompanist. On his next-to-last day as president, William Shawn, the editor of the *New Yorker*, invited him to write something for the magazine: "With time hanging heavy on your hands," Shawn's telegram said, "would you like to try a piece for us on 'Train Thoughts: The Revery of a Man on the Long, Long Journey From Washington, D.C., to Independence.'" Shawn cautioned Truman that "you would be writing on speculation, as this magazine never buys anything sight unseen." There is no record of a response to this offer to write on spec, but as Truman settled in at a new office, a three-room suite on the eleventh floor of the Federal Reserve Bank Building in Kansas City, he began to consider more attractive proposals. He would write a history of his presidency far more substantial than a book he'd published in the spring of 1952: a curious hodge-podge titled *Mr. President*, a compilation of photographs, redacted pre-1949 journal entries, and never-mailed letters, which managed to reignite quarrels with Henry Wallace and Jimmy Byrnes.

In February 1953, *Life* magazine bought the rights to his memoirs for six hundred thousand dollars. Truman wasn't strapped for cash—far from it—but he could use the money and, as a matter of pride, wanted to be paid more than the five hundred thousand dollars that General Eisenhower got for his war memoir, *Crusade in Europe*. His presidential salary had been a taxable hundred thousand dollars a year, but until Congress passed the Former Presidents'

Act, in 1958, ex-presidents received no pension. As an army veteran, however, Captain Truman, who'd retired with the rank of major, was eligible for a monthly benefit of $112.56.

Producing the memoirs, to be published in two volumes by Doubleday, excerpted in *Life*, and syndicated to newspapers, took nearly two vexing years and involved a staff of writers, researchers, and academics. Truman didn't seem to have grasped the writerly task that lay ahead. When asked if he'd give his publisher a rough draft for rewriting, he replied, "There will be no rewriting. It will have to stand on its own feet." As for indemnifying his publisher, he said, "I'm not going to libel anyone. I'm going to tell the truth about those sons of bitches." In early 1954, the *Life* editor Edward K. Thompson visited Kansas City and was worried at seeing only thirty-five pages of editable manuscript, although lots of conversation had been transcribed by interviewers. If Truman would only write "in the simple, lucid, and colorful way he talked," Thompson thought, "we would have no problem." But Truman and his staff were difficult collaborators, the hoped-for "Trumanisms" were a rarity, and after four months, Doubleday sent in a relief team. "I never really appreciated before what is involved in trying to write a book," Truman finally admitted.

Truman asked Dean Acheson to read a draft, an assignment that Acheson took on like a de facto editor. His comments were sharp and instructive, and his occasional impatience led him to scold the author, albeit gently: "You use the cliché, 'striped pants boys in the State Department,'" one note said, addressing a seemingly incurable Truman tic. "I should like to see you change this to 'people in the State Department,' not merely because the phrase is tiresome, but because it gives quite a wrong impression of the tremendous support which you gave to the career service." Some of Acheson's advice had the tone of someone tutoring a slightly backward student; at one point, he told Truman that the manuscript "gives the impression of a two-gun man in the White House shooting with both hands in all directions at the same time." More than once he tried to save Truman from himself, as with his note on Chief Justice Vinson's aborted 1948 mission to Moscow: "These pages . . . seem disingenuous, not wholly frank, unconvincing. The theme is that the Vinson mission had nothing to do with politics, was a good idea as foreign policy, and was spoiled by misunderstanding. Is this supportable? In the first place, no one will believe that it had nothing to do with politics."

There were enough of these pointed suggestions to upset Margaret, who thought her father wasn't being shown proper respect. "I think she probably believed that this is no way to speak to a retired President," David Acheson told me. "I think that she was offended by the tone of equality between Truman and my father in their correspondence and I think she thought her father was a great man and my father was simply a servant." In fact, these comments, and the confidence with which they were expressed, reveal the comfort of their relationship as well as Acheson's enormous sway over Truman. Acheson dedicated his own memoirs to Truman—"The captain with the mighty heart"—but for all that, "my father distrusted Truman's judgment," David Acheson said. "He thought he had too much of the politician in him, would tend to look at things superficially, short term. But I think Dad admired Truman's sense of duty, of obligation. That was very real, and not only very real but in stark contrast to the political values of the day."

The memoirs appeared in two volumes—*Year of Decisions* (dedicated to "The People of All Nations") came out at the end of 1955, followed by *Years of Trial and Hope: 1946–52*, in early 1956. The books, a chronological recounting told mostly in the style of interoffice prose, got respectful but unenthusiastic reviews, and brought into focus a man of complicated motives, wanting to sound plainspoken, defend and embellish his record, settle old scores, and flout his modest upbringing, while demonstrating impressive self-awareness and a talent for self-invention.

2. Positive assessments of Truman's presidency began well before he left the White House. Henry Steele Commager, in a *Look* magazine essay, published in August 1951—when the public Truman was beleaguered by bubbling scandals and an expanding war in Korea—argued the case for history's generous judgment: "Every one of those Presidents whom we now call great were denounced by his contemporaries as a weakling or a tyrant," Commager wrote, and "while critics have belabored Truman for venial sins . . . [he] has gone ahead and chalked up one achievement after another in both foreign and domestic affairs." That's what Dean Acheson emphasized in his summing up—praising the Truman Doctrine, the "1948 grandeur of the Marshall Plan," the Berlin airlift, the creation of NATO, and the intervention in Korea. Those decisions, Acheson wrote, with certitude, "constituted expanding action in truly heroic mold. . . . All of them required rare capacity to decide and act. All of them were decided rightly, and vigorously followed through."

Acheson could have added that, from the time Truman first ran for office, in Jackson County, he understood that the point of being a politician, and the way to keep winning elections, was to improve the lives of his fellow citizens. It made him keep pushing for a national health insurance program, despite formidable opposition. In the early summer of 1950, just before the outbreak of war in Korea, the American Medical Association voted to commit more than a million dollars for newspaper and radio advertising, determined that "socialized medicine would become a dead issue." Truman, as always, persisted. In late 1951, he created the Commission on the Health Needs of the Nation, determined that that something constructive might emerge. A decade later, it did; when Medicare became law, in 1965, President Johnson made it a point to sign the bill in Independence, with Harry and Bess Truman at his side.

Other domestic successes, such as an increase in the minimum wage and an expansion of Social Security benefits, tended to be incremental, but while such programs reflect what Truman cared about, they're not what he's most remembered for. Rather, students of the period—revisionists, post-revisionists, neo-revisionists, and no doubt other -ists—give particular attention to foreign policy and the origins of the Cold War. To revisit their arguments—from those who see Truman as an indispensable world figure, those who fault him for heightening East-West tensions, and those who can't forgive him for having ordered the first use of an atomic bomb—is to be reminded that, in mid-century America, the nation's leaders faced many choices, and that many outcomes were possible. As the Harvard

professor Ernest R. May observed in a survey of this seemingly infinite material, "Some of the scholarly debate about the cold war
has been, underneath, a debate about what *should* have happened.
Some has also been a debate about what *could* have happened." It's
also tempting to wonder what *might* have happened had Roosevelt
completed his fourth term.

A modern reader, who understands why Truman, and the men
around him, chose to act as they did, may feel some satisfaction with
how it all came out; or, because history doesn't come to a full stop,
how it *seems* to have come out. The chilling history of thermonuclear weapons is still being written, but hasn't the world avoided the
ultimate nuclear catastrophe? Senator J. William Fulbright, when he
chaired the Foreign Relations Committee during the Vietnam War,
wrote, disapprovingly, that "more by far than any other factor, the
anti-Communism of the Truman Doctrine has been the guiding spirit
of American foreign policy since the Second World War," but didn't
the Truman Doctrine help stanch the spread of Communism? And
consider what *did* happen: Germany and Japan emerged from the
ruins to become prosperous democracies; Western Europe, for all its
troubles, remains at peace; and the North Atlantic alliance, despite
its enlarged membership, is holding on. At the sixtieth anniversary of
the Korean truce, in 2013, President Barack Obama said, "Korea was
a victory," because "fifty million South Koreans live in freedom—a
vibrant democracy, one of the world's most dynamic economies, in
stark contrast to the repression and poverty of the North." Would
that have happened if the West had shrugged off North Korea's attempt to control the peninsula? From a twenty-first-century vantage
point, it's possible to believe in a happier ending, even the notion
that the two Koreas will someday unite, and lean toward democracy.
A recent visitor to the Demilitarized Zone, stopping at the Dorasan
station, on Seoul's Gyeongui Line, could take note of the Potemkin
boarding platform where a sign says "To Pyongyang."

When Truman reflected on his record, that's more or less how
he saw things. Using the atom bomb in Japan, he would say, saved
hundreds of thousands of lives—sometimes he'd say "millions." As
for Korea, having persuaded himself that he had to choose between

military force and appeasement, he had little doubt that he'd chosen correctly. "The issue," he'd say, "was whether there would be fighting in a limited area now or on a much larger scale later on—whether there would be some casualties now or many more casualties later." Or, as if to expunge any self-doubt: "I'm not sorry for it. Under the same circumstance, I'd do it again." And, with a hint of grandiloquence, when some schoolchildren asked, "Mr. President, sir, what was your most memorable moment in public life?" he replied, "When I had to save the Republic of Korea."

For the United States, Korea was the first war of its kind. Unlike the nation's next Asian war, in Vietnam, this one was unaccompanied by campus protests and political fury. It was sometimes called the "forgotten war," although it's never been forgotten by Koreans, by the Americans who fought there, or by their families. During the conflict, thirty-seven thousand American soldiers, and some four thousand allies, died. At least three times as many were wounded. More than two hundred thousand South Korean soldiers, and three hundred thousand South Korean civilians, were killed, though these numbers fluctuate depending on the source. The number of enemy dead was much larger—possibly a quarter-million North Korean troops, more than a million Chinese, and uncounted civilians, though those statistics too are from several sources, with varying reliability. Like the War Memorial in Seoul, the Victorious Fatherland Liberation War Museum in Pyongyang recalls the ferocity of the conflict. In the South alone, the war left nearly four million refugees, three hundred thousand war widows, a hundred thousand orphans, and ten million separated families. By the end of the winter of 1951, UN officials estimated that there were three million homeless, many of whom became refugees, traveling southward, overwhelming the UN Command, who had orders to shoot if necessary. Massacres of Korean prisoners and civilians, carried out by Koreans on both sides, were not uncommon.

The scorched-earth bombing ordered by General MacArthur was efficiently carried out by General Edward Stratemeyer, the Far East Air Forces commander, and before the air war ended, American planes had dropped 635,000 tons of bombs, including 32,557 tons of napalm. One variation, known as "golden rain," showered soldiers or civilians with this sticky fire. Their screams, it was reported, could be heard from a mile away. The destruction was enough for the deposed General MacArthur, in May 1951, to tell the Senate Committees on Armed Services and Foreign Relations that the war had become a "slaughter such as I have never heard of in the history of mankind." The fighting, he said, has "almost destroyed that nation. . . . I have never seen such devastation," he continued, and "after I looked at that wreckage and those thousands of women and children and everything, I vomited."

Dwight D. Eisenhower had been president for six months when the UN Command and North Korea agreed to an armistice—or, more precisely, an edgy cease-fire. The agreement, signed in Panmunjom, on July 27, 1953, after more than two years of querulous talks, was undoubtedly hastened by the death of Stalin, in early March. Zhou Enlai attended Stalin's funeral, and met with the new Soviet leadership, for whom ending the war was a priority, just as it was for China, which had suffered considerable losses. It had become obvious that a military victory, with acceptable costs, was out of reach, for all sides.

By the time of Panmunjom, what was originally portrayed as an international effort to push the Communist invaders back across the 38th Parallel, seemed an almost irrelevant goal, and a terrible failure, when one considers that it might have been achieved three years earlier, after Inchon, if UN forces had not then pushed across the 38th Parallel, carrying with them General MacArthur's misguided hope of total victory. The post-armistice border separating the two Koreas looked about as it had in 1945, although the 38th Parallel line was to be superseded by the more flexible Military Demarcation Line. That gave a slight territorial advantage to North Korea, which also annexed the city of Kaesong, where peace talks had begun in 1951. Kaesong thus became the only city to change sides. It is not difficult to imagine how all that misery and ruin affected North Korea's founder, Kim Il-sung, and his descendants, and how it shaped their vengeful hatred of the United States.

Eisenhower's reaction to the cease-fire was to say, with a cheerless smile, "The war is over and I hope my son is going to come home soon." Truman said, "About all I can say is that I hope sincerely it will mean peace," adding, a little sourly, "Just signing a truce doesn't mean peace." Those mild statements did not reflect Truman's undiminished anger with Eisenhower. They did, though, reveal his resentment at the blame he'd gotten for this faraway war; worse than that, it was as if Eisenhower was getting credit for negotiations that he'd begun! "Conditions are such that Ike can do no wrong and I can do no right," Truman wrote to Acheson. "If it weren't tragic it would be the best comedy in history."

Syngman Rhee came to the United States a year later. He and his Austrian-born wife were honored with a White House dinner, where they were seated next to Dwight and Mamie Eisenhower. The next day, Rhee was greeted by cheers when he spoke to a joint session of Congress. Those in the chamber, though, did not cheer when Rhee asked the United States to provide air and naval support in a preventive war against Communist China—in other words, to restart the Korean conflict. Although Rhee thanked Truman, Eisenhower, and the military for what they'd done, his gratitude was conditional: He dismissed the "unwise armistice which the enemy is using to build up its strength." He then went to see Truman, in Missouri, although he knew the American visit wouldn't improve his popularity at home, where no statues honor Truman.

3. Truman's White House records were turned over to the federal government, to be stored in what would become the Truman Presidential Library and Museum, situated on U.S. Highway 24, about a mile—walking distance—from the Gates-Wallace house. Despite its somewhat off-putting, semi-monumental exterior, Truman's democratic spirit is unmistakably present, starting with a Thomas Hart Benton mural, *Independence and the Opening of the West*, which frames the interior entrance and exudes a celebratory view of the semi-mythical America of Truman's boyhood. The painting is filled, even overfilled, with ideas, some encouraged during Benton's conversations with Truman, though not Truman's unrealizable wish to see the Louisiana Purchase portrayed. You do see images of Pawnee Indians, freed slaves, trappers, mule skinners, oxen, and, at the top, a pioneer family, with their covered wagons and a guard dog. It is gaudy, triumphant, and, to twenty-first-century sensibilities, a little alarming.

The library, which had great importance for Truman and became the first, and best, of several first-rate presidential research sites, opened in the summer of 1957, in a ceremony that included Herbert Hoover, the only other living ex-president. After the 1932 election, Hoover was snubbed by Roosevelt; Truman, in 1947, in an act of generous inclusiveness, called him back to government service, to help deal with the food shortage in Europe. On a sweltering Midwestern July day, a crowd of ten thousand watched the dedication, along with a guest list that included Chief Justice Earl Warren, Eleanor Roosevelt, Dean Acheson, and a number of congressional leaders. Truman moved his office from Kansas City to the library, and he became a faithful visitor, using a desk imported from Blair House, surrounded by books, tchotchkes, and photographs. Now and then, he stepped out to speak to fortunate tourists and schoolchildren.

If it is possible to fix a time for such an unrecorded transition, it was about then that Truman began to morph into being "Harry Truman," a jaunty, laconic Midwesterner who liked playing himself, someone who could tell a college audience, "Missouri has had a number of notorious characters. The three, I guess, most notorious are Mark Twain, Jesse James, and me." He loved that someone born in a four-room farmhouse next to a mule barn could become president, and happily took on the role of a truth-telling, no-bullshit, give-'em-hell common man, whose decisions had helped to change the world. He never forgot how it was to be a clerk at the Union National Bank, in Kansas City, rushing away from his perch to see a real, living president—Theodore Roosevelt: "He made a good speech," Truman recalled, "but nobody went down to hear him speak, they wanted to see him grin, to see his teeth, which they did."

In 1955, Truman received an honorary degree from Oxford (his diploma was inscribed with his Latinate name, "*Harricum*"), and appeared close to tears when he heard himself described as "Truest of allies, direct in your speech . . . and ever a pattern of simple courage." He dined, in London, with Churchill, Attlee, and Anthony Eden, a prime ministerial trifecta, followed by a lunch with Queen Elizabeth II. At the same time, he could behave like a character out of Mark Twain's *The Innocents Abroad*. He had a chance to meet Pablo Picasso, in Cannes, arranged by the former White House counsel Sam Rosenman, even though Bess had warned Rosenman, "You know what Harry thinks about modern paintings." Truman promised not to "say anything to hurt his feelings," but then, within earshot of Picasso, he wondered how anyone could "rave about those things? They're God-awful!"

Politics still made him cranky. In 1956, he attended the Democratic Convention in Chicago, where he promoted the candidacy of Averell Harriman and made an ineffectual effort to block the renomination of Adlai Stevenson, calling him "too defeatist" to win—in other words, not a Harry Truman. His obduracy was such that an old friend, the Kansas City businessman Thomas Evans, recalled how it worried Bess: "[F]or the only time in my life, I saw her upset, even in tears, pleading with me, 'Tom, can't you do something to stop Harry, he's making a fool of himself.'" Truman skipped the 1960 convention in Los Angeles, when Senator John F. Kennedy was nominated. Kennedy's religion bothered the Missouri Baptist, although it hadn't seemed to trouble him in 1952, when he'd encouraged Brien McMahon to run. "Do you really care about Jack's being a Catholic?" Acheson asked, in a letter written soon after Kennedy narrowly defeated Richard Nixon in the general election. "I never have. . . . Furthermore, I don't think he's a very good Catholic."

Among visitors to the Truman Library was Eisenhower, who stopped by in 1961, a year into his post-presidency. He was planning a library of his own, in Abilene, Kansas, where he was reared, and wanted to see how Truman had managed it. They chatted and looked at artifacts on display, including the globe that had twice gone from Eisenhower to Truman, and a copy of Eisenhower's *Crusade in Europe*, which the general had inscribed "this is the first copy presented to anyone outside my immediate family." The former presidents saluted each other as they said their goodbyes. But although they would meet again, at several funerals, including those for Sam Rayburn, Eleanor Roosevelt, George Marshall, and President Kennedy, there was never much warmth between them. Truman sometimes referred to him as "Glamor Boy," and at a Press Club appearance in November 1961, he said, "Mr. Hoover and I have formed a former Presidents' association. He's president and I'm secretary. The other fellow hasn't been taken in yet." And yet: After they'd seen each other, for what turned out to be the last time—a D-Day anniversary in Kansas City, in 1966—Truman remarked to his former aide David Noyes, "You see how easy it is to like Ike. I like Ike. I guess I always did, but there are times when I wished that he had majored in history."

Round-number birthdays got special attention, and each burnished the reputation of the historic Truman. His seventy-fifth, at the Waldorf-Astoria, was watched on closed-circuit television in sixteen cities. Eleanor Roosevelt, one of the speakers, sketched a sharp-lined portrait of gallantry: "The character of my friend was proved on that terrible day"—the death of her husband. "He was frightened—as he should have been. For no man had ever been placed so abruptly in such a seat of responsibility." She continued, "The decisions he made then shaped the very world we live in today." He returned to Washington for his eightieth, and while he could no longer walk a hundred and twenty steps per minute, he was unflagging for much of an emotional day. He stayed at Blair House, as President Johnson's guest, and returned to the Senate chamber, where he listened to bipartisan praise from more than twenty senators, and got a standing ovation. "If I have many more happy birthdays I shall never have another one like this," he said. When he greeted the Missouri senator Stuart Symington, he held out his left hand and said, "Here, take the arm closest to my heart."

4. Margaret Truman married Clifton Daniel, a *New York Times* editor, on April 21, 1956, in Independence, at the Trinity Episcopal Church, where Harry and Bess had been married, in 1919. But she'd left Independence, for good. Her home was Manhattan, where she'd become a minor celebrity. She appeared on NBC's weekly radio broadcast, *The Big Show* (with Tallulah Bankhead); was a co-host, with Mike Wallace, on a radio program called *Weekday*; and was a "mystery guest" and substitute panelist, on CBS's popular TV show *What's My Line?* She lent her name, though not much more, to twenty-some mystery novels set in Washington, and gave up her ambition to be a serious concert singer. With gratuitous malice, her former coach, Helen Traubel, said that "keeping her on key" had been an "unconquerable difficulty." The Daniels had four children, all boys, born between 1957 and 1966. The in-laws telephoned every Wednesday and Sunday.

When the former president came to town, he stayed at the Carlyle, close to the Daniels' triplex at 830 Park Avenue. New York agreed with him. At the city's seven daily newspapers, every city desk knew when Truman was in residence, and counted on him for colorful copy. Street cleaners would call, "Hi, Mr. President," and taxi drivers would shout, "Give 'em hell, Harry." He'd smile and wave, with reporters in pursuit and photographers ahead, running backward. Edward Robb Ellis, who worked for the *World Telegram and Sun*, recalled Truman "Trudging along with us at his heels," and hearing him say, almost to himself, "You know, after three years I thought all of this would wear off." It might have worn off had Truman, abetted by those trailing reporters, not begun to toss off remarks that seemed calculated to provoke, though perhaps not entirely calculated. Rather, he sometimes sounded as he had during the last months of his presidency, such as when he'd seemed confused about an "ultimatum" he had never sent to Stalin. He was saying things that he'd never said as president, especially when it came to equality for African Americans. For instance, he made clear he didn't approve of the lunch-counter sit-ins in the South, and in March 1960 said, "If anyone came to my store and sat down, I would throw him out. Private business has its own rights and can do what it wants." Three years later, the *New York Times* Metro reporter Gay Talese asked Truman if he thought racial intermarriage would become more common. "I hope not," Truman replied. "I don't believe in it. What's that word about four-feet long? Miscegenation?" He asked, "Would you want your daughter to marry a Negro?" When Talese replied that he'd want his daughter to marry the man she loved, Truman said, "You haven't answered my question," and continued, "Well she won't love someone who isn't her color." Roy Wilkins, the executive director of the NAACP, regarded those comments as "blunt, untimely, and unkind," but he wouldn't permit the seventy-nine-year-old Truman, whom he admired, to efface his record on race relations. "Let him have his breakfast strolls and his free-wheeling quips," Wilkins wrote in a syndicated column. "He can't stop the civil rights clock and his record entitles him to a few errors, however irritating, in his retirement years." In 1962 and 1963, he was interviewed by Merle Miller, whose best-selling book *Plain Speaking: An Oral Biography of Harry Truman* portrayed the former president at his most freewheeling. Among its sensational passages was Truman's purported claim that, during the war, Eisenhower had asked to be relieved of duty so that he could return and marry his reputed lover, Kay Summersby—a dubious allegation, unsupported by Miller's extant taped interviews. The book, useless as reliable history, was published a year after Truman's death.

By the mid-1960s, Truman had begun a slow descent into frailty. His physical decline became a public concern after October 13, 1964, when he slipped in a bathtub at home, hitting his head and breaking two ribs. It didn't sound very serious, but it kept him from traveling to New York for the funeral of Herbert Hoover. It wasn't his first fall. According to the former White House doctor Wallace Graham, he'd been suffering from vertigo, a "Parkinson-like syndrome." He continued to take short, halting walks in his neighborhood, using a cane, but by 1968 he was rarely seen outside, and almost never at the Truman Library. On his eighty-eighth birthday, in May 1972, a group of high school students serenaded him with "Happy Birthday, Mr. President." In December, suffering from lung congestion and an irregular heartbeat, he was admitted to Kansas City's Research Hospital and Medical Center, a five-hundred-bed facility where he spent the last twenty-two days of his life, with his wife and daughter often at his bedside. His room cost $59.50 a day, and was partially paid for by Medicare.

Late on Christmas Day, after Bess and Margaret, both exhausted, had returned to North Delaware Street, Truman slipped into a coma.

He died early the next morning, of what doctors called a "collapse of the cardiovascular system." Mary Jane Truman, then eighty-three, and the only surviving member of the immediate family (John Vivian had died in 1965), had recently been admitted to Research Hospital, after a fall. She was in a room nearby when a nurse told her that her older brother was dead.

A small funeral at the Truman Library included Masonic rites, and among the two hundred and fifty guests were Mrs. Eddie Jacobson, Thomas Hart Benton, John Snyder, and Averell Harriman. Official Washington said its goodbye at the Washington National Cathedral, on January 5, 1973, where the Reverend Francis B. Sayre Jr., Woodrow Wilson's grandson, spoke of Truman as "a fearless man of simple soil . . . earthy, plain, there were no wrinkles in his honesty." The Truman family was represented by Margaret and Clifton Daniel. Beside them was Mamie Eisenhower, who'd sat in the same pew on March 31, 1969, at the funeral of her husband. It had been almost exactly twenty years from the day Truman left office, another occasion to assess his stormy, unsettled presidency.

5. Before Germany's defeat, General Marshall remarked to Lord Halifax, the British ambassador, that "when this war ends, there will have been no example in history of a nation as young as ours having such responsibility thrust upon it. God only knows whether we shall be worthy of it." It's fair to say that they *were* worthy, and responsible, and that much of the credit goes to Harry Truman—and his acquiescence to the urgings of the driven men who surrounded him: Acheson and Marshall, above all, but also James Forrestal, the nation's first defense secretary; James F. Byrnes, his secretary of state for twenty months; Admiral William Leahy, the chief of staff he inherited from Roosevelt; and Averell Harriman, who'd been ambassador to Russia, and much more; Senator Arthur Vandenberg, who had a true conversion to internationalism, the atomic scientists; and the generals of World War II: Eisenhower, Bradley, Ridgway, and MacArthur. Truman's leadership was never stirring; he could be overwhelmed by his duties, and by the pounding that came with the job. But he was steadfast, honorable, sometimes courageous, and deeply in love with his country and its Constitution. He rarely, if ever, wobbled.

Truman and his men were circumscribed by their times; with the choices they faced, Dean Acheson would say, "not only is the future clouded but the present is clouded." Three years before the rise of Senator McCarthy, they couldn't know that a program in which two million federal workers were subjected to loyalty checks would uncover very few disloyal Americans while quickening the Red scare—unintended collateral damage. They faced baffling choices, some of which, such as the use and custody of nuclear weapons, no president had ever faced. They saw no satisfactory alternative to developing a thermonuclear weapon when the nation's Communist rival was doing the same, nor could they come up with a way to stop or slow down an arms race being conducted in secrecy. They couldn't know that what they'd thought would be a limited conflict in a small, Far Eastern country—its outcome bound to be quickly determined by the invincible victors of World War II—could quickly expand and, by drawing in Russia and Communist China, come close to growing into an all-consuming global hot war. In the 1940s and 1950s, they couldn't know that the resolve to contain the expansionist ambitions of Stalin's Russia might mutate into a policy to stamp out all sorts of little wars as well as speculative threats, and that, over the years, each of these little wars and threats—in places like Libya, or Iraq, or Afghanistan, or Vietnam—could grow into lengthy dispiriting struggles.

Truman's successors, who should have learned something from this, nonetheless continued to urge involvement in faraway places that were little understood—an often retold history of feckless endangerment: Lyndon Johnson, who ordered an enormous escalation in Southeast Asia, on the basis of falsehoods; or Richard Nixon, who continued what he knew was an unwinnable conflict, at the cost of many thousands of lives; or George W. Bush, whose administration might have quickly destroyed the Afghanistan-based terrorist group responsible for the 2001 attack on the World Trade Center and the Pentagon, but, failing that, led the United States into the nation's longest conflict—nearly twenty years—and launched a ruinous, destabilizing war in Iraq, on the basis of misinformation, and for motives that remain unclear. One no longer hears, or believes, the sort of thing Dean Acheson wrote in *Present at the Creation*, his engaging, and self-congratulatory, memoir: that "our efforts for the most part left conditions better than we found them."

Truman himself, in the nation's memory, is a larger, far more appealing figure than the man who once occupied the Oval Office; he's the gruff, scrappy "Harry Truman" celebrated by everyone from Nixon to the Bushes to Obama, and the person about whom Eleanor Roosevelt could say, "With every decision he grew until to the entire world he was a towering figure." To his contemporaries and critics, though, he was a besieged, uninspiring leader, a dismal orator who was forced to make rapid, and risky, decisions during a time marked by war scares, petty scandals, and stubborn labor strikes. Truman, as president, filled both roles; if he could never replace the masterful Franklin Roosevelt, he became someone, or *something*, else: a man, burdened by a persistent absence of foresight, whose policies nonetheless brought stability to an unsteady world.

Truman took office just eighty years after the Civil War. A good-hearted visitor from another time, he remained faithful to the lessons and ideas he'd absorbed during a nineteenth-century childhood, from reading about the lives of great men and famous women. He'd learned enough, and thought enough about what he'd learned, to worry about the fragility of his democratic republic. In a 1959 letter to a supporter of the Truman Library, he said that if young people "do not understand and appreciate what they have it will go the way of the Judges of Isreal [sic], the city states of Greece, the great Roman Republic and the Dutch Republic." He understood, and cherished, the task he'd been handed, and if he did not always seem big enough for the job, no one could question the size of the decisions he made while he held it.

Even Truman's adversaries, with few exceptions, found it hard to stay mad at him. Few viewed him with the raw hatred that's been directed toward some of his inheritors. Americans knew this man, or thought they did, and regarded him, as the *New Yorker*'s Richard Rovere would write soon after he left office, with the sort of fondness "that townsmen have for one of their own whom they know to have borne up well under great difficulties." Lippmann was correct in writing that the temper Truman frequently lost was a good temper, and no biographer has captured that with as much skill, and thoroughness, as David McCullough, whose masterful *Truman* celebrated Truman's many virtues, and his communion with the better angels of his compatriots—the idea, as the historian Clinton Rossiter wrote, that he was someone "whom history will delight to remember." Such affectionate regard cannot alter the past, or undo its dreadful misjudgments, but it is bound to affect the outlook of anyone who attempts to revisit a time that was contentious and dangerous, triumphant and tragic. Anyone retelling that story must contend not only with the alarms of the present age but, in the character of Harry S. Truman, with the immeasurable power of sentimental imagination.

Acknowledgments

This is the second book I've done with Priscilla Painton, Simon & Schuster's vice president and editorial director. She's seen me through several drafts with unflagging attention, ingenious suggestions, and constant encouragement—most recently during a time of uprooted households and altered lives. I couldn't have wished for a better editor, or partner. She knows how grateful I am; now, so will anyone who reads this.

It's also my fifth book with Simon & Schuster, where I'm lucky enough to have the support of the multitalented CEO, Jonathan Karp. Whenever friends tell me that there's no editing at American publishing houses, I try to correct them. The help and advice I've received came from many of the best people in the industry, among them senior production editor Lisa Healy, who was painstaking and forbearing. I'm deeply indebted to copy editor Rick Willett; proofreader W. Anne Jones; production editors Martha Schwartz, Sherry Wasserman, and Jason Chappell, all of whom saved me from embarrassing missteps; and indexer Catherine Foster. I've also relied on the exceptionally attentive assistant editor Hana Park

The book took shape after conversations with, among others, Priscilla Painton; the wise Tina Bennett, my friend and agent (of twenty years!); and friends and former colleagues at *The New Yorker*. As with my last book, *Ike and Dick: Portrait of a Strange Political Marriage*, they saw that writing about the Truman presidency was also a way to write about the era of my Washington childhood—a special attraction.

I got lots of help from a wide range of men and women, starting with the archivists at the Harry S. Truman Library and Museum, in Independence, Missouri, who were always conscientious and professional. I was especially appreciative of the advice and counsel I got from Randy Sowell, who could find the solution to just about every historical puzzle; and to Tammy Williams, who helped guide me through the Library's extraordinary collection. Many thanks, too, to supervisory archivist Sam Rushay, David Clark, and Laurie Austin; and a farewell thanks to Judy Turner, who retired from the Library and Museum, but was there at the start of this project.

I'm deeply grateful to Anne Kenney, for many years the immensely capable director of Cornell Libraries. She offered me full access to the library's resources in return for my unindentured service on the Cornell University Library Advisory Committee—a bargain by any measure. Thanks too, to Marcia Tucker, Librarian, Historical Studies-Social Science Library, at the Institute for Advanced Study, in Princeton, who went far out of her way to help.

I couldn't have done this without the resources and knowledgeable staff of the extraordinary New York Public Library; Columbia University's Oral History Archives, at Butler Library; the Seeley G. Mudd Manuscript Library, Princeton University; the Library of Congress; the New-York Historical Society; the Franklin D. Roosevelt Presidential Library and Museum; the Clemson University Library; and the District of Columbia Public Library.

Individual thanks go to a number of remarkable people: The late David Campion Acheson (1921–2018), a unique witness, with whom I had a memorable lunch, followed by telephone calls and an email correspondence; Judge Flora Barth Wolf, the daughter of the *Washington Post*'s editorialist Alan Barth, who has vivid memories of growing in Washington in the years of the Red Scare; Patricia McMahon Fox, the observant daughter of Senator Brien McMahon; Douglas J. Richardson, Chief of Interpretation, the National Park Service, Department of the Interior, who took me through the Truman-Young family farmhouse, in Grandview, Missouri, and passed on some of his immense knowledge of the Truman family; Rachel List, who located an unpublished memoir by her father, the pianist Eugene List, who entertained Truman, Stalin, and Churchill in Potsdam; Peter Wievel and Henriette Harris, new friends in Berlin, who helped make the excursion to Potsdam and Babelsberg especially rewarding; Fredrik Logevall, the foremost chronicler of

America's wars in Southeast Asia (and author of a superb in-progress biography of John F. Kennedy), for his invaluable advice and detailed suggestions after reading my chapters on the Korean conflict; Joe Lelyveld, who wrote the authoritative account of Franklin D. Roosevelt's dying days, and became an astute encourager over dinners and lunches at Barney Greengrass; the China scholar Chen Jian, who answered my questions on Chinese involvement in Korea; the author and travel writer Tom Miller, who alerted me to the engaging memoir of his uncle Edward Harris. More thanks go to manuscript reference librarian Lewis Wyman, at the Library of Congress; James Cross, manuscripts archivist, at Clemson University Libraries; archivists Sarah Cunningham and Nicole Haddad, at the LBJ Library, in Austin, Texas; archivist James W. Zobel, at the Douglas MacArthur Memorial, in Norfolk, Virginia; Keith Call, Special Collections Assistant, Wheaton College; Eric Simonoff, for his early pro bono encouragement; Sandra McElwaine, my onetime colleague at the legendary *Washington Star*, who introduced me to David Acheson; Crary Pullen, who expertly rounded up the photos; the China expert and favorite son, T.A. Frank; and my wife, Diana Crone Frank, who has been the center of my life from the day we met.

Notes

Frequently Used Abbreviations

COHP: Columbia University Oral History Project

FRUS: Foreign Relations of the United States

HM: Henry Morgenthau Diaries (at the Franklin D. Roosevelt Library)

HSTL: Harry S. Truman Library and Museum

LBJL: Lyndon Baines Johnson Library and Museum

LOC: Library of Congress

MHDC: Miscellaneous Historical Documents Collection (at the HSTL)

NYPL: New York Public Library

MT: Margaret Truman

PPP: Post-presidential Papers (at the Truman Library)

PSF: President's Secretary's Files (Truman Papers, at the Truman Library)

YUL: Yale University Libraries

PROLOGUE: The Missourian

ix *"The first time you are in Washington"*: Sherwood, *Roosevelt and Hopkins*, p. 918.

ix *That was not surprising*: "Harry Truman . . . again?," *Ladies' Home Journal*, March 1948, p. 38; *Autobiography*, p. 3.

ix *"What a story in democracy"*: "Truman to Shelve Personal Rule," *New York Times*, April 15, 1945, p. 5.

x *making what he called "jump decisions"*: Heller, *Truman White House*, pp. 98–99.

x *nervously high-strung*: Catledge, *My Life and Times*, p. 71.

x *the "champion axman"*: "Truman Is Champion," *Washington Post*, April 6, 1952, p. B1.

xi *with a hard g*: "Margaret Truman," *New York Times*, January 12, 2008, p. 1.

xii *"He wouldn't be asking"*: HSTL, OH-Elsey, 2-10-64.

xii *"the World as it should be"*: HSTL, PSF, Longhand Notes, ca. December 1947.

xii   *"It is a most amazing spectacle"*: HSTL, PSF, Longhand Notes, 9-20-45.

xii   *Yet he once said:* "Truman Hints He'd Seize Press, Like Steel . . . ," *New York Herald Tribune*, April 18, 1952, p. 1.

xii   *He believed that he understood:* Heller, *Truman White House*, p. 180.

xiii *"Hindsight is not"*: Amos Elon, *The Pity of It All: A History of Jews in Germany, 1743–1933* (New York: Henry Holt, 2003), p. 12.

xiii *Gunther described him:* Gunther, *Inside U.S.A.*, p. 341.

xiii *John is seated:* HSTL, photo, John and Martha on their wedding day; *America* magazine, " 'Mama' Truman and Her Presidential Son," Joseph McCauley, 5-8-16.

xiv   *where she studied music, art, and literature:* Hamby, *Man of the People*, p. 6; Ferrell, *Truman & Pendergast*, p. 6.

xiv   *Before Quantrill:* See, for example, McPherson, *Battle Cry of Freedom*, pp. 784–86; Stiles, *Jesse James*, pp. 50, 70–72.

xiv   *Harry loved to read:* HSTL, Ayers Papers, Box 22, "Statement of the Military Career of Harry Truman."

xiv   *had a special affinity for Gustavus Adolphus:* HSTL, PSF, Longhand Notes of Judge Harry Truman, 5-14-34.

xiv   *"They may look like an ill-considered group"*: Appendix to *Congressional Record*, "The Rise of Pendergast's Protégé, " 9-20-44, p. A4215.

xv   *an ophthalmologist called "flat eyeball"*: HSTL, Daniels Papers, Interview, 7-28-49; Ferrell, *A Life*, p. 10.

xv   *"eat unleavened bread"*: "Harry S. Truman's Turning Point," *Kansas City Star*, May 24, 1931, p. 54.

xv   *"Mothers held him up as a model"*: "Harry Truman, Musician," *New York Times*, June 18, 1950, SM10.

xv   *"He had the most remarkable voice"*: LBJL, Merle Miller, Tape 4. See also Ferrell, *Harry S. Truman*, p. 25; Richard Lawrence Miller, *Truman*, p. 206.

xv   *at the Union National Bank:* "Harry S. Truman's Turning Point," *Kansas City Star*, May 24, 1931, p. 54.

xv   *"I had the best time"*: HSTL, PSF, Longhand Notes, 5-14-34.

xv   *"Just think of me arising"*: HSTL, PSF, Papers Pertaining to Family, Business and Personal Affairs, 12-30-13.

xvi   *Harry's parents slept:* Author's visit, 5-8-2018.

xvi   *The farm did well:* Richard S. Kirkendall, "Harry S. Truman, A Missouri Farmer in the Golden Age," *Agricultural History*, October 1972, pp. 467–83; Hamby, *Man of the People*, p. 27.

xvi   *"I'd never had another"*: HSTL, PSF, Longhand Notes of Judge Harry S. Truman, 5-14-34.

xvi   *With the rank of captain:* HSTL, Ayers Papers, Box 22, "Statement of the Military Career of Harry Truman."

xvi   *"I didn't think it was right"*: HSTL, PSF, Longhand Notes of Judge Harry S. Truman, 5-14-34.

xvi   *He promised that he "wouldn't look"*: HSTL, Ayers Papers, Box 22, "Statement of the Military Career of Harry Truman."

xvii *"the farmer who was threatening"*: MT, *Bess W. Truman*, p. 56.

xvii   *"The bullet came out"*: See also "David Wallace . . . ," *St. Louis Republic*, June 18, 1903, p. 2.

xvii   *That family history:* Multiple sources, but see, particularly, MT, *Bess W. Truman*; also *Kansas City Star*, December 5, 1952.

xvii   *"a fine Jewish boy":* HSTL, PSF, Longhand Notes of Judge Harry S. Truman, 5-14-34.

xvii   *"I'm the boss":* Milligan, *Missouri Waltz*, p. 47.

xviii   *Over the years:* "After Four Years . . . ," *New York Times*, April 10, 1949, SM7.

xviii   *he never officially became a member:* Miller, *Truman*, p. 172.

xviii   *to build superior, hard-surfaced roads:* HSTL, OH-John W. Snyder, 11-8-67.

xviii   *"and efficient administration":* "The Service of Judge Truman," *Kansas City Star*, November 2, 1930, p. 24.

xviii   *"Congressman pays $7,500":* HSTL, Papers Pertaining to Family, Business, and Personal Affairs, Letter to Bess, 4-23-33.

 xix   *He was called a "Pendergast office boy":* HST, *Autobiography*, p. 131; Daniels, *Man of Independence*, p. 172.

 xix   *in the senator's private office:* "Hangs T.J.'s Picture," *Marshfield Mail*, January 17, 1935, p. 1.

 xix   *without moving his lips:* https://www.senate.gov/artandhistory/history/common /generic/SOS_Leslie_Biffle.htm.

 xix   *"Then one discovered":* Acheson, *Sketches from Life*, pp. 131–32.

 xix   *might come from the tap:* William P. Helm, *Harry Truman*, p. 11.

 xx   *"You were anxious about my evenings":* Ferrell, *Dear Bess*, 7-31-39, p. 416.

 xx   *Truman faced another three-way primary:* "Pendergast Again Issue . . . ," *New York Times*, August 4, 1940, p. 62.

 xx   *"I sent word":* HSTL, Jonathan Daniels Papers, Interview, 8-30-49.

 xxi   *"I'll never forget Tuesday night":* Ferrell, *Dear Bess*, 9-9-40, p. 441.

 xxi   *called "preposterous":* "Clark and Truman Back . . . ," *St. Louis Post-Dispatch*, February 25, 1942, p. 3; "Speak Out on Hannegan," *St. Louis Post-Dispatch*, February 28, 1942, p.4.

 xxi   *before wrapping up:* "Army Says It Cut . . . ," *New York Times*, April 15, 1943, p. 17; "Billion-Dollar Watchdog," *Time*, March 8, 1943, pp. 13–15.

 xxi   *"You assure that this is for a specific purpose":* YUL, Stimson Diary, 6-17-43, Reel 8, pp. 121–22.

xxii   *"is being carried out in a wasteful manner":* Stoff and Fanton, *The Manhattan Project*, p. 51.

xxii   *Truman's "ugly letter":* YUL, Stimson Diary, Reel 8, pp. 90–92, 3-10-44.

xxii   *"talks smoothly":* Ibid., 3-13-44, p. 96.

xxii   *"merely carrying out":* Ibid., 3-13-44, p. 93.

xxii   *"One just didn't ask":* Conant, *My Several Lives*, p. 297.

xxii   *friends who hadn't been near him:* Catledge, *My Life and Times*, p. 144; Flynn, *You're the Boss*, pp. 178–79.

xxii   *There had been occasional newspaper stories:* See, for instance, "President Is Recovering," *New York Times*, November 4, 1944, p. 19; "Roosevelt Loses 10 Lb.," *New York Times*, January 18, 1944, p. 40.

xxii *"stamina is far above the average"*: "President's Health Called Better Than Ever," *New York Times*, January 29, 1944, p. 15.

xxii *the prognosis was exceedingly grim*: See, for example, Lelyveld, *His Final Battle*, pp. 96–97; Ferrell, *The Dying President*, p. 23; Walker, *FDR's Quiet Confidant*, note, p. 181; "Clinical Notes on the Illness and Death of President Franklin D. Roosevelt," *Annals of Internal Medicine* (1970).

xxiii *When Roosevelt reappeared*: "Roosevelt Is Back," *New York Herald Tribune*, May 8, 1944, p. 1A.

xxiii *He waited until July 11*: FDR Press Conferences 7-7-44 and 7-11-44, http://www.fdrlibrary.marist.edu; "Roosevelt Talks to Hannegan," *New York Herald Tribune*, July 8, 1944, p. 1; "Roosevelt Expected to Request . . . ," *New York Herald Tribune*, July 12, 1944, p. 1A. See also Ferrell, *Truman in the White House*, pp. 157+. Childs, *Witness to Power*, p. 9.

xxiii *That gave Byrnes control*: Robertson, *Sly and Able*, p. 5.

xxiv *Before the vice presidency*: Macdonald, *Henry Wallace*, p. 42; Walker, *FDR's Quiet Confidant*, p. 177; Michelson, *The Ghost Talks*, p. 197; "'41 Book Cited Silly Letters . . . ," *New York Herald Tribune*, May 4, 1944, p. 11A.

xxiv *The social critic Dwight MacDonald*: Macdonald, *Henry Wallace*, p. 118. See also Alex Ross, "Uncommon Man," *New Yorker*, July 14, 2013.

xxiv *Roosevelt worried*: Weiss, *The President's Man*, p. 193.

xxiv *"opposition to every measure sought by Negroes"*: White, *A Man Called White*, pp. 266–67.

xxv *intelligence and aspiration*: See a celebratory, and not entirely reliable, video portrait of Byrnes, https://www.knowitall.org/video/james-f-byrnes-palmetto-special.

xxv *an "odd, sharply angular face"*: "Sly and Able," *Saturday Evening Post*, July 20, 1940, p. 18.

xxv *the "smartest politician I knew"*: Catledge, *My Life and the Times*, p. 71.

xxv *"more a private language to himself"*: Robertson, *Sly and Able*, p. 7.

xxvi *Roosevelt had also been thinking*: Sherwood, *Roosevelt and Hopkins*, p. 881.

xxvi *and the newspapers had begun to pick up*: See, for instance, " . . . Will Not Dictate Nomination," *New York Herald Tribune*, July 5, 1944, p. 1A.

xxvi *Roosevelt sometimes dodged arguments*: Rosenman, *Working with Roosevelt*, pp. 440–43.

xxvi *"Boys, I guess it's Truman"*: Walker, *FDR's Quiet Confidant*, p. 140.

xxvi *"Hope it will be fun"*: HSTL, MT Diary, 7-17-44.

xxvi *a specially constructed Pullman*: Author's visit, April 16, 2017. The *Ferdinand Magellan* may be seen, and boarded, at the Gold Coast Railroad Museum, in Miami; www.gcrm.org.

xxvi *"If I were a delegate"*: HSTL, Miscellaneous Historical Documents, Box 17, 7-1-44.

xxvi *asked Truman to nominate him*: Daniels, *White House Witness*, p. 239.

xxvii *Margaret in her diary wrote, "Ye Gods!"*: HSTL, MT Diary, 7-19-44.

xxvii *"One thing we forgot"*: Byrnes, *All in One Lifetime*, pp. 226–27.

xxvii *Hannegan later denied*: "Hannegan Decries . . . ," *New York Times*, September 15, 1944, p. 13.

xxvii *"his stock appeared to slip"*: "Democrats Face Many-Sided Battle . . . ," *New York Times*, July 19, 1944, p. 1.

xxvii *"Tell him to go to hell"*: Daniels, *Man of Independence*, p. 232.

xxvii *Truman's initial response*: Donovan, *Conflict and Crisis*, p. xiii.

xxvii *he was "forced into it by Pres. Roosevelt himself"*: HSTL, PSF, Longhand Notes, undated 1952.

xxvii *"in deference to the wishes of the President"*: "Sharp Race Looms . . . ," *New York Times*, July 20, 1944, p. 10.

xxvii *"Next to me was a lobster"*: Nick Clarke, *Alistair Cooke*, pp. 197–98.

xxviii *a "very spiffy affair"*: MT, *Bess*, p. 161; "Large Number at White House," *New York Times*, April 7, 1937, p. 22.

xxviii *saw each other eight times*: See FDR's daily schedule at http://www.fdrlibrary .marist.edu/daybyday.

xxviii *"I don't think I saw Roosevelt but twice"*: Daniels, *Man of Independence*, p. 259.

xxviii *"They didn't tell me anything"*: Wallace, *Diary*, May, 18, 1945, p. 451–52.

xxviii *"I don't think Father thought about him"*: James Roosevelt, *My Parents*, p. 165.

xxviii *he'd refer to Roosevelt as a "fakir"*: HSTL, Papers Pertaining to Family, Business, and Personal Affairs, Letter to Bess, 6-15-46.

xxviii *"The Pres. took his coat off and I had to"*: MT, *Letters from Father*, p. 58.

xxix *They sat on the South Lawn*: "President, Truman Map the Campaign," *New York Herald Tribune*, August 19, 1944, p. 6.

xxix *Truman recounted more of this*: MT, *Letters from Father*, pp. 57–58; Ferrell, *Dear Bess*, pp. 509–10.

xxix *"He's keen as a briar"*: "Democratic Ticket Maps Campaign Plans," *New York Herald Tribune*, August 19, 1944, p. 7.

xxix *"physically he's just going to pieces"*: HSTL, OH-Harry Vaughan; Ferrell, *Dying President*, p. 89; Ferrell, *Dear Bess*, p. 238.

xxix *"played at the wrong speed"*: Thomas Fleming, "Eight Days with Harry Truman," *American Heritage*, August-September 1992.

xxix *The subject of Roosevelt's health*: "Truman Sees Party Victory," *Baltimore Sun*, October 17, 1944, p. 9; "Truman Can't Picture Dewey as President," *New York Times*, October 17, 1944, p. 9.

xxx *He "read his ghostwritten speeches slowly and mechanically"*: Allen and Shannon, *Truman Merry-Go-Round*, p. 14.

xxx *"You can't afford to take a chance"*: "Truman Warns U.S . . . ," *New York Herald Tribune*, October 15, 1944, p. 29.

xxx *"surprised to find Truman"*: Morris, *Let the Chips Fall*, p. 5.

xxx *"and he was playing Mozart"*: "Harry Truman, Musician," *New York Times*, June 18, 1950, SM10.

xxx *seemed, to Truman, to be in pain*: HSTL, PPP, Box 643, Interviews with Truman by David Noyes and William Hillman, 1-25-54.

xxxi *He spoke for six minutes*: "Roosevelt Says . . . ," *New York Herald Tribune*, January 21, 1945, p. 1; Phillips, *Truman Presidency*, p. 1; HSTL, OH-Carleton Kent, 12-21-70.

xxxi *among them Bernard Baruch . . . and Helen Keller*: "Luncheon Marked by Informality," *New York Times*, January 21, 1945, p. 27; *Sunday Star*, January 21, 1945, pp. 1, 6.

xxxi   *"If you have any urgent messages":* HSTL, PSF, 1-22-45.

xxxi   *"These were the things we talked about":* HST, *Mr. Citizen*, p. 165.

xxxii   *the ranking "diners out":* "Truman Dines in Glow," *Kansas City Star*, February 18, 1945, p. 2A.

xxxii   *"Not since the days of Charlie Curtis":* "Vice President Makes Hit with Hostesses," *Washington Post*, February 6, 1945, p. 10.

xxxii   *"one of the most sumptuous feasts since the war":* "Truman Dines in Glow," *Kansas City Star*, February 18, 1945, p. 4; "Mrs. McLean Gives Dinner," *Washington Post*, February 18, 1945, p. S1; "Truman to Social Peak," *Kansas City Star*, February 17, 1945, p. 1.

xxxii   *a dinner . . . at the Sulgrave club:* "President and Mrs. Truman Are Honor Guests . . . ," *Washington Evening Star*, March 9, 1945, p. B3; Mesta, *Perle*, pp. 98, 100–101; JFK Library, OH-Bundy-Neustadt, March, May 1964.

xxxiii   *"the capital's No. 1 social butterfly":* "Capital Makes . . . ," *Chicago Tribune*, March 12, 1945, p. 16.

xxxiii   *"Wow, she's really a sizzler!":* "Lauren Bacall Aids Show," *Washington Post*, February 11, 1945, p. M4; for more on this, see Margaret Truman's talk at the National Press Club, recorded by C-SPAN: https://www.c-span.org/video/?60197 -1/memories-president-truman&start=$].

xxxiii   *"an informed interpreter of Administration policy":* *Christian Science Monitor*, March 9, 1945, p. 18.

xxxiii   *"we could not have found a worse place":* FRUS, Conferences at Malta and Yalta, Log of the Trip, 2-2-45.

xxxiii   *"infested with vermin":* "Clinical Notes on the Illness and Death of President Franklin D. Roosevelt," *Annals of Internal Medicine* (1970).

xxxiii   *"You either have to castrate the German people":* Smith, *American Diplomacy*, p. 121.

xxxiv   *an arrival preceded by rumors:* HSTL, PPP, Box 643, Discussion, Interviewed by Hillman and Noyes, 1-23-54.

xxxiv   *an odd, almost conversational speech:* "Report . . . ," *New York Times*, March 2, 1945, p. 12; "F.D.R. Rambles . . . ," *Chicago Tribune*, March 2, 1945, p. 9.

xxxiv   *Mrs. Roosevelt saw the decision:* Bernard Asbell, in *Mother and Daughter: The Letters of Eleanor & Anna Roosevelt* (New York: Fromm International, 1988), p. 184.

xxxiv   *Truman said it was his suggestion:* HSTL, PPP, Box 643, interviews with HST by David Noyes and William Hillman, 1-25-54.

xxxv   *Truman "looked spick and span":* Drury, *Senate Journal*, pp. 388-90.

xxxv   *asked for a bit of friendly patronage:* HSTL, PSF, Longhand Notes, 4-5-45 and 4-7-45.

xxxv   *"it's my job to get 'em prayed for":* HSTL, Papers of Harry S. Truman Pertaining to Family, Business, and Personal Affairs, Box 688, 4-11-45.

xxxv   *"Turn on your radio":* HST, *Memoirs I*, p. 6.

xxxv   *Truman had otherwise been looking forward to a poker game:* HSTL, OH-Edward McKim, 1-18-64 and 2-16-64.

xxxvi   *"but we'll be a little bit late":* Ibid., 2-16-64 and 1-18-64.

xxxvi   *The call was from Steve Early:* Phillips, *Truman Presidency*, p. 5.

xxxvi *Early asked him to come:* HSTL, Papers of Harry S. Truman Pertaining to Family, Business, and Personal Affairs, Box 688, 4-16-45.

xxxvi *"He just jammed his hat on his head":* "Truman, 60, Takes Oath . . . ," *New York Herald Tribune*, April 13, 1945, pp. 1A, 8.

xxxvi *By then, Early had telephoned:* Levin, *Making of FDR*, p. 428.

xxxvi *It was nearly dark:* Daniels, *Man of Independence*, p. 28.

xxxvi *"Tell us what we can do":* HSTL, Papers of Harry S. Truman Pertaining to Family, Business, and Personal Affairs Box 688, 4-16-45, HST to Mary Jane and Martha.

xxxvi *He telephoned Bess:* MT, *Bess*, p. 249.

xxxvi *"quite a long wait":* YUL, Stimson Diary, 4-12-45, Reel 9, p. 88.

xxxvii *Close by were members:* Daniels, *Man of Independence*, pp. 289–90; "Baffling Biffle . . . ," *Washington Post*, February 25, 1945, p. B6.

xxxvii *Truman looked nervous and pale:* "Truman, 60, Takes Oath . . . ," *New York Herald Tribune*, April 13, 1945, pp. 1A, 8; "Truman Is Sworn In . . . ," *New York Times*, April 13, 1945, p. 1.

xxxvii *At first no one said anything:* Henry Morgenthau Diaries, April 12, 1945.

xxxvii *Secretary of Labor Frances Perkins:* Stettinius, *Diaries*, p. 314; Biddle, *In Brief Authority*, p. 360.

xxxvii *"about an immense project":* HST, *Memoirs I*, p. 10.

xxxvii *in a neighbor's apartment:* Daniels, *White House Witness*, p. 283.

xxxvii *"The desk had been swept clean":* Daniels, *Man of Independence*, p. 27.

xxxviii *"I'm not big enough for this job":* LBJL, OH-Aiken, 10-10-68.

xxxviii *To reporters who'd trailed him:* "Truman's First Word to Press . . . ," *New York Herald Tribune*, April 14, 1945, p. 5.

xxxviii *"Even the declaration of war didn't compare":* HSTL, OH-General William Draper, 1-11-72.

xxxviii *Distracted elevator operators:* Federal Diary, *Washington Post*, April 14, 1945, p. 5.

xxxviii *"I greeted him as an old friend":* HST, *Memoirs I*, p. 33.

xxxviii *"He has not hesitated to gut every friend he had":* Brown, *James F. Byrnes*, pp. 222–23.

xxxviii *"I am so distressed":* New York Times, April 13, 1945, p. 8.

xxxix *"I'm just private citizen James F. Byrnes":* "Byrnes Agrees to Be . . . ," *New York Herald Tribune*, April 14, 1945, p. 1A.

xxxix *Newspaper stories were already suggesting:* "Truman Holds Lengthy Talk . . . ," *Baltimore Sun*, April 15, 1945, p. 1.

xxxix *It included a memorandum:* HSTL, Naval Aide Files, Crimea.

xxxix *"both wisdom and bigness" on Truman's part:* Christian Science Monitor, April 16, 1945, p. 18.

xxxix *Truman once called him:* "Presidential Advisers . . . ," *New York Times*, April 22, 1945, p. E10.

xl *No one stood:* Sherwood, *Roosevelt and Hopkins*, p. 881.

xl *Anna and Elliott Roosevelt:* "Rites at Capital," *New York Herald Tribune*, April 15, 1945, p. 1A.

xl *was being treated at the Mayo Clinic:* "Hopkins Quits to Rest . . . ," *New York Herald Tribune*, July 4, 1945, p. 1a.

xl *The service . . . was over in twenty-three minutes:* "Mrs. Roosevelt Leads Family," *New York Herald Tribune*, April 15, 1945, p. 2; "500,000 Mourners . . . ," *Washington Evening Star*, April 14, 1945, p. 1; "Truman to Hold First Talk . . . ," *Washington Evening Star*, April 15, 1945, p. 6; "White House Scene . . . ," *New York Times*, April 15, 1945, p. 3m; some of the day is on YouTube: https://www.youtube.com/watch?v=Swy07ewx-ds].

xl *Harry Vaughan soon came running:* "White House scene . . . ," *New York Times* April 15, 1945, p. 3.

xl *Byrnes was busy:* "Byrnes Rumored as Successor . . . ," *Atlanta Constitution*, April 17, 1945, p. 2.

xl *Byrnes "never left Truman's side":* Lash, *World of Love*, pp. 184–85.

xl *"clung to him as if they were afraid":* Biddle, *In Brief Authority*, p. 364.

xli *"I know little of the project":* Stoff and Fanton, *The Manhattan Project*, Document 33, Byrnes to FDR, 3-3-44.

xli *The applause was loudest:* "Truman Asks Congress for Its Fullest Aid," *New York Herald Tribune*, April 17, 1945, p. 1A.

xli *"maybe it will come out all right":* HSTL, Papers Pertaining to Family, Business, and Personal Affairs, Box 688, 4-16-45.

xli *a "wholesome sense of inadequacy":* COHP, Steelman, p. 234.

xlii *"I want to keep my feet on the ground":* Truman reportedly to Clark Clifford; Lilienthal, *Journals*, Volume Two, p. 434.

xlii *"I did what I thought was right":* MT, *Where the Buck Stops*, p. 206.

xliii *"We know . . . that what is at stake here":* "Warns Aggressors," *New York Times*, July 20, 1950, p. 1.

xliv *"And poor H.S.T.":* The Papers of Dwight David Eisenhower, Volume 11, Part 5, Chapter 11, pp. 1409–10, 11-6-50.

xliv *" 'I should think he has' ":* Lord Moran, *Churchill: Taken from the Diaries of Lord Moran* (Boston: Houghton Mifflin, 1977), p. 293.

ONE: President Truman

1 *"Just two months ago today":* HSTL, Papers of Harry S. Truman Pertaining to Family, Business, and Personal Affairs, 6-12-45.

1 *"Don't shoot the piano player":* Quoted in "Washington on Review," *Kansas City Star*, October 7, 1945, p. 14A.

1 *"Confusion and uncertainty prevail":* HSTL, Ayers Papers Diary, Box 19, 4-14-45 + 4-16-45.

1 *"a man of bouncing enthusiasms":* New Republic, December 29, 1947, p. 19.

1 *"I have no desire to remain here":* HSTL, Ayers Papers, Diary, Box 19, 4-14-45 + 4-16-45.

2 *"It was a dreadful time":* HSTL, OH-Robert Nixon, 10-19-70.

2 *"I've paid the rent":* HSTL, Papers Pertaining to Family, Business, and Personal Affairs, Box 688, 4-16-45; HSTL, PSF, 6-1-45; "The Palace Guard Changes . . . ," *Newsweek*, April 23, 1945, pp. 32–33.

2 *"intimated any such thing":* John J. McCloy World War II Diaries, July 20, 1945.

2   *"I was handicapped by lack of knowledge"*: HSTL, Truman Papers, PSF, *Diary*, May 6, 1948.

3   *"abnormally equipped with energy"*: "Plenipotentiary-II," *New Yorker*, May 10, 1952, p. 36.

3   *"A country's policies"*: "Plenipotentiary-I," *New Yorker*, May 3, 1952, p. 42.

3   *an ornate maze:* Described by Walter Bedell Smith in *My Three Years in Moscow*, p. 49.

3   *"He greeted me in silence"*: LOC, Harriman Papers, Box 678, April 13, 1945.

3   *The Russians were consumed:* Ibid., April 10, 1945.

4   *"the capacity to make decisions"*: Harriman and Abel, *Special Envoy*, pp. 447–49.

4   *"And keep on sending me long messages"*: HST, *Memoirs I*, pp. 86–88.

4   *"[they] need us more than we need them"*: Harriman and Abel, *Special Envoy*, pp. 447–49; HST, *Memoirs I*, pp. 86–88.

4   *He'd told Stettinius:* Stettinius, *Diaries of Edward R. Stettinius, Jr*, p. 318.

4   *"like people from across the tracks"*: Wallace, *Diary*, p. 451.

4   *"these barbarians"*: LOC, Joseph E. Davies Papers, Box 18, conversation with WAH, 7-17-45.

5   *Molotov . . . who'd stopped in Washington:* "Truman Moves to Establish . . . ," *Christian Science Monitor*, April 16, 1945, pp. 16, 18; "Stalin Sends Molotov . . . ," *New York Herald Tribune*, April 16, 1945, p. 17; "Molotov in . . . ," *New York Herald Tribune*, April 23, 1945, p. 1A.

5   *Molotov was no ordinary foreign minister:* HSTL, OH-Durbrow, 5-31-73; Djilas, *Conversations with Stalin*, p. 62.

5   *"deliberate, composed and tenacious"*: Ibid., pp. 69–71.

5   *When he saw Truman the next day:* HSTL, Daily Appointments of Harry S. Truman, April 23, 1945.

6   *"Carry out your agreements"*: Bohlen, *Witness to History*, pp. 212–13; HST, *Memoirs I*, p. 85.

6   *a change in Truman's tone:* Cheuv, *Molotov Remembers*, p. 55.

6   *"This is rendered imperative"*: Stalin's *Correspondence with Roosevelt and Truman, 1941–1945*, April 23, 1945, pp. 420–21.

6   *"I gave it to him straight"*: LOC, Joseph E. Davies Papers, Box 16, Chrono File, April 17, 1945.

6   *"Molotov was shaken and went pale"*: LOC, Davies Papers, Box 16, Handwritten Notes, Journal, April 30, 1945.

7   *"After the caller left"*: Hechler, *Working with Truman*, p. 53.

7   *"I think it is very important"*: YUL, Stimson Diary, Reel 9, 4-24-45; Truman, *Memoirs I*, p. 85.

7   *They spent about forty-five minutes:* Barton Bernstein, "Reconsidering the Atomic General," *Journal of Military History* (July, 2003).

7   *"the biggest fool thing"*: HST *Memoirs* I, p. 21.

7   *"we were perfecting"*: HST, Ibid., p. 11.

8   *Stimson remembered too:* YUL, Stimson Diary, Reel 9, 4-25-45.

8   *His first impression:* Ibid., April 18, 1945.

8   *evidence of bestiality and cruelty:* The Papers of Dwight David Eisenhower,

Vol. 4, Part 10, Chapter 28, Letter to Marshall, 7-19-45, p. 2623. See also pp. 2616–19.

8   *"an overanticipated thrill":* Berlin, *Washington Despatches 1941–45*, p. 553.

8   *"fading power for evil":* "V-E Spurs Forces . . . ," *New York Times*, May 8, 1945, p. 5.

9   *which Truman proclaimed as a time:* One may watch the speech on YouTube, https://www.youtube.com/watch?v=nV-go1cuzgE].

9   *It was her first time in Washington:* HSTL, Ayers Papers, Box 14, 5-11-45.

9   *"Oh fiddlesticks!":* "Truman's Mother . . . ," *New York Times*, May 12, 1945, p. 15.

9   *He disliked words like "progressive":* Lilienthal, *Journals*, Volume Two, p. 434, quoting Clark Clifford.

9   *found the transition especially hard, even wrenching:* See, for example, Biddle, *In Brief Authority*, p. 365; Berlin, *Letters*, p. 555; Wallace, *Diary*, p. 451.

10   *that Jimmy Byrnes would soon replace him:* "Capital Hears Byrnes May Become . . . ," *Boston Globe*, April 16, 1945, p. 1.

10   *"of distinction and usefulness":* "President Truman," *New York Herald Tribune*, April 17, 1945, p. 25; "Byrnes Declines Position," *Wall Street Journal*, April 18, 1945, p. 4; "Byrnes Rumored . . . ," *Atlanta Constitution*, April 17, 1945, p. 2; *New York Herald Tribune*, April 17 1945, p. 23; *New York Herald Tribune*, April 27, 1945, p. 23; Berlin, *Letters*, 546–47.

10   *He sometimes used the salutation "Dear Harry":* Messer, *End of an Alliance*, p. 66.

10   *Truman began his press conference:* Presidential news conference, May 23, 1945.

10   *Biddle . . . had refused to go along:* Biddle, *In Brief Authority*, p. 365.

11   *"abrupt and undignified":* Ibid.

11   *Truman later remembered:* HST, *Memoirs I*, p. 325.

11   *"knows how to work on the team":* HSTL, PSF, Box 135, handwritten note, April 18, 1945.

11   *Truman's Missouri ally Bob Hannegan:* "Missouri Past and Washington Present," *New York Herald Tribune* August 31, 1949, p. 17.

11   *They'd been neighbors:* Childs, *Witness to Power*, p. 12.

11   *"a lot of nervous energy":* Henry Morgenthau Diaries, 4-1-45.

11   *left "with the distinct feeling":* Ibid., 5-9-45.

11   *a "block head, nut":* Poen, *Strictly Personal*, pp. 76–77 (unsent letter, February 26, 1950).

12   *"The talk around town":* Henry Morgenthau Diaries, 6-1-45.

12   *"the laughing lobbyist":* " 'Kind-to-Hannegan' Week," *Washington Evening Star*, April 2, 1946, p. A-7.

12   *"court jester, adviser, and wire-puller":* "The Mysterious Mr. Allen," *Saturday Evening Post*, January 5, 1946, p. 17; "The Regular Guys," *Time*, August 12, 1946, pp. 17–19.

12   *When Stettinius asked:* Stettinius, *Diary*, Calendar Notes, June 21, 1945, p. 399.

13   *Six of FDR's ten:* "Truman's Ordeal," *Atlanta Constitution*, April 19, 1945, p. 7.

13   *"the sort to be conspicuous good fellows":* Alsop, *Reporter's Trade*, pp. 97–98.

13   *"worthy and honourable mediocrities":* Berlin, *Letters*, pp. 555–58.

13 *he was "rarely relaxed and comfortable":* Clifford, *Counsel to the President,* pp. 69–70.

13 *"Oh you can't leave me":* COHP, Steelman, p. 118.

13 *arthritis and heart ailments:* Hersey, *Aspects of the Presidency,* p. 13.

13 *a "stooped, lean, tired figure":* Allen and Shannon, *Truman Merry-Go-Round,* p. 55.

13 *He was trusted by reporters:* For a closer look, see Walter Davenport, "Charlie Ross, Press Secretary," *Collier's,* November 17, 1945, p. 33; Fletcher Knebel, "We Shall All Miss Him," *Magazine of Sigma Chi,* March 1951, pp. 2–9: HSTL, OH-Elsey, 2-17-64.

14 *"I just want to get the ordeal over with":* HSTL, PSF, Box 190, First Year, Press Conferences, 5-2-45.

14 *"Are you going to go slow today?":* Ibid., 6-13-45.

14 *"When things come to that stage":* Ferrell, *Dear Bess,* p. 515.

TWO: Terminal

15 *"I am getting ready":* HSTL, Papers Pertaining to Family, Business, and Personal Affairs, Box 688, 7-3-45.

15 *"gravely concerned and alarmed":* LOC, Davies Papers, Box 16, 5-13-45.

15 *"with ability and dignity":* Ibid., Diary and Letter to Molotov, 5-2-45.

16 *had asked Jack Warner to make it:* See more on this in Ronald Radosh and Allis Radosh, "A Great Historic Mistake: The Making of 'Mission to Moscow,'" in *Film History* 16, No. 4, "Politics and Film" (2004): 358–77.

16 *"A child would like to sit in his lap and a dog would sidle up to him":* Joseph Edward Davies, *Mission to Moscow* (New York: Simon & Schuster, 1941), p. 312.

16 *"a shallow and politically ambitious man":* "Reflections," *New Yorker,* February 25, 1985, pp. 57–58. See also Kennan's memoir, *At the Century's Ending, Reflections, 1982–1995.*

16 *urged him to meet with Stalin:* LOC, Davies Papers, Box 16, Visit with Truman, 5-13-45.

16 *He suggested Alaska or Siberia:* HSTL, PSF, Longhand Notes, 5-22-45.

16 *the phrase "Iron Curtain":* Sherwood, *Roosevelt and Hopkins,* p. 910.

17 *"I was startled, shocked, and amazed":* LOC, Davies Papers, Box 17, 5-21-45.

17 *"only half in this world":* Moran, *Churchill,* p. 243.

17 *"po dushe"—"from the soul":* Bohlen, *Witness to History,* p. 244.

17 *Truman told Stettinius:* Stettinius, *Diary,* Calendar Notes, pp. 377–78.

17 *"some unshattered town":* Churchill, *Defending the West,* pp. 67, 70.

17 *"Uncle Joe should make some sort of gesture":* HSTL, PSF, Longhand Notes, 5-22-45.

17 *Stalin complained about American "misdeeds":* FRUS, The Genesis of the Conference, The Hopkins Mission to Moscow, pp. 61–62.

18 *"wherever he might be":* FRUS, Memorandum by Bohlen on Hopkins Stalin conversation, May 26, 1945, Potsdam, vol. I, pp. 26+.

18 *Harriman reported:* Ibid.

18 *Davies had been instructed:* LOC, Davies Papers, Box 16, Visit with Truman,

5-13-45; FRUS, Memorandum by Bohlen on Hopkins-Stalin conversation, May 26, 1945, Potsdam, vol. I, p. 65.

18 *becoming "quite emotional":* FRUS, "The Davies Mission to London," pp. 67–68.

18 *Roosevelt and Stalin enjoyed "ribbing" Churchill:* LOC, Davies Papers, Chrono Files, Box 16, 5-13-45; Birse, *Memoirs,* p. 156–56.

18 *"possibly the immediate Peace in real danger":* LOC, Davies Papers, Report to HST, 6-12-45.

19 *"one of the great figures of history":* Moran, *Churchill,* p. 322.

19 *"must now use it":* "New World Hope," *New York Times,* June 27, 1945, p. 1.

19 *"Oh, what a great day in history":* "United Nations Charter Signed," *New York Herald Tribune,* June 27, 1945, p. 1A.

19 *"Yes," Truman replied:* Stettinius, *Diary,* June 25, 1945, pp. 403–4.

19 *He said that . . . Stettinius:* "Stettinius Resigns," *New York Herald Tribune,* June 28, 1945, p. 1A.

19 *without a committee hearing:* "Senate Swiftly . . . ," *New York Herald Tribune,* July 3, 1945, p. 5.

19 *"alters completely the necessary qualifications":* "President Truman," *New York Herald Tribune,* April 17, 1945, p. 25.

20 *could do the job:* "Truman Backed by Growing Public Confidence . . . ," *New York Times,* July 1, 1945, p. 1.

20 *"That's the Reichsmarschall's baton," Charlie Ross informed reporters:* HSTL, PSF, Box 190, First Year.

20 *"I have a successor in mind":* "Morgenthau Out . . . ," *Courant,* July 6, 1945, p. 1; Presidential News Conference, July 5, 1945, https://www.presidency.ucsb.edu/documents/the-presidents-news-conference-412.

20 *and a favorite poker companion:* Clifford, *Counsel to the President,* pp. 69–70.

21 *"How I hate this trip":* HSTL, PSF, Longhand Notes, 7-7-45; HSTL, Papers Pertaining to Family, Business, and Personal Affairs, Box 688, 7-3-45.

21 *"I'm seeing all the good pictures we missed":* H. Freeman Matthews Papers, Correspondence, Box 5, Folder 2, Public Policy Papers, Department of Special Collections, Princeton University Library.

21 *"Right interesting to an artillery man":* HSTL, Papers Pertaining to Family, Business, and Personal Affairs, Box 688, 7-3-45.

21 *"He squeezed facts and opinions out of us":* Murphy, *Diplomat Among Warriors,* p. 269.

21 *"Nearly every memorandum has a catch in it":* HSTL, PSF, Longhand Notes, 6-1-45.

21 *Truman led correspondents:* "Atlantic Trip . . . ," *New York Herald Tribune,* July 11, 1945, p. 3; Leahy, *I Was There,* p. 387.

22 *He conferred every day:* Bohlen, *Witness to History,* pp. 225–26.

22 *"must be stripped of all extraordinary privileges":* Hull, *Memoirs,* Volume 2, p. 1524.

22 *"What has made Japan dangerous":* LOC, Archibald MacLeish papers, Box 4, Memo on Japan, 7-6-45.

22 *But with no one aboard to argue:* Bird, *The Chairman,* p. 250.

22 *The Augusta docked on July 15:* A film of the arrival shows Truman and his

entourage greeted by General Eisenhower, among others. It can be viewed at https://www.ushmm.org/wlc/en/media_fi.php?ModuleId=0&MediaId=219.

23 *"What is Belgrade like?":* Berlin, *Washington Despatches*, p. 557.

23 *Facing the possibility of defeat:* "Churchill Wind-Up," *New York Times*, July 4, 1945, p. 4; "Attlee Bares Site . . . ," *New York Times*, June 16, 1945, p. 1.

23 *six royal and imperial palaces:* "Install Phones . . . ," *Chicago Tribune*, July 5, 1945, p. 9.

23 *selected as the meeting place:* "Potsdam in a Strange Role," *Christian Science Monitor*, July 13, 1945, p. 16.

24 *"an oasis of material comfort":* Astley, *Inner Circle*, pp. 210, 213–14.

24 *amenities that included:* LOC, Joseph Davies Papers, Box 17, 7-13-45.

24 *Truman's "Little White House":* Author's visit.

24 *"His wife works in the neighborhood":* H. Freeman Matthews Papers, Box 5, letter, 7-25-45, Public Policy Papers, Department of Special Collections, Princeton University Library.

24 *"except for the heat and mosquitoes":* YUL, Stimson Diary, 7-15-45, Reel 9.

24 *They'd also very likely bugged the house:* https://www.cia.gov/library/center-for-the-study-of-intelligence/csi-publications/csi-studies/studies/vol49no3/html_files/FDR_Teheran_12.htm.

24 *"a bewilderment of ornate clocks":* "Where Did Stalin Live?," *Baltimore Sun*, August 3, 1945, p. 7.

24 *"a beautiful house":* Winston and Clementine. The Personal Letters of the Churchills (New York: Houghton Mifflin, 1999), p. 532.

24 *There would be no Stalin-Truman meeting:* H. Freeman Matthews Papers, Box 5, Folder 2, 7-25-45, Public Policy Papers, Department of Special Collections, Princeton University Library; Harriman and Abel, *Special Envoy*, p. 484; Murphy, *Diplomat Among Warriors*, p. 268.

25 *"He gave me a lot of hooey":* Ferrell, *Off the Record*, p. 52.

25 *"We should require time":* Moran, *Churchill*, p. 293; Leahy, *I Was There*, p. 399.

25 *"to do a little sightseeing":* Byrnes, *Speaking Frankly*, p. 68.

25 *No one seemed interested:* "Stalin Late . . . ," *New York Herald Tribune*, July 17, 1945, p. 1A.

25 *"There he is, the old one":* Moran, *Churchill*, pp. 288–91.

26 *"it was not hard to distinguish":* Leahy, *I Was There*, pp. 395–96.

26 *"found it hard to believe":* "Alanbrooke, *War Diaries*, p. 705.

26 *"There was a smell of death and decay":* Ismay, *Memoirs*, p. 402. A twenty-minute Russian film provides a remarkable look, in color, at bombed Berlin, as well as Babelsberg, and at the three leaders in Potsdam. There are no subtitles, but they're not needed. https://www.youtube.com/watch?v=CbFGcz22jqA]

26 *the "Hitler balcony":* Leahy, *I Was There*, p. 295.

26 *still "an impressive affair":* John J. McCloy Diaries, July 26, 1945.

26 *at Byrnes's urging, he stayed in the car:* Brown, *James F. Byrnes*, p. 271.

26 *Truman's reflections:* See, for instance, Leahy, *I Was There*, p. 395; Ismay, *Memoirs*, p. 402; and HST Potsdam travel log, 7-16-45, https://history.state.gov/historicaldocuments/frus1945Berlinv02/d710.

26 *"a great world tragedy":* HST, *Memoirs I*, p. 378.

27 *Churchill sat in an adjoining courtyard:* "Stalin Late . . . ," *New York Herald Tribune*, July 17, 1945, p. 1A.

27 *"I'll tell Stalin about this":* Ismay, *Memoirs*, p. 402; Moran, *Churchill*, pp. 288–91.

27 *a "pocketful of Nazi medals":* Elsey, *Unplanned Life*, p. 87.

27 *"so I felt less guilty":* John J. McCloy Diaries, 7-26-45.

27 *a macabre and slightly unsettling prank:* H. Freeman Matthews Papers, Box 6, private memoir, p. 628, Public Policy Papers, Department of Special Collections, Princeton University Library.

27 *This contagious search for keepsakes:* "Hitler's Aerie on Mountain Also Bombed," *New York Herald Tribune*, April 26, 1945, p. 3; "Hitler's Berchtesgaden Turns Into Coney Island," *Christian Science Monitor*, July 5, 1945, p. 8; "Dishes From Hitler's Hideout," *Christian Science Monitor*, June 22, 1945, p. 3.

28 *"saw a flash light up the sky":* "Army Ammunition . . . ," *El Paso Herald Post*, July 16, 1945, p. 34.

28 *"a blind woman . . . saw the light":* Feis, *Between War & Peace*," pp. 165–71.

28 *"who of course were greatly interested":* YUL, Stimson Diary, Reel 9, 7-16-45.

28 *"God give them light!":* John J. McCloy Diaries, 7-16-45.

28 *"must be seen to be imagined":* Memorandum for the Secretary of War, 7-18-45, https://www.atomicheritage.org/key-documents/groves-farrell-watching-trinity #:~:text=The%20whole%20country%20was%20lighted,be%20seen%20 to%20be%20imagined.

29 *"the President was tremendously pepped up":* YUL, Stimon Diary, Reel 9, 7-21-45.

29 *"after Noah and his fabulous ark":* HSTL, Truman Papers, PSF, Diary, 7-25-45.

29 *"the second coming in wrath":* "Remembered Words," *Atlantic*, March 1957, pp. 56–57, cited in FRUS, Potsdam, Stimson-Churchill conversation, 7-22-45.

29 *"And now where are the Russians!!!":* Alanbrooke, *War Diaries*, p. 701.

29 *"little boys with a big red apple":* John J. McCloy Diaries, 7-23-45 and 7-24-45.

THREE: An Unsteady Alliance

30 *"I find it very hard to say what Germany is":* Tehran, Yalta, and Potsdam Conferences, p. 162.

30 *"His escorts bristled":* Elsey, *Unplanned Life*, p. 87.

30 *"I can deal with Stalin":* FRUS, Potsdam Diary, 7-17-45.

31 *the 'old man' had a good heart":* COHP-Wallace, 11-28-45, Volume 24, p. 4,290.

31 *though he "most especially noticed":* HST, *Memoir I*, p. 267.

31 *sensitive about his own height:* Ibid.

31 *"was a very small man":* LBJL, Merle Miller, tape #4.

31 *"It is only the 'little fellow' who are hard to deal with":* LOC, Joseph Davies Papers, Box 18, Journal, "Truman on Little Men," 7-25-45.

31 *"Yet I was the little man":* Acheson and Truman, *Affection and Trust*, p. 365.

31 *"I never saw him increase his pace":* Gromyko, *Memories*, p. 99.

31 *Others noticed that, close up:* Lukacs, *1945: Year Zero*, p. 114; YUL, Stimson Diary, 7-2-45, Reel 9.

32 *"those yellow eyes":* Djilas, *Conversations with Stalin*, pp. 60–61.

32 *"small, dapper and rather twinkly":* http://www.winstonchurchill.org/the-life
-of-churchill/life/an-interview-with-mary-soames.

32 *"old fat Winston":* Truman, *Letters Home*, p. 195.

32 *"He was as near like Tom Pendergast":* Daniels, *Man of Independence*, p. 278.

32 *in Spain or Argentina:* Byrnes, *Speaking Frankly*, p. 68.

32 *"extremely polite":* HST, *Memoirs I*, p. 378.

32 *"an entirely novel form of bomb":* Churchill, *Triumph and Tragedy*, p. 640.

33 *the departed dogs and cats:* Astley, *Inner Circle*, pp. 217–18.

33 *the tight seating around the circular table:* Author's visit, 7-26-17.

33 *"crippled by not knowing":* YUL, Stimson Diary, Reel 9, 7-23-45.

33 *"which I could have the privilege of looking over":* Ibid., 7-18-45 and 7-19-45.

34 *"according to Hoyle or not":* Ferrell, *Dear Bess*, p. 519.

34 *"Churchill talks all the time":* HSTL, Papers Pertaining to Family, Business, and Personal Affairs, Box 688, 7-18-45.

34 *"I've only had one letter":* Ibid.

34 *"I look carefully through every pouch":* Ibid.

34 *"It was a nerve wracking experience":* Ibid.

34 *"walking on air":* Ferrell, *Dear Bess*, p. 519.

34 *"as if he were lecturing a schoolroom":* Abell, *Drew Pearson Diaries*, p. 26.

34 *"I mean business":* HSTL, Papers Pertaining to Family, Business, and Personal Affairs, 7-20-45.

35 *"when I hit him with a hammer":* Ibid., 7-25-45.

35 *"Do be kind to him":* H. Freeman Matthews Papers, excerpts from unpublished autobiography, Public Policy Papers, Department of Special Collections, Princeton University Library.

35 *"chairman of a Board Meeting":* Birse, *Memoirs*, p. 206.

35 *He thought Truman looked "noticeably restless":* Cadogan, *Diaries*, pp. 765–66.

35 *"an angry and outraged bullfrog":* Gillies, *Radical Diplomat*, p. 131.

35 *a "well-ordered mind":* Clayton, *Selected Papers*, p. 139.

35 *"sometimes with flashing anger":* H. Freeman Matthews Papers, unpublished memoir, Box 5, Folder 2, Public Policy Papers, Department of Special Collections, Princeton University Library.

36 *"I believe the Germany of 1886": Tehran, Yalta & Potsdam Conferences*, Second Sitting, July 18, 1945, pp. 161–62.

36 *to ban the press:* Churchill, *Defending the West*, p. 135.

36 *"to stroke down their plumage":* LOC, Joseph E. Davies Papers, Box 18, 7-18-45; Churchill, *Triumph and Tragedy*, p. 650.

36 *"except in silence and secrecy": Winston and Clementine. The Personal Letters of the Churchills* (New York: Houghton Mifflin, 1999), p. 532.

36 *"If one goes outside":* Cadogan, *Diaries*, pp. 771–72.

36 *"the unfortunate result":* "Parley's Secrecy . . . ," *New York Times*, July 19, 1945, p. 5.

37 *Churchill would wear, etc.:* Brown, *James F. Byrnes*, p. 273.

37 *"Our boy was good":* Ferrell, *Dear Bess*, p. 520.

37 *"It was like a wild dream":* List (unpublished memoir), *Playing for the Big Three at Potsdam*.

38   *"There I was, face to face with Stalin"*: Ibid.

38   *"and what's more he understands it"*: Ibid.; see also "List, Pianist, Reveals . . . ," *New York Times*, August 13, 1945, p. 23.

38   *"there are also palaces in Japan"*: "Potsdam Concert," Talk of the Town, *New Yorker*, December 29, 1945, p. 15.

38   *"I'm sick of the whole business"*: Ferrell, *Dear Bess*," p. 520.

38   *"honesty adorns the man"*: Alanbrooke, *War Diaries*, p. 702.

38   *"a country boy from Missouri"*: FRUS, Potsdam Minutes, 7-23-45, pp. 319–20.

38   He'd wanted to do it *"nonchalantly"*: Bohlen, *Witness to History*, p. 237.

39   *"had some doubts whether Stalin had taken it in"*: Eden, *The Reckoning*, p. 635.

39   *"hoped we would make 'good use of it'"*: HST, *Memoirs I*, p. 416.

39   *The Russians weren't fooled*: Cheuv, *Molotov Remembers*, p. 56; Gromyko, *Memories*, pp. 109–10; Zhukov, *Memoirs*, p. 675.

39   *"already thoroughly beaten"*: Forrestal Papers, Box 150, Folder 12, 4-25-47, Public Policy Papers, Department of Special Collections, Princeton University Library.

39   *could be quickly won*: YUL, Stimson Diary, 7-23-45, Reel 9; FRUS, Potsdam Minutes 7-19-46, p. 129.

40   *He then distributed a two-paragraph memorandum*: HSTL, Memorandum, Free and Unrestricted Navigation of International Inland Waterways, Naval Aide Files, Berlin Conference File, 7-23-45.

40   *"Perhaps we can pass over this point now"*: FRUS, Potsdam, 7-24-45, pp. 36–46.

40   *"—or at least some of us will"*: H. Freeman Matthews Papers, unpublished memoir, Box 5, Public Policy Papers, Department of Special Collections, Princeton University Library.

40   *"We have been going at it hammer and tongs"*: Ferrell, *Dear Bess,* July 25, 1945, p. 521.

41   *"It's too bad about Churchill"*: HSTL, Papers Pertaining to Family, Business, and Personal Affairs, Box 688, 7-28-45.

41   *"He knew his English language"*: Truman, *Letters Home*, p. 195.

41   *"We miss you very much here"*: HSTL, Churchill Archives Centre Records, Berlin 7-30, 1945.

41   *Hitler should be added to the list*: FRUS, Potsdam, 7-31-45, p. 526.

42   *"Stalin gave Hitler a gift"*: Berezhkov, *At Stalin's Side*, p. 58.

42   *a matter of "vital importance"*: FRUS, Potsdam, 7-31-45, p. 527.

42   *"Truman could not mistake the rebuff"*: Murphy, *Diplomat Among Warriors*, p. 277; FRUS, the Conference of Berlin (Potsdam Conference), 8-1-45, pp. 577–78.

42   *"Well, that was the President's own idea"*: Mee, *Meeting at Potsdam*, p. 198.

43   *"endearing and disarming"*: Cited by Costigliola, *Roosevelt's Lost Alliances*, p. 363.

43   *"My one regret"*: "Truman Puts Duties Aside to Review Yanks," *Washington Post*, July 24, 1945.

FOUR: "The Basic Power of the Universe"

44   *"this last great action"*: "The Decision to Use the Atom Bomb," *Harper's*, February 1949, p. 107.

44   *"Myrna Alloys"*: Lilienthal, *Journals, Volume Two*, 5-21-47, p. 170.

44   *"we will have given them the chance"*: FRUS, Potsdam Diary, 7-25-45.

44   *"We do not intend"*: HST, *Memoirs I*, p. 351.

45   *"I had made the decision"*: Ibid., pp. 419–20.

45   *"I think it was just accepted"*: Clayton, *Selected Papers*, pp. 128–29; see also Compton, *Atomic Quest*, pp. 238–39.

45   *"a foregone conclusion"*: Compton, *Atomic Quest*, pp. 238–39.

45   *"From the psychological point of view"*: Stoff and Fanton, *The Manhattan Project*, pp. 97–104.

45   *"exclusively a place of homes and art and shrines"*: Ibid., "Compton's Recollections," p. 22.

45   *"the bitterness which would be"*: YUL, Stimson Diary, Reel 9, 7-24-45.

46   *"He & I are in accord"*: HSTL, PSF, *Diary*, 7-25-45.

46   to *"warn Japan into surrender"*: YUL, Stimson Diary, 7-2-45, Reel 9. Lewis Strauss, who later chaired the Atomic Energy Commission, was working in the Navy Department's ordnance bureau and became a special assistant to James Forrestal. He suggested that the bomb first be used on the Nikko Forest, known for an extraordinary grove of cryptomerias—cedar trees, which grow to an unusual height; "It would have been impressive to have used the bomb there. We could have warned all the people to leave. And when they returned and saw that for a mile or more about all these trees had been laid down like the spokes of a wheel from the epicenter of the explosion like a giant windrow, I think this would have been just as convincing and far less dreadful than the destruction of two cities and thousands of non-combatants," HSTL, OH-Strauss, 6-16-71.

46   *the more realistic cost:* Barton Bernstein, "Reconsidering the Atomic General," *Journal of Military History* (July 2003): pp. 908–9.

46   *"in the last analysis, it would control"*: LOC, Davies Papers, Box 19, Atomic Bomb Diary, 7-29-45.

46   *an urgent question:* To continue this argument, see Alperovitz, *Atomic Diplomacy.*

46   *leaving at least a million homeless:* Gordin, *Five Days*, p. 51.

47   *"have become homeless mobs"*: Forrestal Diary, Box 149, Folder 8, 7-7-45, Public Policy Papers, Department of Special Collections, Princeton University Library.

47   *"even if no invasion had been planned or contemplated"*: HSTL, Elsey Papers, Box 71, Japan, "United States Strategic Bombing Survey, Japan's Struggle to End the War, 7-1-46"; Lacey, *Truman Presidency*, p. 180.

47   *"I don't want to have to answer any questions from Stalin"*: Elsey, *Unplanned Life*, p. 91.

47   *"I am very sure"*: HSTL, PSF, Longhand Notes, 8-5,-45.

47   *The king . . . greeted Truman:* HSTL, PSF, Longhand Notes, 8-5-45; there's an interesting film clip at https://www.youtube.com/watch?v=o9l0x5XHfDU.

47   *"It sounds like a professor's dream to me!"*: Leahy, *I Was There*, p. 431; HSTL, PSF, Longhand Notes, 8-5-45.

48   *"talked of most everything, and nothing much"*: HSTL, PSF, Longhand Notes, 8-5-45

48   *"the King was appalled"*: Nicolson, *The Later Years*, August 8, 1945, pp. 31–32.

48 *"took a snort of Haig & Haig"*: HSTL, PSF, Longhand Notes, 8-5-45; HST, *Memoirs I*, p. 413.

49 *"It's time for us to get on home!"*: HST, *Memoirs I*, pp. 421–23.

49 *"I have an announcement to make to you"*: "Truman Bares . . . ," *Chicago Tribune*, August 7, 1945.

49 *"an awful load lifted from our backs"*: A. Merriman Smith, *Thank You, Mr. President*, pp. 257–58.

49 *"If they do not now accept our terms"*: https://www.trumanlibrary.gov/library /public-papers/93/statement-president-announcing-use-bomb-hiroshima.

49 *his index finger guiding him*: https://www.youtube.com/watch?v=U_zyvPW JBbw.

50 *"couldn't tell his wife what he did"*: COHP, Arthur W. Page, pp. 58–61, 6-19-56.

50 *"which I had the distinction of making"*: Ferrell, *Truman in the White House*, p. 59.

50 *"seemed delighted to be back"*: Ibid.

50 *"he could be depended upon"*: Ibid.

50 *"obstinate and bull-headed"*: COHP, Wallace, 11-28-45, Volume 24, p. 4,290.

50 *"impenetrable cloud of dust and smoke"*: *New York Times*, August 7, 1945, p.1, "New Age Ushered."

50 *"literally seared to death"*: "Bomb Killed 'Uncounted Thousands,' " *New York Herald Tribune*, August 9, 1945, p. 1.

51 *"Or will we have to repeat the horror?"*: "The Annihilation of Hiroshima," *New York Herald Tribune*, August 9, 1945, p. 22.

51 *"I am sure that at the end of the world"*: Edward R. Murrow, in his CBS Radio broadcast, http://history.journalism.ku.edu/1940/multimedia/audio/Murrow _broadcasts/47_1945-09-10_915OverHiroshima.mp3.

51 *hid the city from aerial view*: "Nagasaki Flames . . . ," *New York Times*, August 10, 1945, p. 1.

51 *"We indicated that we meant business"*: HST, *Memoirs I*, p. 426.

51 *"not to upset the existing plans"*: Ibid., p. 40; Groves, *Now It Can Be Told*, p. 265.

51 *Groves had "stacked the deck"*: Gordin, *Five Days*, pp. 46–55.

52 *"and they will not like them"*: https://millercenter.org/the-presidency/presiden tial-speeches/august-9-1945-radio-report-american-people-potsdam-confer ence.

52 *"One felt that such news should come"*: Alsop, *To Marietta, from Paris*, August 5, 1945, p. 41.

52 *Bishop G. Bromley Oxnam . . . urged a suspension*: "Oxnam, Dulles Ask Halt . . . ," *New York Times*, August 10, 1945, p. 1.

52 *if Emperor Hirohito could remain on the throne*: "Allies Willing to Retain Hirohito," *New York Herald Tribune*, August 12, 1945, p. 1.

53 *"If they had prevailed"*: Leahy, *I Was There*, p. 434.

53 *"the first official word of surrender"*: "Byrnes First . . . ," *New York Times*, August 15, 1945, p. 4.

53 *The emperor would live on*: "Japan Bows . . . ," *New York Herald Tribune*, August 15, 1945, p. 1a; "Japs Quit Unconditionally," *Washington Post*, August 15, 1945, p. 1.

53 *Pedestrians went crazy:* "Japanese War Ends," *New York Herald Tribune*, August, 15, 1945, p. 1A.

54 *"I'm glad Harry decided to end the war":* "President's Mother Says She's Glad . . . ," *Christian Science Monitor*, August 15, 1945, p. 17.

54 *"The last of our enemies":* "Peace to Britain . . . ," *New York Times*, August 15, 1945, p. 4.

54 *he wanted "to shorten the agony of war":* Radio broadcast, August 9, 1945.

54 *"and not women and children":* HSTL, *Diary*, 7-25-45.

54 *"I had told Stimson":* HST, *Memoirs I*, p. 420.

55 *Most of those killed in Hiroshima and Nagasaki were noncombatants:* Barton Bernstein, "Reconsidering the Atomic General," *Journal of Military History* (July 2003): 905; Bernstein and Matusow, *Truman Administration*, pp. 40–41.

55 *"I pleaded with the Japanese":* *Where the Buck Stops*, pp. 205–6.

55 *"We picked a couple of cities":* https://nsarchive2.gwu.edu/dc.html?doc=3913 572-President-Harry-S-Truman-Handwritten-Remarks-for.

55 *called Oppenheimer a "'cry baby' scientist":* LOC, Oppenheimer Papers, Memorandum from Dean Acheson to HST, 5-7-46.

56 *"The worst thing I ever did":* Schlesinger, *A Life in the 20th Century*, p. 351.

56 *"He didn't like the idea of killing, as he said, 'all those kids'":* Wallace, *Diary*, pp. 473–75.

56 *If Japan's capitulation hadn't come quickly:* Barton Bernstein, "Reconsidering the Atomic General," *Journal of Military History* (July 2003): 906; Gordin, *Five Days in August*, pp. 101–2.

56 *"this is the beginning or the end!":* "A Bomb Epic Had Roots in Iowa," *Washington Post*, February 9, 1947, p. S6.

56 *much of its impressiveness is marred:* "Atomic Bomb Film . . . ," *New York Times*, February 21, 1947, p. 15.

57 *"Even the word is frightening":* Farrar, *Reluctant Servant*, p. 171.

57 *"without limit, without moral containment":* Lilienthal, *Journals*, Volume Two, p. 271.

FIVE: Truman's "Conniver"

58 *"Don't ever let anybody":* HSTL, Papers Pertaining to Family, Business, and Personal Affairs, Box 688, 9-11-45.

58 *the counsel of others:* In late summer 1945, Truman sent a memorandum to each cabinet member, suggesting that, as soon as the "war emergency agencies can be wound up," they all meet for lunch three times a week. It would, he wrote, "give me the opportunity to have the whole cabinet in my complete confidence as to what is going on." He got enthusiastic responses, even from those who must have known that, with such different men and such different agendas, such a plan, however well-meaning, would be pointless. See: HSTL, PSF, Box 134, Cabinet.

58 *"when you punish your dog":* YUL, Stimson diary, Reel 9, p.70, Memorandum of conference with the president, 8-8-45.

58 *he was like "the head boy in a school":* Alsop, *"I've Seen the Best of It,"* p. 268.

59 *"my able and conniving Secretary of State"*: HSTL, PSF, Longhand Notes, 7-7-45.

59 *"as unofficial adviser"*: "Back to the Big Three," *Spectator*, July 6, 1945, p. 175.

59 *"the most honest horse thief he had ever met"*: Wallace, *Diary*, pp. 473–75.

59 *"a very small number of people"*: Institute for Advanced Study, Princeton Seminar, Reel 2, 7-2-53.

59 *"you never knew you had made an impression"*: American Secretaries of State and Their Diplomacy, Vol. XIV, pp. 145–46.

60 *"an asset sometimes"*: HSTL, PSF, Longhand Notes, 7-7-45.

60 *"in full charge of foreign policy"*: HST, *Memoirs I*, p. 599.

60 *"No man probably"*: Ibid., p. 66.

60 *"hated the idea"*: Harriman and Abel, *Special Envoy*, p. 523.

61 *"The balance has been destroyed"*: Scott D. Sagan, "Why Do States Build Nuclear Weapons?" *International Security* (Winter 1996–97): 58.

61 *"Atomic bombs are intended for intimidating the weak-nerved"*: Stalin, *On Post-War International Relations*, p. 13.

61 Byrnes arrived five minutes later: Kennan, *At the Century's Ending*, pp. 286-90.

62 an *"alienated loner"*: Isaacson and Thomas, *The Wise Men*, p. 434.

62 *"large, intense, wide-set"*: Lilienthal, *Journals*, Volume Two, 3-9-47, p. 160.

62 *"slender and good-looking"*: "Mysterious Mr. X," *New York Herald Tribune*, January 4, 1948, p. SM10.

62 had succeeded in creating a *"friendly spirit"*: "Byrnes Is Jubilant," *New York Times*, December 27, 1945, p. 25.

62 usually less fatigued: *American Secretaries of State and Their Diplomacy*, Vol. XIV, pp. 144–46.

62 *"The working hours of the Soviets were hard on me"*: Clemson University, Byrnes Papers, Series 5, Box 12, Folder 2.

62 the *"enormous nervous strain"*: Byrnes, *All in One Lifetime*, p. 340.

63 Harriman's diagnosis: Harriman and Abell, *Special Envoy*, p. 524.

63 *"I used to sit in the cabinet"*: COHP, Steelman, p. 166.

63 a seventeen-page report: HSTL, PSF, Box 134; Byrnes.

63 made it to Kansas City in six hours: "Truman Flies Home . . . ," *New York Times*, December 26, 1945, p. 1.

63 *"you might as well have stayed in Washington"*: MT, *Bess W. Truman*, p. 280.

63 *"I did as I was told"*: Ibid., p. 281.

64 *"No one ever needed help and assistance as I do now"*: Ferrell, *Dear Bess*, p. 523; MT, *Bess W. Truman*, p. 281.

64 *"the fanciest presidential yacht"*: Wallace, *Diary*, December 11, 1945, p. 528.

64 Truman planned to use some of the time: LOC, Leahy Papers, Journal, 12-28-45; COHP, Steelman, p. 166.

65 He informed Byrnes *"as well as I could"*: Institute for Advanced Study, Princeton Seminar, Reel 2, Rewrite Record 2.

65 *"I've got to work on this speech"*: Messer, *End of an Alliance*, p. 155; Acheson Interview, 2-18-55, in Neal, *HST*, pp. 15–16.

65 he was on his way again: Ibid., pp. 156—57.

65 to cancel his radio speech: HSTL, Eben Ayers Papers, Box 15, Diary, 1-2-46.

65   *"wind up our work tomorrow"*: HST, *Memoirs I*, pp. 598–89.

65   *"and not to worry"*: Ibid., p. 601.

65   *"and I don't mean maybe"*: COHP, Steelman, p. 167.

66   *"informs me that he was not consulted"*: LOC, Leahy Papers, Diary, 12-26-45 and 12-28-45.

66   *occasionally drifted into domestic matters:* Marquis Childs, *Washington Post*, March 9, 1946, p. 9.

66   *Byrnes's "appeasement attitude"*: LOC, Leahy Papers, Diary, 2-21-46.

66   *"I was not going to have a policy announced"*: HSTL, Jonathan Daniels Papers, Interview by Daniels in Blair House, 8-30-49.

67   *"was unable to get a satisfactory reply"*: LOC, Leahy Papers, Diary, 12-29-45.

67   *"and he got the trimming of his life"*: COHP, Steelman, pp. 167, 169–70.

67   *Truman told Charlie Ross that he'd approved:* HSTL, Ayers Papers, Box 15, 1-2-46.

67   *To follow Byrnes's schedule:* Robertson, *Sly and Able*, pp. 45–46.

67   *"cold, bleak winter weather"*: LOC, Leahy Papers, Diary, 12-30-45.

67   *in a formal setting:* For example, when he returned from London, in the fall: https://www.youtube.com/watch?v=ybgS6rpXzlg.

67   *like someone who had just mastered English:* Byrnes's speech can be heard at https://www.wnyc.org/story/james-f-byrnes-reports-on-the-big-three-foreign -ministers-conference-at-moscow/.

68   *"It must be recognized"*: *New York Herald Tribune*, December 31, 1945, pp. 1A, 6.

68   *were singing "Auld Lang Syne"*: "Truman Works on Talk . . . ," *New York Herald Tribune*, January 2, 1946, p. 1A.

68   *Truman had had to ask a White House operator:* HSTL, MHDC, Box 27, #891. Archivist Randy Sowell, at the Truman Library, believes that this message went out on December 30.

68   *"Byrnes lost his nerve in Moscow"*: Daniels, *Man of Independence*, pp. 309–11.

68   *"I accepted the invitation to join him"*: Byrnes, *All in One Lifetime*, p. 343.

68   *Truman "only afterward complained"*: Messer, *End of an Alliance*, p. 149.

69   *"basic scientific information for peaceful ends"*: HSTL, PSF, Box 34; see also https://history.state.gov/historicaldocuments/frus1945v02/d235.

69   *Drew Pearson . . . reported:* "Washington Merry-Go-Round," *Washington Post*, January 8, 1946, p. 5.

69   *"somebody just wants to tell a big lie"*: Presidential News Conference, March 14, 1946, https://www.presidency.ucsb.edu/documents/the-presidents-news-conference -447.

70   *"I'm tired of babying the Soviets"*: HSTL, PSF, Longhand Notes, 1-5-46.

70   *"probably the most decisive year"*: LOC, Elmer Davis Radio Scripts, 12-23-45.

SIX: Churchill Makes Mischief

71   *"Finish your question—I'm sorry"*: Presidential News Conference, January 31, 1946, https://www.presidency.ucsb.edu/documents/the-presidents-news-conference -438.

71   *"everything was a little too precise"*: HSTL, OH-Robert Nixon, 10-19-70.

71   *"There is hardly a man in Congress":* "Mr Truman Reorganizes," *Harper's,* January 1946, p. 34.

71   *"poor perplexed little man of the White House":* Berlin, *Letters,* pp. 621 and 628.

72   *"straight-forward, decisive, simple, entirely honest":* Acheson, *Present at the Creation,* p. 104.

72   *"conspirators in the 'Palace Guard'":* HSTL, Papers Pertaining to Family, Business, and Personal Affairs, 9-19-45.

72   *"a dictatorship is the hardest thing":* HSTL, Jonathan Daniels Papers, Interview, 8-30-49.

72   *"absence of illusion of any sort":* Smith, *My Three Years in Moscow,* p. 56.

72   *"prisoner of the Politburo":* https://www.trumanlibrary.gov/library/public-papers /126/rear-platform-and-other-informal-remarks-oregon.

72   *"talked to frankly":* HST, *Memoirs I,* p. 44.

72   to *"leap into an advanced country":* "Stalin Sets a Huge Output," *New York Times,* February 10, 1946, p. 30.

73   *and the quicker it came the better:* Wallace, *Diary,* Januaury 2, 1946, pp. 537–38.

73   *"or words to that effect":* Ayers Diary, 2-5-46, from Ferrell, *Truman in the White House,* p. 135.

74   the *"vigorous foreign policy . . . that we need, in these times":* LOC, Elmer Davis Papers, 1-9-46.

74   *"where he could get a house or find a car":* Lord Halifax Diaries, 8-17-45.

74   *David Reynolds, in his engaging:* Reynolds, *In Command of History,* pp. ix–xx.

75   *"I would be most pleased to introduce you":* Churchill, *Defending the West,* 11-16-45, p. 153.

75   *among them Byrnes and Bernard Baruch:* "Byrnes, Baruch," *New York Herald Tribune,* February 16, 1946, p. 3.

75   *"'clarion calls' regarding the dangers he foresees":* Churchill, *Defending the West,* pp. 157–58.

75   *crockery flew about the cabin:* "Churchill Is the Guest of Truman," *New York Times,* February 11, 1946, p. 1.

75   *"Will you please wire me":* Churchill, *Defending the West,* p. 159.

75   The Ferdinand Magellan *was back in service:* From Gold Coast Railroad Museum, www.gcrm.org.

76   *though he'd not given . . . a preview:* Bullock, *Ernest Bevin,* p. 224.

76   *Admiral Leahy was "enthusiastic":* Attlee, *Twilight of Empire,* pp. 162–63.

76   *He foresaw "forceful objections":* LOC, Leahy Papers, Diary, 1-10-46.

76   *"I could find no fault":* Ibid., 3-2-46.

76   *and, it was reported, did so, flawlessly:* "Truman, Churchill Travel . . . ," *New York Times,* March 6, 1946, p. 1; "Churchill Talks on Peace . . . ," *New York Herald Tribune,* March 5, 1946, p. 1A.

77   *"we had to put a bit of whiskey in it":* HSTL, OH-Harry Vaughan, 1-16-63.

77   *"My sides are sore":* Ferrell, *Off the Record,* pp. 38–39.

77   *Truman's games observed certain customs:* Among many references to Truman's poker habits, and prowess, see HSTL, MHDC, T-Y, Vaccaro, 307; HSTL, OH-Frank Pace Jr.; HSTL, Charles G. Ross Papers, Box 17, 3-7-46; Clifford, *Counsel to the President,* pp. 102–3.

77 *"couldn't seem to get the hang of"*: HSTL, Charles G. Ross Papers, Box 17, 3-7-46.

77 *"a boy's delight in the game"*: Ibid.

77 Clement Attlee thought it was of *"vital importance"*: Attlee, *Twight of Empire*, p. 161.

78 *"and for my wartime colleague, Marshal Stalin"*: "Churchill Hits Red Peril," *Chicago Tribune*, March 6, 1946, p. 14.

79 *"we were all sucked into the awful whirlpool"*: "Text . . . ," *New York Herald Tribune*, March 6, 1946, p. 16. In May 1945, Churchill warned that "an iron curtain is drawn down upon their front. We do not know what is going on behind. There seems little doubt that the whole of the regions east of the line Lubeck-Trieste-Corfu will soon be completely in their hands." See Churchill, *Defending the West*, May 12, 1945, p. 75.

79 *"You might as well talk about a trip to the moon"*: COHP, Wallace, 3-5-46, Volume 29, pp. 4600–4.

79 *did stir things up*: *American Secretaries of State*, Volume XIV, p. 203.

79 *"I have no comment"*: Presidential News Conference; March 8, 1946, https://www.presidency.ucsb.edu/documents/the-presidents-news-conference-440.

80 *"a call to war with the Soviet Union"*: "Stalin Brands Churchill," *Christian Science Monitor*, March 14, 1946, p. 14; "Stalin Takes the Stump," *Time*, March 25, 1946. For more background, see the Roosevelt-Stalin correspondence in Butler, *My Dear Mr. Stalin*, p. 325.

80 *just as he'd introduced Churchill*: Clifford, *Counsel to the President*, p. 108.

80 *The letter was carried to Moscow*: "The Developing Crisis," *New York Herald Tribune*, March 14, 1946, p. 25A; see also Wallace, *Diary*, May 21, 1946, p. 572.

80 *"he would probably be alive today"*: Smith, *My Three Years in Moscow*, pp. 50–52.

81 *"I don't suppose I should kick"*: HSTL, Papers Pertaining to Family, Business, and Personal Affairs, Box 688, 1-30-47.

81 *"she doesn't want to be"*: Ibid., 1-17-47.

81 *would also soon be on her own*: For more on Margaret Truman in that period, see also "The Real Romance," *Time*, February 26, 1951, pp. 39–44; "Why Shouldn't I Sing?," *Saturday Evening Post*, April 22, 1950, pp. 24–95; "Margaret Truman, Career Girl," *New York Times*, September 4, 1946, SM8; "Father's Wish," *Newsweek*, November 17, 1947, p. 26.

81 *"He seemed lonesome"*: HSTL, Ross Papers, Diary, 3-23-46.

81 *"Russia couldn't turn a wheel"*: Ibid., 3-25-46.

SEVEN: The Quick and the Dead

82 *"I've forgotten what they were"*: Harpo Marx and Rowland Barber, *Harpo Speaks!* (New York: Bernard Geis Associates, 1961), p. 15.

82 *"and eventually set up a free world"*: HSTL, PSF, Longhand Notes. The reference to a bill dealing with labor strikes, and the imminence of an auto-industry walkout, suggests this was written in the late summer or early fall of 1945, https://www.trumanlibrary.gov/library/truman-papers/longhand-notes-presidential-file-194April 1953/undated-ca-1945.

83   *on the future of nuclear energy:* "Truman to Give Views Later," *New York Herald Tribune,* September 7, 1945, p. 10A.

83   *catch up within five years:* HSTL, PSF, Atomic Files, Box 174, Cabinet, 9-21-45.

83   *"both futile and dangerous":* HSTL, PSF, Atomic Files, Memorandum Requested by the President (from Acheson), Box 174, 9-25-45.

83   *"an instrument of destruction":* Special Message to the Congress on Atomic Energy, October 3, 1945, https://www.trumanlibrary.gov/library/public-papers /156/special-message-congress-atomic-energy.

83   *the "scientific knowledge that resulted":* News conference, October 8, 1945, https://www.presidency.ucsb.edu/node/230540.

84   *"let's put it that way":* Ibid.

84   *"let them use it":* HSTL, OH-Robert Nixon, 10-22-70.

85   *"to help instead of ruining mankind":* "'Constructive' Group Urged by M'Mahon," *New York Times,* August 10, 1945, p 6.

85   *"development of nuclear physics":* "McMahon asks reexamination . . . ," *Washington Post,* November 1, 1945, p. 7.

85   *use and development of atomic energy:* "Atomic Bomb Rule . . . ," *Hartford Courant,* September 7, 1945, p. 1; "Truman to Give Views Later," *New York Herald Tribune,* September 7, 1945, p. 10A.

85   *A competing bill:* For more on this legislative history, see Byson S. Miller, "A Law Is Passed: The Atomic Energy Act of 1946," *University of Chicago Law Review* 15, No. 4 (Summer 1948): 799–821.

85   *with some frequency:* Truman's meetings with McMahon may be found through his Daily Appointments: https://www.trumanlibrary.gov/calendar/search?com ment_keywords=McMahon&body_value_op=word.

85   *On Woodland Drive:* Telephone interview, by the author, with Patricia McMahon Fox, 9-15-20.

85   *"a short well-groomed gentleman":* "Connecticut's Three-Ring . . . ," *New York Herald Tribune,* October 29, 1950, p. F6; some biographical material is from the McMahon Papers at Georgetown University.

86   *"make himself older":* John D. Lane, Administrative Assistant to McMahon, Oral History Interviews, October 12 and December 6, 2006, Senate Historical Office.

86   *"as it saw fit":* Forrestal, *Diaries,* pp. 133–34.

86   *"not a good match":* Ibid.

86   *"there beckons a place of honor in history":* HSTL, Public Papers of the President, Truman to Brien McMahon, 2-2-46. The Atomic Energy Act of 1946 was a model of legislative integrity and care. In his short history of the act, published in the *University of Chicago Law Review,* Byron S. Miller, concluded that "rarely has a legislative body making its own decisions emerged with a bill reflecting as high a caliber of statesmanship as did the Senate Special Committee."

86   *the Senate voted unanimously:* "Senate Votes Civil Rule," *New York Herald Tribune,* June 2, 1946, p. 2.

86   *"I have always doubted":* Groves, *Now It Can Be Told,* pp. 393–94.

87   *"terrible position we are all in":* Lilienthal, *Journals,* Volume Two, 1-16-46, p. 10.

87   *"The highest hope of the American people":* Speech delivered on October 27, 1945, https://www.trumanlibrary.gov/library/public-papers/178/address-foreign -policy-navy-day-celebration-new-york-city.

87   *a pretty good light-heavyweight boxer:* "On the Other Side of the Moon," *Time,* August 4, 1947, p. 12+; "David Lilienthal Is Dead," *New York Times,* January 15, 1981, p. 1.

87   *the status quo was unacceptable:* For more on this, see "Seven Men on a Problem," *New Yorker,* August 17, 1946, p. 49+; Acheson, *Present at the Creation,* pp. 151–52; Lilienthal, *Journals,* Volume Two, 1-16-46, p. 10; Schwartz, *The Speculator,* p. 492.

88   *Four days later:* Lilienthal, *Journals,* Volume Two, 1-20-46, p. 11.

88   *"a quite new approach":* J. Robert Oppenheimer, *Foreign Affairs,* January 1948, pp. 239–52.

88   *"a crazy kind of finale":* Lilienthal, *Journals,* Volume Two, 3-19-46, p. 30.

88   *"loaded with maleness":* "The Old Man. III-National Kibitzer," *New Yorker,* 1-17-48, p. 33.

88   *"can think of himself":* Schwartz, *The Speculator,* p. 471.

88   *"When I read this news":* Lilienthal, *Journals,* Volume Two, 3-19-46, p. 30; Acheson, *Present at the Creation,* p. 154.

89   *Night sessions were out of the question:* Schwartz, *The Speculator,* p. 491.

89   *"He is really quite an old man":* Lilienthal, *Journals,* Volume Two, 5-19-46, pp. 49–50.

89   *"It is a mystery to me":* Schwartz, *The Speculator,* p. 490.

89   *"there never was a greater egotist":* HSTL, Papers Pertaining to Family, Business, and Personal Affairs Letter to Bess, 6-15-46.

90   *"a secret string-puller, and a major self-promoter":* Lawrenson, *Stranger at the Party,* p. 148; Schwartz, *The Spectacular,* p. 33.

90   *"Only the snapping turtle mouth":* Childs, *Witness to Power,* p. 92.

90   *"I can't hear you":* "President, Baruch . . . ," *New York Times,* March 27, 1946, p. 12.

90   *"he could smell his way through it":* Schwartz, *The Speculator,* p. 491.

90   *Byrnes had then admitted, to Acheson:* Lilienthal, *Journals,* Volume Two, 1-13-46, pp. 58–59.

90   *But to Lilienthal's relief:* Ibid., 6-15-46, pp. 59-60.

90   *praised as imaginative and bold:* "Baruch Plan . . . ," *New York Times,* June 15, 1946, p. 1.

91   *"a rollicking good time":* Kahn, *The World of Swope,"* p. 401.

91   *"in the eighth round":* LOC, Leahy Papers, Diary, 6-20-46.

91   *"It's the policy outlined in the directive":* Presidential News Conference, 6-14 -46, https://www.presidency.ucsb.edu/documents/the-presidents-news-conference -48146.

92   *"He has been too free in answering badgering questions".* HSTL, Ross Papers, Box 17, 2-21-46.

92   *involving some forty thousand people:* Bradley, *No Place to Hide,* pp. xiv–xv.

92   *"is somewhat as if Joe Louis":* "Bikini," *New York Herald Tribune,* June 29, 1946, p. 13.

92 *"more useful information could be obtained"*: LOC, Oppenheimer Papers, JRO to HST, 5-3-46.

92 *"strength of the atomic dictator"*: HSTL, Matthew J. Connelly Papers, Notes on Cabinet Meetings, 3-22-46, https://www.trumanlibrary.gov/node/329902.

92 *he'd decide about the next two:* Ibid.

93 *"in the nature of a laboratory experiment"*: HSTL, Public Papers of the President, April 12, 1946.

93 *where the navy had built a new village:* "Bikini Natives Grieve," *New York Herald Tribune*, May 5, 1946, p. 7.

93 *"We will put our trust in God"*: "Bikini Natives Accept . . . ," *Los Angeles Times*, June 9, 1946, p. 5.

93 *an "awesome, spine-chilling spectacle"*: "Fiery 'Super Volcano' . . . ," *New York Times,* July 1, 1946, p, 1.

93 *"beautiful silver white mushroom top"*: Saltonstall Papers, Bikini Atoll Diary, Massachusetts Historical Society, https://www.masshist.org/features/saltonstall /senator-saltonstall-bikini-atoll.

93 *"rose-purple light"*: Forrestal Diary, Box 150, Folder 3, 7-1-46, Public Policy Papers, Department of Special Collections, Princeton University Library.

93 *Out of some ninety ships:* "11 Ships Lost . . . ," *New York Herald Tribune*, July 2, 1946, p. 1.

94 *"You have made a true contribution"*: "King Invited," *Chicago Tribune*, July 17, 1946, p. 3; "Truman Thanks Bikini . . . ," *New York Times*, July 17, 1946, p. 7.

94 *would be pleased with some military gold braid:* "Bikini's King . . . ," *New York Times*, 7-7-46, p. 7. In September, Hatch, Blandy, and others brought gifts to Truman from the natives of Bikini. HSTL, Daily Appointments of Harry S. Truman, 9-4-46.

94 *"a gigantic dome-shaped mushroom"*: "Ships Bob Around," *New York Times*, July 25, 1946, p. 1.

94 *"It's a fouled-up world"*: Bradley, *No Place to Hide*, p. 104.

94 *"blew up something more essential"*: "Pravda Says . . . ," *New York Herald Tribune*, July 4, 1946, p. 7A.

95 *Truman that day seemed more interested:* HSTL, Matthew Connelly Papers, Cabinet Meeting, 7-26-46.

95 *found Oppenheimer "in deep despair"*: Lilienthal, *Journals*, Volume Two, July 24, 1946, pp. 69–70.

EIGHT: A Season of Disharmony

96 *in a letter to John J. McCloy:* Blum, *Public Philosopher*, November 14, 1946, pp. 490–91.

96 *the trial of twenty-four top Nazis concluded:* "Top Nazis Make Final Pleas," *New York Herald Tribune*, September 1, 1946, p. 1.

96 *twelve by hanging:* "12 Nazi War Leaders Sentenced to Be Hanged," *New York Times*, October 2, 1946, p. 1.

97 *on a German-owned estate in Patagonia:* "Hitler, Eva Reported Landed . . . ,"

Washington Post, July 17, 1945, p. 1; "Hitler Rumors Start to Fly," *New York Herald Tribune*, July 17, 1945, p. 3.

97   *had not died in his bunker:* "Manhunt for Hitler Under Way," *Austin American*, September 9, 1945, p. 1; "Rumors on Hitler Termed Unstable," *Baltimore Sun*, July 21, 1945, p. 1.

97   *Those who waited outside could hear shouts:* "Guilt Is Punished," *New York Times*, October 16, 1946, p. 1.

97   *"vengeance is seldom justice":* "Taft Condemns Hanging," *New York Times*, October 6, 1946, p. 1.

97   *"these remaining malefactors":* "Truman Sees Other Trials," *Baltimore Sun*, October 18, 1946, p. 4.

97   *coast-to-coast service in six hours:* Pan-Am Plans . . . ," *Boston Globe*, September 12, 1946, p. 8; *Boston Globe* September 1, 1946, p. C9; *Washington Post*, October 1, 1946, p. M1; *New York Herald Tribune* September 1, 1946, p. 13; *Chicago Tribune*, September 1, 1946, p. 9.

98   *and Clark Clifford:* Fleeson, "Second Cooks . . . ," *Nation's Business*, March 1947, p. 57.

98   *"in a faintly sacerdotal gesture":* Alsop, *The Center*, p. 164.

98   *"too storybookish to be real":* Allen and Shannon, *Truman Merry-Go-Round* p. 58.

98   *when the heavy ball landed in the water:* "Advisers Board Truman Yacht," *New York Herald Tribune*, September 2, 1946, p. 11.

99   *"as young lads do":* HSTL, OH-Trohan, 10-7-70; a log of Truman's summer cruise can be read at this link: https://www.whitehousehistory.org/a-journey-in to-nowhere.

99   *"possibly the most important federal bureau":* "The Center of Reality," *New Yorker*, March 20, 1948, p. 62.

99   *"in all the peoples of the world":* "Wallace Reveals He Bade . . . ," *New York Times*, September 18, 1946, p. 2.

100 *"a Stalinoid audience":* Macdonald, *Henry Wallace*, p. 107.

100 *the crowd hissed again:* "Peace with Russia," *New York Herald Tribune* September 13, 1946, p. 1; "Wallace Wants Russia . . . ," *New York Times*, September 13, 1946, p. 1.

100 *"I approved the whole speech":* Presidential News Conference, October 12, 1946, at 4 p.m.; https://www.presidency.ucsb.edu/documents/the-presidents-news -conference-430.

100 *tell the "whole truth":* HSTL, Ayers Papers, Diary, Box 15, 10-12-46.

100 *"a bit slow to catch on":* "Truman, Wallace, and Byrnes," *New York Herald Tribune*, September 17, 1946, p. 7A.

101 *Truman had been "trapped" by reporters' questions:* HSTL, Ayers Papers, Diary, Box 19, 10-12-46; Forrestal, *Diaries*, pp. 207–9.

101 *Admiral Leahy told Truman:* LOC, Leahy Papers, Diary, 9-16-46.

101 *Much of this behind-the-scenes intrigue:* "Prior Objection to Wallace Talk . . . ," *New York Times*, September 14, 1946, p. 1.

101 *he had answered "extemporaneously":* Presidential News Conference, September 12, 1946, https://www.presidency.ucsb.edu/documents/the-presidents-news -conference-430.

101 *"would be called a lie"*: Macdonald, *Henry Wallace*. p. 111.

101 *"At this time I have not determined"*: Clemson University, James F. Byrnes Papers, Box 20, Folder 12, 9-15-46.

101 *Byrnes's words were now "at a discount"*: HSTL, Monte Poen Papers, Box 3, handwritten notes, interview with Robert Jackson, ca. 1954.

102 *"speak on this subject again"*: "Wallace Stand . . . ," *New York Times*, September 17, 1946, p. 1; "Dispute Might Force . . . ," *Baltimore Sun*, September 17, 1946, p. 1.

102 *he hadn't intended to damage Byrnes*: Wallace, *Diary*, pp. 614–16.

102 *"every member's business but his own"*: HSTL, PSF, Longhand Notes, 9-16-46, "read to the Sec. of State and discussed-not typed or mailed."

102 *Wallace returned to the White House*: "Truman Silences Wallace," *New York Herald Tribune*, September 19, 1946, p. 1.

102 *"Wallace destroyed it in a day"*: Clemson University, James F. Byrnes Papers, Series 5, Box 20, Folder 12.

102 *"while he is a member of your Cabinet"*: Byrnes, *All in One Lifetime*, pp. 373–74.

102 *"that we can keep peace with Russia"*: "Truman Silences Wallace," *New York Herald Tribune*, September 19, 1946, p. 1.

102 *"had been giving him hell"*: Wallace, *Diary*, pp. 620–24.

102 *"it is a good one"*: HSTL, Papers Pertaining to Family, Business, and Personal Affair, Box 688, 9-18-46.

102 *"fundamentally sound intellectually"*: HSTL, PSF, Longhand Notes, 9-19-46.

102 *Truman would ask Wallace to leave*: Brown, *James F. Byrnes*, p. 350; Clemson University, Byrnes Papers, Series 5, Box 20, Folder 12.

103 *"Of course I hated to do it"*: HSTL, Papers Pertaining to Family, Business, and Personal Affairs, Box 688, 9-20-46.

103 *"I shall continue to fight for peace"*: HSTL, Ayers Papers, Diary, Box 15, 9-20-46; "The President Acts," *New York Times*, September 21, 1946, p. 1; "Truman Puts Secretary . . . ," *New York Herald Tribune*, September 21, 1946, p. 1.

103 *Truman was in a blue mood*: HSTL, Ayers Papers, Diary, Box 15, 9-21-46 and 9-22-46.

103 *"not so quick as his tongue"*: Acheson, *Present at the Creation*, p. 192.

103 *"and full production at home"*: HSTL, Charles Ross Papers, Box 17, Diary, 9-23-46.

104 *"There is no other in the world, I am sure"*: Ibid., Handwritten Notes, 6-25-48.

104 *an "aperient and interesting gossipy talk"*: LOC, Leahy Papers, Diary, 10-2-46.

104 *"the voters decided"*: "Elephant Cavorts . . . ," *New York Times* December 15, 1946, p. 62.

104 *or an actual election*: "Truman Remains Silent as More Urge Him to Quit," *Boston Globe*, November 7, 1946, p. 1.

105 *"wasting the moral and political capital"*: "A personal interview with Stalin," *Look*, February 4, 1947, p. 21+; "Elliott Roosevelt Lands Here, He Criticizes Truman Policies," *New York Herald Tribune*, December 26, 1946, p. 11A.

105 *"I don't think he can be elected"*: Walker, *FDR's Quiet Confidant*, p. 160.

105 *On his arrival*: "The No. 1 No. 2 Man . . . ," *New York Times*, August 25, 1946, SM 95.

105   *"I was the reception committee"*: Acheson, *Present at the Creation*, p. 200; Institute for Advanced Study, Princeton Seminar, Rewrite, Reel 1, 7-2-53; Beisner, *Dean Acheson*, p. 27.

NINE: The Doctrine's Dilemma

106   *"You ask me"*: Vandenberg, *Private Papers*, p. 341.

106   *having to face:* "Truman in Missouri," *Washington Post*, December 26, 1946, p. 1; *New York Herald Tribune*, 12-27, 1946, p. 5, "Truman Back . . . "

106   *"anybody could run the show"*: HSTL, Charles Ross Papers, Box 17, 1-16-47.

106   *"a hell of a place"*: HSTL, PSF, Longhand Notes, 1-6-47.

107   *a hint of other, more serious structural problems:* HSTL, Papers Pertaining to Family, Business, and Personal Affairs, Box 688, 2-13-47.

108   *"everything else would go"*: Institute for Advanced Study, Princeton Seminar, Rewrite, Reel 1, 7-2-53, pp. 134–35.

108   *That . . . wasn't so:* HST Diary, 1-7-46; "Decision Is Sudden," *New York Times*, January 8, 1947, p. 1.

108   *"the born statesman's personal dignity"*: "The Year of the Bullbat," *Time*, January 6, 1947, Cover Story.

108   *"So much for that"*: HSTL, PSF, Longhand Notes, 1-8-47.

108   *"and heartfelt regret"*: Clemson University, J. F. Byrnes Papers, Series 4, Box 17, Folder 19.

109   *"ablest man in the whole gallery"*: HSTL, PSF, Longhand Notes, 1-3-47.

109   *"the great one of the age"*: Ferrell, *Off the Record*, p. 109.

109   *a "one-sided half-smile"*: Lilienthal, *Journals*, Volume Two, June 27, 1947, p. 213.

109   *"the matter under discussion"*: HST, *Memoirs II*, p. 112.

109   *"and communicated force"*: Acheson, *Sketches From Life*, p. 147.

109   *"seem small around him"*: Alsop, *To Marietta*, p. 135.

109   *"I would still be hopeful"*: "Letter From Chungking" *New Yorker*, 3-26-46, p. 85.

110   *was unreachable:* For more on this, see Daniel Kurtz-Phelan's thorough history: *The China Mission: George Marshall's Unfinished War, 1945–1947*.

110   *"It cannot be said"*: "Some believe . . . ," *New York Times*, January 7, 1947, p. 2.

110   *"just to get out of this one!"*: COHP, Eisenhower, pp. 41–42.

110   *"I have been terribly worried"*: The Papers of Dwight David Eisenhower, Vol. 7, Chapter 9, p. 1085, 5-28-46.

110   *"is straightening that one out"*: HSTL, Papers Pertaining to Family, Business, and Personal Affairs, Box 688, 1-19-47.

110   *"would go to hell for pleasure"*: *American Secretaries of State and Their Diplomacy*, Volume XIV, p. 316.

110   *the two were regular lunch companions:* Isaacson and Thomas, *Wise Men*, p. 409.

110   *"No. 1 No. 2 Man"*: "No. 1 No. 2 Man . . . ," *New York Times*, August 25, 1946, p. 95.

111   *"Washington fiddles while Byrnes roams"*: *South Carolina Historical Magazine*, No. 3 (July 1967): 188–90, review by Raymond Moore; Beisner, *Dean Acheson*, p. 27.

111 *"had about driven Dean crazy"*: Lilienthal, *Journals*, Volume Two, March 9, 1947, p. 160.

111 *"He was quite clear"*: Institute for Advanced Study, Princeton Seminar, 7-2-53, pp. 134–35.

111 *"not the master of our foreign policy"*: "Decision Is Sudden," *New York Times*, January 8, 1947, p. 1.

111 *a deputy chief of staff*: The Papers of George Catlett Marshall, Volume 6: "The Whole World Hangs in the Balance," Letter to Robert A. Lovett, 2-6-47.

111 *"Avoid trivia"*: HSTL, Harry B. Price Papers, interview with George Kennan, 2-19-53 (for the Marshall Foundation), https://www.marshallfoundation.org /library/oral-histories/interview-george-f-kennan-february-19-1953/.

111 *"the smoke and crises of current battle"*: Acheson, *Present at the Creation*, p. 214.

111 *"knows more about the Soviet Union"*: Gaddis, *George F. Kennan*, p. 252.

112 *"grand strategy was a new concept"*: Ibid., p. 277.

112 *"even more comprehensive reports"*: MT, *Harry S. Truman*, pp. 346–48.

112 *went to the President's desk*: The entire Clifford-Elsey report may be read at https://www.trumanlibrary.gov/library/research-files/report-american-relations -soviet-union-clark-clifford-clifford-elsey-report.

113 *"Absolute secrecy is necessary"*: Elsey, *Unplanned Life*, p. 143; Clifford, *Counsel to the President*, pp. 123–34; MT, *Harry S. Truman*, pp. 346–48.

114 *"absorb it into the Soviet sphere"*: "The Developing Crisis," *New York Herald Tribune*, March 14, 1946, p. 25.

114 *"tantamount to British abdication"*: Forrestal Papers, Volume 6, Box 150, Folder 10, 2-24-47, Public Policy Papers, Department of Special Collections, Princeton University Library.

114 *"handed the job of world leadership"*: Jones, *Fifteen Weeks*, p. 7.

115 *"were bent on world conquest"*: Ibid., p. 63.

115 *"such a polarization of power"*: HSTL, Meeting Notes, ca. February 1947, J. M. Jones Papers, Subject File, Drafts of Truman Doctrine.

115 *"most of its members will do the same"*: Acheson, *Present at the Creation*, p. 219.

115 *"scare hell out of the country"*: Goldman, *Crucial Decade*, p. 59; HSTL, OH-Loy Henderson, 7-5-73.

116 *"stable, non-Soviet government"*: LOC, Leahy Papers, Diary, 2-27-47.

116 *"It looks not so good though right now"*: HSTL, Papers Pertaining to Family, Business, and Personal Affairs, 2-27-47, letter to Mary Jane Truman.

116 *to defend a weak one*: Truman, *Memoirs II*, pp. 100–1.

116 *"the security of the United States was involved"*: Ibid., pp. 106–7.

116 *"The convergence of massive historical trends"*: Acheson, *Present at the Creation*, p. 220.

117 Elsey's *"methodical mind"*: Clifford, *Counsel to the President*, p. 131.

117 *"to say that he found objections"*: Jones, *Fifteen Weeks*, p. 155; Acheson, *Present at the Creation*, p. 221.

117 *"more grandiose and more sweeping"*: Kennan, *Memoirs*, p. 315.

117 *"no comparable guerrilla movement"*: Ibid., p. 316.

117   *the policy was set:* Jones, *Fifteen Weeks*, p. 155.

117   *"as he was able to get the press to say":* COHP, Steelman, p. 241.

117   *"the evil soil of poverty and strife":* Clifford, *Counsel to the President*, pp. 134–35.

117   *"He can demonstrate that for himself":* Appendix to the Congressional Record, Tribute to Senator Truman, 6-17-40, p. 3925.

117   *"Boy, does he work at it!":* "Truman's Work on Radio Voice Pays Off . . . ," *New York Herald Tribune*, April 27, 1947, p. A2.

117   *"difficulty in reading aloud":* Institute for Advanced Study, Princeton Seminar, Reel 2, Rewrite Record.

117   *Truman could look up from his script:* Mitchell, *Truman and the News Media*, p. 164. Truman's critics could be brutal. A year later, the *New Republic* said "his performance on the air is still that of a faltering schoolboy who has been handed a reader two grades beyond him." ("Truman as Leader," 5-17-48, p. 13).

118   *That got a standing ovation:* "Truman Asks 400 Millions for Greece, Turkey . . . ," *New York Herald Tribune*, March 13, 1947, p. 1.

118   *"free of hesitation or double talk":* Truman, *Memoirs II*, p. 105.

118   *a linguistic gift from Herbert Bayard Swope:* Etymological sleuths might argue that George Orwell was first. He used the term in his essay "You and the Atom Bomb," in October 1945, two months into the atomic age, in which he considered the existence of a nation "which was at once unconquerable and in a permanent state of 'cold war' with its neighbors."

118   *"to be wrong in his facts":* Kahn, *World of Swope*, p. 404.

119   *would help avert a future war:* "Acheson Says War May Be Averted . . . ," *New York Herald Tribune*, March 21, 1947, p. 1A.

119   *no intention to assist just* any *nation that asked for help:* "Bewildered Congress Faces World Leadership Decision," *New York Times*, March 14, 1947, p. 2.

119   *He called Truman's speech "a complete departure":* "Truman Asks 400 Million . . . ," *New York Herald Tribune*, March 13, 1947, p. 1.

119   *"the controlling factor in international relations":* "Taft Condemns Hanging . . . ," *New York Times*, October 6, 1946, p. 1.

119   *"and called the turn":* Jones, *Fifteen Weeks*, p. 12.

119   *"the epochal policy he laid before Congress":* "Truman's 'Anniversary Song' Is More Lilting . . . ," *Washington Post*, April 6, 1947, p.1.

119   *"applied them to the world":* "Democracy's Monroe Doctrine," *Wall Street Journal*, March 13, 1947, p. 4.

120   *"that found themselves in this extremity":* Kennan, *Memoirs*, pp. 319–20.

120   *"to clothe and justify particular actions":* Ibid., p. 322.

120   *known as the Little White House:* Author's visit, April 2017.

120   *"but pleasant splashing":* HSTL, OH-Roger Tubby, 2-10-70, pp. 96–98.

121   *"Your Pop had to tell the world":* MT, *Letters from Father*, p. 90.

121   *"and a huge dose of penicillin":* Saturday Evening Post, April 20, 1950, p. 24+.

121   *"in a prayerful attitude":* "15,000,000 Hear Margaret Truman in Radio Debut," *New York World-Telegram*, March 17, 1947; see also "Miss Truman Makes Radio Debut," *New York Times*, March 17, 1947, p. 1; *New York Herald Tribune*, March 17, 1947, p. 1.

121 *"I wanted to shoot him"*: HSTL, Papers Pertaining to Family, Business, and Personal Affairs, Box 688, 3-22-47.

TEN: Wealth of a Nation

122 *"Can't answer that question"*: Presidential News Conference, 10-16-47, https://www.presidency.ucsb.edu/documents/the-presidents-news-conference-414.

122 *never been happier:* "Acheson Slated . . . ," *New York Times*, May 12, 1947, p. 1.

122 *never risen above twelve thousand dollars:* "Lovett Named to Succeed Acheson," *Baltimore Sun*, May 13, 1947, p. 2.

122 *"perfect information broker"*: Clarke, *Alistair Cooke*, p. 350.

123 *"I was absolutely devoted"*: HSTL, OH-Robert A. Lovett, 7-7-71.

123 *to rein in his heavy smoking:* "Lovett . . . Believed to be Marshall Choice," *Baltimore Sun*, May 13, 1947, p. 2; "Robert Lovett—'Co-pilot at State'" *New York Times*, August 17, 1947, p. 112+; "Marshall's Right-Hand Man," *Washington Post*, May 13, 1947, p.1; "Acheson to Quit . . . ," *New York Times*, May 12, 1947, p. 1.

123 *"that hangs over us and all the world"*: "Cassandra Speaking," *New York Herald Tribune*, April 5, 1947, p. 13.

123 *"millions, even billions" to rebuild Europe:* "U.S. to Study Need of New Aid Abroad," *New York Times*, May 19, 1947, p. 12.

123 *neither of whom wanted to injure their useful alliance:* Jones, *Fifteen Weeks*, p. 236.

124 *"would call 'Operation Rathole'"*: Acheson, *Present at the Creation*, p. 232.

124 *"widen these margins"*: Ibid., pp. 274–81.

124 *"outlines a positive economic program"*: HSTL, Truman and the Marshall Plan, Jones to Lippmann, 5-7-47.

124 *"set to a new tune"*: "Emphasis on Foreign Aid," *New York Times*, May 9, 1947, p. 3.

124 *"a very important démarche"*: HSTL, OH-Leonard Miall, 6-17-64.

124 *never mentioned it:* Marshall Foundation, Kindleberger interview, 9-19-77; Jones, *Fifteen Weeks*, pp. 255–56; HSTL, OH-Miall, June 17, 1964.

125 *led the honorees:* Pogue, *George C. Marshall*, p. 207; *The American Secretaries of State and Their Diplomacy*, Volume XV, pp. 110–11.

125 *"I need not tell you that the world situation is very serious"*: Cray, *General of the Arm*, p. 608.

125 *"may be the touchstone"*: "Europe Must Plot Own Future . . . ," *Boston Globe*, June 6, 1947, p. 1.

125 *a call for "augmented American aid"*: "Marshall Says Europe . . . ," *New York Herald Tribune*, June 6, 1947, p. 1.

125 *"As 'Cure' For Ills"*: "As Cure for Ills," *New York Times*, June 6, 1947, p. 1.

125 *the "crisis" facing the future of bipartisan foreign policy:* "Bipartisan Foreign Policy Now Facing Crisis," *New York Times*, June 8, 1947, p. E3.

126 *"that of civilization in general"*: "Marshall at Harvard," *New York Herald Tribune*, June 14, 1947, p. 13.

126 *"Human misery, begotten of hunger"*: "Eisenhower Says U.S. Aid . . . ," *Baltimore Sun*, June 7, 1947, p. 1.

126 *"civilization, as we know it, will perish"*: "U.S. Is Advised by Eisenhower," *New York Herald Tribune*, June 7, 1947, p. 2; "Eisenhower Bids . . . ," *New York Times*, June 7, 1947, p. 1.

126 *His emphasis, though, was on . . . domestic goals:* https://www.trumanlibrary.gov /library/public-papers/110/address-kansas-city-35th-division-reunion-memorial -service.

126 *"all my clothing was wet"*: LOC, Leahy Papers, Diary, 6-8-47.

126 *Truman was smiling:* "President Truman, Brisk Walker . . . ," *Kansas City Star*, June 7, 1947, p. 3.

127 *"the idea wasn't so much"*: Geroge C. Marshall: *Interviews and Reminiscences*, p. 558.

127 *"social and political disintegration will overwhelm Europe"*: Clayton, *Selected Papers*, Memorandum on the European Crisis, May 27, 1947, p. 202.

127 *Kennan . . . claimed to be "intimately connected"*: George Kennan Papers, Correspondence, Box 99, Folder 7, 4-6-48, Public Policy Papers, Department of Special Collections, Princeton University Library.

127 *"to prevent the complete breakdown of Western Europe"*: Bohlen, *Witness to History*, p. 264.

127 *"The patient is sinking"*: "Marshall's Report . . . ," *New York Times*, April 29, 1947, p. 4.

127 *"and that was the beginning of the talk"*: Pogue, *Interviews and Reminiscences*, p. 559.

127 *"the prologue to the Marshall Plan"*: HST, *Memoirs II*, p. 113.

128 *had all that much to do with it:* Pogue, *Interviews and Reminiscences*, p. 561.

128 *"a whole hell of a lot better"*: Isaacson and Thomas, *Wise Men*, p. 410.

128 *"turn belly up, and die"*: Clifford, *Counsel to the President*, p. 144.

128 *"and never informed the Department of its final form"*: Acheson, *Present at the Creation*, p. 223.

128 *"talking things over"*: Memorandum of interview with the President, 6-16-47: http://marshallfoundation.org/library/digital-archive/6-081-memorandum-in terview-president-june-16-1947/.

129 *helped by Russia's predictable opposition:* See Benn Steil's excellent *The Marshall Plan*, pp. 117–43, for a most useful look at how this played out.

129 *"ahead of reconstruction of Germany's victims"*: "Marshall Plan Criticized . . . ," *New York Herald Tribune*, July 27, 1947, p. 1.

129 *against the "peace-loving nations"*: "Text of address . . . ," *New York Times*, September 19, 1947, p. 18.

130 *"historical state document"*: HSTL, PSF, Longhand Notes, 12-12-47. For news accounts see, among others, "Harriman Reports," *New York Times*, November 9, 1947, p. 1; "Congress Looks at Harriman Blueprint," *Newsweek*, November 17, 1947, p. 25; "Truman Asks 17-Billion . . . ," *New York Herald Tribune*, December 20, 1947, p. 1.

130 *working side by side with Marshall:* NYPL, Sulzberger Papers, Box 46, Folder 24, McCormick letter, 11-7-48.

130 *"I worked on that as hard"*: Pogue, *George C. Marshall*, p. 557.

130 *"starved rats in the ruins"*: Frank, *Ike and Dick*, p. 12.

131   an "attitude of contemptuousness": Forrestal Papers, Volume 7, Box 150, Folder 12, 4-28-47, Public Policy Papers, Department of Special Collections, Princeton University Library.

131   "somehow shrunk into his clothes": Arthur Krock Papers, Box 1, May–June 1947, Public Policy Papers, Department of Special Collections, Princeton University Library.

131   "Marshall and I were in perfect agreement": Truman, Memoirs II, pp. 110–13.

131   "the most provocative work": "The Challenge," Time, March 17, 1947, p. 71+.

131   "a crisis in Western civilization itself ": Ibid.

132   a hundred thousand copies in one year: McNeill, Arnold J. Toynbee, pp. 214–15.

132   "perhaps not less deadly, new weapons": "Whither This World—II," Boston Globe, December 5, 1947, p. 28.

ELEVEN: Strange Interludes

133   transferring from the Library of Congress: Lowenthal, Federal Bureau of Investigation, p. 88.

133   in pursuit of spies and "white slavers": Ibid., pp. 13–14.

134   "'wiretap as much as you can'": "Senators Says F.B.I. . . . ," New York Herald Tribune, February 4, 1942, p. 3.

134   Hoover's "Stork Club playmate": "Derides Excuse," Chicago Tribune, February 4, 1942, p 1.

134   But he was wrong, and soon admitted it: See, for example, "Senators Say F.B.I Had Power to Combat Pearl Harbor Spies," New York Herald Tribune, February 4, 1942, p. 3; "Derides Excuse for FBI Failure in Hawaii Raid," Chicago Tribune, February 4, 1942, p. 1.

135   "the diabolic machinations of sinister figures": HSTL, Stephen J. Springarn Papers, Box 34, Internal Security File, General Loyalties Files, Folder 2 of 3, 2-26-47.

135   Communist ideology is "akin to disease": "F.B.I. Chief Calls U.S. Reds . . . ," New York Herald Tribune, March 27, 1947, p. 1.

135   "They were Commies": Spillane, One Lonely Night, p. 153.

135   The Party's political power was minuscule: Bontecue, Federal Loyalty-Security, p. 9.

135   A number of newspaper stories: "Unprecedented Step . . . ," New York Times, March 23, 1947, p. 1; "Purge Is Ordered . . . ," Baltimore Sun, March 23, 1947, p. 1; "FBI Order Check . . . ," New York Herald Tribune, March 23, 1947, p. 1.

135   The federal workforce employed: Association of the Bar of the City of New York, Report of the Special Committee on the Federal Loyalty-Security Program (New York: Dodd, Mead & Company, 1956), p. 4.

135   it was "a reply to critics": Henry L. Shattuck, The Loyalty Review Board of the U.S. Civil Service Commission, 1947–1953, Proceedings of the Massachusetts Historical Society, Third Series, Vol. 78 (1966), pp. 63–80.

136   "they will become an American Gestapo": Clifford, Counsel to the President, p. 180.

136 *"Edgar Hoover would give his right eye":* HSTL, Letter to Bess, Papers Pertaining to Family, Business, and Personal Affairs, 9-27-47.

136 *"to the outrage of brain-washing":* HST, *Memoirs II,* p. 269.

136 *"a right to be confronted with his accusers":* Ibid., p. 271.

137 *This material went to the FBI:* "U.S. Agencies Begin Loyalty Check . . . ," *New York Herald Tribune,* August 13, 1947, p. 1; "F.B.I. to Begin . . . ," *New York Herald Tribune,* August 18, 1947, p. 13.

137 *"We must all agree":* Bontecue, *Federal Loyalty-Security,* p. 95.

137 *a "disloyal state of mind":* See, for example, "The Loyalty of Federal Employees," *Western Political Quarterly* (March 1949).

137 *"The inevitable effect":* Barth, *Loyalty of Free Men,* p. 129.

137 *"She believed that the F.B.I. was listening":* Flora Barth Wolfe, interview by author, January 9, 2019.

138 *to be tracked down in case of a national emergency:* Navasky, *Naming Names,* p. 23.

138 *"collared by a strong-arm investigator":* Jerry Kluttz, *Washington Post,* Federal Diary, April 16, 1947, p. 6.

138 *they might inquire as to how a person felt:* Harper, *Politics of Loyalty,* pp. 48–49; Bontecue, *Federal Loyalty-Security,* p. 138.

138 *Loyalty boards were interested in reading habits:* Bontecue, *Federal Loyalty-Security,* pp. 138–41.

139 *"the department will be given the benefit of the doubt":* "Purge of State . . . ," *New York Herald Tribune,* October 8, 1947, p. 1.

139 *"such violent reactions to the Loyalty Tests":* Neal, *Eleanor and Harry,* 11-13-47, p. 113.

139 *Truman . . . tried to assure government employees:* "Truman Forbids . . . ," *Washington Post,* November 15, 1947, p. 1.

139 *"no one has a constitutional right to work for the government":* Neal, *Eleanor and Harry,* pp. 114–15.

140 *"Well you didn't have to take the chance did you?":* HSTL, Papers Pertaining to Family, Business, and Personal Affairs, Letter to Bess, 6-30-47.

TWELVE: A Cemetery for Dead Cats

141 *"doesn't let others sleep":* Byrnes, *Speaking Frankly,* p. 212.

141 *"an open invitation to catastrophe":* "Our Armed Forces MUST be Unified," *Collier's Weekly,* 8-26-44, p. 16.

141 *A lot of this had been outlined:* Dorwart, *Eberstadt and Forrestal,* p. 106; see also "The U.S. Outgrows White House," *Wall Street Journal,* October 29, 1945, p. 4; LOC, Leahy Papers, Diary, 1-17-47.

142 *"adamantine insistence":* HSTL, OH-George M. Elsey, 2-10-64.

142 *a high price for not having":* "Truman Urges Merger," *New York Herald Tribune,* January 20, 1945, p. 1; text of Truman message, *New York Times,* December 20, 1945, p. 14.

142 *"What Forrestal kept pressing for":* HSTL, OH-Elsey, 2-10-64.

142 *"The military functions and the civilian decisions":* NSA/47, Hearings on H.R.

2319, Committee on Expenditures, April–June, 1945; July 1, 1947, https://babel.hathitrust.org/cgi/pt?id=umn.31951d03603976d&view=1up&seq=1&q1=132.

142 *Forrestal tried to reassure him:* Forrestal Papers, Box 150, Folder 10, 2-7-47, Public Policy Papers, Department of Special Collections, Princeton University Library.

142 *"I think the whole world knows":* Hearings before the House Committee on Expenditures in the Executive Department, April–June, 1947, p. 132, https://babel.hathitrust.org/cgi/pt?id=umn.31951d03603976d&view=1up&seq=1&q1=132.

143 *"this office will probably be":* Cited by Walter Millis, ed., *The Forrestal Diaries,* p. 299.

143 *in Manhattan and Long Island:* Hoopes and Brinkley, *Driven Patriot,* pp. 44 and 79.

144 *"a small man":* Dos Passos, *The Great Days,* p. 66.

144 *"tight mouth and piercing eyes":* Rogow, *James Forrestal,* p. 247.

144 *sometimes used his column to boost him:* "Forrestal's Rise . . . ," *New York Times,* July 27, 1947, p. 3.

144 *"amazed by his kaleidoscopic activities":* "Jim's Play All Work . . . ," *Washington Post,* July 24, 1947, p. B3.

144 *wanted was a life of "prosperous obscurity":* New-York Historical Society, Lovett Logbook, 9-24-47.

144 *"a lively, kinetic couple":* Alsop, *I've Seen the Best of It,* p. 307.

144 *"what in the world do all you people":* Clifford, *Counsel to the President,* p. 171.

144 *"had begun to detect inner disturbances":* Krock, *Memoirs,* pp. 249–50.

145 *"we would have to face that situation":* The Forrestal Diaries, Cabinet Luncheon, 6-23-47, p. 281.

145 *"tightlipped, concise profanity":* "Army & Navy," *Time,* October 29, 1945, pp. 26–28.

145 *"he'd go out late in the afternoon":* HSTL, OH-Robert Dennison, 9-10-71, 1 of 3.

145 *"I couldn't bring myself":* HSTL, PSF, Longhand Notes, 7-2-47.

146 *"and a wispy mustache":* Alsop, *The Center,* p. 273.

146 *"I turned first to the man":* Clifford, *Counsel to the President,* p. 166.

146 *Souers had been a reservist during the war:* "Souers to Boss Intelligence Unit . . . ," *Washington Post,* January 24, 1946, p. 3.

146 *"It was mutual":* HSTL, OH-Symington, 5-29-81.

146 *"of the most powerful nation":* Rogow, *James Forrestal,* p. 155.

146 *"integrity and spirit of the Navy":* Rogow Papers, Box 3, John T. Connor to Rogow, 7-5-60, Public Policy Papers, Department of Special Collections, Princeton University Library.

146 *his experience in the Missouri National Guard:* The Forrestal, Diaries, July 30, 1945, pp. 415–16.

146 *"the first one who had ever said 'no' to anything":* Ibid., September 18, 1947, p. 318.

147 *"beyond the capacity of any one man":* "Forrestal Opposes Army's Plan," *New York Herald Tribune,* October 23, 1945, p.1.

147   *Stuart Symington said that Forrestal:* HSTL, OH-Symington, 5-29-81.

147   *"mamma is sinking swiftly":* HSTL, Truman Papers, PSF, Diary, 7-26-47.

147   *Truman had gotten similar calls before:* LOC, Leahy Papers, Diary, 5-17-47.

147   *"is not a casual business": The Forrestal Diaries*, pp. 295–96.

148   *"No one knew it":* HSTL, PSF, *Diary*, 7-26-47.

148   *"I knew what he would say":* HSTL, Truman Papers, PSF, Diary, 11-24-52, 5 a.m.

148   *"She was saying goodbye":* MT, *Harry S. Truman*, p. 369.

148   *"no one's looking":* HSTL, Truman Papers, PSF, Diary, 7-28-47; Daily Appointment Sheet for President Harry S. Truman, 7-28-47 and 7-29-47, HSTL, Matthew Connelly Files, Daily Presidential Appointments, 1945–1952.

149   *"from the heart":* https://www.presidency.ucsb.edu/documents/remarks-reporters -following-the-death-tthe-presidents-mother..

THIRTEEN: Minority Reports

150   *"As usual it has been a trying week":* HSTL, Papers of Harry S. Truman Pertaining to Family, Business, and Personal Affairs, Box 688.

150   *"click into place":* Alsop, *The Center*, p. 164.

150   *"the politically advantageous course to follow":* HSTL, Clark Clifford Papers, Memorandum for the President, 11-19-47.

150   *an assistant in the budget office:* "I wrote this and it went to Clark Clifford," Rowe told an interviewer for the Truman Library. See https://www.truman library.gov/library/oral-histories/rowejh#11; Gary Donaldson, *Presidential Studies Quarterly* 23, No. 4 (Fall, 1993), pp. 747–54.

150   *"seized by Clifford":* See Appendix B, in Rowe's oral history: https://www .trumanlibrary.gov/library/oral-histories/rowejhap#appb.

151   *"no more for nigger equality": Journal of Blacks in Higher Education*, No. 26 (Winter, 1999–2000): 28–30. The *St. Louis Post-Dispatch* columnist Marquis Childs later wrote about approaching Truman, on behalf of Agnes Meyer, whose family owned the *Washington Post*, to ask if he'd speak at a dinner for the Wendell Willkie Awards for Negro Journalism. Truman said, " 'Hardly a day goes by that I don't get a letter from that woman or from Eleanor Roosevelt telling me how to handle this job. I get along pretty well with the burr heads . . . until sooner or later I say nigger. I don't see why I shouldn't do it.' And he did." (Childs, *Eisenhower: Captive Hero*, p. 93.)

151   *"Negroes deserve every aid and protection":* Appendix to the Congressional Record, 7-25-40, p. 4546.

151   *"Negroes want justice, not social relations":* Helm, *Harry Truman*, p. 136.

152   *Bess Truman had agreed to be:* "Mrs. Truman Curbs . . . ," *New York Herald Tribune*, October 5, 1945, p. 17.

152   *Hazel Scott . . . was known for performing swing versions of the classics:* Among many extraordinary film clips, this one: https://www.youtube.com/watch?v=2w PZm_aWUuo.

152   *"He got nowhere":* HSTL, Papers of Harry S. Truman Pertaining to Family, Business, and Personal Affairs, Box 688, Letter to Mary Jane Truman, 10-13-47.

152 *Truman was said to have joked:* HSTL, Eben Ayers Papers, Box 14, 10-13-45.

152 *Margaret Truman was to write that her father knew he'd made a mistake:* MT, *Bess W. Truman*, p. 279. For more on this episode see "The Transformation of the Racial Views of Harry Truman," *Journal of Blacks in Higher Education*, No. 26 (Winter, 1999–2000): 28–30; Mitchell, *Truman and the News Media*, p. 193; "D.A.R. 'White Artists Only' . . . ," *New York Herald Tribune*, October 12, 1945, p. 1; "Truman Condemns . . . ," *New York Times*, October 13, 1945, p. 15.

153 *"with the end of his billy":* Read Woodard's affidavit at http://faculty.uscupstate .edu/amyers/deposition.html.

153 *"into my eyeballs":* A detailed account of this—an excerpt from *Unexampled Courage* by Richard Gergel—may be found at https://lithub.com/an-account -of-the-blinding-of-sgt-isaac-woodard-by-the-police-officer-lynwood-shull. For more on this topic, see William E. Leuchtenburg, "The Conversion of Harry Truman," *American Heritage* 42, No. 7 (November 1991; Garth E. Pauley, "Harry Truman and the NAACP: A Case Study in Presidential Persuasion on Civil Rights," *Rhetoric and Public Affairs* 2, No. 2, Special Issue on Civil Rights in the Postmodern Era (Summer 1999): 211–41.

153 *every word of Woodard's affidavit:* One can listen to this and other commentaries here: https://orsonwelles.indiana.edu/collections/show/9.

153 *"push it with everything you have":* HSTL, Tom Clark Papers, Letter to Tom Clark, 9-20-46; Memorandum to David Niles, 9-20-46.

153 *he sounded like a different man:* "Truman Demands We Fight Harder . . . ," *New York Times*, June 30, 1947, p. 1.

154 *"But I believe what I say":* HSTL, Papers of Harry S. Truman Pertaining to Family, Business, and Personal Affairs, Box 688, Letter to Mary Jane Truman, 6-28-47.

154 *"The only limit to an American's achievement":* Address before the NAACP, June 29, 1947; see the text at http://www.presidency.ucsb.edu/ws/index.php ?pid=12686.

154 *"I am going to prove that I do mean it":* White, *A Man Called White* pp. 347–48.

154 *"To Secure These Rights":* See the entire report at https://www.trumanlibrary .gov/library/to-secure-these-rights.

154 *"It is the point at which":* Ibid., p. 7.

155 *"the most courageous and specific":* White, *A Man Called White*, p. 333.

155 *and an end to segregated interstate travel:* "Anti-Lynching Law, Civil Liberties Unit Sought By Truman," *New York Times*, February 3, 1948, p. 1.

155 *"Well, boys, they've fired on Fort Sumter again":* Brown, *James F. Byrnes*, p. 360.

155 *"We either live with the stench or we don't":* "Ban on Segregated Travel Arouses Most Resentment," *Washington Post*, February 9, 1948, p. 1.

155 *"Here's telling President Truman":* "Truman Message on Rights Assailed by Southern Editors," *Baltimore Sun*, February 4, 1948, p. 2.

155 *There was immediate talk of Southern Democrats:* "South Threatens Anti-Truman Drive," *New York Times*, February 4, 1948, p. 1.

155 *would "stab us in the back":* "Thurmond Links . . . ," *Baltimore Sun*, August 12, 1948, p.1; "2 States Join Anti-Truman Bolt," *New York Herald Tribune*, March 2, 1948, p. 1; "Democratic Chief Quits . . . ," *Chicago Tribune*, February 29, 1948,

p. 1; see the full text on the Clemson University Web site at http://tigerprints .clemson.edu/cgi/viewcontent.cgi?article=1303&context=strom.

156 *"bipartisan reactionary war policy"*: "Democrats Scored," *New York Times*, December 30, 1947, p. 1.

156 *"This giant of a man"*: "Wallace Rally Is Likened to Hollywood," *Courant*, October 9, 1947, p. 1, and October 12, 1947, p. D12.

157 *a victory . . . called an "earthquake"*: *New York Herald Tribune*, editorial, February 19, 1948, p. 22; *New York Times*, Krock column, February 19, 1948, p. 22.

157 *"'They're disloyal to their country. Disloyal!'"*: "Truman Denies Slur . . . ," *New York Herald Tribune* March 12, 1948, p. 1.

157 *"It makes good reading in a political year"*: Presidential News Conference, March 11, 1948, http://www.presidency.ucsb.edu/ws/index.php?pid=13126#.

158 *"It seems that some of his best friends"*: NYPL, Sulzberger Papers, Box 80, Memorandum, 5-10-48.

158 *oil was "the life blood of a war machine"*: "Shortage of Oil Threatens Our Defense," *New York Times*, January 20, 1948, p. 1.

158 *"not to see any more of these Jews"*: New-York Historical Society, Robert A. Lovett logbook, Daily Logs, 11-25-47.

158 *"Jesus Christ couldn't please them"*: Wallace, *Diary*, July 30, 1946, p. 607.

159 *"a world wide war between Moslems and Christians"*: LOC Leahy Papers, Diary, 1-17-48.

159 *"passports to nowhere"*: "Hitler's Time Bomb," *New York Herald Tribune*, August 21, 1947, p.22.

159 *just in case it was needed*: New-York Historical Society, Lovett Logbook, 7-22-47 and 8-21-47; "British Return 4,500 Jews . . . ," *New York Herald Tribune*, July 21, 1947, p.1; *New York Herald Tribune*, July 22, 1947, p. 9; "4,406 Exodus Jews Landed, Some Clubbed," *New York Herald Tribune*, September 9, 1947, p. 1; "Hoses, Truncheons Rout Exodus Jews . . . ," *New York Times*, September 10, 1947, p. 1.

160 *"Put an underdog on top"*: HSTL, PSF, Diary, 7-21-47.

160 *"It was our responsibility"*: Sevareid, *Conversations*, p. 71.

160 *no opinion on the matter*: "U.S. Protest," *New York Herald Tribune*, September 11, 1947, p. 1.

160 *and on small fishing boats*: "Almost All Exodus '47," *New York Herald Tribune*, July 19, 1948, p. 1.

160 *"The cross-questioning became more and more rough"*: HSTL, OH-Henderson.

161 *"'How many Arab votes are there in the United States?'"*: HSTL, OH-Connelly, 8-21-68.

161 *"The whole thing is absurd"*: MT, *Harry S. Truman*, pp. 387–88.

161 *"It would be hard to find a truer friend"*: Truman, *Memoirs II*, p. 160.

161 *Jacobson even visited Truman in Key West*: LOC, Leahy Papers, Diaries, 3-15-51.

161 *Jacobson visited the White House a number of times:* HSTL, OH-Granoff, 4-9-69, 9-27-69.

162 *"That isn't like you"*: Truman, *Memoirs II*, pp. 160–1; HSTL, Daily Appointments, 3-13-48.

162 *"I don't think Weizmann's name ever passed our lips"*: HSTL, OH-Granoff.

162   *Weizmann visited the White House:* FRUS, Volume 5, Part 3, p. 737; Daniels, *Man of Independence,* p. 318; HSTL, Connelly Files, Daily Appointments, 5-25-48.

162   *"You two Jews have put it over on me":* Decisions, the Conflicts of Harry S. Truman, Part 6, https://www.trumanlibrary.gov/library/audiovisual-materials /screen-gems/decision-conflicts.

162   *That came as a surprise to delegates:* "UN Staggered . . . ," *New York Herald Tribune,* May 15, 1948, p. 1.

162   *It also followed . . . another unpleasant meeting:* HSTL, OH-Clifford, 2-23-71.

163   *"I asked him to be here":* Clifford, *Counsel to the President,* p. 12.

163   *"I would vote against the President":* Ibid; FRUS, Volume 5, Part 2, 1948, the Near East, South Asia, and Africa, pp. 975–78.

163   *"Marshall glared at CMC":* Clifford, *Counsel to the President,* p. 12.

163   *to cool things down:* HSTL, OH-Clifford, 2-23-71.

163   *"to make him the midwife":* FRUS, Volume 5, Part 2, 5-17-48, pp. 1005–7.

163   *"'deserving of four years more'":* Elsey, *Unplanned Life,* p. 162.

164   *"still the same striped pants conspirators":* HSTL, Papers Pertaining to Family, Business, and Personal Affairs, Box 688, 3-21-48.

164   *a "dangerous influence" over foreign policy:* "'Military Rule' Called Threat," *New York Herald Tribune,* January 29, 1948, p. 1.

164   *"seem to be in agreement in this matter":* LOC, Leahy Diary, 1-29-48.

164   *"two persons are sitting at this desk":* NYPL, Sulzberger Papers, Box 80, Memorandum from Arthur Krock to Sulzberger, 4-8-48.

FOURTEEN: The Frontiers of Hazard

165   *"Our Russian 'friends' seem most ungrateful":* HSTL, Churchill Archives Centre Records, Box No. 1.

165   *seized control of the government:* "Czech Reds Take Over," *New York Herald Tribune,* February 25, 1948, p 1; "Communist Putsch . . . ," *New York Herald Tribune,* February 29, 1948, p. 4; "Czech Reds Seizing Power . . . ," *New York Times,* February 25, 1948, p. 1.

165   *A visitor to Prague:* "The Creeping Terror," *New York Herald Tribune,* November 5, 1947, p. 25.

166   *"Let us please stop talking":* "New World Hope," *New York Times,* June 27, 1945, p. 1.

166   *"The exposed frontiers of hazard":* "Says Peril Nears . . . ," *New York Times,* March 2, 1948, p. 1.

166   *the Communists "have succeeded, by terror":* HSTL, PSF, Box 134, Notes, Meetings, 3-5-48.

167   *"Things look black":* MT, *Letters from Father,* March 3, 1948, pp. 102–8.

167   *"tight as a steel spring":* Forrestal Papers, Vol. 12, Box 151, 8-27-48, Public Policy Papers, Department of Special Collections, Princeton University Library.

167   *"my feeling is real":* The Forrestal Diaries, March 5, 1948, p. 387.

167   *According to Gallup:* Los Angeles Times, October 31, 1947, p. 9.

167   *jumped, or was pushed:* "News Is Delayed," *New York Times,* March 11, 1948,

p. 1; "Masaryk Dies in Plunge, Reds Say Suicide," *New York Herald Tribune*, March 11, 1948, p. 1.

167   *developed a tic:* Cray, *General of the Army*, p. 85.

167   *"barefaced efforts to overthrow the governments of France and Italy":* "Marshall Identifies Russians as Threat to World Stability," *New York Times*, January 13, 1948, p. 1; "E.R.P. Called Bar to Europe Rule by Reds," *New York Herald Tribune*, January 13, 1948, p. 1.

168   *"indicates very plainly what is going on":* "Marshall Charges Czech Reign of Terror," *New York Herald Tribune*, March 11, 1948, p. 1.

168   *"I advise everybody here to be very calm":* "Marshall Czech Statement . . . ," *New York Times*, March 12, 1948, p. 12.

168   *"we should be careful . . . not to let any passions get the better of us":* Presidential News Conference, March 11, 1948, http://www.presidency.ucsb.edu/ws /index.php?pid=13126#.

169   *defense policies of the United States:* https://www.nato.int/archives/1st5years /chapters/1.htm.

169   *"a very good chance of losing it":* The Forrestal, Diaries, "International Situation," March 16, 1948, p. 395.

169   *"without having warned the Congress and the people":* Truman in the White House, pp. 247–8, 3-16-48.

169   *"the maintenance of the future peace":* Hearings Before the House Committee on Expenditures in the Executive Department, April-June 1947, p. 132, https://babel.hathitrust.org/cgi/pt?id=umn.31951d03603976d&view=1u p&seq=1&q1=132 .

170   *"we shall pay the price of war":* The complete text is at https://www.presidency.ucsb .edu/documents/special-message-the-congress-the-threat-the-freedom-europe; and it may be heard at https://www.youtube.com/watch?v=S6_QWZuSz8E.

171   *for war with Russia:* "Democrats Scored," *New York Times*, December 30, 1947, p. 1.

171   *"I'll not buy it":* "Soviet Denounced . . . ," *New York Times*, March 18, 1948, p. 1; "Truman Calls for Draft . . . ," *New York Herald Tribune*, March 18, 1948, p. 1; "Truman in Speech Here Scorns 'Wallace and His Communists,'" *New York Herald Tribune*, March 28, 1948, p. 1.

171   *"rotted harvest of appeasement":* "Truman Rejects Any Wallace Aid," *New York Times*, March 8, 1948, p. 30.

171   *"has found the leak in the White House":* Truman in the White House, 3-18-48, p. 250.

172   *"tends to back up his President":* HSTL, Clifford Files, Memorandum, 11-19-47.

172   *Since the end of the war:* "Marshall Calls for Resistance," *New York Herald Tribune*, September 9, 1948, p. 1.

172   *Admiral Leahy was receiving reports:* LOC, Leahy Papers, Diary, 3-6-48.

172   *considered indefensible:* See: Murphy, *Diplomat Among Warriors*, pp. 310–22, for a firsthand recollection.

172   *"is suffering from internal weakness":* LOC, Leahy Papers, Diary, 6-29-48.

172   *"We aren't going to stand for it":* Connally, *My Name Is Tom Connally*, pp. 329–30.

172   *"and we intend to stay":* "Marshall Says 'We Intend to Stay,'" *New York Herald*

Tribune, July 1, 1948, p. 10; an interesting look at this time, through the eyes of the CIA, may be found here: https://www.cia.gov/library/readingroom /docs/1961-09-01d-A.pdf.

173 *were killed in accidents:* "Soviet Threatens Berlin Lane . . . ," *New York Times*, September 25, 1948, p. 1; https://www.german-way.com/history-and-culture /germany/history-of-germany/the-berlin-airlift/.

173 *General Clay was sure that the airlift could continue:* LOC, Leahy Papers, Diary, 10-21-48.

173 *would require 133 atomic weapons:* Condit, *The Joint Chiefs of Staff*, p. 158; Bowie and Immerman, *Waging Peace*, p. 15. See also Kohn and Harahan, *U.S. Strategic Air Warfare*.

173 *Three "improved" weapons were detonated:* "Three New Atomic Arms," *New York Times*, May 18, 1948, p. 1.

174 *"there's nothing else to do":* Lilienthal, *Journals*, Volume Two, May 18, 1948, p. 342.

174 *"the proper time to drop one":* The Forrestal Diaries, July 15, 1948, p. 458.

174 *"you have made fine progress":* Lilienthal, *Journals*, Volume Two, May 18, 1948, p. 342.

174 *"I appointed good men":* Ibid., p. 343.

FIFTEEN: The Scrapper

175 *"form of American democracy":* Neal, *Miracle of '48* , p. 134.

175 *Doctors at Walter Reed:* Cray, *General of the Army*, p. 655.

175 *a discreet bet on Truman's probable opponent:* Clifford, *Counsel to the President*, p. 173; Rogow Papers, Box 2, Dewey to Rogow, 6-25-59, Public Policy Papers, Department of Special Collections, Princeton University Library, "Forrestal Holds Dangers Lessened," *New York Times*, February 2, 1949, p. 1.

175 *"Now my bath room is about to fall":* HSTL, Papers of Harry S. Truman Pertaining to Family, Business, and Personal Affairs, Box 688, 8-10-48.

176 *"If I felt any better I couldn't stand it":* "President Departs . . . ," *New York Times*, June 4, 1948, p. 1; "Truman Starts . . . ," *New York Herald Tribune*, June 4, 1948, p. 1; Ross, *Loneliest Campaign*, pp. 80–82; "Letter from a Campaign Train," *New Yorker*, October 9, 1948, pp. 69–77.

176 *"There is a melody in his voice":* Nation's Business, June 1948, p. 29.

176 *"He can't do what he wants to":* "Truman Declares Stalin . . . ," *New York Herald Tribune*, June 12, 1948, p. 1; Neal, *Miracle of '48*, p. 26, Rear Platform Remarks, Eugene, Oregon 6-11-48.

176 *"To err is Truman":* The crack was introduced at a Wallace rally. See: "Truman Sold Out to GOP," *Baltimore Sun*, May 14, 1947, p. 1,

176 *"the special-privilege Congress":* "Truman Returns . . . ," *New York Herald Tribune*, June 19, 1948, p. 1.

176 *and passage of the Marshall Plan:* "Vandenberg Retorts . . . ," *New York Herald Tribune*, June 19, 1948, p. 1.

176 *"every whistle stop in the United States":* Hechler, *Working with Truman*, p. 77;

"Declares Truman Assails . . . ," *Washington Post*, June 12, 1948, p. 1; "Truman to Speak at 'Whistle Stops,' " *New York Times*, September 7, 1948, p. 18.

177 *"and need not concern you":* NYPL, Sulzberger Papers, Box 46, Anne McCormick to AHS, 11-7-48.

177 *"Mortimer Snerd, Henry Wallace":* Mortimer Snerd was the ventriloquist Edgar Bergen's dimwitted companion to Charlie McCarthy.

177 *She reminded delegates:* "Republican Exuberance . . . ," *New York Times*, June 22, 1948, p. 3; text of convention speech, *New York Herald Tribune*, June 22, 1948, p. 10; "U.S. Distrust of Democrats . . . ," *Courant*, June 22, 1948, p. 1.

177 *"how small a part":* "Mr. Truman on Tour," *New York Herald Tribune*, September 27, 1948, p. 17.

177 *influence of the "Missouri Gang":* "Truman as Leader," *New Republic*, May 17, 1948, pp. 13–22. (Henry Wallace by then had stepped down as editor.)

178 *Roosevelt's four sons:* "James Roosevelt to Urge . . . ," *Boston Globe*, July 4, 1948, p. C1.

178 *"is definite and positive":* "Eisenhower Rules Self Out," *New York Herald Tribune*, January 24, 1948, p. 1; "Refusal 'Positive,' " *New York Times*, January 24, 1948, p. 1; text of letter, *Washington Post*, January 24, 1948, p. 1.

178 *his entire life had been built:* Forrestal Papers, Volume 9, Box 151, Folder 3, 1-22-48, Public Policy Papers, Department of Special Collections, Princeton University Library.

178 *"you can't miss being President":* Krock, *Memoirs*, 279–80.

178 *"A lot of people like that":* HSTL, PSF, Longhand Notes, 6-18-48.

178 *"Take the Roosevelt clan as an example":* HSTL, Papers of Harry S. Truman Pertaining to Family, Business, and Personal Affairs, Box 688, 3-31-48.

178 *"must be allowed to lead their own lives":* My Day column, 3-30-48; https://www.gwu.edu/~erpapers/myday/displaydoc.cfm?_y=1948&_f=md000927.

178 *"The most dangerous consequences":* Forrestal Diary, Box 151, Volume 10, Folder 3, 3-26-48, Public Policy Papers, Department of Special Collections, Princeton University Library.

178 *victory lay with the reluctant Eisenhower:* "Politics of the Two Parties," *New York Herald Tribune*, July 12, 1948, p. 15; "Mr. Truman and the Democratic Problem," *New York Herald Tribune,* July 13, 1948, p. 25.

179 *"to throw an election":* "Wayward Press," *New Yorker*, August 14, 1948, p. 72.

179 *"I hope we can solve it":* HSTL, Churchill Churchill Archives Centre Records, Box 1, 7-10-48.

179 *and a civilian passenger:* "Berlin Food Plane Crashes," *Baltimore Sun*, July 9, 1948, p. 1.

179 *"with a corn knife":* Interview with Alben W. Barkley, July 23, 1953, Alben W. Barkley Oral History Project, Louie B. Nunn Center for Oral History, University of Kentucky Libraries, https://kentuckyoralhistory.org/ark:/16417/xt7vd n3ztj4U.

179 *had gone missing:* "Democrats Appear to Have Given Up . . . ," *Washington Post*, July 12, 1948, p. 1; "Figures of New Deal Era Missing . . . ," *New York Times*, July 13, 1948, p. 7.

179   *"no professional liberal is intellectually honest"*: HSTL, Truman Papers, PSF, Diary, 7-9-48.

179   *"My 'good' friend, Leslie Biffle"*: Ibid., 7-12-48.

179   *"arise and renounce it"*: Interview with Alben W. Barkley, July 23, 1953, Alben W. Barkley Oral History Project, Louie B. Nunn Center for Oral History, University of Kentucky Libraries, https://kentuckyoralhistory.org/ark:/16417/xt7v dn3ztj40.

180   *"call old man Barkley"*: HSTL, PSF, Diary, 7-12-48.

180   *"I don't want any warmed-over biscuits"*: "Cheering Convention Demands," *Boston Globe*, July 13, 1948, p. 1; "Democrats Cheer Barkley Gibes," *New York Herald Tribune*, July 13, 1948, p. 1.

180   *people at home . . . could experience . . . a political convention*: "What TV Industry Learned," *Boston Globe*, July 4, 1948, p. C1; "Video Fans Clamor for More," *Boston Globe*, July 18, 1948, p. C9.

180   *"Barkley . . . mentions me only casually by name"*: HSTL, PSF, Diary, 7-13-48.

181   *"You shall not crucify the South"*: "Truman Kept Waiting," *New York Herald Tribune*, July 15, 1948, pp. 1–2; "Victory Sweeping," *New York Times*, July 15, 1948, p. 1; "Twilight of the Gods," *New York Herald Tribune*, July 15, 1948, p. 21.

181   *"reduced to such a lonely plight"*: Alsop, *I've Seen the Best Of It*, p. 296.

181   *"a little more fluid than usual"*: HSTL, OH-Graham, 3-30-89.

181   *He promised to call Congress back*: https://www.senate.gov/artandhistory/history /minute/Turnip_Day_Session.htm; "In a Fighting Mood," *New York Times*, July 15, 1948, p. 1.

182   *integrating the military services*: See also Nichols, *A Matter of Justice*, pp. 42–45.

182   *nominated Governor Thurmond*: "Southeners Name Thurmond," *New York Times*, July 18, 1948, p.1.

182   *on a sorrel horse named Nugget*: "Taylor Ends Ride for Peace," *Washington Post*, November 17, 1947, p. 2; "Taylor Bolts Party," *New York Herald Tribune*, February 24, 1948, p. 1.

182   *"I know I can take it"*: Charles G Ross, "How Truman Did It," *Colliers*, December 25, 1948, pp. 13, 87–88.

182   *"and I'm going to give 'em hell"*: "Truman Off on Western Trip . . . ," *New York Times*, September 18, 1948, p. 1.

182   *Truman could only see enthusiastic crowds*: "Will Truman Campaign 'Catch Fire?,'" *New York Herald Tribune*, October 16, 1948, p. 10.

183   *Sometimes he'd invite people to come aboard*: "Letter from a Campaign Train," *New Yorker*, October 9 1948, pp. 69–70; "Truman Literally Gets 'Close' . . . ," *Baltimore Sun*, September 24, 1948, p. 1.

183   *"a traveling circus"*: HSTL, OH-Richard Strout, 2-5-71.

183   *"It has become a stunt"*: "Dewey Is Almost Certain to Win," *New York Herald Tribune*, September 9 1948, p. 1.

183   *forty-five electoral votes from eleven states*: "Southern Revolt . . . ," *New York Times*, September 13, 1948, p.1.

183   *Marshall often looked fatigued*: "Marshall Has an Operation," *New York Times*, December 8, 1948, p. 1.

183   *decided to delay*: Cray, *General of the Army*, p. 655.

183   *"You can't settle it"*: Presidential News Conference, 9-9-48; https://www.presi dency.ucsb.edu/documents/the-presidents-news-conference-371.

184   *"Spend a most pleasant day"*: HSTL, PSF, Diary, 9-11-48.

184   *"feel better although Berlin is a mess"*: Ibid., 9-13-48.

184   *Marshall was sure*: HSTL, Connelly Files, Notes on Cabinet Meetings File, 7-23-48.

184   *he "apparently" told Truman*: Cray, *General of the Army*, p. 655.

184   *something dramatic was needed*: Carr, *Truman Stalin and Peace*, pp. 106, 109; LOC, Leahy Papers, Diary, 9-15-48.

184   *the two of them came up with a scheme*: Krasnoff, *Truman and Noyes*, p. 59.

185   *he hadn't informed his secretary of state*: Ibid.

185   *Truman soon canceled the Vinson plan*: New-York Historical Society, Lovett Logbook, 10-5-48; HSTL-OH, Monte Poen Papers, Box 3, Robert Lovett interview.

185   *"The matter was then dropped"*: HSTL, PSF, Box 53, Vinson, 10-9-48; Pogue, *George C. Marshall*, pp. 407–8; "Marshall on Truman Meeting," *New York Herald Tribune*, October 10, 1948, p. 7.

185   *"I am grateful to you"*: "Vinson Moscow Mission Abandoned . . . ," *New York Herald Tribune*, October 10, 1948, p. 1; "Situation Cleared . . . ," *New York Times*, October 10, 1948, p. 1.

185   *"I hope not"*: HSTL, PSF, Box 53, Memorandum of news conference, 10-9-48.

186   *"avoid a recurrence"*: New-York Historical Society, Lovett Logbook, 10-12-48, telephone call, 10:46 a.m.

186   *Truman was "going to try something else"*: Ibid., 10-22-48, call from Krock, 6 p.m.

186   *"He must be feeling desperate about the campaign"*: Connally, *My Name Is Tom Connally*, p. 331; Vandenberg, *Private Papers*, p. 458.

186   *"cold and cunning men"*: "Calls GOP 'Cunning' . . . ," *New York Times*, September 29, 1948, p. 1.

186   *to pass a "police state program"*: "Taft Declares . . . ," *New York Herald Tribune*, July 29, 1948, p. 1.

187   *"You can throw the Gallup Poll right into the ashcan"*: "Truman Confident . . . ," *New York Times*, October 30, 1948, p. 7.

187   *"and so I decided to come in to town"*: Charles G Ross, "How Truman Did It," *Colliers*, December 25, 1948, pp. 13, 87–88.

SIXTEEN: Office Politics

188   *"apt to come unstuck by Thursday"*: Forrestal, *Diaries*, p. 541.

188   *a formal dance at the Sulgrave Club*: "Arthur M. Hills Give . . . ," *Washington Post*, November 6, 1948, p. B5.

188   *"already was looking for a successor"*: "Barkley Joins President to Plot Program," *Baltimore Sun*, November 10, 1948, p. 1.

188   *"the greatest in the history of this old capital"*: HSTL, Papers Pertaining to Family, Business, and Personal Affairs, , Box 688, 11-7-48.

189   *asked for suggestions to include*: Forrestal Papers, Volume XIII, Box 151, Folder 13, Public Policy Papers, Department of Special Collections, Princeton University Library.

189 *"Where are your cameras?":* "Truman Grows 'Jeff Davis' Beard . . . ," *New York Times,* November 11, 1948, p. 1.

189 *Truman started calling him "Jeeter":* Clifford, *Counsel to the President,* p. 246.

189 *over to touristy Duval Street:* Parks, *Harry Truman and the Little White House,* p. 51.

189 *"He was pretty full of himself, naturally":* HSTL, OH-Robert G. Nixon, 10-28-70.

189 "I gloat! Hear me!": *Stalky & Co.* (London: Macmillan, 1899), p. 14.

190 *the hazards of "flying dual control":* "Flying Dual Control," *New York Herald Tribune,* November 3, 1948, p. 29.

190 *"candidates make election contests":* HSTL, PSF, draft letter, 12-30-48.

190 *majorities in both houses of Congress:* The final electoral vote margin was 303–189, and Truman's popular vote, 24,105,694, surpassed Dewey's by more than two million. Thurmond and Wallace got about the same popular vote—1.1 million—but Thurmond's States Rights Party got 39 electoral votes and Wallace's Progressive Party got none.

190 *"That's the kind of courage":* Vandenberg, *Private Papers,* p. 460.

190 *rather than an ivory tower:* Ferrell, *Truman in the White House,* p. 315; Acheson and Truman, *Affection and Trust,* p. 19.

190 *"Wednesday morning Democrats":* HSTL, Ayers Papers, Box 17, 11-5-48; LOC, Leahy Papers, Diary, 11-3-48–11-5-48.

191 *something more modern could take its place:* "White House Is Closing as Unsafe . . . ," *New York Times,* January 7, 1948, p. 1.

191 *selling president-watching tickets:* "White House Life . . . ," *Washington Post,* November 19, 1949, p. 7.

191 *"to afford good medical care":* State of the Union, January 5, 1949, https://www.presidency.ucsb.edu/documents/annual-message-the-congress-the-state-the-union-21.

191 *"a chance to obtain those services":* "Truman Submits Medical Aid Plan," *New York Times,* April 23, 1949, p. 1; "Health Plan Vote Deferred," *New York Times,* April 28, 1949, p. 19.

192 *"refused to pass anything":* "Giant Pre-Inaugural Studded with Stars," *Los Angeles Times,* January 20, 1949, p. 18.

192 *"defeated by an overwhelming majority":* This famous mimicry is on YouTube at https://www.youtube.com/watch?v=q9WLImeRwOU.

192 *The crowd loved it:* "Truman Jibes at Prophets . . . ," *Washington Post,* January 20, 1949, p. 1.

192 *that included Vinson and General Eisenhower:* HSTL, Daily Sheets, 1-6-49.

192 *Secretary of State Marshall:* "Marshall Has an Operation," *New York Times,* December 8, 1948, p. 1.

192 *on at least three occasions:* Presidential News Conference, December 2, 1948, https://www.presidency.ucsb.edu/documents/the-presidents-news-conference-374.

192 *"You had better be sitting down":* Institute for Advanced Study, Princeton Seminar Files, Acheson Papers, Reel 2, Track 2, 10-10-53.

193 *"It has taken years and years":* "Mr. Secretary," *New Yorker,* November 19, 1949, pp. 49, 59.

193 *"we will surpass in greater liberty":* https://www.trumanlibrary.gov/library/public -papers/19/inaugural-address.

193 *as if Forrestal was being blocked:* "Thousands Fill . . . ," *Washington Post*, January 21, 1949, p. L4.

194 *and waved to the general:* "Biggest Presidential Parade," *New York Herald Tribune*, February 21, 1949, p. 1; "'Ike' in Parade," *Boston Globe*, January 21, 1948, p. 1; "In the Parade . . . ," *New York Times*, January 21, 1949, p. 5.

194 *When Strom Thurmond's car:* "A Happy President," *New York Times*, January 21, 1949, p. 5.

194 *"I could get him to approve anything":* Pogue, *Interviews and Reminiscences,"* 11-15-56, p. 331.

194 *"likely to be the law of the land":* COHP, Royall, 2-2-63, p. 221.

194 *looking more English than American:* Acheson, *Acheson Country*, pp. 25–26.

194 *"The President was almost always inclined":* Institute for Advanced Study, Princeton Seminar Files, Acheson Papers, Reel 2, Track 2, 10-10-53.

195 *where his crew coach was Averell Harriman: American Secretaries of State*, Volume XVI, p. 4.

195 *"his penetrating, almost popping eyes":* "Mr. Secretary, II," *New Yorker*, November 19, 1949, p. 40.

195 *"mustache wax a couple of times a week":* Acheson, *Acheson Country*, pp. 25–26.

195 *"has a personality of its own":* "Mr. Secretary, I," *New Yorker*, November 12, 1949, p. 41.

195 *His mother . . . was Canadian: American Secretaries of State*, Volume XVI, p. 1.

195 *"'You stand for everything that has been wrong'":* Goldman, *Crucial Decade*, p. 125.

195 *"can be as mean as a polecat":* NYPL, Sulzberger Papers, Box 1, Reston to AHS, 1-31-58.

196 *"I suppose I cannot say":* Wheaton College, Malcolm Muggeridge Papers; "Mr. Acheson Brings a New Touch . . . ," *Telegraph*, January 10, 1949; letter from Acheson to Muggeridge, January 18, 1949, 1-10-49, Wheaton College, Malcolm Muggeridge Papers.

196 *"That's Truman's spontaneity for me":* Brandon, *Special Relationships*, p. 67.

196 *"had, in effect, only one foreign policy adviser":* Jespersen, *Interviews with George F. Kennan*, interview with Louis Fischer, 1965, p. 59.

196 *"conniving to run the Presidency":* Acheson and Truman, *Affection and Trust*, pp. 163–64.

197 *"and it's getting more burdensome all the time":* HSTL, OH-Dennison, 9-10-71.

197 *"I don't pass the buck":* HSTL, PSF, Diary, 7-19-48; Ferrell, *Off the Record*, p. 145.

197 *He'd repeatedly dip his fingers:* "Big Boss of the Pentagon," *New York Times*, August 29, 1948, p. SM9.

197 *a program parallel to the Marshall Plan:* https://www.nato.int/archives/1st5years /chapters/1.htm; "U.S. Armed Help for Free Nations," *Christian Science Monitor*, June 12, 1948, p. 1.

197 *"I have informed him that I will be unable to remain":* "Forrestal to Quit During Next Term," *New York Times*, November 15, 1948, p. 1; "Forrestal Says He Won't Serve," *New York Herald Tribune*, November 15, 1948, p. 1.

198   *"The Cabinet is singularly and peculiarly his business"*: "Forrestal Will Stay if Truman Desires," *New York Times*, November 18, 1948, p. 1.

198   *which did include two Florida politicians*: LOC, Leahy Papers, Diary, 11-18-48.

198   *"There is no situation"*: HSTL, Ayers Papers, Box 17, Diary, 5-24-49; *Washington Post*, November 19, 1948, p. 5; "President Gets Forrestal Report," *New York Herald Tribune*, November 19, 1948, p. 1.

198   *felt even more adrift within the Truman orbit*: Forrestal, *Diaries*, pp. 427–28; LOC, Leahy Papers, Diary, 11-18-48; Hoopes and Brinkley, *Driven Patriot*, Hoopes interview with Marx Leva.

198   *a speed record for getting through eighteen holes*: "Big Boss of the Pentagon," *New York Times*, August 29, 1948, p. SM9.

199   *"Jim was all drive"*: Schlesinger, *A Life*, pp. 383–84.

199   *"the failures of professional men to 'get together'"*: The Papers of Dwight David Eisenhower, Volume 10, Part 2, Chapter 4, pp. 461–62, 2-2-49.

199   *Its chief purpose was to relieve the pressure on Forrestal*: Ibid., pp. 466–70, 2-4-49.

199   *Truman agreed to appoint an under secretary*: Ibid., pp. 482–83.

199   *"arch representative of Wall Street imperialism"*: Jack Anderson, *Confessions of Muckraker*, pp. 123.

199   *The holdup had been tabloid-worthy*: "48,000 Gems Taken," *New York Times*, July 3, 1937, p. 32.

199   *"spent the remainder of the night"*: Jack Anderson, *Confessions of a Muckraker*, p. 135; "In the Nation," *New York Times*, February 27, 1945, p 18; Rogow, *James Forrestal*, p. 281; "Friends Link Forrestal . . . ," *Washington Post*, May 23, 1949, p. E1.

199   *"as nervous as a whore in church"*: Abell, *Drew Pearson Diaries*, Janusry 31, 1949, pp. 17–18.

200   *"they have wired it"*: Arthur Krock Papers, Public Policy Papers, Department of Special Collections, Princeton University Library. See also Krock, *Memoirs*, p. 254, where Eberstadt is identified only as "Z."

200   *to report this to the President*: Donovan, *Tumultuous Years*, p. 61.

200   *"When I saw Jim Forrestal was cracking up"*: HSTL, PSF, Longhand Notes, 9-14-50; also, Ferrell, *Off the Record*, pp. 191–93.

200   *among them . . . Harry Vaughan*: "The General's Shadow," *New York Herald Tribune*, March 28, 1949, p. 8.

200   *"a more active member of the Democratic Party"*: "Forrestal to Quit," *New York Times*, March 3, 1949, p. 1; also *Baltimore Sun*, March 3, 1949, p. 3; *Christian Science Monitor*, March 3, 1949, p. 1; *New York Herald Tribune*, March 3, 1949, p. 10; *Chicago Tribune*, March 3, 1949, p. 1.

200   *He'd felt let down*: McFarland and Rolle, *Louis Johnson and the Arming of America*, pp. 99–100.

200   *commander of the American Legion*: "Defense Secretary Forrestal Resigns . . . ," *New York Herald Tribune*, March 4, 1949, p. 1.

200   *"Big, beefy"*: "Paid in Full," *Time*, March 14, 1949, p. 23+ .

201   *"political stalwart and feudist"*: *Saturday Evening Post*, July 30, 1949, p. 26; Donovan, *Tumultuous Years*, p. 61.

201   *also been one of Pearson's informants:* Abell, *Drew Pearson Diaries*, January 13, 1949, p. 9.

201   *summoning outside help:* Rogow, *James Forrstal*, pp. 313–34.

201   *had been Forrestal's alone:* "Forrestal Resigns . . . ," *New York Herald Tribune* March 4, 1949, p. 1.

201   *"as his successor":* Letter from Truman, 7-29-59, quoted by Rogow, *James Forrestal*, p. 313.

201   *same dubious claim:* Ibid.

201   *"Jim, I want to congratulate you on a great public career":* HSTL, Remarks at a Testimonial Dinner for Secretary Forrestal, 3-23-49.

201   *during the Civil War: Louis Johnson and the Arming of America*, p. 150.

202   *"whether I really wanted him to be relieved by Louis Johnson this noon":* HSTL, OH-Dennison, 9-20-71.

202   *"You deserve it, Jim":* "Johnson Sworn In," *Washington Post*, March 29, 1949, p. 1; "Forrestal Gets . . . ," *New York Times*, March 29, 1949, p. 3.

202   *his third Distinguished Service Medal:* LOC, Leahy Papers, Diary, 3-26-49.

202   *"he looked like a man who just could not believe it":* HSTL, OH-Robert G. Nixon, 11-3-70.

202   *"nervous exhaustion" was the preferred term:* "Forrestal Seriously Ill," *Washington Post*, April 7, 1949, p. 3.

202   *"I regret to report that James Forrestal . . . is out of his mind":* China Weekly Review, April 16–49, p. 159; "Forrestal Found Victim of Fatigue," *Baltimore Sun*, April 12, 1949, p.1.

203   *were "coming along fine":* "Truman Pays Visit," *New York Herald Tribune*, April 24, 1949, p. 28.

203   *Forrestal was in room 1618:* "Forrestal Killed . . . ," *New York Times*, May 23, 1949, p. 1.

203   *Truman had planned to attend another Gridiron event:* HSTL, Ayers Papers, Box 17, Diary, 5-22-49; "Stuffing Beaten Out of Shirts . . . ," *Washington Post*, May 22, 1949, p. M1.

203   *"the vicious rules of politics":* "Worry Over Intrigues . . . ," *Washington Star*, May 23, 1949, p. 15.

203   *"trying to make out that he had killed Forrestal":* HSTL, Ayers Papers, Box 17, Diary, 5-23-49.

203   *"I expect to remain a victim of the Washington scene":* "Forrestal Sees Truman . . . ," *New York Herald Tribune*, January 12, 1949, p. 1; Dos Passos, *The Great Days*, p. 233.

SEVENTEEN: "First Lightning"

204   *"develops a flame-thrower to protect himself":* "The Hydrogen Bomb: IV," *Scientific American*, June 1950, p. 11.

204   *the United States "could lick Russia":* Wallace, *Diary*, June 25, 1946, p. 582; he'd been told about this by the *New York Times*'s Felix Belair.

204   *"Moscow came out of the dark ages only in 1917":* HSTL, Jonathan Daniels Papers, Interview with Truman, 8-30-49.

204 *The West's counter-blockade:* For the administration's view of the situation in Berlin, see HSTL, PSF, Box 186, Berlin, "A Report to the National Security Council," 6-12-52.

204 *On the other side:* For a detailed look, see Carolyn Eisenberg's excellent *Drawing the Line,* a study of Cold War politics, and the decision-making that led to the division of Germany in May 1949.

204 *"security and freedom in the North Atlantic Community":* https://www.nato.int /archives/1st5years/chapters/1.htm; Childs, *Witness to Power,* p. 122.

205 *"We are like a group of householders":* https://www.trumanlibrary.gov/library/public -papers/68/address-occasion-signing-north-atlantic-treaty.

205 *"we are now nearer to war":* Ferrell, *Truman in the White House,* 8-31-49, p. 326.

205 *the globe in his office:* Lilienthal, *Journals,* Volume Two, February 14, 1949, p. 471.

205 *"never" be able to build a nuclear bomb:* Truman supposedly said this to J. Robert Oppenheimer. Quoted in Costigliola, *Roosevelt's Lost Alliances,* p. 373.

205 *There was no reason to think that everything would change:* "Acheson States," *New York Herald Tribune,* September 24, 1949, p. 1.

206 *thought it would take twenty:* Conant, *My Several Lives,* pp. 360–61.

206 *"were still censored":* In his book *Atomic Cover-up,* Greg Mitchell recounts much of this history; his disturbing documentary may be watched by linking to gregmitch.medium.com.

206 *"had run down their cheeks":* Hersey, *Hiroshima,* p. 68.

206 *"life on the surface was no longer possible": Dimension X,* 9-15-50, "Hello Tomorrow." https://www.oldtimeradiodownloads.com/sci-fi/dimension-x/hello-tomor row-1950-09-15.

206 *would make him famous:* Frady, *Billy Graham,* p. 201.

206 *"America's Sensational Young Evangelist":* Ibid., p. 191.

207 *"out of a Nordic fairy tale":* Ibid., p. 5.

207 *"I am persuaded that time is desperately short!":* Graham, *Revival in Our Time,* p. 122.

207 *"either revival or judgment":* Frady, *Billy Graham,* p.197.

207 *to call for a "Day of Prayer":* HSTL, General File, Billy Graham, 1-1-50.

208 *"I hope there won't have to be an arms race":* Presidential News Conference, October 6, 1949, http://www.presidency.ucsb.edu/ws/index.php?pid=13323.

208 *be pursued in peacetime:* Peter Galison and Barton Bernstein, "In Any Light: Scientists and the Decision to Build the Superbomb," *Historical Studies in the Physical and Biological Sciences* 19, No. 2 (1989): 272.

208 *to Truman's great displeasure:* "Truman Demands . . . ," *New York Times,* November 26, 1949, p. 1.

209 *stop the "loose talk":* Ibid.

209 *"It is necessarily an evil thing":* FRUS, 1949, National Security Affairs, Foreign Economic Policy, Volume I, pp. 575, 577–79.

209 *"annihilation of any life on earth":* "Einstein Says Hydrogen Bomb May Doom All," *New York Herald Tribune,* February 13, 1950, p. 1.

209 *"dream of total destruction":* "Pandora's Box II," *New York Herald Tribune,* January 4, 1950, p. 25.

209   *"to blow up the earth":* "The Bomb," *New York Herald Tribune,* January 18, 1950, p. 25.

209   *"talk to lying scoundrels":* HSTL, PSF, Truman to McMahon, 1-5-50, cited in Peter Galison and Barton Bernstein, "In Any Light: Scientists and the Decision to Build the Superbomb," *Historical Studies in the Physical and Biological Sciences* 19, No. 2 (1989): 267–347.

209   *"a vast number of civilians":* Ibid., pp. 292–93. For a fuller discussion of the decision process, see Warner R. Schilling, "The H-Bomb Decision: How to Decide Without Actually Choosing," *Political Science Quarterly* (March 1961): 24–46.

210   *"we may already have lost the armaments race":* "Build New Bomb . . . ," *New York Times,* January 28, 1950, p. 6.

210   *to carry atomic bombs to ports all over Europe:* "Urey Fears Entry of Bombs in Ships," *New York Times* February 9, 1950, p. 1.

210   *at the 1925 F Street Club:* https://www.trumanlibrary.gov/calendar/search?comment_keywords=McMahon&body_value_op=word.

210   *"fission bombs might destroy":* FRUS, 1949, Volume I, pp. 588–91.

210   *"fission bombs otherwise needed":* Ibid.

210   *"I don't blitz easily":* Lilienthal, *Journals,* Volume Two, p. 594.

211   *"his chief constables":* HSTL, OH-Sidney Souers, 12-15-54 and 12-16-54.

211   *a final recommendation on the Super:* Ibid., 12-15-54.

211   *"acerbity of Louis Johnson's nature":* Acheson, *Present at the Creation,* pp. 347–48.

211   *the fading chance of international cooperation:* Ibid.

211   *Beyond the "imperative necessity":* FRUS, 1949, National Security Affairs, Foreign Economic Policy, Volume I, p. 595.

212   *"We must protect the President":* Lilienthal, *Journals,* Volume Two, January 31, 1950, p. 630.

212   *"make it just one of those things":* Ibid., p. 625.

213   *he'd made the correct decision:* Ibid., pp. 632–63.; see also Acheson, *Present at the Creation,* p. 349.

212   *"Let's get on with it":* HSTL, OH-Sidney Souers, 12-16-54.

213   *"until a satisfactory plan for international control of atomic energy":* https://www.trumanlibrary.gov/library/public-papers/26/statement-president-hydrogen-bomb.

213   *"When you see something that is technically sweet":* Donovan, *Tumultuous Years,* p. 154.

213   *"reasonably be expected to possess":* FRUS, 1949, Volume I, p. 597.

213   *"and a sad day for the human race":* Lilienthal, *Journals,* Volume Two, February 2, 1950, p. 634.

213   *"tie on your hat":* Ibid.

214   *"except what was stated":* Presidential News Conference, February 2, 1950, https://www.presidency.ucsb.edu/documents/the-presidents-news-conference-580.

214   *effective arms control:* Text of McMahon's address, *New York Times,* February 3, 1950, p. 2.

214 *"highest statesmanship in Christian ethics"*: "M'Mahon Proposes...," *New York Times*, February 3, 1950, p. 1.

215 *"That is the fundamental basis of our foreign policy"*: Presidential News Conference, February 9, 1950, https://www.presidency.ucsb.edu/documents/the-presidents-news-conference-597.

215 *and making just that offer*: "Vandenberg bids...," *New York Herald Tribune*, February 2, 1950, p. 1.

215 *and dangerous balance of power*: For a full discussion of this question, see Barton J. Benstein, "Crossing the Rubicon: A Missed Opportunity to Stop the H-Bomb?," *International Security* (Fall, 1989): 132–60.

215 *"all theory and assumption"*: HST, *Memoirs II*, p. 308.

EIGHTEEN: "A New Fanatic Faith"

216 *"A country which"*: American Diplomacy, p. vii.

216 *Truman also talked about* "Congressional spy hunts": "An Interview With Truman...," *New York Times*, February 15, 1950, p. 1.

217 *allusion to McCarthy... was unmistakable*: Wheeling Intelligencer, February 10, 1950, http://www.advances.umd.edu/LincolnBirthday/mccarthy1950.xml; "Senator McCarthy and His 'Big Three,'" *New York Herald Tribune*, March 5, 1950, p. B1; Childs, "McCarthy's Irresponsible Charges," *Washington Post*, February 23, 1950, p. 9; "Senator to Name 57 Aides," *Los Angeles Times*, February 15, 1950, p. 5; "McCarthy Says He Could Name...," *New York Herald Tribune*, February 21, 1950, p. 1.

217 *a "heavy-shouldered, black-browed man"*: "McCarthy Stirs Bitter Row...," *New York Times*, March 31, 1950, p. 3.

217 *"I've got a pailful of shit"*: Bayley, *Joe McCarthy and the Press*, p. 36.

217 *that the State Department was home to an espionage ring*: "McCarthy Bombshell," *Newsweek*, March 6, 1950, p. 19.

217 *"and saw it come up a gusher"*: Rovere, *Senator Joe McCarthy*, p. 72.

218 *The West could only watch*: For a provocative history of this period, see Dikötter, *Tragedy of Liberation*.

218 *Hiss had been sentenced to prison*: "Hiss Guilty...," *New York Times*, January 22, 1950, p. 1.

218 *of the first United Nations conference*: "New World Hope," *New York Times*, June 27, 1945, p. 1.

218 *"the most abominable of all crimes"*: "No Appeaser, Acheson Says," *New York Times*, January 14, 1949, p. 1; Acheson, *Present at the Creation*, p. 360; "Acheson Values Ethics...," *Christian Science Monitor*, January 26, 1950, p. 1; *Wheeling Intelligencer*, February 10, 1950. Among many books about the Hiss case, Allen Weinstein's *Perjury: The Hiss-Chambers Case* (New York: Knopf, 1979) still stands out.

219 *"I am giving you the facts as I see them"*: Presidential News Conference, from Key West, March 30, 1950, https://www.trumanlibrary.gov/library/public-papers/80/presidents-news-conference-key-west.

219 *"I wish someone had sabotaged it sooner"*: "Truman Terms McCarthy...," *New York Herald Tribune*, March 31, 1950, p. 1.

219 *"that's exactly what they are"*: HSTL, PSF, Box 139, 3-31-50, HST to Acheson.

219 *"Roman Holiday in the House"*: HSTL, Charles Murphy Files, Box 14, Folder 5, 4-29-50.

219 *fell to thirteen billion*: Hastings, *Korean War*, p. 58.

219 "What am I to do?": Childs, *Witness to History*, p. 54.

220 *to listen to his opinion*: "Sullivan Quits; Calls Johnson Action Tragic," *New York Herald Tribune*, April 27, 1949, p. 1.

220 *less reliance on conventional arms*: "Air Force Accused...," *New York Times*, October 8, 1949, p. 1.

220 *submarine-launched guided missiles*: "Truman and the Bomb," *New York Herald Tribune*, February 3, 1950, p. 2.

220 *"the fierce whip of an intense patriotism"*: Alsop and Alsop, *The Reporter's Trade*, p. 15.

220 *Their loathing of Johnson became increasingly personal*: "Mr. Johnson's Untruths," *New York Herald Tribune*, February 13, 1950, p. 13; "The Cost of Mr. Johnson," *New York Herald Tribune*, February 17, 1950, p. 21; "Johnson and the Chiefs," *New York Herald Tribune*, February 20, 1950, p. 17; *New York Herald Tribune*, March 6, 1950, p. 9; "Mr. Johnson's Untruths," *New York Herald Tribune*, March 8, 1950, p. 9.

220 *a "great subterranean struggle"*: "Acheson and Johnson," *New York Herald Tribune*, June 23, 1950, p. 17.

221 *"was verboten, and he raised hell"*: Institute for Advanced Study, Princeton Seminar, Reel 3, 7-23-53, pp. 666–72; HSTL, OH-Paul Nitze, 8-5-75.

221 *"and wept in shame"*: Acheson, *Present at the Creation*, pp., 373–74; HSTL, OH-Nitze, 8-5-75.

221 *"must have been off his rocker at that time"*: HSTL, OH-Freeman Matthews, 6-7-73.

221 *to reexamine "our objectives in peace and war"*: National Security Council Report, "United States Objectives and Programs for National Security," April 14, 1950, https://digitalarchive.wilsoncenter.org/document/116191; Beisner, *Dean Acheson*, pp. 238–41; see also HSTL, OH-Paul Nitze, 8-5-75.

221 *Quick to lose his hot temper: Louis Johnson and the Arming of America*, p. 354.

221 *"mere cussedness": Present at the Creation*, p. 374.

222 *a twenty-three-thousand-word policy guidepost*: https://digitalarchive.wilsoncenter.org/document/116191.

222 *"It can be confidently reported"*: "Truman Must Choose," *New York Herald Tribune*, March 31, 1950, p. 23.

222 *"Unlike previous aspirants to hegemony"*: NSC-68; https//:digitalarchive.wilsoncenter.org/document/116191.

222 *"must rest on the intentions... of other nations"*: Kennan, *Diaries*, p. 226, September 26, 1949.

223 *to "bludgeon the mass mind"*: Acheson, *Present at the Creation*, p. 374.

223 *He wanted the report . . . to get "no publicity":* FRUS, National Security Policy, 1950, p. 235.

224 *"Never has fate been secreted in so unlikely a receptacle":* Institute for Advanced Study, Princeton Seminar, 2-13-54, Reel 2, Track 1.

224 *"a geographical artificiality":* FRUS, Korea, 1950, Vol. VII, p. 504.

225 *"two geographic spheres of influence":* Schoenbaum, *Waging Peace and War*, p. 130.

225 *"securing all of Korea as a satellite":* HSTL, The Korean War and It Origins, "Implementation of Soviet Objectives in Korea," Office of Reports and Estimates 62, 11-18-47.

225 *"with a minimum of bad effects":* FRUS, The Far East and Australasia, Volume VI: Letter from Kenneth Royall to George C. Marshall, 6-23-48.

226 *"which have been imposed upon the people of north Korea":* HSTL, Special Message to Congress, 6-7-49.

226 *carry on the fight to hold the non-Communist South:* "Rhee Insists Our Aid . . . ," *New York Times*, January 21, 1950, p. 5.

226 *"the spearhead of Russian imperialism":* "Secretary Acheson's Views . . . ," *New York Herald Tribune*, January 13, 1950, p. 10.

226 *"attaching them to the Soviet Union":* "Acheson Says U.S. Relies . . . ," *New York Herald Tribune*, January 13, 1950, p. 1; "Four Areas Listed . . . ," *New York Times*, January 13, 1950, p. 1.

226 *"within the realm of practical relationship":* Ibid.

226 *"not within the capabilities of the United States":* James, *Years of MacArthur*, pp. 401–2.

227 *"It was my decision":* Institute for Advanced Study, Princeton Seminar, 2-13-54, Reel 2, Track 3, pp. 1–7.

227 *"that it not be used by a hostile power":* Ibid.

227 *"concrete plans for an attack":* Khrushchev Remembers, *The Glasnost Tapes*, pp. 144–46.

227 *to prevent Communist expansion in Southeast Asia:* HSTL, PSF, NSC, Box 183, 2-27-50, "The Position of the United States with Respect to Indochina"; "U.S. Recognizes Viet Nam . . . ," *New York Times*, February 8, 1950, p. 1; for a particularly valuable history of the region, see Logevall, *Embers of War*.

227 *to combat the threat of "Soviet imperialism":* "U.S. Pledges Aid to France in Indo-China," *New York Herald Tribune*, May 9, 1950, p. 1.

228 *"the Communist tide will spread contagiously":* "Truman Doctrine Held Set by U.S. for Southeast Asia," *New York Times*, May 14, 1950, p. 21.

NINETEEN: A "Border Incident"

229 *"The war came early one morning":* Kim, *The Martyred*, p. 11.

229 *"a telephone call for 'Mr. Rush'":* Alsop, *I've Seen the Best of It*, p. 307; "Why We Went . . . ," *Saturday Evening Post*, November 5, 1951, p. 22.

229 *"this was it":* Alsop and Alsop, *Reporter's Trade*, p. 147; Alsop, *I've Seen the Best*, p. 307.

229   *The news had just come:* HSTL, George M. Elsey Files, Box 71, Korea; Roy E. Appleman, *U.S. Army in the Korean War*, p. 36.

230   *After a stop at the new Friendship Airport:* Beverly Smith, "Why We Went . . . ," *Saturday Evening Post*, November 5, 1951, p. 22.

230   *MacArthur never went out at night:* Haig, *Inner Circles*, p. 20.

230   *was actually a heavy attack:* Acheson, *Present at the Creation*, p. 402; see also, Schnabel and Watson, *Joint Chiefs of Staff*, Volume III, *The Korean War*, Part One, pp. 25–26.

230   *"You can't do a thing tonight":* HSTL, OH-Hickerson, 6-5-73.

231   *"If this keeps up":* Acheson, *Present at the Creation*, pp. 402–4; HSTL, Ayers Papers, Box 17, Diary, 6-29-50; Lilienthal, *Journals*, Volume Three, p. 75.

231   *"this war was a matter of 'Koreans invading Korea'":* Cumings, *Korea's Place in the Sun*, p. 263.

231   *Stalin had wanted to avoid war with the West:* For a concise overview, see Halberstam's *The Coldest Winter*, pp. 48–54.

231   *supported the attack:* Kathryn Weathersby, "To Attack, or Not to Attack? Stalin, Kim Il Sung, and the Prelude to War," *Cold War International History Project Bulletin*, Issue No. 5 (April 1995).

231   *"was on their side":* Chen Jian, "Far Short of a 'Glorious Victory': Revisiting China's Changing Strategies to Manage the Korean War," *Chinese Historical Review* (2018).

231   *"There's a development":* HSTL, OH-Hickerson.

232   *Acheson had regarded Rusk's request:* Acheson, *Present at the Creation*, pp. 431–32; "Acheson Shifts Aides . . . ," *New York Times*, March 28, 1950, p. 4.

232   *"a great historian":* Carr, *Truman Stalin and Peace*, p. 150.

232   *in his gray, West Point bathrobe:* Whitney, *MacArthur: His Rendevous with History*, p. 315.

232   *"It couldn't be, I told myself":* MacArthur, *Reminiscences*, pp. 327–28.

232   *"he appeared to be trying to convince himself":* Manchester, *American Caesar*, pp. 548–49.

233   *was afraid to disturb him on a Sunday:* HSTL, Ayers Papers, Diary, 6-30-50; Blum, *Public Philosopher*, pp. 555–56, Lippmann conversation with Foster Dulles, 8-10-50.

233   *flown out to him:* Haig, *Inner Circles*, pp. 19–20.

233   *calling the "volcanic":* Ibid.

233   *Dulles finally made the MacArthur call himself:* Blum, *Public Philosopher*, pp. 555–56, Lippmann conversation with Foster Dulles, 8-10-50.

233   *"gripped between his teeth":* Allison, *Ambassador from the Prairie*, p. 129.

233   *"with one arm tied behind my back":* Ibid.

233   *"should have his head examined":* Blum, *Public Philosopher*, pp. 555–56, conversation with Foster Dulles, 8-10-50.

223   *more serious than just another incident along the 30th Parallel:* University of Georgia, Dean Rusk Oral History Collection, interviewed by Thomas Schoenbaum, ca. 1985.

234   *As many as eight hundred:* Appleman, *U.S. Army in the Korean War*, pp. 33–34.

234   *By the end of June:* Ibid., p. 35.

234 *"to take Korea seriously"*: H. Freeman Matthews Papers, excerpts from an un-published autobiography, Public Policy Papers, Department of Special Collections, Princeton University Library.

234 *"a little head scratching"*: The Papers of Dwight David Eisenhower, Volume 13, Chapter 10, 7-11-50, p. 1225.

234 *"thought Acheson might call"*: HSTL, Elsey Papers, Box 71, 6-25-50.

234 *"a breach of the peace"*: HSTL, PSF, United Nations Security Council Resolution, 6-25-50.

234 *"as may be necessary to repel the armed attack"*: Schnabel and Watson, *Joint Chiefs of Staff*, Volume III, *The Korean War*, Part One, p. 50.

235 *"It could be a dangerous situation"*: "Truman Cuts His Trip Short," *New York Herald Tribune*, June 26, 1950, p. 1; *New York Times*, June 26, 1950, p. 7.

235 *"brought on the second world war"*: HST, *Memoirs II*, p. 333.

235 *"yessir, we'll let 'em have it"*: HSTL,OH-Webb, 2-20-80.

235 *"the shadow cast by power"*: Acheson, *Present at the Creation*, p. 405.

236 *"a darkening report of great confusion"*: Ibid., p. 406.

236 *"to prevent this kind of situation"*: FRUS, Vol. VII, June 24, 1950, Outbreak of Hostilities, pp. 182–83.

237 *"this action would save the situation"*: Ibid.

237 *"leading most probably to world war"*: Schnabel and Watson, *Joint Chiefs of Staff*, Volume III, *The Korean War*, Part One, p. 50; Manchester, *American Caesar*, pp. 548–49; "Why We Went . . . ," *Saturday Evening Post*, November 5, 1951, p. 22.

237 *"acted without prior instruction from Moscow"*: FRUS, Outbreak of Hostilities, June 24–30, pp. 149–50.

237 *Soviet aerial involvement would come later*: The literature on who wanted what, and to what extent, is immense. See, for instance, FRUS, 1950, Volume 7, "Outbreak of Hostilities," pp. 125–267; "New Russian Documents on the Korean War," *Cold War International History Project (CWIHP) Bulletin*, pp. 30–40; Kathryn Weathersby, "To Attack of Not to Attack?: Stalin, Kim Il Sung, and the Prelude to War," *Cold War International History Project (CWIHP) Bulletin*, No. 5 (Spring 1995), pp. 1–9, https://www.wilsoncenter.org/sites/default/files/media/documents/publication/CWIHP_Bulletin_5.pdf; *World Today* 6, No. 8 (August 1950): 319–30; Joong Keun Lee, *Korean War 1129*, p. 8+; Cumings, *Korea's Place in the Sun*; Goncharov, Lewis, and Litai, *Uncertain Partners*.

237 *"some friends went over and helped them"*: Hastings, *Korean War*, p. 59.

238 *"the attack upon Korea makes it plain"*: HSTL, Statement on the Situation in Korea, 6-27-50.

238 *"without losing too much face"*: HSTL, The Korean War and Its Origins, "Notes Regarding Meeting with Congressional Leaders."

238 *"The old fire horse got a whiff of smoke"*: HSTL, Clifford Files, 6-29-50 and 6-30-50.

238 *"the essence of the Truman policy is to give Russia a free hand"*: "Undeclared War," *Chicago Tribune*, June 28, 1950, p. 18.

239 *"we will have finally terminated for all time"*: "Taft Demands . . . ," *New York Herald Tribune*, June 29, 1950, p. 1.

239   *"the whole moral basis of American foreign policy"*: "New Spirit Felt in Capital," *New York Times*, June 28, 1950, p. 4.

239   *"the cause of peace for the world"*: "Survey Finds 8 of 10 . . . ," *Washington Post*, July 2, 1950, p. M1.

240   *"That is exactly what it amounts to"*: Presidential News Conference, June 29, 1950, http://www.presidency.ucsb.edu/ws/index.php?pid=13544.

240   *"I don't expect to comment on any matter of strategy"*: Ibid.

240   *MacArthur made his first post-attack trip to Korea*: "Air Attack Eluded by MacArthur," *Washington Post*, June 30, 1950, p. 3; Collins, *War in Peacetime*, p. 18.

241   *they could see Seoul burning*: Whitney, *MacArthur: His Rendezvous with History*, pp. 327–28.

241   *"the introduction of U.S. ground combat forces into the Korean battle area"*: FRUS, Volume VII, 1950, "The Outbreak of Hostilities," pp. 248–50.

241   *"all out effort before situation out of hand"*: Ibid., pp. 255–56.

241   *South of the Han*: Appleman, *U.S. Army in the Korean War*, p. 35.

241   *"a clear-cut decision without delay is imperative"*: Schnabel and Watson, *Joint Chiefs of Staff*, Volume III, *The Korean War*, Part One, pp. 51–52.

241   *"fighting Asiatics on the Asiatic mainland"*: Ibid., p. 50.

242   *"and now is the time to call their bluff"*: Elsey, *Unplanned Life*, p. 49.

242   *"Both are prizes Russia has wanted since Ivan the Terrible"*: HSTL, Elsey Files, Korea, Box 71, 6-30-50.

242   *"General MacArthur has been authorized to use certain supporting ground units"*: Schnabel and Watson, *Joint Chiefs of Staff*, Volume III, *The Korean War*, Part One, p. 53.

242   *"built up to heroic stature"*: Truman in the White House, 6-30-50, p. 360.

243   *"not as a Person but as a Personage"*: Marshall Papers, http://marshallfoundation.org/library/digital-archive/to-general-of-the-army-douglas-macarthur-11/.

243   *"an almost superstitious awe"*: Ridgway, *Korean War*, p. 61.

243   *"'an untouchable' whose actions"*: Soffer, *General Matthew B. Ridgway*, pp. 113–14.

243   *"such a damn fool could have gotten to be a general"*: DDEL, *Ann Whitman Diary*, December 4, 1954.

243   *"produce Custers, Pattons, and MacArthurs"*: Ferrell, *Off the Record*, pp. 46–47.

243   *"as a statement of policy to be followed"*: FRUS, Volume I, 1950, National Security Policy, p. 400.

244   *"we played cards"*: Truman in the White House, June 30, 1950, p. 360.

244   *"maybe tomorrow you can make a better one"*: Talking with Harry, pp. 98–99; "How the President Makes Decisions," *New York Times*, October 8, 1950, SM8.

244   *"in the long run, is the correct one"*: Talking with Harry, p. 321.

244   *"without trying to weigh for himself the problems involved"*: Ibid.

244   *"just now beginning to calculate all the risks"*: "Sweating It Out," *Wall Street Journal*, June 30, 1950, p. 4.

244   had *"almost no capacity for abstract thought"*: *New York Times*, "The Undramatic Man of Drama," March 11, 1951, p. 167.

245   *"commend the action by the United States rather than action by the President"*: FRUS, North Korean Offensive, July 1–September 15, 1950, pp. 287–88.

245 *"There is no telling what they'll do"*: HSTL, Elsey papers, cited in Donovan, *Nemesis*, p. 38.

245 *a "gang of armed marauders"*: HSTL,President's Secretary's Files, Box 53; Presidential News Conference June 29, 1950, https://www.presidency.ucsb.edu /documents/the-presidents-news-conference-624.

TWENTY: "The Second Hand of Destiny"

246 *"Every war is ironic"*: Paul Fussell, *The Great War and Modern Memory* (Oxford University Press, 1975), p. 7.

246 *"The Potomac fever registers"*: "It's 1940 Again . . . ," *Washington Post*, July 19, 1950, p. B8.

246 *"like Hitler's re-occupation of the Rhineland"*: "The Great Decision," *New York Herald Tribune*, June 28, 1950, p. 25.

246 *"untied a thousand knots"*: "New Spirit Felt . . . ," *New York Times* 6-18-50, p. 4.

246 *authorized the United States to set up a unified command in Korea*: "Action by Council," *New York Times*, July 8, 1950, p. 1.

246 *Fifty percent of the troops were American*: See the breakdown, in Sheila Miyoshi Jager's *Brothers at War* (New York: Norton, 2013), p. 481.

246 *the "bitter struggle" in Indochina was enough to contend with*: "Action By U.N. . . . ," *New York Times*, July 8, 1950, p. 1.

247 *Leahy foresaw "another 'Dunkirk'"*: LOC, Lehy Papers, Diary, 7-13-50 and 7-14-50.

247 *"Good luck to you, and God bless you and your men"*: Roy E. Appleman, *U.S. Army in the Korean War*, p. 60.

247 *The first GI to die . . . was Private Kenneth Shadrick*: "A Quiet Boy of 19 . . . ," *New York Herald Tribune*, July 8, 1950, p. 4,

247 *any fighting since the Civil War*: Fehrenbach, *This Kind of War*, p. 124.

247 *"flew them over and put them onto the battlefield"*: Dean Rusk Oral History Collection, Rusk interviewed by Thomas Schoenbaum circa 1985; http://russell librarydocs.libs.uga.edu/Rusk_OH_M.pdf.

247 *"for the prize of Pusan"*: Rees, *Korea: The Limited War*, p. 41.

248 *"with Chinese Communist ground elements"*: Schnabel and Watson, *Joint Chiefs*, Volume III, 1950–51, *The Korean War*, Part One, p. 76.

248 *"the problem is to compose and unite Korea"*: Ibid., p. 95; Collins, *War in Peacetime*, pp. 83, 144.

248 *"but a larger audience unseen"*: Ibid., p. 81.

248 *"a sort of creeping emergency"*: Dwight D. Eisenhower Papers, Volume 11, Part V, Chapter 10, 1253, footnote in letter to Lucian King Truscott Jr., 8-1-50.

249 *explosive noises of a nighttime battleground*: Author's visit, February 15, 2018.

249 *"found to be potentially dangerous to the internal security"*: FRUS, 1950–1955, the Intelligence Community, https://history.state.gov/historicaldocuments/frus 1950-55Intel/d16.

250 *"Presumably they are designed to save the lives of American boys"*: "Use of Atom Bomb in Korea Demanded . . . ," *Christian Science Monitor*, July 13, 1950, p. 3.

250 *"would be strongly tempted"*: FRUS, Korea, July 1–September 15, 1950, p. 373.

250 *"We will have to meet the situations as they develop"*: Presidential News Conference, 7-13-50, http://www.presidency.ucsb.edu/ws/index.php?pid=13558.

250 *"We have not achieved a clear and realistic . . . view of our objectives in Korea"*: FRUS, 1950, Korea, Vol. VII, 8-21-50, pp. 623–26.

251 *"and not have to order our terrible weapon turned loose"*: HSTL, Family, Business, and Personal Affairs Papers, 7-12-50.

251 *"what is at stake here is nothing less than our own national security and the peace of the world"*: https://www.trumanlibrary.gov/library/public-papers/194/radio-and-television-address-american-people-situation-korea.

251 *"I recommend that they be removed"*: Special Message to Congress, July 19, 1950, https://www.trumanlibrary.gov/library/public-papers/193/special-message-congress-reporting-situation-korea.

252 *"when is all this going to end?"*: Typewritten note, Charles Ross to Edward A. Harris, accompanying Truman's personal history lesson, 7-19-50, Special Collections Research Center at Syracuse University.

252 *"direct and intimate understanding of foreign countries"*: "House, Hopkins, and Harriman," *New York Herald Tribune*, June 20, 1950, p. 23.

252 *when MacArthur was superintendent at West Point*: HSTL, Korean War File, Box 1, letter from Harriman to J. E. Wiltz, 12-19-75; excerpt from speech at West Point, 9-9-75.

252 *a great admirer of Chiang Kai-shek*: Blum, *Public Philosopher*, pp. 555–56; Lippmann conversation with Foster Dulles, 8-10-50.

252 *Truman wanted Harriman to emphasize*: "Key Aides on Visit," *New York Times*, July 31, 1950, p. 1; "U.S. Awaits Report to Ease Tension," *Baltimore Sun*, August 8, 1950, p. 1; Schnabel and Watson, *Joint Chiefs of Staff*, Volume III, 1950–51, *The Korean War*, Part One, p. 234.

253 *"Nobody shot at me"*: "Harriman Has Closeup Look," *Washington Post*, August 8, 1950, p. 3.

253 *"and would be so recorded in history"*: HSTL, MacArthur, Harriman memo, 8-8-50, Box 111.

253 *"makes me feel sick in my stomach"*: Ibid.

253 *"In a brilliant 2½ hour presentation"*: Memorandum of conversation, 8-8-50, in Tokyo, with Harriman, Ridgway, Almond, and Air Force General Lauris Norstad, FRUS, 1950, Korea, Volume VII, 8-21-50, pp. 540–41.

253 *"For reasons which are rather difficult to explain"*: Truman, *Memoirs II*, pp. 351–53.

254 *"a policy of defeatism and appeasement in the Pacific"*: "U.S. Awaits Report to Ease Tension on MacArthur's Trip," *Baltimore Sun*, August 8, 1950, p. 1; "Official Qualifies Denial . . . ," *Baltimore Sun*, August 9, 1950, p. 1; "MacArthur Assails Gossip Over Trip," *New York Times*, August 10, 1950, p. 1.

254 *"The leg of a girl of twenty"*: Considine, *It's All News to Me*, p. 204.

254 *I am satisfied with what he is doing"*: Presidential News Conference, August 10, 1950, https://www.presidency.ucsb.edu/documents/the-presidents-news-conference-599.

255 *could be achieved "by negotiation"*: "Free Vote Urged . . . ," *New York Times*, August 19, 1950, p. 1.

255 *with a "strictly limited purpose":* Schnabel and Watson, *Joint Chiefs of Staff,* Volume III 1950–51, *The Korean War,* Part One, p. 96.

255 *wrested from its control:* National Security Council Report, NSC 81/1, "United States Courses of Action with Respect to Korea," September 9, 1950, https://digitalarchive.wilsoncenter.org/document/116194.pdf.

255 *"clarify any fogginess in current American thinking":* David Lawrence Papers, 8-24-50, 8-27-50, Public Policy Papers, Department of Special Collections, Princeton University Library; "Text of Talk . . . ," *Chicago Tribune,* August 28, 1950, p. 1; "Deep Policy Clash . . . ," *New York Times,* September 2, 1950, p. 71.

256 *"an order from me":* Institute for Advanced Study, Princeton Seminar, Reel 5, Track 2, February 13, 1954.

256 *"He wants that order sent":* Ibid.

256 *"The President . . . directs that you withdraw your message":* HSTL, Memorandum for the Record, 8-26-1950, Acheson Papers, Secretary of State File.

256 *"I regret to inform you":* "MacArthur 'Directed,'" *New York Times,* August 28, 1950, p. 1.

256 *"The President regards the incident as closed":* "Policy Clash Seen," *New York Times,* August 29, 1950, p. 1.

256 *"their reports were satisfactory":* "Truman Sends MacArthur Copy . . . ," *New York Herald Tribune,* September 30, 1950, p. 1.

257 *disowned and denounced as soon as it was uttered:* "Matthews Favors U.S. War . . . ," *New York Times,* August 26, 1950, p. 1. Matthews quickly apologized.

257 *"Amen, Amen, Amen":* HSTL, PSF, Longhand Notes, 8-15-50.

257 *"a most interesting morning":* Ferrell, *Off the Record,* Truman Diary, September 14, 1950, p. 191.

257 *"to run the whole government":* Ibid.

257 *had put him further on Truman's wrong side:* Stewart Alsop, "Acheson and Johnson," *New York Herald Tribune,* June 23, 1950, p. 17.

258 *a "white-faced and upset" Harriman: Truman in the White House,* p. 361.

258 *later that month:* Presidential News Conferences, 8-3-50, https://www.presidency.ucsb.edu/documents/the-presidents-news-conference-619, and 8-31-50, https://www.presidency.ucsb.edu/documents/the-presidents-news-conference-577.

258 *"is on his way out":* "Sec. Johnson Is on Way Out," *Washington Post,* September 10, 1950, p. M2.

258 *"He said 'Mr. President, I can't talk'":* MT, *Harry S. Truman,* p. 480.

258 *"I handed him a pen and told him to sign it":* Elsey, *Unplanned Life,* p. 196.

258 *"This is the toughest job I have ever had to do":* HSTL, Elsey Papers, Box 72, Memorandum for Record, 9-13-50.

258 *"he said 'You are ruining me'":* HSTL, PSF, Longhand Notes, 9-11-50.

259 *"Somewhat ruefully, I now admit I was right":* "Johnson Resigns . . . ," *New York Herald Tribune,* September 13, 1950, p. 1.

259 *"a happy retirement":* Truman Diary, 9-14-50, in Ferrell, *Off the Record,* p. 192.

259 *"whatever you think is necessary":* Ibid.

259 *"Will you assure the American people":* "Marshall Approved . . . ," *Baltimore Sun,* September 20, 1950, p. 4.

259 *"For two or three weeks now, the fear that has haunted Washington"*: "Letter From Washington," *New Yorker,* September 2, 1950, p. 58.

259 *was aware of "ominous rumblings"*: "China Reds Ponder . . . ," *Christian Science Monitor,* August 30, 1950, p. 1.

259 *the Chinese mainland wasn't being threatened*: "Acheson Says U.S. Is Trying to Keep Peiping Out of War," *New York Times,* August 31, 1950, p. 1.

260 *"I hope that there is no great danger"*: Presidential News Conference, August 31, 1950, http://www.presidency.ucsb.edu/ws/index.php?pid=13602.

260 *"It is your liberty and mine which is involved"*: The text of Truman's September 1, 1950, address may be found at https://www.trumanlibrary.org/public papers/index.php?pid=861.

261 *"falling away to a whisper"*: Whitney, *MacArthur: His Rendezvous with History,* p. 370.

261 *"I can almost hear the ticking of the second hand of destiny"*: For more on MacArthur's speaking style see Duffy and Carpenter, *Douglas MacArthur,* p. 87.

261 *"of his own instinct"*: Hastings, *Korean War,* p. 101.

261 *would not want "to make open war"*: HSTL, Korean War File, Box 6, "38th Parallel," Memorandum, 9-8-50.

261 *"ever to be studied"*: Rees, *Korea,* p. 96.

261 *known as "the professor"*: Hastings, *Korean War,* p. 104; Sandler, *Korean War,* pp. 318–19.

262 *"the war in Korea was decided by an end run"*: LOC, Elmer Davis Papers, script, 10-20-50.

262 *"We love you as the savior of our race"*: "Battle of Korea," *Time,* October 9, 1950, pp. 35–36; Baillie, *High Tension,* p. 224.

TWENTY-ONE: A Meeting on a Small Island

263 *can "go to hell"*: HSTL, Wake Island Conference, from statements made at Wake Island, October 15, 1950, compiled by General of the Army Omar N. Bradley, from notes kept by the conferees.

263 *"ought to know his Commander in Chief"*: Truman, *Memoirs II,* pp. 362–23.

263 *wouldn't be a bad thing*: HSTL, Connelly Files, Daily Appointment Sheets, 9-30-50.

263 *"this would be good public relations"*: HSTL, OH-Charles Murphy, 6-21-69.

264 *"I'll go!" he said*: Elsey, *Unplanned Life,* p. 197.

264 *"our operations militarily in North Korea"*: Schnabel and Watson, *Joint Chiefs of Staff,* Volume III, 1950–1951, *The Korean War,* Part One, p. 99.

264 *"We want you to feel unhampered"*: FRUS, 1950, Korea, 9-16-45 to 11-28-50, p. 826+.

264 *"inconceivable that General Marshall should have arrogated to himself"*: Acheson, *Present at the Creation,* pp. 433–34.

265 *"we will intervene"*: Goncharov, Lewis, and Litai, *Uncertain Partners,* pp. 276–77; Collins, *War in Peacetime,* pp. 172–74; Kaufman, *Korean War,* p. 87.

265 *didn't take these warnings "at face value"*: Nitze, *From Hiroshima to Glasnost,* p. 108.

265 *"that world war might result"*: FRUS, 1950, Korea, 9-16-45 to 11-28-50, pp. 790–91.

265 *"was at once transmitted to General MacArthur":* Truman, *Memoirs II,* pp. 361–62.

265 *"such military supervision as I may direct":* FRUS, September 16, 1950–November 28, p. 796; "War's End Sought," *New York Times,* October 1, 1950, p. 1.

265 *"China's most dangerous enemy":* "South Koreans Drive into North," *Christian Science Monitor,* October 2, 1950, p. 1; "South Koreans Cross 38th Parallel," *New York Times,* October 2, 1950, p. 1.

265 *"to a hazy sun":* "Truman Has Sunbath," *New York Times,* October 2, 1950, p. 23.

266 *"V-K Day":* "Toward V-K Day," *New York Times,* October 15, 1950, p. E1.

266 *"We want to get going":* "Americans Cross Parallel," *New York Times,* October 8, 1950, p. 1; "GI's Cheer Order to Cross Line," *New York Herald Tribune,* October 9, 1950, p. 1.

266 *although he was told to get Pentagon approval:* FRUS, 1950, Korea, 9-16-50 to 11-28-50, p. 915.

266 *surrender the "forces under your command":* "MacArthur Gives Reds an Ultimatum," *New York Times,* October 9, 1950, p. 1.

266 *"America and its accomplice countries":* "Plans for Guerilla Warfare," *New York Times,* October 11, 1950, p. 6; "Premier of North Tells Army," *New York Times,* October 11, 1950, p. 1.

266 *Chinese troops were making their way:* James, *Years of MacArthur,* p. 491.

266 *"every Intelligence Service knows":* *Washington Post,* October 10, 1950, p. B11, "Walter Winchell . . . in New York."

266 *found MacArthur to be a prickly case:* http://www.army.mil/article/46209/the-influence-of-command—general-george-c-marshall-as-mentor/.

266 *shift the venue to Wake Island:* Donovan, *Tumultuous Years,* p. 284; MacArthur, *Reminiscences,* pp. 360–61.

267 *"General MacArthur and I are making a quick trip":* FRUS, September 16, 1950–November 28, 1950, pp. 913–14; "Truman to Fly to Pacific to See MacArthur," *New York Herald Tribune,* October 11, 1950, p. 1; "Truman to Fly to See MacArthur . . . ," *New York Times,* October 11, 1950, p. 1.

267 *"I wanted no part in it":* Acheson, *Present at the Creation,* p. 456.

268 *"seemed really taken aback":* Jurika, *From Pearl Harbor to Vietnam,* pp. 240–41; "The Presidency," *Time,* October 23, 1950, p. 20.

268 *"He shook hands, as an equal":* Hastings, *The Korean War,* p. 122.

268 *"The President wants my views":* HSTL, Korean War File, Box 1, Conversation with MacArthur prior to Truman's arrival.

268 *something "really momentous was to be discussed":* Whitney, *MacArthur: His Rendezvous with History,* p. 386.

269 *"his disgust at 'being summoned for political reasons'":* HSTL, OH-Muccio, 2-18-71.

269 *"with only one shower between":* Ibid.

269 *"that it seemed to be automatic":* Ibid.

269 *"MacArthur is brilliant, theatrical, stern":* "Drama on a Stage," *New York Herald Tribune,* October 15, 1950, p. A3.

269 *they "seemed to hit it off handsomely":* "Truman and MacArthur Agree . . . ," *New York Herald Tribune,* October 15, 1950, p. 1.

269   *"had been in use for twenty years"*: HSTL, Truman Papers, PSF, Diary, 11-25-50.

270   *the driver of the Chevy overheard:* James, *Years of MacArthur*, p, 504; Rees, *Korea*, pp. 117–18.

270   *MacArthur's thoughts about fiscal problems in the Philippines:* Whitney, MacArthur: *His Rendezvous with History*, p. 387.

270   *"Think nothing more about that"*: Ibid.

270   *"Had I not thought so"*: HSTL, Korean War File, Box 7 (Wake Island), Memorandum of Conversation, 10-14-50, written by Rusk and checked with Harriman.

270   *"as though some tremendous event were impending"*: I'm indebted to the late Matthew Aid, an independent researcher who specialized in signal intelligence and the National Security Agency, for alerting me to these messages, which may be found in the MacArthur Memorial Library, in Norfolk, Virginia. See Aid, *Secret Sentry*, p. 33.

271   *"doing irreparable harm to the security and prestige of the United States"*: MacArthur Memorial Library, Papers of Major General Courtney Whitney, Box 5, Folder 14.

271   *"with which I have been connected"*: Ibid.

271   *"they skipped hastily and often disconnectedly"*: James, *Years of MacArthur*, p. 506.

271   *"only fighting to save face"*: HSTL, Wake Island Conference.

271   *"but they are obstinate"*: MacArthur Memorial Library, Colonel Bunker's notes, 10-15-50, p. 1.

272   *"Always," he said:* Ibid.

272   *"do to help the French"*: HSTL, Wake Island Conference.

272   *"we are up against it"*: MacArthur Memorial Library, Colonel Bunker's notes, 10-15-50, p. 16; HSTL, Wake Island Conference.

272   *"We have worked on the French tooth and nail"*: Ibid.

272   *"with the damned French"*: MacArthur Memorial Library, Colonel Bunker's notes, 10-15-50, p. 17.

272   *"would be doing well"*: Ibid., p. 10.

272   *he couldn't understand why China had "gone out on such a limb"*: FRUS, 1950, Volume VII, pp. 961–62; Addendum to Notes on Wake Conference, by Rusk, 10-14-40.

273   *"an authoritative statement of policy"*: Acheson, *Present at the Creation*, p. 452.

273   *"before we get in trouble"*: HSTL, Korean War Collection, Box 1, Letter from Rusk to J. E. Wiltz, 1-12-76.

273   *"This has been a most satisfactory conference"*: James, *Years of MacArthur*, p. 510.

274   *"would make Grant's look like a model of perfection"*: MacArthur, *Reminiscences*, pp. 388–89.

274   *"from the President's publicity man"*: "The General Rose at Dawn," *Time*, October 23, 1950, p. 21+.

274   *"a shining example of gallantry and tenacity"*: MacArthur, *Reminiscences*, pp. 362–63.

274   *"and he gave it to General MacArthur"*: HSTL, OH-Charles Murphy, 6-21-69.

274   *"No field commander in the history of warfare"*: "The General Rose at Dawn," *Time*, October 23, 1950, p. 21+.

274   *Truman had left feeling "highly pleased"*: "Truman Has Rest . . . ," *New York Times*, October 16, 1950, p. 1.

275   *"I've never had a more satisfactory conference"*: Ibid.

275   *"Who was that young whippersnapper"*: HSTL, Korean War File, Box 1, Letter from Muccio to J. E. Wiltz, 2-18-76; Hastings, *Korean War*, p. 123.

275   *"a tendency toward temporizing"*: MacArthur, *Reminiscences*, pp. 363–64.

275   *"a political grandstand play"*: "The General Rose at Dawn," *Time*, October 23, 1950, p. 21+.

275   *and above all on the notes taken by Vernice Anderson*: Philip C. Jessup, "The Record of Wake Island—A Correction," *Journal of American History* 3 (1981): 866–70.

275   *"She kept out of sight for the whole time"*: Jurika, *From Pearl Harbor to Vietnam*, p. 241.

275   *"Without our knowledge"*: Whitney, *MacArthur: His Rendezvous with History*, pp. 391–92.

276   *"was very, very little mystery"*: HSTL, OH-Muccio, 2-18-71.

276   *"I thought everyone knew I was there"*: HSTL, OH-Anderson, 2-2-71.

276   *Colonel Laurence E. Bunker*: Colonel Bunker's notes on the Wake Island Conference, MacArthur Memorial Library. Also, HSTL, OH-Colonel Laurence Bunker.

276   *"an extremely important and historic meeting"*: Philip C. Jessup, "The Record of Wake Island—A Correction," *Journal of American History* 3 (1981): 866–70.

276   *"There is really no mystery about it"*: "Question Period," *Time*, October 30, 1950, p. 23; *New York Herald Tribune*, October 18, 1950, p. 18, text of speech.

277   *"There is no disagreement"*: Presidential News Conference, October 19, 1950, https://www.presidency.ucsb.edu/documents/the-presidents-news-conference-598.

TWENTY-TWO: *Mense Horribilis*

278   *"I was fearful as we climbed"*: Salter, *Gods of Tin: The Flying Years* (New York: Shoemaker and Hoard, 2004). p. 81.

278   *One attacker was shot dead:* "Attempt Foiled," *New York Herald Tribune*, November 2, 1950, p. 1; "President Resting," *New York Times*, November 2, 1950, p. 1. HSTL, Eben Ayers Papers, Box 23, Letter to Jonathan Daniels, 11-6-50; "Two Puerto Rican Revolutionists . . . ," *Baltimore Sun*, November 2, 1950, p. 1.

278   *"Get back!":* "Policeman Yells at Truman," *New York Herald Tribune*, November 2, 1950, p. 3.

278   *"I'm really a prisoner now"*: MT, *Bess W. Truman*, pp. 361–62.

278   *a heightened nervousness that lasted for the remainder of her husband's presidency:* Ibid.

278   *"It's hell to be President"*: HSTL, Truman Papers, PSF, Longhand Note, 10-5-50. (Although this note is dated October 5, specific reference to the assassination attempt means it must have been written after November 1.)

278   *"every war is going to astonish you"*: Eisenhower Press Conference, March 23, 1955, https://www.presidency.ucsb.edu/documents/the-presidents-news-conference-326.

278   *"to pay our troops there a brief visit"*: Truman, *Memoirs II*, p. 363.

279   *"pacification of the entire peninsula"*: Ridgway, *The Korean War*, p. 63.

279 *the men marching north:* Fehrenbach, *This Kind of War*, p. 335. A good, and brief, summary of this operation, by the military historian Spencer C. Tucker, appears on pp. 108–12, in *Encyclopedia of the Korean War.*

279 *"full speed to the Yalu River":* "G.I.'s Racing for Frontier . . . ," *New York Herald Tribune*, November 1, 1950, p. 1.

280 *kept secret for decades:* See, for instance, Stepen Budiansky, *Code Warriors* (New York: Knopf, 2016); *see also* Steven J. Zaloga, "The Russians in MiG Alley," *Air Force Magazine*, February 1991.

280 *the world's first jet-to-jet dogfight:* Sandler, *Korean War*, p. 233; for more detail on these early jet encounters, see Dario Leone, writing for the Aviation Geek Club blog, on September 23, 2016.

280 *the number of Chinese soldiers was unknown:* "Chinese Troops in Korea," *New York Times*, January 5, 1950, p. 152.

280 *dragon's teeth that sprouted into an army:* "The Chinese in Korea," *Wall Street Journal*, November 17, 1950, p. 4.

280 *"with a Communist force":* Appleman, *Disaster in Korea*, p. 5.

280 *bound to intervene:* The author's correspondence with Chen Jian.

280 *"our present sphere of military action":* "MacArthur Assails China Reds' War Entry," *New York Herald Tribune*, November 6, 1950, p. 1.

280 *knew what they were facing:* Ibid., p. 25.

280 *to order General Edward Stratemeyer:* James, *Years of MacArthur*, p. 520.

281 *though not as badly as they had in 1946:* The Democrats kept their 1948 House majority, but held the Senate by just two seats, which created a Republican-Dixiecrat coalition that was not friendly to the Democratic president. See, for example, "Dark Days for President," *New York Herald Tribune*, December 10, 1950, p. A3.

281 *"without his personal and direct understanding of the situation":* Schnabel and Watson, *Joint Chiefs of Staff*, Volume III, 1950–51, *The Korean War*, Part One, p. 126–27; Stratemeyer, *The Three Wars of Lt. Gen. George E. Stratemeyer*, p. 263; James, *Years of MacArthur*, p. 521.

281 *"I told Bradley to give him the 'go-ahead'":* Truman, *Memoirs II*, p. 376.

281 *a fear that "great danger" might result:* HSTL, Korean War File, Box 7, "Hot Pursuit," 11-13-50 and 11-17-50.

281 *an extensive use of napalm:* Sandler, *The Korean War*, pp. 227–78, entry by Elizabeth Schafer.

282 *had become "a military and tactical target":* Stratemeyer, *The Three Wars . . .* p. 258.

282 *obliterated in less than an hour:* "Key Enemy City Leveled," *Washington Post*, November 10, 1950, p. 2G.

282 *"Burn it if you so desire":* Stratemeyer, *The Three Wars . . . ,"* p. 254.

282 *"from starvation and exposure": Strategic Air Warfare: An Interview with Generals Curtis E. LeMay, Leon W. Johnson, David A. Burchinal, and Jack J. Catton* Washington, D.C.: Office of Air Force History United States Air Force, 1988, p. 87

282 *"civilian death toll of more than two million":* Cumings, *Korea's Place in the Sun* p. 289.

282 *and the Harry Vaughans:* HSTL, Daily Sheets, 11-22-50.

283 *"weird bugle calls and whistles":* Donovan, *Nemesis*, p. 305.

283 *"an eerie, very foreign sound":* Halberstam, *Coldest Winter*, p. 26.

283 *"Don't let a bunch of Chinese laundrymen":* Richard W. Stewart, "The X Corps in Korea, December 1950," *Combat Studies Institute*, April 1991.

283 *along a narrow, slippery mountain road:* "Enemy Hit in West . . . ," *New York Times*, December 7, 1950; "Retreat Slows," *New York Times*, December 10, 1950, p. E1.

283 *"All that they possessed in common":* Hastings, *Korean War*, p. 147.

283 *"We face an entirely new war":* Schnabel and Watson, *Joint Chiefs of Staff*, Volume III, 1950–51, *The Korean War*, pp. 148–49.

284 *" 'I know you fellows will work with us on it' ":* "Ten O'clock Meeting," *New Yorker*, April 14, 1951, pp. 51–53.

284 *"We will!":* Ibid., pp. 54–55.

284 *consider declaring a "complete emergency":* HSTL, Eben Ayers Papers, Box 21, Diary, 11-28-50 and 11-29-50.

285 *"to lose face before the enemy":* FRUS, Volume VII, 1950, Notes on NSC Meeting, 11-28-50 pp. 124–46.

285 *"we had won the war and that we could send a Division":* HSTL, PSF, Diary, 11-25-50.

285 *"as a world matter":* FRUS, Volume VII, 1950, Notes on NSC Meeting, 11-28-50, pp. 124–46.

285 *"I don't know how to terminate it":* HSTL, Elsey Files, Box 72, Korea, 11-28-50, 3:05 p.m.

286 *"no nation will be safe or secure":* Presidential News Conference, November 30, 1950, http://www.presidency.ucsb.edu/ws/index.php?pid=13673.

287 *"That happens when it is used":* Ibid.

287 *"A whisper ran along the benches":* "The Wayward Press," *New Yorker*, November 16, 1950, pp. 78–90.

287 *"It is one of our weapons":* Presidential News Conference, November 30, 1950.

287 *"virtual state of panic":* FRUS, Korea, Volume VII, 11-28-50 to 12-31-50; 12-1-50, p. 1276.

287 *"against a colored people":* Ibid., p. 1300.

288 *that is "if we get in the big one":* Stratemeyer, *The Three Wars . . .* , p. 321; "Five-Star Schoolmaster," *New Yorker*, March 10, 1951, p. 49.

288 *"no one can guarantee that war will not come":* "Acheson Declares War Risk Is Grave," *New York Times*, November 30, 1950, p. 1.

288 *Truman the next day asked Congress:* "President in Plea . . . ," *New York Times*, December 2, 1950, p. 1; "President Asks Congress . . . ," *Wall Street Journal*, December 2, 1950, p. 2; *New York Herald Tribune*, December 2, 1950, p. 4, text of message.

288 *a bigger war: New York Times*, 12-2-50, p. 3, "All-Out War Force"

288 *"was not worth a nickel":* HSTL, Korean War Files, Box 7, Folder 24, "Chinese Intervention," Memorandum of Conversation, Notes on Meeting in JCS Conference Room, 12-1-50, by Ambassador-at-Large Philip C. Jessup; see also Schnabel and Watson, *Joint Chiefs of Staff*, Volume III, 1950–51, *The Korean War*, Part One, pp. 155–66.

288 *Western Europe was "our prime concern":* FRUS, Korea Volume VII, 11-28-50 to 12-31-50; 12-1-50, p. 1279.

288 *"must take some punishment from the air"*: Ibid.

288 *"if they can bog us down in Asia"*: Ibid. The CIA memorandum would say that "Soviet rulers have resolved to pursue aggressively their world-wide attack on the power position of the United States . . . regardless of the possibility that global war may result."

289 *"protect our national honor at the same time"*: FRUS, Memorandum from Acheson's assistant Lucius D. Battle, after a 12-2-50 meeting, 12-3-50, p. 1309.

289 *The President agreed with his secretary of state*: Ibid., pp. 1310–11.

289 *who didn't visit Korea*: Halberstam, *Coldest Winter*, p. 475.

289 *issue orders from Tokyo*: Ibid.

289 *"without precedent in military history"*: New York Times, December 2, 1950, p. 4, text of comments.

289 *"Never before has the patience"*: Ibid.

289 *"a state of undeclared war . . . now exists"*: "General critical . . . ," *New York Times*, December 2, 1950, p. 1.

289 *"entire Chinese nation"*: FRUS, Korea Volume VII, 11-28-50 to 12-31-50, p. 1320–22.

290 *"give up the whole of Asia"*: This discussion is recorded in FRUS, Korea Volume VII, Memorandum of Conversation by Ambassador-at-Large Jessup, 12-3-50, p. 1324.

290 *"and seat them in the U.N."*: Ibid., p. 1325.

290 *"but not a disgraceful one"*: Ibid., p. 1324.

290 *"the preservation of your forces"*: Ibid., footnote, p. 1333; Schnabel and Watson, *Joint Chiefs of Staff*, Volume III, 1950–51, *The Korean War*, Part One, p. 162.

290 *without saying a word*: Ridgway *The Korean War*, p. 62.

291 *"was the atmosphere more grim"*: "Washington Grim," *New York Times*, December 4, 1950, p. 1.

291 *"well onto the flypaper"*: Acheson, *Present at the Creation*, p. 481.

291 *an annoyed glance from Attlee*: Ibid.

291 *"I said No!"*: HSTL, Truman Papers, PSF, Diary, 12-5-50.

291 *"singing First World War songs"*: R. W. Johnson, "Already a Member," *London Review of Books*, September 11, 2014, p. 31.

291 *he expected to keep the PM informed*: HSTL, PSF, Attlee Meetings, December 1950; memorandum from James E. Webb to President Truman, 12-14-50.

291 *"The work remains, of course, extraordinarily interesting"*: Farrar, *Reluctant Servant*, pp. 181, 222; HSTL, Charles Ross Papers, Ross to Mary Paxton Keeley, 5-2-50.

292 *rode back to the office*: Elsey, *Unplanned Life*, p. 200.

292 *what he called "the screaming, competitive"*: HSTL, OH-Carleton Kent, 12-21-70.

292 *"I felt like it"*: HSTL, Eben Ayers Papers, Box 17, 12-5-50, 6:25 p.m.

293 *"Charlie Ross died in battle too"*: Farrar, *Reluctant Servant*, pp. 225–26; "Truman to Attend Rites . . . , *Washington Evening Star*, December 6, 1950, p. 1; "Ross: War Casualty," *Washington Evening Star*, December 6, 1950, p. A13; HSTL, Ayers Papers, Box 21, Diary, 12-5-50.

293 *"tears streaming down his face"*: Farrar, *Reluctant Servant*, p. 231, from an interview with Walter W. Ross, August 4, 1964.

294   *The Trumans attended the concert:* Saturday Evening Post April 22-50, p. 24
      "Why Shouldn't I Sing?"
294   *brought Margaret back for four encores:* Washington Evening Star, December 6,
      1950, pp. 5, B3; HSTL,Ayers Papers, Box 21, Diary, 12-5-50.
294   *"one of my better performances":* MT, Harry S. Truman, p. 501.
294   *"She communicates almost nothing":* "Margaret Truman Sings Here Again with
      Light Program," Washington Post, December 7, 1950, p. B13.
295   *"and perhaps a supporter below!":* https://www.trumanlibrary.gov/education
      /trivia/letter-truman-defends-daughter-singing.
295   *The Trib's story noted:* "Truman Berates a Music Critic," New York Herald Tri-
      bune, December 9, 1950, p. 1.
295   *"He took it out and mailed it":* HSTL, OH-Cornelius J. Mara, 6-9-71.
295   *"I worry that one of these days":* Lilienthal, Journals, Volume Three, Decem-
      ber 9, 1950, p. 41.
296   *"we must meet whatever comes—and we will":* HSTL, PSF, Longhand Note,
      12-9-50.
296   *"it looks like World War III is here":* HSTL, Truman Papers, PSF, Diary, 12-9-50.
296   *the "inflated globalism" of the Truman Doctrine:* "The Crisis of Confidence,"
      New York Herald Tribune, December 18, 1950, p. 21.
296   *"the hope of unifying Korea by force":* Schnabel and Watson, Joint Chiefs of
      Staff, Volume III, 1950–51, The Korean War, Part One, p. 171.
297   *"We have to do something about it":* HSTL, Elsey Files, Box 73, National Emer-
      gency Declaration folder.
297   *called a "co-presidency":* Paul G. Pierpaoli, Jr., "Truman's Other War: The Battle
      for the American Homefront, 1950–1953," OAH Magazine of History, Spring
      2000.
298   *Stalin would win the first year "hands down":* "World War III. U.S. Would Win
      It," Wall Street Journal, December 19, 1950, p. 1.
298   *their numerical superiority promised "rapid success":* LOC, Leahy Papers, Diary,
      1-1-51.
298   *"We are on the side of freedom":* HSTL, Korean War File, Box 7, Folder 24,
      "Massive Chinese . . . Intervention."
298   *"to maintain the balance of power across the sea":* Fehrenbach, This Kind of War,
      p. 140.
298   *"to make it a much bigger war":* "Hard Decisions and Old Wisdom," New York
      Herald Tribune, December 7, 1950, p. 27.

TWENTY-THREE: "Voice of God"

299   *"to put the full thesis out":* Committees on Armed Services and the Committee
      on Foreign Relations, "Military Situation in the Far East," May 5, 1951, p. 301.
299   *and snarled traffic:* "Sleet, Rain . . . ," Washington Post, February 1, 1951, p. B1.
299   *"and we're getting stronger every day":* Lilienthal, Journals, Volume III, Janu-
      ary 30, 1951, p. 71.
300   *on his way to see his son:* "General Walker," Washington Post, December 26,
      1950, p. 8.

300 *Ridgway's nickname:* Halberstam, *Coldest Winter*, pp. 491–92.

300 *"this present telegram is not repeat not":* HSTL, Korean War File, Box 7, Folder 24, Message to General MacArthur, 1-13-51.

301 *"If we are not in Korea to win":* "'Second Front' in Asia . . . ," *New York Herald Tribune*, February 13, 1951, p. 13.

301 *"There is no substitute for victory":* Bernstein and Matusow, *The Truman Administration*, pp. 454–45.

301 *is the only realistic choice:* FRUS, Volume VII, Korea and China, 1951, Part 1, 2-11-51, pp. 165–66, "Outline of Actions Regarding Korea." Rusk's purposely implausible options included withdrawal without conditions and regime change in China.

301 *"for a broader settlement":* FRUS, Volume VII, Draft Text of Presidential Statement on Korea, 3-21-51, pp. 253–54.

301 *was being pursued:* Ibid., p. 251.

301 *"Recommend that no further military restrictions be imposed":* "Washington and MacArthur Clash . . . ," *New York Times*, March 25, 1951, p. 1; "Joint Chiefs Tell MacArthur . . . ," *New York Times*, March 27, 1951.

302 *"imminent military collapse":* FRUS, Volume VII, Korea, 1951; pp. 265–6.

302 *that "the general had to go":* Schnabel and Watson, *Joint Chiefs of Staff*, pp. 212–13.

302 *"a challenge to the authority of the President":* HST, *Memoirs II*, pp. 441–42.

302 *"It's the lousiest trick":* MT, *Harry S. Truman*, p. 371.

302 *"he could transform the Korean War into a major conflict":* Goulden, *Korea*, p. 477.

302 *"a general war against China":* HSTL, OH-Charles Burton Marshall, 6-21-89 and 6-23-89.

302 *"MacArthur's real aim was to expand the war":* Nitze, *From Hiroshima to Glasnost*, p. 109.

303 *"The Chinese would soon starve or surrender":* MacArthur, *Reminiscences*, p. 384.

303 *would face "certain death or slow deformity":* "Truman Urged to Stop War by New Atomic Aid," *New York Herald Tribune*, April 17, 1951, p. 1; "Atomic Death Belt," *New York Times*, April 17, 1951 p. 1.

303 *"and the area beyond not sacrosanct":* HSTL, PSF, General File, Box 209, Korea-Lowe, 3-16-51.

303 *face no more than a private rebuke:* "M'Arthur Rebuke by Truman Likely," *New York Times*, April 8, 1951, p. 1.

304 *"The situation with regard to the Far Eastern general":* HSTL, Truman Papers, PSF, Diary, 4-5-50.

304 *"and maybe the beginning of World War III":* "Truman Soften U.S. War Scare," *Christian Science Monitor*, April 5, 1951, p. 1.

304 *"not all of them Communist Chinese":* FRUS, Volume VII, footnote, p. 313. See also "Joint Chiefs of Staff Confer . . . ," *New York Times*, April 9, 1951, p. 9; Hechler, *Working with Truman*, pp. 176, 179; "White House Rebuffs MacArthur," *New York Herald Tribune*, May 7, 1951, p. 1; "Strong Allied Forces Cross Parallel," *Baltimore Sun*, April 5, 1951, p. 1; "Showdown on MacArthur Near," *New York Herald Tribune*, April 10, 1951, p. 1.

304 *"last four years, I will say"*: Presidential News Conference, April 5, 1951, https:// www.presidency.ucsb.edu/documents/the-presidents-news-conference-539.

304 *"For the first time in my military career"*: "MacArthur Quoted as Protesting 'Wraps,'" *Washington Post*, April 6, 1951, p. 10.

305 *"must be recalled"*: HSTL, Truman Papers, PSF, Diary, 4-6-51.

305 *"before the Cabinet meets"*: Ibid., and 4-7-51.

305 *He didn't tell them what was in the offing:* Ibid., 4-8-51.

305 *an "imminent showdown" with MacArthur:* "Joint Chiefs of Staff Confer . . . ," *New York Times*, April 9, 1951, p. 1.

305 *"In the Pentagon as well"*: Ridgway, *The Korean War*, p. 62.

305 *When messages like that came in:* Halberstam, *Coldest Winter*, p. 475.

306 *offered congratulations:* Ridgway, *The Korean War*, p. 158.

306 *"so I'll repeat it"*: HSTL, OH-Frank Pace, 2-17-72.

306 *"'Belt him a couple for me, Roger'"*: Hechler, *Working with Truman*, p. 180.

306 *"letters of abuse by the dozens"*: HSTL, Truman Papers, PSF, Diary, 4-10-51.

306 *at one point falling, briefly, to 16 percent:* "Truman's Popularity Is in Another Decline," *New York Times*, April 8, 1951, p. 151; "Increase Noted in Popularity," *Washington Post*, April 14, 1951, p. 29,

307 *"We do not want to widen the conflict"*: "The Little Man Who Dared," *Time*, April 23, 1951, p. 24.

307 *"the son of a bitch should be impeached"*: "Action of M Day," *Time*, April 23, 1951, p. 24; "What They Said," Ibid., p. 28.

307 *"It's too bad those Puerto Ricans"*: Hechler, *Working with Truman*, p. 181.

307 *"That is not the function of a soldier"*: HSTL,PSF, Box 11, News of the World, NBC, 4-11-51.

307 *"did not agree with that policy"*: https://www.trumanlibrary.gov/library/public-papers /77/statement-and-order-president-relieving-general-macarthur-his-commands.

307 *"a worse double-crosser than . . . McClellan"*: Elsey, *Unplanned Life*, pp. 204–6.

307 *"one of our greatest military commanders"*: Ibid.

308 *"the responsibility of the Department of State"*: "Agreement and Disclosure," *New York Herald Tribune*, April 24, 1951, p. 2.

308 *"It seems that at the present time"*: LOC, Leahy Papers, Diary, 4-11-50.

308 *"'Jeannie, we're going home at last'"*: Whitney, *MacArthur: His Rendezvous with History*, p. 472.

308 *"I think this has been his finest hour"*: Willoughby, *MacArthur*, p. 423.

308 *"was entirely himself"*: Ridgway, *The Korean War*, p. 266.

308 *"such callous disregard for the ordinary decencies"*: MacArthur, *Reminiscences*, p. 395.

309 *"Well, that was simple"*: "MacArthur in Capital . . . ," *New York Times*, April 19, 1951, p. 1.

309 *without "the permission of the President"*: "Flies U.S. in 8 Hours," April 19, 1951, p. 1.

309 *a warm April day:* "Washington's Distaff Side," *Washington Post*, April 20, 1951, p. C1.

309 *the legislators clapped and cheered:* Ibid.

310 *"a hurricane of emotion swept the chamber"*: "Cheers, Tears Greet Speech," *New York Herald Tribune*, April 20, 1951, p. 1.

310 *"the last ten minutes"*: Lilienthal, *Journals*, Volume Three, April 10, 1951, p. 143.

310 *that it rivaled Churchill*: LOC, Leahy Papers, Diary, 4-19-51.

310 *"we heard the voice of God"*: *Historically Speaking* 12, No. 2 (April 2011): 37–40.

310 *the "greatest crowd in Washington's history"*: "550,000 . . . ," *Washington Post*, April 20, 1951, p.1.

311 *He was very much surprised. [laughter]*: Presidential News Conference, May 3, 1951; http://www.presidency.ucsb.edu/ws/index.php?pid=14078.

311 *MacArthur had not been consulted*: "Johnson Testifies Acheson Inspired Korea Intervention," *New York Times*, June 15, 1951, p. 1; "Johnson Tells of 'Pressure' . . . ," *New York Herald Tribune*, June 15, 1951.

311 *without a formal report*: "Hearings to End," *New York Herald Tribune*, June 19, 1951, p. 1; "MacArthur Hearings End," *New York Times*, June 26, 1951, p. 1.

311 *"would be an anticlimax to the hearings"*: Schnabel and Watson, *Joint Chiefs of Staff*, Volume III, 1950–51, *The Korean War, Part One*, p. 256.

311 *"a conspiracy so immense"*: To read the entire speech, see Speeches and Debates of Senator Joe McCarthy, 1950–1951, Reprint from the Congressional Record, https://babel.hathitrust.org/cgi/pt?id=uc1.c049728219&view=1up&seq=4.

312 *"right into the hands of the Russians"*: https://www.trumanlibrary.gov/library/public-papers/138/address-tullahoma-tenn-dedication-arnold-engineering-development-center.

312 *"people rubber-necked, and started leaving"*: HSTL, PSF, Box 111 (MacArthur), telegram, 6-15-51.

312 *"His Texas trip was a dud"*: HSTL, Truman Papers, PSF, Longhand Notes of President Harry S. Truman, 6-21-51.

TWENTY-FOUR: "The Mess in Washington"

313 *"to advance himself a point or two"*: A letter to Archie Butt's sister-in-law, Mrs. Lewis F. B. Butt, April 8, 1909, in Archie Butt, *Taft and Roosevelt: The Intimate Letters of Archie Butt* (New York: Doubleday, Doran and Company, Inc., 1930), p. 42.

313 *at a bombing and gunnery range*: "Atomic Boom Town . . . ," *New York Times*, February 11, 1951, p. 159; "Nevada Atom Test . . . ," *Los AngelesTimes*, January 28, 1951, p.1; "2d Atomic Blast . . . ," *New York Times*, January 29, 1951, p.1; "Las Vegas Warned . . . ," *New York Herald Tribune*, February 5, 1951, p. 9.

313 *"the mountains disappeared as if by magic"*: "Blast of Atom Bomb Thrills . . . ," *Los Angeles Times*, February 7, 1951, p. 26; "Tests of Atomic Artillery Indicated," *New York Times*, February 7, 1951, p. 1.

313 *The explosions left traces*: "Harmless Radioactivity in Snow . . . ," *New York Herald Tribune*, February 3, 1951, p. 1.

313 The Beast from 20,000 Fathoms: https://www.scripts.com/script/the_beast_from_20%2C000_fathoms_19740.

314 *"It is fantastic what can happen"*: "Civilization in Grave Peril . . . ," *Washington Post*, September 5, 1951, p.1; " 'Fantastic Weapon' Talk Contains Much Fantasy," *New York Times*, September 16, 1951, p. E10.

314 *"endless nibbling aggressions"*: Dean, *Forging the Atomic Shield*, pp. 28–29.

314 *tested a second atomic bomb:* The second bomb had a yield of thirty-eight kilotons, nearly twice as much as First Lightning, https://nuclearweaponarchive .org/Russia/Sovwpnprog.html.

314 *"an intelligently planned atomic attack"*: Dean, *Forging the Atomic Shield*, p. 159.

314 *a better name was needed:* Ibid., p. 160.

314 *on the drawing board:* Ibid., p. 161.

315 *"You nice people have saved my life"*: David Acheson, interview with author, April 7, 2015, Washington, D.C.; *Acheson Country*, p. 147.

315 *David Acheson is certain she wasn't there:* David Acheson, email exchange with author, April 11, 2018.

315 *"Bess spent the summer of 1951"*: MT, *Bess W. Truman*, p. 374.

315 *conversation turned to the subject of wartime:* *Acheson Country*, pp. 148–50; HSTL, President's Daily Appointments, 7-8-51.

315 *"We're going the other way"*: Sandler, *Korean War*, pp. 307–8.

315 *"the fighting and dying"*: Halberstam, *Coldest Winter*, p. 628.

316 *"This is the final chance"*: HSTL, Truman Papers, PSF, Longhand Notes, 1-27-52.

316 *led by events:* See, for example, "Portrait of a Stubborn Man," *New York Times*, April 22, 1951, p. 173.

317 *a family vacation in Guatemala:* "Vaughan Says . . . ," *New York Herald Tribune*, July 7, 1949, p. 1.

317 *"welcomed everyone, like a friendly puppy"*: Hechler, *Working with Truman*, p. 5.

317 *promoting Louis Johnson:* "Missouri Past . . . ," *New York Herald Tribune*, August 31, 1949, p. 17.

317 *a judgeship in Wisconsin:* "The General's Shadow," *New York Herald Tribune*, March 28, 1949, p. 15.

317 *hers was "a lemon"*: MT, *Bess W. Truman*, p. 347.

317 *never denied doing the favors:* HSTL, Eben Ayers Papers, Box 20, Diary, 8-12-49, 8-13-49; "Vaughan Says FBI . . . ," *New York Times*, September 1, 1949, p. 1; *New York Herald Tribune*, August 31, 1949, p. 10, text of prepared statement.

317 *were being conducted by Democrats:* "Missouri Past and Washington Present," *New York Herald Tribune*, August 31, 1949, p. 17; "Vaughan Is Named in Race Track Deal . . . ," *New York Times*, August 10, 1949, p. 1; "Vaughan Admits Deep-Freeze Gifts . . . ," *New York Times*, August 14, 1949, p. 1.

318 *Fulbright saw it as "just a loan"*: "Fulbright Plans . . . ," *New York Herald Tribune*, January 2, 1950, p. 16.

318 *"had the support of the right politicians"*: *Harper's*, January 1, 1952, pp. 27–33.

318 *Eventually, "five percenters," "deep freezes," and "mink coats"*: "Two Democrats Hurt the Party," *New York Herald Tribune*, February 4, 1951, p. A3; *New York Herald Tribune*, 2-6-51, p. 15, "Truman Asked to Dismiss Aid . . . "; *New York Times*, 3-3-51, p. 1, "Senators Accuse R.F.C. of Politics in Loan Dealings."

318 *"What seems to be new"*: "Fulbright Urges Moral Drive," *New York Herald Tribune*, March 28, 1951, p. 1.

318 *"this asinine report"*: Presidential News Conference, February 8, 1951, https://www.presidency.ucsb.edu/documents/the-presidents-news-conference-563.

319 *especially if the accused was someone . . . like William M. Boyle Jr*: "Boyle Is Named as Recipient of Fee," *Washington Post*, July 26, 1951, p. 1; "Boyle's Role in R.F.C. Loan to Be Probed," *New York Herald Tribune*, August 26, 1951, p.1; Alsop Bros., "Missouri Past and Washington Present," *New York Herald Tribune*, August 31. 1949, p. 17.

319 *he'd personally "examined the facts"*: "No Impropriety in RFC Case . . . ," *Washington Post*, August 10, 1951, p. 1; http://www.presidency.ucsb.edu/ws/index.php?pid=13874.

319 *"most loyal body of civil servants in the world"*: *New York Herald Tribune*, August 15, 1951, p. 10, text of Truman address.

319 *had been hired while Hannegan was in charge*: "The Tax Thieves of 1951," *New Republic*, November 11, 1951.

319 *by firing the assistant attorney general*: "The Friendliest People," *Time*, December 10, 1951; "President Removes Tax Chief . . . ," *New York Times*, November 17, 1951, p. 1.

320 *"Son, I'll never forget you"*: "McGrath Says He's Paying Penalty . . . ," *Washington Post*, April 2, 1951, p. 1.

320 *referring to "the mess in Washington"*: Dunar, *Truman Scandals*, p. 357, note 41; Dwight D. Eisenhower Library, Robert Humphreys Papers.

320 *when he accepted the assignment*: "Newbold Morris Names . . . ," *New York Times*, February 2, 1952, p. 1; "Newbold Morris Heads Clean-Up . . . ," *New York Herald Tribune*, February 2, 1952, p. 1; Morris, *Let the Chips Fall*, p. 3.

320 *"I felt a sudden twinge"*: Morris, *Let the Chips Fall*, p. 4.

320 *"a Shakespearean drama"*: Ibid., p. 34.

321 *"meant business"*: Ibid., p. 13.

321 *"employees at the top"*: Ibid., p. 14.

321 *"a stench in the nostrils of the Lord"*: "Immorality Rampant Here, Graham Says," *Washington Post*, 2-2-52, p. 8.

321 *an inquisitive fifteen-page questionnaire*: HSTL, Miscellaneous Historical Documents Collection, #160, K–M; see also Morris's account, in *Let the Chips Fall*, pp. 14, 26–27.

321 *Morris subsequently announced the appointment*: "Big Questionnaire by Morris Ready," *New York Times*, March 17, 1952, p. 12.

321 *Although he'd welcomed Morris*: "Mr. Morris Goes to Washington," *New Yorker*, 4-19-52, p. 121+.

322 *would not consent to any of this*: Morris, *Let the Chips Fall*, p. 29.

322 *refusing to obey a president's executive order*: HSTL, PSF, Box 135, McGrath folder, 4-1-52.

322 *before the President stepped away*: "McGrath Threatens to Quit . . . ," *New York Times*, April 3, 1952, p. 1.

322 *"it will not be quoted by me"*: Presidential News Conference, April 3, 1952, http://www.presidency.ucsb.edu/ws/index.php?pid=14446.

323 *"I can't answer that question":* Ibid.; "Upsets Come Fast," *New York Times,* April 4, 1952, p. 1; "McGrath Out Too, After Ousting Morris," *New York Herald Tribune,* April 4, 1952, p. 1.

323 *"began to rip things open":* "Fiasco," *New York Herald Tribune,* April 7, 1952, p. 17.

323 *"impeccable celebrity":* Ibid.

323 *"no trouble finding me":* Morris, *Let the Chips Fall,* p. 37.

324 *"I am most sincerely, your friend":* HSTL, Truman Papers, PSF, letter to Mc-Grath, 4-17-52.

324 *"It should not be done":* HSTL, PSF, Longhand Notes, 4-16-50; LOC, Leahy Papers, Diary, 3-20-52; Rigdon, *White House Sailor,* p. 267; "President Seen Favoring Stevenson," *Washington Post,* January 19, 1952, p. 7.

324 *Eisenhower, who'd gone on leave:* See, *"Ike and Dick,"* pp. 22–23; Greenstein, p. 160.

324 *defeated by Franklin Pierce, a Democrat:* Presidential News Conference, January 10, 1952, https://www.trumanlibrary.gov/library/public-papers/7/presidents-news-conference-0.

324 *"your judgment and your patriotism":* Ferrell, *Off the Record,* p. 220.

325 *"of transcendent importance":* Dwight David Eisenhower Papers, Volume 12, Part 3, 1-1-52, pp. 830–31.

325 *his Senate Crime Committee:* "Tennessee Crusader Tackles Crime," *New York Times,* July 30, 1950, SM5.

325 *"the battle against corruption":* "Kefauver Out for Presidency," *New York Herald Tribune,* January 24, 1952, p. 1.

325 *"Senator Cow Fever":* HSTL, Truman Papers, PSF, Longhand Notes, 12-25-52.

325 *out of thirty-three thousand cast:* "Eisenhower Defeats Taft," *New York Times,* March 12, 1952, p. 1.

325 *"not be an open convention":* Presidential News Conference, March 20, 1952, https://www.presidency.ucsb.edu/documents/the-presidents-news-conference-key-west-0.

325 *"most utterly meaningless speech I have ever heard":* Schlesinger, *Journals,* p. 3.

326 *and didn't think he could either:* MT, *Bess W. Truman,* p. 379.

326 *"more for it than any other President":* "Truman Will Not Run Again," *New York Herald Tribune,* March 30, 1952, p. 1; *New York Times,* March 30, 1952, p. 64, text of Truman speech.

326 *"They applauded with really macabre enthusiasm":* Schlesinger, *Journals,* p. 3.

TWENTY-FIVE: Dubious Battles

327 *"Well I never promoted a fight":* Margaret Truman, interviewing her parents, on CBS's *Person to Person,* May 27, 1955; MT *Souvenir,* p. 349.

327 *went on strike:* "Steel Talks Fail," *New York Times,* April 4, 1952, p. 1; "Truman Orders Seizure of Steel Industry . . . ," *Wall Street Journal,* April 9, 1952, p. 2.

327 *"our domestic economy into chaos":* Radio and television address from the White House, 10:30 p.m., April 8, 1952, https://www.trumanlibrary.gov/library/public-papers/82/radio-and-television-address-american-people-need-government-operation.

327   *"to give them a big boost in prices":* Ibid.; see also Marcus, *Truman and the Steel Seizure*, pp. 83–84.

328   *"the dirtiest job he had ever given anyone":* Sawyer, *Concerns of a Conservative Democrat*, p. 257.

328   *a "valid case" to consider impeachment:* "Taft Urges Steps to Remove Truman," *New York Times*, April 18, 1952, p. 14.

328   *When a presiding judge sided:* "Court Backs Truman . . . ," *New York Herald Tribune*, April 10, 1952, p. 1.

329   *"That's the answer":* "Truman Hints He'd Seize Press, Like Steel . . . ," *New York Herald Tribune*, April 18, 1952, p. 1; Presidential News Conference, April 17, 1952, https://www.presidency.ucsb.edu/documents/the-presidents-news-conference -500.

329   *"we were in the midst":* Presidential News Conference, April 24, 1952, https://www.presidency.ucsb.edu/documents/the-presidents-news-conference-531.

329   *"meet a situation of that kind":* Ibid.

329   *"And that . . . can only be done":* Ibid.

330   *"How could such a jumble":* "State of the Nation," *Christian Science Monitor*, April 25, 1952, p. 1. Truman, though, did not revise his version of history. Speaking to Columbia University students in 1960, he said, "A short time after the Germans surrendered in Trieste, Tito announced that he was going to occupy the city. I called Eisenhower, and Marshall, and the Chief of Naval Operations, and I asked the Commanding General of the Armed Forces in Europe how long it would take to get three divisions to the Brenner Pass. He needed, he told me, a couple of days. I asked the Chief of Naval Operations how long it would take to bring the Mediterranean Fleet into the Adriatic. He said about three days. I said to Tito, 'Come over, Tito, I'll meet you at the Brenner Pass in about three days,' and he didn't come. When Stalin refused to move out of Iran at the time agreed, I sent him word I would move the fleet as far as the Persian Gulf. He got out. That was all part of the foreign policy to save the Free World." From *Truman Speaks*, p. 71.

331   *"I don't intend to answer any questions":* Presidential News Conference, May 1, 1952, https://www.presidency.ucsb.edu/documents/the-presidents-news-conference -535.

331   *The only person to speak:* "High Court Is Told 'War' Justifies . . . ," *New York Times*, May 14, 1952, p. 1; "The Steel Debate . . . ," *Wall Street Journal*, May 13, 1952, p. 1; "High Tribunal Sharp . . . ," *New York Herald Tribune*, May 13, 1952, p. 1; Marcus, *Truman and the Steel Seizure*, pp. 166–69.

331   *He compared the seizure:* https://supreme.justia.com/cases/federal/us/343/579 /case.html.

331   *Chief Justice Vinson . . . read his dissent aloud:* "Justice Black Writes Opinion . . . ," *Wall Street Journal*, June 3, 1952, p. 2; "Supreme Court Voids Steel Seizure . . . ," *New York Herald Tribune*, June 3, 1952, p. 1; Marcus, *Truman and the Steel Seizure*, pp. 195–227.

331   *the strike resumed:* "Next Move in Crisis . . . ," *New York Times*, June 3, 1952, p. 1.

331   *He asked Congress for legislation:* Special Message to Congress, June 10, 1952, http://www.presidency.ucsb.edu/ws/?pid=14152.

332   *valuable book on the case:* Marcus, *Truman and the Steel Seizure*.

332 *"because he was too 'shaky'"*: MT, *Bess W. Truman*, p. 385.

332 *"My good friend Alben"*: HSTL, Truman Papers, PSF, Longhand Notes, 7-7-52.

333 *Truman must have confided his plans:* HSTL, Daily Appointment Calendar.

333 *"will cut you up"*: "John D. Lane: Administrative Assistant to McMahon," Oral History Interviews, October 12 and December 6, 2006, Senate Historical Office.

333 *McMahon soon withdrew:* See, for instance, "McMahon's Candidacy Leads the Way," *Hartford Courant*, January 22, 1952, p. 1, and "Truman Man Quits Illinois Primary," *Louisville Courier-Journal*, January 26, 1952, p. 1.

333 *"it is at all likely"*: "Draft Would Be Accepted," *Hartford Courant*, April 7, 1952, p. 22.

333 *"Murph"*: Hersey, *Aspects of the Presidency*, p. 15.

333 *the Cleveland-Stevenson ticket:* Miller, *Rise to Power*, p. 18.

333 *"One dishonest public official"*: "The 'Reluctant' Democrat," *Wall Street Journal*, March 11, 1952, p 10.

333 *"feels the need of a little warmth"*: "Sir Galahad & the Pols," *Time*, January 28, 1952, pp. 16–18.

334 *"outside the frame of machine politics"*: COHP, Childs (Stevenson Project), p. 69.

334 *"a gay person"*: Martin, *Adlai Stevenson of Illinois*, Volume I, pp. 86–87.

334 *killed a sixteen-year-old girl:* Ibid., pp. 41–42.

335 *"It's impossible for me to evaluate"*: Ibid., p. 43; Ives and Dolson, *My Brother Adlai*, pp. 72–73.

335 *locked his records in an office cabinet:* Martin, *Adlai Stevenson of Illinois*, Volume 1, p. 528.

335 *Stevenson's "greatest charm"*: Ball, *The Past Has Another Pattern*, pp. 111–14.

335 *"who arrived in my old Chevrolet"*: Ibid., pp. 113–14.

336 *"He apparently was flabbergasted"*: HSTL,Truman Papers, PSF, Longhand Notes, 7-11-52.

336 *"How could I?"*: Presidential News Conference, January 24, 1952, https://www.presidency.ucsb.edu/documents/the-presidents-news-conference-519.

336 *"That possibility is so remote"*: "Stevenson Says Possibility . . . ," *Washington Post*, January 25, 1952, p. 2.

336 *"and run into the Korean War"*: Ball, *The Past Has Another Pattern*, p. 129.

336 *"I am sure God Almighty will guide me"*: HSTL, Truman Papers, PSF, Longhand Notes, 3-4-52.

337 *"the high regard he already had for you"*: Martin, *Adlai Stevenson of Illinois*, Volume 1, pp. 541–42; HSTL, OH-Charles Murphy, 7-15-69; Phillips, *The Truman Presidency*, pp. 417–19.

337 *"and they have my utmost gratitude"*: "Stevenson Asserts He Couldn't Accept . . . ," *New York Times*, April 16, 1952, p. 1; Martin, *Adlai Stevenson of Illinois*, Volume 1, p. 561.

337 *"This is the hardest thing"*: Ibid., p. 56.

337 *"his radio voice has the magical quality"*: "Stevenson and the Independent Voter," *Harper's*, April 1952, p. 64.

337 *"I wonder if I have to issue a Gen. Sherman"*: cited in Martin, *Adlai Stevenson of Illinois*, Volume 1, p. 575.

337 *he "is too damn coy"*: Ibid., p. 577.

338 *to remain at Walter Reed for five days:* For a closer look at this episode, see Samuel W. Rushay, Jr., "The President Is Very Acutely Ill," *Prologue* 44, No. 2 (Fall 2012).

338 *"and his color not as bright":* HSTL, Ayers Papers, Box 21, 7-21-52—7-24-52.

338 *and edging upward:* Ibid.

338 *Truman watched some of the Chicago proceedings:* "Truman Reported Stevenson Backer," *New York Times*, July 23, 1952, p. 10; *New York Times* "Big Ovations Mark . . . ," July 25, 1952, p. 1.

339 *"No enemy nation could have inflicted more damage":* "Truman Summons Fairless and Murray . . . ," *Wall Street Journal*, July 24, 1952, p. 2.

339 *to discuss a settlement:* Ibid.; Marcus, *Truman and the Steel Seizure*, p. 252.

339 *"this should lead to a speedy resumption":* "Steel Accord Agreed On," *New York Herald Tribune*, July 25, 1952, p. 1.

339 *"conniving and scheming":* "Stevenson Gaining," *New York Times*, July 24, 1952, p. 1.

339 *"Why would it embarrass me?":* There are at least two versions, recalled by Truman, of this conversation. See HST, *Memoirs II*, p. 496, and HST, *Mr. Citizen*, pp. 77–78.

TWENTY-SIX: Bad Chemistry

340 *"In private life Mr. Daubeny":* Anthony Trollope, *Phineas Finn* (Oxford World Classics, New Edition, 2011), p. 70.

340 *"We will carry on the fight":* Address in Chicago, July 26, 1952, https://www.trumanlibrary.gov/library/public-papers/218/address-chicago-democratic-national-convention.

340 *" 'Thy will be done' ":* https://www.presidency.ucsb.edu/documents/address-accepting-the-presidential-nomination-the-democratic-national-convention-chicago-0.

340 *"lofty and literary":* HSTL, Ayers Papers,Files, Box 21, 7-25-52.

341 *"I'm not a prima donna":* HSTL, Truman Papers, PSF, Longhand Notes, 7-11-52.

341 *that history would treat him well:* "President's Popularity Inches Up," *Washington Post*, May 11, 1952, p. B1.

341 *"such a good friend":* Statement from 7-28-52, https://www.trumanlibrary.gov/library/public-papers/219/statement-president-death-senator-brien-mcmahon.

341 *"this demagogic dumb bell would make!":* HSTL, Truman Papers, PSF, Longhand Notes, 7-7-52.

341 *"I vetoed that":* HSTL, Truman Papers, PSF, Longhand Notes, 7-11-52. Although Truman dated this July 11, it refers to a meeting from July 26.

342 *"I am going to bed":* "Tapping of Sparkman . . . ," *Washington Post*, July 27, 1952, p. M3.

342 *"installed a I.V. set":* HSTL, Truman Papers, PSF, Longhand Notes, 7-11-52.

342 *"he's a peach":* "Sparkman Is Stevenson's," *New York Herald Tribune*, July 27, 1952, p. 1.

342 *"If it is worth anything to you":* Martin, *Adlai Stevenson of Illinois*, Volume 1, p. 607.

342 *"I am grateful beyond expression"*: Ibid.

342 *"He asked me and I turned it down"*: Ibid., p. 608; see Alice and Michael Arlen's *The Huntress*, for a fuller, though not wholly satisfying, look at the Stevenson-Patterson relationship.

342 *"pink right down to her underwear"*: Greg Mitchell, *Tricky Dick and the Pink Lady* (New York: Random House, 1998), p. 170.

343 *"traitors to the high principles"*: *Los Angeles Times*, October 28, 1952, p 2+; Ferrell, *Off the Record*, p. 341; Frank, *Ike and Dick*, p. 52.

343 *It didn't take long for Truman to get the idea*: "Top Strategy Plans," *Baltimore Sun*, August 13, 1952, p. 1; "Stevenson, Truman Discuss Campaign," *New York Times*, August 13, 1952, p. 1; "Truman Talks to Stevenson," *New York Herald Tribune*, August 13, 1952, p. 1.

343 *"Stevenson's attitude toward the President"*: Truman, *Memoirs II*, p. 498.

343 *blaming "both sides"*: "Holds Steel Case Mishandled," *New York Times*, August 19, 1952, p. 15.

343 *he "was seeking to disassociate himself"*: HST, *Memoirs II*, p. 498.

343 *"I can only give my best"*: "Letter to Editor Disavows Making Commitments to Truman, Others," *Washington Post*, August 17, 1952, p. M1.

343 *"This mess is the inevitable"*: "Texts of . . . ," *New York Times*, September 3, 1952, p. 22.

344 *No comment*: Presidential News Conference, August 21, 1952, http://www.presidency.ucsb.edu/ws/index.php?pid=14232; "Truman Says Democrats . . . ," *New York Herald Tribune*, August 22, 1952, p. 1.

344 *"that's all it can run on"*: "Truman Says Democrats . . . ," *New York Herald Tribune*, August 22, 1952, p. 1.

344 *"a big blot or 'mess'"*: Truman, *Memoirs II*, p. 498.

344 *"were talking through his hat"*: "Mess in Washington," *Washington Post*, August 22, 1952, p. 18.

344 *"Dad never really warmed"*: MT, *Bess W. Truman*, p. 389.

344 *"Therefore I shall remain silent"*: HSTL, Truman Papers, PSF, Unsent Draft Letter from Truman to Stevenson, undated; "Stevenson's 'Knighthoods' Worry," *Washington Post*, August 4, 1952, p. B1; "Stevenson Selects Political Amateur . . . ," *New York Times*, August 9, 1952, p. 1; "'I'm Amateur . . . ,'" *Chicago Tribune*, September 10, 1952, p. 2.

345 *"men of little faith"*: https://www.presidency.ucsb.edu/documents/address-chicago-the-democratic-national-convention.

345 *"We are going to survive"*: *New York Herald Tribune*, September 22, 1952, p. 12, text, cited in Alsop and Alsop, *Reporter's Trade*, p. 189.

345 *"When it seemed to me almost too late"*: Truman, *Memoirs II, p. 499*. See also "Truman Will Widen . . . ," *New York Times*, September 6, 1952, p. 1; "Truman to Stump," *New York Times*, September 13, 1952, p.1; Stewart Alsop, "Truman Champs at Bit," *New York Herald Tribune*, September 14, 1952, p. A7; "Truman's Role," *Wall Street Journal*, September 16, 1952, p. 1.

345 *rarely taken time off*: "Joseph Short . . . ," *Baltimore Sun*, September 19, 1952, p. 1.

345 *"I shall place loyalty to my country"*: "Byrnes to Vote for Eisenhower," *New York Herald Tribune*, September 19, 1952, p. 1; text, p. 13.

345 *"We've got a great leader"*: Leviero, "Politics Hath No Fury . . . ," *New York Times*, October 12, 1952, p. E3.

345 *"suddenly turned toward me"*: Eisenhower, *Crusade in Europe*, p. 444.

346 *"I told 'Ike' again"*: LOC, Davies Papers, Box 18, Excerpt from Letter Home, 7-23-45.

346 *"I think he is one of the great men"*: Presidential News Conference, August 9, 1951, https://www.presidency.ucsb.edu/documents/the-presidents-news-conference-561.

346 *"that is his business"*: That news conference, on January 10, 1952, had an unusual amount of good humor and laughter, and its spirit was captured here in a rare video: https://www.youtube.com/watch?v=xERa44M6UOE.

346 *"He's as fine a man as ever walked"*: Presidential News Conference, May 1, 1952, https://www.presidency.ucsb.edu/documents/the-presidents-news-conference-535.

346 *"snollygosters" had taken control of Eisenhower*: "Truman Declares Eisenhower Is Dupe . . . ," *New York Times*, October 2, 1952, p. 1.

346 *"Why, this fellow don't know"*: Rovere, *Affairs of State*, p. 72.

347 *"to dwarf any in the previous history of man"*: "Marshall U.S. Foe, M'Carthy Charges," *New York Times*, June 15, 1951, p. 3; "Sen. McCarthy Says Marshall Lost Peace . . . ," *New York Herald Tribune*, June 15, 1951, p. 6;.

347 *"I have been privileged for thirty-five years"*: Hughes, *Ordeal of Power*, p. 42.

347 *Eisenhower later denied what was obviously true*: For a bit more on this, see Kenneth W. Thompson (Editor), *The Eisenhower Presidency: Eleven Intimate Perspectives of Dwight D. Eisenhower* (Lanham, Maryland: University Press of America,1984), pp. 31–32. Also Eisenhower, *Mandate for Change*, pp. 318–19.

347 *"made President Truman as mad as anything"*: HSTL, OH-Charles Murphy, 7-25-69.

347 *Truman began to sound personally offended*: "Truman Declares General Betrays . . . ," *New York Times*, October 8, 1952, p. 1; "Truman Brands Ike 'Unfit,'" *Washington Post*, October 8, 1952, p. 1; "Eisenhower Scores President . . . ," *New York Times*, October 2, 1952, p. 1.

348 *"If we cannot win the war"*: "Eisenhower Wants Koreans to Bear . . . ," *New York Times*, October 3, 1952, p. 1.

348 *it was wrong for Eisenhower to turn on it*: "President Bitter," *New York Times*, October 5, 1952, p. 1.

348 *he "has been my military adviser"*: "President Invites Plans to End War . . . ," *New York Times*, October 17, 1952, p. 1.

348 *"noisy, harmless blanks"*: "General Ridicules . . . ," *New York Herald Tribune*, October 5, 1952, p. 1.

349 *"I shall go to Korea"*: "Eisenhower Says He Will Go to Korea . . . ," *New York Herald Tribune*, October 25, 1952, p. 1.

349 *"That's the speech that will beat us"*: McKeever, *Adlai Stevenson*, p. 44.

349 *"No man had less right to use this crisis"*: Truman, *Memoirs II*, pp. 501-2.

349 *"it lies in Moscow"*: "Stevenson Advises Rival . . . ," *New York Times*, October 26, 1952, p.1.

349 *"more than all of these combined"*: *New York Herald Tribune*, October 8, 1952, p. 16, text of Detroit speech.

349 *He'd done so, he said:* "Truman Releases Secret Document . . . ," *New York Times,* November 3, 1952, p. 1.

350 *"I thought we had lost the election":* Truman, *Memoirs II,* pp. 502, 504.

350 *the "dead weight of the immediate past":* "Truman Shows Ire in Wake of Defeat," *Washington Post,* December 16, 1952, p. 16.

350 *"what President Roosevelt and he were trying to do":* HSTL, Ayers Papers, Box 21, 11-8-52.

350 *"the whole world was on fire":* "First H-Bomb . . . ," *Washington Post,* November 9, 1952, p. 1; "Island Vanishes . . . ," *Los Angeles Times,* November 11, 1952, p. 1; "Flash Is Described," *New York Times,* November 17, 1952, p. 1.

350 *"It's a boy":* https://nsarchive2.gwu.edu/coldwar/interviews/episode-8/teller1 .html.

TWENTY-SEVEN: The Bitter End

351 *"I can't help but dream out loud":* https://www.presidency.ucsb.edu/documents /the-presidents-farewell-address-the-american-people.

351 *Then he flew to Washington:* "Cheering Crowds Welcome General," *New York Times,* November 19, 1952, p. 1; *Washington Post,* January 19, 1952, p. 3, sidelights of big parade; "Eisenhower Briefed . . . ," *Chicago Tribune,* November 19, 1952, p. 1.

351 *The general . . . brought along:* HSTL, Ayers Papers, Box 21 11-18-52.

351 *"certainly no 'love feast'":* Lodge, *As It Was,* p. 31.

352 *"if you still desire to go to Korea":* MT, *Harry S. Truman,* p. 549.

352 *"not very graciously":* HSTL, Truman Papers, PSF, Longhand Notes, 11-20-52.

352 *"I think all this went into one ear":* Ibid.

352 *"I don't just mean to me either":* MT, *Where the Buck Stops,* p. 62.

352 *"on a matter that caught his attention":* Acheson, *Present at the Creation,* p. 707.

352 *"if I can stand sitting next to him":* Hughes, *Ordeal of Power,* p. 54.

353 *"I let it go":* "Lone Photographer Tells How He Made Two Smile," *New York Times,* November 19, 1952, p. 18.

353 *He wore a hooded parka:* "A Three-Day Tour," *New York Times,* December 6, 1952, p.1.

353 *"How difficult it seems to be":* *New York Times,* December 6, 1952, p. 4, Korea statement.

353 *"has a great deal to say about that":* Jurika, *From Pearl Harbor to Vietnam,* p. 237.

353 *He'd even put himself in the running:* "MacArthur Cheered Wildly," and text, *New York Times,* July 8, 1952, pp. 1, 8. MacArthur's speech may be viewed on C-SPAN, https://www.c-span.org/video/?3985-1/gen-douglas-macarthur-key note-address.

354 *"a clear and definite solution":* "M'Arthur Reveals He Has Peace Plan," *New York Times,* December 6, 1952, p. 13; "MacArthur Claims Clear and Definite War Solution," *Baltimore Sun,* December 6, 1952, p. 1.

354 *"a failure of policy there":* "Eisenhower Asks MacArthur . . . ," *New York Times,* December 10, 1952, p. 1.

354   *"got there just at the end"*: "Mrs. Wallace Is Dead," *Kansas City Star*, November 5, 1952, p. 1.

355   *"To hell with them"*: HSTL, Truman Papers, PSF, Longhand Notes, 12-6-52.

355   *ought to present that plan "at once"*: "Truman Asks MacArthur . . . ," *New York Herald Tribune*, December 11, 1952, p. 1.

355   *"Any decent man would have done it"*: Presidential News Conference, December 11, 1952, http://www.presidency.ucsb.edu/ws/index.php?pid=14356.

356   *"I hope some good"*: Ibid.

356   *a "much more important decision"*: "Korea 'Most Terrible," *Washington Post*, December 27, 1952, p. 1; "Truman Reviews 8 Years . . . ," *New York Times*, December 27, 1952, p. 1; "Truman in Farewell Interview," *New York Herald Tribune*, December 27, 1952, p. 1.

356   *"I think Russia would like"*: "Truman Says Soviet Wants U.S. in All-Out Asian War," *New York Times*, December 28, 1952, p. 1.

356   *"the war of the future"*: "Truman Bids Stalin Drop . . . ," *New York Times*, January 8, 1953, p. 1; http://www.presidency.ucsb.edu/ws/index.php?pid=14379&st=&st1=.

357   *"When history says"*: Harry S. Truman, "The President's Farewell Address to the American People," January 15, 1953, https://www.trumanlibrary.gov/library/public-papers/378/presidents-farewell-address-american-people; HSTL, Eben Ayers Papers, Box 21, 1-15-53.

357   *"the assurance of a warm place"*: "The Truman Farewell," *New York Herald Tribune*, January 16, 1953, p. 16.

357   *"it was a good temper that he was losing"*: "Farewell to Truman," *New York Herald Tribune*, January 19, 1953, p. 17.

358   *"I hope they will never cut"*: http://www.presidency.ucsb.edu/ws/index.php?pid=14391.

358   *"we have a most pleasant visit"*: HSTL, Truman Papers, PSF, Longhand Notes, 1-20-53.

358   *The Trumans had invited the Eisenhowers*: Truman, *Mr. Citizen*, p. 19.

358   *"Mr. Eisenhower sat still"*: "Greatest Tribute to Truman," *Washington Evening Star*, January 21, 1953, p. A19.

358   *"it was a shocking moment"*: McCullough, *Truman*, p. 921.

359   *"I was glad I wasn't in that car"*: West, *Upstairs*, p. 113.

359   *Martin "changed the subject"*: HSTL, Truman Papers, PSF, Longhand Notes, 1-20-53.

359   *"My son had been upset"*: Eisenhower, *Mandate for Change*, pp. 100–1.

359   *"I wonder what s.o.b"*: HSTL, OH-Dennison, 11-2-71; "Truman Ordered Eisenhower Son . . . ," *New York Herald Tribune*, January 23, 1953, p. 1.

359   *Truman didn't hesitate to accept*: See also Ferrell, *Off the Record*, March 20, 1953, p. 289.

360   *"smiled in paternal fashion"*: "Air of Solemnity," *Washington Post*, January 21, 1953, p. 1.

360   *to offer him a lift*: Author's interview with Patricia McMahon Fox, May 5, 2020.

360   *"every year it's going to be better"*: David Acheson, interview by author, in Washington, D.C., April 9, 2015; Acheson, *Present at the Creation*, p. 721.

360   *"Never anything like it"*: HSTL, Truman Papers, PSF, Longhand Notes, 1-20-53.

361   *"I will never forget this"*: "I'm Mr. Truman . . . ," *New York Herald Tribune*, January 21, 1953, p. 1; "Truman, Too, Gets His Blaze of Glory," *New York Times*, January 21, 1953, p. 1.

361   *"amid cheers & tears"*: HSTL, Truman Papers, PSF, Longhand Notes, 1-20-53.

361   *stopping on the way for dinner at a Hot Shoppe*: HSTL, Ayers Papers, Diary, Box 21, 1-20-53.

361   *"It seems just the same"*: "Jaunty Ex-President Takes Usual Walk . . . ," *Washington Evening Star*, January 21, 1953, p. 1.

361   *"It was the pay-off"*: HSTL, Truman Papers, PSF, Longhand Notes, 1-20-53.

EPILOGUE: Citizen Truman

363   *"no one would pay the slightest attention"*: Truman, *Mr. Citizen*, p. 22.

363   *a front-gate lock controlled from inside*: MT, *Souvenir*, p. 335.

363   *as a six-year-old*: HSTL, Truman Papers, PSF, Longhand Notes, 2-5-53.

363   *"I am not convinced Russia has the bomb"*: "Truman Thinks Soviets Haven't . . . ," *Atlanta Constitution*, January 27, 1953, p. 1.

363   *"I was quoting the President"*: HSTL, OH-Robert Nixon, 10-29-70.

364   *guilty of "reprehensible misrepresentations"*: "Truman Draws Rebuke," *New York Herald Tribune*, January 10, 1953, p. 4.

364   *"a dry news hole"*: "Truman imposes Gag . . . . ," *New York Herald Tribune*, February 1, 1953, p. 91.

364   *Margaret's piano accompanist*: "Truman Rejects Job Offers," *New York Times*, January 25, 1953, p. 1.

364   *"never buys anything sight unseen"*: NYPL, New Yorker Archives, Box 526, Shawn to HST, telegram, 1-19-53.

364   *with Henry Wallace and Jimmy Byrnes*: The book referred to "Mr. X," unmistakably Wallace, who "wants us to disband our armed forces, give Russia our atomic secrets and trust a bunch of adventurers in the Kremlin Politburo." It also included the angry, unsent letter to Byrnes, from 1946, when Byrnes returned from the foreign ministers conference in Moscow; and it claimed that Truman had read it aloud to Byrnes—which Byrnes, angrily, denied.

364   *bought the rights to his memoirs*: "Truman Discloses Sale of Memoirs . . . ," *New York Times*, February 22, 1953, p. 1.

364   *wasn't strapped for cash*: A 2021 story in *New York* magazine questioned "myths" about Truman's finances. https://nymag.com/intelligencer/2021/07/the-truman -show.html.

364   *for his war memoir,* Crusade in Europe: Thompson, *A Love Affair with Life . . .* , p. 165.

365   *As an army veteran*: "Gen. Vaughan to Retire . . . ," *Washington Post*, January 18, 1953, p. 9.

365   *a staff of writers, researchers, and academics*: Krasnoff, *Truman and Noyes*, pp. 112–13.

365   *"have to stand on its own feet"*: "Truman Discloses Sale of Memoirs . . . ," *New York Times*, February 22, 1953, p. 1.

365   *"those sons of bitches"*: Thompson, *A Love Affair with Life* . . . , p. 165.

365   *"we would have no problem"*: Ibid., p. 166

365   *"I never really appreciated"*: Elson, *World of Time Inc*, p. 299.

365   *"I should like to see you change this"*: Acheson and Truman, *Affection and Trust*, July 21, 1955, p. 79.

365   *"gives the impression of a two-gun man"*: Ibid., July 18, 1955, p. 99.

366   *"had nothing to do with politics"*: Ibid., pp. 105–6.

366   *"and my father was simply a servant"*: David Acheson, telephone interview with author, April 8, 2015. David Acheson told me that Margaret Truman Daniel stood in the way of publishing her father's correspondence with Acheson. "I discussed it with her several times," Acheson wrote in a May 2015 email. "She was adamant and not very polite, or reasoned, about it. That is why a 1953–1971 correspondence wasn't published until after her death." Mrs. Daniel died in early 2008; *Affection and Trust: The Personal Correspondence of Harry S. Truman and Dean Acheson, 1953–1971* was published in 2010.

366   *"captain with the mighty heart"*: Acheson, *Present at the Creation*.

366   *"That was very real"*: Telephone interview with David Acheson, April 8, 2015.

366   *"Every one of those Presidents"*: *Look*, August 18, 1951, pp. 60+; reprinted in the Congressional Record of August 15, 1951, pp. A5146–48.

367   *"and vigorously followed through"*: Acheson, *Present at the Creation*, p. 731.

367   *"would become a dead issue"*: "A.M.A. Sets $1,100,00 Ad Drive," *New York Times*, June 27, 1950, p. 1.

368   *"Some of the scholarly debate"*: May, *America's Cold War Strategy*, pp. 89–90.

368   *At the sixtieth anniversary*: https://obamawhitehouse.archives.gov/the-press-office /2013/07/27/remarks-president-60th-anniversary-korean-war-armistice.

368   *"To Pyongyang"*: Author's visit, February 18, 2018.

369   *"or many more casualties later"*: Truman farewell speech, January 15, 1953, https://www.trumanlibrary.gov/library/public-papers/378/presidents-farewell -address-american-people.

369   *"I'd do it again"*: LBJL, Merle Miller, tape #5.

369   *"When I had to save the Republic of Korea"*: Robert Sherrod, "A Day in a Former President's Busy Life," *Saturday Evening Post*, June 13, 1964, p. 15.

369   *During the conflict, thirty-seven thousand*: Allan R. Millett, in Tucker, *Encyclopedia of the Korean War*, p. 101.

369   *depending on the source*: Ibid.

369   *Like the War Memorial in Seoul*: http://www.koreakonsult.com/Attraction_Pyon gyang_war_museum_eng.html.

369   *and ten million separated families*: Lee, *Korean War 1129*, pp. 567–69. Many books and monographs deal with this subject. For a broader, and occasionally horrifying, view, see Conway-Lanz, *Collateral Damage*, also Hwang, *Korea's Grievous War*.

369   *to shoot if necessary*: Conway-Lanz, *Collateral Damage*, pp. 112–13.

370   *could be heard from a mile away*: Sandler, *The Korean War*, entry by Elizabeth Schafer, pp. 227–28.

370 *"I vomited"*: FRUS, Senate Foreign Relations and Armed Services committee hearings, May, 1951, "Military Situation in the Far East," Part I, p. 81.

370 *suffered considerable losses:* Cold War International History Project Bulletin, Woodrow Wilson Center, "New Evidence on Cold War Crises, Russian Documents on the Korean War," https://www.wilsoncenter.org/sites/default/files/media/documents/publication/CWIHPBulletin14-15_p4.pdf.; see also Chen Jian, "Far Short of a 'Glorious Victory': Revisiting China's Changing Strategies to Manage the Korean War," *Chinese Historical Review* (2018).

370 *an almost irrelevant goal:* http://nationalinterest.org/blog/the-buzz/why-the-korean-war-was-one-the-deadliest-wars-modern-history-20445; *Asia-Pacific Journal* 7 (March 16, 2009): 1+.

371 *"The war is over":* "President Is Happy," *New York Times*, July 27, 1953, p. 1. See also Frank, *Ike and Dick*, p. 73.

371 *"Just signing a truce doesn't mean peace":* "Truman Expresses Hope . . . ," *New York Times*, July 27, 1953, p. 2; "Truman Warns . . . ," *New York Times*, July 27, 1953, p. 8.

371 *"the best comedy in history":* Acheson and Truman, *Affection and Trust*, December 26, 1953, pp. 42–43.

371 *to restart the Korean conflict:* "Congress silent . . . ," *New York Herald Tribune*, July 29, 1954, p. 1.

371 *"using to build up its strength":* Text of Rhee's Address . . . ," *New York Times*, July 29, 1954, p. 2.

371 *from the Gates-Wallace house:* "Key to Dynamic Period," *Kansas City Star*, July 7, 1957, p. 1.

372 *the Louisiana Purchase portrayed:* HSTL, OH-Thomas Hart Benton (4-21-64, pp. 51–2).

372 *on a sweltering Midwestern July day:* See YouTube clip of the dedication at https://www.youtube.com/watch?v=dCpRu3vnu2I.

372 *"Missouri has had a number of notorious characters":* Truman Speaks, p. 3.

372 *"He made a good speech":* LBJL, Merle Miller, tape #4.

373 *"pattern of simple courage":* "Truman Sheds a Tear," *Chicago Tribune*, June 21, 1956, p. C12; "Oxford Honors . . . ," *New York Times*, June 21, 1956, p. 1.

373 *lunch with Queen Elizabeth II:* "Truman Guest of Eden," *New York Times*, June 26, 1956, p. 10.

373 *"They're God-awful!":* Truman, *Letters Home*, p. 265.

373 *"too defeatist" to win:* "The Political Dagger," *New York Times*, August 15, 1956, p. 12; HSTL, PPP, Adlai Stevenson., 8-16-56.

373 *"'he's making a fool of himself'":* HSTL, OH-Thomas Evans, 12-19-63.

373 *"I don't think he's a very good Catholic":* Acheson, *Affection and Trust*, p. 252, 11-20-60.

373 *"this is the first copy":* HSTL, OH-Samuel H. Montague, 10-30-92.

374 *as "Glamor Boy":* Thompson, *A Love Affair with Life* . . . , p. 166.

374 *"hasn't been taken in yet":* "Salty Truman . . . ," *New York Herald Tribune*, November 3, 1961, p. 10.

374 *"You see how easy it is to like Ike":* Krasnoff, *Truman and Noyes*, pp. 105–6.

374   *"The decisions he made":* "Truman Is Toasted . . . ," *New York Times*, May 9, 1959, p. 1.

374   *"If I have many more":* "My First Eighty Years," *Saturday Evening Post*, June 13, 1964, pp. 16–18.

374   *"take the arm closest to my heart":* "Truman, 80, Feted . . . ," *New York Times*, May 9, 1964, p. 1; "Truman Remains the Same," *Los Angeles Times*, May 13, 1964, p. A6; "Truman on 80th . . . ," *Baltimore Sun*, January 9, 1964, p. 1.

374   *Margaret Truman married Clifton Daniel:* "Margaret Truman to Wed . . . ," *New York Herald Tribune*, March 13, 1956, p. 1; "This Gentleman Preferred an Extra Special Blonde!," *Washington Post*, March 18, 1956, p. F1; "Margaret Truman . . . ," *New York Herald Tribune*, April 22, 1956, p. 1; "Margaret Weds . . . ," *Chicago Tribune*, April 22, 1956, p. 1.

375   *CBS's popular TV show:* What's My Line? MT, *Souvenir*, p. 335; see: https://www.youtube.com/watch?v=_2l-Sl9jwBQ.

375   *an "unconquerable difficulty":* "Helen Traubel Sorry . . . ," *Boston Globe*, December 23, 1958, p. 1.

375   *The in-laws telephoned:* "Secrets of a Happy Man . . . ," *Boston Globe*, August 27, 1961, p. A5.

375   *"Give 'em hell, Harry":* Thompson, *Love Affair with Life* . . . , p. 162.

375   *"Trudging along with us at his heels":* Ellis, *Diary of the Century*, pp. 239–41.

375   *"Private business has its own rights":* "Truman Hits Sit-downs . . . ," *Los Angeles Times*, March 20, 1960, p. 25.

376   *"someone who isn't her color":* "Truman Opposes Biracial Marriage," *New York Times*, September 12, 1963, p. 30. Murray Kempton, a New York columnist (and much more), followed up the Talese story, and wrote: "It seemed sensible to call the old man and ask him if his remarks had been accurately transcribed. 'Sure,' Truman answered, 'I asked this fellow whether he'd want his daughter to marry a nigger, etc., and etc.'" Kempton, *Rebellions, Perversities*, pp. 424–26; See also HSTL, Sidney Souers Papers, letter, 9-19-63; "Truman Stirs a New Storm," *Baltimore Sun*, September 16, 1963, p. 5; "Truman Denounces Rights 'Busybodies,'" *St. Louis Post-Dispatch*, September 16, 1963.

376   *"Let him have his breakfast strolls":* "Truman's Record, Not Remarks . . . ," *Los Angeles Times*, April 26, 1965, p. A5.

376   *a year after Truman's death:* For a thorough discussion of this, see Francis Heller's "Plain Faking," in the May-June issue of *American Heritage*; https://www.americanheritage.com/plain-faking.

376   *He continued to take short, halting walks:* "A Step Less Brisk," *Globe and Mail*, May 9, 1969, p. 10.

376   *"Happy birthday, Mr. President":* "Truman Is Serenaded," *New York Times*, May 9, 1972, p. 46.

376   *paid for by Medicare:* "Truman . . . Is Dead," *New York Times*, December 27, 1972, p. 1.

377   *had recently been admitted:* Ibid.

377   *A small funeral:* "Truman Buried . . . ," *New York Times*, December 29, 1972, p. 1.

377 *Official Washington said its goodbye:* "Last Respects Paid Truman," *Washington Post*, January 6, 1973, p. 1.

377 *"shall be worthy of it":* Halifax, *Fullness of Days*, p. 305.

378 *"the present is clouded":* Sevareid, *Conversations*, p. 72.

378 *for motives that remain unclear:* See, for example, the *Washington Post*'s "Afghanistan Papers" report, in mid-December 2019.

379 *"better than we found them":* Acheson, *Present at the Creation*, p. 728.

379 *"a towering figure":* "Truman Is Toasted . . . ," *New York Times*, May 9, 1959, p. 1.

379 *"and the Dutch Republic":* Samuel W. Rushay, Jr., Prologue, *Harry Truman's History Lessons* 41, No. 1 (Spring 2009); https://www.archives.gov/publications/prologue/27009/spring/truman-history.html.

379 *"borne up well under great difficulties":* Rovere, *Affairs of State*, p. 70.

380 *"history will delight to remember":* cited in Rosenman, *Presidential Style*, p. 513.

Sources

Harry Truman's presidency started off with victories over Nazi Germany and Japan, and the first use of a nuclear weapon in war. His last years in office were dominated by the mislabeled "forgotten war" on the Korean peninsula, a conflict that, more than ever, is a rich, perplexing subject for those gripped by the past and worried about the future. Those who approach Truman's life and times—guided, as I was, by the sources that follow—will discover why this deceptively simple man, a child of the nineteenth century, has such a firm grip on the twenty-first century.

Bibliography

Abell, Tyler (editor). *Drew Pearson Diaries. 1949–1959*. New York: Holt, Rinehart and Winston, 1974.

Abels, Jules. *The Truman Scandals*. Chicago: Henry Regnery Company, 1956.

Acheson, David C. *Acheson Country*. Foreword by David McCullough. New York: W. W. Norton, 1993.

Acheson, Dean. *Among Friends. Personal Letters of Dean Acheson*. Edited by David S. McLellan and David C. Acheson. New York: Dodd, Mead, 1980.

———. *Present at the Creation. My Years in the State Department*. New York: W. W. Norton, 1969.

———. *Sketches From Life of Men I Have Known*. New York: Harper & Brothers, 1961.

Acheson, Dean, and Harry S. Truman, *Affection and Trust: The Personal Correspondence of Harry S. Truman and Dean Acheson, 1953–1971*. Introduction by David McCullough. New York: Alfred A. Knopf, 2010.

Aid, Matthew M. *The Secret Sentry: The Untold History of the National Security Agency*. New York: Bloomsbury Press, 2009.

Alanbrooke, Field Marshall Lord. *War Diaries 1939–1945*. Edited by Alex Danchev and Daniel Todman. London: Weidenfeld & Nicolson, 2001.

Allen, George E. *Presidents Who Have Known Me*. New York: Simon & Schuster, 1960.

Allen, Robert S., and William V. Shannon. *The Truman Merry-Go-Round*. New York: Vanguard Press, 1950.

Allison, John M. *Ambassador From the Prairie, or Allison Wonderland.* Boston: Houghton Mifflin, 1973.

Alperovitz, Gar. *Atomic Diplomacy: Hiroshima & Potsdam.* (Expanded and Updated Edition). New York: Elisabeth Sifton Books-Penguin Books, 1965, 1985.

Alsop, Joseph, and Stewart Alsop. *The Reporter's Trade.* New York: Reynal & Company, 1958.

Alsop, Joseph, and Turner Catledge. *The 168 Days.* Garden City, New York: Doubleday, 1938.

Alsop, Joseph W. With Adam Platt. *"I've Seen the Best of It": Memoirs.* New York: W. W. Norton, 1992.

Alsop, Stewart. *The Center: People and Power in Political Washington.* New York: Harper & Row, 1968.

Alsop, Susan Mary. *To Marietta from Paris, 1945–1960.* Garden City, New York: Doubleday, 1975.

The American Secretaries of State and Their Diplomacy. Volume XIV. New York: Cooper Square Publishers, 1965. E. R. Stettinius, Jr., by Richard L. Walker. James F. Byrnes, by George Curry.

The American Secretaries of State and Their Diplomacy. Volume XV. Ferrell, Robert H. (editor). George C. Marshall as Secretary of State, 1947–1949.

The American Secretaries of State and Their Diplomacy. Volume XVI. New York: Cooper Square Publishers, 1972. Ferrell, Robert H. (editor). Smith, Gaddis. Dean Acheson.

Anderson, Jack, and Ronald W. May, *McCarthy: The Man, the Senator, the "Ism."* London: Victor Gollancz, Ltd., 1953.

Anderson, Jack. *Confessions of a Muckraker.* With James Boyd. New York: Random House, 1979.

Andrews, Bert. *Washington Witch Hunt.* New York: Random House, 1948.

Appleman, Lt. Col. Roy E. *Disaster in Korea: The Chinese Confront MacArthur.* College Station: Texas A&M University Press, 1989.

Appleman, Roy E. *U.S. Army in the Korean War: South to the Naktong, North to the Yalu (June–November, 1950).* Washington, D.C.: Office of the Chief of Military History, Department of the Army, 1961.

Arlen, Alice, and Michael J. Arlen, *The Huntress: The Adventures, Escapades, and Triumphs of Alicia Patterson.* New York: Pantheon, 2016.

Association of the Bar of the City of New York. *Report of the Special Committee on the Federal Loyalty-Security Program.* New York: Dodd, Mead, 1956.

Astley, Joan Bright. *The Inner Circle: A View of War at the Top.* London: Hutchinson, 1971.

Attlee, Clement. *Twilight of Empire: Memoirs of Prime Minister Clement Attlee.* As set down by Francis Williams. New York: A. S. Barnes, 1961.

Baillie, Hugh. *High Tension: The Recollections of Hugh Baillie.* New York: Harper & Brothers, 1959.

Baime, A. J. *The Accidental President: Harry S. Truman and the Four Months That Changed the World,* New York: Mariner Books, 2018.

Ball, George W. *The Past Has Another Pattern: Memoirs*. New York: W. W. Norton, 1982.

Barkley, Alben W. *That Reminds Me—*. Garden City, New York: Doubleday & Company, 1954.

Barth, Alan. *The Loyalty of Free Men*. With a Foreword by Zechariah Chafee Jr. New York: Viking, 1951.

Bayley, Edwin R. *Joe McCarthy and the Press*. Madison: University of Wisconsin Press, 1981.

Beale, Betty. *Power at Play: A Memoir of Parties, Politicians and the Presidents in My Bedroom*. Washington, D.C.: Regnery Gateway, 1993.

Beisner, Robert L. *Dean Acheson: A Life in the Cold War*. New York: Oxford University Press, 2006.

Bell, Jack. *The Splendid Misery: The Story of the Presidency and Power Politics at Close Range*. Garden City, New York: Doubleday, 1960.

Berezhkov, Valentin M. *At Stalin's Side: His Interpreter's Memoirs from the October Revolution to the Fall of the Dictator's Empire*. New York: Birch Lane Press, 1994.

Berger, Meyer. *The Story of the New York Times, 1851–1951*. New York: Simon & Schuster, 1951.

Berle, Adolf. *Navigating the Rapids*. New York: Harcourt Brace Jovanovich, 1973.

Berlin, Isaiah. *Letters 1928–1946*. Edited by Henry Hardy. Cambridge: Cambridge University Press, 2004.

———. *Washington Despatches 1941–45*. Edited by H. G. Nicholas. Chicago: University of Chicago Press, 1981.

Bernstein, Barton J., and Allen J. Matusow (editors). *The Truman Administration: A Documentary History*. New York: Harper & Row, 1966.

Beschloss, Michael. *Presidents of War: The Epic Story from 1807 to Modern Times*. New York: Crown, 2018.

Biddle, Francis. *In Brief Authority: From the Years with Roosevelt to the Nürnberg Trial*. Garden City, New York: Doubleday & Company, 1962.

Bird, Kai. *The Chairman: John J. McCloy, The Making of the American Establishment*. New York: Simon & Schuster, 1992.

Bird, Kai, and Martin J. Sherwin. *American Prometheus: The Triumph and Tragedy of J. Robert Oppenheimer*. New York: Alfred A. Knopf, 2005.

Birse, A. H. *Memoirs of an Interpreter: Behind the Scenes with Churchill's Interpreter at the Big Three Conferences*. Foreword by Sir Anthony Eden. New York: Coward-McCann, 1967.

Blum, John Morton (editor). *Public Philosopher: Selected Letters of Walter Lippmann*. New York: Ticknor & Fields, 1985.

Bohlen, Charles E., with Robert H. Phelps. *Witness to History*. New York: W. W. Norton, 1973.

Bontecou, Eleanor. *The Federal Loyalty Security Program*. Ithaca, New York: Cornell University Press, 1953.

Bowie, Robert R., and Richard H. Immerman. *Waging Peace: How Eisenhower Shaped an Enduring Cold War Strategy*. New York: Oxford University Press, 1998.

Bradley, David. *No Place to Hide*. Boston: Little, Brown, 1948.

Brandon, Henry. *Special Relationships: A Foreign Correspondent's Memoirs from Roosevelt to Reagan*. New York: Macmillan, 1988.

Brands, H. W. Jr. *Cold Warriors: Eisenhower's Generation and American Foreign Policy*. New York: Columbia University Press, 1988.

Brands, H. W. *The General vs. the President: MacArthur and Truman at the Brink of Nuclear War*. New York: Doubleday, 2016.

Brinkley, Douglas, and Townsend Hoopes. *Driven Patriot: The Life and Times of James Forrestal*. New York: Alfred A. Knopf, 1992.

Brown, Walter J. *James F. Byrnes of South Carolina: A Remembrance*. Privately published, 1992.

Bruns, Roger A. *Billy Graham: A Biography*. Westport, CT: Greenwood.

Bullock, Alan. *Ernest Bevin: Foreign Secretary*. New York: W. W. Norton, 1983.

Burns, James MacGregor. *Roosevelt: The Soldier of Freedom*. 1940–1945. New York: Harcourt Brace Jovanovich, 1970.

Bush, Vannevar. *Science: The Endless Frontier*. Washington, D.C.: National Science Foundation, 1945.

Butler, Susan (editor). *My Dear Mr. Stalin: The Complete Correspondence Between Franklin D. Roosevelt and Joseph V. Stalin*. Foreword by Arthur M. Schlesinger Jr. New Haven, Connecticut: Yale University Press, 2005.

Byrnes, James F. *All in One Lifetime*. New York: Harper & Brothers, 1958.

———. *Speaking Frankly*. New York: Harper & Brothers, 1947.

Cadogan, Alexander. *The Diaries of Sir Alexander Cadogan, 1938–1945*. Edited by David Dilks. New York: G. P. Putnam's Sons, 1971.

Campbell, Tracy. *Short of the Glory: The Fall and Redemption of Edward F. Pritchard Jr.* Lexington: University Press of Kentucky, 1998.

Carr, Albert Z. *Truman Stalin and Peace*. Garden City, New York: Doubleday, 1950.

Catledge, Turner. *My Life and the Times*. New York: Harper & Row, 1971.

Chace, James. *Acheson: The Secretary of State Who Created the American World*. New York: Simon & Schuster, 1998.

Channon, Henry. *Chips: The Diaries of Sir Henry Channon*. Edited by Robert Rhodes James. London: Weidenfeld & Nicolson, 1967.

Cheuv, Felix. *Molotov Remembers: Inside Kremlin Politics*. Conversations with Felix Cheuv. Edited with an introduction and notes by Albert Resis. Chicago: Ivan R. Dee, 1993.

Childs, Marquis. *Eisenhower: Captive Hero*. New York: Harcourt, Brace, 1958.

———. *Witness to Power*. New York: McGraw-Hill, 1975.

Churchill, Winston. *Defending the West: The Truman-Churchill Correspondence, 1945–1960*. Edited with an Introduction by G. W. Sand. Westport, Connecticut: Praeger, 2004.

———. *Triumph and Tragedy*. Boston: Houghton Mifflin, 1953.

Clarke, Nick. *Alistair Cooke: The Biography*. London: Weidenfeld & Nicolson, 1999.

Clay, Lucius D. *The Papers of General Lucius D. Clay, Germany 1945–1949*. Volume One and Volume Two. Edited by Jean Edward Smith. Bloomington: Indiana University Press, 1974.

Clayton, Will. *Selected Papers of Will Clayton*. Edited by Frederick J. Dobney. Baltimore: Johns Hopkins Press, 1971.

Clifford, Clark, with Richard Holbrooke. *Counsel to the President: A Memoir*. New York: Random House, 1991.

Collins, J. Lawton. *War in Peacetime: The History and Lessons of Korea*. Boston: Houghton Mifflin, 1969.

Colville, John. *The Fringes of Power: Downing Street Diaries*, Volume Two: *1941–April, 1955*. New York: W. W. Norton, 1985.

Compton, Arthur Holly. *Atomic Quest. A Personal Narrative*. New York: Oxford University Press, 1956.

Conant, James B. *My Several Lives: Memoirs of a Social Inventor*. New York: Harper & Row, 1970.

Condit, Kenneth W. *The Joint Chiefs of Staff and National Policy*, Volume II: *1947–1949*. Washington, D.C.: Office of the Chairman of the Joint Chiefs of Staff, 1995.

Connally, Tom, as told to Alfred Steinberg. *My Name Is Tom Connally*. New York: Thomas Y. Crowell, 1954.

Considine, Bob. *It's All News to Me: A Reporter's Deposition*. New York: Meredith Press, 1967.

Conway-Lanz, Sahr. *Collateral Damage: Americans, Noncombatants Immunity and Atrocity After World War II*. New York: Routledge, 2006.

Cooke, Alistair. *A Generation on Trial: U.S.A. v. Alger Hiss*. New York: Alfred A. Knopf, 1950.

———. *Reporting America*. New York: Overlook Press, 2008.

Costigliola Frank. *Roosevelt's Lost Alliances: How Personal Politics Helped Start the Cold War*. Princeton, New Jersey: Princeton University Press, 2012.

Cray, Ed. *General of the Army: George C. Marshall, Soldier and Statesman*. New York: Touchstone, 1990.

Crosswell, D. K. R. *Beetle. The Life of General Walter Bedell Smith*. Lexington: University Press of Kentucky, 2010.

Cumings, Bruce. *The Korean War: A History*. New York: Random House, 2011.

———. *Korea's Place in the Sun: A Modern History*. New York: W. W. Norton, Updated Edition, 2005.

Daniel, Clifton Truman. *Dear Harry, Love Bess: Bess Truman's Letters to Harry Truman 1919–1943*. Kirksville, Missouri: Truman State University Press, 2011.

Daniels, Jonathan. *The Man of Independence*. Philadelphia: J. B. Lippincott, 1950.

———. *White House Witness, 1942–1945: An Intimate Diary of the Years with F.D.R.* New York: Doubleday, 1975.

Dean, Gordon E. *Forging the Atomic Shield: Excerpts from the Office Diary of Gordon E. Dean*. Edited by Roger M. Anders. Chapel Hill: University of North Carolina Press, 1987.

Dikötter, Frank. *The Tragedy of Liberation: A History of the Chinese Revolution 1945–1957*. New York: Bloomsbury Paperback, 2018.

Djilas, Milovan. *Conversations with Stalin*. New York: Harcourt, Brace & World, 1962.

Dobbs, Michael. *Six Months in 1945: From World War to Cold War.* New York: Alfred A. Knopf, 2012.

Donovan, Robert J. *Conflict and Crisis: The Presidency of Harry Truman, 1945–1948.* New York: W. W. Norton, 1977.

_____. *Tumultuous Years: The Presidency of Harry S. Truman 1949–1953.* New York: W. W. Norton, 1982.

_____. *Nemesis: Truman and Johnson in the Coils of War in Asia.* New York: St. Martins-Marek, 1984.

Dorwart, Jeffery M. *Eberstadt and Forrestal: A National Security Partnership, 1909–1949.* College Station: Texas A&M University Press, 1991.

Dos Passos, John. *The Great Days.* New York: Popular Library, 1959.

Drury, Allen. *A Senate Journal, 1943–1945.* New York: McGraw-Hill, 1963.

Duffy, Bernard K., and Ronald H. Carpenter. *Douglas MacArthur: Warrior as Wordsmith.* Westport, Connecticut: Greenwood Press, 1997.

Dunar, Andrew J. *The Truman Scandals and the Politics of Morality.* Columbia: University of Missouri Press, 1984.

Dyke, Richard W., and Francis X. Gannon. *Chet Holifield: Master Legislator and Nuclear Statesman.* Lanham, Maryland: University Press of America, 1996.

Eden, Anthony. *The Reckoning.* Boston: Houghton Mifflin, 1965.

Eisenberg, Carolyn. *Drawing the Line: The American Decision to Divide Germany, 1944–1949.* New York: Cambridge University Press, 1997.

Eisenhower, Dwight D. *At Ease: Stories I Tell to Friends.* Garden City, New York: Doubleday, 1967.

_____. *Crusade in Europe.* Baltimore: Johns Hopkins University Press, 1997.

_____. *Mandate for Change: The White House Years, 1953–1956.* Garden City, New York: Doubleday, 1963.

Ellis, Edward Robb. *A Diary of the Century: Tales from America's Greatest Diarist.* Introduction by Pete Hamill. New York: Union Square Press, 2008.

Elsey, George McKee. *An Unplanned Life: A Memoir.* Columbia: University of Missouri Press, 2005.

Elson, Robert T. *The World of Time Inc.: The Intimate History of a Publishing Enterprise, 1941–1960.* New York: Atheneum, 1973.

Evans, Hugh E. *The Hidden Campaign: FDR's Health and the 1944 Election.* Armonk, New York: M. E. Sharpe, 2002.

Farrar, Ronald T. *Reluctant Servant: The Story of Charles E. Ross.* Columbia: University of Missouri Press, 1969.

Fehrenbach, T. R. *This Kind of War: A Study in Unpreparedness.* New York: Macmillan, 1963.

Feis, Herbert. *Between War and Peace. The Potsdam Conference.* Princeton, New Jersey: Princeton University Press, 1960.

_____. *Japan Subdued: The Atomic Bomb and the End of the War in the Pacific.* Princeton, New Jersey: Princeton University Press, 1961.

Ferrell, Robert H. *Choosing Truman: The Democratic Convention of 1944.* Columbia: University of Missouri Press, 1994.

_____. *The Dying President: Franklin D. Roosevelt 1944–1945*. Columbia: University of Missouri Press, 1998.

_____. *Harry S. Truman: A Life*. Columbia: University of Missouri Press, 1994.

_____. *Truman & Pendergast*. Columbia: University of Missouri Press, 1999.

Ferrell, Robert H. (editor). *Dear Bess: The Letters from Harry to Bess Truman 1910–1959*. New York: W. W. Norton, 1983.

_____. *Off the Record: The Private Papers of Harry S. Truman*. New York: Harper & Row, 1980.

_____. *Truman in the White House: The Diary of Eben E. Ayers*. Columbia: University of Missouri Press, 1991.

Flynn, Edward J. *You're the Boss*. New York: Viking, 1947.

Forrestal, James. *The Forrestal Diaries*. Edited by Walter Millis. New York: Viking, 1951.

Foster, Mark S. *Henry J. Kaiser: Builder in the Modern American West*. Austin: University of Texas Press, 1989.

Frady, Marshall. *Billy Graham: A Parable of American Righteousness*. Boston: Little, Brown, 1979.

Freeland, Richard M. *The Truman Doctrine and the Origins of McCarthyism: Foreign Policy, Domestic Politics, and Internal Security, 1946–1948*. New York: Alfred A. Knopf, 1972.

Frank, Jeffrey. *Ike and Dick: Portrait of a Strange Political Marriage*. New York: Simon & Schuster, 2013.

Gabler, Neal. *Winchell: Gossip, Power and the Culture of Celebrity*. New York: Alfred A. Knopf, 1994.

Gaddis, John Lewis. *The Cold War: A New History*. New York: Penguin Press, 2005.

_____. *George F. Kennan: An American Life*. New York: Penguin Press, 2011.

George C. Marshall. Interviews and Reminiscences for Forrest C. Pogue. Lexington, Virginia: George C. Marshall Research Foundation, 1991.

Gergel, Richard. *Unexampled Courage: The Blinding of Sgt. Isaac Woodard and the Awakening of President Harry S. Truman and Judge J. Waties Waring*. New York: Sarah Crichton Books, 2019.

Gilbert, Martin. *Never Despair: Winston S. Churchill 1945–1965*. London: Heinemann, 1988.

Gillies, Donald. *Radical Diplomat: The Life of Archibald Clark Kerr, Lord Inverchapel, 1882–1951*. London and New York: I. B. Tauris, 1999.

Goldman, Eric F. *The Crucial Decade—and After: America, 1945–1960*. New York: Vintage, 1960.

Goncharov, Sergei N., John W. Lewis, and Xue Litai. *Uncertain Partners: Stalin, Mao, and the Korean War*. Stanford, California: Stanford University Press, 1993.

Gordin, Michael D. *Five Days in August: How World War II Became a Nuclear War*. Princeton, New Jersey: Princeton University Press, 2007.

_____. *Red Cloud at Dawn: Truman, Stalin, and the End of the Atomic Monopoly*. New York: Farrar, Straus and Giroux, 2009.

Goulden, C. *Korea: The Untold Story of the War*. New York: Times Books, 1982.

Graham, Billy. *Revival in Our Time: The Story of the Billy Graham Evangelistic Campaign*. Wheaton, Illinois: Van Kampen Press, 1950.

Greenberg, David. *Republic of Spin: An Inside History of the American Presidency*. New York: W. W. Norton, 2016.

Greenstein, Fred I. *The Hidden-Hand Presidency*. New York: Basic Books. 1982.

Grew, Joseph C. *Turbulent Era: A Diplomatic Record of Forty Years, 1904–1945*. Edited by Walter Johnson. Boston: Houghton Mifflin, 1952.

Griese, Noel L. *Arthur W. Page: Publisher. Public Relations Pioneer. Patriot*. Atlanta: Anvil Publishers, 2001.

Griffith, Robert. *The Politics of Fear: Joseph R. McCarthy and the Senate*. Amherst: University of Massachusetts Press, 1987.

Gromyko, Andrei. *Memories*. London: Hutchinson, 1989.

Groves, General Leslie M. *Now It Can Be Told*. New Introduction by Edward Teller. New York: Da Capo, 1962, 1983.

Gunther, John. *Inside U.S.A.* New York: Harper & Brothers, 1947.

Haig, Alexander M. Jr., with Charles McCarry. *Inner Circles: How America Changed the World, A Memoir*. New York: Warner Books, 1992.

Halberstam, David. *The Coldest Winter: America and the Korean War*. New York: Hyperion, 2007.

———. *The Fifties*. New York: Villard Books, New York, 1993.

Halifax, Lord. *Fullness of Days*. New York: Dodd, Mead, 1957.

Hamburger, Philip. *Matters of State: A Political Excursion*. Washington, D.C.: Counterpoint, 2000.

Hamby, Alonzo L. *Man of the People: A Life of Harry S. Truman*. New York: Oxford University Press, 1995.

Harden, Blaine. *King of Spies: The Dark Reign of America's Spymaster in Korea*. New York: Viking, 2017.

Harper, Alan D. *The Politics of Loyalty: The White House and the Communist Issue, 1946–1952*. Westport, Connecticut: Greenwood Press, 1969.

Harriman, W. Averell, and Elie Abel. *Special Envoy to Churchill and Stalin, 1941–1946*. Edited by Charles A. Miller. New York: Random House, 1975.

Harris, Edward A. *Autobiography of a Reporter*. New Market, Virginia: Upper House Books, 2016.

Harry S. Truman: Memorial Tributes Delivered in Congress. Washington: Government Printing Office, 1973.

Hassett, William D. *Off the Record with F.D.R. 1942–1945*. Westport, Connecticut: Greenwood Press, 1980.

Hastings, Max. *The Korean War*. New York: Simon & Schuster, 1987.

Hechler, Ken. *Working with Truman: A Personal Memoir of the White House Years*. New York: G. P. Putnam's Sons, 1982.

Heller, Francis H. (editor). *The Truman White House: The Administration of the Presidency, 1945–1953*. Lawrence, Kansas: Regents Press, 1980.

Helm, Edith Benham. *The Captains and the Kings*. With a foreword by Mrs. Franklin D. Roosevelt. New York: G. P. Putnam's Sons, 1954.

Helm, William P. *Harry Truman: A Political Biography*. New York: Duell, Sloan and Pearce, 1947.

Henderson, Deirdre (editor). *Prelude to Leadership: The European Diary of John F. Kennedy, Summer 1945*. Introduction by Hugh Sidey. Washington, D.C.: Regnery, 1995.

Herken, Gregg. *The Georgetown Set: The Friends and Rivals in Cold War Washington*. New York: Alfred A. Knopf, 2014.

Hersey, John. *Aspects of the Presidency: Truman and Ford in Office*. Introduction by Robert A. Dahl. New York: Ticknor & Fields, 1980.

_____. *Hiroshima*. New York: Alfred A. Knopf, 1946.

Higgins, Marguerite. *War in Korea: The Report of a Woman Combat Correspondent*. Photographs by Carl Mydans and others. Garden City, New York: Doubleday, 1951.

Hillman, William. *Mr. President: The First Publication from the Personal Diaries, Private Letters, Papers and Revealing Interviews of Harry S. Truman*. Pictures by Alfred Wagg. New York: Farrar, Straus and Young, 1952.

Hitchcock, William I. *The Age of Eisenhower: America and the World in the 1950s*. New York: Simon & Schuster, 2019.

Hogan, Michael J. *A Cross of Iron: Harry S. Truman and the Origins of the National Security State, 1945–1954*. New York: Cambridge University Press, 1998.

Hoopes, Townsend. *The Devil and John Foster Dulles*. Boston: Atlantic-Little Brown, 1973.

Huff, Col. Sid, with Joe Alex Morris. *My Fifteen Years with General MacArthur*. New York: Paperback Library, 1964.

Hughes, Emmet John. *The Ordeal of Power*. New York: Atheneum, 1963.

Hull, Cordell. *The Memoirs of Cordell Hull*. Volume II. New York: Macmillan, 1948.

Huntington, Samuel P. *The Soldier and the State: The Theory and Politics of Civil-Military Relations*. Cambridge: Harvard University Press, 1981.

Hwang, Su-kyoung. *Korea's Grievous War*. Philadelphia: University of Pennsylvania Press, 2016.

Isaacson, Walter, and Evan Thomas. *The Wise Men: Six Friends and the World They Made*. New York: Simon & Schuster, 1986.

Ismay, Hastings. *The Memoirs of General the Lord Ismay*. London: William Heinemann, 1960.

Ives, Elizabeth Stevenson, and Hildegarde Dolson. *My Brother Adlai*. New York: William Morrow, 1956.

James, D. Clayton. *The Years of MacArthur, Volume III: Triumph & Disaster, 1945–1964*. Boston: Houghton Mifflin, 1985.

Jespersen, T. Christopher (editor). *Interviews with George F. Kennan*. Jackson: University Press of Mississippi.

Jones, Joseph M. *The Fifteen Weeks*. New York: Viking, 1955.

Judis, John N. *Genesis: Truman, American Jews, and the Origins of the Arab/Israeli Conflict*. New York: Farrar, Straus and Giroux, 2014.

Jurika, Stephen Jr. (editor). *From Pearl Harbor to Vietnam: The Memoirs of Arthur W. Radford*. Stanford, California: Hoover Institution Press, 1980.

Kahn, E. J. Jr. *The World of Swope*. New York: Simon & Schuster, 1965.

Kaufman, Burton I. *The Korean War: Challenges in Crisis, Credibility, and Command*. New York: Alfred A. Knopf, 1988.

Kempton, Murray. *America Comes of Middle Age*. Boston: Little, Brown, 1963.

———. *Rebellions, Perversities, and Main Events*. New York: Times Books, 1994.

Kennan, George F. *At the Century's Ending: Reflections, 1982-1995*, New York: W. W. Norton, 1996.

———. *Kennan Diaries*. Edited by Frank Costigliola. New York: W. W. Norton, 2014.

———. *Memoirs, 1925–1950*. Boston: Atlantic Little, Brown, 1967.

Khrushchev Remembers. Translated and edited by Strobe Talbott. With an Introduction, Commentary and Notes by Edward Crankshaw. Boston: Little, Brown, 1974.

Khrushchev Remembers, The Glasnost Tapes (Vol. 3). With a Foreword by Strobe Talbott. Translated and Edited by Jerrold L. Schecter with Vyacheslav V. Luchkov. Boston: Little, Brown, 1990.

Kim, Richard E. *The Martyred*. New York: George Braziller, 1964.

Kirkendall, Richard S. (editor). *Harry's Farewell: Interpreting and Teaching the Truman Presidency*. Columbia: University of Missouri Press, 2004.

———. *The Truman Period as a Research Field*. Columbia: University of Missouri Press, 1974.

Klara, Robert. *The Hidden White House*. New York: St. Martin's Press, 2013.

Knox, Donald. *The Korean War: An Oral History, Pusan to Chosin*. New York: Harcourt Brace Jovanovich, 1985.

Kofsky, Frank. *Harry S. Truman and the War Scare of 1948: A Successful Campaign to Deceive the Nation*. New York: St. Martin's Press, 1993.

Kohn, Richard H. and Joseph P. Harahan. *Strategic Air Power*. An Interview with Generals Curtis E. LeMay, Leon W. Johnson, David A. Burchinal, and Jack J. Catton. Washington, D.C.: Office of Air Force History. United States Air Force, 1988.

Krasnoff, Sidney O. *Truman and Noyes: Story of a President's Alter Ego*. West Palm Beach, Florida: Jonathan Stuart Press, 1997.

Krock, Arthur. *Memoirs: Sixty Years on the Firing Line*. New York: Funk & Wagnalls, 1968.

Kurtz-Phelan, Daniel. *The China Mission: George Marshall's Unfinished War, 1945–1947*. New York: W. W. Norton, 2020.

Lacey, Michael J. (editor). *The Truman Presidency*. Cambridge: Woodrow Wilson International Center for Scholars and Cambridge University Press, 1989.

Lait, Jack, and Lee Mortimer. *Washington Confidential*. New York: Crown, 1951.

Lash, Joseph P. *A World of Love: Eleanor Roosevelt and Her Friends, 1943–62*. Garden City, New York: Doubleday, 1984.

———. *From the Diaries of Felix Frankfurter*. With a biographical essay and notes by Joseph P. Lash. New York: W. W. Norton, 1975.

Lasser, William. *Benjamin V. Cohen: Architect of the New Deal*. Preface by Arthur Schlesinger, Jr. New Haven, Connecticut: Yale University Press, 2002.

Latham, Earl. *The Communist Controversy in Washington: From the New Deal to McCarthy*. Cambridge, Massachusetts: Harvard University Press, 1966.

Lawrenson, Helen. *Stranger at the Party: A Memoir*. New York: Random House, 1975.

Leahy, William D. *I Was There: The Personal Story of the Chief of Staff to Presidents Roosevelt and Truman Based on His Notes and Diaries Made at the Time*. New York: McGraw-Hill, 1950.

Lee, Joong Keun. *Korean War 1129*. Seoul, ROK: WooJung Publishing, 2015.

Leffler, Melvyn P. *A Preponderance of Power: National Security, the Truman Administration, and the Cold War* (Stanford Nuclear Age Series). Stanford, California: Stanford University Press, 1993.

Lelyveld, Joseph. *His Final Battle: The Last Months of Franklin Roosevelt*. New York: Alfred A. Knopf, 2016.

Levin, Linda Lotridge. *The Making of FDR: The Story of Stephen T. Early, America's First Modern Press Secretary*. Amherst, New York: Prometheus, 2008.

Lilienthal, David E. *The Journals of David E. Lilienthal, Volume Two: The Atomic Energy Years, 1945–1950*. New York: Harper & Row, 1964.

_____. *The Journals of David E. Lilienthal*, Volume Three: *Venturesome Years, 1950–1955*. New York: Harper & Row, 1966.

Lippmann, Walter. *The Cold War: A Study in U.S. Foreign Policy*. New York: Harper & Brothers, 1947.

List, Eugene. *Playing for the Big Three at Potsdam*. Unpublished manuscript, ca. 1974.

Lodge, Henry Cabot. *As It Was*. New York: W. W. Norton, 1976.

Logevall, Fredrick. *Embers of War*. New York: Random House, 2012.

_____. *JFK. Coming of Age in the American Century*. New York: Random House, 2020.

Lowenthal, Max. *The Federal Bureau of Investigation*. New York: William Sloane, 1950.

Lukacs, John. A New History of the Cold War. New York: Anchor Books, 1966.

_____. *1945: Year Zero, The Shaping of the Modern Age*. Garden City, New York: Doubleday, 1978.

MacArthur, Douglas. *Reminiscences*. New York: McGraw-Hill, 1964.

Macdonald, Dwight. *Henry Wallace: The Man and the Myth*. New York: Vanguard, 1947.

_____. *A Moral Temper: The Letters of Dwight Macdonald*. Edited with an Introduction by Michael Wreszin. Chicago: Ivan R. Dee, 2001.

Manchester, William. *American Caesar: Douglas MacArthur, 1880–1964*. Boston: Little, Brown, 1978.

Marcus, Maeva. *Truman and the Steel Seizure Case: The Limits of Presidential Power*. New York: Columbia University Press, 1977.

Martin, John Bartlow. *Adlai Stevenson of Illinois*. Garden City, New York: Doubleday, 1976

_____. *Adlai Stevenson and the World*. Garden City, New York: Doubleday, 1976.

Mastny, Voytech. *Russia's Road to the Cold War: Diplomacy, Warfare, and the Politics of Communism, 1941–1945*. New York: Columbia University Press, 1979.

May, Ernest R. (editor). *America's Cold War Strategy: Interpreting NSC 68*. Boston: Bedford/St. Martin's, 1993.

McCullough, David. *Truman*. New York: Simon & Shuster, 1992.

McFarland, Keith D., and David L. Roll. *Louis Johnson and the Arming of America*. Bloomington and Indianapolis: Indiana University Press, 2005.

McKeever, Porter. *Adlai Stevenson: His Life and Legacy*. New York: William Morrow, 1989.

McNeill, William H. *Arnold J. Toynbee: A Life*. New York: Oxford University Press, 1989.

McPherson, Harry. *A Political Education: A Washington Memoir*. Boston: Houghton Mifflin, 1988.

McPherson, James M. *Battle Cry of Freedom: The Civil War Era*. New York: Oxford University Press, 1988.

Mee, Charles L. Jr. *Meeting at Potsdam*. New York: M. Evans, 1975.

Menand, Louis. *The Free World: Art and Thought in the Cold War*. New York: Farrar, Straus and Giroux, 2021.

Merson, Martin. *The Private Diary of a Public Servant*. New York: Macmillan, 1955.

Messer, Robert L. *The End of an Alliance: James F. Byrnes, Roosevelt, Truman, and the Origins of the Cold War*. Chapel Hill: University of North Carolina Press, 1982.

Mesta, Perle, with Robert Cahn. *Perle: My Story*. New York: McGraw-Hill, 1960.

Michelson, Charles. *The Ghost Talks*. New York: G. P. Putnam's, 1944.

Miller, Merle. *Plain Speaking: An Oral Biography of Harry Truman*. New York: Berkley Publishing Corporation,1974.

Miller, Richard Lawrence. *Truman: The Rise to Power*. New York: McGraw-Hill, 1986.

Milligan, Maurice M. *Missouri Waltz: The Inside Story of the Pendergast Machine by the Man Who Smashed It*. New York: Charles Scribner's Sons, 1948.

Miscamble, Wilson D. *From Roosevelt to Truman: Potsdam, Hiroshima, and the Cold War*. New York: Cambridge University Press, 2007.

Mitchell, Franklin D. *Harry S. Truman and the News Media: Contentious Relations, Belated Respect*. Columbia: University of Missouri Press, 1998.

Monk, Ray. *Oppenheimer. A Life Inside the Center*. New York: Doubleday, 2012.

Moran, Lord (Charles McMoran Wilson). *Churchill: Taken from the Diaries of Lord Moran*. Boston: Houghton Mifflin, 1966.

Morris, Newbold, in collaboration with Dana Lee Thomas. *Let the Chips Fall: My Battles Against Corruption*. New York: Appleton-Century-Crofts, 1955.

Murphy, Robert. *Diplomat Among Warriors*. Garden City, New York: Doubleday, 1964.

Navasky, Victor S. *Naming Names*. New York: Viking, 1980.

Neal, Steve. *Harry & Ike: The Partnership That Remade the Postwar World*. New York: Scribner, 2001.

Neal, Steve (editor). *Eleanor and Harry: The Correspondence of Eleanor Roosevelt and Harry S. Truman*. New York: Scribner, 2002.

_____. *HST: Memories of the Truman Years*. Foreword by Clifton Truman Daniel. Carbondale: Southern Illinois University Press, 2003.

_____. *Miracle of '48: Harry Truman's Major Campaign Speeches & Selected Whistle-Stops*. Carbondale: Southern Illinois University Press, 2003.

Nelson, W. Dale. *The President Is at Camp David*. Syracuse, New York: Syracuse University Press, 1995.

Neustadt, Richard E. *Presidential Power*. New York: Signet, 1964.

Nichols, David A. *A Matter of Justice: Eisenhower and the Beginning of the Civil Rights Revolution*. New York: Simon & Schuster, 2007.

Nicolson, Harold. *The Later Years, 1945–1962*, Volume III of *Diaries and Letters*. New York: Atheneum, 1968.

Nitze, Paul H., with Ann M. Smith and Steven E. Rearden. *From Hiroshima to Glasnost: At the Center of Decision, A Memoir*. New York: Grove Weidenfeld, 1989.

Offner, Arnold A. *Another Such Victory: President Truman and the Cold War, 1945–1953*. Stanford, California: Stanford University Press, 2002.

Parks, Arva Moore. *Harry Truman and the Little White House in Key West*. Miami, Florida: Centennial Press, 1999.

Patterson, James T. *Mr. Republican*. Boston: Houghton Mifflin, 1972.

Pearson, Drew. *Washington Merry-Go-Round: The Drew Pearson Diaries, 1960–1969*. Edited and with an introduction by Peter Hannaford, foreword by Richard Norton Smith. Lincoln, Nebraska: Potomac Books, 2015.

Phillips, Cabell. *The Truman Presidency: The History of a Triumphant Succession*. New York: Macmillan, 1966,

Poen, Monte M. (editor). *Strictly Personal and Confidential. The Letters Harry Truman Never Mailed*. Boston: Little, Brown, 1982.

Pogue, Forrest C. *George C. Marshall: Statesman, 1945–1959*. New York: Viking, 1987.

Powers, Thomas. *The Man Who Kept the Secrets: Richard Helms and the CIA*. New York: Pocket Books, 1981.

Price, Harry Bayard. *The Marshall Plan and Its Meaning*. Ithaca, New York: Cornell University Press, 1955.

Rearden, Steven L. *Council of War: A History of the Joint Chiefs of Staff, 1942–1991, Washington, D.C.*: Joint History Office, 2012.

Redding, Jack. *Inside the Democratic Party: An Informal Account of What Went On Behind Scenes in Recent Campaigns, by an Insider*. With a foreword by J. Howard McGrath. Indianapolis: Bobbs-Merrill, 1958.

Rees, David. *Korea: The Limited War*. New York: St. Martin's Press, 1964.

Reston, James. *Deadline*. New York: Random House, 1991.

Reynold, David. *In Command of History: Churchill Fighting and Writing the Second World War*. New York: Random House, 2005.

Rhodes, Richard. *Dark Sun: The Making of the Hydrogen Bomb*. New York: Simon & Schuster, 1995.

Ridgway, Matthew B. *The Korean War: How We Met the Challenge, How All-Out Asian War Was Averted, Why MacArthur Was Dismissed, Why Today's War Objectives Must Be Limited*. New York: Doubleday, 1967.

Ridgway, Matthew, as told to Harold H. Martin. *Soldier: The Memoirs of Matthew B. Ridgway*. New York: Harper & Brothers, 1956.

Rigdon, William M., with James Derieux. *White House Sailor*. Garden City, New York: Doubleday, 1962.

Roberts, Chalmers M. *The Washington Post: The First 100 Years*. Boston: Houghton Mifflin, 1977.

Robertson, David. *Sly and Able: A Political Biography of James F. Byrnes*. New York: Norton, 1994.

Rogow, Arnold A. *James Forrestal: A Study of Personality, Politics, and Policy*. New York: Macmillan, 1963.

Roosevelt, Anna and Eleanor. *Mother and Daughter: The Letters of Eleanor & Anna Roosevelt*. Edited by Bernard Asbell. New York: Coward, McCann & Geoghegan, 1982.

Roosevelt, James, with Bill Libby. *My Parents: A Differing View*. London: W. H. Allen, 1977.

Rosenman, Samuel I. *Working with Roosevelt*. New York: Harper & Brothers, 1952.

Rosenman, Samuel, and Dorothy Rosenman. *Presidential Style*. New York: Harper & Row, 1976.

Ross, Irwin. *The Loneliest Campaign: The Truman Victory of 1948*. New York: New American Library, 1968.

Rovere, Richard H. *Affairs of State: The Eisenhower Years*. New York: Farrar, Straus and Cudahy, 1956.

———. *Arrivals and Departures: A Journalist's Memoirs*. New York: Macmillan, 1976.

———. *Senator Joe McCarthy*. Cleveland Ohio: Meridian, 1960.

Rovere, Richard H., and Arthur M. Schlesinger Jr. *The General and the President*. New York: Farrar, Straus and Young, 1951.

Sand, G. W. *Truman in Retirement: A Former President Views the Nation & the World*. South Bend, Indiana: Justice Books, 1993.

Sandler, Stanley (editor). *The Korean War: An Encyclopedia*. New York and London: Garland, 1995.

Sawyer, Charles. *Concerns of a Conservative Democrat*. Carbondale and Edwardsville: Southern Illinois University Press, 1968.

Sayre, Nora. *Running Time: Films of the Cold War*. New York: Dial Press, 1982.

Scarborough, Joe. *Saving Freedom: Truman, the Cold War, and the Fight for Western Civilization*. New York: Harper, 2020.

Schlesinger, Arthur M. Jr. *Journals 1952–2000*. New York: Penguin Books, 2007.

———. *A Life in the 20th Century: Innocent Beginnings, 1917–1950*. New York: Houghton Mifflin, 2000.

Schnabel, James F., and Robert J. Watson. *The Joint Chiefs of Staff and National Policy*. Volume III, *1950–1951. The Korean War*. Part One. Washington: Office of Joint History, 1998.

Schoenbaum, Thomas J. *Waging Peace & War: Dean Rusk in the Truman, Kennedy & Johnson Years*. New York: Simon & Schuster, 1988.

Schwartz, Jordan A. *The Speculator: Bernard M. Baruch in Washington, 1917–1965*. Chapel Hill: University of North Carolina Press, 1981.

Sevareid, Eric. *Conversations with Eric Sevareid*. Washington, D.C: Public Affairs Press, 1976.

Sherwood, Robert E. *Roosevelt and Hopkins: An Intimate History*. New York: Harper and Brothers, 1948.

Smith, A. Merriman. *Thank You, Mr. President: A White House Notebook*. New York: Harper & Brothers, 1946.

Smith, Gaddis. *American Diplomacy During the Second World War, 1941–1945*. Second Edition. New York: Alfred A. Knopf, 1985.

Smith, Richard Norton. *Thomas E. Dewey and His Times*. New York: Simon & Schuster, 1982.

Smith, Walter Bedell. *My Three Years in Moscow*. Philadelphia: J. B. Lippincott, 1950.

Soffer, Jonathan M. *General Matthew B. Ridgway: From Progressivism to Reaganism, 1895–1993*. Westport, Connecticut: Praeger, 1998.

Solomon, Burt. *The Washington Century: Three Families and the Shaping of the Nation's Capital*. New York: William Morrow, 2004.

Southard, Susan. *Nagasaki: Life After Nuclear War*. New York: Viking, 2015.

Spillane, Mickey. *I, the Jury*. New York: Signet, 1948.

———. *One Lonely Night*. New York: Signet, 1951.

Stacks, John F. Scotty. *James B. Reston and the Rise and Fall of American Journalism*. New York: Little, Brown, 2003.

Stalin, J. V. *On Post-War International Relations*. London: Soviet News, 1947.

———. *Stalin's Correspondence with Roosevelt and Truman, 1941–1945*. New York: Capricorn Books, 1965.

State Department Employee Loyalty Investigation. Washington, D.C.: United States Government Printing Office, 1950.

Steele, Ronald. *Walter Lippmann and the American Century*. Boston: Atlantic-Little, Brown, 1980.

Steil, Benn. *The Marshall Plan: Dawn of the Cold War*. New York: Simon & Schuster, 2018.

Stettinius, Edward R. *Diaries of Edward R. Stettinius, Jr.* Edited by Thomas M. Campbell and George C. Herring. New York: New Viewpoints, 1975.

Stiles, T. J. *Jesse James: Last Rebel of the Civil War*. New York: Alfred A. Knopf, 2002.

Stimson, Henry L., and McGeorge Bundy. *On Active Service in Peace and War*. New York: Harper & Brothers, 1947, 1948.

Stoff, Michael B., and Jonathan F. Fanton. Edited by R. Hal Williams. *The Manhattan Project: A Documentary Introduction to the Atomic Age*. New York: McGraw-Hill College, 1990.

Stone, I. F. *The Truman Era*. Introduction (1972) by Robert Sklar. New York: Random House, 1953.

Stratemeyer, George. *The Three Wars of Lt. Gen. George E. Stratemeyer: His Korean*

War Diary. Edited by William T. Y'Blood. Washington, D.C.: U.S. Government Printing Office, 1999.

Strum, Philippa. *Louis D. Brandeis: Justice for the People*. New York: Schocken, 1984.

Stuart, Graham H. *The Department of State: A History of Its Organization, Procedure, and Personnel*. New York: Macmillan, 1949.

Sulzberger, C. L. *A Long Row of Candles: Memoirs and Diaries (1934-1954)*. New York: Macmillan, 1969.

Sweeney, Michael S. *Secrets of Victory: The Office of Censorship and the American Press and Radio in World War II*. Chapel Hill, North Carolina: University of North Carolina Press, 2001.

Tanenhaus, Sam. *Whittaker Chambers*. New York: Random House (Modern Library Edition), 1998.

The Tehran, Yalta & Potsdam Conferences. Documents. Moscow: Progress Publishers, 1969.

Thompson, Edward K. *A Love Affair with Life & Smithsonian*. Columbia: University of Missouri Press, 1995.

Thompson, Kenneth W. (editor). *Portraits of American Presidents,* Volume II, *The Truman Presidency: Intimate Perspectives*. Lanham, Maryland: University Press of America, 1984.

Thompson, Nicholas. *The Hawk and the Dove: Paul Nitze, George Kennan, and the History of the Cold War*. New York: Henry Holt, 2009.

Trohan, Walter. *Political Animals: Memoirs of a Sentimental Cynic*. Garden City, New York: Doubleday, 1975.

Truman, Harry S. *The Autobiography of Harry S. Truman*. Edited by Robert H. Ferrell. Columbia: University of Missouri Press, 1980.

_____. *Truman Speaks*. New York: Columbia University Press, 1960.

_____. *Letters Home by Harry Truman*. Edited by Monte M. Poen. New York: G. P. Putnam's Sons, 1984.

_____. *Mr. Citizen*. New York: Bernard Geis Associates, 1960.

_____. *The Truman Memoirs,* Volume One: *Year of Decisions*. Garden City, New York: Doubleday, 1955.

_____. *The Truman Memoirs,* Volume Two: *Years of Trial and Hope*. Garden City, New York: Doubleday, 1956.

Truman, Margaret. *Bess W. Truman*. New York: Macmillan, 1986.

_____. *Harry S. Truman*. New York: William Morrow, 1973.

_____. *Souvenir*. New York: McGraw-Hilly, 1956.

Truman, Margaret (editor). *Letters from Father: The Truman Family's Personal Correspondence*. New York: Arbor House, 1981.

_____. *Where the Buck Stops: The Personal and Private Writings of Harry S. Truman*. New York: Warner Books, 1989.

Truman: Talking with Harry, Candid Conversations with President Harry S. Truman. Edited and with commentary by Ralph E. Weber. Wilmington, Delaware: Scholarly Resources, 2001.

Tucker, Spencer C. (editor). *Encyclopedia of The Korean War: A Political, Social, and Military History*. Foreword by John S. D. Eisenhower. New York: Checkmark, 2002.

Tully, Grace. *F.D.R. My Boss*. New York: Charles Scribner's Sons, 1949.

Tye, Larry. *Demagogue: The Life and Long Shadow of Senator Joe McCarthy*. New York: Houghton Mifflin Harcourt, 2020.

Vandenberg, Arthur H. Jr. (editor). *The Private Papers of Senator Vandenberg*. Boston: Houghton Mifflin, 1952.

Walker, Frank C. *FDR's Quiet Confidant: The Autobiography of Frank C. Walker*. Edited by Robert H. Ferrell. Niwot: University Press of Colorado, 1997.

Wallace, Henry A. *The Diary of Henry A. Wallace, 1942–1946*. Edited by John Morton Blum. Boston: Houghton Mifflin, 1973.

Ward, Patricia Dawson. *The Threat of Peace: James F. Byrnes and the Council of Foreign Ministers, 1945–1946*. Kent, Ohio: Kent State University Press, 1979.

Weinstein, Allen. *Perjury: The Hiss-Chambers Case*. New York: Alfred A. Knopf, 1978.

Weiss, Stuart L. *The President's Man: Leo Crowley and Franklin Roosevelt in Peace and War*. Carbondale and Edwardsville: Southern Illinois University Press, 1996.

West, J. B., with Mary Lynn Kotz. *Upstairs at the White House: My Life with the First Ladies*. New York: Open Road, 2016.

White, Walter. *A Man Called White*. New York: Viking, 1948.

Whitney, Courtney. *MacArthur: His Rendezvous with History*. New York: Alfred A. Knopf, 1955.

Whyte, William H. Jr. *The Organization Man*. New York: Doubleday Anchor Books, 1956.

Williams, Herbert Lee. *The Newspaperman's President: Harry S. Truman*. Chicago: Nelson-Hall, 1984.

Willoughby, Major General Charles A., and John Chamberlain. *MacArthur 1941–1951*. New York: McGraw-Hill, 1954.

Yergin, Daniel. *Shattered Peace: The Origins of the Cold War and the National Security State*. Boston: Houghton Mifflin, 1977.

Zhukov, Georgy. *The Memoirs of Marshal Zhukov*. New York: Seymour Lawrence/Delacorte, 1971.

Selected Magazine and Journal Articles

Abbott, Roger S. "The Federal Loyalty Program: Background and Problems." *American Political Science Review* (June 1948): 486–99.

Alexander, Jack. "Stormy New Boss at the Pentagon." *Saturday Evening Post*, July 30, 1949, p. 26+

Alsop, Joseph, and Robert Kintner. "Sly and Able, the Real Leader of the Senate, Jimmy Byrnes." *Saturday Evening Post*, July 20, 1940, p. 18.

Alsop, Joseph, and Stewart Alsop. "If War Comes." *Saturday Evening Post,* September 11, 1948, p. 15.

Alsop, Stewart, and Dr. Ralph Lapp. "Can the New A-Bomb Stop Troops in the Field?" *Saturday Evening Post*, September 9, 1951, p. 20.

Anders, Roger M. "The Atomic Bomb and the Korean War: Gordon Dean and the Issue of Civilian Control." *Military Affairs*, January 1988, p. 1.

Armstrong, Charles K. "The Destruction and Reconstruction of North Korea, 1950–1960." *Asia-Pacific Journal* 7 (March 16, 2009).

Baldwin, Hanson W. "Big Boss of the Pentagon." *New York Times Magazine*, August 29, 1948, p. SM9+.

Barth, Alan. "F.D.R. As a Politician." *Harper's*, February 1945, p. 241+.

———. "How Good Is an FBI Report?" *Harper's*, March 1954. p. 25+.

Bazelon, David T. "The Faith of Henry Wallace: The Populist Tradition in the Atomic Age." *Commentary*, January 1947.

Bernstein, Barton J. "Crossing the Rubicon: A Missed Opportunity to Stop the H-Bomb?" *International Security* 14, No. 2 (Fall 1989): 132–60.

———. "Looking Back: Gen. Marshall and the Atomic Bombing of Japanese Cities." *Arms Control Today*, November 2015, pp. 32–36.

———. "Reconsidering the 'Atomic General': Leslie R. Groves." *Journal of Military History*, July 2003, p. 883.

Bird, Kai, and Max Holland. "The Tapping of 'Tommy the Cork.'" *Nation*, February 8, 1986, p. 1+.

Bliven, Bruce. "Death in the Air." *New Republic*, February 2, 1948, p. 17.

Bolles, Blair. "Corruption in Washington, and What Lies Behind It." *Harper's*, January 1952, pp. 27–33.

Bundy, McGeorge. "Imperatives of Foreign Policy." *Foreign Affairs*, November 1952, pp. 1–14.

Burke, John P. "The National Security Advisor and Staff: Transition Challenges." *Presidential Studies Quarterly* (June, 2009): 283+.

Callaghan, John, and Mark Phythian. "Intellectuals of the Left and the Atomic Dilemma in the Age of the US Atomic Monopoly, 1945–1949." *Contemporary British History*, October 2015, pp. 441–63.

Casey, Steven. "White House Publicity Operations During the Korean War, June 1950–June 1951." *Presidential Studies Quarterly* (December 2005): 691–97.

Chen, Jian. "Far Short of a "Glorious Victory: Revisiting China's Changing Strategies to Manage the Korean War." *Chinese Historical Review*, September 2018, pp. 1–22.

Clayton, William L. "GATT, the Marshall Plan, and OECD." *Political Science Quarterly* (December 1963): 493–503.

Coffin, Tris. "The MacArthur Rebellion." *New Republic*, May 14, 1951, pp. 11–13.

Conway-Lanz, Sahr. "Beyond No Gun Ri: Refugees and the United States Military in the Korean War." *Diplomatic History*, January 2005, pp. 49–81.

DeVoto, Bernard. "The Easy Chair. Foul Birds Come Abroad." *Harper's*, July 1951, p. 48.

———. "Stevenson and the Independent Voter." *Harper's*, April 1952, p. 62+.

Dingman, Roger. "Atomic Diplomacy During the Korean War." *International Security*, Winter 1988-1989, pp. 50–91.

Donaldson, Gary A. "Who Wrote the Clifford Memo? The Origins of Campaign Strategy in the Truman Administration." *Presidential Studies Quarterly* (Fall 1993): 747–54.

Eldridge, David. " 'There Is Hope for the Future': Retrospective Visions of the Bomb in 1950s Hollywood." *Historical Journal of Film, Radio and Television*, August 2006, pp. 295–309.

Emerson, Thomas I., and David M. Helfeld. "Loyalty Among Government Employees." *Yale Law Journal*, December 1948, p. 1.

Fischer, John. "The Lost Liberals. Can They Find a New Road Map?" *Harper's*, May 1947, p. 385.

———. "Mr. Truman's Politburo." *Harper's*, June 1951, p. 29.

———. "Mr. Truman Reorganizes." *Harper's*, January 1946, p. 26.

———. "Truman and Co., Limited." *Harper's*, July 1949, p. 19+.

Fleming, Thomas. "Eight Days with Harry Truman." *American Heritage*, July/August 1992.

Frank, John P. "Fred Vinson and the Chief Justiceship." *University of Chicago Law Review*, January 1953, p. 212+.

Gehman, Richard B. "Imagination Runs Wild." *New Republic*, January 17, 1949, p. 15.

Geselbracht, Raymond H. "Creating the Harry S. Truman Library: The First Fifty Years." *Public Historian*, Summer 2006, pp. 37–78.

Green, Paul S. "That Funny Fat Man." *New Republic*, February 29, 1947, p. 19.

Hamburger, Philip. "Mr. Secretary-I." *New Yorker*, November 12, 1949, p. 39+.

———. "Mr. Secretary-II." *New Yorker*, November 19, 1949, p. 58+.

Hersey, John. "Letter From Chungking." *New Yorker*, March 16, 1946, p. 80+.

———. "Profiles. The Old Man. III-National Kibitzer." *New Yorker*, November 17, 1948, p. 30+.

———. "A Reporter at Large: Hiroshima," *New Yorker*, August 23, 1946.

Hershberg, James G. Translations by Vladislav Zubok. "New Evidence on Cold War Crises: Russian Documents on the Korean War." *Cold War International History Project Bulletin*, Woodrow Wilson Center, No. 14 and 15 (Winter 2003, Spring 2004): 1–11

Hoover, J. Edgar. "A Comment on the Article 'Loyalty Among Government Employees.' " *Yale Law Journal*, February 1949, p. 401.

Huie, William Bradford. "The Terrible Tempered Mr. Truman." *Cosmopolitan*, April 1951, pp. 32–35, 118–19.

Jarman, Rufus. "Washington's Worst Politician." *Saturday Evening Post*, July 24, 1948, p. 20+.

Jervis, Robert. "The Impact of the Korean War on the Cold War." *Journal of Conflict Resolution*, December 1980, p. 563+.

Jessup, Philip C. "The Record of Wake Island—A Correction." *Journal of American History*, March 1981, pp. 866–70.

Johnson, R. W. "Already a Member." *London Review of Books*, September 11, 2014, p. 31.

Kahn, E. J. Jr. "Letter From Korea." *New Yorker*, April 21, 1951, p. 122+.

———. "Plenipotentiary-I." *New Yorker*, May 3, 1952, p. 41+.

———. "Plenipotentiary-II." *New Yorker*, May 10, 1952, p. 36+.

Kaplan, Lawrence S. "The United States and the Origins of NATO, 1946–1949." *Review of Politics*, April 1969, p. 210+.

Kennan, George F. "Containment Then and Now." *Foreign Affairs*, Spring 1987, pp. 885–90.

———. "Russia and the United States." *New Republic*, June 26, 1950, pp. 12–16.

Knebel, Fletcher, and Charles W. Bailey II. "Hiroshima: The Decision That Changed the World." *Look*, June 7, 1960, pp. 25–29.

Lang, Daniel. "The Center of Reality." *New Yorker*, March 20, 1948, p. 62+.

———. "Seven Men on a Problem." *New Yorker*, August 17, 1946, p. 49+.

Lang, Michael. "Globalization and Global History in Toynbee." *Journal of World History*, December 2011.

Lasch, Christopher. "The Cold War, Revisited and Re-Visioned." *New York Times Magazine*, January 14, 1968, p. SM26+.

Lawrence, W. H. "Truman—Portrait of a Stubborn Man." *New York Times Magazine*, April 22, 1951, p. SM8+.

Lehrman, Hal. "Partition in Washington: An Inquiry." *Commentary*, January 1948, p. 205+.

Leuctenburg, William E. "Give 'Em Harry." *New Republic*, May 21, 1984. pp. 22–27.

Leviero, Anthony. "How the President Makes Decisions." *New York Times Magazine*, October 8, 1950, p. SM8+.

Liebling, A. J. "Five-Star Schoolmaster-1." *New Yorker*, March 3, 1951, p. 38+.

———. "Five-Star Schoolmaster-2." *New Yorker*, March 10, 1951, p. 40+.

Lindley, Ernest K. "The Bomb—Test and Control." *Newsweek*, July 29, 1946, p. 25.

———. "The Burial of the 38th Parallel." *Newsweek*, Ocotber 9, 1950, pp. 23, 25.

Lippmann, Walter. "The Cold War." *Foreign Affairs*, Spring 1987, pp. 869–84.

Lutzker, Michael A. "Presidential Decision Making in the Korean War: The British Perspective." *Presidential Studies Quarterly* (Fall 1996): 978.

Martin, John Bartlow, and Eric Larrabee. "The Drafting of Adlai Stevenson." *Harper's*, October 1, 1952, pp. 35–43.

McMahon, Brien. "The Control of Atomic Energy." *Proceedings of the Section of International and Comparative Law* (American Bar Association), 10-28-46 and 10-29-46, pp. 12–16.

Miller, Byron S. "A Law Is Passed: The Atomic Energy Act of 1946." *University of Chicago Law Review*, Summer 1948, pp. 799–821.

"My Daughter Married a Negro." *Harper's*, July 1951, pp. 36–40.

New Republic. "After the Wallace Dismissal." September 30, 1946, p. 395.

———. "Editorial: If Not Truman, Who?" March 17, 1948, p. 27.

———. "A Fourth Term with Whom?" January 31, 1944, p. 134.

———. "In the Dark." March 1, 1948, p. 5.

———. "Truman as Leader." May 17, 1948, p. 13.

———. "Truman or MacArthur—the Choice in Asia." September 11, 1950, p. 5.

———. "The Victory." November 13, 1944, p. 611.

———. "Washington Wire—One Year After." May 20, 1946, p. 715.

———. "Mobilizing Short of War." December 25, 1950, p. 5.

Newsweek. "Communists: McCarthy Bombshell." March 6, 1950, p. 19.

———. "Farewell to Mr. Citizen." January 8, 1973, pp. 12–15.

———. "McCarthy vs. Acheson." March 13, 1950, p. 21.

O'Brien, David M. "He Travels Fastest Who Travels Alone." *Journal of Supreme Court History,* 2012, p. 305+.

Oppenheimer, J. Robert. "International Control of Atomic Energy." *Foreign Affairs,* January 1948, pp. 239–52.

Osborne, John. "Men at War: The Ugly War." *Time,* August 21, 1950.

Pace, J. Bradley. "The Diary of Police Officer Max Gould Recalls Truman's Return to Independence." *JCHS Journal,* Summer 2014, p. 10.

Pauley, Garth E. "Harry Truman and the NAACP: A Case Study in Presidential Persuasion on Civil Rights." *Rhetoric and Public Affairs* (Special Issue on Civil Rights in the Postmodern Era), Summer 1999, pp. 211–41.

Pickering, Lt. Col. Trent A. "A Nuclear Dilemma: Korean War Déjà Vu." (Master's Thesis), U.S. Army War College.

Pierpaoli, Paul G., Jr. "Truman's Other War: The Battle for the American Homefront, 1950–1953." *OAH Magazine of History,* Spring 2000, pp. 15–19.

Podhoretz, Norman. "Truman and the Idea of the Common Man." *Commentary,* January 1956, p. 469.

Radosh, Ronald, and Allis Radosh. "A Great Historic Mistake: The Making of 'Mission to Moscow.'" *Film History, Politics and Film,* 2004, pp. 358–77.

Rhodes, Richard. "Harry's Last Hurrah." *Harper's,* January 1970, p. 48+.

Richards, Miles S. "James F. Byrnes on Foreign Policy." *South Carolina Historical Magazine,* January 1991, pp. 34–44.

Roberts, Geoffrey. "Stalin at the Tehran, Yalta, and Potsdam Conferences." *Journal of Cold War Studies,* Fall 2007, pp. 6–40.

Roosevelt, Elliott. "A Personal Interview with Stalin." *Look,* February 4, 1947, pp. 21–24.

Rosenberg, David Alan. "American Atomic Strategy and the Hydrogen Bomb Decision." *Journal of American History,* June 1979, pp. 62–87.

Rovere, Richard H. "A Reporter at Large: Mr. Morris Goes to Washington." *New Yorker,* April 19, 1952, p 121+.

———. "Truman After Seven Years." *Harper's,* April 1952, pp. 27–33.

Rushay, Samuel W. Jr. "The President Is Very Acutely Ill, Harry S. Truman's Illness of July 1952." *Prologue,* Fall 2012.

Sagan, Scott D. "Why Do States Build Nuclear Weapons?: Three Models in Search of a Bomb." *International Security,* Winter, 1996–97, pp. 54–86.

Samii, Kuross A. "Truman Against Stalin in Iran: A Tale of Three Messages." *Middle Eastern Studies,* January 1987, pp. 95–107.

Schilling, Warner R. "The H-Bomb Decision: How to Decide Without Actually Choosing." *Political Science Quarterly* (March 1961): 24–46.

Shils, Edward. "The Failure of the United Nations Atomic Energy Commission: An Interpretation." *University of Chicago Law Review*, Summer 1948, pp. 855–76.

Smith, Beverly. "Why We Went to War in Korea." *Saturday Evening Post*, November 10, 1951, p. 22+.

Snow, Edgar. "The Stalin Truman Faces." *Saturday Evening Post*, June 30, 1945, p. 20+.

Stewart, Richard W. "The X Corps in Korea, December 1950." *Combat Studies Institute*, April 1991.

Stimson, Henry L. "The Decision to Use the Atomic Bomb." *Harper's*, March 1947, p. 97+.

Strout, Richard. "The Education of Harry Truman." *New Republic*, October 16, 1950, p. 19.

Sylvia, Ronald D. "Presidential Decision Making and Leadership in the Civil Rights Era." *Presidential Studies Quarterly* (Summer 1995): 391+.

Szilard, Leo. "America, Russia and the Bomb." *New Republic*, October 31, 1949.

Time. "The Administration. The Regular Guys." August 12, 1946.

Time. "The Barkley Incident." March 6, 1944.

————. "Billion-Dollar Watchdog." March 8, 1943 (Cover Story).

————. "Catalytic Agent." January 11, 1943.

————. "The Consequences." July 10, 1950.

————. "Democrats: Harry's Happy Hour." August 20, 1956.

————. "Education: The Challenge." March 17, 1947.

————. "Foreign Relations: Two Voices." September 4, 1950.

————. "The Man from Missouri." November 6, 1944.

————. "Illinois: Sir Galahad & the Pols." January 28, 1952.

————. "National Affairs: Action on M-Day." April 23, 1951.

————. "National Affairs: Little Helper." August 15, 1949.

————. "National Affairs: The Neutralizer." March 17, 1952.

————. "National Affairs: New Policy, New Broom." March 29, 1948.

————. "National Affairs: Patriot's Reward." May 30, 1949 pp. 15–16.

————. "The Press: Thirty Seconds over Truman." February 4, 1946.

————. "United Nations: The Vishinsky Approach." September 29, 1947.

————. "Wake Island." October 23, 1950.

Thurmond, Strom. "President Truman's So-Called Civil Rights Program." (Radio Address), Strom Thurmond Collection, Clemson University, March 17, 1948.

Trachtenberg, Marc. "A 'Wasting Asset': American Strategy and the Shifting Nuclear Balance, 1949–1954." *International Security*, Winter 1988–89, pp. 5–49.

"The Transformation of the Racial Views of Harry Truman." *Journal of Blacks in Higher Education*, Winter 1999–2000), pp. 28–30.

Truman, Harry S. "My First Eighty Years." *Saturday Evening Post*, June 13, 1964, p. 15.

Truman, Margaret, as told to Stanley Frank. "Why Shouldn't I Sing?" *Saturday Evening Post*, April 22, 1950, p. 24.

Vandenberg, Gen. Hoyt S. "Air Power's Decisive Role in Europe." *Look*, October 9, 1951, pp. 29–34.

Variety. "Atom Test 'Goes TV.'" February 27, 1951, p. 1.

———. "Danny Kaye Sparks D.C. Correspondents Shindig . . ." March 9, 1949, p. 2.

Wallace, Henry. "The Attack on Human Rights." *New Republic*, August 11, 1947, p. 14.

———. "Farewell and Hail!" *New Republic*, July 9, 1948, p. 14.

———. "The Truman Doctrine—or a Strong UN." *New Republic*, March 31, 1947, p. 12.

Warner, Albert L. "How the Korea Decision Was Made." *Harper's*, June 1951, p. 99+.

Weathersby, Kathryn. "To Attack of Not to Attack? Stalin, Kim Il Sung, and the Prelude to War." *Cold War International History Project Bulletin*, Woodrow Wilson Center, Issue No 5 (Spring 1995): 1–9.

Wechsler, James A., and Nancy F. Wechsler. "The Road Ahead for Civil Rights. The President's Report One Year Later." *Commentary*, January 1948, p. 297.

Weintraub, Stanley. "North Korea and the Bomb." *Military Review*, January–February 2000, p. 20.

Williams, Herbert Lee. "I Was Truman's Ghost." *Presidential Studies Quarterly* (Spring 1982): 256–59.

Wiltz, John Edward. "Truman and MacArthur: The Wake Island Meeting." *Military Affairs*, December 1978, p. 169+.

York, Herbert F. "The Debate Over the Hydrogen Bomb." *Scientific American*, October 1975, pp. 106–13.

Young, Ken. "Revisiting NSC 68." *Journal of Cold War Studies*, Winter 2013, pp. 3–33.

Young, Marilyn. "Reflections on the Korean War and Its Armistice." *Journal of Korean Studies*, Fall 2013, pp. 403–6.

Oral Histories (OH)

From the Harry S. Truman Library

Dean Acheson

George E. Allen

Vernice Anderson

R. Gordon Arneson

Eben Ayers

James P. Aylward

Edward Barrett

Lucius Battle

David C. Bell

Jack Bell

Thomas Hart Benton

Richard Bolling

Raymond K. Brand
Col. Lawrence E. Bunker
Turner Catledge
Tom C. Clark
Clark Clifford
Matthew Connelly
E. Clifton Daniel
Donald Dawson
Robert L. Dennison
William Draper
Elbridge Durbrow
George M. Elsey
Thomas Evans
Edward T. Folliard
Dr. Wallace Graham
A. J. Granoff
W. Averell Harriman
Walter Hehmeyer
Loy Henderson
T. Willard Hunter
Joseph E. Johnson
U. Alexis Johnson
Judge Marvin Jones
Carleton Kent
Charles P. Kindleberger
Marx Leva
Robert A. Lovett
Max Lowenthal
Cornelius J. Mara
Charles Burton Marshall
H. Freeman Matthews

Edward McKim
Leonard Miall
Samuel A. Montague
John J. Muccio
Charles Murphy
Philleo Nash
Paul Nitze
Robert M. Nixon
Rachel Odum
Frank Pace Jr.
Arthur W. Page
Edwin W. Pauley
Irving Perlmeter
James E. Riddleberger
Samuel I Rosenman
Dean Rusk
William Rigdon
Mrs. Joseph Short
John W. Snyder
Sidney W. Souers
Lewis L. Strauss
John R. Steelman
Richard Strout
Stuart Symington
Walter Trohan
Roger Tubby
Harry H, Vaughan
James E. Webb
White House Staff (Charles S. Murphy, Richard E. Neustadt, David H. Stowe, James E. Webb)

Columbia University Oral History Project

Marquis Childs (Stevenson Project)
Jonathan Daniels
Ferdinand Eberstadt
Dwight D. Eisenhower
Robert A. Lovett

Arthur W. Page
Kenneth Royall
John R. Steelman
Henry A. Wallace

University of Kentucky Libraries

Alben W. Barkley Oral History Project

University of Georgia

Dean Rusk Oral History Collection

Archival Collections

Harry S. Truman Library and Museum, Independence, Missouri

Dean Acheson Papers
Eben Ayers Files (papers include his diary)
Churchill Archives Centre Records
Tom Clark Papers
Clark M. Clifford Files
Matthew H. Connelly Files
Jonathan Daniels Papers
Robert L. Dennison Files
George M. Elsey Files
Thomas Fleming Papers
Robert Hannegan Papers
W. Averell Harriman Papers
Ken Hechler Files
Joseph M. Jones Papers
Charles S. Murphy Files
Richard E. Neustadt Files
Monte Poen Papers
Harry Bayard Price Papers
Charles Ross Papers
Sidney Souers Papers
Stephen J. Spingarn Files
John R. Steelman Files
Adlai Stevenson File
Daily Appointments of Harry S. Truman (Daily Sheets)
Map Room File, 1945
Naval Aide to the President Files, 1945–53
National Security Council Files, 1947–53
Korean War File, 1947–52 (Boxes 6, 7)
The Korean War and Its Origins

Margaret Truman Diary
Papers Pertaining to Family, Business, and Personal Affairs
Post Presidential Files (PPP, Box 643; Memoirs)
President's Secretary's File (PSF), which includes Truman Diary
PSF, General Files, Box 209 (Korea-Frank Lowe)
Miscellaneous Historical Documents Collection (MHDC, various boxes)
PSF General File: Louis Johnson memoranda; memo on loyalty board conduct; memo on Wallace resignation; exchange with Byrnes; Korea meetings
PSF, NSC Atomic Files (Boxes 174, 176)
PSF, Longhand Notes, Presidential File, 1944–1953 (Boxes 274–276)
PSF, Longhand Notes, Post-Presidential File, 1953–1955 (Box 276)
Truman and the Marshall Plan

Dwight D. Eisenhower Presidential Library, Abilene, Kansas

Anne Whitman Diary Series (Box 1)
Alfred M. Gruenther Papers, 1941–83
Robert Humphreys Papers
C. D. Jackson Papers (Box 69)

Franklin D. Roosevelt Presidential Library, Hyde Park, New York

William D. Hassett Papers (Diary), Boxes 17, 22
President's Personal File (Truman), 6297–6353

John F. Kennedy Presidential Library and Museum, Cambridge, Masschusetts

Oral History: McGeorge Bundy, interviewed by Richard Neustadt, March 1964 and May 1964

Library of Congress (Manuscript Division), Washington, D.C.

Joseph and Stuart Alsop Papers
Henry Brandon Papers
Joseph Davies Papers
Elmer Davis Papers
Averell Harriman Papers
Harold Ickes Papers (Diary)
William Leahy Papers (Diary, 1945–51)
Clare Boothe Luce Papers
Archibald MacLeish Papers
Evalyn Walsh McClean Papers
J. Robert Oppenheimer Papers
Robert Taft Papers

Lyndon Baines Johnson Library

Merle Miller tape recordings for *Plain Speaking*
George Aiken (oral history)

Yale University Library

Henry M. Stimson Papers

Clemson University Libraries, Special Collections, Clemson, South Carolina

James F. Byrnes Papers
Walter Brown Papers

Public Policy Papers, Department of Special Collections, Princeton University Library

Bernard Baruch Papers
Ferdinand Eberstadt Papers
James Forrestal Papers (Diary)
Emmet Hughes Papers
George Kennan Papers (Diary)

Arthur Krock Papers
David Lawrence Papers
H. Freeman Matthews Papers
Arnold A. Rogow Papers

New York Public Library

A. H. Sulzberger Papers
The New Yorker Archives

New-York Historical Society

Robert A. Lovett Logbook (Records of Brown Brothers Harriman, Series V, Partners'
    Papers, Subseries E.ii, Daily Logs while Under Secretary of State, 1947–1949)

Institute for Advanced Study

Princeton Seminar Files

Wheaton College

Malcolm Muggeridge Papers

MacArthur Memorial Library, Norfolk, Virginia

Colonel Bunker's Notes on the Conference Between President Truman and General
    MacArthur, Wake Island, October 15, 1950

Syracuse University

The Special Collections Research Center (formerly the George Arents Research Library for Special Collections)

Helpful Online Resources

The number of online resources, and their range, expands by the minute; explore them at your peril and pleasure. I made considerable use of the New York Public Library, the New York Society Library, Cornell University Libraries, and the Hathi Trust. Other valuable portals, not all of them free, include:

Foreign Relations of the United States (FRUS): https://search.library.wisc.edu/digital/AFRUS

The Papers of Dwight David Eisenhower (subscription required): https://eisenhower.press.jhu.edu

Presidential New Conferences, dating back to Calvin Coolidge: https://www.presidency.ucsb.edu/statistics/data/presidential-news-conferences

A digital record of hundreds of local newspapers (subscription required): www.newspapers.com

Parliamentary debate in the United Kingdom: https://hansard.parliament.uk

John J. McCloy Diaries: https://www.amherst.edu/library/archives/holdings/john-j.-mccloy-world-war-ii-diaries

Lord Halifax Diaries: https://dlib.york.ac.uk/yodl/app/collection/detail?id=york%3a810133&ref=browse

Papers of George Catlett Marshall, Volume 6: *The Whole World Hangs in the Balance*: https://www.marshallfoundation.org/library/collection/marshall-papers/volume6-the-whole-world-hangs-in-the-balance/#!/collection=340.

The endlessly entertaining, enlightening, and sometimes fragmented video record of our past: www.youtube.com

Illustration Credits

1. Harry S. Truman Library
2. Harry S. Truman Library
3. Harry S. Truman Library
4. Harry S. Truman Library
5. Harry S. Truman Library
6. AP/Shutterstock
7. Harry S. Truman Library
8. Harris & Ewing/Harry S. Truman Library
9. Harry S. Truman Library
10. Harry S. Truman Library
11. United States Army Signal Corps/ Public Domain/Harry S. Truman Library
12. United States Army Signal Corps/Public Domain/Harry S. Truman Library
13. United States Army/Public Domain/Harry S. Truman Library
14. Hathon M. Fields/Harry S. Truman Library
15. Harry S. Truman Library
16. Harry S. Truman Library
17. George Skadding/The Life Picture Collection via Getty Images
18. Bettmann/Getty Images
19. Harry S. Truman Library
20. Harry S. Truman Library
21. Department of State/Public Domain/Harry S. Truman Library
22. Harry S. Truman Library
23. Jeff Brodhead/Monroe County Public Library, Key West, Florida/Harry S. Truman Library
24. Popperfoto via Getty Images

Index

Page numbers beginning with 381 refer to endnotes.

ABC, 121, 153, 180
Abernethy, Thomas G., 155
Acheson, Alice, 79, 111, 315
Acheson, David, 194, 195, 315, 366
    Margaret Truman and, 463
Acheson, Dean Gooderham, xix, 160,
    232, 254, 282, 298, 352, 378–79
  appointed Secretary of State,
    192–93
  on Byrnes, 59, 107–8
  Byrnes and, 63, 64–65, 90, 111
  on China, 226
  and China's entry into Korean War,
    280–81, 288, 290
  and China's threat to enter Korean
    War, 259–60, 265, 272
  Delta Council speech of, 124, 127
  on economic support for Greece
    and Turkey, 115, 118–19, 123–24
  Eisenhower and, 352
  Elsey and, 241–42
  foreign policy shaped by, xliii, 196,
    222–23, 239; see also Cold War;
    Korean War; Marshall Plan;
    Truman Doctrine
  Hiss and, 218, 259
  on HST, 71–72, 103, 117, 291,
    367
  HST and, 79, 105, 111, 218–19,
    224, 234, 235–36, 238, 284,
    291, 314–15, 360, 372, 373, 377
  HST's correspondence with, 55,
    371, 373, 463
  and HST's memoirs, 365–66

HST's reliance on, xi, xliii, 111,
    116, 194–95, 196, 244, 366,
    377
  Indochina and, 227
  Johnson's contentious relationship
    with, 211, 220–21, 230–31,
    236, 256, 257–58, 311
  Kennan and, 117, 222, 250
  on Korea, 224, 226–27, 235–38,
    245
  Korean War and, xliii, 196, 230,
    241–42, 250, 259–60, 265, 272,
    280–81, 285, 287–91, 300, 301,
    305, 308
  Lilienthal and, 87–88, 111
  McCarthy and, 218, 284
  on Marshall, 109, 111, 128, 264
  Marshall Plan and, 127–28
  memoir of, 221, 366, 379
  Muggeridge on, 195–96
  National Press Club speech of,
    226–27, 231
  Nixon and, 343
  NSC-68 and, 222–23, 226
  in resignation as Undersecretary of
    State, 122–23
  Reston and, 110–11, 122, 195,
    239
  Sandy Springs farm of, 230,
    314–15
  on Soviet atomic weapons, 205–6
  on Soviet intentions, 115, 224,
    226, 285
  Taft and, 239

Acheson, Dean Gooderham (*cont.*)
on U.S. atomic weapons, 83,
87–88, 211–12
Vandenberg and, 123
and Wake Island Conference, 267,
273
Acheson, Edward Campion, 195
Acheson, Eleanor Gertrude
Gooderham, 195
Acheson, Patricia, 315
Acheson-Lilienthal Committee, 88
Acheson-Lilienthal report, 88, 90, 214
Affair of State, An (Frank), 133
African Americans, 150, 151
HST's commitment to economic
equality for, xii, 151, 156
HST's shifting attitude toward, xx,
151, 153–54, 156, 180–81, 375,
417, 465
lynchings of, 153, 155
Aiken, George, xxxviii
Alanbrooke, Lord, 26, 29
Alien and Sedition Acts, 217
Allen, George E., 12, 152
Allen, Robert S., xxx, 98
Allison, John W., 233, 250
Almond, Edward, 233, 283
Alsop, Joseph, 13, 58–59, 73, 126,
181, 190, 209, 214, 220, 229,
232, 257, 258
Alsop, Stewart, 13, 98, 126, 150,
181, 190, 209, 214, 220, 222,
257, 258
Alsop, Susan Mary, 52, 109
American Civil Liberties Union,
138
American Labor Party, 157
American Legion, 200, 319
American Medical Association, 367
"American Relations with the Soviet
Union" (Clifford), 112–14
American Society of Newspaper
Editors, 328–29
Anderson, Marian, 152
Anderson, Vernice, 275–76

Anglo-Soviet-Iranian Treaty (1942),
331
anti-Communism, ix, 368
of Acheson, 195
of Hoover, 134–35
of Nixon, 342–43
Appleman, Roy, 234, 280, 282
arms race, 208–10, 211, 215, 378
see also Cold War
Arvey, Jacob, 349
Associated Press, 352
Astley, Joan Bright, 24
Atlanta Constitution, 104
Atomic Development Authority, 88,
91
atomic energy, 83
civilian vs. military control of,
85–86, 91, 95, 174, 378
Atomic Energy Act (1946), 86, 92,
95, 404
Atomic Energy Commission, UN,
88–89
Atomic Energy Commission (AEC),
U.S., 57, 95, 99, 174–75, 206,
314, 397
General Advisory Committee of,
209
Radiation Laboratory of, 210
thermonuclear weapons and, 209,
213
atomic weapons, xli, 7–8, 39, 45, 49,
61, 82, 314
considered for Korean War, 248,
249–50, 286–88, 290, 291, 303,
314
HST on, xlii, 29, 49, 56, 84–85,
95, 173–74, 212–13, 314, 368
and HST's order to use on Japan,
ix–x, 44–45, 47, 54–55, 173,
356, 357, 367, 368; *see also*
Hiroshima; Nagasaki
international control issue of, 87,
95, 213, 214
Soviet development of, 205–7,
210, 363, 378

Soviet testing of, 314
thermonuclear, *see* thermonuclear
   weapons
Truman Committee and, xxi
UN and, 69, 78–79
U.S. development of, xxi–xxii
U.S. monopoly in, 74, 116, 173
U.S. testing of, 7, 27–29, 38–39,
   51, 92–95, 173, 313
Attlee, Clement, 50, 76, 77, 87,
   290–92, 294
   in British elections of 1945, 41–42
   HST and, 41, 84, 290–91, 373
   at Potsdam Conference, 23, 41
Augusta, USS, 21, 22, 37, 47–48, 49,
   50
Austin, Warren, 245–55, 281
Axis powers, 68, 124
Ayers, Eben, 1, 50, 73, 100, 169,
   190, 340
   HST and, 243–44, 338, 361
Ayers, Mary, 361

Bacall, Lauren, xxxiii
Bacher, Robert Fox, 173
Baillie, Hugh, 262, 289
Ball, George, 335, 337
Baltimore *Sun*, 24
Barkley, Alben, xix, 104, 123,
   179, 192, 203, 285, 332,
   359–60
   in election of 1948, 179–80, 181,
      188, 189, 200
   HST's friendship with, 134, 179,
      305
Barth, Alan, 137
Baruch, Bernard, xxxi, 75, 82, 118
   FDR and, xxiii, 90
   HST and, 89, 90
   UN speech of, 90, 91, 95, 207–8,
      214 15
   as U.S. representative to UNAEC,
      88–90, 95
BBC, 124
Beatty, Morgan, 307

Beginning or the End, The (film),
   56–57
Bendiner, Robert, 244
Benton, Thomas Hart, 371–72, 377
Bentsen, Lloyd, 249
Bergheim, Myrtle, 292–93
Berlin, Isaiah, 8, 13, 71
Berlin, Occupied, 26–27, 183–84,
   197
   Churchill's sightseeing in, 25–27
   counter-blockade in, 204
   HST's sightseeing in, 25–26
Berlin Airlift, 172–73, 179, 329, 367
Berlin Blockade, 172–73, 204
Bernstein, Barton J., 46
Bevin, Ernest, 76
   in Council of Foreign Ministers,
      60–61
   at Potsdam Conference, 41
Biddle, Francis, xl, 10–11, 143
Biffle, Leslie L., xix, xxxvii, xxxviii,
   179, 189, 203
Big Show, The (NBC radio broadcast),
   374–75
Bikini Atoll, U.S. nuclear tests near,
   92–95, 406
Bilbo, Theodore G., 156, 177
Bird, Kai, 22
Birse, A. H., 35
Black, Hugo, 73, 151, 328
   Youngstown decision of, 331
Blair House, 2, 130, 191, 235, 245,
   278, 279, 282, 311, 333, 335,
   374
Blandy, W. H. "Spike," 93–94, 406
Boettiger, Anna Roosevelt, xxix,
   xxxi, xl
Bohlen, Charles "Chip," 5, 13, 17,
   21, 42–43, 73, 127
   at Potsdam Conference, 24, 38
Bolles, Blair, 318
Bonesteel, Charles H. "Tick," 224–25
Bontecue, Eleanor, 138
Bormann, Martin, 96
Boston Globe, 125

Bowman, Wellborn, 148
Boyle, William M., Jr., 319
Bradley, David, 94
Bradley, Omar N., 221, 230, 291, 311
    honorary Harvard degree of, 125
    HST and, 184, 281, 284, 377
    Korean War and, 236, 247, 281,
        284, 288, 289–90
    on thermonuclear bomb, 211, 213
    at Wake Island Conference, 267,
        276
Brandt, Raymond P., 104
Braun, Eva, 27, 96–97
Brewster, Owen, 250
Bricker, John W., xxx
Bridges, Styles, 359
Brinkley, Douglas, 143
Brown, Walter, 102–3
Brown Brothers-Harriman, 123
Brussels Pact (1948), 169, 197
Buchenwald concentration camp, 8
Bulgaria, 61, 65, 67–68, 69, 99, 129
Bulletin of the Atomic Scientists,
    Doomsday Clock of, 206
Bunker, Laurence E., 276, 309
Bureau of Internal Revenue, 319
Bureau of Investigation (BOI), 133–34
Burns, James H., 221
Burton, Harold, 328
Bush, George W., 378, 379
Bush, Vannevar, 83, 206
Butler, Hugh, 195
Butt, Archie, 313
Byrnes, James Francis "Jimmy," x,
        14, 19, 22, 47–48, 59, 75, 88,
        110–11, 194, 196, 297, 377
    Acheson and, 63, 64–65, 107–8,
        111
    Acheson on, 59, 107–8
    appointed Secretary of State, 19
    appointed to the Supreme Court,
        xxv
    atomic bomb program and, xli,
        xlii, 7–8, 28, 46
    Bikini tests opposed by, 92–93

on Churchill's Fulton speech, 76
in Council of Foreign Ministers,
        60–62, 87
elected governor of South
        Carolina, 108
FDR and, xxiii–xxv, xxvii, xxxi
on Forrestal, 141
HST's relationship with, xxvi–
        xxvii, xxxviii–xxxix, xl, 10,
        59–60, 62, 63, 64–65, 66–70,
        107, 345, 364, 462
HST's reliance on, 28, 58–59
and Japan's terms of surrender, 22
Leahy on, 54–65, 66
Moscow communiqué of, 63, 65,
        68–69
NBC radio speech of, 62–63,
        64–65, 67–68
at 1946 Paris Peace Conference,
        99, 101
at Potsdam Conference, 21–22, 32,
        34, 42, 59
resignation of, 107–8, 122
segregationist views of, xxiv
in Senate, xxv
shorthand used by, xxv, xxxix
Stalin and, 59, 146
Stimson and, 33
and surrender of Japan, 53
as *Time*'s Man of the Year, 108
as U.S. congressman, xxv
vice-presidential ambitions of,
        xxiii–xxvii, 58, 63, 103
and Wallace's MSG speech, 101–2
at Yalta Conference, xxxi, xxxix, 59
Byrnes, Maude Busch, 64

Cabinet, of FDR, 13, 143
Cabinet, of HST, 14, 20, 95, 102,
        145, 189, 244, 247, 360
    as incohesive group, 145–46, 399
    see also specific secretaries
Cadogan, Alexander, 35, 36
Cairo Conference (1943), 224
Cambodia, 227

Canada, 84, 281
Canin, Stuart, 37
Carr, Albert Z., 184, 232
Casey, Richard and Ethel, 79
Catledge, Turner, xxv, xxvii
Caudle, Theron Lamar, 319–20
CBS, 51, 180, 184, 250, 298
Central Intelligence Agency (CIA),
    145, 225, 447
Central Intelligence Group (CIG),
    145–46, 211
*Challenge of the Fifties, The—Years of
    Crisis,* (CBS program), 298
Chamberlain, John, 280
Chambers, Whittaker, 131, 218
Chang, John M., 261
Chen Jian, 231
Chiang Kai-shek, 60, 109, 116,
    217–18, 231, 239, 300
  at Cairo Conference, 224
  and Korean War, 242
  MacArthur and, 252–53
Chicago Sun-Times, 104
Chicago Tribune, xxxiii, 13, 99, 134,
    189, 238
Childs, Marquis, 23, 66, 90, 219,
    334, 417
China:
  civil war in, 109, 116, 218, 231
  Korean border with, 279
China, Nationalist, 60, 231, 300
  seated on UN Security Council,
    234, 252
  see also Formosa
China, People's Republic of, 224,
    259
  founding of, 217, 231
  Great Terror in, 217
  in Korean War, 280, 282–84, 289,
    296–97, 307, 378
  in threat to enter Korean War,
    259–60, 264–66, 308
  U.S. relations with, 264–65
Chinese People's Volunteer Army
    (CPVA), 280, 282

Christian Science Monitor, xxxiii,
    183, 259
Churchill, Clementine, 24, 36, 74–75
Churchill, Mary, 32
Churchill, Randolph, 144
Churchill, Winston, x, 50, 73–74, 75
  on atomic bomb, 29
  Baruch and, 75
  in British election of 1945, 18, 23,
    35, 40–41, 74
  at Cairo Conference, 224
  FDR and, 84
  Fulton speech of, 74–80
  on HST, xliv, 25
  HST and, 18, 24, 38, 75, 76–77,
    79, 165, 373
  HST on, 25, 32, 41
  HST's correspondence with, 179
  ill health of, 23
  Iron Curtain phrase of, 16, 78, 403
  1946 U.S. trip of, 74–81
  at Potsdam Conference, 23, 24–26
  on Stalin, 19, 72
  at Tehran Conference, 17
  in tour of Occupied Berlin, 26–27
  at Yalta Conference, xxxi,
    xxxiii–xxxiv, 17
Cincinnati Enquirer, xxxii
Civilization on Trial (Toynbee), 132
civil rights, 180–81
  HST and, 153–55, 180, 338, 376
Civil Service Commission, 136, 137
Clark, Tom, 145, 153, 192, 199
  appointed Attorney General, 11
  joined the Supreme Court, 328
  Youngstown case and, 328
Clark-Kerr, Archibald, 35, 42
Clay, Lucius Dubignon, 167, 173
Clayton, William, 45, 101
  Marshall Plan and, 127
Clifford, Clark, 66, 76, 98, 116–17,
    120, 146, 160, 186, 189, 238
  HST and, 64, 120, 128, 136,
    162–63, 176
  Marshall and, 162–63

Clifford, Clark (*cont.*)
  political memo of Rowe and,
    150–51, 171–72
  and recognition of Israel, 162–63
  Soviet threat assessment of Elsey
    and, 112–14, 223
Clifford, Marnie, 188
Cold War, x, 122, 219, 368
  Acheson on, 222
  Swope's coining of term, 118, 130,
    411
  see also arms race; United States,
    Soviet relations with
Collier's, 141
Collins, Lawton, 230, 236, 241, 248,
    256, 288
  MacArthur and, 270–71
  at Wake Island Conference, 267, 270
Columbia University:
  Eisenhower as president of, 177,
    194, 324
  HST's speech at, 455
Commager, Henry Steele, 366–67
Committee for Economic
    Cooperation for Europe, 127
Communism, Communists, 60,
    113, 117, 119, 227, 250, 253,
    300–301
  Chinese, 109, 217–18, 231, 239,
    242, 248, 252, 259–60, 264,
    280, 289, 297, 300, 304, 371
  Czechoslovakian, 165–66, 168
  East German, 172, 179, 183, 204
  Greek, 115
  HST on, 120–21, 136, 166, 235,
    351, 356
  North Korean, xliii, 223, 225–26,
    235, 236, 238, 247–48, 255,
    265, 279, 303, 370
  Stevenson on, 349
  see also anti-Communism
Communism, Communists, Soviet,
    xxxix, 100, 171, 184, 264, 378
  Acheson and, 226
  Marshall Plan and, 130, 132, 170

Communism, Communists, U.S., 150,
    157, 171
  Federal Employee Loyalty Program
    and, 135–36
  Hoover and, 134–35
  McCarthy and, 218–19
Communist bloc, 204
  see also Eastern Europe
Compton, Arthur Holly, 45
Conant, James B., xxii, 88, 125
Congress, U.S., 125, 147, 170, 176
  Atomic Energy Act and, 86, 92,
    404
  Democratic control of, 104, 190
  FDR's March 1, 1945 address to,
    xxxiv
  HST's April 16, 1945 address to,
    xli
  HST's civil rights message to, 155
  HST's March 12, 1947 address to,
    116–18, 119, 120, 131, 168,
    228; *see also* Truman Doctrine
  HST's March 17, 1948 address to,
    168–70
  HST's Special Message on nuclear
    energy to, 83
  Joint Committee on Atomic Energy
    of, 86, 208, 214, 332, 341, 364
  MacArthur's address to, 309–10
  Republican control of, 104, 106,
    128, 176, 177
Congress of Industrial Organizations
    (CIO), xxvii, 339
Connally, Tom, 128, 172, 186, 238
Connelly, Matthew, 160–61
Considine, Bob, 254
Cooke, Alistair, xxvii
Coolidge, Calvin, 331
corruption and domestic scandals
    linked to HST, xi, 316–24, 379
Council of Foreign Ministers, 33, 40,
    60–61, 87
Cray, Ed, 184
Crimean Conference, The (Byrnes),
    xxxix

Crowther, Bosley, 56
Crusade in Europe (Eisenhower),
    345, 365, 373
Cumings, Bruce, 231, 282
Curry, George, 59
Cutler, Robert, 243
Czechoslovakia, 129
    Communist takeover in, 165–66,
        168, 170

Daniel, Clifton, 375, 377
    Margaret Truman's marriage to, 374
Daniels, Jonathan, xx, xxvii, xxviii,
    xxxvi, xxxvii–xxxviii, 32, 66,
    204
Daughters of the American
    Revolution (DAR), 152–53
Davies, Joseph E., 15–16, 18, 24, 27,
    32, 121
    HST and, 6, 15–17, 35, 346
Davis, Elmer, 70, 74, 261–62
Davis, John W., 331
Day, Price, 24
Dean, Gordon, 314
Defense Department, U.S., x, 224,
    247, 257
    Forrestal and, 145–47, 198–99
    inception of, 141
    State Department tensions with,
        220–21, 230–31
    thermonuclear weapons and, 209
    see also War Department, U.S.
Delta Council, 124, 127
Democratic National Committee, 318
Democratic National Conventions:
    of 1900, xv
    of 1944, xxvi–xxvii, 263–64, 320
    of 1948, 155, 179–82
    of 1952, 338–42
    of 1956, 373
    see also elections, U.S.
Democratic National Finance
    Committee, 200–201
Democrats, Democratic Party, xxii,
    316, 344

in election of 1946, 104
in election of 1948, 445
House controlled by, 104, 190,
    445
Senate controlled by, 104, 190
Democrats, Southern, 151, 155,
    165
    in election of 1948, 155, 177,
        181–82, 183
Dennison, Robert L., 6–7, 145,
    196–97, 201–2, 359
desegregation:
    of federal workforce, 182
    of military, 182
De Voto, Bernard, 337
Dewey, Thomas E.:
    in election of 1944, xxx, 232
    in election of 1948, 175, 177, 183,
        426
Dimension X radio drama, 206
Djilas, Milovan, 5, 32
domestic policy, U.S., 126, 177,
    181–82
    Fair Deal, 191, 193
    minimum wage increase and, 367
    national health insurance program
        and, xii, 126, 191, 367
    organized labor and, *see* labor,
        organized
domino theory, 114
Donahue, Libby, 326
Donovan, Robert J., 269
Doomsday Clock, 206
Dos Passos, John, 143–44, 203
Douglas, Helen Gahagan, 342
Douglas, Paul, 214
Douglas, William, 179, 328
Drummond, Roscoe, xxxiii, xxxix,
    188, 330
Drury, Allen, xxxv
Dulles, John Foster, 52, 232–33, 237,
    244, 353
    HST and, 242
    MacArthur and, 233, 242
DuMont, 180, 208

Early, Stephen T., xxiii, xxxvi,
10–11
Eastern Europe, 129, 204
Soviet influence in, 61, 69, 78
see also specific countries
Eberstadt, Ferdinand, 142, 199–200
Eden, Anthony, 39, 40, 373
Einstein, Albert, 164, 209
Eisenhower, Dwight D., 8, 22, 261,
274, 278, 364
appointed NATO commander, 324
as Columbia University president,
177, 194, 324
death of, 377
election of 1948 and, 178
in election of 1952, 342, 343,
348–50, 360
Forrestal's friendship with, 178,
192, 199
globe given to HST by, 114, 205,
245, 352, 373
HST and, x–xi, xliv, 39, 110,
324–25, 377
HST's deteriorating relationship
with, 345–48, 351–53, 355–56,
358–59, 371, 373–74
Korean War and, 347–48, 349,
370–71
Korea trip of, 349, 353
MacArthur and, 234, 243, 274,
354
McCarthy and, 346–47
Marshall and, 110
Missouri speech of, 126
Eisenhower, John, 353, 359
Eisenhower, Mamie, 360, 371, 377
elections, British, of 1945, 18, 23,
35, 40–41
elections, U.S.:
of 1900, xv
of 1944, xxvi, xxx, 263–64
of 1946, 99, 104–5, 128, 177, 217
of 1948, 123, 155–56, 175–76,
184, 186–87, 200, 291, 426,
445

of 1950, 263, 281
of 1952, 320, 325, 332, 342–45,
348–50
see also Democratic National
Conventions; Republican
National Conventions
Elizabeth II, Queen of England,
HST's lunch with, 373
Ellis, Edward Robb, 375
Elon, Amos, xiii
El Paso Herald-Post, 28
Elsey, George McKee, 27, 116–17,
142, 163, 292
Acheson and, 241–42
HST and, 47, 245, 263–64
Soviet threat assessment of Clifford
and, 112–14, 223
England, see Great Britain
Eniwetok Atoll:
first atomic bomb test on,
173
thermonuclear test near, 350
Europe, 224, 368
post-war rebuilding of, xii, 116,
123, 127; see also Marshall
Plan
World War II devastation of,
22–23, 130
European Recovery Act (1948), see
Marshall Plan
Evans, Thomas, 373
Evening Star (Washington), 203,
293, 295
Executive Order 9835, see Federal
Employee Loyalty Program
Executive Order 9980, 182
Executive Order 9981, 182
Exodus 1947 (steamer), Jewish
refugees on, 159–60

Fair Employment Practices
Commission, 155
Fairless, Benjamin, 339
Farrar, Ronald, 292, 293
Farrell, Thomas F., 28, 29

"Favoritism and Influence" (Senate subcommittee report), 318
Federal Bureau of Investigation (FBI):
  Federal Employee Loyalty Program and, 136–38
  Hoover and, xxxii, 134
  HST and, xi, 136
Federal Council of Churches of Christ in America, 52, 232
Federal Employee Loyalty Program, xi, 135, 136–38, 378
  HST and, 136, 150
Fehrenbach, T. R., 247, 279, 298
Ferdinand Magellan rail car, xxvi, 75–76
  HST's 1948 campaign trips on, 175–76, 182–83
  HST's post-presidential trip home in, 359, 361
Fermi, Enrico, 208, 209
Finder, Leonard, 178
Finland, 99
Fischer, John, 71
Fleeson, Doris, 12, 258, 293, 358
Fleming, Thomas, 161
Flynn, Ed, xxv–xxvi, xxxi
Folliard, Edward, 119, 176, 179
Foreign Office, British, 160
foreign policy, U.S., 80, 123, 141–42, 256
  Acheson's shaping of, xliii, 196, 222–23, 239
  containment in, 73, 130, 146, 378
  HST on, 116, 215, 219
  HST's initial lack of knowledge about, 2
  and Marshall's Harvard commencement speech, 124–25
  National Security Act and, 142
  and recognition of Israel, 162
  and support for Greece and Turkey, 115, 117, 118–19, 124, 128, 169, 176, 212–13, 245, 329, 357

U.S. nuclear monopoly and, 74, 116
  see also Cold War; Marshall Plan; NSC-68 policy paper; Truman Doctrine
Foreign Relations of the United States, 33
Former Presidents' Act (1958), 364
Formosa (Taiwan), 227, 236, 237, 255, 270, 277, 290
  MacArthur's trip to, 252, 253–54
Forrestal, James Vincent, 14, 20, 39, 73, 86, 143–45, 169, 174, 188, 193, 198–99, 220, 349, 397
  appointed Secretary of Defense, 147, 148
  at Bikini nuclear test, 93
  breakdown and suicide of, 202–3
  Byrnes on, 141
  and Clay cable, 167
  Distinguished Service Medal awarded to, 202
  Eberstadt's friendship with, 199–200
  Eisenhower's friendship with, 178, 199
  Hopkins's friendship with, 143
  HST and, 144–45, 146, 176, 183–84, 188, 192, 196–98, 377
  increasing instability of, 192, 199–200
  and Japan's surrender, 46–47, 111
  Lovett and, 158
  on Palestine partition, 158
  and reorganization of military and foreign policy establishment, 142, 146–47
  resignation of, 200–202
  Vaughan and, 175, 317
Forrestal, Josephine Ogden, 143, 144, 188, 199, 202
Frady, Marshall, 207
France, 204, 227, 281

Frank, Hans, 96
Frank, Pat, 133
Frankfurter, Felix, 195, 229, 328
Frazer, Joseph W., 317
Fuchs, Klaus, 213, 218
Fulbright, J. William, 104, 299,
    317–18, 368
Fuller, Helen, 319
Funk, Walther, 96
Fussell, Paul, 246

Gaddis, John Lewis, 112
Gallup, 167, 187, 239, 320
Gannett News Service, 333
Garner, John Nance, xix, xxxii
Gaud, William, 73
Georges, Harvey, 352
George VI, King of England, 40–41
    HST and, 47–48
Georgia, lynchings in, 153
Germany, Federal Republic of, 204,
    368
Germany, Nazi, 129
    surrender of, 8, 357
Germany, Occupied, 172
    post-war boundaries of, 23
    see also Berlin, Occupied
"Gods of Tin" (Salter), 278
Goebbels, Joseph, 18
Gordin, Michael D., 51
Gore, Albert, Sr., 303
Göring, Hermann, 20, 27, 96
Goulden, Joseph C., 302
Graham, Billy, 206–7, 321
    HST and, 207, 338, 376
Graham, Frank E., 48
Graham, Wallace, 181, 293, 354
Grand Alliance, xi, 16, 18, 82
    see also Potsdam Conference;
        Tehran Conference; Yalta
        Conference
Grandview, Mo., 53–54, 121
    Truman family farm in, xiv, xv–xvi,
        127, 148, 234
Granoff, Abraham, 162

Great Britain:
    diminishing sphere of influence of,
        114
    Korean War and, 281
    Occupied Germany and, 204
    as partner in Manhattan Project, 84
    World War II's economic toll on, 25
Great Days, The (Dos Passos), 144,
    203
Great War and Modern Memory, The
    (Fussell), 246
Greece:
    British support withdrawn from,
        114, 115, 131
    U.S. economic support for, 115,
        117, 118–19, 124, 128, 169,
        176, 212–13, 245, 329, 357
Gridiron Club, 55, 104, 203
Griswold, Erwin, 335
Gromyko, Andrei, 31, 91, 94
Groves, Leslie R., 7, 51, 56, 86, 206
    Acheson-Lilienthal Committee and,
        88
Gruenther, Alfred, 234
Gunther, John, xiii
Guomindang, 231
    see also Chiang Kai-shek; China,
        Nationalist

Haig, Alexander, 233
Halberstam, David, 283, 305, 315
Halifax, Lord, 64, 74, 114, 377
Hamburger, Philip, 195
Hannegan, Robert E., xx–xxi, xxxv, 9
    FDR and, xxiii, xxvii
    HST and, xl, 11
    tax-collector scandal and, 319
Harding, Warren G., xxx, 1
Harper's, 71, 318, 337
Harriman, Edward Henry, 3
Harriman, W. Averell, 60, 67, 80,
    110, 195, 257–58, 274, 332,
    352, 377
    appointed Secretary of Commerce,
        103, 252

Byrnes and, 62–63
as chair of President's Committee
    on Foreign Aid, 129, 130
FDR's relationship with, 3, 4, 17
HST and, 284, 377
MacArthur and, 252–53, 268, 305
Marshall Plan administered by, 252
in 1956 presidential campaign, 373
on Russia, 3–5
Stalin and, 3–4
at Wake Island Conference, 267,
    270, 276
Harris, Edward A., 251–52
Harvard, 124
Marshall's commencement speech
    at, 124–26
Hastings, Max, 261, 268, 283
Hatch, Carl, 94, 406
health insurance, HST's attempts to
    nationalize, xii, 126, 191, 237
Hearst, 13, 206, 254
Henderson, Loy A., 158, 160, 265
Hersey, John, 206, 283–84, 297
Hickenlooper, Bourke B., 364
Hickerson, John D., 231
Hill, Lister, 181
Hillman, Sidney, xxvii
Hirohito, Emperor of Japan, 22, 52
Hiroshima, atomic bombing of,
    48–49, 50–51, 54–55, 83, 206
Hiss, Alger, 218, 343
Acheson and, 218, 259
Hitler, Adolf, 8
Berchtesgaden retreat of, 27
myths about post-WWII life of,
    17–18, 32, 41, 96–97
Ho Chi Minh, 227
Hoffman, Clare, 142
Holmes, Oliver Wendell, Jr., 223
Hoopes, Townsend, 143
Hoover, Herbert, 317, 333, 359
HST and, 372, 374
Hoover, J. Edgar, xxxii, 249
BOI and, 133–34
Communist witch hunt of, 134–35

FBI and, xxxii, 134
HST and, 134, 136
Hopkins, Harry L., ix, xxxix, 18, 252
Forrestal's friendship with, 143
ill health of, xl, 17
Stalin and, 17, 32, 72
House of Representatives, U.S., 155
Armed Services Committee of, 202
Armed Services subcommittee of,
    158
Committee on Expenditures in the
    Executive Branch of, 142
Committee on Un-American
    Activities of, 134–35, 217
Democratic control of, 104, 190,
    445
Foreign Affairs Committee of,
    118–19, 167
HST's interest in, xviii–xix
Republican control of, 104, 106,
    128, 177
Select Committee on Foreign Aid
    of, 130
Hughes, Emmet John, 347, 348, 352
Hull, Cordell, 22
Hume, Paul, 294–95
Humphrey, Hubert Horatio, 181
Hungary, 99
Hurley, Patrick J., 60, 109, 136

Ickes, Harold, 20, 143
immigration quotas, 150
Independence, Mo., xiii, xvii, 19,
    350, 361, 367, 374
HST's childhood school in, xv,
    293
HST's home in, 63, 81, 105,
    106, 230, 234–35, 315, 317,
    363
Truman Presidential Library and
    Museum in, 371–72
Independence (presidential plane),
    267, 268, 342, 351
Independence and the Opening of the
    West (Benton), 371–72

Indochina, 227, 246, 250, 272
Inside U.S.A. (Gunther), xiii
Institute for Advanced Study, 223
Iran, 115, 224
Iraq, 378
Isaacson, Walter, 62
Ismay, Hastings, Lord 26
Israel:
 HST and, 158–59
 U.S. recognition of, xii, 162–64
Italy, 99, 115, 145, 168, 329
Ives, Elizabeth Stevenson "Buffie,"
 334–35

Jackson, Robert, 101, 137
 Nuremberg war crimes trials and,
 101
 Youngstown case and, 328, 331
Jackson County, Mo., 14, 143,
 367
 HST elected judge in, xviii
 HST's early life in, xiii
Jackson Daily News, 155
Jackson Examiner, xvii
Jacobson, Edward "Eddie":
 HST's friendship with, xvii, 161
 and partition of Palestine, 161–62
Jacobson, Mrs. Edward, 377
James, D. Clayton, 271
Japan:
 atomic bombing of, ix–x, 44–45,
 47, 54–55, 173, 356, 357, 367;
 see also Hiroshima; Nagasaki
 incendiary bombs dropped on,
 46–47, 51
 Pearl Harbor attack of, xxi, 45
 Russia's declaration of war against,
 52
 surrender of, 52–53, 56
 terms of surrender for, 22, 44–45,
 51; *see also* Potsdam Declaration
Japan-Korea Protocol, 224
Jefferson-Jackson Day Dinner,
 155–56
Jenner, William Ezra, 259

Jews, Judaism, 150
 HST and, 157–60
Jim Crow, 155
Jodl, Alfred, 8
Johnson, Edwin C., 85, 208–9, 212,
 214
Johnson, Louis, 202, 230, 311
 Acheson and, 220–21, 230–31,
 236, 256, 257
 appointed Secretary of Defense,
 200–201, 202, 258–59
 HST and, 235, 255–56, 257–58
 HST's firing of, 258–59
 ill health of, 221
 Korean War and, 237, 241, 242
 on military spending, 219–20,
 257
 NSC Special Committee on
 thermonuclear weapons and,
 211–12
 Pearson and, 201
 on Soviet nuclear weapons, 205
 Vaughan and, 317
Johnson, Lyndon B., 249–50, 367,
 374, 378
Joint Chiefs of Staff, 211, 221, 230,
 302, 311
 Korean War and, 236, 245, 247,
 260–61, 264, 279, 281, 284–85,
 289–90, 296, 301, 349
 MacArthur and, 260–61, 264, 266,
 270, 279, 281, 289, 290, 309
 MacArthur relieved of duty by, 305
 TROJAN war plan of, 173
Jones, Joseph M., 114, 115, 117,
 119, 124, 128
Juda, King of Bikini Atoll, 93–94
Justice Department, U.S., 10, 133,
 138, 145
 Attorney General's List of
 Subversive Organizations at, 138
 Criminal Division of, 85
 HST and, 153
 and Morris's questionnaire,
 321–22

Kahn, E. J., Jr., 3
Kaiser-Frazer Corporation, 317–18
Kaltenborn, H. V., 192
Kansas City, Mo., xvii–xviii
Kansas City Star, ix, xv, xviii, xxxii
Kefauver, Estes, 325
    HST and, 325, 341
    in presidential campaign of 1952,
        325, 333, 338, 339
Kempton, Murray, 465
Kennan, George, 16, 61, 62, 67, 129,
        196, 216, 221, 222–23
    Acheson and, 117, 250
    Korean War and, 250
    Long Telegram of, 73, 111, 130
    and Marshall Plan, 127
    on Soviet threat, 117, 146, 222
    State Department Policy Planning
        Staff run by, 111–12, 117, 127
    on Truman Doctrine, 119–20
Kennedy, John F., 217, 351
    assassination of, 374
    in elections of 1960, 373
Key West, HST in, *see* Little White
    House
Khrushchev, Nikita, 227, 370
Kim, Richard E., 229
Kim Il-Sung, 225, 227, 260, 370
    Stalin's support for war plans of,
        227, 237, 280
King, Mackenzie, 84, 87
Kistiakowsky, George, 51
Kluttz, Jerry, 138
Know-Nothing movement, 217
Korea, 61, 224, 279
    Acheson and, 226–27
    Demilitarized Zone of, 368
    HST appropriation bill for, 225–26
    Japanese annexation of, 224
    Japanese incursions in, 224
    Japan Korea Protocol and, 224
    Military Demarcation Line in, 370
    Soviet designs on, 225
    38th Parallel as boundary between
        North and South in, 224, 250

    see also North Korea; South
        Korea
Korean War, x, xliii, 230–34,
        242–45, 247–48, 315, 320, 341,
        367, 378
    Acheson and, xliii, 196, 230,
        235–36, 241–42, 259–60, 272,
        280–81, 285, 286, 290
    armistice in, 368, 370
    armistice talks in, 315, 347
    atomic weapons considered for,
        248, 249–50, 286–88, 290, 291,
        303, 314
    China's entry into, 280, 282–84,
        289–90, 296–97, 378
    China's threat to enter, 259–60,
        272
    Chinese deaths in, 369
    HST and, xliii, 234–35, 236–40,
        241, 250–51, 260, 265, 272,
        276–77, 283–84, 286, 296, 299,
        307, 356, 368–69, 371
    Inchon landing in, 260–62, 271,
        279, 283, 303
    Joint Chiefs of Staff and, 236, 245,
        247, 260–61, 264, 279, 281,
        284–85, 289–90, 296, 301, 349
    Korean deaths in, xliii, 234, 282,
        369
    MacArthur and, 242, 246, 252–53,
        255, 260–62, 264–66, 272,
        279–80, 282–85, 289, 290, 303,
        369
    napalm used in, 281–82, 369–70
    NSC and, 284–85
    Rusk and, 229, 231–32, 449
    Russian support for North Korea
        in, 234, 237, 246, 247, 280, 378
    38th Parallel in, xliii, 233, 234,
        239, 248, 255, 260, 264–65,
        271, 279, 301, 370
    UN and, xliii, 230, 234, 246, 250,
        261, 279–80, 282–83, 300, 308,
        348, 369
    U.S. deaths in, xliii, 247, 348, 369

Krock, Arthur, 144, 164
  HST interview of, 216–17, 223–24
Ku Klux Klan, HST and, xviii
Kurchatov, Igor, 39, 61

labor, organized, 82, 343
  Byrnes and, xxiv, xxvii
  HST and, 177, 379
  Western Union strike and, 327
  see also steelworkers strike
Labor Department, U.S., 10
Labour Party, British, 23
La Guardia, Fiorello, xxx, 8
Lapp, Ralph, 204
Lascelles, Alan, 48
Lash, Gertrude, xl
Laurence, William L., 93
Lawrence, David, 203, 255
Lawrence, Kans., 1854 massacre in,
  xiv
Lawrenson, Helen, 89–90
League of Nations, 157–58
League of Women Shoppers,
  138
Leahy, William, 47, 53, 67, 68,
  91, 102, 120, 126, 172, 203,
  283, 298, 310
  antipathy toward Russia of, 26,
  66, 113
  on atomic weapons, 7, 86
  on Byrnes, 64–65, 66
  on China, 116
  on Churchill's Fulton speech,
  76
  Distinguished Service Medal
  awarded to, 202
  FDR and, 66
  HST and, 21, 64, 101, 104, 211,
  247, 377
  HST's reliance on, 28, 58, 70,
  164
  on Korean War, 308
  on partition of Palestine, 159
  at Potsdam Conference, 21–22,
  34

Lehman, Herbert H., 214
LeMay, Curtis, 46, 282
Lend-Lease program, 3, 4
Leviero, Anthony, 244, 274–75
Liebling, A. J., 179, 287
Life, 74, 364, 365
Lilienthal, David, 57, 87, 88–89,
  174, 210, 213, 310
  Acheson and, 87–88, 111
  appointed chairman of AEC, 57, 99
  HST and, 295, 299, 300
  on NSC Special Committee on
  thermonuclear weapons,
  211–12
  Oppenheimer and, 95
  on thermonuclear weapons, 209
Lima News (Ohio), 350
Lippmann, Walter, 10, 55, 89, 92,
  96, 100, 114, 123, 124, 126,
  127, 177, 178–79, 190, 252,
  296, 298, 308, 357, 379–80
List, Eugene, 37–38, 107
Little White House (Key West), HST
  at, 120–21, 161, 165, 188–90,
  197–98, 218, 317, 324, 325
Lodge, Henry Cabot, Jr., 351
London Telegraph, 196
Long Telegram, of Kennan, 73, 111,
  130
  HST and, 112
Look, 105, 366
Los Alamos, N.Mex., atomic
  weapons lab at, 7, 173, 213
Los Angeles Times, 350
Lovett, Robert Abercrombie, 159,
  280
  appointed Undersecretary of State,
  123
  and Clay cable, 167
  Forrestal and, 144, 158, 202
  HST and, 185, 186, 338–39
  Korean War and, 288
  on Marshall, 123
  and recognition of Israel, 163
  resignation of, 193

Lowe, Frank E., 303
Lucas, Scott W., 245
Luce, Clare Boothe, 177
Luce, Henry, 177

MacArthur, Arthur, IV, 309, 312
MacArthur, Douglas, 232, 236, 238,
   269, 299, 302–3, 304
  Chiang and, 252–53
  Collins and, 270–71
  congressional address of, 309–10
  Distinguished Service Medal
    awarded to, 274
  Dulles and, 233, 242
  Eisenhower and, 234, 243, 274,
    354
  Formosa trip of, 252, 253–54
  Harriman and, 252–53, 268
  HST and, 242, 243, 255–56, 264,
    277, 300, 302, 304, 308, 309,
    310–11, 355, 377
  HST's deference toward, x–xi,
    243, 308
  HST's Wake Island meeting with,
    266–67, 268, 269–75, 285,
    304–5
  insubordination of, 255–56, 300,
    301–2, 304
  Joint Chiefs and, 260–61, 264,
    266, 270, 279, 281, 289, 290,
    309
  on Korean issue, 226
  Korean War and, 242, 246, 248,
    252–53, 255, 260–62, 264–66,
    272, 279–80, 282–85, 287–88,
    289, 290, 303, 369
  Korea trip of, 240–41
  McCarthy and, 311–12
  Marshall and, 264, 267, 309
  Martin and, 301, 304
  memoirs of, 302–3
  Muccio and, 269, 275
  political ambitions of, 243, 263,
    273–74, 353–54
  relieved of duty, 305–8, 311

  Ridgway on, 279, 300, 305
  stature of, 243, 300, 303, 305
  as supreme commander in post-war
    Japan, 67, 226, 230, 232
  Vaughan and, 309
  VFW letter of, 255–56, 269, 270,
    304
MacArthur, Jean, 233, 252, 274,
   308–9, 312
McCarthy, Joseph, 378
  Acheson and, 284
  Eisenhower and, 346–47
  HST and, 218–19, 307
  on MacArthur dismissal, 311–12
  Marshall and, 259, 312, 347
  and Soviet nuclear weapons, 218
  Wheeling speech of, 217, 218
McCloy, John, 2, 22, 27, 29, 96
McCormack, John W., 219
McCormick, Robert "Colonel," 13
McCullough, David, 358, 380
MacDonald, Dwight, xxiv, 100,
  101
McGrath, J. Howard, 209, 320
  HST and, 320, 322, 323–24
  HST's firing of, 322–23
  Morris and, 320, 321–22
McIntire, Ross T., xxii
McLean, Evalyn Walsh, xxxii
MacLeish, Archibald, 22
McMahon, Brien, 209, 314
  atomic energy and, 85–86, 214–15,
    332–33
  death of, 341
  HST and, 85, 209, 210, 214–15,
    341
  in presidential campaign of 1952,
    332–33, 373
  thermonuclear weapons and, 209,
    210
McMahon, Patricia, 86
McMahon, Rosemary, 360
McMahon Act, see Atomic Energy
    Act (1946)
Manchester, William, 232

Manchester Guardian, xxvii
Manchester Union Leader (New
    Hampshire), 178
Manchuria, 226, 281, 304
Manhattan Project, xxi–xxii, 7, 56,
    84, 86, 209
Mao Zedong, 109, 116, 217–18, 239
    see also China, People's Republic of
Mara, Cornelius, 295
Marcus, Maeva, 332
Marshall, Charles Burton, 302
Marshall, George Catlett, 5, 22, 56,
    114, 122, 145, 163, 166, 172,
    178, 188, 194, 222, 291, 311,
    359–60, 377
    Acheson and, 109, 264
    appointed Secretary of Defense,
        259
    appointed Secretary of State, 108–9
    appointed special envoy to China,
        60, 109–10, 217, 259
    on atomic bomb target choice, 46
    Clifford and, 162–63
    death of, 374
    on defense spending, 219–20
    on economic support for Greece
        and Turkey, 115
    Eisenhower and, 110
    Harvard commencement speech of,
        124–26, 127–28, 129
    honorary Harvard degree of,
        125
    HST and, 109, 116, 163, 169, 176,
        183–84, 185, 197, 257, 266,
        284, 377
    HST's deference toward, x–xi, 58,
        159, 164, 194
    and Jewish refugees, 160
    kidney ailment of, 175, 183, 184,
        192
    Korean War and, 280, 288–89, 301
    on Lovett, 123
    MacArthur and, 264, 267, 305,
        309
    McCarthy and, 259, 312, 348
    Moscow talks of, 130–31
    at Paris UN General Assembly
        talks, 184–85
    in resignation as Secretary of State,
        193
    on Soviet ambitions, 167–68
    Stalin and, 131
    on U.S. recognition of Israel,
        162–63
    Vandenberg and, 123
Marshall Plan, xii, xlii, xliv, 127, 166,
    168, 184, 197, 357, 367
    Harriman's administration of, 252
    HST and, 128, 130–31, 132
    passed by Congress, 170, 176
    Soviet opposition to, 129
Martin, John Bartlow, 334–35
Martin, Joseph W., Jr., 300–301, 359
    MacArthur and, 301, 304
Martyred, The (Kim), 229
Marx, Harpo, 82
Masaryk, Jan, 165–66
    death of, 167–68, 205
Masaryk, Tomas, 165
Masons, HST as member of, xvi,
    xviii, 377
Matthews, Francis P., 256–57
Matthews, H. Freeman "Doc," 21,
    221, 234
    at Potsdam Conference, 24, 35,
        40
    on Stalin, 35
Matthews, T. S., 333
Maverick, Maury, 312
May, Andrew Jackson, 85
May, Ernest R., 368
Mayer, Louis B., 56
May-Johnson bill, 85
Medicare, 367, 376
Mee, Charles, 42
Merin, Ruth, 334
Merz, Charles, 158
Messer, Robert, 68
Mesta, Perle, xxxii
Meyer, Eugene, 164

Miall, Leonard, 124–25
military, U.S.:
    and civilian control of atomic
        energy, 85–86, 91, 95, 174, 378
    desegregation of, 182
    HST's reorganization of, 141–42,
        146
    unmatched power of, ix, 9, 132,
        169, 211
    Vandenberg Resolution and, 197,
        204–5
    see also Korean War
military spending, U.S.:
    defense budget and, 219–21, 257
    NCS 68 and, 222
Miller, Merle, 376
Miller, Richard Lawrence, xviii
Milligan, Jacob, xx
Milligan, Maurice, xx, 10
Milwaukee Journal, 217
minimum wage, 126, 367
Minton, Sherman, Youngstown case
    and, 328, 331
Mission to Moscow (Davies), 16
Missouri:
    HST as Senator from, see Senate,
        U.S., HST in
    see also Grandview, Mo.;
        Independence, Mo.; Jackson
        County, Mo.
Molotov, Vyacheslav:
    in Council of Foreign Ministers,
        60–61
    Davies and, 15
    HST and, 5–6, 50
    at Potsdam Conference, 41
    Stalin and, 5
    and U.S. acquisition of atomic
        weapons, 39
Mongolia, 226
Monroe Doctrine, 119
Montreux Convention (1936),
    40
Moran, Charles McMoran Wilson,
    Lord, xliv, 25

Morgenthau, Ellie, 11
Morgenthau, Henry, Jr., xxxvii, 10,
    143
    FDR's relationship with, 11
    HST and, 11–12, 159
    resignation of, 20
Morris, Newbold:
    corruption investigation by, 320–22
    HST and, 320–21, 323
    McGrath and, 320, 321–22
Moynihan, Daniel Patrick, 118
Mr. President (Truman), 364
Muccio, John, 230, 233, 241,
    275–76
    MacArthur and, 269, 275
Muggeridge, Malcolm, 195–96
Murphy, Charles S., 263, 274, 322
    Stevenson and, 336–37
Murray, Philip, 339
Murrow, Edward R., 51
My Brother Adlai (Ives), 335

NAACP, xxiv, 376
    HST's 1947 speech to, 151, 154,
        180
Nagasaki, atomic bombing of, 51, 52,
    55, 56, 85, 206, 209
National Association of
    Manufacturers, 354
National Colored Democratic
    Association, 151
National Defense Research Council,
    83
National Guard, HST in, xv, xvi, 13,
    146, 161
National Labor Relations Act (1935),
    85
National Old Trails Road Association,
    xviii
National Press Club, Acheson's
    speech at, 226–27, 231
National Press Club Servicemen's
    Canteen, xxxiii
National Security Act (1947), 142,
    147–48, 169, 259

National Security Agency (NSA),
    MacArthur and, 302
National Security Council (NSC),
    183, 211, 227, 244
  inception of, 141–42, 149
  Korean War and, 284–85
  NSC-68 paper of, 222–23, 226,
    236
  NSC-81 report of, 255
  Special Committee on
    thermonuclear weapons of,
    211–12
Nazis, Nuremberg war crimes trials
    of, 96–97
NBC, 180, 192, 206307
  Eleanor Roosevelt's program on,
    209
New Deal, xli
  HST's support for, x, xii, 9, 126
New Republic, 156, 319
Newsweek, 122
New York Daily News, 340
New Yorker, 3, 182, 195, 206, 259,
    283, 297, 364, 379
New York Herald Tribune, 51, 53, 68,
    79, 125, 157, 189–90, 269, 307,
    309–10, 323, 357
New York Times, xxv, xxvii, xxxi,
    xxxv, 20, 36, 56, 93, 101, 108,
    125, 144, 157, 164, 168, 169,
    183, 195, 216, 227, 244, 274,
    303, 325, 347, 374, 375
New York World, 89
New York World-Telegram, 121
Nicolson, Harold, 48
Niebuhr, Reinhold, 56
Nitze, Paul, 221, 222, 265, 297, 302
Nixon, Richard M., 130, 217, 378,
    379
  Acheson and, 343
  in election of 1952, 342, 350
  in election of 1960, 373
  Red-hunting by, 342–43
Nixon, Robert G., 189, 202
Noland, Ethel (HST's cousin), 278

North Atlantic Treaty (1949), 204–5
North Atlantic Treaty Organization
    (NATO), xii, xliv, 204, 205, 329,
    357, 367, 368
  Eisenhower appointed commander
    of, 324
North Korea, 223
  Chinese border with, 279
  Russian influence in, 224, 225,
    227, 231
  South Korea attacked by, xliii,
    229–30; see also Korean War
  Soviet border with, 279
  U.S. naval blockade of, 242
  see also Korea; South Korea
Norweb, Raymond Henry, 75
Noyes, David, 184, 374
NSC-68 policy paper, 222, 223, 226,
    236, 243, 296, 297
NSC-81 report, 255, 264
Nuremberg, Nazi war crimes trials in,
    96–97

Obama, Barack, 368, 379
Office of Defense Mobilization,
    297
Office of Economic Stabilization,
    xxiii, 20
Office of Strategic Services, 141
Office of War Mobilization, xxii,
    xxxviii, xli, 297
Operation Crossroads, 92–93, 173
Operation Overlord, xxiii
Oppenheimer, J. Robert:
  Acheson-Lilienthal Committee and,
    88
  honorary Harvard degree of, 125
  HST and, 55–56, 92
  Lilienthal and, 95
  on thermonuclear weapons, 213
Oregon Journal, 343
Orient Coal Mine explosion, 336
Orwell, George, 130, 411
"Our Armed Forces MUST Be
    Unified" (Truman), 141

Oxford, HST's honorary degree
from, 372–73
Oxnam, G. Bromley, 52

Pace, Frank, Jr., 229, 241, 242, 306
at Wake Island Conference, 267,
273, 276
Page, Arthur W., 49–50
Palestine, British Mandate of, 150,
157–58, 159
HST and, 158–61
partition of, 158–66; *see also* Israel
Panikkar, K. M., 264–65
Paris Peace Conference (1946), 99
Patterson, Alicia, Stevenson and, 337,
342
Patterson, Robert P., 74, 142–43,
145, 169
Pearl Harbor, Japan's attack on, xxi
Pearson, Drew, 34, 69, 157, 160,
199, 200, 201, 202–23, 258,
316
Pendergast, Thomas Joseph "T.J.,"
72, 316
gerrymandering by, xviii, 10
as HST's political patron, xvii–
xviii, xix, 1
tax evasion convictions of, xx
Pepper, Claude, 121, 198
Perkins, Frances, xxxvii, 10, 13, 143
Phillips, Cabell, xxxi, 20
Phineas Finn (Trollope), 340
*Plain Speaking: An Oral Biography of
Harry Truman* (Miller), 376
PM, 326
Pogue, Forrest, 194
Poland, post-war border issue of,
xxxiv, 6, 17, 23, 30, 33, 42, 61
Ponselle, Rosa, xxxii–xxxiii
Potsdam Conference (1945), 18–19,
21–24, 30–31, 33 39, 40, 357,
393
Black Sea Straits issue in, 115
German war reparations issue in,
33, 42

HST at, 30–40, 43, 176
HST's international waterways idea
in, 39–40, 42
Nazi war crimes issue in, 33, 41
Poland's post-war boundary and
governance issue in, 23, 33, 42
Potsdam Declaration, 22, 44, 224
Powell, Adam Clayton, Jr., 152
Pravda, 80, 94–95
Present at the Creation (Acheson),
379
Presidential Commission on the
Health Needs of the Nation, 367
Presidential Succession Act (1947),
19
President's Committee on Foreign
Aid, 129, 130
President's Temporary Commission
on Employee Loyalty, 135–36
press, 31, 36, 124, 195, 212, 254,
258
HST and, xii, 13, 55, 83–84, 182,
189, 269, 274, 286–87, 288,
290, 329, 354–55, 361
see also White House press
corps; *specific journalists and
publications*
Progressive Party, U.S., 182, 426

Quantrill, William Clarke, xiv

Rabi, Isidor, 209
Radford, Arthur W., 353
at Wake Island Conference, 267,
268, 272, 275
Rayburn, Sam, xix, xxxv, 304
death of, 374
HST's friendship with, 11, 305
Reconstruction Finance Corporation
(RFC), 317, 319
Reed, Stanley, 328
Rees, David, 247, 261
Reinsch, Leonard, 117
Remington Rand, 353
Reminiscences (MacArthur), 308

Renown, HMS, 47–48
Republican National Conventions:
of 1948, 177, 180
of 1952, 342, 354
see also elections, U.S.
Republicans, Republican Party, 150
in election of 1946, 104
in election of 1952, 320, 346
House controlled by, 104, 106,
128, 177
Senate controlled by, 104, 106,
128, 177, 445
Republic of Korea, *see* South Korea
Reston, James "Scotty," 101, 108,
122, 124, 125–26, 168, 215,
246, 290–91
Acheson and, 110–11, 195, 239
Reynolds, David, 74
Rhee, Syngman, 225, 226, 250, 262,
263, 353, 371
Ridgway, Matthew, 243, 253, 290,
300, 305–6, 315, 377
on MacArthur, 279, 300, 305,
308
Ringler, Paul, 217
Rio Branco, Gastão do, 270–71
Roberts, Roy, ix
Robertson, David, xxv
Robeson, Paul, 138, 156
Romania, 17, 61, 65, 67–68, 69,
99
Roosevelt, Eleanor, xxxi, xxxiv, xl, 2,
11, 151, 154, 209, 372, 417
DAR and, 152
death of, 374
and election of 1948, 178, 179
Federal Employee Loyalty Program
and, 138–39
Harriman's relationship with, 3
on HST, 105, 374, 379
HST and, xxxvi, 138–39
Stevenson's friendship with, 334
Roosevelt, Elliott, xl, 104–5
Stalin interview by, 105
Roosevelt, Franklin, Jr., 178

Roosevelt, Franklin D., xx, 58, 200,
264, 317, 379
Baruch and, xxiii, 90
Cabinet of, 13, 143
at Cairo Conference, 224
Churchill and, 84
in election of 1944, xxiii, xxx–xxxi
fourth-term vice-president issue of,
xxiii–xxviii
Harriman's relationship with, 3
HST on, xxix
HST's relationship with, xxviii–
xxix, xxxi, 2
illness and death of, ix, xxii–xxiii,
xxix, xxx, xxxvi, xxxix–xl
Leahy and, 66
March 1, 1945 congressional
address of, xxxiv
1945 inaugural address of, xxxi
polio of, xxxiv, xxxv
at Tehran Conference, xxxiii–
xxxiv, 17, 33
at Yalta Conference, xxxi, xxxiii,
5, 17, 33
Roosevelt, James, xxviii, xxxi, 79
Roper, Elmo, 183, 190
Rosenman, Samuel, xxvi, 98, 373
Ross, Charles, 50, 66, 76, 77, 83,
101, 120, 203, 252, 345
appointed Press Secretary, xv, 13
HST and, 64, 65, 67, 80–81, 84,
91–92, 98, 100, 103–4, 148,
171, 176, 187, 203, 258, 291,
293, 295
at Potsdam Conference, 36, 291
press briefings of, 20, 53, 75, 168,
198, 256, 291, 292, 293
sudden death of, 292–93, 295
Rossiter, Clinton, 380
Rovere, Richard, 182–83, 217, 259,
379
Rowe, James H., political memo of
Clifford and, 150, 171
Royall, Kenneth, 194, 359
Royster, Vermont, 119, 244

Rusk, David Dean, 224–25, 250
  Korean War and, 229, 231–32,
    241, 247, 261, 272, 280, 301,
    449
  at Wake Island Conference, 263,
    267, 270, 271, 272, 273, 276
Russell, Richard, 311, 332, 338
Russia, *see* Soviet Union

Sacred Cow (presidential plane), 63
St. Louis Post-Dispatch, xxi, 13, 104,
    251, 293, 333, 337, 417
Salter, James, 278
Saltonstall, Leverett, 93
Saturday Evening Post, xxv
Sawyer, Charles, 328, 331
Sayre, Francis B., Jr., 377
Schlesinger, Arthur, Jr., 56, 199, 326
Schloss Cecilienhof, Potsdam
    Conference sessions in, 32–33,
    43
Schoenbaum, Thomas J., 225
Schwartz, Jordan A., 89, 90
Scott, Hazel, 152
Scripps Howard, 13
Sebald, William, 241
Selective Service law, 332
Semipalatinsk-21 (Soviet nuclear test
    site), 205
Senate, U.S.:
  Armed Services Committee of,
    311, 370
  Banking and Currency Committee
    of, 317
  Democratic control of, 104, 190
  Foreign Relations Committee of,
    104, 115, 128, 166, 172, 210,
    238, 311, 368, 370
  HST in, x, xiii, xix–xxii, xxviii,
    xxix, 1, 10, 141, 219, 318
  Labor and Public Welfare
    Subcommittee of, 191
  MacArthur's testimony before,
    370
  McCarthy and, 217

  McMahon's atomic energy speech
    to, 214
  Military Affairs Committee of, 147
  Republican control of, 104, 106,
    128, 177, 445
  Special Committee to Investigate
    Crime in Interstate Commerce
    of, 325
  Special Committee to Investigate
    the National Defense Program
    of, *see* Truman Committee
  Vandenberg Resolution and, 197
Seoul, 225, 230, 236, 262, 353, 368
  North Korean capture of, 229,
    233–34, 241
  War Memorial in, 240, 248–49,
    369
  see also South Korea
Sevareid, Eric, 298, 358
Shannon, William V., xxx, 98
Shawn, William, 364
Sherman, Forrest, 241, 256
Sherwood, Robert, xl, 143
Shirer, William L., 129
Short, Dewey, 310
Short, Joseph R., 322, 356
  appointed Press Secretary, 306
  death of, 345
  press briefings of, 309, 338
Smith, Merriman, 49
Smith, Oliver P., 261, 283
Smith, Walter Bedell, 80, 111, 288
  HST's reliance on, 164
Snyder, John W., 87, 128, 193, 284,
    317, 319, 361, 377
  HST's friendship with, 98–99, 145,
    186, 200, 363
Social Security, 126, 367
Society for the Advancement of
    Management, 123
Souers, Sidney W., 21, 212, 213
  appointed director of CIG, 145–46
  HST and, 146, 210–11, 249
"Sources of Soviet Conduct, The"
    (*Foreign Affairs* article), 129–30

Southeast Asia, 227, 378
  see also specific countries
Southern California, University of,
    Dean's speech to, 314
South Korea, 368
  North Korean attack on, xliii,
    229–30; see also Korean War
  U.S. influence in, 224, 225
  see also Korea; North Korea;
    Seoul
South Korean Army, 241
South Korean Mission, 237
Soviet Union:
  Acheson and, 115, 224, 285, 290
  atomic weapons developed by,
    205–7, 210, 218, 363
  Black Sea Straits and, 40, 70,
    114–15
  broken agreements of, xxiv, xxxiv,
    4, 113, 166, 223–24
  Clifford and Elsey's threat
    assessment of, 112–14
  declaration of war against Japan of,
    52, 224
  East Europe controlled by, 61, 69,
    78
  Harriman's distrust of, 3
  HST on, 4, 170, 204, 223–24
  Korean border with, 279
  Marshall Plan opposed by, 129
  North Korea influence of, 224,
    225, 227, 231
  North Korea war support by, 234,
    237, 245, 247, 280
  Poland's post-war border and,
    xxxiv, 6, 17
  Stalin's ambitions for, 72–73, 447
  UN boycott by, 234, 246
  and United Nations, xxxix
  U.S. relations with, x, 15–16, 42,
    61, 72, 112–13; see also Cold
    War
  World War II losses of, 129
Spaatz, Carl A., 44, 51
Sparkman, John J., 342, 343

Spectator, 59
Spellman, Francis Cardinal, 170–71
Spillane, Mickey, 135
Stalin, Joseph, x, xliii, 5, 17, 19, 31,
    35, 68, 72–73, 184
  in agreement to join war against
    Japan, 39
  broken agreements of, xxxiv, 4,
    113, 166
  Byrnes and, 65
  on Churchill's Fulton speech,
    80
  death of, 370
  Elliott Roosevelt's interview with,
    105
  Harriman's meeting with, 3–4
  Hitler myth propagated by, 17–18,
    32, 41–42, 96–97
  Hopkins and, 17
  on HST, 72
  HST and, 6, 30, 34–35, 38–39, 40,
    42, 78, 80, 146, 329, 330
  HST on, 30–31, 32, 50, 72, 165,
    176, 224
  ill health of, 24, 32, 41, 80, 131
  Kim Il-Sung's war plans supported
    by, 227, 231, 237, 380
  Marshall and, 131
  Molotov and, 5
  on Poland's post-war borders,
    xxxiv, 6, 17–18, 30
  at Potsdam Conference, 23, 30,
    32–38, 41
  purge trials by, 23, 31, 129
  Tito and, 205
  and U.S. possession of atomic
    weapons, 39, 61
  at Yalta Conference, xxxi,
    xxxiii–xxxiv
Stark, Lloyd, xx
State-Defense Review Group, 221
State Department, U.S., x, 22, 59, 60,
    72, 73, 167, 334
  anti-Zionist sentiment at, 158
  China policy of, 284, 300

and Communist expansion in
    Southeast Asia, 227
Defense Department tensions with,
    220–21, 230–31
Federal Employee Loyalty Program
    and, 138–39
HST and, 10, 21, 58, 110, 164,
    365
Korean War and, 230, 237, 265
MacArthur and, 253–54
McCarthy and, 217
near Eastern and African affairs at,
    158
Office of Northeast Asian Affairs
    of, 233
Policy Planning Staff of, 111–12,
    117, 127, 221, 265, 302
salaries at, 122
Vietnam and, 227
State of the Union speeches:
    of 1946, 64, 68
    of 1949, 191
    of 1952, 356
States Rights Party, U.S., 426
Steelman, John, 63, 65, 67, 117, 120
steelworkers strike, 327, 338–39,
    341, 379
    HST's seizure of steel mills in, xii,
        327–28, 331, 339, 343
    settlement of, 339
    Supreme Court case in, 328, 331,
        339
Steptoe & Johnson, 200
Stettinius, Edward R., xxxvii, 3, 5,
    11, 14
    appointed chief representative to
        UN, 19
    Hiss case and, 218
    HST and, 19
    at UN San Francisco conference, 12
Stevenson, Adlai (grandfather), 333
Stevenson, Adlai Ewing, II, 326, 349
    A. Patterson and, 337, 342
    Ball and, 335, 337
    childhood trauma of, 334–35

as disinclined to run for presidency,
    335–37, 338, 340
Eleanor Roosevelt's friendship
    with, 334
in election of 1952, 332, 333–37,
    343–45
in election of 1956, 373
HST and, 333, 335–36, 337–38,
    339, 340, 341, 342, 343, 373
Murphy and, 336–37
Stevenson, Ellen Borden, 334
Stimson, Henry L., xxxvi, 8, 14, 20,
    22, 44, 74, 83, 200
    Byrnes and, 33
    on Hiroshima atomic bomb, 48–49
    HST and, xxxvii, 7, 58
    at Potsdam Conference, 24, 33
    on safeguarding Kyoto, 45–46
    Truman Committee and, xxi–xxii
    and U.S. atomic bomb program,
        xxi–xxii, 28–29, 45, 54, 55
Stone, Harlan F., xxx, xxxvii, 87
Stratemeyer, Edward, 280, 282, 287,
    369
Strauss, Lewis L., 206
    on atomic bomb target choice, 397
    on thermonuclear weapons, 209,
        213
Strickler, Mrs. Thomas J., 121
Strout, Richard, 183
Study of History, A (Toynbee),
    131–32
Sullivan, John L., 220
Sulzberger, Arthur H., 157–58
Sulzberger, C. L., 227–28
Summersby, Kay, 376
Sunday Times (London), 61
"Super" bomb, see thermonuclear
    weapons
Supreme Court, Youngstown case in,
    328, 331
Swope, Herbert Bayard, 89, 90, 130,
    411
Symington, Stuart, 146, 147, 184,
    374

Taft, Robert, 97, 119, 176, 186
    Acheson and, 239, 257
    on Korea crisis, 238–39
    in presidential campaign of 1948,
        177
    in presidential campaign of 1952,
        328, 342, 354
Taft-Hartley Act (1947), 328
Talese, Gay, 374–75, 465
Taylor, Glen, 182
Tehran Conference (1943), xxxiii–
    xxxiv, 17, 24
Teller, Edward, 208, 350
Tennessee, lynchings in, 153
Tennessee Valley Authority, 87
Thayer, Mary Van Rensselaer, 144
thermonuclear weapons, 208, 368
    AEC and, 209, 213
    HST and, 209, 210–11, 212–13,
        221–22
    NSC Special Committee on,
        211–12
    U.S. decision to develop, 209–11,
        219, 221–22, 378
    U.S. tests of, 350, 356
This Kind of War (Fehrenbach), 247
Thomas, Evan, 62
Thompson, Edward K., 365
Thurmond, Strom, 155–56, 194
    in election of 1948, 182, 183, 426
Time, xxi, 108, 131, 145, 177, 218,
    275, 306, 333, 347
Tito, Josip Broz, 205, 455
Tokyo Radio, 50–51
Tory Party, British, 40
Toynbee, Arnold, 131–32
Traubel, Helen, Margaret Truman's
    study with, 293–94, 375
Treasury Department, U.S., 352
Trohan, Walter, 99
Trollope, Anthony, 340
Truman, Elizabeth Virginia Wallace
    "Bess" (HST's wife), xxvii,
    xxviii, xxxi–xxxii, xxxvi–xxxvii,
    16, 50, 121, 176, 230, 278, 282,

    294, 317, 332, 360, 361, 367,
        376
    DAR and, 152–53
    at FDR's funeral service and burial,
        xl
    HST's correspondence with,
        xv–xvi, xx, 14, 15, 34, 38, 40,
        63–64, 72, 251
    HST's courtship and marriage to,
        xvi, xvii, 127, 374
    HST's relationship with, xi,
        xviii–xix, xxix, xxxiii, 21,
        63–64, 106, 140, 182–83, 198,
        230, 325–26, 357, 373
    Madge Wallace's relationship with,
        xvi–xvii, 121, 315
Truman, Harry S.:
    approval ratings of, xii–xiii, 177,
        306, 360
    assassination attempt against, 278,
        291
    business ventures of, xvii
    casual indiscretions of, 9–10, 73,
        83–84, 176, 196
    character of, x, xii, xli, 43, 72, 83,
        218, 232, 269, 338, 356, 366,
        377–78, 380
    Confederate ancestry of, xiv,
        151
    in decision not to run for third
        term, 324, 325–26, 337
    diary of, xxvii, 17, 29, 54, 60, 67,
        77, 82, 108–9, 148–49, 159,
        179, 180, 184, 197, 243, 257,
        278, 285, 295–96, 304, 305,
        306, 315–16, 332, 336, 341,
        358, 361
    as early riser, 50, 139, 358
    Farewell Address of, 351, 357
    finances of, 364–65
    first jobs of, xv
    high fever and hospitalization of,
        338
    history's assessment of, 366–68,
        377–80

idiosyncratic reading of history by,
  xi, xxx, 39–40, 107, 166–67,
  251, 329
illness and death of, 376–77
inland waterways proposal of,
  39–40, 42–43, 52, 70
insecurities and doubts of, x,
  xxxviii, xli
memoirs of, 54, 65, 109, 116, 136,
  279, 349, 364–66
myopia of, xv, 21
piano playing by, xv, xxx, xxxii–
  xxxiii, 38, 43, 50
poker playing by, 12, 20, 67, 77,
  82
post-presidential years of, 363–77
public addresses of, xxx, 8–9, 52,
  118, 168, 251, 260, 296–97,
  307
quick decisions made by, x, xliii, 8,
  11, 103, 244, 379
reading by, xiv–xv, 81
self-inflating recollections of, xxvii,
  6–7
75th birthday of, 374
as sharp dresser, ix, xxxii, xxxv,
  xxxvi–xxxvii, 71, 181, 189,
  315
stilted public speaking manner of,
  xxx, 8–9, 117, 379
temper of, xi, 159–60, 294–95,
  316, 327, 379
vertigo of, 376
Truman, John Anderson (HST's
  father), xiii–xiv, xvi, xvii
  in Democratic Party politics, xiii,
    xv
  temper of, 327
Truman, John Vivian (HST's
  brother), xiv, xvi, 148, 234,
  377
Truman, Martha Ellen Young (HST's
  mother), xiii–xiv, xvi, 16
  college attended by, xiv
  fractured hip of, 121, 149

HST's correspondence with, xxxv,
  xli, 2, 34, 41, 58, 102, 103, 110,
  116
HST's relationship with, 9, 54,
  121, 149
illness and death of, 147–49
Truman, Mary Jane (HST's sister),
  xiv, xvi, 16, 148, 234, 377
  on HST, 151
  HST's correspondence with, xxxv,
    xli, 2, 15, 34, 41, 58, 102, 103,
    110, 116, 150, 154, 164, 175,
    178
Truman, Mary Margaret "Marg"
  (HST's daughter), xi, xxvii,
  xxix, xxxvi, 16, 113, 176,
  183, 294, 315, 320, 361, 366,
  376
  children of, 375
  Clifton Daniel's marriage to, 374
  David Acheson and, 463
  diary of, xxvi
  at FDR's funeral service and burial,
    xl
  on HST, 152–53, 161, 332, 344
  HST's correspondence with,
    xxviii–xxix, 28, 41, 120–21,
    166–67, 205
  at HST's funeral, 377
  HST's relationship with, 2, 63, 81,
    106, 198, 278, 302, 327, 357
  radio and television appearances
    of, 374–75
  singing career of, 81, 121, 140,
    293–95, 375
Truman (McCullough), 380
Truman administration, x, xxxix, 74,
  163, 298, 344
  alleged corruption in, 316–24,
    379
  atomic weapons and, *see* atomic
    weapons; thermonuclear
    weapons
  Loyalty Program and, *see* Federal
    Employee Loyalty Program

Truman administration (*cont.*)
    see also domestic policy, U.S.;
        foreign policy, U.S.; *specific
        departments and secretaries*
Truman & Jacobson Haberdashery,
    xvii, 161
Truman Committee, xxi, xxvi, 8,
    129, 141, 219, 168, 303
Truman Doctrine, 116–17, 119–20,
    124, 126, 132, 244, 296, 368
    Acheson and, 196, 367
    Southeast Asia and, 228, 296
    Soviet opposition to, 129
Truman Presidential Library and
    Museum, 371–72, 373, 376,
    379
    HST's funeral service at, 377
Tubby, Roger, 306, 307
    appointed Press Secretary, 356
Tully, Grace, xxxi, 73
Turkey:
    Black Sea Straits and, 40, 70,
        114–15
    British support withdrawn from,
        114, 115, 131
    U.S. economic support for, 115,
        119, 124, 128, 169, 176,
        212–13, 329, 357

Ukraine, xxxix, 31
Ulam, Stanislaw, 208
Union National Bank, HST's job at,
    xv, 372
unions, see labor, organized
United Nations, xxxiii, xxxix, 277,
    290
    Atomic Energy Commission of,
        88–89
    atomic weapons and, 69, 78–79,
        84, 94
    Baruch's speech to, 90, 91, 95,
        207–8, 214–15
    charter of, 19, 232
    Committee on Palestine of, 160
    founding of, xii, 19

General Assembly of, xxxix, 183,
    266
HST and, 287
Korean War and, xliii, 230, 234,
    236, 238, 242, 246, 250,
    254–55, 261, 271, 279–80,
    282–83, 287, 300, 308, 348
and partition of Palestine, 160–62
and Poland's post-war border and
    governance issue, 17
San Francisco conference of, 5, 17,
    166, 218
Security Council of, 234, 242, 246,
    252
Soviet boycott of, 234, 246, 252
Soviet Union and, xxxix
Vishinsky's speech to, 129
United Press, 49
United States:
    Chinese relations with, 264–65
    domestic policy of, see domestic
        policy, U.S.
    economic power of, ix
    foreign policy of, see foreign policy,
        U.S.
    Israel recognized by, xii, 162–64
    in Korean War, see Korean War
    military power of, ix, 9, 132, 169,
        173, 211
    Soviet relations with, x, 15–16, 42,
        61, 72, 112–13; see also Cold
        War
United States, USS, 220
United States Steel Corp., 339
United States Strategic Bombing
    Survey, 47
Urey, Harold C., 209–10
U.S. News & World Report, 255, 256,
    289, 343

Vandenberg, Arthur, 64, 104, 106,
    115, 123, 128, 186, 190, 215
    HST and, 176, 377
    Marshall Plan and, 130, 166,
        170

Vandenberg, Hoyt, 248, 280, 290
Vandenberg Resolution, 197, 204
Van Horne, Harriet, 121
van Vogt, A. E., 133
Vaughan, Harry Hawkins, xxxvi, 75, 76, 120, 193, 200, 282, 303, 319
  Forrestal and, 175
  HST's friendship with, xxix, xl, 1, 58, 64, 98, 176, 316
  MacArthur and, 309
  Senate investigation of, 316–17
  Stalin and, 30
Veterans Administration, 138
Veterans of Foreign Wars, MacArthur's letter to, 255–56, 269, 270
Victorious Fatherland Liberation War Museum (Pyongyang), 369
Viet Minh, 227
Vietnam, 227, 236, 378
Vietnam War, 120, 368, 369
Vinson, Fred, 104, 192, 193, 202, 317, 332, 360, 361
  appointed Chief Justice, 87
  appointed Secretary of the Treasury, 20
  HST's friendship with, 20, 184, 305
  proposed Russia trip of, 184–85, 216, 365–66
  Youngstown case and, 328, 331
Vishinsky, Andrei Y., 129
Vogue, 143

Wage Stabilization Board, 339
Wagner Act (1935), 85
Wake Island Conference, 263
  abrupt ending of, 273
  HST's and MacArthur's meeting at, 266–67, 268, 269–75, 285, 304–5
  HST's arduous trip to and from, 267–68, 276–77
Walker, Frank, xxvi, xxxv, 9, 105

Walker, Walton H., 300
Wallace, David W., suicide of, xvii
Wallace, Henry Agard, x, xxxii, 4, 20, 63, 73, 79, 110, 121, 143
  appointed Secretary of Commerce, xxx
  in election of 1948, 156–57, 171, 177, 182, 426
  FDR and, xxiii–xxiv, xxvi
  HST and, 50, 56, 99–100, 102, 158, 171, 462
  HST's firing of, 103, 156
  HST's relationship with, xxviii, 10, 364
  MSG speech of, 99–101, 185
  at New Republic, 156
  Soviets, sympathy for the, xxiv, 100–101
Wallace, Margaret Gates "Madge" (HST's mother-in-law), xvi–xvii, 315
  Bess's relationship with, xvi–xvii, 121
  death and burial of, 354
  HST's relationship with, xvii, 354
Wall Street Journal, 119, 244, 280, 297–98
War Department, U.S., 21, 50, 86, 112, 138
  Legislative and Liaison Division of, 243
  Operations Division of, 225
  see also Defense Department, U.S.
War Industries Board, 89
War Memorial (Seoul), 240, 248–49, 369
Warren, Earl, 177, 372
Washington Daily News, 295
Washington Post, x, xxxii, 119, 137, 138, 164, 176, 179, 258, 294, 304, 310, 344, 417
Washington Times-Herald, 295
Webb, James E., 235
Weekday (radio program), 375

Weiss, USS, 98
Weizmann, Chaim, 161–62, 163
Wendell Willkie Awards for Negro
     Journalism, HST's speech at,
     417
Werth, Alexander, 61
West, J. B., 359
Western Union strike, 327
What's My Line? (TV show), 375
Wherry, Kenneth, 219
White, Walter, xxiv, 151, 153, 154,
     155
Whitehead, Don, 94
White House, structural problems of,
     107, 175, 190–91
White House Correspondents' dinner
     (1945), xxxv
White House press corps:
   HST's news conferences and,
     10, 20, 69, 71, 79, 83–84, 91,
     100–101, 157, 168, 207–8,
     218–19, 239–40, 256, 277, 304,
     306, 310–11, 322–23, 328–30,
     331, 334, 355, 357–58
   HST's relationship with, 13–14,
     149, 157, 189, 214, 218
   Ross's briefings to, 20, 53, 75, 168,
     198, 256, 291, 292, 293
   Ross's relationship with, 13, 83,
     293
   Short's briefings to, 309, 338
White Russia, xxxix
Whitney, Courtney, 232, 241, 308
   at Wake Island Conference, 268,
     269–70, 275
Wilkins, Roy, 376
William A. Read & Co., 143
Williamsburg (presidential yacht), 64,
     65, 66, 67, 98–99, 103, 128,
     263, 292
Willkie, Wendell, xxix–xxx
Wilson, Charles Edward, 154–55, 297

Wilson, Woodrow, xxx, 132
Winchell, Walter, 134, 199, 266
Windsor, Edward, Duke of, 53
Wolf, Flora Barth, 137
Woodard, Isaac, Jr., 153
World News Round-Up radio
     program, 250
World of Null-A, The (van Vogt), 133
World Telegram and Sun, 375
World War I, HST's service in, xvi,
     xvii, xxix, 127, 133, 161, 303,
     365
World War II, ix
   devastation of Europe in, 22,
     22–23, 130
   German surrender in, 8, 357
   Jewish death toll in, 96
   Operation Overlord in, xxiii
   Soviet death toll in, 23
   see also Japan
Wyche, Cecil, 155

Yalta Conference (1945), xxxi, 17,
     24
   Poland's post-war border issue in,
     xxxiv, 5, 42
   reparations issue in, xxxiii
Year of Decisions (Truman), 366
Years of Trial and Hope: 1946–52
     (Truman), 366
"You and the Atom Bomb" (Orwell),
     411
Young, E. Merl and Lauretta,
     318
*Youngstown Sheet & Tube Company
     v. Sawyer,* 328, 331, 339
Young-Truman family farm, xiv,
     xv–xvi, 127, 148, 234
Yugoslavia, 129, 205

Zhou Enlai, 264–65, 272, 370
Zionists, Zionism, 158

About the Author

Jeffrey Frank was a senior editor at *The New Yorker*, the deputy editor of *The Washington Post*'s Outlook section, and is the author of *Ike and Dick: Portrait of a Strange Political Marriage*. He has published four novels, among them the Washington Trilogy—*The Columnist*, *Bad Publicity*, and *Trudy Hopedale*—and is the coauthor, with Diana Crone Frank, of a new translation of Hans Christian Andersen stories, which won the 2014 Hans Christian Andersen Prize. He is a contributor to *The New Yorker*, and has written for *The New York Times*, *The Washington Post*, *The Wall Street Journal*, *The Guardian*, *Bookforum*, and *Vogue*, among other publications.